The Reading Commitment

The Reading Commitment

MICHAEL E. ADELSTEIN
UNIVERSITY OF KENTUCKY

JEAN G. PIVAL
UNIVERSITY OF KENTUCKY

HARCOURT BRACE JOVANOVICH, INC.
NEW YORK   SAN DIEGO   CHICAGO   SAN FRANCISCO   ATLANTA

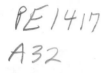

Cover art by Anna Kopczynski

ISBN: 0-15-575570-6

Library of Congress Catalog Card Number: 77-93818

Printed in the United States of America

PREFACE

This collection of essays and poems is designed primarily to give composition students interesting, effective, workable writing models. But most teachers of writing often teach reading skills in addition to rhetorical techniques. However, because of the emphasis on composition, this subsidiary teaching of reading has often been haphazard and unstructured—more by accident than by design. Thus in *The Reading Commitment* we set out to alert students to the specific relationships that exist between efficient, critical reading and effective writing. The selections in *The Reading Commitment* were therefore chosen for their readability and interest for students with a broad spectrum of reading abilities and for their potential usefulness in teaching the critical reading skills that contribute to better writing.

The Introduction sets up a three-step reading approach: Pre-Reading, Analytical Reading, and Reflecting. The questions that precede and follow each selection are based on this method. Each of the three steps emphasizes reading skills that can be applied to the development of good writing habits. The "Pre-Reading" device of finding the subject of a piece and the author's approach to it can help students see the importance of planning their papers in the pre-writing phase. The "Analytical Reading" step emphasizes a close analysis of structure and content. The suggested steps in the "Reflecting" process—Point, Organization, Support, Synthesis, and Evaluation—all stress the rhetorical considerations common to both reading and writing. The "From Reading to Writing" assignments are designed to relate the reading techniques to suggested student themes.

Because an awareness of overall structure is essential to both reading and writing, nearly all of the essays appear in their original, uncut form. Some, like Sally Carrighar's narrative and the description by Annie Dillard, though they are excerpted from longer works, can stand as independent essays. A few, such as Robert Lipsyte's definition of "SportsWorld," are entire chapters of books. All are well unified, however, and are appropriate for discussion in a single class period; occasionally, two related short pieces could be assigned. A wide variety of models is provided—more than ninety in all—so that instructors will have the opportunity to choose those most interesting and most suitable for their students.

We have deliberately limited ourselves to selections that are contemporary in character. They are written in the style and language that students

v

will be expected to emulate; thus, they serve as more practical models than "classic" essays from eighteenth- and nineteenth-century writers. In addition, we agree with the advocates of experiential writing that students write best about contemporary subjects that are pertinent to their experience—for example, personal development, values, education, conservation, sports—that are of enduring interest, and about which students have some prior knowledge. Because we also believe that novice writers can profit from an acquaintance with the rhetorical strategies of professional writers, the book includes many selections by nationally acclaimed authors who are masters of contemporary idiom: writers such as Maya Angelou, Isaac Asimov, Saul Bellow, Wendell Berry, Gwendolyn Brooks, John Ciardi, E. B. White, and Tom Wolfe. These and all the other writers represented in this collection have published successful books or articles that have appeared in leading national magazines.

The Instructor's Manual that is available to users of this textbook suggests answers to the questions accompanying each selection and offers advice on discussion techniques and on motivating students to write. The manual also includes a syllabus correlating *The Reading Commitment* with *The Writing Commitment,* for instructors who want to use the two together. Finally, there are an alternative table of contents arranged according to the rhetorical strategies used in the selections and a bibliography of works dealing with the teaching of reading and writing.

We are indebted to many people for their contributions. For their careful and valuable criticism of the manuscript, we thank Stephen H. Goldman of the University of Kansas, Dougald McMillan and Robert B. Siegle of the University of North Carolina, Gary Tate of Texas Christian University, Don L. Toburen of Butler County Community College, and Clemewell Young of Manchester Community College. For advice, guidance, and friendly encouragement, we are most grateful to Eben Ludlow, our superb editor, and Cecilia Gardner, our capable manuscript editor, as well as to Cathy Fauver, Susan Stoecker, and all the others at Harcourt Brace Jovanovich who helped with myriad tasks. We also wish to thank our colleagues at the University of Kentucky who offered suggestions for workable selections, particularly Alfred L. Crabb, Jr., David Godfrey, Theresa Scahill, and Dale Mathews. And special plaudits must go to Marilyn Fox, Myrna Andersen, and Abderrazak Dahmane for their contributions to this book. But the greatest debt of gratitude we owe to our patient and long-suffering spouses, Carol and Joe, for additional years of bookish neglect.

CONTENTS

2 The Informative Voice: Descriptive Writing   111

3 The Explanatory Voice: Expository Writing 201

4 The Argumentative Voice: Persuasive Writing 331

5 The Critical Voice: Writing About Literature, Television, and Film 443

Critical Analysis of Theme   465

Critical Analysis of Technique   482

Assessment of Reading and Writing Skills: Critical Writing   486

THEMATIC TABLE OF CONTENTS

Youth

The Reading Commitment

Introduction

WHY READ?

In 96 percent of American households there is at least one television set, which is turned on for an average of more than six hours a day. Thus it is not surprising that many young people read little and poorly. You can't learn to drive well except by driving. The same principle applies to reading: you can't learn to read well if you watch television too much and read too little. Of course, many people blame the schools for low reading scores. "Back to basics" is as popular a refrain as the lyrics of the latest gold record.

But the controversy over whether the "basics" of reading should be taught by the phonic-alphabetic or the "look–say" methods misses the point. The true basic problem is that young people don't spend their time reading. They seem to have lost the motivation to read. That may be because they fail to realize the value of the printed word: the information, enjoyment, and enrichment that reading provides.

We read not only to satisfy our curiosity about others—TV stars, film celebrities, jet setters, sports heroes and heroines—but to improve ourselves. Most of us would like to be healthier, wealthier, happier, sexier, thinner, or wiser. Many articles and books offer advice about varied subjects: ways to earn more money and manage it prudently; ways to select a career, mate, or used car; or ways to win everything from friends to a better job. We hope that reading for information in books and articles will help us live the good life—free of problems, cares, and worries.

In addition, we turn to the printed word for facts and figures both to satisfy our own craving for specific detail (note the popularity of the *Guinness Book of World Records*) and to impress others with our knowledge. Why else do sports fans load up with truckloads of data, such as batting averages and total yards gained rushing, if not to show off their knowledge?

And so the printed word—in newspapers, magazines, and books—provides information about sports and politics and hobbies and consumer tips and celebrity gossip and vacation ideas and other appealing subjects. Reading provides information that interests us and that makes us interesting.

1

Besides serving a practical purpose, reading provides sheer pleasure. It's fun to read for fun. Even with television so accessible and offering a similar escape, reading for enjoyment persists. Readers turn to all kinds of stories—tales of love, adventure, romance, war, and science fiction—for the pleasure of mentally leaving their humdrum lives and participating in the thrilling experiences depicted on the printed page. Reading has not only survived the Age of Television but with the advent of the relatively inexpensive and nearly always available paperback, it has boomed among adults. Why?

One answer is that reading offers more than televiewing does. As a reader, you can choose what you want from an almost infinite variety of printed stories. You can decide when you want to read instead of being confined to a network schedule. You can read anywhere—in a tent, bus, subway, plane, beach chair, or bed. And you can derive a more intimate pleasure from the printed word than from the television screen. Settling down comfortably, picking up a book or magazine, and entering its special world is a private act that leaves you alone with your feelings and thoughts. Absent are the polished tones of announcers, the canned laughter of studio soundtracks, the noisy interruptions of commercials, the disconcerting background music. Watching television is like traveling by bus—being part of a group, leaving the driving to others, going where they wish and when they choose. Reading is like traveling in your own car—stopping and starting as you like, taking side trips, arriving at your destination quickly or slowly.

And reading provides the pleasures of the imagination. John Keats, the English poet, referred to this form of enjoyment when he wrote that "heard melodies are sweet, but unheard ones are sweeter." Television provides the "heard" melodies, showing in close-ups and with fine fidelity how everyone looks and sounds. Reading furnishes the sweeter "unheard" melodies, allowing readers to imagine for themselves the world of the printed page. This difference may account for television's general inability to do justice to a novel or short story. Usually, something is missing when the printed word is transferred to the screen; this something may well be the personal imaginative experience that reading provides. Surely this is what Bruno Bettelheim, the noted psychoanalyst, meant when he said that "a good book at once stimulates and frees the mind," while television merely captures it.

In addition to offering information and enjoyment, reading can enrich our lives. Television appeals mainly to the eyes and ears, reading to the mind. Occasionally television presents meaningful dramas and documentaries, but most of the time it offers a bland diet of fast-food hamburgers, Coke, and french fries—little to stick with you and nourish you from one day to the next. Reading provides the necessary vitamins and proteins that strengthen the mind, providing wisdom: an understanding of self and others, human relationships, and the nature of the world we inhabit. The printed page offers a unique opportunity to meet a more experienced and intelligent person—alive or dead—who provides a special insight into life or a different vision of the world.

Reading enables us to enrich our minds with the best that has been thought and said since the dawn of civilization. At our fingertips are such literary and philosophical giants as Homer, Plato, Aristotle, Shakespeare, Cervantes, Voltaire, Dostoevsky, Marx, Freud, and Joyce. Or we can turn to significant contemporary writers, many of whom are represented in this book: Margaret Mead, the renowned anthropologist; Saul Bellow, the Nobel Prize-winning novelist; Rachel Carson, the revered biologist; Gilbert Highet, the eminent classicist; E. B. White, the respected essayist; Milton Friedman, the Nobel Prize-winning economist; and Gloria Steinem, the noted feminist, to mention only a few.

To extend your mind and to broaden your understanding is to acquire a new way of seeing and knowing that will increase your awareness of yourself, of others, and of life itself. Naturally, reading is not the only means to this end; much can be learned from experience. But you cannot experience everything yourself, and you can be bruised and scarred in the process. Experience is a slow and painful teacher. The printed page offers more wisdom at less cost. There the experiences of the finest minds over the centuries are preserved to enrich you with their insights and their understanding of life. All their learning, joys, sorrows, and hopes await you if you read—and comprehend what you read.

The last point—to comprehend what you read—requires that you read actively, intelligently, and critically. That's one objective of this book: to help you read better and enjoy it more. We'd like to turn you off television a bit and turn you on to reading. Now don't get us wrong: we enjoy television, and spend many hours before our sets to relax. But we also read—for at least several hours a day—to stretch our minds, because the information, enjoyment, and enrichment we derive from reading lead to a more stimulating and fuller life.

Another objective of this book, to return to basics, is to help you improve your writing. Truly, reading well usually results in writing well. "A writer," according to Saul Bellow, "is a reader moved to emulation." Just as you can improve your playing of tennis or basketball or the violin by watching professionals, so you can improve your writing by analyzing how professional writers present their ideas clearly, interestingly, and convincingly. More about this subject—how reading helps writing—will come later in this book.

Now that we have had our say about reading, perhaps we should conclude with the words of a famous author, Virginia Woolf, from her essay "How Should One Read a Book?" To fellow readers she wrote of her fantasy about Judgment Day when the avid readers of the world appear with "the great conquerors and lawyers and statesmen" to receive their reward. She prophesied that

the Almighty will turn to Peter and will say, not without a certain envy when He sees us [the readers] coming with our books under our arms, "Look, these need no reward. We have nothing to give them here. They have loved reading."

We hope this book will help you to love reading, too.

HOW TO READ BETTER

Obviously, you can read. But like most college students, you'd probably like to improve your reading: you'd like to be able to concentrate better, to read faster, to remember more of what you've read, and to analyze and evaluate it more effectively. You may have already found that college professors expect you to read, understand, remember, and draw inferences from assignments of fifty to one hundred pages for each of their class meetings. How can you cope with this heavy reading load?

To begin, you should be aware that there are at least three levels of reading. The first, which might be termed basic reading, you learned in elementary school, where you became acquainted with the alphabet, mastered some system of word or phonetic perception, and gradually acquired a basic vocabulary.

Another level of reading, which might be termed analytical, involves understanding the full meaning and implications of a written sentence or passage. This level requires not merely a passive act of word recognition, but an active attempt to determine the total message and experience being conveyed. Analytical reading consists of perceiving the central idea, relating subordinate ideas to it, understanding the key words, realizing the logical assumptions, and discerning the reasons supporting the ideas.

The third level, evaluative reading, consists of formulating a critical judgment about the written work. Evaluative reading requires a questioning attitude, one that constantly challenges the logic of the written statement, searches for the writer's prejudices, weighs the significance of the points, attacks the evidence, considers the stylistic effectiveness of the writing, and then relates the ideas and feelings to other views about the subject.

As a college student, you should have few problems with basic reading. But you may feel that your analytical reading skills need to be improved. You can test yourself on this memorable sentence from the Declaration of Independence:

We hold these truths to be self-evident, that all men are created equal, that they are endowed by their Creator with certain unalienable rights, that among these are life, liberty, and the pursuit of happiness.

You should be familiar with the vocabulary here except for *unalienable,* the archaic form of our modern word *inalienable,* used here with *rights* in the sense of "rights not to be taken away from anyone." With that explanation, you should fully understand the sentence.

But do you? For example, exactly what are the self-evident truths and what do they mean? Are you aware that the sentence has a cause-and-effect structure: all men are created equal because all men are endowed by their Creator with certain unalienable rights. Looking at the effect ("all men are created equal"), did you wonder about the word *men?* Did you assume that it referred only to adult males? Or does it include females, young people, non-Americans? And when you read the word *created,* did you wonder whether men or people could be created equal but then could lose their equality? Is there anything to indicate that people, having been born equal, should continue to be equal throughout their lives? Which brings us to the word *equal.* In what sense are people equal? We know that human beings by virtue of their genetic makeup are not equal physically or mentally, and we realize that not all babies have the same opportunities, either socially, culturally, or materially. Exactly what, then, does the word *equal* mean in this context?

Turning next to the cause—the self-evident truth about unalienable rights—we discover that three are specified: life, liberty, and the pursuit of happiness. The right of *life* seems simple to understand: it means that no one can take away another's life. But what about the death penalty? Does a murderer also have an "unalienable" right to life? Does an unborn fetus? Does an incurably ill patient maintained on life-supporting machines? And exactly what does *liberty* mean? Freedom from taxes, from service in the armed forces, from driving restrictions, from arrest for smoking marijuana? But perhaps even more complicated is *pursuit of happiness.* Let us assume that *happiness* requires personal definition, people deciding to what extent it involves wealth or peace of mind or something else. What then about *pursuit?* What is specifically implied in the right to *pursue,* or *seek,* happiness?

Our purpose in wrestling with this sentence is to illustrate the questioning attitudes involved in analytical reading. As you may realize, the sentence is not a simple one, but mature readers should be able to analyze its structure and realize its implications. Acquiring this skill is difficult, requiring patience and concentration and may be a lifelong venture, as Henry David Thoreau stated in *Walden:*

To read well, that is, to read true books in a true spirit, is a noble exercise, and one that will task the reader more than any exercise which the customs of the day esteem. It requires a training such as athletes underwent, the steady intent almost of the whole life to this object.

Indeed, just as athletes improve their ability in golf, tennis, basketball, and other sports through detailed instruction, grueling practice, and personal evaluation, you may similarly improve your reading skills.

In this Introduction and in the introduction to each part of the book, you will find some instruction to improve your reading; in the main sections of the book, you will discover well-written, contemporary, interesting selections for reading practice; and with each essay you will find questions that will allow you and your instructor to evaluate your comprehension and to help you relate the reading skills to your writing. Except for a few poems included for special reasons, we have tried to choose challenging and stimulating prose pieces written for mature readers. Hard-cover books are generally designed for such readers, as are most popular magazines, such as *Time, Newsweek, Redbook,* and *Sports Illustrated.* Reading the selections in this book should not only interest you but also benefit you—by enlarging your mind, increasing your awareness, expanding your understanding, stimulating ideas for writing, and showing you how to proceed in your own papers.

STEPS IN THE READING PROCESS

PRE-READING

The reading process should begin not with the first words on the first page but with a prior survey called pre-reading. Its purpose is to prepare you for reading: to let you know what you're about to find so that you can adjust yourself accordingly. It's like getting ready for a trip by going over the route and learning about some of the key places, or planning for a football game by studying the past records of the teams and familiarizing yourself with their players, formations, game strategies. You can get more out of a book or article by preparing for reading it. But how?

With a book or textbook, the title and subtitle should provide some inkling of its contents, as should the publisher's statements, which may appear on the front or back of the jacket, inside the jacket-flaps, or on the front or back cover of a paperback book. The table of contents provides a handy outline, while the index offers a listing of the particulars covered. Equally important is the preface or foreword, which many readers unfortunately ignore, but which writers use for stating their purpose and the background of the book. Also, you might flip through the opening and closing chapters: the former usually announces the problem or issue the book will deal with; the latter will often provide a summary. Finally, any printed biographical information about the author may prove helpful.

Pre-reading the selections in this book is somewhat similar. The titles, subtitles and the brief biographical sketches usually provide clues. Then division and subdivision headings, if there are any, can help. Opening and closing paragraphs are especially valuable because they usually contain key ideas. Skimming the first few sentences of other paragraphs can also be rewarding, often disclosing important points or revealing a summary, both being occasionally introduced by a number. For instance, note the clue furnished by the word *two* in the first sentence of the following paragraph:

So there are two rival explanations for the falling turnout at the Presidential polls. Maybe it is because of the way the news comes across through TV and the other media. Maybe it is because of the discouraging state of today's world.

—Ithiel de Sola Pool, "Why Don't People Vote?"
TV Guide, 23 October 1976, p. 6.

This short paragraph in the middle of the article summarizes the ideas and helps you to remember the "two rival explanations."

Another pre-reading clue may take the form of a question that the writer poses and then answers in several following paragraphs; for example:

What can these courses in ethics accomplish? One objective is to help students become more alert in discovering the moral issues that arise in their own lives. . . .

Another major objective is to teach students to reason carefully about ethical issues. . . .

A final objective of these courses is to help students clarify their moral aspirations. . . .

—Derek C. Bok, "Can Ethics Be Taught?"
Change, October 1976, p. 28

Note how the opening question, the numbered sentence, and the opening sentences of the subsequent paragraphs present the main ideas. Pre-reading may not always reveal important information in such an accessible form, but it can often provide direction and purpose to your reading.

ANALYTICAL READING

The second step in the reading process is similar to effective listening, requiring many of the same skills. Think of the written page as a person speaking. Constantly react by mentally asking the writer: What's the point here? Does it make sense? Is it important? How is each point related to the main one and to the previous one? What are some of the key words? Also, anticipate what the writer may say—just as you often do in a conversation—and compare the statements with your own ideas.

Obviously, to question and to compare ideas requires that you concentrate on the printed page instead of daydreaming about your social life, finances, or other personal affairs. The best way of forcing yourself to concentrate and of avoiding the need to reread paragraphs or pages is to have a pencil or high-light marker in hand. With either of these, you will actively look for key words or important sentences to note. We prefer a pencil because in addition to underlining, you can more easily write comments or marks in the margin, and bracket or circle words or allusions whose meaning you cannot understand from context and need to look up. In addition, you can signal reasons or causes and emphasize key points by writing appropriate numbers in the margins or by drawing arrows or similar markers. By actively involving yourself in analytical reading, you will concentrate better and comprehend more.

REFLECTING

So much for pre-reading and analytical reading. Now for the third step: reflecting. This process involves not only thinking about what you have read but also evaluating it. To help you achieve these objectives, you might want to follow our five-question approach, easily remembered by the acronym POSSE. Yes, in reading you're actually hunting—not for desperadoes, obviously, but for ideas and implications in the reading material. POSSE provides you with a systematic process to follow in the form of a series of questions:

1. What is the **P**oint of the selection? In other words, what is the theme, thesis, or controlling idea?
2. How are the ideas **O**rganized? Do they follow a chronological, spatial, cause-effect, or other pattern?
3. How are the ideas **S**upported? Are examples, illustrations, facts, reasons, testimony, or other evidence offered?
4. How can these ideas be **S**ynthesized, or compared or contrasted with my own or other people's experiences and ideas about the subject?
5. How should I **E**valuate the ideas? How clearly, concisely, convincingly, and effectively are the ideas stated? How important are they?

The first three questions focus on reviewing what you've learned from pre-reading and analytical reading. You should be able to state the author's main idea in your own words, describe the organizational pattern, and point out the supporting evidence used. One way to think about this review is to conceive of it as a reply to a friend who has asked you what you read, what it was about, what the main ideas were, and how they were substantiated. If you cannot respond to these questions fully, then you need to reread the work, searching for the answers. Only after you have grasped fully the point, organization, and support should you proceed to the final two questions.

The first of these questions, relating to synthesis, asks you to compare and contrast the written ideas with your own experiences and ideas or with those of other people to gain a broader understanding of the subject and the importance of the author's contribution. You may, of course, know so little about some subjects that you are unable to relate to the ideas. If so, then you cannot synthesize. But if you have had any personal experience with the subject, either directly or indirectly, then you can compare and contrast. If you have just finished reading a review about a film you have seen or have read other reviews about, then you can synthesize. Or if you have read an article about high school vandalism, experienced it in your school, or discussed it with your friends, then you can relate these views to the author's. But, on the one hand, you should realize that your experience may not be typical; on the other hand, you need not feel awed by a work just because it is printed. Recognize your limitations, yet be prepared to disagree when you can find solid reasons and evidence for doing so.

Then you are ready for the most complex of all the reading tasks—evaluation. Of course, you probably do this naturally. When you finish a book or article, you usually have some reaction. You know the extent to which you found it enjoyable, interesting, significant, useful, or beautiful. In talking to friends, you may recommend it or not. A good evaluation is based on your reaction, but it also requires that you have sound reasons for your opinion.

What's initially difficult is determining what standards to apply: obviously, an article about planting tomatoes cannot be evaluated by the same criteria as an argument against the death penalty. Another problem is that standards are not quantitative (based on, say, the number of words or paragraphs) but qualitative, depending on the reader's taste and experience both with the subject itself and with writing in general. For example, judging a review of a new rock album requires some knowledge about rock music standards and some acquaintance with other such reviews.

Consequently, an evaluation is not only a personal reaction but a critical one. As a person, you have certain private and emotional responses conditioned by your past life. As a critic, you should strive to be fair, informed, impartial, objective. Consequently, it would be perfectly understandable for you to cry or be moved emotionally at a movie but to deplore it afterward for being too sentimental. As an example, you may be stirred by the death of a boy's dog in the film, but as a critic, you may realize after reflecting that this scene was cheap, trite, and unnecessary. The same "split personality" approach—personal and critical—applies to reading a personal narrative, a descriptive essay, or an argument. You may dislike it or disagree with it for personal reasons, but then praise it because you realize its value and effectiveness.

Evaluation should be attempted only after you understand the work completely, having analyzed it carefully and reflected on it fully. We stress this point because in our experience, students often tend to dismiss lightly any written work that requires effort. We hope you will realize that many complex ideas cannot be stated simply. Therefore, you should make a reasonable attempt to understand what authors have written before faulting their work. Be certain that you have made the commitment that mature reading demands.

In evaluating, you are on safe ground when you point out in what ways the written material is based on misinformation, incomplete information, or faulty logic. Or you may question whether the generalizations are sound, the evidence sufficient, or the solution practical. By evaluating the written work on these and similar terms, you are basing your judgment on more objective and widely accepted reasons than if you relied solely on your personal taste and response. Consequently, you will be reading and reacting with more insight, intelligence, and sophistication.

It is easier to discuss these three steps in the reading process—pre-reading, analytical reading, and reflecting—than to inform you exactly how to proceed. The best learning is in the doing. In the following pages, we provide you with examples of personal, descriptive, expository, argumentative, and critical writing to acquaint you with the characteristics of these rhetorical forms, to provide you with models for your own writing, and to present you with reading samples that should interest, stimulate, and challenge you. In the introduction to each part of the book, we make suggestions for developing the pertinent pre-reading, analytical reading, and reflecting techniques. In addition, we offer questions at the end of each selection to help you improve your reading skills. But it is up to you to apply our suggestions—to make the reading commitment.

FROM READING TO WRITING

You might well ask at this point, "Why is all this information necessary or helpful in writing?" Contrary to folklore, good writing rarely results from spontaneous, original inspiration. The truth is that good writers don't reinvent the wheel, don't devise a whole new technique of writing every time they produce a new work. True, they learn from their own past experiences, but they also profit from writers whose works they admire. They become voracious readers, learning consciously and unconsciously from everything in print. They learn to read not only with an eye to form, to language use, and to style, but to utilize other writers' techniques in their own writing. They know that writing is a problem-solving endeavor—often a slow and painful one because each problem must be solved anew. Thus, because they reveal how others have solved some of the problems you face in your own writing, critical reading skills and habits can be valuable to you as a writing tool.

As you read good writing, try to develop a sensitivity to strategies that you can adapt and imitate in your own writing. Also, as you learn to analyze other writing, to note its merits and discern its weaknesses, you will become more critical and concerned about your own writing. As you watch good tennis players or guitarists play, you learn from them. And as you read and analyze good writing, you learn from it. In this way, your reading can help to improve your writing.

PART 1

The Intimate Voice: Personal Writing

Personal writing is the most intimate and informal of all writing. Addressed to one's self or a few close friends or a limited group of sympathetic readers, it is like the free and easy conversation between two close friends, the warm exchange among guests at a small dinner party, or the chatty after-dinner speech delivered to an informal, congenial gathering of people. The primary aim is to entertain, to strike responsive emotional chords, rather than to inform or persuade. Consequently, the form is usually narrative, the writer telling a story or relating an incident. Because there is little need for the precise word choice and the objective clarity required in informative writing, the writer chooses language for its interest, color, and spontaneity. And because personal writing appeals primarily to the reader's emotions, relating observations and events that are common to human experience, writers find that dialogue and sensory description are techniques especially helpful to their purpose.

Consequently, it is not surprising that the voice projected in this kind of writing is closer to informal spoken language than we find in any other form. The authors of personal writing try to sound like themselves—honestly and authentically using their own voices, free of the disguise and formality often used in speaking to strangers. When this honest and natural quality is achieved, the writers themselves are revealed: we learn something about them as private people—age, sex, aspirations, secret longings, insecurities, values, responses to other people. Perhaps the closest, most intimate introduction to the writer is achieved in reading diaries and journals, where writers usually note their own thoughts for their own personal satisfaction and enjoyment. Less revealing, perhaps, is the self-portrait painted for the reader in letters and autobiographical narrative or anecdote, where the writer may engage in some role-playing. Least intimate of all the forms of personal writing is the personal essay, which often has the purpose of informing as well as entertaining.

KINDS OF PERSONAL WRITING

DIARIES, JOURNALS, AND LETTERS

Because diaries, journals and letters are written close to the time of the event, they may more nearly capture the essence of the diarist. This characteristic is most vividly noticeable in the selection from Anne Morrow Lindbergh's diaries: written in her first year at college, it reveals the voice of an eager, bubbly young woman.

The Lindbergh piece and the other selections from journals demonstrate another characteristic of journal writing: vivid, concrete details that recreate the experience for us. Although the episode is recounted only very briefly, we see the Eskimo dance that Mrs. Lindbergh describes; we share the intimate reading of poetry with Sylvia Plath and her friend; we find Alan H. Olmstead's collie pup as appealing as he does; we can sense the cold misery of the rain that falls on Michael Parfit's sleeping bag; we walk with Lady Bird Johnson into the yard of an Appalachian cabin. Achieving richness of detail and reproducing authenticity of voice are the main concerns of the diarist writing diary entries or letters to intimates or of journalists writing to a friendly audience. Otherwise, the form is generally free and individual. As diarists, then, we can try our hand at any kind of writing that suits our fancy—narrative, essay, or even intimate poetry, such as haiku.

AUTOBIOGRAPHICAL NARRATIVE

Autobiographical narrative is not quite so free as diary writing. Because it is written to a broader audience, it needs to be tighter in organization. Like fiction, autobiographical narrative has a unifying action or situation limited by a span of time. The action can consist of a single episode, as in the selections from *I Know Why the Caged Bird Sings* and *All God's Dangers*. The latter piece tells of the risks run by a courageous black man during a shopping trip of just a few hours to a racially bigoted small town. The action can also span a longer time, the writer recounting in sequence a number of related experiences, as in Sally Carrighar's account of her summer in the Canadian woods. Finally, two related incidents that happen far apart in time can be narrated, as in the story of how the young son of Ernest Hemingway lied in order to impress his famous father and how, long afterward, the father still felt pain and disappointment.

But whether the action is limited to one single episode or to a series of related ones, it does serve as a unifying device for autobiographical narrative. And although time may be handled in other ways, the simple chronological treatment, moving from an earlier time to a later one, is perhaps the most common and effective organizational scheme.

PERSONAL ANECDOTES

The characteristics of autobiographical narrative are also features of personal anecdotes, except that the anecdote is limited to one action or episode, a brief period of time, and little character development. As readers, we have a better perception of Sally Carrighar in the selection from *Home to the Wilderness* than of the anecdote teller of "A Night on the Moors with the Brontë Family." In narrative, character development is essential; in anecdote, the main emphasis is on the action itself and character development is only incidental.

PERSONAL ESSAY

Most formalistic of all forms of personal writing is the personal essay. Generally, personal essays are strongly thematic; that is, their unity is achieved through a main idea or thread of recurring experiences. Ralph Schoenstein's essay, for instance, comments on the many times that first his grandfather and then he himself worried over things beyond their control; Leo Rosten explains his lifetime love of reading by threading together accounts of numerous times when he was forced into random reading.

The main purpose of a personal essay, however, is not merely to tell a story, but is to comment or to give one's personal reactions to recurring events or situations. The chronological order that can effectively organize a single happening can become cumbersome in discussing numerous situations and the relationships between them. Therefore, writers of personal essays provide a unifying or focusing statement to guide the reader—a statement that introduces the subject and reflects the writer's attitude toward that subject. Sometimes this sentence opens the essay, as in Rosten's "A good book makes my nostrils quiver"; other writers may place the focusing statement at the end of an introductory paragraph or two; but it almost always appears early in the essay and guides the readers on their way through the subject, at the same time establishing the writer's tone.

The personal essay, unlike expository or argumentative writing, frequently reflects a voice that is casual, amused, ironic, sometimes carrying a tone of mock seriousness. Even when the tone is serious, the subject matter of the personal essay—a situation that is irritating or disconcerting, perhaps, but certainly not earthshaking—keeps the essay from being weighty and ponderous.

TACTICS FOR READING PERSONAL WRITING

PRE-READING

In the Introduction to this book, we recommended that you follow certain pre-reading procedures, such as thinking about the title, then skimming the opening and closing paragraphs. Obviously, these procedures are a little difficult to follow in the reading of short personal writing. Often, as in diary entries and letters, there is no title, and you certainly don't want to diminish the pleasure of reading a narrative by learning the outcome before you actually read the selection. But there are some things you can do to prepare yourself to read a piece of personal writing intelligently.

Remembering that there is a thematic relationship between the title and the content of what follows it, and if there is a title, you might examine it with these questions in mind:

1. Are there words in the title I don't know the meaning of? For instance, one selection is entitled "A Night on the Moors with the

Brontë Family"; are you sure that you know what a *moor* is? If not, look it up in the dictionary. Knowing that *moor* is the British term for an open, swampy wasteland will not only help you get into the mood of the story but also establish its location.

2. If names appear in the title, do you know anything about the people or places referred to? Again, the dictionary may give sufficient information. For instance, the dictionary will tell you that the Brontës were a family of English writers; what their names were; and the dates of their lives. We can see from these dates that all were dead by 1855, and that knowledge makes us realize that a story called "A Night on the Moors with the Brontë Family" must be about ghosts. Further information about the Brontës from an encyclopedia would also be helpful.

Once you have scrutinized the title, look for information about the essay. As we suggested in the Introduction, background information is sometimes provided between the title and the opening paragraph, or sometimes in a footnote. This material can give you an idea about what kind of person the writer is, maybe even about the situation described in the article. If it is a book, follow our earlier suggestion to read the dust jacket or the flyleaf.

You may be wondering whether these preliminary steps are necessary. Remember, this procedure is intended to add to your appreciation of the work. It is like tasting a new food dish: you often want some knowledge of the ingredients before you wolf down the whole thing. Similarly, you will probably enjoy your reading more if you taste the content first, preparing your mind to get maximum satisfaction and nourishment from the work. And this brings us to the final step in the pre-reading process—skimming the opening paragraph. If the work is well written, you should glean some idea of the situation, the mood the writer wants to project, the time context, and perhaps an introduction to some of the characters. Now you are ready to read!

ANALYTICAL READING

Many proficient readers prefer to go through a narrative twice: first for the enjoyment and suspense of the plot, then to make themselves aware of more subtle aspects of the work. Other readers would rather absorb everything in one sitting. Whichever method is preferred, critical readers train themselves to get more out of narrative writing than just the story. Certainly, they are aware of the sequence of events, but they are also sensitive to the tone projected by the narrator, to the relationships between characters and between events, and to the influence of the events on individual characters. In addition, critical readers look for developments that signal shifts in the action or that foreshadow the outcome. Sorting these out as they read can lead to their complete satisfaction at the end of the story; they do not feel confused or cheated by the outcome of the story because they failed to respond to some signal the writer gave.

So far we have talked of reading narrative writing in general. Because personal writing relies so heavily on narrative—because accounts of events appear so often in letters, diary entries, personal narratives, autobiographical anecdotes, and even personal essays—it is similar in many respects to fictional narrative. Thus we can apply many of the same reading tactics to personal writing that we do to fiction. Essentially, all narrative involves these questions:

WHO are the characters?
WHAT happens in the narrative? WHAT are the relationships of the characters?
WHEN does the action take place?
WHERE does the action take place?
HOW does the writer organize the telling of the event?

If you follow the pre-reading suggestions, chances are you will know the time period of the action (WHEN) and the location (WHERE) before you start to read. But you must read the whole work to find the answers to the other questions. So, as you read, keep these questions in mind and remember to underline key passages to aid you in your analysis:

1. Who is the writer/narrator? Who are the other characters? What kind of people are they? What are their relationships to one another?
2. What is the tone—the attitude of the writer toward the events, situation, or subject (especially in a personal essay)?
3. How do the events and the characters' reactions to them reveal something about the kind of people they are?
4. What is the relationship of events to one another? What was the purpose of revealing certain events and characters to us?

REFLECTING

When you have read through the work, you are ready to enter the third stage of the reading process—reflecting on what you have read. As we indicated in the Introduction, this is the time to: summarize the content in order to make sure you have assimilated or digested the material; to determine how the writer organized the work and how he or she supported the points made; to synthesize and evaluate. Let's see how our POSSE approach can help to search out a critical method for evaluating personal writing.

*What is the **P**oint of the selection?* With the possible exception of the personal essay, instruction is not usually the main purpose of personal writing. Even so, the reader often leaves a work of personal narrative with new knowledge, fresh insight, or a broadened understanding of human nature. The reader can share vicariously any lesson learned by the narrator—the shame felt by a son who seeks approval from his father by dishonest means or the conclusions about living things reached by a young girl after she kills a porcupine for no reason. If there is an insight implicit in the story, then you should be able to summarize the work, stating that point.

How is the material *Organized?* Most narrative, as we have said, is organized by chronological sequence. If you found that the story moves easily from one event to the next, you can be sure that the writer has provided clues to the time sequence for you, as on page 74, paragraph 18 of the selection by Maya Angelou: *"Before* the girls got to the porch . . . ," "They came *finally* . . . ," "*At first* . . . ," "*Then* one . . . ," "*Another* said. . . ." Skim each selection after reading, making yourself aware of such signals. Eventually, the use of these devices will become second nature to you and will be useful in both your reading and your writing.

How are the ideas *Supported?* Support in other forms of writing is achieved by using examples, citing authority, and the like. But personal writing, particularly narrative, does not lend itself to these techniques. True, the personal essay often contains them, but autobiographical narrative uses other devices to support the writer's views or attitudes. An important contribution to this support is made by the tone or voice projected in the work. A look at the language chosen by the writer at critical points in the narrative can reveal personal attitudes toward the subject. Note, for example, Anne Morrow Lindbergh's vivid language when she refers to her schoolwork (pages 20–21, paragraphs 2, 6): "coils are tightening," "it hounds me doggedly." Her word choice convinces you that she finds the work demanding. In "The Road Less Traveled," note how Michael Parfit's analogy between backpacking and the excitement and sadness of leaving home sets up the ambivalent attitude toward backpacking that is apparent throughout his essay. And observe how Alan Olmstead's language in describing his puppy reveals his affection for her: "A lovely, gentle little lady."

Another question to ask yourself about the writer is this: Do I find the voice relaxed, honest, natural, and informal? Word choice is not the only factor in creating voice—sentence structure and length can also contribute. Fairly simple sentences, numerous sentence fragments, and dialogue sentences help create a familiar voice, while longer, more complex sentences project an air of formality and distance. Thus, the voice the author assumes in writing can lend the same kind of support as it does in a speech before an audience.

How can this work be *Synthesized* with my own or other people's ideas on the same subject? A good way to synthesize personal narrative is to use the technique we often practice in conversation. When we are in a group of people telling stories and anecdotes, one story usually leads to another. Think of how often you have heard such phrases as "That reminds me of the time . . ." and "Speaking of baseball, remember the game. . . ." When that happens, we are synthesizing the elements of the conversation, relating them thematically to similar episodes in our own experience or the experience of others. Likewise, something in a piece of personal writing—the subject, the tone, one of the characters—may remind us of a similar element in another piece. Comparison of the two leads to a synthesis that deepens our understanding of each.

How do I Evaluate the selection? This step should be the simplest of all. All of us can readily define our emotional reaction to a work. If you've followed the other steps outlined here, you should have little trouble giving specific reasons why you liked, disliked, or were unmoved by the selection.

FROM READING TO WRITING

Moving from reading to writing in any particular medium is somewhat like changing from spectator to participant. A basketball game or a piano concert looks easy when someone else is making all the necessary moves and coping with the techniques of the process. So too in reading personal writing. It is easy to become so caught up in a gripping narrative or an entertaining personal essay that you are not conscious of the "moves" of the writer. But when you yourself start to write, you wish that you had been more observant in your reading. Developing the kind of reading habits that we have suggested can help you make the transition from watcher to doer—from reader to writer. As you become aware of the tactics that writers of good narrative use, you can transfer these to your own writing problems. If you make yourself conscious of how the writers in this book have handled problems of organization, sentence strategies, word choice, dialogue, and establishment of tone, then you should begin to see ways to employ these in your writing—not in blind imitation, but as a general model for expressing your own imaginative and writing powers.

Diaries, Journals, and Letters

FROM BRING ME A UNICORN
Anne Morrow Lindbergh

BIOGRAPHICAL SKETCH

Anne Morrow Lindbergh was born in Englewood, New Jersey, in 1906. She graduated from Smith College in 1927, and married Charles A. Lindbergh in 1929. Following the kidnapping and murder of their young son in 1932 and the notoriety surrounding that tragedy, the Lindberghs moved to England. Their return to the United States, on the outbreak of World War II, was marked by renewed notoriety surrounding Lindbergh's opposition to U.S. involvement in the war. Besides her letters and diaries, Mrs. Lindbergh's published works include Listen: The Wind, A Gift from the Sea, *and a novel,* Dearly Beloved.

PRE-READING

1. On the basis of the biographical sketch, what benefits do you think Mrs. Lindbergh gained from preserving a diary and collection of letters written when she was young?

2. Check the dates of the selection. Approximately how old is the writer?

3. Read the first paragraph of the letter. What is the mood of the writer?

[Northampton, April 22, 1925]

Mother darling—

¹ I am terribly sorry not to have written for so long but it has been so frantically crowded and I have been very discouraged and I couldn't bear to write "from the depths"!

² It is a little better now. The work seems to be piling up frightfully and the coils are tightening. Finals are pushing from the other side and it gives you a permanent hounded feeling.

³ And I'm *not* doing any outside things. Not a thing! Really. I don't see anyone that isn't in my classes or in my house and all the time that's not spent at classes is spent studying. Perhaps I get stale.

FROM Anne Morrow Lindbergh, *Bring Me a Unicorn: Diaries and Letters of Anne Morrow Lindbergh, 1922-28* (New York: Harcourt Brace Jovanovich, 1971, 1972), pp. 20-21. Copyright © 1971, 1972 by Anne Morrow Lindbergh. Reprinted by permission of Harcourt Brace Jovanovich, Inc.

⁴ Writing for Miss Kirstein takes *hours,* too. And it needs consecutive hours. I haven't any consecutive hours except at night and on Sunday. Sunday is always one long stretch of work from morning until quite late, without even the break of going to classes.

⁵ I do wish I had some alibi for such inefficiency—something like having appendicitis or being in love, or brain fever—but I haven't *any* excuse—I am a healthy contented sane creature but I seem to work like molasses.

⁶ I think a great deal of it is because I can't seem able ever to drop it from my mind and get away from it and come back refreshed. That is awfully silly of me, but wherever I go I take it all with me—all the paraphernalia of work—mental paraphernalia. I look at a birch tree through a mist of gym shoes, course cards, alarm clocks, papers due, writtens, laundry boxes, choir practices, bills, long themes, and *exams*—etc. It hounds me doggedly and I think much too much about it and it makes me discouraged, and when I'm discouraged I can't do *anything.* This sounds so much worse than it is. I really shouldn't get discouraged. It is just because I can't see anything outside of college. It is so absorbing that it has loomed all out of proportion and I feel cut off from everything else.

⁷ But, Mother, in spite of this torrent of complaints, I love it—I really do—and I wouldn't stop for anything in the world. I've never had anything like it before. It is thrilling and absorbing and wonderful.

⁸ *I'm not taking any writing course* [next year]. Do you think that's awful? Of course there will be a good deal of writing in Eng. 19, and reports to make and write in the History. The reason I'm not taking it is that I won't have time to do them all as fully as I want to, if I do. Besides, I've learned from Miss Kirstein's course that (thrilling as she and it are) I really need more to think about and less to write about. Nothing I write has any backbone to it and it won't have until I absorb more. Do you think it's very silly?

ANALYTICAL READING

1. What do you suppose Lindbergh means by "from the depths" in the first paragraph? What change enables her to write the letter?

2. What does Lindbergh blame for the "permanent hounded feeling" she experiences (paragraph 2)? Are the teachers too demanding? Is she incapable of meeting the standards of Smith College? Or does she perceive some other failing in herself?

3. Evidently Lindbergh knew her mother would be disappointed about her not taking a writing course in the following year. How does Lindbergh attempt to justify her decision?

4. Does Lindbergh introduce a new and separate subject in the last paragraph about next year, or is the subject related to the preceding paragraph or some other idea in the letter?

REFLECTING

Point: What does Lindbergh hope to make her mother realize? Try to summarize the central idea or theme in one sentence. Which of Lindbergh's sentences best states this idea?

Organization: Does Lindbergh ramble on and on in the letter, or is there some general organizational plan? How is paragraph 6 organized and developed? What is the effect of ending with a question?

Support: Refer to specific words, sentences, and fragments that establish the natural, informal voice of the writer. Is Lindbergh convincing about her real attitude toward college? Why and how? In this text, several of the words are italicized. How did they appear in her handwritten letter? Explain the use of brackets in the first sentence of paragraph 8.

Synthesis: Do you or your friends share any of Lindbergh's feelings about the first year at college? Do you need consecutive hours for writing? Discuss the implications of the sentence in paragraph 8: "I really need more to think about and less to write about."

Evaluation: Is Lindbergh's letter interesting, sincere, and natural? Is there a conversational effect to it? Does she make her main point convincingly?

FROM READING TO WRITING

1. Write a letter home or to a friend explaining in detail some problem of adjusting to college, a job, life in a dorm or away from home, or some other new experience. Try to capture Lindbergh's friendly, conversational tone.

2. Write a letter to your parents about some decision that you know will not please them. Try to make them understand your reasons.

3. Write a letter to a favorite high school teacher or coach about your initial reaction to college. Imagine as you write that you are having a face-to-face conversation.

4. Write a letter to your parents about how difficult it is to study because there are so many exciting things going on outside of class, such as getting to know new and interesting people, attending meetings, and the like.

THE BEGINNING OF A CAREER
Sylvia Plath

BIOGRAPHICAL SKETCH

Sylvia Plath (1932–1963) was born in Boston, Massachusetts, educated at Smith, and attended Cambridge University in England on a Fulbright scholarship. There she married the English poet Ted Hughes. She is best known for her autobiograph-

FROM Sylvia Plath, *Letters Home: Correspondence 1960–63*, ed. Aurelia Schober Plath (New York: Harper & Row, 1975), pp. 86–90. Copyright © 1975 by Aurelia Schober Plath. Reprinted by permission of Harper & Row, Publishers, Inc.

ical novel, The Bell Jar, *which dealt with her depression and was published after her suicide. Her highly regarded poetry appeared in three volumes:* The Colossus *(1960) and the posthumous* Ariel *(1965) and* Uncollected Poems *(1965). Because of her impressive poetry, her concern about women's oppression, and her tragic death, she has gained a wide following. In these letters she writes to her mother, Aurelia Plath, who encouraged her to become a writer.*

PRE-READING

1. Read the biographical sketch. To whom are the letters addressed?

2. Check the dates on the letters. How many days are involved? How old was Plath at the time?

3. Read the first paragraph below. Where is Plath at the time of the writing? What is the situation?

The Belmont Hotel, Cape Cod
June 11, 1952

¹ Your amazing telegram [*telegram announcing $500* Mademoiselle *prize for "Sunday at the Mintons',"* which I forwarded*] came just as I was scrubbing tables in the shady interior of The Belmont dining room. I was so excited that I screamed and actually threw my arms around the head waitress who no doubt thinks I am rather insane! Anyhow, psychologically, the moment couldn't have been better. I felt tired—first night's sleep in new places never *are* peaceful—and I didn't get much! To top it off, I was the only girl waitress here, and had been scrubbing furniture, washing dishes and silver, lifting tables, etc. since 8 a.m. Also, I just learned since I am completely inexperienced, I am not going to be working in the main dining room, but in the "side hall" where the managers and top hotel brass eat. So, tips will no doubt net much less during the summer and the company be less interesting. So I was beginning to worry about money when your telegram came. God! To think "Sunday at the Mintons' " is *one* of *two* prize stories to be put in a big national slick!!! Frankly, I can't believe it!

² The first thing I thought of was: Mother can keep her intersession money and buy some pretty clothes and a special trip or something! At least I get a winter coat and extra special suit out of the Mintons. I *think* the prize is $500!!!!!!!!!

³ ME! Of all people! . . .

⁴ So it's really looking up around here, now that I don't have to be scared stiff about money . . . Oh, I say, even if my feet kill me after this first week, and I drop 20 trays, I will have the beach, boys to bring me beer, sun, and young gay companions. What a life.

⁵ Love, your crazy old daughter. (Or as Eddie said: "One hell of a sexy dame"!)

x x x Sivvy

* Aurelia Plath's note.

June 12, 1952

⁶ No doubt after I catch up on sleep, and learn to balance trays high on my left hand, I'll feel much happier. As it is now, I feel stuck in the midst of a lot of loud, brassy Irish Catholics, and the only way I can jolly myself is to say, "Oh, well, it's only for a summer, and I can maybe write about them all." At least I've got a new name for my next protagonist—Marley, a gabby girl who knows her way around but good. The ratio of boys to girls has gotten less and less, so I'll be lucky if I get tagged by the youngest kid here. Lots of the girls are really wise, drinking flirts. As for me, being the conservative, quiet, gracious type, I don't stand much chance of dating some of the cutest ones . . . If I can only get "in" as a pal with these girls, and never for a minute let them know I'm the gentle intellectual type, it'll be O.K.

⁷ As for the *Mlle* news, I don't think it's really sunk in yet. I felt sure they made a mistake, or that you'd made it up to cheer me. The big advantage will be that I won't have to worry about earning barely $300 this summer. I would really have been sick otherwise. I can't wait till August when I can go casually down to the drug store and pick up a slick copy of *Mlle*, flip to the index, and see ME, one of two college girls in the U.S.!

⁸ Really, when I think of how I started it over spring vacation, polished it at school, and sat up till midnight in the Haven House kitchen typing it amidst noise and chatter, I can't get over how the story soared to where it did. One thing about *Mlle* college fiction—although that great one last year by the Radcliffe girl was tremendous and realistic—I remembered the first issue I read where there were two queer part-fantasies, one about the hotel the woman kept for queer people, and the other about an elderly married couple. So I guess the swing of the pendulum dictated something like good old Henry and Elizabeth Minton. Elizabeth has been floating around in my head in her lavender dress, giggling very happily about her burst into the world of print. She always wanted to show Henry she could be famous if she ever worked at it!

⁹ One thing I am partly scared and partly curious about is Dick's reaction when he reads the story in print. I'm glad Dick hasn't read it yet, but Henry started out by being him and Elizabeth me (and they grew old and related in the process). But nevertheless I wonder if Dick will recognize his dismembered self! It's funny how one always, somewhere, has the germ of reality in a story, no matter how fantastic . . .

¹⁰ I get great pleasure out of sharing it [*her feeling about the story*] with *you*, who really understand how terribly much it means as a tangible testimony that I *have* got a germ of writing ability even if *Seventeen* has forgotten about it. The only thing, I probably won't have a chance to win *Mlle* again, so I'll try for a guest editorship maybe next year or my senior year, and set my sights for the *Atlantic*. God, I'm glad I can talk about it with you—probably you're the only outlet that I'll have that won't get tired of my talking about writing . . .

[11] Speaking again of Henry and Liz, it was a step for me to a story where the protagonist isn't always ME, and proved that I am beginning to use imagination to transform the actual incident. I was scared that would never happen, but I think it's an indication that my perspective is broadening.

[12] Sometimes I think—heck, I don't know why I didn't stay home all summer, writing, doing physical science, and having a small part-time job. I could "afford" to now, but it doesn't do much good to yearn about that, I guess. Although it would have been nice. Oh well, I'll cheer up. I love you.

Your own Sivvy

June 15, 1952

Dear Mother,

[13] . . . Do write me letters, Mommy, because I am in a very dangerous state of feeling sorry for myself . . . Just at present, life is awful. *Mademoiselle* seems quite unreal, and I am exhausted, scared, incompetent, unenergetic and generally low in spirits . . . Working in side hall puts me apart, and I feel completely uprooted and clumsy. The more I see the main hall girls expertly getting special dishes, fixing shaved ice and fruit, etc., the more I get an inferiority complex and feel that each day in side hall leaves me further behind . . . But as tempted as I am to be a coward and escape by crawling back home, I have resolved to give it a good month's trial—till July 10 . . . Don't worry about me, but do send me little pellets of advice now and then.

June 24, 1952

[14] . . . Last night I went on a "gang" birthday party at the "Sand Bar" where we sang and talked for a few hours. There were about forty of us kids from the hotel. I managed by some magic to get myself seated next to a fellow in his first year at Harvard Law—and he was just a dear . . . The best part was when we came back. It was a beautiful clear starry night, and Clark went in to get me two of his sweaters to wear because it was cold, and brought out a book of T. S. Eliot's poems. So we sat on a bench where I could just barely read the print, and he put his head in my lap and I read aloud to him for a while. Most nice. The only thing is I am so inclined to get fond of someone who will do things with me like that—always inclined to be too metaphysical and serious conversationally—that's my main trouble . . . So glad to hear the check from *Mlle* is real. I hardly could believe it. Just now I am mentally so disorganized that I can't retain knowledge or think at all. The work is still new enough to be tiring, what with three changes a day into uniforms, and I am so preoccupied by mechanics of living and people that I can't yet organize and assimilate all the chaos of experience pouring in on me. In spite of everything, I still have my good old sense of humor and manage to laugh a good deal of the time . . . I'll make the best of whatever comes my way.

ANALYTICAL READING

1. Is the tone of these letters reminiscent of that in Anne Morrow Lindbergh's letter? Are there similarities in the writing techniques?

2. Would you classify the language as formal or informal? Cite examples from the work to support your choice.

3. What is the relationship between "Sivvy" and her mother? How is this revealed?

REFLECTING

Point: Is there one subject or theme that runs through all four letters? Are there other ideas common to all the letters? Discuss.

Organization: In the first letter, how does Plath organize the material? What devices does she use to move the discussion from one paragraph to the next?

Support: What methods does Plath use to support her points? How does she achieve a conversational style?

Synthesis: The letters dwell on Plath's adjustment to her new situation. Relate this to the Lindbergh selections. Does it seem odd that a girl with such a poetic nature should be so concerned about money? Why or why not?

Evaluation: Did you find the letters interesting? Why or why not? Do they sound natural or affected? Do you find any clue in the letters to Plath's suicide eleven years later?

FROM READING TO WRITING

1. Write a letter about a current problem to someone you feel is completely sympathetic to you.

2. Write a letter to someone close to you concerning a recent triumph you've had, such as an A grade, a job advancement, or a part in a play. Try to write as if you were telling the person about it face to face.

AN OLD MAN'S JOYS AND FEARS
Alan H. Olmstead

BIOGRAPHICAL SKETCH

Alan H. Olmstead (1910–   ) became editor of the Manchester Evening Herald *in 1941 and also wrote a triweekly column for other Connecticut papers, including* The Connecticut Yankee, *which still features his column. In addition, he is*

FROM Alan H. Olmstead, *Threshold: The First Days of Retirement* (New York: Harper & Row, 1975), pp. 57–63, 113–114. Copyright © 1975 by Alan H. Olmstead. Reprinted by permission of Harper & Row, Publishers, Inc.

the author of several unsigned essays for The New Yorker's *"Talk of the Town"*
section. During the first six months of his recent retirement, he kept a diary—
published under the title Threshold—*to record "some of the disappointments,*
pleasures, and reflections of a new traveler into that state of joblessness sometimes
known as the Golden Age."

PRE-READING

1. From the biographical sketch, what do you find out about Olmstead's situation
    as he starts the journal? Why do you think the name of the book is *Threshold*?

2. From the titles of the individual entries, what can you guess about the nature of
    their content? Are you sure you know the meanings of *euphoria* and *via?*

Old Man's Puppy

Thursday, Oct. 26

¹ After some noonday carpentry, which gave a rough finish to the dog
house, and an afternoon of search which ranged from the Connecticut Humane Society's kennels to a final pet shop in Hartford, we came home with a
puppy—a dark-faced, relatively unmarked shepherd-collie. She is, we hope,
essentially the same dog we have always had on the place. Within five seconds
of being put down on her new home ground, she had the heart of whichever
one of us she ran to with tail wagging in a beginning of all the games she and
we were going to play together. Still, this was not the usual kind of puppy
homecoming. Hitherto, much of the tenderness of bringing a new puppy
home was rooted in the fact that the puppy was being brought home to a
child. The child and the puppy would grow up together, in mutual happy
innocence, until they came to that tragic parting of the ways resulting from
the difference in their life spans. The death of the dog who had once been
their puppy—that was often, for the children, their first introduction to the
ineffably sweet sadness of death, an emotional experience which at once awed
and absorbed them by its compulsive, convulsive powers. This time, although
SJ is home for vacation and was reenacting her own previous bringing home
of her first puppy, this was not another child's puppy. It was an old man's
puppy which came home today. The games she gets to play will be old man's
games. He is to be her chief companion, and she will have to listen as he
whispers to her some of his old man's problems. There is a different strain of
sentiment in this kind of relationship, because now the life span of the puppy
and the life span of the human being paired with the puppy have just about
an equal number of years to run, if both are lucky. She is a lovely, gentle little
lady, and we hope to find her a happy kind of name, one fit for a companion-
ship to the end of a journey.

Euphoria, Via Yo-Yo

Friday, Oct. 27

2 There is no better therapy than that of building a dog house, and no better healer of the spirit than a puppy. Between the two, those doldrums— that spell of depression in which, feeling myself lashed by the world and its circumstance into a series of petty defeats, I also began lashing myself—have disappeared. The human spirit can stand only so much of one kind of feeling and then turns and twists, by whatever process it may take, by whatever degree of irrationality may be required, to something different. The dog house stands there, in front of the garage, a momentarily successful enterprise created by saw and hammer and nails. The puppy, still uneasy about unknown worlds, still flatteringly in love with the person it knows best in place of its mother, plays safely in the yard, away from the damage it might do gardens, away from the lifelong danger waiting for it out in the street. If a recovery of the spirit is inevitable and is going to happen anyway, these are at least substantive ingredients for the change. But the truth is that if it hadn't been a dog house and a puppy it would have been something else which produced this turn from depression to euphoria. Strip it down to its essential movements, and the human mood is as complicated as a yo-yo.

Afraid of Halloween

Tuesday, Oct. 31

3 The fear of the unknown is most powerful among the very young and the very old. With the very young the great curative, curiosity, usually comes to the rescue. With old people there is almost no curiosity as to which particular young neighborhood identity may be hiding beneath the Halloween mask at the door. With old people there is a dread, in this era of violence, of the possible appearance of tricksters a little older and meaner than children. With old people there are magnified memories, from past Halloweens, of such things as the soft vegetables splattered against the door, or the homemade bomb exploded in the mail box, or of the night long ago when adult friends, in playful mood, played their roles so well we didn't realize who they were until they had been hulking large and strange inside our home for too many strained minutes. But the real trouble with old people on Halloween is that there are no young people inside the house to go to the door, to play the guessing game with the tots, to muster the spirit to answer and mingle in the challenges of Halloween. So there comes the time when, instead of having jack-o'-lanterns burning in the window, the people in the house sit huddled into their deepest chairs, down below window-sill level, with as few lights as possible showing anywhere and no outside light at all, and try to let a television program distract their minds from the possible imminence of a knock on

some door. Tonight the shameful, craven story was this: sitting in such fear, neither of us moved immediately when the one knock of the evening—a timid, two-thump-only knock—did come, and by the time one of us got to the door and turned on the outside light, what must have been a very small goblin had gone. We felt sorry for the small goblin, but more sorry for ourselves.

To You Coming After

Saturday, Dec. 16

[4] Entry after entry, day after day, reveals this diarist totally wrapped up in the narrowing perceptions of his own particular station in life. Has he nothing to offer except this gossipy exchange of pensioner experience with other "Golden Agers"? Is this the most that life is about—to get this far, and then play the last few innings of the game from a contemplative wheel chair? What if there stumble into this diary some younger people not looking for pensioner experience, but drawn by love or curiosity to see what it may be like, between these covers? Has the old man nothing to say to or for them? Yes, indeed, all you who are coming after, and here is a slice of it. One of the sweet sadnesses very high in the feeling of all us older ones is that of a worried affection for all the younger people who are still strung out in the struggle along the path, who do not know their ending, or how they are going to make it. Every birth that comes after one is at once a miracle and a cruelty; one rejoices in the new life; one anticipates the sorrow the innocence thus born must inevitably encounter. One has to feel guilty, some of the time, for ever having helped bring anybody into this sadistic world. So I, the diarist, am sad for all you young people, the ones I know and love and those I merely observe, and I have this wish for all of you, that life may be as kind to you as it can, and that you all, for your part, may be as kind to one another as you can. I wish mercy upon you all, and joy that is seasoned with proportion and sense so it won't decay on you, and I beg of you not to expect too much happiness from any source. At the same time I fiercely enjoin you not to be too cautious in guarding yourself against those moments of beauty and tenderness, or those instincts for perceiving potential nobility and dignity in the human behavior, which keep lingering on from your childhood. You have to learn to take all things together, layering and reflecting one upon another, compensating, marrying, conserving, spending, juggling, borrowing—and never take any final verdict from either evidence or experience but keep playing the possibility that some day, if you are lucky, you may end up loving and wishing well to the humanity in everybody. You may then discover that however you audit the human experience, it somehow manages to come out a plus, too, like people. Run along, now, to your young busyness, to your terrible maturity, to your first blank awarenesses of the end, but with your options of the spirit always open, to whichever of the ages of man is next for you.

ANALYTICAL READING

1. What is the general tone of the selections? Compare it with that of the Lind-bergh and Plath selections. Do you feel that the writer of this journal is ad-dressing a specific or general audience? Why?

2. What is the writer's attitude toward his dog? toward children? toward young people? toward retirement? How does he communicate this?

3. What kind of person do you think the writer is? Support your answer by citing specific passages that illuminate his personality.

REFLECTING

Point: Is there a message or philosophy contained in the selections? If so, is it one from which all readers can benefit, or just retired people?

Organization: How does the writer organize the individual entries? Does each contain its own unity of idea? Discuss. What theme holds them all together? Describe the effect of the last sentence in each.

Support: Does Olmstead use contrast and comparison in supporting his theme? If so, where and how?

Synthesis: Do these selections also deal with adjustment? Compare them with the Lindbergh and Plath selections. Does Olmstead make you more aware of your relationship to your pet and your Halloween experiences? Does Olmstead regret old age? Or does he accept it and if so, how?

Evaluation: What do you think of the advice given to young people? Which selec-tion did you like the best? the least? Why? Do you find Olmstead's writing to be mature, interesting, perceptive, and sincere? Justify your opinion by citing examples.

FROM READING TO WRITING

1. Write a journal entry about an experience that represented a transition in your life. Try to write it so that it not only helps you to better understand your feelings but also might help someone else to make a similar adjustment.

2. Write a journal entry about your acquisition of a new pet. If possible, write several sequential entries, tying them together with a common theme.

3. Try to analyze why Halloween was exciting to you as a child. Was it only the candy you received that appealed to you?

THE ROAD LESS TRAVELED
Michael Parfit

BIOGRAPHICAL SKETCH

Michael Parfit (1947–   ) was born in London and grew up in England, the United States, and Brazil. In 1971 he graduated from the University of Southern California with a degree in journalism. Parfit began free-lance writing in 1971 and

FROM Michael Parfit, "The Road Less Traveled," *The New York Times Magazine,* July 25, 1976, pp. 12, 16–17, 19, 22. © 1976 by The New York Times Company. Reprinted by permission.

since then has published in The New York Times, *the* Christian Science Monitor, *and the* Wall Street Journal. *He is also a regular contributor to* New Times.

PRE-READING

1. What does the title mean to you? As you read, see how close your meaning is to Parfit's.

2. Skim the first paragraph. Does it give you an idea of what the subject is? How does it relate to the title?

3. What in the biographical sketch hints that Parfit might prefer independence and solitude?

[1] Discovering backpacking is a bit like leaving home for the first time. There's a mixture of pain and new freedom, and your family is not sure it approves. The comparison is imperfect, of course; the pain of the hike is only physical, and from backpacking you always return. But there's a root similarity. In wilderness, as in that first apartment, you find independence that you didn't know was there.

[2] Consider the core experience, shared even by Colin Fletcher, whose book "The Complete Walker" is still the best how-to in the backpacking field. You have come to the end of a dirt road in mountainous country. Beyond the fringe of the road's end is an understory of laced willows, thorned wild roses and gooseberry, out of which rise trees hung with moss. This, you realize, is the extent of man's reach; beyond here is the territory of the weasel, the rat, the bear, the rattlesnake and—who knows?—the wolf. Beyond here you dare not travel.

[3] Then, just as you secure these boundaries in your mind and turn away, the brush parts, and there appears a human being of normal stature who calmly states that he or, just as likely, she has been back in there for a week. It's like an unexpected door opening in stone. It happened to me in the California Sierras in 1968, and though the person was a vegetarian who looked and talked like an oboe and appeared somewhat off his feed, the jolting of vision that he produced opened a new concept of spaciousness and freedom in me which, after a few hundred miles of subsequent back-country travel, I retain.

[4] So today, Monday, I am preparing a pack for a trip into a minor wilderness about 100 miles north of Los Angeles. The place I am going is not a mecca like California's John Muir Trail or the Eastern states' Appalachian Trail, so I won't call unnecessary attention to it by name as if its qualities were rare. It's just an empty place of mountain, desert and river valley, preserved largely because a century of settlers found it inhospitable, and I'll be spending four days there—not much time, but enough to slake my restlessness.

[5] As if to assert its domain, the urban life I am temporarily quitting rushes around me as I pack: film to buy, letters to write, errands to attend to in advance, people to call. I calm this storm of preparation by chanting a kind

of rosary, a list supplied, thoughtfully, by a backpacking store that sells all the items the list requires. In beads, it would dangle to the floor. "Pocketknife, snakebite kit, adhesive tape, aspirin, insect repellent, compass, matches, needles, fishhooks, string, rope, pliers, mirrors, sleeping bag, ground cloth, foam mattress, short pants, long pants, poncho, toilet paper, hat, rope, cooking pots, primus stove, food, tent . . ."

[6] Civilization, which has contributed the aluminum-frame belted backpack to ease wilderness travel, has now gone the other way by providing useless weight in the form of guidebooks that detail wilderness routes. The books are complete with graphs of trail ups and downs which resemble fever charts and have a vaguely similar function, expressing degrees of sweat. Fine for office daydreams, but destructive of mood and mystery in the manner of fluorescent tubes hung in catacombs. This way, ladies; please mind the abyss.

[7] I will take, instead, the ultimate symbol, a topographic map. And I will flout the list and leave my six-pound, two-person tent behind. This is my tribute to the wilderness prophet John Muir, founder of the Sierra Club, who carried only dried bread and tea in a burlap sack. Besides, in this wilderness, in this season, it absolutely never rains.

[8] Tuesday morning. A beginning. Like a kid crying "Salvation!" I expect a miracle from the first steps, a sudden relief of worldly burdens the first time I turn a corner and cut away from the road. It never happens. I have put on the pack, 35 pounds, tied on Vibram-soled boots, crossed a small river called the Manzana, walked for an hour and a half and so far feel only continued restlessness, the urge to push faster than my new weight will let me, and, from a fold of sock, the start of a little pain. Perhaps it's like meditation, or tennis, the inner game: Ask too much of it and you lose it all, double-faulting into the wind. There's more release than grasp in the sport, and it all comes slowly, like the accumulating miles.

[9] The trail winds along the Manzana, named after apple trees but lined with oaks. It is summer, the dry season in this part of the country, and the river is low and warm, making its way languidly from pool to pool, thick with algae the color of straw. There are small, hungry trout in these pools, and when I stop for a drink they gather around my immersed fingers and nibble at my nails and my ring. The sensation is strange, like being kissed by tiny people, and it creates a false but delightful feeling of communication.

[10] I flip a white pebble in the pool and watch them fight over it, then share some crumbs of my "gorp," a mixture of nuts, raisins, granola and M&M's, which they devour like piranhas. Most of them, of course, will die as the river shrivels in the summer's heat, so there's no point in becoming too attached. Still, when the sun finally persuades me to remove my boots and swim in the pool, the little trout kiss my feet.

[11] Later, drying on a rock, I study the "topo" map, a maze of contour lines speckled with interesting names: Cold Spring, Manzana Narrows, Big Cone Spruce Camp, White Ledge, Hurricane Deck, Sulphur Spring, Sweetwater

Canyon, the Sisquoc River. The last holds more promise than just the ring of its Chumash Indian name: It is the heart of this wilderness, and so becomes my goal.

[12] You begin a backpack determined to subvert normal, goal-oriented existence to the point of walking onward with nowhere to go, and then you find that goals are necessary to keep you going. Without them, you'd sit down on a rock after a mile, pant, and eat all your gorp. So I find my devotion to reaching the Sisquoc grows as my body tires.

[13] I am climbing, weaving back and forth up a slope covered with manzanita, the red-skinned savage bush, and dry grass, on which occasional scarlet buglers, small elongated wildflowers, blare silent messages to invisible bees. I had forgotten, as I always do, that the most intense experience of a backpack is its labor. I am not spending my day examining the sublime filigree of nature; I'm spending it in toil, sweat running down my back and in my eyes, watching only the dust of the trail a yard ahead, not for the detail of its diatomaceous soil, but for loose obstacles.

[14] But here is an interesting paradox. The longer I trudge, committing myself to the achievement of the Sisquoc, and the more important the goal becomes to the maintenance of the hike, the less it really matters, except as a device, like a shoehorn to pry me out of laziness and get me moving. If I rest a minute, the desire to get there fidgets at my ankles, but once I'm up and hurting, it disappears in the intensity of the moment.

[15] In the end there is a summit—White Ledge—and I remove the pack and lie back on hot white sandstone. As I luxuriate upon it—who would have thought stone could be so comfortable?—here, too, is a kind of communication. I do not condone talking to plants (except in whispers), much less to rock, but for a short time up here I feel a kind of physical unity with the earth which, I suspect, could be described as mystical and thus robbed of meaning. I am an Aquarius on stone made by a sea, smoothed by rain. Rock and water, uplifted, tearing down, rebuilding, one grain at a time. For a moment here as I lie in hot darkness under my hat, the relationship seems alive beneath me, and my role somehow a participant, but the feeling escapes me. Perhaps it is just a delusion of fatigue; as my body recovers, the Sisquoc, now visible down the canyon, beckons again.

[16] I skid down inclines in matted chaparral of greasewood, more pleasantly known as chemise, and manzanita, through a transition zone of grass, dry and white in the late-afternoon light, into the belly of the canyon. Here, although the creek that slithers over bedrock has already gone south for the year, is a green confusion. The naturalist in me, an amateur of near incompetence, delights and rebels in the same acre. . . .

.   .   .

[17] On Wednesday I reach the Sisquoc, hiking down White Ledge canyon in avenues of chaparral to a camp 13 miles from the nearest road, and, temporarily out of goals, I enter the best and least time-conscious period of back-

packing. Now I can relieve myself of the pack's burden and settle in, attending to numerous small and agreeable tasks. I gather firewood—bits of dry manzanita and Digger-pine cones sticky with resin which burn with a hot red flame and a smell of oil. I reorganize my pack, taking out my nesting cooking pots and a box of rice for this evening's meal.

[18] A backpacking menu is a study in lightness. An incredible selection of freeze-dried foods is available in the multitude of backpacking stores now sprouting up everywhere like mushrooms in damp soil. You can even get freeze-dried strawberry ice cream, if you must. But I usually stick to one-pot meals that stick to me. I don't go as far as some backpackers in my obsession with ounces, cutting the margins off maps and the handle off my toothbrush, but simplicity is part of the joy.

[19] After unrolling my three-pound Dacron sleeping bag and my foam pad—much warmer and only slightly less comfortable than an air mattress— I prospect for a sleeping spot, a pleasant job which involves several periods of prone contemplation. Having thoroughly tested a level bit of ground near an oak, I spend the rest of the day hiking packless down the river, fishing for trout with small, gray flies and considerable success. The river is low, small enough to cross on dry stones, but it pools up under sandstone and shale cliffs, and here the 10-inch trout gather in clear green water to feed. It's like fishing in an aquarium and requires no effort.

[20] In fact, in comparison with yesterday's sweat, this whole day seems to be an orgy of ease, of heavy-lidded laziness in the sun. I have no responsibility but the maintenance of my own life, so this is deeper than ordinary relaxation, which I usually take fitfully against a background of impending decisions. I sit on stones, listen to water, walk, wade, catch fish, and dawdle, while the day slips away. And when I return to camp at dusk with half a dozen trout on a willow-branch stringer, I am happily weary and ready for sleep. "When my days are over," an anonymous backpacker has written the wilderness register near my camp, "bury me here." I can imagine no purer rest.

[21] As the sun drops like a comet into a bank of clouds over White Ledge, I eat rice and trout so fresh they curl in the pan, and I savor the solitude. . . .

· · ·

[22] I go to sleep content, with only the company of mice rustling in oak leaves and frogs on the river singing in rhyme, but late that night I am awakened by a sound I have heard too often: the soft patter—as meaningful as an adder's hiss—of rain.

[23] My inner clock immediately rusts into immobility, and I prepare for a long, slow dawn. How many times have I done this—gone out into dry country with only faith in the forecast as my shelter? And how many times has it rained? . . .

[24] Few of the minor regrets of life are as poignant as wishing you had brought a tent. In gentle rain like this, dampness accumulates slowly with an

inexorable lack of mercy, giving you enough time for anticipation and remorse before engulfing you in simple misery.

[25] Tonight, though, I go through all the preliminaries without the catharsis: Before enough rain has fallen to penetrate the sleeping bag, the storm pauses and I go back to sleep, humid but fundamentally dry. And when I awake to an earthenware sky, I have enough time to find a small cave before the rain returns.

[26] In and out of sunshine, the rest of the trip drifts toward its end. But on the last day, Friday, I am caught by a new compulsion: to get out, back to the city. Ease has aged, and suddenly I am wondering, What's been going on out there in the human turmoil, what's the news? Without a radio, which would be sacrilege, I'm as remote as a star, and anything can happen. Some friends went backpacking for two weeks in early August 1974; you know what they missed. When they came out and the papers were talking about President *Ford,* they felt like Rip van Winkle. In this sense, backpacking amplifies the pace of life by showing you how much goes on while you're away. Often, instead of returning from the back country filled with a new serenity, I come out scrabbling to catch up. In the wilderness, as well as outside, change commands, and this valley is full of the evidence of fire and flood, but compared to the land the human metabolism flashes like gunpowder in the flint-shadowed pan.

[27] So I hustle away over White Ledge and back down the Manzana, knowing, in the end, that backpacking is little more than a partial escape—a retreat into the simplicity of hard work and physical pleasure which allows you to cheat on those taxes levied against you by civilization that you pay in pace and pressure. If you want to retain your hold on what we pompously call reality, you have to come back, hang the pack in the shed like a husk of skin and again confront the 20th century. So if you think of backpacking as salvation, it'll disappoint you. All it does is offer a small door in stone, marked Visitors Only, into another world.

ANALYTICAL READING

1. As you read, did you make yourself aware of the events in each day? Can you outline them?

2. Can you describe the place that Parfit chose for the trip?

3. Is Parfit's account written only for himself or to a larger audience? What part does his tone and word choice play in revealing his concept of audience?

4. Does he make use of figurative language such as analogy, simile, or metaphor? Cite some examples.

5. Were you aware of the variety of sentence structure? If not, examine paragraph 8 and discuss the sentences in it.

6. Did you learn anything about backpacking? equipment? cooking techniques? What does information such as this contribute to this article?

7. What is the writer's attitude toward backpacking? How does the first paragraph set this up?

8. Can you give the meaning of the following words: *topographic, catacombs, abyss, chaparral, filigree, paradox, orgy*? Why is the word *orgy* particularly appropriate?

9. Explain the paradox the author mentions in paragraph 13.

REFLECTING

Point: Summarize in one sentence what you think the message of the article is. How does Parfit create interest in the opening paragraphs?

Organization: Obviously, the author uses chronological organization. But does he find other ways to organize some of the material? Demonstrate.

Support: Can you find specific sentences that act as support to the main point Parfit makes about backpacking? How does he support the attitude set up in the opening paragraph? What details suggest that he is writing to an audience that has little experience with backpacking?

Synthesis: Does Parfit's trip remind you of a backpacking or camping trip you have taken yourself or heard about? How?

Evaluation: What was your reaction to the work? Did you find it interesting, dull, informative? Can you support your emotional reaction by citing specific evidence? How effective is the last paragraph? What is your attitude toward the writer?

FROM READING TO WRITING

1. Write a journal entry about an event you plan for next weekend. Try to emulate Parfit's inclusion of instructional materials without making it into a "how-to" paper. Experiment with fresh, figurative language.

2. If you've kept a journal of a trip taken in the past, choose three or four consecutive entries and revise them for a general audience.

3. Write about your first trip away from home: your preparations, your apprehensions, your feelings of strangeness, your disappointments, your pleasant experiences, your realizations. You might, for example, write about a trip with the Scouts or the Sierra Club, a trip to the beach, high school class trips.

A DAY IN APPALACHIA
Lady Bird Johnson

BIOGRAPHICAL SKETCH

Lady Bird (Claudia) Johnson (1912–   ) was born in Texas. She received Bachelor of Arts and Bachelor of Journalism degrees from the University of Texas. In 1934 she married Lyndon Baines Johnson, who became President in 1963. In

FROM Lady Bird Johnson, *A White House Diary* (New York: Holt, Rinehart & Winston, 1970), pp. 493–99. Copyright © 1970 by Claudia T. Johnson. Reprinted by permission of Holt, Rinehart & Winston, Publishers.

addition to performing the duties of the wife of a national politician, she has owned and operated a radio-TV station in Austin, Texas, and since her husband's death has managed several cattle ranches. She has been active in conservation, beautification, and humanitarian projects, receiving many awards and honors for her work. A White House Diary, *in which this entry appears, is an account of her years as First Lady.*

PRE-READING

1. What historical importance can you infer from the title of the book from which this entry was taken?

2. Does the biographical sketch indicate that this trip is part of a pattern in the writer's life?

3. Skim the first two paragraphs. What can you tell about the purpose of the entry? What group of people is Mrs. Johnson writing about? What time of the year is it?

Tuesday, March 14

Asheville, North Carolina
¹ Today was the fullest, most dramatic day of our three-day trip through Appalachia to see Lyndon's programs on education translated into people. John Gardner, Secretary of Health, Education and Welfare, accompanied us. We woke early in the lovely mountain resort residence of the Governor of North Carolina where Governor and Mrs. Dan Moore were our hosts. Mrs. Moore had suggested that we have breakfast at the dining room table. I was down a bit late for delicious ham and grits and hot biscuits, and could with clear conscience throw caution to the wind because I was going to need all the strength I could get today.
² Then into Trailways buses—two busloads—including Dick Graham, Director of the Teacher Corps, school officials, and more than forty press members. It was a two-hour drive, and they briefed us as we went along on the history, purpose, and operation of the Teacher Corps. The heart of it seems to be to put really good teachers in direct contact with the most needy students, such as you would find at Rio Grande City, Texas, or in Harlem or in the landlocked hills of western North Carolina.
³ Youngsters with a certain amount of rearing and family background can get along with a teacher on a thirty-to-one ratio. But where the school is the principal resource of the children, the only hope is for more teachers, and in that treadworn phrase, for more dedicated ones, to give each child personal attention. One teacher said that since the Teacher Corps had come, for the first time in his life "I've been teaching—not just policing a schoolroom full."
⁴ Mrs. Moore bravely went every mile. People were lined up along the street, waving and smiling, and a great number of flags were out. Always, always, that gives me a lift of the heart.

⁵ We stopped first at the Sylva-Webster High School—a consolidated school—actually out in the country. The entire student body was lined up along the highway and we couldn't bear just to pass them by, so we stopped, got out, and greeted them.

⁶ The road wound up and up into the Appalachian Mountains—breathtakingly beautiful, still in the grip of winter, thickly wooded with balsam and other evergreens, hickory and hardwoods, and whole masses of rhododendron and laurel. Rushing mountain streams came tumbling down in cascade, and then flowed down the valley in swift, clear little rivers, sometimes spanned by walking bridges leading over to a house across the hollow. The maples were just budding in the valleys and halfway up the mountains, making a red tracery, a promise of spring.

⁷ At Canada Township the paved road ended and we got into three smaller schoolbuses for the winding, narrow dirt road to the Mathises' house. This was the family we were going to visit to see just what effect the Teachers Corps had on individuals, to show the raw material the Teachers Corps students had to work with—the background from which they came.

⁸ At first I had flinched at the idea. It sounded like an insensitive exposure of their poverty, a crass use of them. Liz had visited Canada Township and talked with Gertie Moss, the principal. She had come back convinced, and had convinced me, that if we were really to show what the Teachers Corps did, this was the best way. As for the Mathises, and all those like them in the hills and hollows, they were, for all their poverty, proud, hospitable, deeply interested, not in the least overwhelmed at the thought of our visit.

⁹ So there we were, walking down the little trail among the hemlock and rhododendron—Gertie Moss and I leading the crowd—hopping on stepping stones over Needy Creek (well-named), bending over to go through a rail fence into the yard where the Mathis family was lined up to meet us. Mr. Mathis, a grizzled wood cutter in his forties, and Mrs. Mathis greeted me with lively interest. Their seven children, from about six to nineteen, lined up around them in front of their two-room wooden shack in the hollow. A hound dog lounged in the yard, a few chickens scratched. There was one lone apple tree and some discarded rubber tires in which flowers had grown last summer.

¹⁰ They had a ten-acre farm and they made less than two thousand dollars a year, from that part-time work, wood cutting. But they had kept the seven children in school most of the time. All of them were small for their ages, and all of them had bad teeth. Every time a mouth opened, you knew that to go into the world and get a job, they would have to have not only training, a skill, but also a dentist.

¹¹ Mrs. Mathis asked us in, very brightly and comfortably. They really were glad to see us and apparently did not feel invaded by the army of fifty or more television and newspaper reporters in the front yard. Inside we met her elderly mother in her eighties, Mrs. Minnie Alexander. There were several sofas covered with throws, all with the springs nearly out, a potbellied stove

and a curtain that led to the back bedroom, where presumably, there were beds, although I am sure four or five of the family must have slept on those sofas.

¹² I had feared the conversation would be strained, but it wasn't. I asked if there were fish in these beautiful mountain streams. Mr. Mathis said, "Yes, mountain trout." There was a TV set. We talked about each other's favorite program. And Mr. Mathis said hospitably, "When the President comes on, we just kept him right on, listen to him just like it was a program."

¹³ Mrs. Mathis told us what a job it was to get the children off to school in the morning. And then, most important of all, she talked about the Teachers Corps. "It's grand. The children like the ones at school. We met them when we were up there at a meeting one night." Then she asked, "Do you have a garden on your ranch?" And I talked about our corn and tomatoes, and she about their corn, cabbage, and beans.

¹⁴ There were John Gardner and Liz and I and a pool reporter and all the Mathises in the tiny room. I gave her packages of preserves and honey from the LBJ Ranch, wrapped incongruously in the elegant embossed paper of the White House. Mrs. Mathis told me, with a lively spirit, that I ought to see the country in the springtime when the apple tree was in bloom and later when the rhododendron was out.

¹⁵ What keeps these people in the hills? It's beautiful country, but is it love of the land, or fear of the outside?

¹⁶ We all walked up to the schoolbus and the Mathises piled in with us, and we rode back to the long, low, brick structure that is the result of consolidating six one-room schoolhouses in as many hollows, bringing together 105 students where all eight grades are taught by four teachers.

¹⁷ As we came up the hill, we saw floating above the school the Stars and Stripes and beside it the flag of North Carolina. I felt a sudden, fierce elation. The school was the hope of the community—probably the only hope these mountain people had to acquire a skill that would enable them to go out into the world and make a living. And if you acquired a skill and wanted to stay here in these beautiful hills, what was there to do? School teaching, but what else? It was a grim, wracking problem. You looked at the people and the houses, and you felt the place was a dead end, that several generations of living here had had a self-defeating, brutalizing effect.

¹⁸ There was a ceremony in front of the school underneath the flags. The Glee Club sang "America, the Beautiful" and naturally, "Nothing Could Be Finer than to Be in Carolina." And then the children did a square dance, and I greeted the Head Start students.

¹⁹ The high point of the day was introducing the Job Corps Teachers— three men and a plump, sweet-faced woman, Mrs. Ramsey, who was their leader. Gertie Moss made a welcoming talk, and I answered, haltingly but earnestly, trying to look into the eyes of first one youngster on the right and then another one on the left or some bearded father in overalls out front. I tried to tell them how important it was that they stay in school. "There is no

more important journey you can take than your daily journey into the classroom." One of the children, I had heard, walks two and a half miles before he catches the schoolbus at 7. Often he leaves home by lantern light and has to use the lantern before he reaches home in the evening.

20 With only about twelve hundred members of the Teachers Corps in all the far-flung places like Canada Township, it's a mighty little David for a mighty big Goliath and the legislation is coming up soon. Unless Congress votes the $12 million appropriation, the Teachers Corps will expire in June. I hope we can "walk it across the stage" to expose it to the public and hopefully win support for it.

21 We went inside the school and watched the Teachers Corps in operation. In one room they were using visual-aid machines for faster reading. In another room Mr. Whitmire was cutting the hair of eight-year-old Bobby Carroll Owen. After-hours he cut their hair—"We're a long ways away up here." Gertie Moss had told me the nearest telephone is eleven miles away and nobody in Canada Township gets a newspaper. One intern was giving remedial reading. Another was working with cards with the primer class. I heard they'd put on a Christmas play—the first time ever. And they'd started teaching basketball.

22 Mrs. Moss led me into the cafeteria, and I had a full plate of tasty chicken casserole and green beans, salad, a roll, and dessert. The children also had milk. Mrs. Moss said to me, as though the food were coming to her or her very own family, "Oh, yes, that is one of the things the government has done. We give them a good hot lunch here. And then we serve oatmeal and milk to about thirty of the children who don't have anything at home before they come."

23 By 1:30 we were in cars leaving Canada Township. All that marks it on the main highway is the Mountain Ridge Baptist Church, Brown's General Store, and its heart—the school. I felt as if I understood my country better and also had made a real friend when I shook Gertie Moss' hand. Then we were off down the mountain to Western Carolina College at Cullowhee (an Indian name which means valley of the lilies).

24 We stopped in front of Hunter Library where the President, Dr. Paul Reid, met us, and went inside to meet the staff of this thirty-six hundred-student college. A few years ago there were only six hundred students. Everywhere you looked a new building was going up. Now 65 percent of the teachers in the mountain schools of North Carolina are from Western Carolina College.

25 The reason for this trip was to bring public exposure to the eighteen major measures that Lyndon and the Congress have been able to pass to advance education. At the dedication of the Library, Ruth Graham (Mrs. Billy Graham) gave the invocation. John Gardner made an excellent short speech. Then I made a brief reference to the fact that federal participation in education is not exactly new, going back as far as 1785 in the Land Ordinance, the land grant colleges of the 1860's, and the GI Bill of Rights of our own day. "So

that these things that we are seeing—the Teachers Corps, federal funds for Hunter Library, and new student loan programs, all these programs—are in an old and honored American tradition." I told how Lyndon, whenever he is asked which of his accomplishments he is proudest of, always answers what he's been able to do for education. I ended with a quote from Thomas Wolfe: "To every man his chance—to every man, regardless of his birth, his shining, golden opportunity—to every man the right to live, to work, to be himself, and to become whatever thing his manhood and his vision can combine to make him—this, seeker, is the promise of America."

26 We left for Asheville and were back at the Governor's beautiful western residence a little past 5. I had a real rest—more than an hour. And then up and dressed and ready to go with Secretary John Gardner and Mrs. Moore to Lee Edwards High School for a visit to an adult education class sponsored by the Asheville-Buncombe Technical Institute. Buncombe is a well-known name around here. That talkative, old-time politician was a native of this area, and he added a word to our language.

27 I walked into a class in basic English—thirty or more students, mostly white. The principal had told me that they ranged in age from eighteen to eighty-two and that in the last two years fifty-five hundred Asheville citizens had enrolled! Here the teacher was Mrs. Mildred Smith, a Negro, bright, unruffled, who kept drawing diagrams on the board and getting her class to parse sentences while the battery of cameras and writers moved in. After about ten minutes Mrs. Smith asked me to come up and say a word to the class. It was easy to salute their determination, their get-up-and-go, their drive to go back to school, to make a richer life for themselves and obtain a better job. One of their members stood and responded. He asked me to take back their thanks to the President for this program.

28 Out in the hall where all the other classes had gathered, I saw a great many Negroes, the majority middle-aged, some old. The women outnumbered the men. Liz asked one of them what she did. She said, "I'm a domestic, and I need to know how to read to do my job better." In its different way, this had been one of the most stirring things of the whole trip.

29 From the high school we went to the airport. I walked along the fence shaking hands, and then with a last good-by to Mrs. Moore, I was in the plane that brought us to Nashville and our old and dear friends, Buford and Catherine Ellington, Governor of Tennessee.

30 At last gratefully to bed in the beautiful Tennessee Governor's Mansion. What a day this had been! I wondered about the Mathises and where those seven children would be thirty years from now. Sadly, you are inclined to think the only solution is to get educated and get out, but you wonder why man has managed so ineptly. It's beautiful country and yet on those who live there, generation in and generation out, inter-marrying, the isolation has had a stultifying effect.

31 I hoped it had been good for the newspaper people—their seeing the face of America. It certainly had for me. A young journalism student at North

Carolina College had asked me the inevitable question, "What is it like to be First Lady?" A day like today is the essence of what it is like! One gets to know one's country better. It's a cram course in geography, sociology, and people.

ANALYTICAL READING

1. As you read the diary entry, were you aware of Mrs. Johnson's tone? How did she feel toward the people she met?

2. What did you learn about the physical characteristics of the countryside around Asheville, North Carolina? the schools? the homes? Were you aware of the contrasts between the rich and the poor indicated in the diary entry?

3. As you read, what kind of picture did you form of the narrator? How does this relate to your previous conception of her as a person? Does this say anything about the value of keeping a journal?

4. As you read, did you get any insight into Mrs. Johnson's attitudes toward her husband and his work?

5. As you read, you should have been aware that although much of the entry is narrative in form—chronologically organized from one event to the next—Mrs. Johnson also used description and explanation. Can you cite some examples of the latter two devices?

REFLECTING

Point: What do you think the main point is? Where is it first expressed? Does the writer express other convictions? If so, how are they related to her main point?

Organization: Draw up a brief outline of Mrs. Johnson's schedule. How does it reflect the organizational scheme of the entry?

Support: How do Mrs. Johnson's descriptions contribute to the support she provides for her points? Discuss the effectiveness of the opening sentence. Does it spoil or enhance the account?

Synthesis: Have you had any experience with the Teachers Corps or other government-funded special educational program? If so, how did it compare with Mrs. Johnson's experience? Do you agree or disagree with her conviction of the need for such programs?

Evaluation: Did you find the diary entry effective? biased? convincing? Did you feel that the tour was carefully planned and that Mrs. Johnson's impressions would have been different if her visit had been a surprise? Be able to support your opinions.

FROM READING TO WRITING

1. Visit a special educational facility on campus or in your community, taking notes as you go. Then write a journal entry similar to Mrs. Johnson's: not simply a recounting of the sequence of events, but an evaluation of the situation as well.

2. Tour a depressed neighborhood in your city and then write a journal entry that could be published in the campus newspaper.

3. In the third paragraph, what did the teacher mean who stated that for the first time he had "been teaching—not just policing a schoolroom full"? Write a paper explaining to what extent one of your teachers served mainly as a "police officer," and why.

FOUR HAIKU

PRE-READING

Look up the word *haiku* in the dictionary. As you read, compare the haiku included here with the characteristics given in the dictionary definition.

Old grass clippings sulk
under the damp of sprinklers
and cling to wet feet

Eve Bangerter, 17, Provo, Utah

Robin pulling for
his side of the worm while the
apple stands neutral.

Debbie Whalen, 19, Davenport, Iowa

Poor forsythia,
alone, first flower of spring
in need of a friend.

Nancy Lubars, 14, Clark, N.J.

Sharp sunlight shatters
translucent liquid green and
finds a shy goldfish.

Debbie Gainer, 19, Hamburg, Pa.

ANALYTICAL READING

1. All poetry, especially haiku, attempts to create images. Were you aware of mental pictures forming as you read? What did particular words contribute?

2. Good narrative and descriptive writing is characterized by verbs that "work"— that do more than verbs like *be, have,* and *seem,* which simply connect other sentence parts. How do the verbs in these haiku contribute to the description?

REFLECTING

Point: One of the aims of haiku writing is to produce a sensory image that somehow triggers an intellectual response, that makes a comment about life. Do you think that there is a point or message implicit in any of these haiku? Explain.

Organization: The seventeen-syllable haiku is usually organized into three lines of five, seven, and five syllables. Check the selections to see if they fit this scheme.

Support: In haiku writing, support depends primarily on choosing words that most effectively enhance the image. Do words such as *damp, wet, neutral, alone,* and *shy* act as support?

Synthesis: Do the images in the haiku recall any experiences of your own? Do the poems make them more vivid and meaningful?

Evaluation: Which of the four haiku did you find most effective? Why?

FROM READING TO WRITING

Try your hand at writing some haiku. Remember that they are most effective if they are pure imagery. Try not to make direct comments; let the images say it for you.

Personal Narrative

MADELINE
Loren Eiseley

BIOGRAPHICAL SKETCH

Loren Eiseley (1907–1977) was born in Lincoln, Nebraska, and received a Ph.D. in anthropology from the University of Pennsylvania, where he served as head of the Anthropology Department, dean, and curator of the University's museum. The recipient of many national and international honors and awards, a frequent lecturer, and a member of numerous scholarly organizations, government task forces, and boards of directors, he wrote innumerable articles for scientific journals and national magazines. His verse and prose have appeared in many literary anthologies. Among his most highly respected books are The Immense Journey *(1957),* Darwin's Century *(1958), and* Francis Bacon and the Modern Dilemma *(1963).*

PRE-READING

1. From skimming the first paragraph, can you guess what the narrative will be about? What kind of cat is a "prima donna"? Do you imagine the story about her will be light and entertaining or somewhat serious? Why?

2. From the biographical sketch, do you imagine Eiseley to be serious, playful, matter-of-fact, or what?

¹ Maddy was what we called her familiarly. Madeline was her real name and she was a prima donna and a cat—in that order. Maddy was a cat that bowed, the only one I have ever encountered. She is part of my story, what one might call the elocution or stage part. We patronized each other. Maddy performed her act, and I assumed the role of her most ardent admirer. In discharging this duty I learned a great deal from Maddy, my patroness, whom I here acknowledge.

² I have known a good many cats in my time—some that scratched, some that bit, some who purred, and even one who, by my standards at least, talked. I liked Maddy, I suppose, because we had so much in common. Maddy was an isolate. Maddy lived with three other more aggressive and talented animals who took the major attention of my host. Maddy, by contrast, was not

FROM Loren Eiseley, *All the Strange Hours: The Excavation of a Life* (New York: Charles Scribner's Sons, 1975), pp. 133–37. Copyright © 1975 by Loren Eiseley. Excerpt from "Madeline" is reprinted by permission of Charles Scribner's Sons.

so much antisocial as shy, when you came to know her. She wandered a little forlornly in back rooms and concealed herself under furniture, or in a recess above the fireplace.

³ Maddy, in short, wanted a small place in the sun which the world refused to grant her. She was at heart simply a good-natured ginger cat in a world so full of cats with purrs less hoarse that Maddy, like many of us, had learned to slink obscurely along the wall and hope that she might occasionally receive a condescending pat. Nothing was ever going to go quite right for Maddy. In this we reckoned without poor Maddy's desperation. She discovered a talent, and I, at least, among her human friends, was appalled at how easily this talent might have gone unguessed, except for a chance episode and an equally uncanny tenacity on Maddy's part. Maddy learned to bow.

⁴ Perhaps you may think, as a human being, that this is a very small accomplishment indeed. Let me assure you that it is not. On four feet it is a hard thing to do and, in addition, the cat mind is rarely reconciled to such postures. No one among us in that house, I think now, realized the depths of Maddy's need or her perception.

⁵ It happened, as most things happen, by accident, but the accident was destined to entrap both Maddy and ourselves. She was ensconced in her favorite recess upon the mantle of the fireplace, watching us, as usual, but being unwatched because of the clever gyrations of one of her kindred down on the floor. At this point, Mr. Fleet, our host, happened to stoop over to adjust a burning log in the fireplace.

⁶ Easing his back a moment later, he stood up by the mantle and poked a friendly finger at Maddy, who came out to peer down at the sparks. She also received an unexpected pat from Mr. Fleet. Whether by design or not, the combination of sparks and the hand impinging upon her head at the same time caused Maddy to execute a curious little head movement like a bow. It resembled, I can only say, a curtsey, an Old World gesture out of another time at the Sun King's court.

⁷ Maddy both hunched her forefeet and dropped her head. All she needed to complete the bow was a bonnet or a ribbon. Everyone who saw applauded in astonishment and for a few moments Maddy, for once, was the center of attention. In due course that would have been the end of the matter, but a severe snowstorm descended over our part of the state. We were thus all housebound and bored for several days. This is where Maddy's persistence and physical memory paid off; on the next night upon the mantle she came out of her own volition, and bowed once more with precisely similar steps. Again everyone applauded. Never had Madeline received such a burst of affectionate encouragement. If there were any catcalls they could only have come from her kin beneath the davenport. Her audience was with her. Maddy seized her opportunity. She bowed three times to uproarious applause. She had become the leading character in the house. The event had become memorable. Maddy, no more than a dancer, would forget the steps and the graceful little nod of the head. It became an evening routine.

[8] I have said that in the end both Maddy and her audience were entrapped. It happened in this way: finally the snow went away and we, all except Maddy, tried to resume our usual nocturnal habits—the corner bar, the club, the book. But the bow had become Maddy's life. She lived for it; one could not let her down, humiliate her, relegate her unfeelingly to her former existence. Maddy's fame, her ego, had to be sustained at any cost, even if, at times, her audience was reduced to one. That one carried, at such times, the honor of the house. Maddy's bow must be applauded. Maddy would be stricken if her act began to pall.

[9] To me the act never did pall. More than once I gave up other things to serve as a substitute audience. For, you see, I had come to realize even then that Maddy and myself were precisely alike; we had learned to bow in order to be loved for our graceless selves. The only difference was that as a human being living in a more complex world it had taken me longer to develop the steps and the routine. I talked for a living. But to talk for a living, one must, like Maddy, receive more applause than opprobrium. One must learn certain steps.

[10] I was born and grew up with no burning desire to teach. Sea captain, explorer, jungle adventurer—all these, in my childhood books, had been extolled to me. Unfortunately my reading had not included the great educators. Thus upon completing my doctorate I had no real hope in those still depressed times of 1937 of finding a university post. While I was casting about for a job among newspaper folk of my acquaintance, word came that I had been proffered a position at the University of Kansas.

[11] Most of the midwestern universities of that period had joint departments of sociology and anthropology, or at best one tame anthropologist who was expected to teach in both fields. When I appeared that fall before my first class in introductory sociology I realized two things as I walked through the door. I did not dare sit down. I did not dare use my notes for anything but a security blanket to toss confidently on the table like a true professor. The class was very large. A sizable portion of the football squad was scattered in the back row. I was, I repeat, an isolate like Maddy. If I ever lost that audience there would be chaos. The class met every day in the week.

[12] Each night I studied beyond midnight and wrote outlines that I rarely followed. I paced restlessly before the class, in which even the campus dogs were welcome so long as they nodded their heads sagely in approval. In a few weeks I began to feel like the proverbial Russian fleeing in a sleigh across the steppes before a wolf pack. I am sure that Carroll Clark, my good-natured chairman, realized that a highly unorthodox brand of sociology was being dispensed in his domain, but he held his peace. By then everything from anecdotes of fossil hunting to observations upon Victorian Darwinism were being hurled headlong from the rear of the sleigh. The last object to go would be myself. Fortunately for me, the end of the semester came just in time.

[13] At the close of the first year I had acquired, like Madeline the ginger cat, some followers. I had learned figuratively to bow and I was destined to

keep right on bowing through the next thirty years. There was no escape. Maddy had taught me how necessary it was that one's psyche be sustained. An actor, and this means no reflection upon teaching, has to have at least a few adoring followers. Otherwise he will begin to doubt himself and shrink inward, or take to muttering over outworn notes. This is particularly true in the case of a cat who has literally come out of nowhere to bow under everyone's gaze on a fireplace. Similarly I had emerged as a rather shy, introverted lad, to exhort others from a platform. Dear Maddy, I know all you suffered and I wish I could think you are still bowing to applause. You triumphed over your past in one great appreciative flash. For me it has been a lifelong battle with anxiety. . . .

ANALYTICAL READING

1. What is the relationship between the cat and the narrator? Is Maddy merely a pet?

2. Is the story really about Maddy, or is it about the narrator?

3. How does the author use analogy, or unusual comparison?

4. Is there any evidence that the writer has a sense of humor?

5. What kind of self-image does the writer project as a teacher and as a person?

REFLECTING

Point: Does Eiseley draw a conclusion only about his own life, or does the message extend to all of us? Summarize the message in the narrative.

Organization: This selection is in two parts. Indicate where the division occurs. What device does Eiseley use to make the transition? How does he sustain focus throughout? How does he link the two parts?

Support: How does the comparison between Maddy's learning to bow and Eiseley's learning to teach support the main point of the article? What specific details help?

Synthesis: It is sometimes said that pets take on the characteristics of their owners. Do you think this happens here? Has it happened to you?

Evaluation: Did you find that the selection effectively revealed Eiseley's character? Does the character in the narrative fit the conception of him that you derived from the biographical sketch? What devices help the reader to "know" the narrator? What makes this famous man appear so human?

FROM READING TO WRITING

1. Write an autobiographical narrative about your relationship with a pet.

2. Write an autobiographical narrative about your learning to play a role, perhaps modeling your behavior after older adults.

TO MAKE PAPA PROUD
Gregory H. Hemingway, M.D.

BIOGRAPHICAL SKETCH

Gregory H. Hemingway (1931–   ), the youngest son of Ernest Hemingway, lives and practices medicine in New York. He is not a professional writer, but his book Papa: A Personal Memoir *wins high praise from Norman Mailer, in the foreword to the book, for its "remarkable achievement" in portraying the real Ernest Hemingway. Other critics have hailed his ability for recapturing the bittersweet father-son relationship.*

PRE-READING

1. From the title of the book and the biographical sketch, what kind of relationship would you expect to find between Gregory and his famous father?

2. Skim the first two paragraphs. What task has the father set for the son? How would you react to such instruction from your father?

3. What is the setting? How old do you think the son is at the time of the story?

¹ That summer in Havana I read papa's favorites, from *Huckleberry Finn* to *Portrait of the Artist as a Young Man:* like him, I sometimes had two or three books going at the same time. Then papa steered me to the short story masters, Maupassant and Chekhov. "Don't try to analyze—just relax and enjoy them."

² "Now," papa said one morning. "Try writing a short story yourself. And don't expect it to be any good."

³ I sat down at a table with one of papa's fine-pointed pencils and thought and thought. I looked out the window, and listened to the birds, to a cat crying to join them; and to the scratch of my pencil, doodling. I let the cat out. Another wanted in.

⁴ I went to papa's typewriter. He'd finished with it for the day. Slowly I typed out a story and then took it to him.

⁵ Papa put his glasses on, poured himself another drink, and read, as I waited. He finished it and looked up at me. "It's excellent, Gig. Much better than anything I could do at your age. Only change I'd make is here," and he pointed to the line about a bird falling from its nest and finding, miraculously, that if it flapped its wings, it wouldn't crash on the rocks below.

⁶ "You've written . . . 'All of a sudden he realized he could fly.' Change 'all of a sudden' to 'suddenly.' Never use more words than you have to—it detracts from the flow of action." Papa smiled. I hadn't seen him smile at me like that for a long time. "But you've won the lottery, pal. Writing takes study,

FROM Gregory H. Hemingway, M.D., *Papa: A Personal Memoir* (Boston: Houghton Mifflin, 1976), pp. 104–07. Copyright © 1976 by Gregory H. Hemingway. Preface copyright © 1976 by Norman Mailer. Reprinted by permission of Houghton Mifflin Company.

discipline, and imagination. You've shown me with this that you have the imagination. And if you can do it once, you can do it a thousand times. Imagination doesn't leave you for a long time, maybe never. Dostoyevsky was fifty-seven when he wrote *Crime and Punishment.*

[7] "God, I used to get sad in Key West when people sent me their work and I could tell after reading one page that they didn't have it and never would. I answered every goddamn letter, usually saying that writing well was mainly a matter of luck, that to be given a great talent was like winning a million-to-one lottery; and if you weren't blessed, all the study and self-discipline in the world wouldn't mean a thing. If their letter had something like 'Everybody says I'd make a great engineer but what I really want to do is write,' I'd answer, 'Maybe everybody isn't wrong and you'll probably make an excellent engineer and then forget all about writing and be delighted you never went into it.'

[8] "I wrote hundreds of letters like that and I was getting a dollar a word in those days.

[9] "Later, when there were even more letters, I shortened my answers to 'Writing is a tough trade. Don't get mixed up in it if you can help it.' They probably thought, 'That conceited son of a bitch probably hasn't even read my stuff. But because he can write, he makes a big exclusive thing of it.'

[10] "The important thing is, Gig, that now I can teach *you* because you have the tools. And, in all immodesty, I know a lot about the trade.

[11] "I've wanted to cut down for a long time. The writing doesn't come so easily for me anymore. But I'll be just as happy helping you as doing it myself. Let's have a drink to celebrate."

[12] Only once before can I remember papa being as pleased with me— when I tied for the pigeon-shooting championship. And he was confident that there was another winner in the family when I entered the short story for a school competition and won first prize.

[13] Turgenev should have won the prize. He wrote the story. I merely copied it, changing the setting and the names, from a book I assumed papa hadn't read because some of the pages were still stuck together.

[14] I didn't feel like a winner and wondered how long it would be before papa found out that the only creative contribution I had made to the story was to alter "suddenly" to "all of a sudden."

[15] Fortunately I wasn't around when papa discovered my plagiarism. It got back to me that someone asked him if his son Gregory wrote. "Yes," he replied, with gusto and sparkle, flashing that "say cheese" smile he sometimes affected. "Gregory writes an occasional bad check." And, of course, everyone laughed.

[16] Someone in that crowd might have thought, "What a brutal bastard to make such a callous wisecrack about his son. I guess all those stories I've heard about him being a hard-shell bully are true."

[17] Hard-shelled, yes, but I helped make that shell.

ANALYTICAL READING

1. When in the story do you first suspect the plagiarism?

2. As you read, did you feel vicarious guilt? How does the dialogue between father and son help the reader to feel the son's guilt? Is the writer's use of dialogue more effective than simply telling the reader that he felt guilty?

3. In what other ways do we learn of the son's feelings of guilt? Is the last paragraph effective? Why?

4. What do you learn of the relationship between the writer and his father?

5. Is the language used in the dialogue realistic? Discuss, citing examples. Is there any significance in the father's reference to the son as "Gig" early and "Gregory" later?

REFLECTING

Point: Do you think this selection is only an interesting personal narrative about a son and his famous father, or does it also serve as a moral lesson?

Organization: Where in the narrative does the point of the story become clear? Can you construct a three-part sentence outline that reveals the organizational structure? Does the fact that the plagiarism is not admitted until late in the selection add to or detract from the narrative? Is the one-sentence conclusion effective? Why?

Support: Hemingway uses two incidents to indicate or dramatize the damage done by his plagiarism. What are they? How do "Papa" Hemingway's remarks about writing submitted to him and about his own writing contribute to the narrative?

Synthesis: Can you recall a time when one of your actions made you ashamed afterwards? Does young Hemingway's shame arise from public exposure or because of his love for his father? Is the son reevaluating his father's reputation?

Evaluation: Do you think the ending is effective? Can you suggest another way of handling it? What would be the effect of omitting the last two paragraphs? Can you understand why the son might be motivated to plagiarize? Can you understand and perhaps excuse him?

FROM READING TO WRITING

1. Think of a time when you were humiliated or embarrassed by one of your actions or decisions. Write about it in narrative form, relying heavily on dialogue and events to provide an example from which others might learn.

2. Write about an incident in which you did something that you hoped would win approval from someone. Be sure to reveal the relationship involved. Avoid telling your audience how you felt in so many words. Before you write, work out a skeletal organizational scheme similar to the one you found in the Hemingway narrative.

GOD'S DANGERS IN TOWN
Theodore Rosengarten

BIOGRAPHICAL SKETCH

All God's Dangers *is a remarkable book, an oral history in the words of Nate Shaw, a cotton farmer from Alabama. While a Ph.D. candidate at Harvard University, Theodore Rosengarten won an Ethnic Studies grant from the Ford Foundation which enabled him to interview on tape the eighty-five-year-old Shaw. In the 1930's Shaw joined a sharecroppers union and later, in a shootout with people trying to break up the union, he shot at a sheriff. For that offense, he spent twelve years in prison under often brutal conditions, but managed to retain his independent spirit. The quality of that spirit comes through in this selection from the book.*

PRE-READING

1. After reading the biographical sketch, what might you expect the language in the selection to be—casual and conversational, formal and stiff, or what?

2. From the title of the book, what do you expect from the narrative?

3. The first few paragraphs set up the situation. What is it? Does the narrator imply trouble?

¹ One day I told my wife, "Darlin, I'm goin to Apafalya to get me a load of cotton seed hulls for my cows and some meal."

² She said, "Darlin, you goin to town, I want you to get Rachel and Calvin some shoes"—they was the two oldest.

³ Told her, "All right. I'll do that."

⁴ She didn't know what number they wore but here's what she done: she went and took the measure of their foots and told me to get em shoes just a little longer than the measure from the heel to the toe. Well, I was fully determined to do it—and that was some of my first trouble.

⁵ I drove into Apafalya, hitched my mules, and walked into Mr. Sadler's store to get some shoes for the children first thing; then I was goin to drive on down to the carbox at the depot and load me a load of hulls and meal. Had my cotton bodies on my wagon—

⁶ I went on into Mr. Sadler's store and there was a big crowd in there. The store was full of white people and two or three colored people to my knowin. And there was a crippled fellow in there by the name of Henry Chase—Mr. Sadler had him hired for a clerk, and several more, maybe three or four more clerks was in there and some was women clerks. I walked in the store and a white lady come up to me and asked me, "Can I wait on you?"

⁷ I told her, "Yes, ma'am, I wants a couple of pair of shoes for my children."

FROM Theodore Rosengarten, *All God's Dangers: The Life of Nate Shaw* (New York: Alfred A. Knopf, 1974), pp. 162–70. Copyright © 1974 by Theodore Rosengarten. Reprinted by permission of Alfred A. Knopf, Inc.

⁸ And she took the measures and went on to the west side of the store and I went on around there behind her. She got a ladder, set it up, and she clumb that ladder and me standin off below her. There was a openin between the counters—and I was standin down there, just out of the way of the little swing-door and she was searchin from the front of that store nearly down to where I was.

⁹ And this Chase fellow, he was kind of a rough fellow and it was known—a heap of his people there in town didn't like him. So she was busy huntin my shoes and she'd climb that ladder and take down shoes, measurin em, and she'd set em back up if they wouldn't do, didn't come up to that straw measure. And she was just rattlin around there, up the ladder and down it, and this here Chase fellow was standin off watchin. After a while he come around there, showin his hatred, showin what he was made of, that's all it was. And there was a old broke down—it had been cut in two at the bottom— a old, tough brogan shoe sittin there on the counter, a sample, you know. And he walked through there by me to get behind that counter where she was. I was standin on the outside waitin on her patiently, weren't sayin nothin. And he didn't like that white lady waitin on me, that just set him afire—I knowed it was that; I'd never had no dealins with him, no trouble with him noway— and he remarked, "You been in here the longest—" right in my face.

¹⁰ I said, "No sir, I haven't been in here but just a little while."

¹¹ The white lady spoke up too; said, "No, he hasn't been here very long. I'm tryin to find him some shoes."

¹² He said, "You been in here the longest, you too hard to suit."

¹³ I said, "No sir, all I'm tryin to do is buy me some shoes to match the measure for my children's foots."

¹⁴ She said, "No, he hasn't been here but a short while."

¹⁵ Good God, when she said that he grabbed that old shoe up—he didn't like her to speak up for me—grabbed that shoe up and hit at my head with it. I blocked his lick off. Well, when I blocked his lick off—he'd a hit me side the head with that old shoe, or on the face; no doubt he woulda cut me up—he throwed that shoe down. He seed he couldn't hit me with it, I was goin to block him off. He dropped that shoe back down on the counter and out from between there he come and run down to the low end of the store. And Mr. Sadler kept shovels, hoes, plow tools, and every kind of thing down there, on the low end, back end of the store. Chase runned down there and picked him up one of these long-handled shovels and he whirled around and come back—he just showed that he was given to split me down with that shovel. He come back—he begin to get close to me and I sort of turned myself to him one-sided.

¹⁶ I said, "Don't you hit me with that shovel"—told him to his head, didn't bite my tongue—"don't you hit me with that shovel."

¹⁷ He wouldn't say nothin. Just stood there and looked at me, wouldn't move up on me. Kept that shovel drawed, lookin at me, lookin at me, lookin at me. I just dared him to hit me with that shovel—I never told him what I'd

do and what I wouldn't. Well, he stood there and let into cussin. He disregarded that white lady, just stood there with that shovel on him, cussin me, lookin like all he wanted was a chance. I'd a turned my head and he'd a hit me, looked like from the way he acted.

[18] All right. We got up a loud talk and all the people in the store noticed it. After a while, a fellow by the name of Howard Crabtree—old Dr. Crabtree was a horse doctor and this was his son—runned up there and started his big mouth. And this cripple man Chase tellin me all the time, "Get out of here, you black bastard. Get out of here." Tryin to run me out the store and I hadn't done a thing to him.

[19] And this Crabtree, he runned up, "Naw, he aint goin to hit you, but goddamnit, get out of here like he tells you."

[20] I said, "Both of you make me get out. Both of you make me get out."

[21] Couldn't move me. The white lady had done disbanded and got away from there. I stood my ground when this here Howard Crabtree runned up and taken Chase's part. I said, "I ain't gettin nowhere. Both of you make me get out."

[22] Chase runned back and put the shovel where he got it from and down the aisle on the far side of the store he went. And there was a ring of guns there, breech-loaders. I kept my eyes on him, watchin him. I weren't goin nowhere. The white lady went on back to huntin my shoes after Chase left from there—he come out from the back of the store and went on down to where that ring of guns was, sittin right in the front as you go in the door. And he grabbed up one of them single barrel breech-loaders—that's when a white man befriended me and several more done so until I left town. There was a white gentleman clerkin in there, Mr. Tom Sherman—I seed this here Henry Chase grab that gun and break it down, run his hand in his pocket and take out a shell and put it in there. Totin shells in his pocket so if anything happened that he needed to shoot somebody—picked up a gun and broke it down and unbreeched it and run his hand in his pocket, pulled out a shell and stuck it in there, then breeched it back up and commenced a lookin for a clear openin to shoot at me. I just considered it for a bluff—he weren't goin to shoot me there in that man's store, surely. And I watched him close, he jumpin around lookin, first one way then the other, holdin that gun in his hands, lookin. And Mr. Tom Sherman just quit his business when he seed Chase drop a shell in that gun, walked right on up to him and snatched the gun away. Chase didn't resist Mr. Sherman—that was a heavy-built man. Mr. Sherman took that gun out of his hands, unbreeched it, took that shell out of it, set the gun back in the ring and stood there by that ring of guns. Out the store Chase went.

[23] Well, by that time, the white lady done got my shoes. I turned around and paid her for em. She wrapped em nice and I took the shoes and went on out the back door—it was handy; I come in the back door and I went back out it. I didn't go down the front. Chase'd gone out of there and I didn't want no trouble with him.

²⁴ So, out the back door I went and I turned to the left and walked on out in the middle of the street, goin to my wagon. And when I got out to where I could see clear, Aunt Betsey Culver, Uncle Jim Culver's second wife, was sittin in the street on a buggy. Uncle Jim was over there by Sadler's store, he seed all that happened there. I walked up to the buggy and howdyed with my auntie—didn't talk about that trouble neither. I just set my shoes in the foot of the buggy and was standin there talkin with her. And after a while I happened to look down the street and here come that cripple Chase fellow— he was a young fellow too, and he walked in kind of a hoppin way, one leg drawed back—and the police was with him, old man Bob Leech, settle-aged white man. They was lookin for me and they come up to me quick. Chase pointed at me and said, "That's him, standin right yonder; that's him, standin there at that buggy."

²⁵ Old man Leech walked up to me, looked at me, looked me over. And by me standin kind of sideways at Chase in the store, he done went and told the police that I acted just like I had a pistol in my pocket. Well, he never did see my hand. I had on a big heavy overcoat that day, just what the weather called for. So, he pointed me out to the police; police walked on up to me but wouldn't come right up to me, not very close.

²⁶ He said, "Consider yourself under arrest."

²⁷ I looked at him, said, "Consider myself under arrest for what?"

²⁸ "Uh, consider yourself under arrest."

²⁹ I asked him again, "Consider myself under arrest for what?"

³⁰ "That's all right; that's all right."

³¹ Come up to me and patted me, feelin for a gun. I said, "You want to search me"—I just grabbed that big overcoat and throwed it back—"search me, search me, just as much as you please. Search me."

³² He got up close enough to run his hands around me, feelin my hip pockets. He didn't find no gun. I had no gun, I didn't tote no gun around thataway. He said—he talked kind of through his nose, funny. And I called him in question about every word he spoke to me. He said, "Well, c'mon go with me."

³³ I said, "Go with you where?"

³⁴ "Gowanup-t-th-maya-uvtawn."

³⁵ I couldn't understand him.

³⁶ "Gowanup-t-th-maya-uvtawn."

³⁷ I said, "To the mayor of town?"

³⁸ He talkin thataway and I couldn't hardly understand him, talkin through his nostrils, looked like. I understood him but I just kept him cross-talked. Well, I started not to go—my mind told me, 'Go ahead with him, don't buck him.'

³⁹ He carried me on down the street and hit the left hand side of town goin in—left my shoes in my uncle's buggy. And I went on. Got down there and went up the stairs—the stairsteps come down to the walkway. The mayor of town was upstairs. And by golly, when I got up there, who was the mayor

of town? Doctor Collins! Dr. Collins knowed me well, been knowin me a long time. Walked on into his office and old man Leech, the police, spoke to him. And before he could say anything, Dr. Collins seed who was with him. He said, "Why, hello. What you doin with Shaw up here?"

⁴⁰ "Well, him and Henry Chase got into it down there in Sadler's store."

⁴¹ Dr. Collins said, "Um-hmm." Dr. Collins was a pretty heavy-built man himself. He said, "Well, Mr. Leech, where is Chase?"

⁴² "He down there in town somewhere, in the streets."

⁴³ "Um-hmm."

⁴⁴ "And they got into it in Sadler's store."

⁴⁵ "Mr. Leech, go down there and get Chase and bring him up here."

⁴⁶ The old police went down and got Chase, brought him up there. He come up hip-hoppin, hip-hoppin—that's the way he walked, doin just that-away every step he took. Chase said, when he got up there, "Hi, Doc."

⁴⁷ Dr. Collins said, "Howdy, Henry."

⁴⁸ I was standin there listenin. He said, "Henry, did you and this darky—" he wouldn't say nigger neither; that was a white man, and there was some more of em in this country wouldn't call you nigger. Dr. Collins said, "Henry, did you and this darky get into it down there in Sadler's store?"

⁴⁹ He said, "Yeah." But wouldn't tell nary a thing he done, uncalled for. "He was down there in Sadler's store—" wouldn't tell what I was waitin on or nothin, just told what he wanted Dr. Collins to know— "was down there in Sadler's store and we got into it"—wouldn't tell him what we got into it about—"and I told him to get out of there and he gived me a whole lot of impudent jaw."

⁵⁰ Dr. Collins said, "Um-hmm. Who seed that beside you, Henry?"

⁵¹ "Well, Howard Crabtree seed it."

⁵² And the whole store seed it but none of em weren't busyin theirselves with it. Mr. Tom Sherman seed it and he went and took that gun away from him. Dr. Collins said, "Um-hmm. Well, go down, Mr. Leech, and get Howard Crabtree and bring him up here."

⁵³ Chase said, "And he kept his hand behind him like he had a gun in his hip pocket."

⁵⁴ Crabtree walked up with his big-talkin self. Dr. Collins said, "Crabtree, did you see this darky and Henry Chase get into it down there in Sadler's store?"

⁵⁵ "I did. I did. I seed it every bit."

⁵⁶ "Well, Crabtree, would you—"

⁵⁷ "He had his hand behind him—" told the same lie Chase told—"had his hand behind him and he kept a tellin Chase not to hit him, better not hit him, and givin up a lot of other impudent jaw."

⁵⁸ Dr. Collins said, "Um-hmm. Crabtree, would you swear that he had his hand in his hip pocket?"

⁵⁹ "No, no"—he jumped back then—"no, I wouldn't swear he had his

hand in his hip pocket, but he looked like he had it in there. I don't know where his hand was, he had on that big overcoat."

⁶⁰ "Um-hmm," Dr. Collins said, "Um-hmm."

⁶¹ Dr. Collins knowed me well. Never gived nobody no trouble, tended to my business, let other folks alone, I didn't meddle in things. And at that time I had a good name, right there in Apafalya, I'd been there since I was a little boy up till I was grown and after.

⁶² Dr. Collins said, "Well, the little old case don't amount to nothin. I'm just goin to throw it out."

⁶³ After Crabtree told him he wouldn't swear I had my hand in my hip pocket, Dr. Collins asked me, "Shaw, did you have a pistol?"

⁶⁴ I said, "No, Doctor, I aint seed a pistol in I don't know when. I had no pistol."

⁶⁵ Chase allowed to him, "He went out the back way; he coulda carried it out there and stashed it."

⁶⁶ Well, good devil, just as sure as my Savior's at his restin place today, I didn't have no pistol, never thought about no pistol.

⁶⁷ All right. They whirled and left from up there when Dr. Collins said he was just goin to throw the little case out. And when they started out, I started out right behind em. Dr. Collins throwed his finger at me—"Shaw, this way; Shaw, Shaw."

⁶⁸ I was lookin back at him and I stopped. He said, "Just be yourself and stay up here a few minutes; that'll give em time to get away from down there, clear em out, then you can go."

⁶⁹ I just made myself at home, stood there. After a while, Dr. Collins said, "Well, you can go ahead now. Mess don't amount to nothin nohow, that's the reason I throwed it out."

⁷⁰ When I got down the stairsteps onto the walkway, there was Mr. Harry Black, man I had done my guano dealin with, and there was a fellow went around there in Apafalya, heap of folks called him Tersh Hog—that was Mr. Bob Soule, went for a cousin to Cliff Soule. He lived out about a mile from Apafalya and he didn't take no backwater off nobody. If a thing weren't right, he were goin to fix it right. Some of em didn't like him because they had to pass around him, white folks. And I seed him walk the streets right there in Apafalya with his pistol in his—just like a law, only he'd carry his pistol in his coat pocket, and that handle was hangin out over the pocket. Didn't nobody give Mr. Bob Soule no trouble in Apafalya and nowheres else he went. So, Mr. Bob Soule was standin there at them steps when I come down, and Mr. Harry Black and Mr. Ed Hardy—I knowed them definitely and there was a couple more of em, bout five altogether standin there when I come down. They said, "Hello, Nate. Hello, Nate."

⁷¹ I stopped and spoke to em polite and they was polite to me. Well, Uncle Jim Culver had done stood there too at the bottom of the steps while his trial business was goin on and he heard them white men speak this: "If that nigger

comes down from up there with any charges against him, we goin to paint this damn place red."

[72] I didn't know—I didn't hear em say it. Uncle Jim told me, "They was standin there for a purpose. I done stood here and listened at em. Said, 'If that nigger comes down from up there with any charges against him, we goin to paint this damn place red.' "

[73] All of em knowed me well: I'd traded with Mr. Harry Black and Mr. Ed Hardy and they had passed confidence with me. And Mr. Bob Soule, he loved justice. When I walked down amongst em, all of em, I knowed em, looked in their faces, standin huddled there where the stairway hit the walkway. They was satisfied. They left there when I left.

[74] Uncle Jim added his advice: "Things are hot here, son. Now you go on up the street and get your mules and wagon and turn around and go on back home."

[75] I said to myself, 'The devil will happen before I do that.'

[76] And he said, "Don't come back, don't come back through town. Go on home. Take your mules and go on home now."

[77] I went on up there and pulled my mules back and hitched the traces and untied em from the post they was hitched to—both of em hitched to the same post and them inside traces dropped—set up on my wagon and went just as straight, just as dead straight right back down through Apafalya as I could go. Uncle Jim was standin there and he told some fellow, "There that boy goin right back through town and I told him to get his mules and wagon and go on back home."

[78] But I was game as a peacock. I just went straight to his buggy and got my shoes out and carried em to my wagon, hitched my mules back, crawled up in the wagon over them high bodies, right down dead through town I went. And when I got down close to where the railroad runned under that bridge there in Apafalya I turned to my left and went on down to the depot. Loaded my hulls and meal—and when I left, I had a straight way right out from there up the back streets of town toward home.

[79] One day after that, Uncle Jim got at me bout goin back down through town. I told him, "I aint no rabbit, Uncle Jim. When a man's mistreated thataway and he got friends and they proves it, he don't need to be scared. Of course, it's a dangerous situation and if I'd a been guilty of anything, I'd a took low."

[80] There was a old colored fellow down at the door at Sadler's store the whole time this ruckus was goin on inside. Mighta been inside himself at the start but he runned out if he was; he acted like he runned out. And he stood where he could see me. And do you know he just stood there and beckoned to me that whole time, he beckoned to me to run out. That just roused the whole store up. The old man tickled me. He was a pretty heavy-built old man and he weren't as high—his head, he could have walked under a tall horse and never touched it. Heavy-built old colored man. And he had on one of these old

frock-tail coats and it hit him just below the knee and it was cut back like a bug's wings. And he just stood there and bowed and beckoned for me to run out there. And every time he'd bow, that old coat would fly up behind him and when he straightened up it would hit him right back there below the bend in his legs. Tickled me, it tickled me. I thought it was the funniest thing I ever saw. He was scared for me and wanted me to run out of there. I didn't run nowhere. I stood just like I'm standin today—when I know I'm right and I aint harmin nobody and nothin else, I'll give you trouble if you try to move me.

ANALYTICAL READING

1. Does the narrator's language contribute to or detract from the authenticity of the account? Cite examples.

2. As you read, were you aware of the relationships of the characters to one another? How are these revealed in the narrative?

3. Is it more accurate to describe the narrator as aggressive and militant or as respectful and courageous?

4. Where does the incident take place? Is the setting important?

5. What do you think is the turning point of the story?

REFLECTING

Point: Is the purpose of the narrative simply to dramatize the brutality of some whites toward blacks? Is there more than one main point? How does the narrator communicate his message to the reader?

Organization: What is the organizational pattern? Do you think it is characteristic of narrative writing? Is it violated by the last paragraph? If so, why?

Support: What events and human relationships help to support the narrator's points in the story? What particular words and phrases help to make the story realistic?

Synthesis: How does this story compare with others like it, such as *Roots* or the selection by Maya Angelou (pages 71–75)? Would you say that this story makes a comment about the human spirit? How do you account for Shaw's courage?

Evaluation: How did you react emotionally to the story? Do you think the narrator demonstrates self-pity in telling about the incident? Illustrate. How does the narrator show that some white people treat him fairly?

FROM READING TO WRITING

1. Using as much dialogue as possible, write a narrative about an incident in your own life when you were placed in some kind of danger.

2. Write a personal narrative about a time when you had unexpected difficulty in making a purchase, returning something, or complaining about some defect.

UNUSUAL WRITING LESSONS
Robert M. Pirsig

BIOGRAPHICAL SKETCH

Robert M. Pirsig (1928–   ) was born in Minneapolis, Minnesota, graduated from Montana State University, where he later served as an instructor in English composition before taking a similar position at the University of Chicago. He has also worked as a technical writer for several companies and served as an official of the Zen Meditation Center in Minneapolis. In 1974, he was awarded a Guggenheim fellowship. Since the publication in 1974 of Zen and the Art of Motorcycle Maintenance, *which has become a favorite on college campuses, he has written articles for several periodicals. The book is an autobiographical narrative of his motorcycle journey across the United States with his young son. But it is also a journey back to sanity and regaining of values. In this selection and throughout the book, Pirsig uses the name Phaedrus for the old personality he is trying to leave behind.*

PRE-READING

1. From the title of Pirsig's book and the biographical sketch, do you expect the book to be unconventional? Why? What does the incongruous pairing of an Oriental religion and motorcycles tell you about Pirsig's mind?

2. Skim the first two paragraphs. Pirsig talks of Quality in the first paragraph and begins the narrative in the second. Can you assume from this that his personal experience will somehow relate to Quality? What catches the reader's interest in the opening paragraphs and suggests the main idea of the selection?

[1] Today now I want to take up the first phase of his [Phaedrus'] journey into Quality, the nonmetaphysical phase, and this will be pleasant. It's nice to start journeys pleasantly, even when you know they won't end that way. Using his class notes as reference material I want to reconstruct the way in which Quality became a working concept for him in the teaching of rhetoric. His second phase, the metaphysical one, was tenuous and speculative, but this first phase, in which he simply taught rhetoric, was by all accounts solid and pragmatic and probably deserves to be judged on its own merits, independently of the second phase.

[2] He'd been innovating extensively. He'd been having trouble with students who had nothing to say. At first he thought it was laziness but later it became apparent that it wasn't. They just couldn't think of anything to say.

[3] One of them, a girl with strong-lensed glasses, wanted to write a five-hundred-word essay about the United States. He was used to the sinking feeling that comes from statements like this, and suggested without disparagement that she narrow it down to just Bozeman [Montana].

FROM Robert M. Pirsig, *Zen and the Art of Motorcycle Maintenance* (New York: William Morrow & Co., 1974), pp. 190–94, 270–72. Copyright © 1974 by Robert M. Pirsig. Reprinted by permission of William Morrow & Company, Inc.

⁴ When the paper came due she didn't have it and was quite upset. She had tried and tried but she just couldn't think of anything to say.

⁵ He had already discussed her with her previous instructors and they'd confirmed his impressions of her. She was very serious, disciplined and hard-working, but extremely dull. Not a spark of creativity in her anywhere. Her eyes, behind the thick-lensed glasses, were the eyes of a drudge. She wasn't bluffing him, she really couldn't think of anything to say, and was upset by her inability to do as she was told.

⁶ It just stumped him. Now *he* couldn't think of anything to say. A silence occurred, and then a peculiar answer: "Narrow it down to the *main street* of Bozeman." It was a stroke of insight.

⁷ She nodded dutifully and went out. But just before her next class she came back in *real* distress, tears this time, distress that had obviously been there for a long time. She still couldn't think of anything to say, and couldn't understand why, if she couldn't think of anything about *all* of Bozeman, she should be able to think of something about just one street.

⁸ He was furious. "You're not *looking!*" he said. A memory came back of his own dismissal from the University for having *too much* to say. For every fact there is an *infinity* of hypotheses. The more you *look* the more you *see*. She really wasn't looking and yet somehow didn't understand this.

⁹ He told her angrily, "Narrow it down to the *front* of *one* building on the main street of Bozeman. The Opera House. Start with the upper left-hand brick."

¹⁰ Her eyes, behind the thick-lensed glasses, opened wide.

¹¹ She came in the next class with a puzzled look and handed him a five-thousand-word essay on the front of the Opera House on the main street of Bozeman, Montana. "I sat in the hamburger stand across the street," she said, "and started writing about the first brick, and the second brick, and then by the third brick it all started to come and I couldn't stop. They thought I was crazy, and they kept kidding me, but here it all is. I don't understand it."

¹² Neither did he, but on long walks through the streets of town he thought about it and concluded she was evidently stopped with the same kind of blockage that had paralyzed him on his first day of teaching. She was blocked because she was trying to repeat, in her writing, things she had already heard, just as on the first day he had tried to repeat things he had already decided to say. She couldn't think of anything to write about Bozeman because she couldn't recall anything she had heard worth repeating. She was strangely unaware that she could look and see freshly for herself, as she wrote, without primary regard for what had been said before. The narrowing down to one brick destroyed the blockage because it was so obvious she *had* to do some original and direct seeing.

¹³ He experimented further. In one class he had everyone write all hour about the back of his thumb. Everyone gave him funny looks at the beginning of the hour, but everyone did it, and there wasn't a single complaint about "nothing to say."

[14] In another class he changed the subject from the thumb to a coin, and got a full hour's writing from every student. In other classes it was the same. Some asked, "Do you have to write about both sides?" Once they got into the idea of seeing directly for themselves they also saw there was no limit to the amount they could say. It was a confidence-building assignment too, because what they wrote, even though seemingly trivial, was nevertheless their own thing, not a mimicking of someone else's. Classes where he used that coin exercise were always less balky and more interested.

[15] As a result of his experiments he concluded that imitation was a real evil that had to be broken before real rhetoric teaching could begin. This imitation seemed to be an external compulsion. Little children didn't have it. It seemed to come later on, possibly as a result of school itself.

[16] That sounded right, and the more he thought about it the more right it sounded. Schools teach you to imitate. If you don't imitate what the teacher wants you get a bad grade. Here, in college, it was more sophisticated, of course; you were supposed to imitate the teacher in such a way as to convince the teacher you were not imitating, but taking the essence of the instruction and going ahead with it on your own. That got you A's. Originality on the other hand could get you anything—from A to F. The whole grading system cautioned against it.

[17] He discussed this with a professor of psychology who lived next door to him, an extremely imaginative teacher, who said, "Right. Eliminate the whole degree-and-grading system and then you'll get real education."

[18] Phaedrus thought about this, and when weeks later a very bright student couldn't think of a subject for a term paper, it was still on his mind, so he gave it to her as a topic. She didn't like the topic at first, but agreed to take it anyway.

[19] Within a week she was talking about it to everyone, and within two weeks had worked up a superb paper. The class she delivered it to didn't have the advantage of two weeks to think about the subject, however, and was quite hostile to the whole idea of eliminating grades and degrees. This didn't slow her down at all. Her tone took on an old-time religious fervor. She begged the other students to *listen*, to understand this was really *right*. "I'm not saying this for *him*," she said and glanced at Phaedrus. "It's for *you*."

[20] Her pleading tone, her religious fervor, greatly impressed him, along with the fact that her college entrance examinations had placed her in the upper one percent of the class. During the next quarter, when teaching "persuasive writing," he chose this topic as a "demonstrator," a piece of persuasive writing he worked up by himself, day by day, in front of and with the help of the class.

[21] He used the demonstrator to avoid talking in terms of principles of composition, all of which he had deep doubts about. He felt that by exposing classes to his own sentences as he made them, with all the misgivings and hang-ups and erasures, he would give a more honest picture of what writing was like than by spending class time picking nits in completed student work

or holding up the completed work of masters for emulation. This time he developed the argument that the whole grading system and degree should be eliminated, and to make it something that truly involved the students in what they were hearing, he withheld all grades during the quarter.

.   .   .

²² This road keeps on winding down through this canyon. Early morning patches of sun are around us everywhere. The cycle hums through the cold air and mountain pines and we pass a small sign that says a breakfast place is a mile ahead.

²³ "Are you hungry?" I shout.

²⁴ "Yes!" Chris [Pirsig's eleven-year-old son] shouts back.

²⁵ Soon a second sign saying CABINS with an arrow under it points off to the left. We slow down, turn and follow a dirt road until it reaches some varnished log cabins under some trees. We pull the cycle under a tree, shut off the ignition and gas and walk inside the main lodge. The wooden floors have a nice clomp under the cycle boots. We sit down at a tableclothed table and order eggs, hot cakes, maple syrup, milk, sausages and orange juice. That cold wind has worked up an appetite.

²⁶ "I want to write a letter to Mom," Chris says.

²⁷ That sounds good to me. I go to the desk and get some of the lodge stationery. I bring it to Chris and give him my pen. That brisk morning air has given him some energy too. He puts the paper in front of him, grabs the pen in a heavy grip and then concentrates on the blank paper for a while.

²⁸ He looks up. "What day is it?"

²⁹ I tell him. He nods and writes it down.

³⁰ Then I see him write, "Dear Mom:"

³¹ Then he stares at the paper for a while.

³² Then he looks up. "What should I say?"

³³ I start to grin. I should have him write for an hour abour one side of a coin. I've sometimes thought of him as a student but not as a rhetoric student.

³⁴ We're interrupted by the hot cakes and I tell him to put the letter to one side and I'll help him afterward.

³⁵ When we are done I sit smoking with a leaden feeling from the hot cakes and the eggs and everything and notice through the window that under the pines outside the ground is in patches of shadow and sunlight.

³⁶ Chris brings out the paper again. "Now help me," he says.

³⁷ "Okay," I say. I tell him getting stuck is the commonest trouble of all. Usually, I say, your mind gets stuck when you're trying to do too many things at once. What you have to do is try not to force words to come. That just gets you more stuck. What you have to do now is separate out the things and do them one at a time. You're trying to think of what to *say* and what to say *first* at the same time and that's too hard. So separate them out. Just make a list of all the things you want to say in any old order. Then later we'll figure out the right order.

[38] "Like what things?" he asks.

[39] "Well, what do you want to tell her?"

[40] "About the trip."

[41] "What things about the trip?"

[42] He thinks for a while. "About the mountain we climbed."

[43] "Okay, write that down," I say.

[44] He does.

[45] Then I see him write down another item, then another, while I finish my cigarette and coffee. He goes through three sheets of paper, listing things he wants to say.

[46] "Save those," I tell him, "and we'll work on them later."

[47] "I'll never get all this into one letter," he says.

[48] He sees me laugh and frowns.

[49] I say, "Just pick out the best things." Then we head outside and onto the motorcycle again.

[50] On the road down the canyon now we feel the steady drop of altitude by a popping of ears. It's becoming warmer and the air is thicker too. It's good-bye to the high country, which we've been more or less in since Miles City.

ANALYTICAL READING

1. What is Pirsig's tone? How do you think he feels toward his students? toward his son? Support your opinion by citing examples.

2. What seems to be Pirsig's main concern about his students' writing? What devices does he use to deal with their problems? with his son's problem?

3. The incidents in the narrative parallel a development of ideas in the writer's mind. Show the relationship between the incidents and the new ideas.

4. Compare the language of the opening paragraph with that of the rest of the narrative. Which is more concrete? What do you think is the effect of less abstract language? How do you feel about the author referring to himself as *he* instead of *I*?

5. What did you learn about teaching and teachers as you read the selection?

6. Explain what the statement "The more you *look* the more you *see*" means in the selection.

REFLECTING

Point: Does Pirsig make more than one point in the narrative? What? Do you think he makes a point about Quality? If so, what is it?

Organization: The excerpt has almost a double organizational scheme: one is the chronological order of the narrative, the other is a progression of points made about freshman English and the grading system. Outline the two and express their relationship to each other.

Support: Does the narrative sufficiently support the points made by Pirsig? Do you feel that he makes a strong case for Quality as "a working concept"? Discuss.

Is ample evidence offered to show that schools teach students to imitate? Does it seem natural that a class would be hostile to the idea of eliminating grades?

Synthesis: How do the instructions that Pirsig gives to his student, and his son relate to your own experiences in composition classes? How do you react to his recommendations about the grading system? To what extent do you feel compelled to agree with your teachers?

Evaluation: Compare the effectiveness of this narrative with that of the Hemingway and Eiseley selections. Specifically, compare whether the ending of each re-solves the problem raised in each.

FROM READING TO WRITING

1. Write a short narrative about a personal experience that illustrates the state-ment, "The more you *look* the more you *see*."

2. Write an account of a brief activity that you engage in almost daily, but never look at closely. Provide as much detail as possible. Suggestions: walking a path that you take every day to class; standing in line for a meal at the dorm; the routine you follow in getting ready for studying or for a date.

3. Write a narrative showing how students do or do not cater to the whims of college or high school teachers.

A WILDERNESS EXPERIENCE
Sally Carrighar

BIOGRAPHICAL SKETCH

Sally Carrighar was born in Cleveland, Ohio. She won immediate fame with her first book, One Day on Beetle Rock, *published in 1944. Her works, most of them dealing with nature and man's relationship to it, have earned her a reputation as a naturalist and conservationist. Other books include* One Day at Teton Marsh, Icebound Summer, Wild Heritage, *and* Home to the Wilderness, *from which this selection comes.*

PRE-READING

1. From the title of Carrighar's book, what would you expect her attitude toward the wilderness to be?

2. After skimming the first paragraph, what do you know of the situation? Note Sally Carrighar's age at the time of the narrative. Was this a new experience for her?

FROM Sally Carrighar, *Home to the Wilderness* (Boston: Houghton Mifflin, 1973), pp. 89–97. Copyright 1944 by Sally Carrighar. Copyright © 1973 by I.C.E. Limited. Reprinted by permission of Hough-ton Mifflin Company.

¹ As amazing as miracles was a morning in June the year that I was fifteen and woke up in a tent on an island in Canada. We had arrived by lake steamer the previous night and, tired after the long trip from Kansas City, had gone straight to bed. Now it was daylight. I got up quickly, quietly and slipped out to see this new world.

² The tent was a short way back from the shore with a path leading down to a little dock. I walked to the end of it. Ripples were gently rearranging the pebbles along the beach but the lake was smooth. Its wide and beautiful surface, delicate silver-blue, streamed with a mist that disappeared as I watched, for the light of the early sun, splintering on the tops of the mainland evergreen trees, was starting to fall on the mist and dissolve it. Curiously the lake's level surface seemed to be moving in alternate glassy streams, right and left, an effect that sometimes occurs on quiet water, I don't know why.

³ The bay in front of the dock was framed by the shores of the mainland, which curved together from both sides to meet in a point. At that vertex another island, rocky and tall, rose from the water. It looked uninhabited; and although a few cabins were scattered along the mainland, between and behind them was unbroken forest. It was my first sight of a natural wilderness. Behind our tent too, and several other tents here and a house in their midst, was the forest. Over everything, as pervasive as sunshine, was the fragrance of balsam firs. It was aromatic and sweet and I closed by eyes and breathed deeply to draw in more of it.

⁴ Voices from some of the tents meant that others were stirring. At the house wood smoke rose from the chimney, another redolent fragrance mingling soon with the smell of bacon frying. It is a combination familiar to everyone who has known woodland mornings. There would be talk at breakfast, the meeting with strangers—a loss. The sunrise across the wild northern lake seemed a kind of holiness that human chatter was bound to destroy a little. The water, so still and lucent, beyond it the dark mystery of the forest, and the firs' fragrance: for this sacred experience, enjoyed alone, I would get up at dawn every day during that summer.

⁵ We would be here for three months with my father joining us for July. Neither of my parents had been here before but friends, the Wymans from Painesville, had written to say that they knew of this island in the Muskoka Lakes and suggested our spending some weeks there together. After three summers in Kansas City, where the temperature day and night can stay above ninety, we were going to get away somewhere, and since my father had not been back to his native Canada for some time, the Wymans' idea appealed to my parents.

⁶ On the island were five or six visiting families. Some had children of whom only one was a girl near my age. She would turn out to be very lively, never happy unless she was engaged in some boisterous game. I thought of her as an enemy. The family who owned this tiny resort were named White. They had several grown sons and a daughter. One of the sons, Dalton, nineteen, was just back from Montreal where he had won the junior world championship in canoeing. He was dark-haired and tall, with a puckish smile, to me

that year probably the most glamorous youth in the world. One could never, of course, hope to be friends with him.

⁷ At the back of the house were a large vegetable garden, two or three sheds and an old boat with grass growing up through its timbers. Past them one reached a thicket. I pushed through it that first afternoon, into the woods beyond.

⁸ The brush was thinner here but the trees grew densely. I wandered on, memorizing some landmarks: this boulder, this berry bush, this fallen log. I looked back. All had disappeared! It was a different grove when one turned around.

⁹ The house was no longer in sight and my heart beat faster. I was lost! But one couldn't get lost on an island, although this one was large, three and a half miles long. It was only necessary to find the shore, mostly rocky and wild, and follow it back. But I still felt lost and curiously afraid.

¹⁰ The trees, vaguely and strangely, were menacing. Not in any park, cemetery or pasture had I ever been so entirely enclosed by trees. These were massive, like giants. One surrounded by them felt helpless. They spread above, forming together a cavelike dark. They were presences. *Which way had I come*—where was the shore!

¹¹ Fear of trees is an old reaction, still a familiar emotion on primitive levels. Eskimos camping among trees, found along Northern rivers, dare not settle down beneath one for the night until they have stood off and thrown a knife into its trunk. Many other tribes have been awed by trees. If a branch has been broken off, if its bark has been damaged, or in the case of having to fell it, an apology would be made to a tree. The blood of a slaughtered animal was brushed onto it, or it was given a drink of water. In the Punjab, a former province of India, human sacrifices were made to a certain tree every year. Trees and groves in many parts of the world have been considered sacred.

·   ·   ·

¹² In the Canadian woods I didn't believe consciously that a tree might be hostile. I was just strangely uneasy there in the eerie atmosphere of the grove. One can name this dread and call it claustrophobia, which probably is an ancient fear. A prehistoric man might have felt trapped in dense woods, and recently Sir Frank Fraser Darling, the eloquent conservationist, has said that many modern people are afraid of a wilderness, which is why they are so willing to see it destroyed. Anyway I was slightly alarmed by that island forest, and although I was rather eager to know what was there I couldn't force myself to continue farther.

¹³ My going and coming were noted, for I met Dalton on the way back and he said, "You didn't stay in the woods very long."

¹⁴ "I was getting lost." He smiled with amusement.

¹⁵ There were always three or four canoes pulled up on the beach. One day I got one of them out on the water and was floundering around in it when Dalton came down to the dock. He called, "Try to bring it back to the beach and I'll show you how to paddle." I sat in the bow facing him as with his

strong, quick stroke he shot us out onto the lake. There he gave me the first lesson, demonstrating the right way to hold the paddle, how to turn it so smoothly in pulling it back that a canoe doesn't vary its course by an inch. "Line up the prow with some tree on the shore," he said, "and don't let it swing either side off the trunk." In shallow water again we changed places and awkwardly I tried to put into practice what he had demonstrated. A skill, a start in learning a new skill—inspiring prospect—from this young man who himself was dedicated to perfecting a skill: was it possible that we might have something in common?

¹⁶ The Whites had a piano. It was in the sitting room of the house and I could no more stay away from it than I could have gone without food. My frequent playing must have been a trial to some of the other guests, especially a violinist who practiced several hours a day in his tent (a situation I didn't remind him of when I met him years later in San Francisco where he was teaching the young Yehudi Menuhin). But Dalton enjoyed my music. He used to come and stand at one end of the piano with his elbow on top, listening and watching.

¹⁷ He gave me more paddling lessons and after a while I too could hold a canoe's prow on the trunk of a shoreline tree. In the afternoons I went out with him in his racing canoe, as ballast he said, while he kept up his training. His canoe was a little sliver of a thing with graphite all over the outside to make it slip through the water faster. In Montreal he had paddled a mile in four minutes and seven seconds, a record which probably has been beaten many times, but when he dipped in his paddle, his canoe leapt away like a dolphin.

¹⁸ He landed us on the mainland one day and said, "Let's take a little walk." With a companion one could enjoy a forest. Besides, the trees here were of varying heights, they didn't form caves. It was an intricate scene, everything was prolifically growing—and dying. The ground was a litter of brown leaves and fir needles and sticks. It was unkempt compared with a park but fascinating.

¹⁹ All around us was limber movement. The grasses and wildflowers bent quivering in the flow of the breeze and the trees above were a green ruffling commotion. Their leaves, as they tossed and swung, seemed to be cutting the sky into bits, to be scattered as scraps of sunlight along the ground.

²⁰ Birds were lacing the air, in and out of the trees and bushes. One on the ground was jumping forward and scratching back through dead leaves and one, also searching for insects, was spiralling upon a tree trunk, pressing its stiff, short tail on the bark as a prop. At that time, in June, most of the birds would be feeding young, Dalton said, and they had to work all day catching insects for them. Besides this bright movement of wings, then, there must be thousands of tinier creatures doing whatever insects do on a summer afternoon: a world everywhere *alive.*

²¹ Dalton seemed to have realized that I knew almost nothing about what was here and was showing me things: a porcupine's tracks, a bee tree, a fox's

burrow. He knocked on a tree and a flying squirrel poked its little head out of a hole. It was all wonderful, even exciting, but strange.

²² We came out on a small elevation. Below was a meadow brimful of yellow-green sunlight. Perhaps this was the pleasantest way to enjoy a forest: with trees and brush at your back but a wide escape if anything should approach from behind. Unmentionable were wolves, bears. (They may have been there in fact. That forest is now built up but resorts not far away advertise that guests can hear wolves baying.) Dalton had brought his rifle. Was he just thinking of shooting something for fun, or was the gun for protection?

²³ The thought of escape was still there. Compare a park: only a few, spaced-out trees were allowed to grow, their dead branches were pruned away, the flowers were all in neat beds, the grass was kept mowed, never allowed to become weeds or "grasses." All controlled, therefore safe.

²⁴ Here the plants grew their own way and the animals went their own way—one might appear anywhere, any time. No one knew what might happen—did happen, for there were dead broken trees among the live ones. Everything was wild—naturally. That was the meaning of forests of course, that they were wild. Therefore unpredictable.

²⁵ Yet the wilderness was a beautiful, even enchanting place with its graceful movement and active life. Even underfoot if one scratched away the brown leaves as the bird had done, one might come upon small, secret lives. But might there be things that would bite? I had heard of tarantulas. With a feeling of cowardice, shrinking back, I wanted to leave, to return to the wide placid lake. And then I did something which made it seem that, on nature's terms, I had no right to be here at all.

²⁶ Dalton said, "Look!" Pointing: "There's a porcupine in the crotch of that tree over there." One of the wild inhabitants of this forest, only medium sized for an animal, sat on the branch, his back a high curve, with his quills raised and bristling. He might be lying like that to let the sunshine come into his fur, warm down to his skin. He looked sleepy. Dalton handed the rifle to me and said, "Let's see if you can hit it."

²⁷ He showed the way the gun should be held, braced against my shoulder, how to sight the target along the barrel. "Now pull the trigger back with your right hand—slowly, just squeeze it." I pulled the trigger and with astonishment saw the porcupine fall to the ground.

²⁸ Dalton was full of praise. "Very good! I didn't think you could do it." We went down along the side of the meadow. Beneath the tree lay the porcupine, limp and still. Even his fur and quills were that, lifeless now. Looking smaller, this was the little creature who, a few moments earlier, had been up on the bough wrapped in sunshine, enjoying life. I burst into tears.

²⁹ Dalton went over alone the next day and drew out the quills and brought them to me to decorate the basket of scented sweet-grass that I, like all the women, was making. I gave them away. . . .

³⁰ I never returned to the mainland forest alone, but by midsummer I'd made my own a small peninsula on the island. Paddling along its shore one

morning I had tied the canoe to a tree overhanging the lake and sat in its shade doing embroidery. The point—it was the southern tip of the island— was narrow, not more than fifty yards wide. Through its trees I could see across to the bay on the other side and the center was open, with a thin cover of grass and wildflowers among sun-warmed rocks. It looked perfectly safe and I went ashore to investigate.

[31] There was no trail leading away from here, the point seemed private, peculiarly mine, and it pleased me very much. I came back the next day and then other days. Sometimes I walked about but more often sat under one of the trees, which were firs and quivering aspens, listening to the songs of the birds and watching them and a squirrel who was always there. I had a wonderful feeling—I had had it too with the chipmunk—that I was acceptable here, that I was liked, for they made little overtures even before I started feeding them bits of bread. Perhaps it helped that I talked to them.

[32] Gradually, a few moments one day, more moments the next, being there in that small safe woodland began to seem almost the same experience as making music, as the way, when I played the piano, I *was* the music, my physical body feeling as if it dissolved in the sounds. I could say my dimensions then were those of the melodies and the harmony that spread out from the piano in all directions. I had no consciousness of my individual self.

[33] Tenuously, imperfectly that Canadian summer, the same thing happened when I would walk around the peninsula, unafraid. It was not a wide going out and out, as with music, but again by losing myself—this time by becoming identified with whatever I was especially aware of. It happened first with a flower. I held a blue flower in my hand, probably a wild aster, wondering what its name was, and then thought that human names for natural things are superfluous. Nature herself does not name them. The important thing is to *know* this flower, look at its color until the blueness becomes as real as a keynote of music. Look at the exquisite yellow flowerettes in the center, become very small with them. *Be* the flower, be the trees, the blowing grasses. Fly with the birds, jump with the squirrel!

[34] Finally I spent every morning there. No one knew where I had gone.

ANALYTICAL READING

1. In this narrative, Sally Carrighar moves from being a stranger to becoming a part of the wilderness. Trace the steps in this progress.

2. In her descriptions of the Canadian island, to what senses does Carrighar appeal? Illustrate.

3. How does Carrighar use comparison in the selection? How do these comparisons help to explain the killing of the porcupine?

4. What kind of person was Dalton? Do you think he and the writer were similar?

5. What is Carrighar's relationship to Dalton? Does that relationship help to explain the killing of the porcupine? Why does she say that she "never, of course, hoped to be friends with him"?

6. Can you give the meaning of these words: *lucent, redolent, claustrophobia, graphite?*

7. Reread the eight paragraphs (18-25) preceding the encounter with the porcupine. How do they heighten the horror of killing the porcupine? Why does she shoot it?

REFLECTING

Point: What point does Carrighar make about the relationship of humans with the wilderness? How does it relate to the attitudes toward trees that she mentions?

Organization: Does Carrighar rely mainly on chronological organization? Support your answer. Divide the narrative into several main sections, showing their functional relationships. For example, what purpose does the paragraph about the piano serve?

Support: Discuss Carrighar's use of the following to support her message: (1) description, (2) her experiences with animals, (3) her feelings about trees and flowers.

Synthesis: Compare the message in the last paragraph with Pirsig's recommendation to his student. Relate Carrighar's experiences with Parfit's.

Evaluation: Do you find Carrighar's language effective? Does she create images? List some sentences that strike you as especially effective. Be able to justify your choices. Does she convince you of her changed attitude toward being alone in the woods? Do you grow to share her reverence toward nature?

FROM READING TO WRITING

1. Some of Carrighar's sentences create images in much the same way as haiku do. Choose several sentences and, using her words, shape them into seventeen-syllable haiku. You will have to delete unnecessary words.

2. Write a narrative about a time in your own life when hurting or killing an animal gave you a new awareness of life and your relationship to other creatures.

3. Describe your own first awareness of the beauty of nature or your first feelings of oneness with it. Avoid flowery generalities; try to be as specific in your statements as Carrighar is.

GRANDMOTHER'S ENCOUNTER
Maya Angelou

BIOGRAPHICAL SKETCH

Maya Angelou (1928–   ) was born in St. Louis. She started her career as a dancer and toured Europe and Africa in Porgy and Bess *and has had acting roles in* Cabaret for Freedom *and Genet's* The Blacks. *More recently, she played Kunta*

FROM Maya Angelou, *I Know Why the Caged Bird Sings* (New York: Random House, 1969), pp. 26–32. Copyright © 1969 by Maya Angelou. Reprinted by permission of Random House, Inc.

Kinte's grandmother in the TV version of Roots. *A civil rights activist, she worked with Martin Luther King, Jr., and the Southern Christian Leadership Conference and has taught and lectured in a number of universities. Her most recent book is* Gather Together in My Name, *a continuation of the book from which this selection is taken,* I Know Why the Caged Bird Sings.

PRE-READING

1. What relationship do you see between the title of the book the selection comes from and the information in the biographical sketch?

2. From skimming the first paragraph, what do you expect the selection to be about? Who is the main character?

¹ "Thou shall not be dirty" and "Thou shall not be impudent" were the two commandments of Grandmother Henderson upon which hung our total salvation.

² Each night in the bitterest winter we were forced to wash faces, arms, necks, legs and feet before going to bed. She used to add, with a smirk that unprofane people can't control when venturing into profanity, "and wash as far as possible, then wash possible."

³ We would go to the well and wash in the ice-cold, clear water, grease our legs with the equally cold stiff Vaseline, then tiptoe into the house. We wiped the dust from our toes and settled down for schoolwork, cornbread, clabbered milk, prayers and bed, always in that order. Momma was famous for pulling the quilts off after we had fallen asleep to examine our feet. If they weren't clean enough for her, she took the switch (she kept one behind the bedroom door for emergencies) and woke up the offender with a few aptly placed burning reminders.

⁴ The area around the well at night was dark and slick, and boys told about how snakes love water, so that anyone who had to draw water at night and then stand there alone and wash knew that moccasins and rattlers, puff adders and boa constrictors were winding their way to the well and would arrive just as the person washing got soap in her eyes. But Momma convinced us that not only was cleanliness next to Godliness, dirtiness was the inventor of misery.

⁵ The impudent child was detested by God and a shame to its parents and could bring destruction to its house and line. All adults had to be addressed as Mister, Missus, Miss, Auntie, Cousin, Unk, Uncle, Buhbah, Sister, Brother and a thousand other appellations indicating familial relationship and the lowliness of the addressor.

⁶ Everyone I knew respected these customary laws, except for the powhitetrash children.

⁷ Some families of powhitetrash lived on Momma's farm land behind the school. Sometimes a gaggle of them came to the Store, filling the whole room, chasing out the air and even changing the well-known scents. The children crawled over the shelves and into the potato and onion bins, twanging all the

time in their sharp voices like cigarbox guitars. They took liberties in my Store that I would never dare. Since Momma told us that the less you say to white-folks (or even powhitetrash) the better, Bailey and I would stand, solemn, quiet, in the displaced air. But if one of the playful apparitions got close to us, I pinched it. Partly out of angry frustration and partly because I didn't believe in its flesh reality.

⁸ They called my uncle by his first name and ordered him around the Store. He, to my crying shame, obeyed them in his limping dip-straight-dip fashion.

⁹ My grandmother, too, followed their orders, except that she didn't seem to be servile because she anticipated their needs.

¹⁰ "Here's sugar, Miz Potter, and here's baking powder. You didn't buy soda last month, you'll probably be needing some."

¹¹ Momma always directed her statements to the adults, but sometimes, Oh painful sometimes, the grimy, snotty-nosed girls would answer her.

¹² "Naw, Annie . . ."—to Momma? Who owned the land they lived on? Who forgot more than they would ever learn? If there was any justice in the world, God should strike them dumb at once!—"Just give us some extra sody crackers, and some more mackerel."

¹³ At least they never looked in her face, or I never caught them doing so. Nobody with a smidgen of training, not even the worst roustabout, would look right in a grown person's face. It meant the person was trying to take the words out before they were formed. The dirty little children didn't do that, but they threw their orders around the Store like lashes from a cat-o'-nine-tails.

¹⁴ When I was around ten years old, those scruffy children caused me the most painful and confusing experience I had ever had with my grandmother.

¹⁵ One summer morning, after I had swept the dirt yard of leaves, spear-mint-gum wrappers and Vienna-sausage labels, I raked the yellow-red dirt, and made half-moons carefully, so that the design stood out clearly and mask-like. I put the rake behind the Store and came through the back of the house to find Grandmother on the front porch in her big, wide white apron. The apron was so stiff by virtue of the starch that it could have stood alone. Momma was admiring the yard, so I joined her. It truly looked like a flat redhead that had been raked with a big-toothed comb. Momma didn't say anything but I knew she liked it. She looked over toward the school principal's house and to the right at Mr. McElroy's. She was hoping one of those commu-nity pillars would see the design before the day's business wiped it out. Then she looked upward to the school. My head had swung with hers, so at just about the same time we saw a troop of the powhitetrash kids marching over the hill and down by the side of the school.

¹⁶ I looked to Momma for direction. She did an excellent job of sagging from her waist down, but from the waist up she seemed to be pulling for the top of the oak tree across the road. Then she began to moan a hymn. Maybe not to moan, but the tune was so slow and the meter so strange that she could

have been moaning. She didn't look at me again. When the children reached halfway down the hill, halfway to the Store, she said without turning, "Sister, go on inside."

[17] I wanted to beg her, "Momma, don't wait for them. Come on inside with me. If they come in the Store, you go to the bedroom and let me wait on them. They only frighten me if you're around. Alone I know how to handle them." But of course I couldn't say anything, so I went in and stood behind the screen door.

[18] Before the girls got to the porch I heard their laughter crackling and popping like pine logs in a cooking stove. I suppose my lifelong paranoia was born in those cold, molasses-slow minutes. They came finally to stand on the ground in front of Momma. At first they pretended seriousness. Then one of them wrapped her right arm in the crook of her left, pushed out her mouth and started to hum. I realized that she was aping my grandmother. Another said, "Naw, Helen, you ain't standing like her. This here's it." Then she lifted her chest, folded her arms and mocked that strange carriage that was Annie Henderson. Another laughed, "Naw, you can't do it. Your mouth ain't pooched out enough. It's like this."

[19] I thought about the rifle behind the door, but I knew I'd never be able to hold it straight, and the .410, our sawed-off shotgun, which stayed loaded and was fired every New Year's night, was locked in the trunk and Uncle Willie had the key on his chain. Through the fly-specked screen-door, I could see that the arms of Momma's apron jiggled from the vibrations of her humming. But her knees seemed to have locked as if they would never bend again.

[20] She sang on. No louder than before, but no softer either. No slower or faster.

[21] The dirt of the girls' cotton dresses continued on their legs, feet, arms and faces to make them all of a piece. Their greasy uncolored hair hung down, uncombed, with a grim finality. I knelt to see them better, to remember them for all time. The tears that had slipped down my dress left unsurprising dark spots, and made the front yard blurry and even more unreal. The world had taken a deep breath and was having doubts about continuing to revolve.

[22] The girls had tired of mocking Momma and turned to other means of agitation. One crossed her eyes, stuck her thumbs in both sides of her mouth and said, "Look here, Annie." Grandmother hummed on and the apron strings trembled. I wanted to throw a handful of black pepper in their faces, to throw lye on them, to scream that they were dirty, scummy peckerwoods, but I knew I was as clearly imprisoned behind the scene as the actors outside were confined to their roles.

[23] One of the smaller girls did a kind of puppet dance while her fellow clowns laughed at her. But the tall one, who was almost a woman, said something very quietly, which I couldn't hear. They all moved backward from the porch, still watching Momma. For an awful second I thought they were going to throw a rock at Momma, who seemed (except for the apron strings) to have

turned into stone herself. But the big girl turned her back, bent down and put her hands flat on the ground—she didn't pick up anything. She simply shifted her weight and did a hand stand.

²⁴ Her dirty bare feet and long legs went straight for the sky. Her dress fell down around her shoulders, and she had on no drawers. The slick pubic hair made a brown triangle where her legs came together. She hung in the vacuum of that lifeless morning for only a few seconds, then wavered and tumbled. The other girls clapped her on the back and slapped their hands.

²⁵ Momma changed her song to "Bread of Heaven, bread of Heaven, feed me till I want no more."

²⁶ I found that I was praying too. How long could Momma hold out? What new indignity would they think of to subject her to? Would I be able to stay out of it? What would Momma really like me to do?

²⁷ Then they were moving out of the yard, on their way to town. They bobbed their heads and shook their slack behinds and turned, one at a time:

²⁸ " 'Bye, Annie."

²⁹ " 'Bye, Annie."

³⁰ " 'Bye, Annie."

³¹ Momma never turned her head or unfolded her arms, but she stopped singing and said, " 'Bye, Miz Helen, 'bye, Miz Ruth, 'bye, Miz Eloise."

³² I burst. A firecracker July-the-Fourth burst. How could Momma call them Miz? The mean nasty things. Why couldn't she have come inside the sweet, cool store when we saw them breasting the hill? What did she prove? And then if they were dirty, mean and impudent, why did Momma have to call them Miz?

³³ She stood another whole song through and then opened the screen door to look down on me crying in rage. She looked until I looked up. Her face was a brown moon that shone on me. She was beautiful. Something had happened out there, which I couldn't completely understand, but I could see that she was happy. Then she bent down and touched me as mothers of the church "lay hands on the sick and afflicted" and I quieted.

³⁴ "Go wash your face, Sister." And she went behind the candy counter and hummed, "Glory, glory, hallelujah, when I lay my burden down."

³⁵ I threw the well water on my face and used the weekday handkerchief to blow my nose. Whatever the contest had been out front, I knew Momma had won.

³⁶ I took the rake back to the front yard. The smudged footprints were easy to erase. I worked for a long time on my new design and laid the rake behind the wash pot. When I came back in the Store, I took Momma's hand and we both walked outside to look at the pattern.

³⁷ It was a large heart with lots of hearts growing smaller inside, and piercing from the outside rim to the smallest heart was an arrow. Momma said, "Sister, that's right pretty." Then she turned back to the Store and resumed, "Glory, glory, hallelujah, when I lay my burden down."

ANALYTICAL READING

1. How old is the narrator? What kind of relationship does she have with her grandmother?

2. Were you aware of the language used? How does Maya Angelou indicate regionalisms and dialect variations in the story? Do these characteristics add authenticity to the narrator's voice? Refer to specific expressions: why, for example, is *powhitetrash* one word?

3. What do the first four or five paragraphs contribute to the narrative?

4. What is the tone in the story? Does it shift? When? If so, does this contribute to our knowledge of the narrator's feelings? Does the foreshadowing in paragraph 15 add to or detract from the account?

5. What do you find out about the physical environment and the way the characters lived? How is this information revealed?

6. What do you think the narrator learned from the episode? Why did she draw the heart in the dust? Has the incident affected her attitude toward the children?

REFLECTING

Point: What do you think the message is? Does the reader gain some understanding as the narrator does? Do you think the reader might learn things that the narrator is unaware of?

Organization: Does Maya Angelou use only a chronological organization? What do the opening paragraphs do for the overall organization of the story?

Support: How does Maya Angelou use the following to support the message in the story: the action, the emotional response of the narrator, the language, the images?

Synthesis: In what ways is this story related to the Nate Shaw selection? to other stories you may have read or know about (*Roots,* for example)? Contrast the reactions of the young and old black women. How do you account for the differences?

Evaluation: Did you find the situation believable? Why? Does the ending come close to excessive sentimentality? If you planned to present this narrative as a play, how would you have it end? Does the incident suggest realistically the threat that the blacks felt from the whites? Is it effectively depicted here?

FROM READING TO WRITING

1. Write a short narrative about a situation that somehow threatened you or a person close to you. Without making direct moralistic statements, try to write the story so that the reader can infer a moral lesson about human relationships.

2. Describe an experience you have had involving a bully, using dialogue and perhaps trying to explain the cause or causes of your characters' actions.

Autobiographical Anecdote

A NIGHT ON THE MOORS WITH THE BRONTË FAMILY
Scott Hume

BIOGRAPHICAL SKETCH

Scott Hume was born in Cleveland, Ohio, in 1950. He received his undergraduate education at Denison University, and is a graduate student in the English department of the University of Chicago.

PRE-READING

1. From the title and the biographical sketch, what kind of story do you expect this to be?

2. What do you learn about the narrator in the opening paragraph?

3. What is a moor? Do you associate the word with any other stories you have read? If so, what kind of stories were they?

¹ I am not the sort who sets much store in the supernatural. Postboxes do not become witches, shadows demons, in the loneliness of a full-mooned Halloween, nor do I suffer the superstitious gladly. But late one night on a Yorkshire moor, I was given a lesson in tolerance.

² My wife, Mary, and I were on a motor tour of England last fall. Her interest in Victorian political history and mine in Victorian literature had kept us moving about the country, visiting the homes of Disraeli, Dickens and other personal "shrines." One of my choices during our planning for the trip had been to visit Haworth, tucked among the folds of the Yorkshire countryside and found on only the most detailed maps. Haworth had produced three of the most remarkable 19th-century literary imaginations: the Brontë sisters.

³ No matter that this tiny village has since become famous—we had the feeling of having stumbled upon it, even though it was our precise destination. The 20 miles that separate it from the soot-blackened town of Bradford to the south is a peopleless stretch of hilly grazing land, scrub vegetation and sheep.

FROM *The New York Times*, October 31, 1976, Section 10, p. 1. © 1976 by The New York Times Company. Reprinted by permission.

One drives up over one more hill and Haworth suddenly appears like some somber Brigadoon.

⁴ The town is arranged along one principal street, which moves determinedly up along the side of a hill, stopping at the top where town merges again into moor. It is a village that might have been taken wholly from an Edward Gorey drawing: Dark stone and airless quiet. A few shops, a post office/bookstore, a few small inns. Spare and compact as though the land begrudges the space it takes.

⁵ The day we spent there touring the sights was overcast and damp. We walked respectfully through the Parish Church of St. Michael and All Angels, cold and simple, where the Rev. Patrick Brontë had been parson. We toured the Haworth Parsonage where the widower clergyman had raised his daughters Charlotte, Emily and Anne, and his rakehell son, Branwell. We paused to look at the sofa upon which Charlotte died at age 39, at that outliving her sisters and brother.

⁶ We ate a pleasant dinner at a small candle-lit restaurant, discussing the family over lager and lamb. We said what every visitor to Haworth must say: Being in that lonely town makes the stormy passions of "Wuthering Heights," the strange gothicism of "Jane Eyre," the moody introversion of "The Tenant of Wildfell Hall," all seem much more understandable.

⁷ We walked outside into an incredibly dark night. There were no street lamps in Haworth, and very little other light after dark. It is a town that retreats into itself early in the evening. A wind which must have swelled close to 30 miles an hour at times roared up over the hill and across the moor with such swirling fury that we had almost to yell to be heard at arm's length.

⁸ Perhaps it was the cumulative effect of 12 hours spent in the sobering atmosphere of the village. Perhaps it was the discussion of the dark novels and mad Branwell over beers. Or perhaps it was just that imp of the perverse that causes travelers to overcome their normal reservations and seek adventures around which later to memorialize their travels. Whatever the reason, standing in the dark and the wind, I suggested to Mary that we take a walk out on the moor in search of the ghost of Catherine Earnshaw or whatever or whoever else might still linger there.

⁹ The imp attacks different travelers at different moments; Mary resisted, wisely pointing out that it was pitch black, that we had no way of knowing what was out there or how to get around, and that it was probably private property anyway. She didn't need to add the most compelling caution of all: It was damned eerie out there in the dark. But nothing summons bravado like the misgivings of a companion, and I repeatedly assured her that there was no need to worry.

¹⁰ She finally agreed to join me, and we started across the fields, stumbling on the dark and uneven ground. I could not resist the temptation to add to the Halloweenish feel of the night by suggesting that I heard voices in the wind or by suddenly stopping in half-mock fright.

[11] We climbed to the top of a hill and stood swaying with the wind, saying nothing but peering across the black moor and blacker sky.

[12] "Charlotte! Emily! Anne! Branwell!" I called out. There was no echo, no response.

[13] I would have called again, but Mary spoke up: "Will you please stop trying to scare me? It's weird enough here without that. Let's go back."

[14] So we started our return to Haworth. We had walked only a short way when Mary stopped short.

[15] "What is that?"

[16] "Are you going to try to scare me now?" I laughed.

[17] "No, really. Listen."

[18] I didn't take her seriously until I felt it, too. The ground was rumbling beneath us. We turned—and saw four horses, shadows in the night, spring over the hill behind us. There was no question in which direction they were coming and none who they were.

[19] "It's the Brontës!" I screamed with a nervous laugh as we ran away as fast as we could across the fields. We could hear the sound of their hooves, following us no matter how we twisted and turned.

[20] Mary tripped, rolled and was up and running again in one move.

[21] Just as they were almost upon us we dove over the stone wall that separated the moor from the road from which we had strayed. Laughing, wide-eyed, out of breath, we looked at each other in disbelief. Had we really seen them? Yes! There really had been four of them! Too strange!

[22] When we picked ourselves up, the horses were still on the other side of the wall. Tired too, their breath shot out of their nostrils into the wind. There was a moment when we all faced each other in silence. Then they were gone again over the hills.

[23] I still do not believe in the supernatural, but neither do I make fun of those who do.

ANALYTICAL READING

1. This, like all anecdotes, really involves a single incident. What is it?

2. How does Hume establish a mood and a setting for the incident? Cite examples of language use that contribute to the mood and setting.

3. What words demand that the reader have specialized knowledge of the Brontës?

4. How did the experience modify the narrator's attitudes?

5. Unlike narrative, the anecdote is primarily concerned with the action. Is that true here? How much do you find out about the two characters involved? What does the description of the day and dinner add to the story?

REFLECTING

Point: What does the narrator learn from the experience? Does the reader learn it as well?

Organization: Although the story is presented chronologically, Hume gives many details about earlier activities in the day. What is the effect? How much time elapses altogether?

Support: The author relies strongly on references to the Brontës' novels for support of descriptive statements. What is the danger of relying too heavily on readers' prior knowledge? What details suggest that the writer is telling the truth?

Synthesis: How does this tale compare to other ghost stories you know about— "The Legend of Sleepy Hollow" or "The Hound of the Baskervilles," for instance? Have you had a similar experience with a "haunted house" or other spooky place?

Evaluation: Do you think this is an effective ghost story, or could it have been written with greater suspense? What changes would you suggest? Do you accept as valid the motivation for Mary and Scott's walk on the moor? What traditional devices are used here?

FROM READING TO WRITING

1. Almost all of us have experienced an eerie situation or have heard someone tell "true" ghost stories. Write one as a short anecdote, concentrating on the action rather than on the characters and their reactions.

2. Write an anecdote about a visit to a place that frightened you. Make the audience experience the terror you felt.

3. Do you believe in ghosts? Write a narrative showing (not just telling) why you do.

JAMES DICKEY'S GLORY

James Dickey

BIOGRAPHICAL SKETCH

James Dickey (1923–   ) was born in Atlanta, graduated from Vanderbilt University (where he played football) with B.A. and M.A. degrees, and flew more than a hundred combat missions in World War II. Now a professor of English at the University of South Carolina, he has worked in advertising, has been poet in residence at several schools, and served as a consultant in poetry to the Library of Congress for two terms. He is the author of numerous books of poetry, including Buckdancer's Choice, *which won the National Book Award in 1966. Among his many prose works are several books of literary criticism and critical articles, and the novel* Deliverance, *which was a Literary Guild selection and was made into a popular movie.*

FROM *Esquire,* October 1976, p. 81. © 1976 by Esquire, Inc. Reprinted by permission of Esquire Magazine.

PRE-READING

1. From the biographical sketch, what would you expect Dickey's "glory" to be?

2. From the title and the first paragraph, how would you identify the "glory"?

¹ In 1940 I was a senior in high school. My main sport was football, but my preference was really track. I was a big strong animal who could run fast, and I gloried in this fact. My conference, though I lived in Atlanta, was not the conference in which the big Atlanta high schools competed. I ran in the North Georgia Interscholastic Conference, or N.G.I.C., as it was popularly known. The high-hurdles event, which was my specialty, was often held on grass, up the middle of a football field. This was the case at the 1940 N.G.I.C. meet. We qualified in the afternoon, all of us trying hard but not so hard as to tire ourselves out for the night's final. In the trials I lost to a fine hurdler from Canton, Georgia, and then went out with him, soaked with shower water, and got a cheeseburger. I felt that I had not run well, that my start had been bad, that I had not been able to get a good grip on the turf with my spikes, that I had been too high over the hurdles, that my finish had been poor. But my conqueror had set a new N.G.I.C. record, and he should have.

² When I suited up for the finals, though, I was ready. I felt that I had come to run. It was a cool night, and there were several hundred people in the stands, and, when they called the hurdles final, a great many people were clustered about the finish line, where the tape glimmered with ghostly promise for the winner. I ran in the next lane from the boy from Canton. We shook hands: a new friendship, a fierce rivalry, for I knew he would give no quarter, and I knew damn well that I wasn't planning to give any. We got down on the blocks. Before us was a green sea of grass with faint line stripes from spring practice across it. I concentrated on getting as much pressure on my legs as I could. I would try to get off well, though I was too big to hope for a really fast start. The gun cracked, and we were gone. I paid no attention to where anyone else was but concentrated on form and on picking up speed between hurdles. But I could dimly sense the Canton boy. At the fifth hurdle I could tell that we were dead even.

³ The finish-line crowd was coming at us like a hurricane. I concentrated on staying low over the hurdles and made really good moves on the next three. I began to edge him by inches, and by the next two hurdles I thought that if I didn't hit the next two I'd make it. I also said to myself, as I remember, *don't* play it safe. Go low over the last stick, and then give it everything you've got up the final straight.

⁴ But I did hit the last hurdle. I hit it with the inner ankle of my left foot, tearing the flesh to the bone, as I found out later, and the injury left a scar which I bear to this day. However, my frenzied momentum was such that I won by a yard, careening wildly into the crowd after the tape broke around my neck. I smashed into the spectators and bowled over a little boy, hitting straight into his nose with my knee. He lay on the smoky grass crying, his

nose bleeding, and I came back, blowing like a wounded stallion, everybody congratulating me on a new N.G.I.C. record. But I went to the boy, raised him up in my arms, wiped the blood from his nose, tried to comfort him, and kissed him. That raising-up of an injured, unknown child was the greatest thing that I have ever gleaned from sports.

ANALYTICAL READING

1. What does Dickey mean by "glory"? How does it compare to your preconceived notions?

2. How old do you think Dickey was at the time of the incident? Where did it take place?

3. Is there an ironic twist at the ending of the story? How does Dickey prepare the reader for it?

4. How does Dickey use description to heighten the sense of total concentration?

5. As you read, were you aware of how Dickey uses sentence structure to emphasize the speed and urgency of the race? Review the second paragraph describing the race, listing the length and kinds of sentences you find there.

REFLECTING

Point: Does the story make a statement about human priorities? Discuss.

Organization: Except for the first paragraph, the story is arranged chronologically. What purpose does the first paragraph serve?

Support: In questions 4 and 5 above, you looked at the description and sentence techniques. Do these also serve as support? How? What specific details make the selection vivid? How effective are such images as "The finish-line crowd was coming at us like a hurricane" and "I came back, blowing like a wounded stallion"?

Synthesis: Compare Dickey's experience with Sally Carrighar's. What do they have in common? How are they different?

Evaluation: Did the story hold your suspense and interest? Why? Would the story have been more or less successful if Dickey had explained why the raising up of the child was so important to him? How does the ending flatter the reader?

FROM READING TO WRITING

1. Write an anecdote about a time when you participated in a competitive event and things turned out differently than you had expected.

2. Write an anecdote titled "_____'s Glory," putting your name in the blank.

3. Write an anecdote about how sports contributed to the development of your character.

THE PERFECT PICTURE
James Alexander Thom

BIOGRAPHICAL SKETCH

James Alexander Thom, a native of Indiana and a graduate of Butler University (Indianapolis), has been a police reporter, feature writer, and financial editor for the Indianapolis Star *and an editor of the revived* Saturday Evening Post. *Now a free-lance writer, he has been a contributor to* Reader's Digest, National Geographic, *and* The Country Gentleman. *His novels include* Spectator Sport *(1978) and one he is currently working on that is based on the Revolutionary War. At present he is a lecturer in the school of journalism at Indiana University.*

PRE-READING

1. From the title, what profession would you expect the narrator to be in?

2. After skimming the first paragraph, what do you know of the narrator and the plot?

3. Describe the tone the writer establishes in the opening paragraph.

¹ It was early in the spring about 15 years ago—a day of pale sunlight and trees just beginning to bud. I was a young police reporter, driving to a scene I didn't want to see. A man, the police-dispatcher's broadcast said, had accidentally backed his pickup truck over his baby granddaughter in the driveway of the family home. It was a fatality.

² As I parked among police cars and TV-news cruisers, I saw a stocky, white-haired man in cotton work clothes standing near a pickup. Cameras were trained on him, and reporters were sticking microphones in his face. Looking totally bewildered, he was trying to answer their questions. Mostly he was only moving his lips, blinking and choking up.

³ After a while the reporters gave up on him and followed the police into the small white house. I can still see in my mind's eye that devastated old man looking down at the place in the driveway where the child had been. Beside the house was a freshly spaded flower bed, and nearby a pile of dark, rich earth.

⁴ "I was just backing up there to spread that good dirt," he said to me, though I had not asked him anything. "I didn't even know she was outdoors." He stretched his hand toward the flower bed, then let it flop to his side. He lapsed back into his thoughts, and I, like a good reporter, went into the house to find someone who could provide a recent photo of the toddler.

⁵ A few minutes later, with all the details in my notebook and a three-by-five studio portrait of the cherubic child tucked in my jacket pocket, I went toward the kitchen where the police had said the body was.

⁶ I had brought a camera in with me—the big, bulky Speed Graphic which used to be the newspaper reporter's trademark. Everybody had drifted back out of the house together—family, police, reporters and photographers. Entering the kitchen, I came upon this scene:

⁷ On a Formica-topped table, backlighted by a frilly curtained window, lay the tiny body, wrapped in a clean white sheet. Somehow the grandfather had managed to stay away from the crowd. He was sitting on a chair beside the table, in profile to me and unaware of my presence, looking uncomprehendingly at the swaddled corpse.

⁸ The house was very quiet. A clock ticked. As I watched, the grandfather slowly leaned forward, curved his arms like parentheses around the head and feet of the little form, then pressed his face to the shroud and remained motionless.

⁹ In that hushed moment I recognized the makings of a prize-winning news photograph. I appraised the light, adjusted the lens setting and distance, locked a bulb in the flashgun, raised the camera and composed the scene in the viewfinder.

¹⁰ Every element of the picture was perfect: the grandfather in his plain work clothes, his white hair backlighted by sunshine, the child's form wrapped in the sheet, the atmosphere of the simple home suggested by black iron trivets and World's Fair souvenir plates on the walls flanking the window. Outside, the police could be seen inspecting the fatal rear wheel of the pickup while the child's mother and father leaned in each other's arms.

¹¹ I don't know how many seconds I stood there, unable to snap that shutter. I was keenly aware of the powerful story-telling value that photo would have, and my professional conscience told me to take it. Yet I couldn't make my hand fire that flashbulb and intrude on the poor man's island of grief.

¹² At length I lowered the camera and crept away, shaken with doubt about my suitability for the journalistic profession. Of course I never told the city editor or any fellow reporters about that missed opportunity for a perfect news picture.

¹³ Every day, on the newscasts and in the papers, we see pictures of people in extreme conditions of grief and despair. Human suffering has become a spectator sport. And sometimes, as I'm watching news film, I remember that day.

¹⁴ I still feel right about what I did.

ANALYTICAL READING

1. What do we learn of the narrator's feelings about the assignment? about the old man? What words indicate the writer's sympathy and emotional involvement?

2. As you read, were you aware of the devices the writer used to indicate the time sequence? Check back to find examples.

3. Unlike the writers of many of the other narrative selections, Thom uses very little dialogue. What advantage can you see in this?

4. The descriptions in the anecdote are often photographic. Choose one that you think has strong pictorial characteristics and analyze how that effect is achieved.

REFLECTING

Point: The writer makes a rather obvious point. Summarize it in one sentence. Where in the article is it presented? How is the reader prepared for it?

Organization: How is the story organized? Draw a simple outline of the time elements in the story. Has the author eliminated unnecessary details to focus on the scene with the child and grandfather?

Support: How do the detailed descriptions help to support the message of the story? Discuss the effectiveness of the phrase "island of grief" (paragraph 11)?

Synthesis: The story involves a conflict between professional and personal ethics. Does Dickey's narrative relate to this conflict?

Evaluation: This story could easily have been handled as a sentimental tear-jerker or as an obvious moral sermon. Does the writer avoid these traps? Justify your opinion. Did the writer do right? Did he have a responsibility to newspaper readers? What about comparable episodes today on television?

FROM READING TO WRITING

1. Write in anecdote form about an episode in your life that involved a moral decision. Indicate how you feel today about the decision you made.

2. Write about a time when the demands of a job, sport, or other activity conflicted with your personal ethics.

THE ALARM CLOCK
Mari Evans

BIOGRAPHICAL SKETCH

Mari Evans is a native of Toledo, Ohio. Formerly an assistant professor at Indiana and Northwestern universities, she has lectured and read her poetry at many colleges, and also served as a consultant to the National Endowment for the Arts. Among her many honors and awards are a John Hay Whitney fellowship, a Woodrow Wilson Foundation grant, and the first annual award in 1970 of the Black Academy of Arts and Letters for her book, I Am a Black Woman. *She has written several other books, including some for juveniles, and has contributed to numerous journals.*

FROM *I Am a Black Woman* (New York: William Morrow & Co., 1970). Reprinted by permission of the author.

PRE-READING

1. In order to realize all the possible relationships of the title to the poem, think about the possible meanings of "alarm."

2. From the biographical sketch, what general subject might you expect the poem to deal with?

Alarm clock
sure sound
loud
this mornin' . . .
remind me of the time   5
I sat down
in a drug store
with my
mind
away far off . . .   10
until the girl
and she was small
it seems to me
with yellow hair
a hangin'   15
smiled up and said
"I'm sorry but
we don't serve
you people
here"   20
and I woke up
quick
like I did this mornin'
when the
alarm   25
went off . . .
It don't do
to wake up
quick . . .

ANALYTICAL READING

1. What kind of person is "I"? How does the poet depend upon the American experience to identify the narrator? Do you think "I" is a man or woman? Does it matter?

2. What is the situation in the poem? Does the poem fit into the category of "anecdote"?

3. What seems incongruous about the white girl's statement? How does the poet contribute to this effect.

4. Discuss the poem's use of analogy.

5. How would you characterize the speaker's dialect in the poem?

6. How many meanings of *alarm* do you find in the poem?

REFLECTING

Point: What is the message in the poem? How is it made?

Organization: Does the writer use flashback organizational technique? Discuss.

Support: Does the description of the white girl help to support the message?

Synthesis: How does the poem relate to the Nate Shaw selection? the Maya Angelou selection? Is it true that "it don't do to wake up quick"?

Evaluation: Is the analogy handled effectively? In forming an opinion about the poem, examine the form carefully; what words are repeated? Why does the poet give such importance to her daydreaming?

FROM READING TO WRITING

1. Making use of some of the writing techniques that you found in reading Evans' poem, write an anecdote poem. Try to imitate Evans' method of using sparse descriptions with carefully selected words to set the setting and situation.

2. Write about a memorable incident in your own life—first as a prose anecdote, then as an anecdote poem.

3. Write about an incident when you were suddenly and suprisingly confronted by reality.

TO DEFEND THE RIGHTS
OF THE HELPLESS
Eunice Shriver

BIOGRAPHICAL SKETCH

Eunice Shriver was born in Massachusetts, a daughter of Joseph P. and Rose Kennedy. She obtained a degree in sociology from Manhattanville College of the Sacred Heart and an M.S. in sociology from Stanford University. She follows the Kennedy tradition of active participation in public affairs; her particular interests are the rehabilitation of mentally retarded people, women criminals, the handicapped, and juvenile delinquents. In addition, she has taken an active part in the political campaigns of her three brothers, John F., Robert, and Edward, and of her husband, Sargent Shriver.

FROM *Redbook*, April 1976, p. 65. Copyright © 1976 by The Redbook Publishing Company.

PRE-READING

PRE-READING

1. Does the title indicate that this article might be more than simply the relating of an anecdote? Is there an argumentative edge to the title—a sense that the writer will attempt to "sell" an idea?

2. From the biographical sketch, why do you think the first paragraph is especially effective as an attention-getting device?

[1] The experience that made me proudest to be an American had nothing to do with politics, power or patriotism.

[2] It happened last summer. At 6 p.m. on August 7, 1975, I was in Mount Pleasant, Michigan, to attend the Fourth International Special Olympics for the mentally retarded, most of them children, some of them adults. I stood outside Perry Stadium, greeting some of the 3,200 competitors who were massed there under bright flags and banners, waiting for the ceremonies to start. They had come from 30 states and eight countries. I saw many in wheel chairs, dozens on crutches. Some had cerebral palsy, many were mongoloid; all were slower in thought than what we have decreed to be "normal" in our society.

[3] I thought about the great courage of these people, the agonizing effort and determination that had brought them all the way to this Michigan town. I hoped fervently that the Special Olympics would somehow prove to be an exciting, significant and memorable experience in their lives.

[4] Then as I walked into the brightly lighted stadium I saw something I'll never forget: 20,000 people—total strangers to the mentally retarded—had filled every seat. They had come to tell the contenders that they were loved, wanted, admired. This was no condescending "benefit" audience. Here were farmers, factory workers, storekeepers, housewives—most of them conservative Midwesterners who do not readily show their emotions. But as the band began to play and the competitors entered the stadium these people cheered their heads off.

[5] "They like us!" exclaimed a ten-year-old girl from Connecticut as she marched in with her delegation. It was true. For the next four days the cheering never stopped.

[6] Away from the stadium, moreover, the people of Mount Pleasant pitched in to make the retarded children and adults welcome in every way. They took them into their homes, exchanged names and addresses, gave them souvenirs, assisted them in the Olympic events. One thousand Mount Pleasant teen-agers adopted as "brothers and sisters" boys and girls whose differences from their hosts were startling and even disturbing. Fifty nearby communities made them guests of honor for a day.

[7] When it was all over, one young Michigan woman wrote to me: "I saw and heard and did things that I shall never forget as long as I live. It was the most satisfying thing I have ever done in my life." Another young volunteer told me, "I got so excited when I saw one boy running the two-twenty-yard

dash on crutches that I ran along with him for the whole race. I felt I was a part of him."

[8] President Kennedy once said that a nation's greatness can be measured by the way it treats its weakest citizens. At Mount Pleasant I saw and felt how great America can be.

[9] Still, I know that in many places in our country we have not yet learned to accept people who are different. We have not learned that the rights of the helpless must be defended even more vigorously than those of the powerful. Not every community is Mount Pleasant, and mentally retarded individuals are not cheered or welcomed everywhere. They are often rejected by their community, isolated, put in institutions, experimented upon, forgotten. Until we see clearly the common value of all people—bright or dull, strong or weak, fortunate or deprived—we fail to honor the essential American idea; and more deeply, in denying the humanity of others we are destroying it in ourselves.

[10] But Mount Pleasant, Michigan, was different, and in that joyous stadium on that August night I saw America at its greatest, and I was deeply proud.

ANALYTICAL READING

1. Does Shriver allow the situation itself to create a sympathetic attitude? Note that there is little description of the participants. Does this help to keep the article from becoming overly sentimental?

2. What advantage is achieved by Shriver's emphasis on the responses of the audience, rather than on the actions of the participants?

3. What purpose does the anecdote serve? Is it merely to tell a story?

REFLECTING

Point: What is the message in the story? Can you pick out one sentence that summarizes it?

Organization: The article is divided into two parts. What are they?

Support: Does Shriver depend only on the anecdote to support her point? If not, what else is used? How does she convey the mood of the people of Mount Pleasant?

Synthesis: How does this anecdote compare with Thom's narrative about the "perfect picture"? How does it compare with the treatment of handicapped children in your community?

Evaluation: This article was written as part of the bicentennial celebration. Do you think the patriotic emphasis weakens or strengthens it as a piece of writing? Justify your opinion. Do you feel that the next-to-last paragraph adds to or detracts from the selection?

FROM READING TO WRITING

1. Write an essay that makes a moral point by relying mainly on an anecdote that illustrates it.

2. Write an anecdote about an episode involving some kind of heroic or courageous action.

3. Write a narrative praising or criticizing people for the way they behaved at some event, such as a basketball loss, a graduation, or a lecture.

Personal Essay

LOOK FOR THE RUSTY LINING
Ralph Schoenstein

BIOGRAPHICAL SKETCH

Ralph Schoenstein (1933–   ) was born in New York and earned a B.A. from Columbia University. He has been active as a television writer-producer and journalist. His nonfiction sports story "A Giant Fan's Lament" won him the Grantland Rice Memorial Award in 1962. He has written many books, the most recent of which are Wasted on the Young *(1974) and* Booze Book *(1974). His humorous essays have appeared in numerous magazines and anthologies.*

PRE-READING

1. Of what popular saying is the title a rephrasing? What do you expect the title to contribute to the tone of this personal essay?

2. After skimming the first paragraph, indicate the sentence that you think is the focusing statement—the one that introduces the subject to the reader?

3. From skimming the first paragraph, do you expect this to be a serious essay? What sets the tone?

¹ My grandfather's hobby was worrying, and although hobbies are not usually thought of as being inheritable, I am a talented worrier, too. My grandfather's glum genes, which skipped my merry father, have reflowered in me as a major, all-purpose anxiety. A few weeks ago, for example, I learned that collapsing stars called black holes may soon suck up all the matter in the universe. Because I read this in *Vogue*, I hoped at first that the black holes were some kind of fad—a celestial pop event like Kohoutek or UFOs—but then I saw that the author of the article had been twice a visting Member at the Institute for Advanced Study, in Princeton, and I knew that another crisis was at hand. Ominously, the Institute is just down the street from where I do *my* worrying.

² The end of the universe should have been a splendid challenge for a gifted worrier like me, but mostly it upset me in a new and worrisome way, because it made me realize that I was spread too thin. When I found the

FROM *The New Yorker*, February 3, 1975, p. 31. Reprinted by permission. © 1975 by the New Yorker Magazine, Inc.

black-hole story, I hadn't nearly come to the end of an earlier wonderful worry of mine about the polar ice cap melting and raising the level of the Atlantic Ocean enought to submerge the entire East Coast. I had been thinking of moving my family to Saskatchewan, but now that I was falling behind in my worrying, I had to worry if Saskatchewan might be tastier for a black hole than Princeton. On the other hand, Princeton was closer to those African killer bees that have been inexorably moving north from Brazil—the ones that made me decide not to visit Central America last winter. The bees are getting very close to Central America, and Panama may be the only place where there is a chance to turn them back. Of course, even if it had only butterflies, Panama would still be a worrisome vacation spot for me, because it is said to be riddled with as much anti-American feeling as Boston.

³ In these terrible days, I often think of my grandfather, who was a nervous wreck in a simpler and happier time. His worries were transient and nicely manageable: When would Mel Ott start hitting again? When would Eleanor Roosevelt collapse from too much traveling around? When would the Third Avenue "L" rust away? I miss him, but he is lucky not to be alive and worrying today. I don't think he could have handled all the terrors that keep testing my sanity; he might even have surrendered and become an optimist, thus forfeiting the hobby he loved.

⁴ He was my inspiration when I was a boy—a worrier to look up to. He used to visit me in my room, where he would examine my homework and then shake his head and say, "You'll never get through medical school with spelling like this."

⁵ "But these are brand-new words," I would tell him in a worried way. "Spelling is harder this year than it was in the second grade."

⁶ He would sigh and say, "I don't know. I'm not even sure you should be a doctor at all. I just read that they have the highest rate for dropping dead."

⁷ My grandfather's quaint worries about me and Mel Ott and Eleanor Roosevelt are enough to make a contemporary worrier weep with envy. I wonder what he would have done if he had read a recent prediction by Gunnar Myrdal that the American economy could utterly collapse within five years—just before the Eastern tidal wave but shortly after the arrival of the bees. Probably he would have adopted something like my own advanced worrying posture and learned to make room for each new worry by letting it trump one of the old ones. For example, when I read about the inundation of the East I forgot about my overdue Bloomingdale's bill; when I read Gunnar Myrdal's warning I decided to stop worrying about what would happen if Connecticut ever ran out of antiques. When I heard about the bees I eased off my worry about a root canal of mine and let the Panama Canal replace it on the Top Twenty.

⁸ What a list! Something old and something new, something cosmic yet something trivial too, for the creative worrier must forever blend the pedestrian with the immemorial. If the sun burns out, will the Mets be able to play their entire schedule at night? If cryogenicially frozen human beings are ever

revived, will they have to re-register to vote? And if the little toe disappears, will field goals play a smaller part in the National Football League?

[9] Actually, I've never had a worry as worrisome as the universe-destroying black holes. I mean, the universe is where I do all my worrying, and if it suddenly disappears I may not be able to relocate. My only hope comes from a first principle of worry that I have learned in a lifetime of anxiety; i.e., some of the biggest problems are half of a self-cancelling pair. A nice example is that dreaded polar ice cap, which some scientists say isn't starting to melt at all but instead will shortly begin to enlarge rapidly, giving birth to a new ice age that soon will cover the entire United States. I worried about this ice layer from last February 9th until about Labor Day, by which time my worry about the price of bottom round had reduced it to the size of a rink. Lately, however, I have turned my mind back to the ice again, and I have been worrying about the fact that you cannot have ice that is growing and melting at the same time. One of these terrors is a dud, and the job of the dedicated worrier is to find out which one it is.

[10] Applying this principle to the black holes, I wonder if there may not be some white holes in space as well—pretty, glowing things that won't digest a universe but may prefer to spit it out again. All I need is a new flash from the Institute about one of these, and then perhaps I will be able to start worrying about chinch bugs and the male menopause and all the other gentle terrors my grandfather could endorse.

[11] Is that the right way to spell "chinch bugs"?

ANALYTICAL READING

1. Does the writer sustain the tone set in the opening paragraph? How?

2. What "how-to" suggestions for worrying does Schoenstein offer? How do these contribute to the overall tone?

3. How does the last paragraph contribute to the effectiveness of the essay?

REFLECTING

Point: Do you think the writer is advocating that we all should worry, or that we worry too much, or what? Discuss. Is there any suggestion about "the good old days" as opposed to the present?

Organization: Outline the organization of the personal essay by summarizing the main point of each paragraph. How do these relate to the focusing statement?

Support: Recall some of the specific things that Schoenstein and his grandfather worry about. How do these contribute to the organization?

Synthesis: Does this essay touch on your own experiences? Do you tend to worry needlessly? Would it help to be able to scoff at your own worries? Do you know people who always worry? What present-day real worries have been omitted from the essay? Why?

Evaluation: Do you think the writer effectively sustains the point of view throughout? Discuss. What contribution does the character of the grandfather make to
   the account?

FROM READING TO WRITING

1. Make a list of your own persistent worries, categorize them into different types,
    and then write a humorous personal essay about them. Remember to avoid a
    heavy touch; choose words carefully to maintain a gentle sarcasm.

2. Choose an annoying or puzzling habit that you or someone close to you has.
    Summarize it in one sentence that can serve as the focusing statement and
    write a brief personal essay about it. Try for an amused but affectionate tone.

THE MAGIC POWER OF WORDS
Thomas H. Middleton

BIOGRAPHICAL SKETCH

   *Thomas Middleton (1926–   ), after his graduation from Princeton, became
an actor and has appeared in both film and stage plays. During rehearsals he began
to work Double-Crostic puzzles to kill time; later he started to create them himself.
For the last ten years his Double-Crostic has been a regular feature of the* Saturday
Review. *In addition, he writes a regular column, "Light Refractions," which reflects
his fascination with word meanings and usage.*

PRE-READING

1. What does the word "magic" conjure up in your mind? Can you think of words
    that have had "magic power" for you?

2. From the opening paragraph, what kind of words do you expect the essay to
    deal with?

   [1] There was a distressing story in the newspaper a few months ago. I
wish I'd clipped it out and saved it. As it is, I can only hope I remember it
fairly accurately. There was a group of people who wanted a particular dictionary removed from the shelves of the local library because it contained a lot of
obscenity. I think they said there were sixty-five or so dirty words in it. Some
poor woman who was acting as a spokesman for the group had a list of the
offending words, which she started to read aloud at a hearing. She managed to
read about twenty of them before she started sobbing uncontrollably and
couldn't continue.
   [2] I'm sure I could have read off the entire list. I'm equally sure I'd have
been somewhat embarrassed at reading some of the words out loud at a

FROM *Saturday Review*, 11 December 1976, p. 90. Copyright © 1976 by the Saturday Review Corporation.

hearing. Today, there are undoubtedly many people—both men and women—who could have managed the whole thing without a trace of a qualm. But the fact is that we'd not all be doing the same thing. For me, it would mean enunciating words whose connotations might range from the completely inoffensive to the quite unpleasant, with a good sprinkling of the ludicrous in between.

3 For those who could read the list with no feeling of uneasiness, the words would be "only words."

4 While I don't like anything about the idea of removing any dictionaries from any libraries, I can sympathize with the woman who broke down. For her, the words were not "only words": they were horrifying things with their own terrible power, and they were too much for her.

5 There is power in spoken words. Some of the power is not unlike magic. The fact that the power may (or may not) be all in our minds does not diminish its effect.

6 Most people probably don't know that if you tell someone your dream before breakfast, it will come true, but my mother told me that almost as soon as I was old enough to put my dreams into words. So all my life I've been telling my good dreams before breakfast and saving the nightmares for later. It wasn't until I was well into my twenties that I finally realized that this superstition was not at all widespread. In fact, I haven't met anyone outside of my immediate family who has ever heard of it. Maybe my mother made it up. It is, nevertheless, a minor instance of the magic power of the spoken word.

7 One of the major instances of this power is the widely held belief in the efficacy of knocking wood. If, for example, the old heap hasn't had to go to the garage for repairs in almost a year, you'd better not mention the fact out loud, or you'll need a new clutch and a new set of rings that evening—unless you knock wood.

8 When I was in college, one of the psychology professors told us, in a lecture on superstition, that even among men of science who knew that super-stitions were only superstitions and should not be taken seriously, knocking wood was a very common practice. He made me feel better, because though I may fool around with other superstitions (dreams before breakfast, etc.), "knock wood" is one superstition I take absolutely seriously. I've walked under ladders; I ignore black cats; I've put a hat on a bed; even as a child, I stepped on many a crack, smug in the conviction that I would not thus break my mother's back; I've even spilled salt without tossing some over my shoul-der; but if I were to say something like, "I haven't had a bad cold in over three years," I wouldn't be able to breathe regularly until I'd knocked wood.

9 Obviously, it's all right to *think* about how well things have been going. Just don't express your thoughts in words, where there is magic.

10 Countless generations have been taught, practically as soon as they could speak, that enunciating certain words constitutes a giant step toward hell and that speaking or chanting other words or combinations of words is a big help along the road to salvation or spiritual bliss; one man's nonsense syllable is another's path to peace.

[11] While the power of traditionally shocking words to shock is at an all-time low, at least in the United States, and many of us have decided that words are only words and are not in themselves either good or bad, it is still hard for me to imagine anyone for whom there are not some words with almost supernatural connotations, whether the words be Om, O Lord Our Father, Holy Mary, Hare Krishna, or a simple statement of faith in one's carburetor.

[12] As one who has to find wood to knock in order to minimize the negative effects of his own words, I certainly can't fault someone who is overpowered by a collection of—to her—hideous taboos taken from a dictionary.

ANALYTICAL READING

1. Middleton treats the account in the newspaper as an opening anecdote. What does this contribute to the essay?

2. Where does Middleton place his focusing statement?

3. Do you think Middleton intended to instruct his audience about words or simply to comment on some superstitions concerning them? Discuss. How does he feel about the people attacking the dictionary?

4. As you read, were you aware of the devices Middleton used to hold the essay together? Review the essay, noting how he moves from one paragraph to the next and how he repeats words that have to do with his subject.

REFLECTING

Point: Does Middleton's point have to do with what words mean or with what people *think* they mean? Explain.

Organization: How does Middleton use the final paragraph to pull the essay together? How effective is the opening anecdote?

Support: What examples does Middleton use to support his statements? How effective are the examples in sustaining interest in the essay?

Synthesis: Does the essay relate to some situations you recalled from the title at the pre-reading stage? Are magic words employed in folk tales, comic strips, movie cartoons, transcendental meditation? Should a dictionary list all words, or should certain kinds of words be omitted?

Evaluation: Compare this personal essay with Schoenstein's. Which do you find more effective? Why? Has Middleton given you any new understanding about language? If so, what?

FROM READING TO WRITING

1. Write an essay about some superstitions you developed as a young child that are still with you. Try opening the essay with an anecdote.

2. Write an essay that recounts how you learned that certain words were unacceptable in some social situations.

3. In J. D. Salinger's novel *Catcher in the Rye,* young Holden Caulfield tries to erase a dirty word written on a wall. Relate this action to Middleton's essay.

4. Write a personal essay recounting times when you have noticed that masculine gender words, such as *spokesman* or *chairman,* seemed to exert the "magical" effect of stereotyping.

A BOOK WAS A BOOK
Leo Rosten

BIOGRAPHICAL SKETCH

Leo Rosten (1908–   ) was born in Lodz, Poland, immigrated to the United States in his youth, and received a Ph.D. from the University of Chicago and another from the London School of Economics and Political Science. He was a consultant to many government commissions during World War II, a special editorial advisor for Look *magazine, and a lecturer at numerous universities. In addition to several screenplays written under the pseudonym of Leonard Ross, he has written under his own name a collection of essays; several novels, including* The Education of H*Y*M*A*N K*A*P*L*A*N, *a comic story based on his experiences teaching English part-time to adult immigrants in a night school; and a delightful dictionary-like work,* The Joys of Yiddish. *Rosten is now a regular contributor to* Saturday Review.

PRE-READING

1. The title is comparable to other expressions in the language such as "A rose is a rose," "A beer is a beer," "A tree is a tree." Does this imply an undiscriminating attitude? How?

2. How does the first paragraph establish subject? tone? reader interest? Do you think after reading the first paragraph that the title implies that a book was only a book or that a book was a Book?

¹ A good book makes my nostrils quiver. In all other respects, I like to think, I am a clean, wholesome American boy. The memory of Lou Gehrig brings a lump to my throat; a well-shaped limb brings a gleam to my eye; but a good book makes my nostrils quiver.

² It is not that my nostrils are especially quiverable. They quiver because, for reasons you soon shall hear, a book triggers the most delicious associations in my mind between reading and (of all things) pickles. Dill pickles.

³ "*Dill* pickles?" you echo. "What on earth do books have to do with pickles?"

⁴ I'm glad you asked that.

FROM Leo Rosten, *The Many Words of Leo Rosten* (New York: Harper & Row, 1964), pp. 3–6. Copyright © 1962 by Leo Rosten. Reprinted by permission of Harper & Row, Publishers, Inc.

⁵ In my youth, I lived on the west side of Chicago. It offered all who inhabited that rough-and-tumble section of the city the vitality of life: crowds, noise, challenge, conflict, camaraderie, sidewalk poets, alley crooks, front-step seminars—plus the priceless dream of someday moving to a nicer neighborhood. This is a life and a dream that my children, raised in antiseptic California and genteel Connecticut, have been cruelly deprived of.

⁶ In those days, the Chicago public library used to establish outposts of civilization in depositary branches scattered around the city. The closest depot from which I could get free books was located at the rear of a seedy stationery store near Kedzie Avenue on Twelfth Street, which no campaigns by civic improvementeers could get us to call "Roosevelt Road." The man who ran the stationery store received a fee, I suppose, for the use of the dreariest twenty square feet of his premises.

⁷ To the golden, magical promise of that stationery store I would race in breathless excitement from George Howland school several afternoons a week. Neither hail nor fire nor pestilence, nor even Chicago's weather, could slow me down. I ran to my Eldorado in order to pick up such books as might have been deposited there, ear-marked for me, by a truck from the central library in that far-off sector of wealth and lake-front we called Downtown.

⁸ To order a book, under the neighborhood depositary system, you first consulted a card catalogue at the rear of the stationery (or dry goods, candy, novelty) store. On a slip of coarse brown paper, with the majestic words CHICAGO PUBLIC LIBRARY printed on top, you wrote your name and address, and then, in the columns provided, listed the call numbers of the books you wanted to get.

⁹ All the brown slips from all the depositary branches went to the central library, where the slaves who toiled in the stacks would go down the lists of numbers. If the first number on your list was not on the shelves of the stacks, the cellar gnomes would draw a contemptuous line through that number and proceed to the next. Since I could never be sure that the books I most yearned for would be available, I soon learned to list ten, twenty, even thirty numbers. The faceless lackeys at Michigan and Randolph never would send thirty books, of course, or even twenty, or even ten. They usually meted out no more than two to a customer. In any case, several days after listing my numbers on those library slips, I would race back to the stationery store for the treasures I might have drawn in this strange lottery.

¹⁰ Now the Lord, as we all know, doth move in mysterious ways. In my case, I think He received a special celestial pleasure in afflicting the guys in the stacks with astigmatism or hallucinations whenever they got to the brown slip on which I had so carefully, so legibly, so lovingly printed the numbers of the books I most coveted.

¹¹ For instead of receiving, say, number 712.8T, a piece of glory I could rattle off in my sleep as *Dave Porter in the Philippines,* I would get instead, say, number 912.8T, which is *The Prickle-Edged Flora of the Lower Sudan,* or 782.8R, a racy gem entitled *Aunt Polly's System for Tatting Antimacassars,* or even 742.5B, a

dandy little thriller about the drainage problems of the Mosquito Coast. (The Mosquito Coast is that strip of Honduras and Nicaragua I hope to hell I never see.)

[12] Well, a man going mad from thirst is not likely to reject a bottle of wine because of its vintage; I, a book-starved lunatic of no discrimination whatso-ever, read any book that fell into my hot little hands. I would be bitterly disappointed, of course, to discover that I had been gulled once more, that the malevolent cabal downtown had not sent me a single book out of the thirty immortal numbers I had listed—books by the great Burt L. Standish, the peerless Frank Packard, the masterly Sax Rohmer, the incomparable Joseph Altsheler. But if I was to be denied the joy of chortling over the antics of *The Red-Headed Outfield*, or cliff-hanging on the exploits of Dr. Fu Manchu, or cheering that matchless modern Robin Hood, Jimmy Dale—then, by heaven, *The Prickle-Edged Flora of the Lower Sudan* it would be. And it was.

[13] Between my passion to read anything and the statistical aberrations of the pixies in the library's nether regions, I managed to stuff my mind with information about as odd, exotic, pointless and useless as you are likely to find in the brain-pan of any bibliophile of my generation. It is not that I have a particularly retentive memory: I am not even blessed with the kind of mental-ity that latches on to simple facts like my bank balance, or the name of my daughter's latest suitor, or when it was my wife told me to be sure and turn off the oven. It is just that through some perverse arrangement of cells my brain seizes with joy upon such bits and pieces of culture as these:

[14] Nicolas Lancret left 780 paintings.

[15] Sirutel is a river in Rumania. (I'll bet you thought it was a syrup that provides "stomach regularity"—Leturis spelled backward.)

[16] In Borneo, they call 1.36 pounds of anything a Catty.

[17] The sawfly often is wingless.

[18] The Esopus Creek Dam is 252 feet high.

[19] In 1905, our Secretary of the Navy was a man named Bonaparte—Charles J. Bonaparte, to be exact.

[20] I have spent my life walking around with junk like that in my head, hoping that one of these days someone will come right out and ask me how many gametes are in a zygote, or in what year the Diet of Worms convened, or who played third base for the infamous Black Sox. I sometimes dream of dazzling beautiful duchesses in Mayfair with just such nuggets of knowl-edge—tossed off, need I say, with the most casual of airs and the most memo-rable aplomb. At dinner parties on Park Avenue I sometimes smile inscrutably as I drop the name of Ethelred the Unready into the table talk, or the diameter of the rose window at Chartres, or the great, undying name of Bonehead Merkel—but no one seems to care about erudition any more. In fact, people tend to draw away from me when I ruminate aloud about Philander Smith College, which you probably didn't know is in Little Rock.

[21] I have learned to enjoy these things just for themselves. It enlivens many a solitary walk for me to chuckle to myself over the sudden recollection

that it was in 1811 that Tecumseh, that noble Shawnee, decided to make a stand against the white man, or that "monoecious" denotes the presence of *both male and female flowers on the same plant.*

²² My experiences at that stationer's shop, so many years ago, taught me (apart from such nonsense) that there are rare and wonderful surprises to be found in the random. The book picked up to browse in, the side street taken just because you feel like it, the bus ride to no place in particular, the pedestrian stopped with a question to which you already know the answer ("How do I get to Fort Knox?")—in these random encounters with the unknown I have often found unexpected and delightful rewards.

²³ I sometimes think that in exchange for the priceless treasures it supplies, every library ought to set aside one day a year for Random Reading. Everyone who comes into the library on Random Day would be invited to reach into a huge barrel filled with books, pull out a volume at random—and read it. I should like to be on the committee that chooses the masterpieces, neglected by passing fads and debased tastes, that would go into those barrels.

²⁴ Barrels. That brings me back to pickles, from which I have strayed. Why does a good book make my nostrils quiver? Because whenever I left the stationery store, my eyes and mind glued to whatever book I had not ordered, there would be wafted into my nostrils a most pungent and provocative smell—a whiff of garlic and dill. I can't be sure whether the pickle barrel from which it came was concealed behind the stationer's counter, to satisfy some secret, shameless appetite of his, or whether that ambrosian scent came from the grocery store next door. But what does it matter? Just give me a good book and a pickle, or an olfactory facsimile of same, and I am in heaven. Even the gross deadweight tonnage of Liberia's tankers cannot intrude on my ecstasy.

ANALYTICAL READING

1. How does Rosten maintain an atmosphere of excitement and wonder throughout the essay? What words contribute to this effect?

2. Notice how Rosten is able to describe a place vividly by piling up descriptive words in one sentence—for instance, paragraph 5, where he describes the west side of Chicago. Find other examples.

3. What function does the lengthy description of the library system serve?

4. As you read, were you able to determine from context the meaning of *pestilence, Eldorado, gnomes, malevolent, cabal, aberrations, bibliophile?*

5. What effect does Rosten achieve by reciting items of trivial information? How does it contribute to the subject of the essay?

6. How does Rosten relate his book experiences to other facets of life?

REFLECTING

Point: Is the point of the essay simply that reading for the joy of reading is sufficient?

Organization: How does Rosten use pickles as an organizational device? Does the reference to pickles early in the essay serve another function? How is the essay organized?

Support: Point out the various devices Rosten uses to support the main message in the essay. Show how the details make the account more interesting and convincing.

Synthesis: Compare Rosten's childhood passion for books with a childhood enthusiasm you had. What purpose do you think such interests might serve? When you rummage around in the library, do you share Rosten's belief in random reading?

Evaluation: From the essay, what would you say is Rosten's attitude toward reading? Does he tell you this directly or by the way the essay is written? Discuss. Does he generate more enthusiasm in you about reading? What do you think of Rosten's voice—is it too informal?

FROM READING TO WRITING

1. Allow yourself about fifteen minutes to write about a favorite childhood pastime. Write as quickly as possible, trying to get down all your ideas.

2. Revise the essay you produced in exercise 1 by replacing all the ordinary words with provocative, colorful words, using them to create a consistent tone throughout.

3. Recreate in an essay your own experiences in the library with the card catalogue, librarians, and books.

TERRY PICKENS, NEWSBOY
Studs Terkel

BIOGRAPHICAL SKETCH

Studs Terkel (1912–   ), born in New York City, has a law degree from the Chicago Law School but has always worked in the communication field; he has been an actor in soap operas, a sports commentator, and a disc jockey, and has conducted on-the-spot interviews all over the world. Like Working, *his two previous books,* Division Street: America *and* Hard Times, *were best sellers.* Working *is a collection of taped interviews in which people discuss their attitudes toward their work.*

PRE-READING

1. Does the word *newsboy* in the title suggest any irritating experiences that might be common to all people who deliver papers? List a few before reading.

2. Does the first paragraph give an indication of the newsboy's attitude toward his job?

¹ I've been having trouble collecting. I had one woman hid from me once. I had another woman tell her kids to tell me she wasn't home. He says,"Mom, newsboy," She says (whispers), "Tell him I'm not home." I could hear it from the door. I came back in half an hour and she paid me. She's not a deadbeat. They'll pay you if you get 'em. Sometimes you have to wait . . .

² If I don't catch 'em at home, I get pretty mad. That means I gotta come back and come back and come back and come back until I catch 'em. Go around about nine o'clock at night and seven o'clock in the morning. This one guy owed me four dollars. He got real mad at me for comin' around at ten o'clock. Why'd I come around so late? He probably was mad 'cause I caught him home. But he paid me. I don't care whether he gets mad at me, just so I get paid.

³ I like to have money. It's nice to have money once in a while instead of being flat broke all the time. Most of my friends are usually flat broke. I spent $150 this summer. On nothing—candy, cokes, games of pool, games of pinball. We went to McDonald's a couple of times. I just bought anything I wanted. I wonder where the money went. I have nothing to show for it. I'm like a gambler, the more I have, the more I want to spend. That's just the way I am.

⁴ It's supposed to be such a great deal. The guy, when he came over and asked me if I wanted a route, he made it sound so great. Seven dollars a week for hardly any work at all. And then you find out the guy told you a bunch of bull. You mistrust the people. You mistrust your customers because they don't pay you sometimes.

⁵ Then you get mad at the people at the printing corporation. You're supposed to get fifty-seven papers. They'll send me forty-seven or else they'll send me sixty-seven. Sunday mornings they get mixed up. Cliff'll have ten or eleven extras and I'll be ten or eleven short. That happens all the time. The printers, I don't think they care. They make all these stupid mistakes at least once a week. I think they're half-asleep or something. I do my job, I don't see why they can't do theirs. I don't like my job any more than they do.

⁶ Sunday mornings at three—that's when I get up. I stay up later so I'm tired. But the dark doesn't bother me. I run into things sometimes, though. Somebody's dog'll come out and about give you a heart attack. There's this one woman, she had two big German shepherds, great big old things, like three or four feet tall. One of 'em won't bite you. He'll just run up, charging, bark at you, and then he'll go away. The other one, I didn't know she had another one—when it bit me. This dog came around the bush. (Imitates bark-

ing.) When I turned around, he was at me. He bit me right there (indicates scar on leg). It was bleeding a little. I gave him a real dirty look.

⁷ He ran over to the other neighbor's lawn and tried to keep me from gettin' in there. I walked up and delivered the paper. I was about ready to beat the thing's head in or kill it. Or something with it. I was so mad. I called up that woman and she said the dog had all its shots and "I don't believe he bit you." I said, "Lady, he bit me." Her daughter started giving me the third degree. "What color was the dog?" "How big was it?" "Are you sure it was our yard and our dog?" Then they saw the dogs weren't in the pen.

⁸ First they told me they didn't think I needed any shots. Then they said they'd pay for the doctor. I never went to the doctor. It wasn't bleeding a whole lot. But I told her if I ever see that dog again, she's gonna have to get her papers from somebody else. Now they keep the dog penned up and it barks at me and everything. And I give it a dirty look.

⁹ There's a lot of dogs around here. I got this other dog, a little black one, it tried to bite me too. It lunged at me, ripped my pants, and missed me. (With the glee of W.C. Fields) I kicked it *good*. It still chases me. There are two black dogs. The other one I've kicked so many times that it just doesn't bother me any more. I've kicked his face in once when he was biting my leg. Now he just stays under the bushes and growls at me. I don't bother to give him a dirty look.

¹⁰ There was these two other dogs. They'd always run out in the street and chase me. I kicked them. They'd come back and I'd kick 'em again. I don't have any problems with 'em any more, because they got hit chasin' cars. They're both dead.

¹¹ I don't like many of my customers, 'cause they'll cuss me if they don't get their papers just exactly in the right place. This one guy cussed me up and down for about fifteen minutes. I don't want to repeat what he called me. All the words, just up and down. He told me he drives past all those blank drugstores on his blank way home and he could stop off at one of 'em and get a blank newspaper. And I'm just a blank convenience.

¹² I was so mad at him. I hated his guts. I felt like taking a lead pipe to him or something. But I kept my mouth shut, 'cause I didn't know if the press guy'd get mad at me and I'd lose my route. You see, this guy could help or he could hurt me. So I kept my mouth shut.

¹³ A lot of customers are considerate but a lot of 'em aren't. Lot of 'em act like they're doing you such a favor taking the paper from you. It costs the same dime at a drugstore. Every time they want you to do something they threaten you: (imitates nasty, nasal voice) "Or I'll quit."

¹⁴ What I really can't stand: you'll be collecting and somebody'll come out and start telling you all their problems. "I'm going to visit my daughter today, yes, I am. She's twenty-two, you know." "Look here, I got all my sons home, see the army uniforms?" They'll stand for like half an hour. I got two or three like that, and they always got something to say to me. I'll have like two hours wasted listening to these people blabbin' before they pay me. Mmm, I don't

know. Maybe they're lonely. But they've got a daughter and a son, why do they have to blab in my ear?

¹⁵ A lot of the younger customers have had routes and they know how hard it is, how mean people are. They'll be nicer to you. They tend to tip you more. And they don't blab all day long. They'll just pay you and smile at you. The younger people frequently offer me a coke or something.

¹⁶ Older people are afraid of me, a lot of them. The first three, four weeks—(muses) they seemed so afraid of me. They think I'm gonna rob 'em or something. It's funny. You wouldn't think it'd be like this in a small town, would you? They're afraid I'm gonna beat 'em up, take their money. They'd just reach through the door and give me the money. Now they know you so well, they invite you in and blab in your ear for half an hour. It's one or the other. I really don't know why they're afraid. I'm not old, so I wouldn't know how old people feel.

¹⁷ Once in a while I come home angry, most of the time just crabby. Sometimes kids steal the paper out of people's boxes. I lose my profits. It costs me a dime. The company isn't responsible, I am. The company wouldn't believe you probably that somebody stole the paper.

¹⁸ I don't see where being a newsboy and learning that people are pretty mean or that people don't have enough money to buy things with is gonna make you a better person or anything. If anything, it's gonna make a worse person out of you, 'cause you're not gonna like people that don't pay you. And you're not gonna like people who act like they're doing you a big favor paying you. Yeah, it sort of molds your character, but I don't think for the better. If anybody told me being a newsboy builds character, I'd know he was a liar.

¹⁹ I don't see where people get all this bull about the kid who's gonna be President and being a newsboy made a President out of him. It taught him how to handle his money and this bull. You know what it did? It taught him how to hate the people on his route. And the printers. And dogs.

ANALYTICAL READING

1. This account was recorded by Studs Terkel on a tape recorder. Is there anything about the language and sentence structure that indicates its oral nature? Why are some comments in parentheses?

2. What characteristics of autobiographical narrative did you find? Why is this selection closer in form to a personal essay?

3. Do the examples contribute to Pickens' conclusion?

4. How old do you think Pickens is? On what evidence do you base your guess?

REFLECTING

Point: What is the message? Where is it expressed? What is its purpose?

Organization: Even though it is an interview, the essay does have unity and structure. Trace the kinds of experiences Pickens talks about and point out how they are related. How does he move from one to the next?

Support: Outline the main points made and the devices that support and embellish them.

Synthesis: Have you had a job in which you had contact with the public? Were your experiences similar to Pickens'? Compare this essay with Sylvia Plath's account of her experiences as a waitress (pp. 23–25). What did you know previously about being a newsboy? What did you learn about it from this essay?

Evaluation: Do you think the use of dialogue adds interest? Does the essay hold your interest? Why? Does the voice of the narrator seem authentic? Is he convincing? How typical do you think his experience is?

FROM READING TO WRITING

1. Add an opening paragraph to the interview to give it a suitable focusing statement. Be sure to imitate the voice of the narrator.

2. Write an essay about the irritations or satisfactions you experienced in a job you have had.

Assessment of Reading and Writing Skills: Personal Writing

Step 1

Read the essay that follows with the aim of understanding and recalling the important ideas. When you finish, note how long it took you to read the selection. Then close your book and write a summary of the important information without referring again to the essay. Indicate also your impression of the tone and word choice of the writer. You will be allowed 7 to 10 minutes to write; your instructor will establish the limit and tell you when the time is up.

A BOSTON TERRIER
E. B. White

I would like to hand down a dissenting opinion in the case of the Camel ad which shows a Boston terrier relaxing. I can string along with cigarette manufacturers to a certain degree, but when it comes to the temperament and habits of terriers, I shall stand my ground.

The ad says: "A dog's nervous system resembles our own." I don't think a dog's nervous system resembles my own in the least. A dog's nervous system is in a class by itself. If it resembles anything at all, it resembles the New York Edison Company's power plant. This is particularly true of Boston terriers, and if the Camel people don't know that, they have never been around dogs.

The ad says: "But when a dog's nerves tire, he obeys his instincts—he relaxes." This, I admit, is true. But I should like to call attention to the fact that it sometimes takes days, even weeks, before a dog's nerves tire. In the case of terriers it can run into months.

I knew a Boston terrier once (he is now dead and, so far as I know, relaxed) whose nerves stayed keyed up from the twenty-fifth of one June to the sixth of the following July, without one minute's peace for anybody in the

FROM E. B. White, *One Man's Meat* (New York and London: Harper & Brothers, 1944), pp. 69-70. Copyright 1939 by E. B. White. Reprinted by permission of Harper & Row, Publishers, Inc.

family. He was an old dog and he was blind in one eye, but his infirmities caused no diminution in his nervous power. During the period of which I speak, the famous period of his greatest excitation, he not only raised a type of general hell which startled even his closest friends and observers, but he gave a mighty clever excuse. He said it was love.

"I'm in love," he would scream. (He could scream just like a hurt child.) "I'm in love and I'm going *crazy*."

Day and night it was all the same. I tried everything to soothe him. I tried darkness, cold water dashed in the face, the lash, long quiet talks, warm milk administered internally, threats, promises and close confinement in remote locations. At last, after about a week of it, I went down the road and had a chat with the lady who owned the object of our terrier's affection. It was she who finally cleared up the situation.

"Oh," she said, wearily, "if it's that bad, let him out."

I hadn't thought of anything as simple as that myself, but I am a creature of infinite reserve. As a matter of record, it turned out to be not so simple— the terrier got run over by a motor car one night while returning from his amorous adventures, suffering a complete paralysis of the hip but no assuagement of the nervous system; and the little Scotty bitch returned to Washington, D. C., and a Caesarian.

I am not through with the Camel people yet. Love is not the only thing that can keep a dog's nerves in a state of perpetual jangle. A dog, more than any other creature, it seems to me, gets interested in one subject, theme, or object, in life, and pursues it with a fixity of purpose which would be inspiring to Man if it weren't so troublesome. One dog gets absorbed in one thing, another dog in another. When I was a boy there was a smooth-haired fox terrier (in those days nobody ever heard of a fox terrier that *wasn't* smooth-haired) who became interested, rather late in life, in a certain stone. The stone was about the size of an egg. As far as I could see, it was like a million other stones—but to him it was the Stone Supreme.

He kept it with him day and night, slept with it, ate with it, played with it, analyzed it, took it on little trips (you would often see him three blocks from home, trotting along on some shady errand, his stone safe in his jaws). He used to lie by the hour on the porch of his house, chewing the stone with an expression half tender, half petulant. When he slept, he merely enjoyed a muscular suspension: his nerves were still up and around, adjusting the bed clothes, tossing and turning.

He permitted people to throw the stone for him and people would. But if the stone lodged somewhere he couldn't get to he raised such an uproar that it was absolutely necessary that the stone be returned, for the public peace. His absorption was so great it brought wrinkles to his face, and he grew old before his time. I think he used to worry that somebody was going to pitch the stone into a lake or a bog, where it would be irretrievable. He wore off every tooth in his jaw, wore them right down to the gums, and they became mere brown vestigial bumps. His breath was awful (he panted night and day) and his eyes were alight with an unearthly zeal. He died in a fight with another dog. I have always suspected it was because he tried to hold the stone in his mouth all through the battle. The Camel people will just have to take my word for it: that dog was a living denial of the whole theory of relaxation. He was a paragon of nervous tension, from the moment he first laid eyes on his slimy little stone till the hour of his death.

The advertisement speaks of the way humans "prod" themselves to endeavor—so that they keep on and on working long after they should quit. The inference is that a dog never does that. But I have a dog right now that can prod himself harder and drive himself longer than any human I ever saw. This animal is a dachshund, and I shall spare you the long dull inanities of his innumerable obsessions. His particular study (or mania) at the moment is a black-and-white kitten that my wife gave me for Christmas, thinking that what my life needed was something else that could move quickly from one place in the room to another. The dachshund began his research on Christmas eve when the kitten arrived "secretly" in the cellar, and now, five months later, is taking his Ph.D. still working late at night on it, every night. If he could write a book about that cat, it would make *Middletown* look like the work of a backward child.

I'll be glad to have the Camel people study this animal in one of his relaxed moods, but they will have to bring their own seismograph. Even curled up cozily in a chair, dreaming of his cat, he quivers like an aspen.

Step 2

Read the following essay as quickly as you can without sacrificing your comprehension of the material. You will have a maximum of 2 minutes, 20 seconds (200 words per minute) to glean as much information as you can. If you finish before time is called, note how long it took you to read the selection. Again, close your book and write a summary of the essay, including a statement about the tone and word choice. You will have 7 to 10 minutes for this task.

A PROPERLY TRAINED MAN IS DOG'S BEST FRIEND
Erma Bombeck

My name is Murray Bombeck and I'm a guest columnist.

I'm a 3½-month-old Yorkshire Terrier.

There are a lot of dogs who are wondering whether they want to own a person. They like people. They're fun to be around, but are they worth all the fuss and bother?

FROM Erma Bombeck, "At Wit's End," *Louisville Courier-Journal*, September 24, 1976, p. B6. Copyright 1976 by Field Enterprises, Inc. Courtesy of Field Newspaper Syndicate.

I felt the same way when a few months ago I observed this couple. Their dog (another Yorkshire) had just been killed and, frankly, they were a psychological mess. During the interview, they kept calling me "Harry" (the deceased dog's name) and the woman kept swooping me off the floor and crying in my fur. They would take a lot of training.

First nights are generally a disaster. At 11 o'clock at night, just when things are beginning to cook, they turn off the lights and go to bed. (I had been warned by other person owners that this would happen.) I tried to keep them on their feet all night but things like this happen. Old habits are hard to break.

Another thing you have to know about people is that you have to keep them busy or they drive you crazy. Every time I ate a houseplant, they were there. When I chewed on shoes, they were there. They were smothering me. Once, when I went into the white living room to go to the bathroom, she came in, swooped me up, ran around hysterically finding a key to the back door, opened it up and heaved me out onto the grass.

You cannot imagine what turned her on.

When I "performed" she jumped up and down and clapped her hands while summoning three other people from the house to observe. I felt like a fool.

The hardest part of training a person, however, is discipline. You have to be firm with people or they'll run all over you. When they want to play by grabbing your nose, at first you just walk off, but when they pursue it, you just sink your teeth into their hands. They may look shocked and hurt at first, but you'll eventually have a person you don't have to be ashamed to take places.

And, lastly, be careful the first time you take them out in public. They wander away from you. I don't recommend a leash, but leave them in the car a few times and they'll shape up.

Everything you've heard about people is true. They're messy. They're tempermental and they're hard to train.

But in the evening when you're tired and they scratch behind your ears . . . or when you're beat from the sun and they let you play in the garden hose . . . or when you're sick and they put you on the sofa . . . they're worth it. People make great pets.

Step 3

Without looking back at the two essays, write a paragraph or two in which you evaluate them and explain how their ideas or issues are related. You may refer to your summaries, but not to the essays. Time: 10 minutes.

The
Informative Voice:
Descriptive Writing

2

In many ways, writing description is like painting a picture. The writer must approach the task with the same skills of perception that the artist has—the ability to look at an object, a person, or a scene and to reproduce it in vivid detail. There is, however, one notable difference in the two media. A painting appeals to the physical eye; written description to the mind's eye. Thus, while painters can often create the illusion of a tree or a building with a single brush stroke, writers must rely upon a number of well-chosen words that not only depict the image they wish to project but often convey an emotional response as well. Although the two media are different in many ways, both painting and descriptive writing share the need for detail—specific, concrete, colorful particulars. Where the artist paints with tints and strokes, the writer paints with words and phrases.

Therefore, to be most effective, descriptive writing demands that the writer select words carefully, being sensitive to all their subtle variations of meaning and to the way words sound together. Just as a painting can be marred by combining jarring colors or brushing too bold a stroke, so too can descriptive writing be flawed by a word that violates the imagery or the tone.

Another way that writers create descriptive pictures is by using comparison or analogy. An extended comparison is especially helpful when the writer is describing something that may be outside the reader's experience. Comparing the subject to something familiar can help the audience "see" it better. However, comparisons need not be lengthy to accomplish this. Figurative language devices such as simile, metaphor, and personification can make lively, effective comparisons with a single word or a short phrase. Remember, a simile uses *like* or *as;* a metaphor implies a comparison; personification ascribes human characteristics to nonhuman objects. For Example:

Simile: ". . . the very grand old elms *like gray broomstraws."* (Edmund Wilson, *Upstate*)

Metaphor: "I drove across the *upraised thumb* of Idaho." (John Steinbeck, *Travels with Charley*)

Personification: "Lying in my bed under the *weeping night* . . ." (John Steinbeck, *Travels with Charley*)

Creating word pictures, then, is the primary aim of descriptive writing. It can be as objective, factual, and impersonal as a scientist's report or a view under a microscope, designed primarily to give the reader specific information about an object, a place, or a person. Or it can be subjective, impressionistic, personal, fashioned as much to reflect the writer's feelings about the object being described as to supply information. These two approaches can be seen in a comparison of the wood duck in Jack Denton Scott's article (page 146, paragraphs 7–8) with that of the ducks in S. Dillon

Ripley's "The View from the Castle" (pages 151–52, paragraphs 2–5). Borrowed from a naturalist's handbook, Scott's description is precise and complete—you could paint a detailed portrait of a wood duck merely using his details. Ripley's highly subjective or personal description, however, emphasizes those details necessary to convey the sense of beauty, grace, and serenity derived from watching the ducks on the pond.

Writers can employ these sensory possibilities in many ways. Complete articles or essays can be purely descriptive, with the main purpose to describe something in vivid detail. This is the case with most of the selections included in this section of the text. Descriptive passages may also be used to add to the setting or atmosphere in narrative, to help explain a situation in expository writing, or to provide a vivid proof in argument. They can even introduce an explanatory or persuasive essay, as does Marilyn Kluger's article "A Time of Plenty." Regardless of its purpose, descriptive writing has distinctive characteristics that should be considered whether you are reading or writing it.

KINDS OF DESCRIPTIVE WRITING

PERSONAL DESCRIPTION

Personal description strives to be subjective. Words are chosen for their emotive qualities; the writer's voice bears the mark of the distinctive individual behind the pen—a person who is angry, sympathetic, amused, or awed about the subject. Addressing a less specialized audience than factual description reaches, writers of personal description usually seek some opening device to attract the reader's attention. Avon Neal's opening line in "Scarecrows Provide an Antic Art Form" *hooks* the reader by referring to a folktale about the perfect scarecrow, while Tom Wolfe's "A Sunday Kind of Love" starts with the most provocative single word in the language—*love.*

FACTUAL DESCRIPTION

Assuming that readers have an established interest in the subject, writers of factual description, unlike writers of personal description, do not feel compelled to provide an attention-arousing device—a hook to attract the reader. Already interested in the subject, the reader wants a no-nonsense, complete, factual description that supplies all the pertinent information. The reader usually does not expect or even want the writer's personal impressions about the subject. Thus, the voice of the writer tends to be matter-of-fact and serious, using vocabulary that may be scientific or technical and aimed at a specialized audience.

MIXED DESCRIPTION

Often, description cannot be categorized exclusively as personal or factual, but combines features of both. The resulting mixed description frequently includes impressionistic and subjective passages; it may also tailor the factual descriptions so that they highlight a mood or tone the writer wishes to create, or illustrate a judgment being made. Saul Bellow's factual description of the Illinois landscape in "Illinois Journey," for instance, adds to the mood of monotony he creates. Rachel Carson's objective descriptions of beaches in "Our Ever-Changing Shore" heightens her expression of concern for the preservation of the environment.

CHARACTER SKETCH

Descriptions of people are called character sketches and can be as varied as any other description. A character sketch can be entirely factual, as in a police description of a wanted criminal; it can be subjective—the writer's impressions of another person; or, as is frequently the case, it can be a mixture of the two. In addition, a sketch can either describe a particular person or a personality type. As you might expect, a character sketch of a *person* limits the writer to the physical and personality traits of that individual. A character sketch of a *type,* however, demands that the writer search for traits shared by the people who exemplify the type. Leo Durocher's description of Babe Ruth's physical appearance, for example, is appropriate in a character sketch of this particular baseball hero, but would not be suitable in a character sketch of the baseball hero as a type.

TACTICS FOR READING DESCRIPTIVE WRITING

PRE-READING

Many of the techniques you practiced in reading the personal writing in Part One will apply as well to reading descriptive writing. Certainly, you can profit from the habit of analyzing the title, reading any background material supplied, and skimming the opening paragraphs. But with description, you can follow our suggestion in the Introduction to the book that you also skim the closing paragraph. Knowing the ending of a description, unlike knowing how a narrative ends, will not detract from your satisfaction; on the contrary, you may gain added insight into the writer's attitudes toward the subject. Noting, for instance, that Jack Denton Scott's descriptive essay on the wood duck (pages 145–49) ends with approval of conservation measures can help you to appreciate better the hunter's personal admiration for wood ducks in an otherwise objective description. Or realizing from the last paragraph in the Rachel Carson selection (pages 156–60) that she considers the sea "the last outpost," you can be prepared before a full reading for the tone of awe and concern that pervades the description and accounts for its main point and its subjectivity.

ANALYTICAL READING

In reading description, you can add to the skills emphasized in reading personal writing. Certainly you want to maintain a perception of the writer's voice and of the subtle shades of meaning in the words used. As you read, underline or mark descriptive passages that are especially effective, noting fresh, image-evoking adjectives or metaphors. Look for statements throughout that may reveal the writer's purpose in writing the description—to inform, to share a beloved person or place with others, or to record an image of a person or place for posterity. Sentences that shed light on such questions can help you to gain a sense of the purpose and organization of the essay, if you relate them to the opening or focusing statement.

Sentence structure may demand more concentration from you in description than in personal narrative. You should become aware of the more complex sentences used to convey numerous descriptive details; however, this consciousness of sentence strategy need not interfere with your train of thought as you read.

Most important, remember that descriptive writing is meant to be sensory. So let yourself go and enjoy to the fullest the vicarious experience the writer sets up for you: see the details of the setting, smell the odors, and hear the sounds. If you are able to project yourself into the description, then you will be reading effectively and meaningfully.

REFLECTING

Point. Like personal essays, descriptions often begin with a statement indicating the writer's purpose. This is often a summary of the main point the writer wishes to make. It should be supported throughout the essay and is often reinforced, restated, or rephrased in the closing paragraph. Wilma Dykeman uses this device in "Miss May" (pages 168–69) to make her point that a teacher like Miss May is an asset to any community. The sentence in the opening paragraph, "Any city or community can ill afford to lose the likes of her," is rephrased in the final line, "We can ill afford to lose her instruction."

Organization. Like narrative writing, description can be arranged chronologically; however, the most frequent organizational device is spatial. A writer must describe a bird's plumage, for instance, by moving from one area of the body to another. The description moves in space (left to right, front to back), not in time. Occasionally, a description will have both chronological and spatial organization, as in Frank Goodwyn's poem, "Twenty-Point Buck" (page 119). Time does pass in the poem, but the emphasis is on the spatial arrangement of the deer, the woods, and the hunter. Chronology is secondary in importance; in fact, the spatial arrangement creates a timeless, "frozen" image.

Support. Support in description is achieved almost exclusively by word painting—the piling up of descriptive words and phrases. Obviously, some sentence structures are better suited to this kind of stockpiling than others. The short, simple sentences often used in personal narrative dialogue would be inefficient, resulting in needless repetition of information. Compound sentences, strung across the page like beads by *and,* could create a monotonous style, one that would be likely to intrude on the reader's consciousness and interfere with the reading process.

Many modern writers find that a useful sentence type for handling a multitude of detail is the cumulative sentence, in which most of the basic information is given first, followed by a string of specific details. This basic sentence structure permits an amazing amount of variety. Here are three examples from John Steinbeck's *Travels with Charley* illustrating just a few of the possibilities. The basic information (main clause) is italicized in each:

> *The bed was lumpy,* the walls dirty yellow, the curtains like the undershirt of a slattern. (All details added after the main clause; all treated in similar sentence structures.)
>
> His dark, shining *hair was a masterpiece of overcombing,* the top hair laid back and criss-crossed with long side strands that just cleared the ears. (Details added before the subject *hair* and at the end of the main clause in random structures.)
>
> Just under the ridge of a pass, *I stopped for gasoline in a little* put-together, do-it yourself *group of cabins,* square boxes, each with a stoop, a door, and one window, and no vestige of a garden or gravel paths. (Details added before the main clause, before the subject *group of cabins,* and at the end of the main clause.)

Useful as the cumulative sentence is, it is certainly not the only sentence device employed by writers to present many details. Any sentence structure repeated over and over results in poor writing style. But used with care, the cumulative sentence does permit readers to follow easily the flow of the sentence, and does enable writers to add many vivid supporting details.

Synthesis. Effective description, like effective personal narrative, should strike some responsive chord in each reader. A well-written description of a favorite duck pond or a memorable teacher should remind you of the same or similar experience or memory against which a comparison or contrast can be made. In order to assimilate a written work completely, you should also be able to compare and contrast it with other essays you have read so that you can become aware of the organizational strategies and the word choices that make a description a unique, individual piece of work.

Evaluation. As with personal writing, your emotional response will be uniquely yours. You will react most strongly when reading descriptions of places or people that evoke your own experiences. But to be the kind of critical reader we outlined in the Introduction to the book, you should also be able to support your emotional response by citing specific traits that a work has—traits that are characteristic of that particular kind of writing. Is Gordon A. Reims' description of Maine lobstermen (pages 178–81), for instance, effective simply because he admires these colorful people, or does his organization, his word pictures of the trappings of the trade, his description of the hard sea life that they share contribute to the reader's response? When you can state in detail the reasons why you like or dislike a descriptive essay, you have become a critical evaluator of description.

FROM READING TO WRITING

Points that we have stressed about reading description can be utilized in your own writing assignments:

1. *Organization.* Somewhere in your opening paragraph, include an opening, focusing statement that signals your reader what your subject is and how you feel about it. Then, before you write, think about how you wish to handle the organization and point of view. If it is a static description of a place or person, spatial arrangement is necessary, but where should you start? If your essay involves an incident or passage of time, how should you combine chronological and spatial organization? Also, do you need to attract the reader's interest in the opening paragraphs? And should your description be factual, personal, or mixed?

2. *Voice and language.* Decide in your early paragraphs which voice you wish to assume and try to keep it consistent throughout. You might remember that establishing a consistent voice is difficult even for experienced writers and may require adjustment in revision. As you look over your first draft, be alert for shifts in tone or in levels of usage. Experiment with words. Of all the forms of prose writing, description usually allows you the greatest freedom and creativity in language. Don't be satisfied until you have found the best combination of words to portray precisely what you wish to describe. Remember, you are not just *telling about* your subject, but *recreating* it—with all its sights, sounds, odors, tastes, and tactile feelings. As you play with the words, experiment also with sentence structure; try your hand at various cumulative sentences to include additional details. Remember, writing can be dull or it can be fun; it is fun only when you experiment and create.

Personal Description

TWENTY-POINT BUCK
Frank Goodwyn

BIOGRAPHICAL SKETCH

Frank Goodwyn (1911–   ) grew up on a Texas ranch as a cowboy, spending his summers in cow camps and his winters at the ranch school. He has a Ph.D. from the University of Texas, and his teaching assignments have included the ranch school he attended, Colorado University, Northwestern, and the University of Maryland, where he has been since 1950. His published works include two novels, The Magic of Limping John *and* The Black Bull, *three books of nonfiction, and numerous articles in academic journals in the fields of Spanish and folklore. He has been the recipient of the J. Frank Dobie Fellowship in Southwestern Literature, the Julius Rosenwald Fellowship, and Best Book of the Year awards for his two novels.*

PRE-READING

1. What significance would the title have for a hunter looking for a trophy?
2. How does the first line of the poem establish a setting, the season, and the general subject?

> His spread of antlers strikes the frozen branches
> And flings a shower of ice across his back,
> And as he leaps into the deeper brush,
> His tail, a bouncing fluff of cotton, shrinks
> Away. The woods fall silent as before,   5
> With shadowy, cold, haphazard barriers
> For subtle, silent things to hide behind.
>
> The icy coating, shattered into chips,
> Grows back together soon. The crystals merge
> To one bright, spangled glaze around the twigs,   10
> Over the fallen leaves and brittle bark.
>
> The hunter pauses, shrugs and shakes his head.
> The tracks are covered fast. The daylight fades.

FROM *Journal of Popular Culture*, Vol. 9, No. 3 (Winter 1975), p. 261. Reprinted in Frank Goodwyn, *Poems About the West*, copyright 1976 by the Potomac Corral of The Westerners, and used by permission of the publishers.

ANALYTICAL READING

1. As you read, were you aware of the imagery? How is the imagery created? Cite specific examples.

2. Is the narrator part of the action? Is the narrator critical of the hunter or sympathetic? Defend your answer.

3. What words help to convey the sense of cold winter?

4. Did you notice the verbs in the poem? How do they contribute to the description?

5. Do you think the final three words convey a meaning beyond the literal one? If so, what? Support your answer from the content of the poem.

REFLECTING

Point: Is there a "message" in the poem, or is it merely a vivid description of a moment in time?

Organization: Does the poet use chronological or spatial organization or a combination of the two? Do the last three words contribute to the organization?

Support: What function do you think the second verse fulfills? Would the point of the poem be supported without it?

Synthesis: Compare the "action" described here with that in paragraph 17 of the Carrighar article (page 68). Do you think the poem expresses the majesty and supremacy that the title implies?

Evaluation: What imagery in the poem did you find most effective? least effective? Why? How did the experience of the poem affect you—were you moved, involved, concerned?

FROM READING TO WRITING

1. Describe a single action that you have observed as you walked on campus or in a park—an encounter between a dog and a squirrel; two birds fighting over territory; a dog or child playing in a fountain; a student throwing a Frisbee or a snowball. Concentrate on creating images. Write in either paragraph or free-verse form.

2. Retell the incident in the poem in paragraph form, without destroying the sharp imagery of the poem.

FALL COMES IN ON ROLLER SKATES
Anne Rivers Siddons

BIOGRAPHICAL SKETCH

Anne Rivers Siddons, who was born in Atlanta, Georgia, has a B.A. degree in commercial art, with a minor in English, from Auburn University. She is presently the senior editor of Atlanta Magazine *and a contributing editor to* Georgia Magazine. *She has published two books,* Heartbreak Hotel *(available in paperback), and* John Chancellor Makes Me Cry *(1975). In addition, she has contributed articles to such magazines as* Redbook, House Beautiful, *and* Gentlemen's Quarterly.

PRE-READING

1. What is your reaction to the title? What tone is established by the title?

2. After skimming the first five paragraphs, what statement can you make about the use of the title in the opening section?

[1] "How do you know when fall gets here?" a five-year-old of my acquaintance asked her mother and me on a Sunday afternoon last year. We were sitting on the edge of her parents' pocket-sized swimming pool, dangling our feet in the exhausted September water. The temperature was 92 degrees.

[2] "Fall is when the leaves are red and the air is nippy and you get to wear your new wool clothes," said her mother. "In fact, fall starts officially next week."

[3] The child, taking in the used-green leaves and the heat miasma uncoiling from the patio, clearly regarded this as another piece of adult propaganda and rewarded us with the level stare children reserve for kittenish adult excesses. Wool was a patent insanity in anybody's book, and bright foliage and tart mornings were light-years away from her back yard.

[4] It was most probably a rhetorical question. Children know when autumn comes, almost to the hour. Some small signal forever lost to adults trips the delicate interior alarm clock that is built into children somewhere behind their ribs. It isn't leaves going bright, or cool mornings. Those come later. Fall comes when you stop doing the summer things and start doing the fall ones.

[5] When I was small, fall came in on roller skates. Somewhere in the last burning days of August, a morning came when we met under the oak tree in my front yard—as we had every morning that summer—and the skates were there. Jangling in bicycle baskets. Thumping over skinny shoulders like outsized epaulettes. Skate keys sprouted amulet-like around reedy necks, on shoelaces or grimy twine. There had been no previous agreement to put away the rubber-tire slingshots and the gut-spilling softballs. The alarm clock had simply, for each of us, gone off sometime in the dreamless night.

FROM *Atlanta Magazine,* October 1969. Reprinted by permission of Atlanta Magazine and the author.

⁶ For the rest of fall, up until the lowering winter met us on the way home from school and robbed us of the light, skating was the autumn thing that we did. We went in swooping flights down sidewalks and streets, always with our parents' "Be *careful!*" thrumming in our ears, drunk on our own momentum, giddy on wind and wheels. The very small ones of us, restricted to front walks, windmilled on treacherous feet and looked with awe and hate at the flying phalanxes of big kids streaming by, trailing immortality like a bright comet's tail. The more accomplished of us were allowed to skate as far as the shuffleboard court on the high school playground—smooth, seamless, utopian skating.

⁷ We came to know every street, every sidewalk, by the burring skirr our skates made on them; they spoke to us in a hundred voices, through the soles of our feet. Each of us, every fall, ruined a pair of shoes with too-tight skate clamps. Knees were scabbed until Christmas.

⁸ School started somewhere in the yellowing days, and we went back to the rows of scarred desks that left forearms perpetually bruised with the ghosts of last year's ink. We were strange to each other for a little while in those first days, even though we'd been together like litters of kittens for a whole summer. Reluctant to be laid by, the jealous summer still tugged at our hair and tickled behind closed eyelids.

⁹ But soon we were the spawn of chalk and cloakrooms again, creatures of a thousand rituals, and the wild summer children were gone. Tans went mustardy and flaked under an onslaught of starch. Big colts' feet, bare and winged like Hermes's all summer, were earthbound as Clydesdales' in clunk-ing new saddle oxfords. Rasping new sweaters began to feel good in the morn-ings as we jostled and quarreled to school, flanked by an honor guard of trotting dogs. But the sweaters were shed in the still-hot noons and left to grieve in balls, stuffed into our desks. By the time the real cold set in, and the hated coats and leggings were brought out of cedar chests, the sweaters were frail and used, forgotten until spring behind Blue Horse notebooks.

¹⁰ Summer was a time of good things to eat, of course, but it is the taste of autumn that I remember. Wild, smoky, bittersweet things ripened in the bronze afternoons, and the glazed mornings bit them to exotic sharpness. Preposterous yellow persimmons grew on a tree in the schoolyard, and if you got a good one, the taste was incredible, wonderful, like a topaz melting on your tongue. Too-ripe ones were truly dreadful, tasting just like their overripe peers which had burst and gone to yellow slime on the ground looked, sly and sickened. Too-green ones would pucker your mouth to acid flannel for the rest of the day.

¹¹ Scuppernongs hung on an old broken arbor on my grandfather's farm; huge, green, gold-dusted things that were surely the sweetest fruits autumn ever gave a greedy child. Flinty little Yates apples lay on the ground under the old trees in the ruined orchard, each one worth one bite of pure, winy nectar before you noticed half a worm. Sweet potatoes, newly dug from their sand

hills and roasted in my grandmother's black coal stove, were honey and smoke, too rich to finish.

[12] But pomegranates were the Grail.

[13] It seems that pomegranates always hung over my childhood autumns. And they were always forbidden fruit. Just as Persephone was imprisoned six months in the underworld for eating pomegranates, so I was regularly placed under house arrest for stealing Mrs. Word's next-door pomegranates. On the outside, Mrs. Word's pomegranates were tough and leathery and rosy and enormous. On the inside, when you broke them open, the rows of rose-quartz crystals were Kubla Khan's toys. I don't think I ever really liked the strange Persian taste to them, but I stole enough of them to keep a Bronx fruit stand in business. Like Everest, they were there. One of the worst moments in my life to this day was the time my mother apprehended me at my black business and marched me, mewling like a cornered kitten, into Mrs. Word's impeccable parlor to confess and seek forgiveness. It was, of course, granted.

[14] As the fall wore on, mornings were born silver, and bleeding sunsets came earlier, and rumbling furnaces came alive in basements. We melted, with a winter-long stench, the soles of our saddle oxfords, standing over hot-air registers. The Southeastern Fair wheeled by in a technicolor blur of saw-dust and cotton candy and forbidden midway shows where, the big kids said, ladies took their clothes off. Halloween smelled of the wet, burnt insides of pumpkins and was terrible with an atavistic terror in front of the fire in our living room, where my father read me the witches' speech from *Macbeth*. I remember one magic night in October when I was plucked up out of sleep, wrapped in a quilt, and taken outside in our back yard to watch a meteor shower. Warm on my father's shoulder, but with everything strange and too big and not like our back yard at all, I watched as the very sky above me wheeled and arced and bloomed. It was, I thought, something God arranged for me because He knew my father.

[15] Soon ice crystals bristled in red clay, waiting to be scrunched under the loathsome galoshes. Saturdays and Sundays, which had been vast blue bowls to whoop and tumble in, so full of joy that little gold specks pin-wheeled behind your eyelids when you closed them, turned gray and howled. We did smeary things with stubbly, useless scissors and paste—does anyone remember the forbidden peppermint taste of library paste?—and drove our parents wild, whining plaintively about the eternities of our heavy days.

[16] We listened, with much the same look as my young friend beside the swimming pool, to their patient recounting of the fun we'd have next spring, when we could go outside again. But that was next year, a different digit on a new calendar. And between us and spring, as the fall came down like a black window shade, was a long, whirling winter place where anything could happen.

[17] Even Christmas. But that's another story.

ANALYTICAL READING

1. What purpose do you think the first four paragraphs serve? Do the last two paragraphs relate to that purpose?

2. What part is played by the definition of "fall" in paragraph 4?

3. Point out descriptive phrases that you found especially effective. Can you analyze the devices used by the writer?

4. Find examples of metaphor and simile in the essay. Can you say that the use of figurative language is a strong element of Siddens' style of writing?

5. Find examples of cumulative sentences that you found especially effective in providing vivid details.

6. Explain the following words and phrases: "heat miasma," "scuppernongs," "pomegranates," "amulet-like," "flying phalanxes," "winged like Hermes's," "earthbound as Clydesdales'."

7. How does the writer use color imagery to contrast summer, fall, and winter?

REFLECTING

Point: How does the title tie in with the focusing statement of the essay? What do you think the writer's point is? Does it have anything to do with a contrast between the viewpoints of adults and children?

Organization: Is the organization chronological, spatial, or a combination of the two? How important is time in the essay? How is it handled?

Support: How do the descriptions of children's activities help to reinforce the association of roller-skating with fall? How do the figurative language and the color imagery in the essay help to support the main idea? What senses are appealed to besides sight?

Synthesis: As you read, did you recall activities in your own life that have seasonal significance—sports, childhood games, farm or yard chores, hiking? Discuss. Do you know Keats' "Ode to Autumn"? If so, compare its description with the essay's.

Evaluation: How effective did you find the essay? Were you able to recreate in your own mind the things described in the essay? If so, what writing tactics contributed to that?

FROM READING TO WRITING

1. Using the form of Siddons' title as a focusing point, write a short essay that vividly describes an activity that has seasonal importance, or did when you were a child: Fall (summer, spring, winter) came (comes) in on

    ――――――――――――――――――― .

2. Write a description of an activity that you as a child viewed in a different way than did your parents. It could be an activity that you considered exciting, but that your parents thought dangerous, such as swimming in a forbidden swim-

ming hole or hitching sled rides on cars; or something you did that your parents simply found maddening, such as the way you ate mashed potatoes or waded through mud puddles.

SCARECROWS PROVIDE AN ANTIC ART FORM

Avon Neal

BIOGRAPHICAL SKETCH

Avon Neal, born in Indiana in 1922, holds a Master of Fine Arts degree from Siquieros College. He has worked with the Metropolitan Museum of Art and at the Smithsonian Institution. Awarded Ford Foundation Grants in 1962–1964, Neal has developed the ancient Oriental art of ink rubbing into a contemporary print technique. He is the co-author of Archaic Art of New England Gravestones *and author of several books on rubbings, folk figures, and the recent* When Shall We Three Meet Again.

PRE-READING

1. From the title, what would you expect this essay to deal with? What does the word *antic* imply?

2. What information in the biographical sketch explains the title and Neal's particular slant on the subject?

3. What is accomplished in the first four paragraphs? Do you think that the final paragraph may contain a clue about the writer's point of view about scarecrows?

[1] Somewhere in the annals of American folklore there is a tale about the farmer who made a scarecrow so fearsome in appearance that crows not only left his crops alone but brought back corn they had stolen years before. It is the kind of story that appeals to those who wage continuous battle against not only crows but other garden pests as well.

[2] From Man's earliest efforts to protect his crops he has relied upon scarecrows. Created in his own image and more often than not dressed in his own cast-off clothing, these intimidating minions stand guard while he is attending to other chores. They range from simple stick figures draped with old gunny sacks to elaborate sartorial masterpieces, some of them fit for display in a museum.

[3] There is evidence to show that when Columbus set foot on this continent, Indians were using scarecrows to keep vigil over their cornfields. The

FROM *Smithsonian*, September 1976, pp. 115–18. Copyright 1976 by the Smithsonian Institution.

Colonists used them extensively as they heeded the planter's adage and dropped five kernels into each hill of corn, "one for the woodchuck, one for the crow, one for the cutworm and two to grow."

[4] Stories abound about tramps who have replenished their wardrobes at the expense of scarecrows. During the late Victorian era it was not unusual for a field effigy to spring full-blown from last year's outmoded Sunday best, and it was the lucky vagabond who plundered him. A present-day tramp, however, would be hard put to come away with anything wearable from some of our contemporary scarecrows which, more than likely, consist of spin-offs from modern technology—strips of metal foil, garish reflectors, tin cans, plastic doodads, glass baubles, aluminum pie tins, and all things that flash and glitter in the sunlight or jangle as they clink together at the slightest breeze, supposedly to the terror of crows.

[5] In former times when scarecrows were meant to be more utilitarian than ornamental, most were erected plain and practical. A ragged black coat flapping in the wind was enough to keep crows at bay, and a sweaty work shirt hung over a fence post discouraged the nocturnal forays of deer. Because of Man's inherent desire to decorate, scarecrows finally have evolved into the quaint field figures that populate our countrysides today.

[6] It is remarkable how many scarecrows end up looking like the people who made them. This phenomenon has often been sheepishly noted by passersby who have hailed a friend from a distance, only to learn upon pulling alongside that they were addressing a newly constructed scarecrow. More than one hill-country feud has been avoided when closer scrutiny revealed that the supposed slight of an unreciprocated "Howdy, neighbor" came from a stoic scarecrow instead of a peevish farmer.

[7] Such resemblances are no doubt coincidental, owing to the maker's having used his own discarded garments. A portly farmer may hang a ragged coat and a pair of triple-patched overalls on a post and stuff them with straw until their seams split and their buttons pop; a skinny person sticks a sparsely clothed, Slim Jim figure in his field.

[8] A woman in Massachusetts used her deceased husband's old clothes to construct a scarecrow for her vegetable patch. After a few days, however, she removed it, explaining that it was most disconcerting when she passed her kitchen window and caught a fleeting glimpse of it out of the corner of her eye; the familiar slouch and loose garments flapping in the breeze reminded her too much of her late spouse striding through the corn.

[9] Although farm folk have tried all sorts of devices to trick crows, they still face the same problems as did their pioneering forebears. Only now, in this age of automobiles and other mechanical contrivances, crows seem much bolder for they are no longer terrified by sudden blasts of noise or flashes of light. In spite of all the racket-makers, bright flashers, clanging pan lids, whirligigs, dangling metal strips that tinkle and clatter in the breeze, decoy owls, waving streamers, explosive fireworks, obnoxious scents, alarms and electronic gadgets that go off at irregular intervals, and other Rube Goldberg contraptions employed to drive them off, wildlife of one kind or another con-

tinue to exact their annual tribute from farms, just as they have since tilling of the soil began.

¹⁰ It is interesting to note that women turn their creative talents to the art of scarecrow construction as often as do men, although the majority of their creations are male. Children are the most spontaneous, while summer folk contribute more in the way of decoration. Many of the finest scarecrows are built by immigrants from Europe, generally older people of peasant stock who brought the tradition with them from Germany, France, Italy, Portugal, Poland, or other countries steeped in this rural custom. They take great pleasure in planting their rude mannequins in just the right places in their vegetable gardens and in arranging with meticulous care every detail of dress for their effigies.

¹¹ There is no end to the reasoning people use to justify their scarecrows; some are defensive, others good-natured and indulgent when asked. Most bestow affectionate titles on them, names like The Duke, Slim Jim, Skinny Minnie, and in one case a lady, herself a summer refugee from city life and, no doubt, fashionable hairdressers, christened her outrageously frazzle-topped garden figure Gorgeous Gussie. A rather dour upstate New Yorker simply gave his creation the grim sobriquet "It."

¹² A housewife in southern Connecticut insists upon filling her garden each year with whimsical figures and rearranging them every few days because, as she explains it, woodchucks cause her the most trouble and "they don't like it when things get changed about."

¹³ Another woman, an elderly Vermonter, claimed that the bedraggled scarecrow in her tiny, well-kept garden was "just plain useless when it comes to scaring off crows and other critters," but she liked it because "the poor old thing is such good company."

¹⁴ Scarecrows are ephemeral creatures, rarely lasting beyond their season in the sun. Most often they land on the rubbish heap, entwined in garlands of withered squash vines or stacked with the bean poles beside a garden wall. The skeleton may be broken into lengths to warm the hearth some frosty evening when the harvest is in.

¹⁵ It is safe to say that practical people don't put much faith in scarecrows. That all-too-familiar scene of crows perched on the outstretched arms of a guardian of crops belies any notion of infallibility. Nevertheless, scarecrows continue to be the nostalgic quintessence of rural life.

ANALYTICAL READING

1. What does Neal say about how people identify with their scarecrows? Point out examples used to illustrate this point.

2. In paragraph 9, how does Neal make the reader aware of devices other than scarecrows? Is the writer's purpose merely to list them? Discuss. Has this purpose been mentioned earlier? If so, point out the sentence.

3. In paragraph 10, Neal classifies the kinds of scarecrows made by different kinds of people. What kinds of people are mentioned, and how does the discussion relate to earlier attempts to link scarecrow creations to personality?

4. Do the last four paragraphs illustrate the writer's discussion of the scarecrow as "an art form"?

5. What advantage does the writer gain from the use of direct quotes in paragraphs 12 and 13?

6. Does Neal rely on reader knowledge of the general appearance of scarecrows? Discuss the descriptive technique used in the article.

REFLECTING

Point: Do you think the title can be used as a summary of Neal's point? What other ideas might be added? What audience is Neal writing to, and how does this affect the point of view?

Organization: Is the overall organization chronological, spatial, or some other? Do individual descriptions have spatial arrangement? Make a brief outline of the parts of the essay.

Support: Point out places where the discussion of examples has been designed to support a particular point.

Synthesis: From this discussion of the scarecrow as a folk art, can you see relationships to figures made for other purposes, such as effigies for homecoming games or parades? What features do they share with scarecrows?

Evaluation: Did you find that the essay lived up to the expectations you developed in your pre-reading? Why or why not? Has the writer convinced you to some extent that scarecrow-making today is indeed a folk art form?

FROM READING TO WRITING

1. Write an essay describing the mannequins or effigies made for the homecoming festivities at your high school or college.

2. Write an article describing a folk art common in your section of the country— for example, hex signs, bottle trees, Halloween jack-o'-lanterns, decorated rural mailboxes.

A SUNDAY KIND OF LOVE
Tom Wolfe

BIOGRAPHICAL SKETCH

Tom Wolfe was born in Richmond, Virginia, in 1931, earned a B.A. degree (cum laude) *from Washington and Lee University and a Ph.D. from Yale University in 1957. He has written for a number of newspapers, among them the* Washington

FROM Tom Wolfe, *The Kandy-Kolored Tangerine-Flake Streamline Baby* (New York: Farrar, Straus & Giroux, 1965), pp. 256–61. Copyright © 1963, 1964, 1965, by Thomas K. Wolfe, Jr. Copyright © 1963, 1964, 1965 by New York Herald Tribune, Inc. Reprinted with the permission of Farrar, Straus & Giroux, Inc.

Post, *the* New York Herald Tribune, *and* New York *magazine. He has been a contributing editor of* New York *since 1968. His new journalistic style has won him two Washington Newspaper Guild awards. Wolfe defines the "new journalism" as a "nonfiction form that combines the emotional impact" of fiction, the "analytical insights" of scholarly writing, and the "deep factual foundation of 'hard reporting.'" His published works include:* The Kandy-Kolored Tangerine-Flake Streamline Baby *(1965),* The Painted Word *(1975), and* Mauve Gloves and Madmen, Clutter and Vine *(1977).*

PRE-READING

1. What does the title suggest? Would the omission of the words "kind of" make any difference?

2. Skim the first paragraph. What direction is suggested in the opening sentences, particularly by the fragment, "Still, the odds!"?

¹ Love! Attar of libido in the air! It is 8:45 A.M. Thursday morning in the IRT subway station at 50th Street and Broadway and already two kids are hung up in a kind of herringbone weave of arms and legs, which proves, one has to admit, that love is not *confined* to Sunday in New York. Still, the odds! All the faces come popping in clots out of the Seventh Avenue local, past the King Size Ice Cream machine, and the turnstiles start whacking away as if the world were breaking up on the reefs. Four steps past the turnstiles everybody is already backed up haunch to paunch for the climb up the ramp and the stairs to the surface, a great funnel of flesh, wool, felt, leather, rubber and steaming alumicron, with the blood squeezing through everybody's old sclerotic arteries in hopped-up spurts from too much coffee and the effort of surfacing from the subway at the rush hour. Yet there on the landing are a boy and a girl, both about eighteen, in one of those utter, My Sin, backbreaking embraces.

² He envelops her not only with his arms but with his chest, which has the American teen-ager concave shape to it. She has her head cocked at a 90-degree angle and they have their eyes pressed shut for all they are worth and some incredibly feverish action going with each other's mouths. All round them, tens, scores, it seems like hundreds, of faces and bodies are perspiring, trooping and bellying up the stairs with arteriosclerotic grimaces past a showcase full of such novel items as Joy Buzzers, Squirting Nickels, Finger Rats, Scary Tarantulas and spoons with realistic dead flies on them, past Fred's barbershop, which is just off the landing and has glossy photographs of young men with the kind of baroque haircuts one can get in there, and up onto 50th Street into a madhouse of traffic and shops with weird lingerie and gray hair-dyeing displays in the windows, signs for free teacup readings and a pool-playing match between the Playboy Bunnies and Downey's Showgirls, and then everybody pounds on toward the Time-Life Building, the Brill Building or NBC.

³ The boy and the girl just keep on writhing in their embroilment. Her hand is sliding up the back of his neck, which he turns when her fingers

wander into the intricate formal gardens of his Chicago Boxcar hairdo at the base of the skull. The turn causes his face to start to mash in the ciliated hull of her beehive hairdo, and so she rolls her head 180 degrees to the other side, using their mouths for the pivot. But aside from good hair grooming, they are oblivious to everything but each other. Everybody gives them a once-over. Disgusting! Amusing! How touching! A few kids pass by and say things like "Swing it, baby." But the great majority in that heaving funnel up the stairs seem to be as much astounded as anything else. The vision of love at rush hour cannot strike anyone exactly as romance. It is a feat, like a fat man crossing the English Channel in a barrel. It is an earnest accomplishment against the tide. It is a piece of slightly gross heroics, after the manner of those knobby, varicose old men who come out from some place in baggy shorts every year and run through the streets of Boston in the Marathon race. And somehow that is the gaffe against love all week long in New York, for everybody, not just two kids writhing under their coiffures in the 50th Street subway station; too hurried, too crowded, too hard, and no time for dalliance. Which explains why the real thing in New York is, as it says in the song, a Sunday kind of love.

⁴ There is Saturday, but Saturday is not much better than Monday through Friday. Saturday is the day for errands in New York. More millions of shoppers are pouring in to keep the place jammed up. Everybody is bobbing around, running up to Yorkville to pick up these arty cheeses for this evening, or down to Fourth Avenue to try to find this Van Vechten book, *Parties*, to complete the set for somebody, or off to the cleaner's, the dentist's, the hairdresser's, or some guy's who is going to loan you his station wagon to pick up two flush doors to make tables out of, or over to some place somebody mentioned that is supposed to have fabulous cuts of meat and the butcher wears a straw hat and arm garters and is colorfully rude.

⁵ True, there is Saturday night, and Friday night. They are fine for dates and good times in New York. But for the dalliance of love, they are just as stupefying and wound up as the rest of the week. On Friday and Saturday nights everybody is making some kind of scene. It may be a cellar cabaret in the Village where five guys from some place talk "Jamaican" and pound steel drums and the Connecticut teenagers wear plaid ponchos and knee-high boots and drink such things as Passion Climax cocktails, which are made of apple cider with watermelon balls thrown in. Or it may be some cellar in the East 50's, a discotheque, where the alabaster kids come on in sleeveless minksides jackets, tweed evening dresses and cool-it Modernismus hairdos. But either way, it's a scene, a production, and soon the evening begins to whirl, like the whole world with the bed-spins, in a montage of taxis, slithery legs slithering in, slithery legs slithering out, worsted, piqué, grins, eye teeth, glissandos, buffoondos, tips, par lamps, doormen, lines, magenta ropes, white dickies, mirrors and bar bottles, pink men and shawl-collared coats, hatcheck girls and neon peach fingernails, taxis, keys, broken lamps and no coat hangers. . . .

⁶ And, then, an unbelievable dawning; Sunday, in New York.

[7] George G., who writes "Z" ads for a department store, keeps saying that all it takes for him is to smell coffee being made at a certain point in the percolation. It doesn't matter where. It could be the worst death-ball hamburger dive. All he has to do is smell it, and suddenly he finds himself swimming, drowning, dissolving in his own reverie of New York's Sunday kind of love.

Anne A.'s apartment was nothing, he keeps saying, and that was the funny thing. She lived in Chelsea. It was this one room with a cameo-style carving of a bored Medusa on the facing of the mantelpiece, this one room plus a kitchen, in a brownstone sunk down behind a lot of loft buildings and truck terminals and so forth. Beautiful Chelsea. But on Sunday morning by 10:30 the sun would be hitting cleanly between two rearview buildings and making it through the old no man's land of gas effluvia ducts, restaurant vents, aerials, fire escapes, stairwell doors, clotheslines, chimneys, skylights, vestigial lightning rods, mansard slopes, and those peculiarly bleak, filthy and misshapen backsides of New York buildings, into Anne's kitchen.

[8] George would be sitting at this rickety little table with an oilcloth over it. How he goes on about it! The place was grimy. You couldn't keep the soot out. The place was beautiful. Anne is at the stove making coffee. The smell of the coffee being made, just the smell . . . already he is turned on. She had on a great terrycloth bathrobe with a sash belt. The way she moved around inside that bathrobe with the sun shining in the window always got him. It was the atmosphere of the thing. There she was, moving around in that great fluffy bathrobe with the sun hitting her hair, and they had all the time in the world. There wasn't even one flatulent truck horn out on Eighth Avenue. Nobody was clobbering their way down the stairs in high heels out in the hall at 10 minutes to 9.

[9] Anne would make scrambled eggs, plain scrambled eggs, but it was a feast. It was incredible. She would bring out a couple of these little smoked fish with golden skin and some smoked oysters that always came in a little can with ornate lettering and royal colors and flourishes and some Kissebrot bread and black cherry preserves, and then the coffee. They had about a million cups of coffee apiece, until the warmth seemed to seep through your whole viscera. And then cigarettes. The cigarettes were like some soothing incense. The radiator was always making a hissing sound and then a clunk. The sun was shining in and the fire escapes and effluvia ducts were just silhouettes out there someplace. George would tear off another slice of Kissebrot and pile on some black cherry preserves and drink some more coffee and have another cigarette, and Anne crossed her legs under her terrycloth bathrobe and crossed her arms and drew on her cigarette, and that was the way it went.

[10] "It was the *torpor*, boy," he says. "It was beautiful. Torpor is a beautiful, underrated thing. Torpor is a luxury. Especially in this stupid town. There in that kitchen it was like being in a perfect cocoon of love. Everything was beautiful, a perfect cocoon."

¹¹ By and by they would get dressed, always in as shiftless a getup as possible. She would put on a big heavy sweater, a raincoat and a pair of faded slacks that gripped her like neoprene rubber. He would put on a pair of corduroy pants, a crew sweater with moth holes and a raincoat. Then they would go out and walk down to 14th Street for the Sunday paper.

¹² All of a sudden it was great out there on the street in New York. All those damnable millions who come careening into Manhattan all week weren't there. The town was empty. To a man and woman shuffling along there, torpid, in the cocoon of love, it was as if all of rotten Gotham had improved overnight. Even the people looked better. There would be one of those old dolls with little flabby arms all bunched up in a coat of pastel oatmeal texture, the kind whose lumpy old legs you keep seeing as she heaves her way up the subway stairs ahead of you and holds everybody up because she is so flabby and decrepit . . . and today, Sunday, on good, clean, empty 14th Street, she just looked like a nice old lady. There was no one around to make her look slow, stupid, unfit, unhip, expendable. That was the thing about Sunday. The weasel millions were absent. And Anne walking along beside him with a thready old pair of slacks gripping her like neoprene rubber looked like possibly the most marvelous vision the world had ever come up with, and the cocoon of love was perfect. It was like having your cake and eating it, too. On the one hand, here it was, boy, the prize: New York. All the buildings, the Gotham spires, were sitting up all over the landscape in silhouette like ikons representing all that was great, glorious and triumphant in New York. And, on the other hand, there were no weasel millions bellying past you and eating crullers on the run with the crumbs flaking off the corners of their mouths as a reminder of how much *Angst* and *Welthustle* you had to put into the town to get any of that out of it for yourself. All there was was the cocoon of love, which was complete. It was like being inside a scenic Easter Egg where you look in and the Gotham spires are just standing there like a little gemlike backdrop.

¹³ By and by the two of them would be back in the apartment sprawled out on the floor rustling through the Sunday paper, all that even black ink appliquéd on big fat fronds of paper. Anne would put an E. Power Biggs organ record on the hi-fi, and pretty soon the old trammeler's bass chords would be vibrating through you as if he had clamped a diathermy machine on your solar plexus. So there they would be, sprawled out on the floor, rustling through the Sunday paper, getting bathed and massaged by E. Power Biggs' sonic waves. It was like taking peyote or something. This marvelously high feeling would come over them, as though they were psychedelic, and the most commonplace objects took on this great radiance and significance. It was like old Aldous Huxley in his drug experiments, sitting there hooking down peyote buttons and staring at a clay geranium pot on a table, which gradually became the most fabulous geranium pot in God's world. The way it curved . . . why, it curved 360 d-e-g-r-e-e-s! And the clay . . . why, it was the color of the earth itself! And the top . . . It had a r-i-m on it! George had the same feeling.

Anne's apartment . . . it was hung all over the place with the usual New York working girl's modern prints, the Picasso scrawls, the Mondrians curling at the corners . . . somehow nobody ever gets even a mat for a Mondrian print . . . the Toulouse-Lautrecs with that guy with the chin kicking his silhouette leg, the Klees, that Paul Klee is cute . . . why, all of a sudden these were the most beautiful things in the whole hagiology of art . . . the way that guy with the chin k-i-c-k-s t-h-a-t l-e-g, the way that Paul Klee h-i-t-s t-h-a-t b-a-l-l . . . the way that apartment just wrapped around them like a cocoon, with lint under the couch like angel's hair, and the plum cover on the bed lying halfway on the floor in folds like the folds in a Tiepolo cherub's silks, and the bored Medusa on the mantelpiece looking like the most splendidly, gloriously b-o-r-e-d Medusa in the face of time!

[14] "Now, that was love," says George, "and there has never been anything like it. I don't know what happens to it. Unless it's Monday. Monday sort of happens to it in New York."

ANALYTICAL READING

1. What sentence did you underline that might serve as the thesis sentence for the essay?

2. What is the setting for the first part of the essay? What is its importance?

3. What appears to be the narrator's attitude toward the young lovers?

4. Why do you think there is no specific mention of Tuesday or Wednesday?

5. What details did you find most descriptive?

6. At the beginning, Anne's apartment is described in one way; at the end, in another. Are these factual or personal descriptions? Explain.

7. Is "cocoon of love" an apt metaphor? Why? What other figures of speech help to create a vivid description? What passages did you mark as being especially effective?

8. Does "real love" occur only on Sunday? Explain.

REFLECTING

Point: Is Wolfe describing New York, love, young and older lovers, or what?

Organization: The essay is organized chronologically; but what other rhetorical devices provide the basic organizational pattern? Would it have been more effective to have started with Sunday and then moved on through the other days? And to have explicitly described George and Anne's love instead of describing how they spent their Sundays?

Support: Point out several cumulative sentences and show how they contribute to describing the scene. How does Wolfe use only Thursday morning, Friday night, and Saturday to convey a sense of the entire week besides Sunday?

Synthesis: Is the subway scene anything like some comparable scene at high school or on a college campus? Is the essay confined only to readers who know New

York, or can any reader feel and participate in the experience it describes? Is "torpor" a luxury to people everywhere? To young as well as older people? Could you guess from context what *torpor* means?

Evaluation: Was Wolfe effective in portraying the peace and beauty and completeness of a Sunday kind of love? Why? Is the essay too limited in scope, pertaining only to New York City? Does the selection fit Wolfe's definition of the "new journalism" quoted in the biographical sketch? Discuss. How effective are the introductory and closing paragraphs?

FROM READING TO WRITING

1. Write a paper comparing a description of the real and the artificial in, for example, restaurants, church services, classes, homes. Try to emulate Wolfe's style of writing.

2. Write about different manifestations of love in real life, films, books, or television shows, presenting the settings and actions vividly. Establish a fairly general audience.

A TIME OF PLENTY
Marilyn Kluger

BIOGRAPHICAL SKETCH

Marilyn Kluger and her husband run a successful mail-order business—The Country Store—in Newburgh, Indiana. Although their home is in Newburgh, they and their teen-aged sons spend part of each year in Vermont. Besides articles on food and crafts, she has published The Joy of Spinning *(1971) and* The Wild Flavor *(1973), a recipe book on preserving wild foods; she is currently working on* Preserving Summer's Bounty, *to be published by M. Evans and Company.*

PRE-READING

1. Could the title be misleading today and, if so, in what way? How do the first two sentences establish the scene and the subject of the essay?

2. The essay appeared in the magazine *Gourmet.* What does this indicate the subject might be?

¹ Thanksgiving Day on our Indiana farm has always meant an epic of cookery for the women, a day of quail hunting for the men, and unstinted feasting for all who sit at our table to partake of the bountiful meal that symbolizes the end of another growing season and the gathering in of the year's crops. In my childhood the Thanksgiving feast was not an occasion for

a full-scale reunion with our many relatives, although we were never without company for dinner. Extra places were laid at the table for my maternal grandparents and perhaps for an aunt and uncle, some cousins, or visiting hunters. And usually among our guests were the hired hands who worked steadily, sometimes even on Thanksgiving Day, to complete my father's harvest before the end of Indian summer and the advent of bad weather.

² It was my parents' custom year round to rise before dawn, as soon as the roosters began their crowing. On ordinary days I was only dreamily aware of the hen house cacophony and the muffled sounds of morning activity that drifted up to my bedroom under the eaves. But on such a special day as Thanksgiving the scents arising from below the stairway were especially tantalizing and the louder noises from the kitchen were different from the everyday sounds of breakfast preparation. It was not a day when Mother tiptoed in the kitchen so that the rest of the household could sleep. Was that the rattling of the turkey roaster? Would the enormous bird vanish into the oven while I drowsed? The impending activities of the day and the lure of the kitchen were enough to rouse even the most incurable sleepyhead from a featherbed.

³ On the last Thursday in November I could stay in bed only until the night chill left the house, hearing first the clash of the heavy gates in the huge black iron range, with its flowery scrolls and nickeled decorations, as Mother shook down the ashes. Then, in their proper sequence, came the sounds of the fire being made—the rustle of newspaper, the snap of kindling, the rush of smoke up the chimney when Mother opened the damper, slid the regulator wide open, and struck a match to the kerosene-soaked corncobs that started a quick hot fire. I listened for the bang of the cast-iron lid dropping back into place and for the tick of the stovepipe as fierce flames sent up their first heat, then the sound of the lid being lifted again as Mother fed more dry wood and lumps of coal to the greedy new fire. The duties of the kitchen on Thanksgiving were a thousandfold, and I could tell that Mother was bustling about with a quicker step than usual.

⁴ Outside beneath my window my father whistled for Queen, our English setter. At the sound of his whistle, my brothers, who were sleeping in the next room, would begin to mumble and stir. Their ears were as acutely attuned to my father's whistle as mine were to the kitchen noises. Jim and Harold did not want to be left behind, tardily finishing their chores, when Dad strode out across the fields with the gun on his shoulder and Queen at his side. And I did not want to miss the goings-on in the kitchen, where Mother, Grandmother, and Aunt Emma would cook and visit all morning, telling interesting stories and creating delicious foods for the harvest feast.

.   .   .

ANALYTICAL READING

1. In what ways is Thanksgiving Day for this family different from other days?

2. About how old is the narrator?

3. About how many people would you guess are at the dinner table? Explain.

4. How do the activities of the women differ from those of the men?

5. Which senses are appealed to in the essay? Refer to specific sentences.

REFLECTING

Point: Does the writer merely describe Thanksgiving morning, or does she also provide some symbolic element? These paragraphs provide background for a longer article; what would you expect the rest of the article to deal with?

Organization: How does the opening paragraph fit into the organization of the rest of the essay? How are the second and third paragraphs related?

Support: How are cumulative sentences used to recreate the Thanksgiving Day? What sentence or sentences—cumulative or not—do you think provide a vivid description of the morning? Is the language used that of an adult, a child, or a mixture of both? Cite examples.

Synthesis: Can you compare the essay with some childhood festive occasion or family tradition of your own? What memories do the descriptions bring to mind?

Evaluation: Does the lengthy opening sentence detract from the essay? Does the final paragraph about the writer's brothers violate the unity of the kitchen scene? Is she successful in making you feel part of the household, in experiencing what the day meant to her? If so, to what writing devices do you attribute this success?

FROM READING TO WRITING

1. Write a similar essay describing an eventful occasion in your family, perhaps Christmas dinner, a Passover seder, or annual reunion. Be certain not to focus on your personal feelings but on the sights, sounds, odors, tastes, and tactile (touch) sensations that you recall.

2. In the same vein, describe a past or present ordinary day, perhaps early morning in your household, with every member of the family following a set routine.

Factual Description

FROM ON THE BALL
Roger Angell

BIOGRAPHICAL SKETCH

Born in New York City in 1920, Roger Angell earned a B.A. degree from Harvard University in 1942. He has written for and been editor of a number of magazines, including Holiday *and* The New Yorker. *He has also found time to be active in community affairs, serving as a trustee of Sydenham Hospital and being active in an administrative role in the New York Civil Liberties Union. His numerous articles and books include* The Stone Arbor *(1961),* The Summer Game *(1972), and* Five Seasons: A Baseball Companion *(1977). Since 1956 he has been a general contributor to* The New Yorker.

PRE-READING

1. In what way does the title aptly describe this selection and in what way does it gain your attention?

2. At what point in the opening sentences do you fully realize the subject of the piece?

[1] It weighs just over five ounces and measures between 2.86 and 2.94 inches in diameter. It is made of a composition-cork nucleus encased in two thin layers of rubber, one black and one red, surrounded by a hundred and twenty-one yards of tightly wrapped blue-gray wool yarn, forty-five yards of white wool yarn, fifty-three more yards of blue-gray wool yarn, a hundred and fifty yards of fine cotton yarn, a coat of rubber cement, and a cowhide (formerly horsehide) exterior, which is held together with two hundred and sixteen slightly raised red cotton stitches. Printed certifications, endorsements, and outdoor advertising spherically attest to its authenticity. Like most institutions, it is considered inferior in its present form to its ancient archetypes, and in this case the complaint is probably justified; on occasion in recent years it has actually been known to come apart under the demands of its brief but rigorous active career. Baseballs are assembled and hand-stitched in Taiwan

FROM "On the Ball," *The New Yorker*, October 4, 1976, p. 90. Reprinted by permission. © 1976 by The New Yorker Magazine, Inc.

(before this year the work was done in Haiti, and before 1973 in Chicopee, Massachusetts), and contemporary pitchers claim that there is a tangible variation in the size and feel of the balls that now come into play in a single game; a true peewee is treasured by hurlers, and its departure from the premises, by fair means or foul, is secretly mourned. But never mind: any baseball is beautiful. No other small package comes as close to the ideal in design and utility. It is a perfect object for a man's hand. Pick it up and it instantly suggests its purpose; it is meant to be thrown a considerable distance—thrown hard and with precision. Its feel and heft are the beginning of the sport's critical dimensions; if it were a fraction of an inch larger or smaller, a few centigrams heavier or lighter, the game of baseball would be utterly different. Hold a baseball in your hand. As it happens, this one is not brand new. Here, just to one side of the curved surgical welt of stitches, there is a pale-green grass smudge, darkening on one edge almost to black—the mark of an old infield play, a tough grounder now lost in memory. Feel the ball, turn it over in your hand; hold it across the seam or the other way, with the seam just to the side of your middle finger. Speculation stirs. You want to get outdoors and throw this spare and sensual object to somebody, or, at the very least, watch somebody else throw it. The game has begun. . . .

ANALYTICAL READING

1. Is this description personal, factual, or both? Explain using specific references to the selection.

2. Discuss the statement: "Like most institutions, it is considered inferior in its present form to its ancient archetypes."

3. What is the purpose of including the sentence about "a true peewee"? Explain fully the phrase "by fair means or foul."

4. This excerpt from a longer article is not divided into paragraphs. Where might the author have started a new paragraph or new paragraphs?

5. What is the author's tone? Explain your answer.

REFLECTING

Point: What is the purpose of the initial sentences? Which sentence did you underline as the thesis sentence?

Organization: Analyze the selection, showing the relationship of the parts.

Support: Do the details provide reasonably sufficient evidence for the writer's conclusion about a baseball? Point out where a cumulative sentence has been used to present numerous facts. Do the details about baseballs suggest to you that the author is an authority? If so, why is that important?

Synthesis: Is the selection sexist, appealing only to men and failing to interest and arouse enthusiasm in women? Have you ever looked hard at or thought much about a baseball before? Do you gain a new or fresh insight from reading the selection?

Evaluation: Is Angell's viewpoint and attitude contagious? Do you feel as he does in the closing line, or can you at least understand how he would feel this way? If so, how has he enabled you to share his attitude? This paragraph opens an article about types of players and their attitudes toward baseball; in light of that knowledge, what do you think of the approach used?

FROM READING TO WRITING

1. Write a factual description of some common subject, such as one side of a penny, the palm of your hand, a matchbook, a shoe, or a watch. Then write a personal description of it, bringing out your feelings and thoughts. It need not be something you like; you might select your alarm clock and describe how you react to its raucous ring early in the morning.

2. Write a paper similar to Angell's piece, describing an object, such as a basketball, tennis ball, backpack, bicycle, or stereo. Avoiding a revelation about your emotional reactions to the subject, give as many factual details as possible. You may wish to obtain some information from the library.

FROM CARPENTER ANTS
T. C. Schneirla

BIOGRAPHICAL SKETCH

T(heodore) C(hristian) Schneirla (1902–68) was born in Bay City, Michigan, and received the B.S., M.S., and Sc.D. degrees from the University of Michigan. An authority on Eciton, or army ants, he explored their habits in the jungles of Mexico, Trinidad, and the Panama Canal Zone. From 1947 to 1968 he was curator of the department of animal behavior of the American Museum of Natural History in New York. He was the author of Animal Psychology, *the co-author, with L. C. Craft, of* Experiments in Psychology, *and a contributor to* Encyclopaedia Britannica, Twentieth Century Psychology, *and* Philosophy for the Future. *Schneirla's numerous articles appeared in such periodicals as* Natural History, Scientific American, *and* Psychological Review.

PRE-READING

1. From skimming the first and last paragraphs, what particular activity of the carpenter ants do you expect to be described?

2. Is the tone personal or impersonal? Explain. What kind of description does this suggest?

3. Is any special attempt made in the introductory paragraph to interest readers, to arouse their curiosity, or attract their attention?

[1] The colonies of the black species *C. pennsylvannicus* and its subspecies *C. ferrugineus* of the American temperate zone may grow to be fairly large. There may be as many as a few thousand workers, a single reproductive female (the queen), a brood of varying make-up, according to the season, and at certain times of year a considerable number of young winged males and queens. As with many other species of *Camponotus*, the workers (or neuter females) are polymorphic; that is, they range in size and type from the large and robust workers-major to the smallest, the workers-minor. The queen is readily distinguished from the workers by her great size, her large head and bulging thorax, and by the high polish she generally acquires from the almost incessant licking and stroking of her body by workers.

[2] Colonies that have weathered the hazard of their first two or three years are usually able to produce reproductive individuals—the large winged males and females. The late summer brood of males and females, after emerging from their large cocoons, usually remain in their parent nests through the winter, huddled in clusters with the hibernating workers within the inner recesses of their catacomb-like shelter. They make their exodus early in the following warm season, in late spring or early summer as a rule. If the occupants of a house have been unaware of a flourishing *Camponotus* colony within the foundation beams, the discovery is likely to come on some warm day in late spring, when from some chink in the molding a whole host of males and numerous females may come out into the room.

[3] In the open, the winged males and females spill out of their home nests on the warm and bright days from May into July and soon take to the air in a mating flight. This results in the fertilization of many of the females. In contrast to the large-eyed but tiny-headed males, which cannot survive long as solitary individuals after the flight, many of the inseminated queens return to some woody surface or to the earth and are able to establish themselves. Fascinating and unsolved problems are presented both by their behavior and their physiology, which seem to change markedly after fertilization has taken place.

[4] When a fertilized queen descends from her flight, she drops or bites off her wings, then soon becomes photo-negative. That is to say, she is markedly light-shy, whereas before fertilization she was light-positive, as indicated by upward spiraling toward light in the mating flight. As a result of this change, when the newly fertilized queen reaches a sheltered dark place, she settles down. If accidentally exposed to light, she again promptly disappears from view. In the northern states, if you pull strips of bark from logs and stumps in the late spring, you are likely to expose one or more newly established *Campo-notus* queens. Each is in a little cell ringed around with a wall of wood fibers set up by the queen herself. Or she may find her way into the deserted burrow of a tunneling wood beetle in which she comes to rest at some turning. She may perish through seasonal vissicitudes or through the invasion of her cell by ants or other predatory insects. Otherwise, however, the young queen can survive

by living on her own tissues and can found a colony through her own resources.

[5] Her now degenerating wing muscles and the fat bodies with which she
is abundantly equipped provide nourishment for her and her first brood. For,
unlike the colony-founding queen of some Australian ants of primitive poner-
ine species, which leave their cells and forage about, thereby procuring food
for themselves and for their first brood, the *Camponotus* queens remain seques-
tered and have no food except what is available from their own bodies. On
this special "reducing diet," the queen soon begins to lay eggs, and with this
substance she can feed the larvae which presently appear.

[6] That the first brood is not lavishly fed by the queen is evident from the
very small stature of the few workers that appear in the first lot. They are all
of the worker-minor caste. However, these diminutive workers may succeed
in consolidating the young colony by slowly extending the nest and by foraging in the environs, bringing in food that is used to replenish the queen's
reserves and feed the additional brood. If the first pygmy workers do not carry
out such work effectively, the colony is likely to perish. If they work well, the
population grows and the nest is extended into wood and earth. As soon as the
first workers have appeared and are busy in the nest, the queen turns to
producing eggs as her exclusive task. Thereafter she labors no more except in
this important capacity as egg-making machine.

ANALYTICAL READING

1. On the basis of the first paragraph, do you think Schneirla is writing to a highly
   scientific audience? Why or why not? Why are Latin terms used?

2. In what sentence in paragraph 3 does the writer's tone change? Explain the
   function of this sentence in relation to the paragraphs that follow it.

3. Where does Schneirla indicate he is interested not only in describing the carpenter ants but also in alerting readers to their possible presence? Explain why
   you think he does this.

4. What are the two main problems confronting the queen and her new colony?

REFLECTING

Point: What is the main activity that Schneirla describes in this selection? Summarize this activity in a sentence or two.

Organization: What organizational plan is followed? Does this plan start with the
   second or third paragraph? Justify your answer.

Support: How does Schneirla define terms that may be too technical for his readers? Point to examples. Why is the information about the males subordinated
   in the third sentence of paragraph 3? What is the function of the final sentence
   in paragraph 4? What purpose does the contrast in paragraph 5 serve?

Synthesis: What did you find most interesting in the selection? Is there any relationship between the queen's first offspring and the child of a human family?

Has reading the selection affected your attitude toward ants? Is there any possible analogy between the queen and her workers, and some husbands and wives?

Evaluation: Although you may not have been interested in carpenter ants, did you find the selection well organized, clearly written, and informative? Were sufficient details provided? Was the author's voice appropriate, authoritative, objective?

FROM READING TO WRITING

1. Write a factual description of some animals, such as ants or birds building a nest, fish swimming in a tank, birds at a feeder or tugging a worm out of the ground, dogs getting acquainted, or cats fighting.

2. Write a factual description of some advertisement, such as one about cars, liquor or beer, apparel, or some food or other product. Submit the advertisement with your paper.

3. Describe some routine campus activity, such as students leaving a class, entering the library, chaining their bicycles. Be factual and objective.

TERROR AT TINKER CREEK
Annie Dillard

BIOGRAPHICAL SKETCH

Annie Dillard grew up in Pittsburgh, Pennsylvania, and attended Hollins College. Since 1956 she has lived in Roanoke Valley, Virginia, the location of Tinker Creek. A journalist and a poet, she has been a contributing editor to Harper's *magazine and a columnist for the Wilderness Society. In addition to* Pilgrim at Tinker Creek, *from which this selection is taken, she has published a book of poems,* Tickets for a Prayer Wheel, *and the recent* Holy the Firm.

PRE-READING

1. What word in the title of the book gives a clue as to Dillard's attitude toward the Tinker Creek area? Explain.

2. From the biographical sketch, what kind of attitude would you expect her to have about nature?

3. What does the first paragraph reveal about the kind of person Dillard is? What is the subject of this selection from her book's first chapter?

FROM Annie Dillard, *Pilgrim at Tinker Creek* (New York: Harper's Magazine Press, Harper & Row, 1974), pp. 5–6. Reprinted by permission of the author.

[1] A couple of summers ago I was walking along the edge of the island to see what I could see in the water, and mainly to scare frogs. Frogs have an inelegant way of taking off from invisible positions on the bank just ahead of your feet, in dire panic, emitting a froggy "Yike!" and splashing into the water. Incredibly, this amused me, and incredibly, it amuses me still. As I walked along the grassy edge of the island, I got better and better at seeing frogs both in and out of the water. I learned to recognize, slowing down, the difference in texture of the light reflected from mudbank, water, grass, or frog. Frogs were flying all around me. At the end of the island I noticed a small green frog. He was exactly half in and half out of the water, looking like a schematic diagram of an amphibian, and he didn't jump.

[2] He didn't jump; I crept closer. At last I knelt on the island's winterkilled grass, lost, dumbstruck, staring at the frog in the creek just four feet away. He was a very small frog with wide, dull eyes. And just as I looked at him, he slowly crumpled and began to sag. The spirit vanished from his eyes as if snuffed. His skin emptied and drooped; his very skull seemed to collapse and settle like a kicked tent. He was shrinking before my eyes like a deflating football. I watched the taut, glistening skin on his shoulders ruck, and rumple, and fall. Soon, part of his skin, formless as a pricked balloon, lay in floating folds like bright scum on top of the water: it was a monstrous and terrifying thing. I gaped bewildered, appalled. An oval shadow hung in the water behind the drained frog; then the shadow glided away. The frog skin bag started to sink.

[3] I had read about the giant water bug, but never seen one. "Giant water bug" is really the name of the creature, which is an enormous, heavy-bodied brown beetle. It eats insects, tadpoles, fish, and frogs. Its grasping forelegs are mighty and hooked inward. It seizes a victim with these legs, hugs it tight, and paralyzes it with enzymes injected during a vicious bite. That one bite is the only bite it ever takes. Through the puncture shoot the poisons that dissolve the victim's muscles and bones and organs—all but the skin—and through it the giant water bug sucks out the victim's body, reduced to a juice. This event is quite common in warm fresh water. The frog I saw was being sucked by a giant water bug. I had been kneeling on the island grass; when the unrecognizable flap of frog skin settled on the creek bottom, swaying, I stood up and brushed the knees of my pants. I couldn't catch my breath.

[4] Of course, many carnivorous animals devour their prey alive. The usual method seems to be to subdue the victim by downing or grasping it so it can't flee, then eating it whole or in a series of bloody bites. Frogs eat everything whole, stuffing prey into their mouths with their thumbs. People have seen frogs with their wide jaws so full of live dragonflies they couldn't close them. Ants don't even have to catch their prey: in the spring they swarm over newly hatched, featherless birds in the nest and eat them tiny bite by bite.

ANALYTICAL READING

1. What initially attracted Dillard to the "small green frog"? Why was she so horrified?

2. Is there any indication that the frog feels pain? What explanation for this does Dillard offer?

3. Do you think the contrast in tone between the first paragraph and the second adds to the horror? Explain. How does Dillard achieve that contrast through the content of the two paragraphs?

4. Does the last paragraph help relieve the horror the author establishes? Why or why not?

REFLECTING

Point: State in one sentence what you think Dillard tries to illustrate in this vivid description.

Organization: Discuss the organization. Why is it effective for Dillard to describe the event exactly as it happened before she explains about the water beetle?

Support: Pick out images and comparisons that you find especially effective and that you think help to support the writer's purpose or point.

Synthesis: Did you share the experience with Dillard? Have you too witnessed natural phenomena about which you could say "I couldn't catch my breath"? Discuss.

Evaluation: Although this is essentially a factual description, Dillard is able to inject her own emotional reaction to the phenomenon. Select some words and phrases that reveal her attitudes. Discuss the various techniques—language, organization, content—that you found contributed most to your emotional reaction to the description.

FROM READING TO WRITING

1. Describe in detail a natural phenomenon that you have observed and that affected you. As Dillard does, let the straight, factual description express your reaction to the situation.

2. Write a factual description of your pet or of a plant you have in your room. Try to let your readers see it vividly enough to be able to draw a reasonably accurate sketch of it.

3. Go to a quiet spot on campus or near your home—a wooded area or a pond—and observe an encounter between two creatures. Describe the incident, using the kind of vivid detail that Dillard does.

Mixed Description

THE WONDROUS WOOD DUCK
Jack Denton Scott

BIOGRAPHICAL SKETCH

Jack Denton Scott, born in West Virginia in 1915, is well known as a novelist, naturalist, essayist, world traveler (fourteen trips around the world), travel writer, and author of books in many fields. Formerly a syndicated columnist for the New York Herald Tribune, *he is also the author of several award-winning children's books. Among his better-known works are* Elephant Grass, *a novel;* Spargo, *a mystery story;* Forests of the Night *and* Passport to Adventure, *travel adventure books;* The Duluth Mongoose, Canada Geese, *and* Discovering the American Stork, *books on natural history; and* The Complete Book of Pasta, Feast of France *(with Antoine Gilly), and* Mastering Microwave Cooking *(with Maria Luisa Scott), cookbooks. In addition, Scott has written more than 2,000 magazine articles.*

PRE-READING

1. How do the title and the opening paragraphs suggest what the essay is about and what the author's attitude is?

2. How does the closing paragraph give a slightly different perspective on the author's attitude?

¹ It was like watching a rainbow break into segments, then have those beautifully hued pieces float so close that you could almost reach out and touch them. But rainbows vanish as you get closer to them, and their colors fade, as if the sight of them was the vision in a dream. And rainbows don't have feathers, and they don't fly.

² What was happening to me was one of those rare wildlife experiences that make a duck hunter lay his shotgun beside him in the blind and watch, hypnotized. It was a fall day, close to the hour of dusk, the light just beginning to go over a small woodland lake in upstate New York. That last light has a splintering, a penetrating effect, not unlike the bursting glow of a log in a fireplace before the fire puffs its last. It spotlighted the trees which were walled around the area.

FROM *Sports Afield with Rod & Gun,* July 1976, pp. 46–47, 62–66. Copyright 1976 by The Hearst Corporation.

³ Wood ducks were flighting in to roost on the lake, the drake dandies leading the way, the dying light catching their plumage in a fire-burst of color. More remarkable even than the color of these most beautiful of all ducks was the dexterity of their flight, equalled only by that of the ruffed grouse and the woodcock. No other duck can dodge and thread its way through trees the way the wood duck can.

⁴ They came on swift, silent wings, gliding through the treetops as if guided by radar, twisting, turning, never touching a twig in that thick growth of trees that surrounded the lake.

⁵ It was a spectacular acrobatic performance that few duck hunters who hunt the big waters ever see, for wood ducks prefer small, isolated bodies of water near woodland where they roost at night. Naturalists claim that wood ducks are noisy, making a variety of calls as they fly, everything from a squeal to a loud *hoo-eek*. The first wood ducks I ever saw made no sound. They were too busy at their business of landing in the center of that small lake before darkness blanked out their world. And although they made that flight through the trees look as simple as flapping a wing, it had to take some doing.

⁶ That was a long ago day when wood ducks made a bird watcher out of a duck hunter. I had been told what to expect, but never can the telling equal the seeing of these ornate wildfowl that flash by like twinkling jewels.

⁷ I sat there and tried to identify those colors as they passed so close to me that I could see the white ring around the female's eyes. Comparing their colors to that of a rainbow may be poetic but it is lazily fudging the matter, not giving these peacocks of the waterfowl world their due. Naturalist Robert Ridgway did it better than I could.

⁸ Ridgway noted that the wood duck drake has a crested head of metallic green, purple and violet, relieved by a pure white line extending backward from the angle of the upper mandible along each side of the crown and upper border of the crest; another from behind the eye backward along the lower edge of the crest, and two much broader transverse bars crossing the cheeks and sides of the neck, respectively, confluent with a white throat patch. Upper parts are chiefly velvety black, varied with metallic hues of bronze, purple, blue and green; chest is rich chestnut glossed with reddish purple and marked with triangular white spots. Sides of the breast are crossed with a broad pure white bar with a deep black one behind it. Sides and flanks are delicately waved with black on a buff ground, and the outer feathers are beautifully ornamented with broad crescentic bars of white and black; the abdomen is white, the bill painted with jet-black, milk-white, lilac, red, orange and yellow.

⁹ The hen isn't exactly dowdy, but her brown feathers almost pale her into insignificance beside the gaudy male "waterfowl in wedding raiment," which his scientific name *Aix sponsa* means roughly translated. But watching a female swimming on a woodland pond without benefit of drake places her in a different perspective. She has a white ring around her eye, her crest, smaller than the male's, is glossed with green, her back shines with bronze and green-

ish purple and her breast is buff. In fact, she is prettier than any other female duck.

[10] Seeing your first flock of wood ducks come in to spend the night on an isolated lake is akin to secretly watching a great artist dab his brush in the paints on his palette and then slash color on the blank of canvas. It is dramatic, and it is unnerving.

[11] But to look beyond beauty is to discover that this 20-inch-long, 1½-pound duck is a plucky personality with characteristics and assets that rank it high in the wildfowl hierarchy. Belonging to the clan *Anatidae* of ducks, geese and swans, and the subfamily *Anatinae* of dabbling ducks, mallard, gadwalls, black ducks, teal and widgeons, it is the only member of that tribe to nest in trees. It also differs from the other ducks in that it seldom flies south of our borders; it is native only to North America, and long before the words "endangered species" became part of our language the wood duck, which was on the edge of extinction, made such a strong comeback that now it is the most common breeding wildfowl in the eastern United States. Today it is believed that we have a stable population of 3½-million wood ducks.

[12] That population explosion is a success story with few parallels, involving farsighted men and a helpful public, among other factors. About a century ago wood ducks were at least as plentiful as they are now, with large populations in the eastern United States and on the West Coast. But by the early 1900s a combination of factors almost wiped out our most beautiful wildfowl. Their numbers were reduced so drastically that naturalists claimed that there were more wood ducks in Belgium than in the United States. And that small population was bred by bird fanciers from a few pairs imported from this country.

[13] Hunting was partially responsible for the decline. Despite the fact that as early as 1901, A. K. Fisher of the Biological Survey sounded a warning asking for strong protective measures, and some eastern states quickly passed laws protecting wood ducks, the slaughter continued. Laws weren't strictly enforced, spring shooting and unregulated hunting continued. Fishermen also contributed to the downfall of the wood duck, with flytiers offering $4 for a skin of a male duck, from which the famous Gordon, Cahill and Hendrickson trout flies were made.

[14] But major habitat loss may have been the greatest decimator. Lumbering wiped out vast tracts of forests which had provided both nesting and food, and enormous areas of marshland were drained by agricultural interests. All factors combined to just about finish the wood duck.

[15] Finally Congress, which had been urged for a decade to take action, moved, passing in 1913 the hotly contested Migratory Bird Law, which directed the Department of Agriculture not only to draft but to enforce laws protecting all migratory birds. One of those laws wisely limited wildfowl shooting to 3½ months a year. Then, in 1918, President Woodrow Wilson, also after much urging by enlightened conservationists, signed his name to the Migratory Bird Treaty Act, empowering the government to bear down even

more on the hunting of migratory birds. Concurrently, the United States and Canada abolished all wood duck hunting. These laws remained in effect until 1941, when the wood ducks made their classic comeback. More than law, however, helped bring about that remarkable wood duck rebirth. In wetland wood duck habitat all across the country, people erected thousands of nesting boxes to replace the felled trees.

16 Today, wildlife management programs suggest that the practice of giving the wood duck a helping hand with its nesting continue, noting that it is farsighted insurance for both duck hunter and bird watcher. They add that lack of tree nest cavities, presence of nest predators and competition from other cavity nesters, keep down wood duck production. Properly built and placed, artificial nest boxes can help offset these natural limitations.

17 A mated pair search for a nest-tree together, preferring hollow trees close to water. Ideally, the three should be near water that is 25 percent open and 75 percent plant-covered. This type of water usually abounds in insects and small marine life which is very important to the growing young. Dense overhead cover is liked for the security it offers, and the water is necessary protection and feeding ground until the young are able to fly. Marshy areas are ideal, for they also offer screened sections that the ducks use to safely laze and preen.

18 The nest hole in the hollow tree may be close to the ground or as high as 60 feet. The female, weighing about 1¼ pounds, a slim 18 inches long, has no difficulty squeezing through a hole four inches in diameter. She prefers small holes that most predators can't enter. Pileated woodpeckers, the size of a large pigeon, with an enormous bill, chisel out many a wood duck nest hole. But the wood duck is cautious in selecting her nest, and often has competition from squirrels, raccoons, opossums, owls, starlings, even wasps and bees. If an ideal hole is occupied, she continues her search, never fighting for possession. A man-made nest box is readily used, if located properly, with the female sometimes returning to it for her decade of life. She does little to any nest except evenly distribute the debris in it to properly cradle the eggs.

19 Once the nest is selected, the female enters it the following dawn, the drake close by. Within an hour, the first egg is laid, and the female then joins the male in a short flight. The hen lays one egg every day, until her clutch of eight to 15 is complete. After she lays the sixth egg, she begins removing down from her breast, so much that it finally blankets and insulates all of the eggs. With the laying of the last egg incubation begins, the hen handling it alone. She is not immediately abandoned by the flashy drake, meeting him every day when she leaves the nest for short periods to feed and preen and join other wood ducks that have gathered at a good feeding area.

20 But by the time the eggs are incubated in about 30 days, the drake has left his mate and joined other irresponsible dandies, and it is her chore to raise the young. She broods the ducklings for a day, then begins a remarkable performance: Cautiously, she sits half in and half out of the hole, looking for danger. When all is clear, she flies to the ground and begins a soft, beseeching

clucking, until a duckling appears in the hole, peeping loudly. Whether she waits below on water or ground, the ducklings never hesitate but leap out of the nest, splashing on the water or bouncing on the ground. Rarely are they injured. When all of the dark-brown-and-buff ducklings are out of the nest, they join their mother, in a tight cluster, if on water, or in a line if she leads them across land to water. At a day old, they can swim well and dive deeply enough to escape some enemies.

[21] However, bringing this family out of the nest isn't all that simple. Predators range from raccoons, snakes, minks and squirrels to crows and starlings, all of which prey on the eggs, some even eating the young in the nest.

[22] If the hen has chosen her nest site well, where water and shoreline offer food and protection, by the time the young are three days old they are actively feeding themselves on all kinds of insect life. If the habitat is right, perhaps eight out of 12 ducklings will survive, but mortality is high, big turtles and mink taking many and only about 42 percent reach flight age.

[23] Eight weeks after they bravely leaped from the nest out into the world the ducklings can fly. At this time they are fully feathered, but males can only be identified by their red eyes, which grow a deeper red as they age. By October the young wood ducklings are in full plumage and difficult to distinguish from adults. From this point on, plant life of many varieties (everything from acorns to wild grapes) is their main food.

[24] At this time, flocks gather in small family groups all across the eastern half of the country, as far north as southern Canada, preparing for migration, which is actually a gradual shifting of the eastern population to South Atlantic and Gulf states. (There also is a small population in the Pacific Northwest and California.) It is a leisurely migration about which little is known, with the ducks seeking shallow water, rarely flighting to salt water. Isolated swampland is the usual roosting area at night, where they gather in flocks of anywhere from 100 to thousands. Two biologists counted 5400 wood ducks in one square mile near Green Island, Iowa.

[25] Although their migration is slow and seemingly aimless, wood ducks are strong fliers and have been clocked at over 50 miles an hour, which they were doing with apparent ease. Thus, they are sporty birds and offer exciting shooting by drifting rivers in canoes, johnboating through swamps, wading old beaver ponds, jump shooting along rivers and creeks. Dedicated wood duck hunters claim that the sport combines that of grouse, woodcock and quail shooting, with the wood duck out-pointing the other three game birds in wariness and in flying. Despite the bright dress of the drake, wood ducks are also masters at camouflage and inhabit terrain that offers easy vanishing points.

[26] Today, because of concerned conservationists, proper laws and the birds' own resourcefulness and parental responsibility, there are enough wood ducks for duck hunters to harvest 1 million every season without upsetting the population balance.

ANALYTICAL READING

1. The writer begins with a description of an experience. Is it a recent one? What effect did it have on him? What do you think was Scott's purpose in relating this experience?

2. Why is there a reference to naturalist Robert Ridgway? How does his description of the wood duck differ from Scott's?

3. What is significant about the wood ducks besides their beauty?

4. What factors were responsible for the almost complete elimination of the wood ducks? What helped to preserve them?

5. What is the main mating problem of the wood ducks?

6. Does the author approve or disapprove of the hunting of wood ducks? Justify your answer with references to specific sentences.

REFLECTING

Point: Is the essay concerned mainly about describing the ducks, hunting them, or preserving them?

Organization: What are the main divisions of the essay? Would a factual description of the wood duck have provided a more effective introduction? What function does the closing paragraph perform? How are Ridgeway's descriptions in paragraphs 8 and 9 organized?

Support: What does the analogy to a rainbow in paragraph 1 contribute to the essay? the one about watching an artist in paragraph 10? What is the author's tone? How is it revealed? Point out sentences you underlined because you felt that they contributed mainly to either the factual or personal description of the wood duck.

Synthesis: What does Scott assume about readers' knowledge of wood ducks? Can you appreciate the essay even though you may not be interested in animals or wildlife? If so, how has the author attracted your interest? Do you feel any differently about conservation laws and restrictions after having read the essay?

Evaluation: To what extent has the author accomplished his purpose? Is the mixture of personal and factual description effective? Have you gained any insight into the natural laws, habits, and struggles of wildlife? If you think the essay is successful, explain how the author has created and sustained your interest and influenced your views.

FROM READING TO WRITING

1. Write a mixed description of a plant you have been growing or of some object in your room, such as a chair, painting, or bureau.

2. Write a similar description about some interesting prepared food, such as a Big Mac, a Caesar salad, an ethnic dish, or a casserole.

THE VIEW FROM THE CASTLE
S. Dillon Ripley

BIOGRAPHICAL SKETCH

S. Dillon Ripley was born in New York City in 1913. Besides a Ph.D. from Harvard University and an LL.D. from Yale University, he has received honorary degrees from many universities, including Cambridge University and Brown University. As a director of various corporations, foundations, and museums, Ripley has headed many scientific expeditions to the South Pacific, Southeast Asia, India, and Nepal. He has been president of the International Council of Bird Preservation and Chairman of the World Wildlife Fund. Currently, he is a professor at Yale University and active in the Smithsonian Institution. Among his many works on birds and wildlife is his most recent, Paradox of the Human Condition *(1975).*

PRE-READING

1. What does the title suggest to you?

2. From the biographical sketch, what would you expect Ripley to write about? Would you consider him an authority? Why?

3. Skim the opening paragraph. Which sentence best indicates what is to follow?

[1] After sunset, these fall evenings, there is a time of twilight on the ponds when the senses are quickened as the light fails. Hearing sharpens, one smells more keenly, the eyes seem to adjust to reduced light reflection even as pools of darkness gather between the trees. I used to love this time on our duck ponds, for then imagination wakens and one senses again the life of the hunter. But now our feelings are mixed with dread, for a new predator has been added to the roster of mink, raccoon, fox and stray dog that our fences guard against.

[2] Beyond the first ponds is a bench, and here I can sit and watch in the gloaming. Ducks and geese coursing over the water leave behind a variety of v-shaped ripples and deliquescing colors, pinks to reds to mauves to purples. Some v's are narrow—a single wood duck on an errand of its own; others are a series of expanding trails—a family group of small geese, sailing effortlessly in line. Two larger geese junket by, tails higher, necks lower, sleepily pushing along.

[3] But suddenly the spell is broken, drowsiness is gone. We are alert, all of us. Why? No sound, no smell, but distant motion—or is it? It's hard to tell; birds are all on the water now, all looking in one direction, beginning a slow drifting movement, as if mesmerized. At the end of the pond there is a big boulder sticking out of the water, gray against the limpid purple. And, yes,

FROM *Smithsonian*, November 1976, p. 6. Copyright 1976 by the Smithsonian Institution.

there's a shape on top, quite still—no darting mink or deliberate raccoon, just still and tall. It can only be a great owl, silent, motionless, come on velvet wings like a wraith. I dare not move, for the owl's eyes are five to ten times more light-receptive than my own.

⁴ The ducks and geese seem riveted on the owl, as I am. Like some cloaked Mephistophelian figure the predator decoys his prey, for they are drifting toward the boulder, seemingly spellbound. The owl does not move. I cannot see if it even blinks. As we all watch, a blurred movement comes from behind. Without a sound a second owl sweeps low over the water, strikes with outstreched feet at a duck, and glides away, its talons locked in the back of the helpless bird.

⁵ It is over in an instant and I am powerless. With cries of alarm, ducks and geese dart in all directions in panic. The hypnotist flies off to join its mate, and I can only marvel at the drama which has deprived us of one of our small supply of breeding canvasback ducks. From being very uncommon a generation ago, great horned owls have become locally more visible on the East Coast, perhaps because with the spread of the suburbs have come untended woodland, town dumps and a plethora of rats and skunks to feed upon. Now our ducks are threatened in a manner that fences cannot cure. The subsiding ripples of the pond seem like wavelets in a mirage as our rare birds disappear—canvasbacks, ring-necks, Hawaiian ducks, teal, all carefully nurtured on our ponds and formerly secure.

⁶ The succession of life itself, the changes in the ratio of predator to prey, the ebb and flow of species—all this is a marvel in nature, no matter how painful in the eye of the beholder. Like life itself, change is the only surety. And so who will win? Perhaps the owls will, for their power is great, their adaptability more breathtaking than anyone could know.

ANALYTICAL READING

1. Why did the author formerly love this time of year on the duck ponds? What does he mean by "the imagination wakens and one senses again the life of the hunter" (paragraph 1)? Is this statement ironic? Why?

2. At the end of paragraph 3, why does Ripley "dare not move"?

3. How does the author account for the presence of the great horned owls?

4. Explain the final paragraph, discussing the ideas and implications in each sentence.

REFLECTING

Point: This selection mainly uses description but includes narration and exposition. Identify uses of each method and explain how all relate to the author's main idea.

Organization: How is the essay organized? Be certain to account for the function of the opening and closing paragraphs.

Support: Point out the many appeals to the senses. Discuss the following verbs or verbals in paragraph 2: *coursing, sailing, junket by.* Is there a contrast between the author's vocabulary and his voice (note "*deliquescing* colors" in paragraph 2)? How do the questions in paragraph 3 enhance the effect of tension? Point out effective figures of speech that you think add support to the essay—for example, "like a wraith" in paragraph 3 and "Like some cloaked Mephistophelian figure" in paragraph 4. Explain your choices.

Synthesis: Can you relate some experience of your own to this one: a cat attacking a bird, or a dog a cat? Do you share the author's view that such things are "a marvel in nature"? How does Ripley's descriptive essay compare to Jack Denton Scott's (pages 145–49)?

Evaluation: Can you understand the reasons for the author's views in the final paragraph? What has contributed to his conclusion that the owls may win? What makes the episode so vivid and dramatic?

FROM READING TO WRITING

1. Describe vividly some natural change that has occurred around your home, such as drought, an invasion of blackbirds or squirrels, or environmental pollution that threatens wildlife.

2. Write a before-and-after description of the changes that take place in a scene with the arrival of an intruder. You might consider writing about the quiet on a street before the touring ice cream wagon arrives, the locker room before and after players arrive, a dorm on a weekday and then on the weekend.

ILLINOIS JOURNEY
Saul Bellow

BIOGRAPHICAL SKETCH

Saul Bellow was born in a suburb of Montreal, Canada, in 1915. Nine years later his family, immigrants from Russia, moved to Chicago. Bellow first attended the University of Chicago, then transferred to and graduated from Northwestern University with honors in sociology and anthropology; he did graduate work in anthropology at the University of Wisconsin. Currently Professor of the Committee on Social Thought at the University of Chicago, he received the Nobel Prize for Literature in 1976. The best known of Bellow's many written works—which include stories, one-act plays, essays, reviews, translations—are his major novels: The Adventures of Augie March *(winner of the National Book Award for Fiction, 1953);* Henderson the Rain King; Herzog *(winner of the National Book Award, 1964);* Mr. Sammler's Planet *(winner of the National Book Award, 1970); and* Humboldt's Gift *(winner of the Pulitzer Prize, 1975).*

FROM *Holiday*, March 1976, pp. 31, 62. Copyright © 1957 by Saul Bellow. Reprinted by permission of Russell & Volkening, Inc. as agents for the author.

PRE-READING

1. What do the title and first sentence suggest about what Bellow plans to discuss? Does the phrase "at first appear monotonous" imply that he will probably take a contrary view in the article?

2. How helpful is the first sentence of the last paragraph?

3. From the biographical sketch, would you expect Bellow to be interested in the scenery from the standpoint of its beauty or as a human environment? Explain.

[1] The features of Illinois are not striking; they do not leap to the eye but lie flat and at first appear monotonous. The roads are wide, hard, perfect, sometimes of a shallow depth in the far distance but so nearly level as to make you feel that the earth really is flat. From east and west, travelers dart across these prairies into the huge horizons and through cornfields that go on forever; giant skies, giant clouds, an eternal nearly featureless sameness. You find it hard to travel slowly. The endless miles pressed flat by the ancient glacier seduce you into speeding. As the car eats into the distances you begin gradually to feel that you are riding upon the floor of the continent, the very bottom of it, low and flat, and an impatient spirit of movement, of overtaking and urgency passes into your heart.

[2] Miles and miles of prairie, slowly rising and falling, sometimes give you a sense that something is in the process of becoming, or that the liberation of a great force is imminent, some power, like Michelangelo's slave only half released from the block of stone. Conceivably the mound-building Indians believed their resurrection would coincide with some such liberation, and built their graves in imitation of the low moraines deposited by the departing glaciers. But they have not yet been released and remain drowned in their waves of earth. They have left their bones, their flints and pots, their place names and tribal names and little besides except a stain, seldom vivid, on the consciousness of their white successors.

[3] The soil of the Illinois prairies is fat, rich and thick. After spring plowing it looks oil-blackened or colored by the soft coal which occurs in great veins throughout the state. In the fields you frequently see a small tipple, or a crazy-looking device that pumps oil and nods like the neck of a horse at a quick walk. . . . Along the roads, with intervals between them as neat and even as buttons on the cuff, sit steel storage bins, in form like the tents of Mongolia. They are filled with grain. And the elevators and tanks, trucks and machines that crawl over the fields and blunder over the highways—whatever you see is productive. It creates wealth, it stores wealth, it is wealth.

[4] As you pass the fields, you see signs the farmers have posted telling in short code what sort of seed they have planted. The farmhouses are seldom at the roadside, but far within the fields. The solitude and silence are deep and wide. Then, when you have gone ten or twenty miles through cornfields with-

out having seen a living thing, no cow, no dog, scarcely even a bird under the hot sky, suddenly you come upon a noisy contraption at the roadside, a system of contraptions, rather, for husking the corn and stripping the grain. It burns and bangs away, and the conveyor belts rattle. . . .

⁵ When you leave, this noise and activity are cut off at one stroke: you are once more in the deaf, hot solitude of trembling air, alone in the cornfields.

⁶ North, south, east and west, there is no end to them. They line roads and streams and hem in the woods and surround towns, and they crowd into back yards and edge up to gas stations. An exotic stranger might assume he had come upon a race of corn worshipers who had created a corn ocean; or that he was among a people who had fallen in love with infinite repetition of the same details, like the builders of skyscrapers in New York and Chicago who have raised up bricks and windows by the thousands, and all alike. From corn you can derive notions of equality, or uniformity, massed democracy. You can, if you are given to that form of mental play, recall Joseph's brethren in the lean years, and think how famine has been conquered here and superabundance itself become such a danger that the Government has to take measures against it.

⁷ The power, the monotony, the oceanic extent of the cornfields do indeed shrink up and dwarf the past. How are you to think of the small bands of Illini, Ottawas, Cahokians, Shawnee, Miamis who camped in the turkey grass, and the French Jesuits who descended the Mississippi and found them. When you force your mind to summon them, the Indians appear rather doll-like in the radiance of the present moment. They are covered in the corn, swamped in the oil, hidden in the coal of Franklin County, run over by the trains, turned phantom by the stockyards. There are monuments to them . . . throughout the state, but they are only historical ornaments to the pride of the present. . . .

ANALYTICAL READING

1. What main impressions about Illinois do you derive from the description?

2. What sense perceptions has Bellow primarily relied on?

3. What is the purpose of referring to the Indian tribes?

4. What is the writer's attitude toward the changed landscape? Does it represent progress to him? How does he seem to feel about New York and Chicago?

REFLECTING

Point: Which sentence best summarizes the essay? How would you express the author's dominant impression of and attitude toward Illinois?

Organization: Can you discern an overall pattern? What is the specific subject of paragraph 4 and how is it organized? What function does paragraph 5 serve? How is paragraph 6 organized?

Support: How well educated an audience is Bellow writing to? Explain with references to particular passages. What figures of speech are particularly effective? Discuss some, such as, "nods like the neck of a horse at a quick walk" (paragraph 3); "like the builders of skyscrapers" (paragraph 6); "the Indians appear rather doll-like" (paragraph 7).

Synthesis: Have your views about Illinois been changed? If so, how? Do you share the author's views about the Indians of Illinois? Do his descriptions reflect your answer to question 3 under "Pre-reading" (page 154)?

Evaluation: How clear and convincing is Bellow's description of his Illinois journey? How complete is it? Does it gain or lose by the inclusion of references to Indians? What specific features of the selection help to make it effective or ineffective?

FROM READING TO WRITING

1. Describe your own state, giving readers your personal impression but being careful to support it with many details.

2. Describe your college to a high school student who would like to picture it and learn about its physical atmosphere but who is unable to visit it.

FROM OUR EVER-CHANGING SHORE
Rachel Carson

BIOGRAPHICAL SKETCH

Rachel Carson (1907–1964), an author and scientist with an M.A. from Johns Hopkins University, worked with the United States Fish and Wildlife Service from 1936 to 1952. Her second book, The Sea Around Us *(1951), earned her a worldwide reputation as a naturalist. In the 1960's she became very concerned about the effect of DDT and other pesticides on fish and bird life. Her book on the subject,* Silent Spring *(1962), created an international controversy and was instrumental in the subsequent banning of DDT.*

PRE-READING

1. What does the title suggest? Are you familiar with conservationist Rachel Carson and her work? If so, what attitude toward nature might you expect to find in the selection?

2. What words or phrases in the first and last paragraphs provide clues to the subject?

FROM Rachel Carson, "Our Ever-Changing Shore," in Paul Brooks, *The House of Life: Rachel Carson at Work* (Boston: Houghton Mifflin, 1972), pp. 218–24. Copyright © 1972 by Paul Brooks. Reprinted by permission of Houghton Mifflin Company. The article originally appeared in *Holiday* Magazine, July 1958, © 1958 by The Curtis Publishing Company.

[1] The shore means many things to many people. Of its varied moods the one usually considered typical is not so at all. The true spirit of the sea does not reside in the gentle surf that laps a sun-drenched bathing beach on a summer day. Instead, it is on a lonely shore at dawn or twilight, or in storm or midnight darkness that we sense a mysterious something we recognize as the reality of the sea. For the ocean has nothing to do with humanity. It is supremely unaware of man, and when we carry too many of the trappings of human existence with us to the threshold of the sea world our ears are dulled and we do not hear the accents of sublimity in which it speaks.

[2] Sometimes the shore speaks of the earth and its own creation; sometimes it speaks of life. If we are lucky in choosing our time and place, we may witness a spectacle that echoes of vast and elemental things. On a summer night when the moon is full, the sea and the swelling tide and a creature of the ancient shore conspire to work primeval magic on many of the beaches from Maine to Florida. On such a night the horseshoe crabs move in, just as they did under a Paleozoic moon—just as they have been doing through all the hundreds of millions of years since then—coming out of the sea to dig their nests in the wet sand and deposit their spawn.

[3] As the tide nears its flood dark shapes appear in the surf line. They gleam with the wetness of the sea as the moon shines on the smooth curves of their massive shells. The first to arrive linger in the foaming water below the advancing front of the tide. These are the waiting males. At last other forms emerge out of the darkness offshore, swimming easily in the deeper water but crawling awkwardly and hesitantly as the sea shallows beneath them. They make their way to the beach through the crowd of jostling males. In thinning water each female digs her nest and sheds her burden of eggs, hundreds of tiny balls of potential life. An attending male fertilizes them. Then the pair moves on, leaving the eggs to the sea, which gently stirs them and packs the sand about them, grain by grain.

[4] Not all of the high tides of the next moon cycle will reach this spot, for the water movements vary in strength and at the moon's quarters are weakest of all. A month after the egg laying the embryos will be ready for life; then the high tides of another full moon will wash away the sand of the nest. The turbulence of the rising tide will cause the egg membranes to split, releasing the young crabs to a life of their own over their shallow shores of bays and sounds.

[5] But how do the parent crabs foresee these events? What is there in this primitive, lumbering creature that tells it that the moon is full and the tides are running high? And what tells it that the security of its eggs will somehow be enhanced if the nests are dug and the eggs deposited on these stronger tides of the moon's cycle?

[6] Tonight, in this setting of full moon and pressing tide, the shore speaks of life in a mysterious and magical way. Here is the sea and land's edge. Here is a creature that has known such seas and shores for eons of time, while the stream of evolution swept on, leaving it almost untouched since the days of the trilobites. The horseshoe crabs in their being obliterate the barrier of time.

Our thoughts become uncertain: is it really today? or is it a million—or a hundred million years ago?

[7] Or sometimes when the place and mood are right, and time is of no account, it is the early sea itself that we glimpse. I remember feeling, once, that I had actually sensed what the young earth was like. We had come down through spruce woods to the sea—woods that were dim with drifting mists and the first light of day. As we passed beyond the last line of trees onto the rocks of the shore a curtain of fog dropped silently but instantly behind us, shutting out all sights and sounds of the land. Suddenly our world was only the dripping rocks and the gray sea that swirled against them and occasionally exploded in a muted roar. These, and the gray mists—nothing more. For all one could tell the time might have been Paleozoic, when the world was in very fact only rocks and sea.

[8] We stood quietly, speaking few words. There was nothing, really, for human words to say in the presence of something so vast, mysterious, and immensely powerful. Perhaps only in music of deep inspiration and grandeur could the message of that morning be translated by the human spirit, as in the opening bars of Beethoven's Ninth Symphony—music that echoes across vast distances and down long corridors of time, bringing the sense of what was and of what is to come—music of swelling power that swirls and explodes even as the sea surged against the rocks below us.

[9] But that morning all that was worth saying was being said by the sea. It is only in wild and solitary places that it speaks so clearly. Another such place that I like to remember is that wilderness of beach and high dunes where Cape Cod, after its thirty-mile thrust into the Atlantic, bends back toward the mainland. Over the thousands of years the sea and the wind have worked together to build this world out of sand. The wide beach is serene, like the ocean that stretches away to a far-off horizon. Offshore the dangerous shoals of Peaked Hill Bars lie just beneath the surface, holding within themselves the remains of many ships. Behind the beach the dunes begin to rise, moving inland like a vast sea of sand waves caught in a moment of immobility as they sweep over the land.

[10] The dunes are a place of silence, to which even the sound of the sea comes as a distant whisper; a place where, if you listen closely, you can hear the hissing of the ever mobile sand grains that leap and slide in every breath of wind, or the dry swish of the beach grass, writing its endless symbols in the sand.

[11] Few people come out through that solitude of dune and sky into the vaster solitude of beach and sea. A bird could fly from the highway to the beach in a matter of minutes, its shadow gliding easily and swiftly up one great desert ridge and down another. But such easy passage is not for the human traveler, who must make his slow way on foot. The thin line of his footprints, toiling up slopes and plunging down into valleys, is soon erased by the shifting, sliding sands. So indifferent are these dunes to man, so quickly do they obliterate the signs of his presence, that they might never have known him at all.

[12] I remember my own first visit to the beach at Peaked Hill Bars. From the highway a sandy track led off through thickets of pine. The horizon lay high on the crest of a near dune. Soon the track was lost, the trees thinned out, the world was all sand and sky.

[13] From the crest of the first hill I hoped for a view of the sea. Instead there was another hill, across a wide valley. Everything in this dune world spoke of the forces that had created it, of the wind that had shifted and molded the materials it received from the sea, here throwing the surface of a dune into firm ridges, there smoothing it into swelling curves. At last I came to a break in the seaward line of dunes and saw before me the beach and the sea.

[14] On the shore below me there was at first no sign of any living thing. Then perhaps half a mile down the beach I saw a party of gulls resting near the water's edge. They were silent and intent, facing the wind. Whatever communion they had at that moment was with the sea rather than with each other. They seemed almost to have forgotten their own kind and the ways of gulls. When once a white, feathered form drifted down from the dunes and dropped to the sand beside them none of the group challenged him. I approached them slowly. Each time I crossed that invisible line beyond which no human trespasser might come, the gulls rose in a silent flock and moved to a more distant part of the sands. Everything in that scene caused me to feel apart, remembering that the relation of birds to the sea is rooted in millions of years, that man came but yesterday.

[15] And there have been other shores where time stood still. On Buzzards Bay there is a beach studded with rocks left by the glaciers. Barnacles grow on them now, and a curtain of rockweeds drapes them below the tide line. The bay shore of mud and sand is crossed by the winding trails of many periwinkles. On the beach at every high tide are cast the shells and empty husks of all that live offshore: the gold and silver shells of the rock oysters of jingles, the curious little half decks or slipper shells, the brown, fernlike remains of Bugula, the moss animal, the bones of fishes and the egg strings of whelks.

[16] Behind the beach is a narrow rim of low dunes, then a wide salt marsh. This marsh, when I visited it on an evening toward the end of summer, had filled with shore birds since the previous night; and their voices were a faint, continuous twittering. Green herons fished along the creek banks, creeping at the edge of the tall grasses, placing one foot at a time with infinite care, then with a quick forward lunge attempting to seize some small fish or other prey. Farther back in the marsh a score of night herons stood motionless. From the bordering woods across the marsh a mother deer and her two fawns came down to drink silently, then melted back into their forest world.

[17] The salt marsh that evening was like a calm, green sea—only a little calmer, a little greener than the wide sheet of the bay on the other side of the dunes. The same breeze that rippled the surface of the bay set the tips of the marsh grasses to swaying in long undulations. Within its depths the marsh concealed the lurking bittern, the foraging heron, the meadow mouse running down long trails of overarching grass stems, even as the watery sea concealed the lurking squids and fishes and their prey. Like the foam on the beach when

the wind had whipped the surface waters into a light froth, the even more delicate foam of the sea lavender flecked the dune barrier and ran to the edge of the marsh. Already the fiery red of the glasswort or marsh samphire flickered over the higher ground of the marsh, while offshore mysterious lights flared in the waters of the bay at night. These were signs of approaching autumn, which may be found at the sea's edge before even the first leaf shows a splash of red or yellow.

[18] The sea's phosphorescence is never so striking alongshore as in late summer. Then some of the chief light producers of the water world have their fall gatherings in bays and coves. Just where and when their constellations will form no one can predict. And the identity of these wheeling stars of the night sea varies. Usually the tiny glittering sparks are exceedingly minute, one-celled creatures, called dinoflagellates. Larger forms, flaring with a ghostly blue-white phosphorescence, may be comb jellies, crystal clear and about the size of a small plum.

[19] On beach and dune and over the flat vistas of salt marsh, too, the advancing seasons cast their shadows; the time of change is at hand. Mornings, a light mist lies over the marshes and rises from the creeks. The nights begin to hint of frost; the stars take on a wintry sparkle; Orion and his dogs hunt in the sky. It is a time, too, of color—red of berries in the dune thickets, rich yellow of the goldenrod, purple and lacy white of the wild asters in the fields. In the dunes and on the ocean beach the colors are softer, more subtle. There may be a curious purple shading over the sand. It shifts with the wind, piles up in little ridges of deeper color like the ripple marks of waves. When first I saw this sand on the northern Massachusetts coast, I wondered about it. According to local belief the purple color comes from some seaweed, left on the shore, dried, and reduced to a thin film of powder over the coarser particles of sand. Years later I found the answer. I discovered drifts of the same purple color amid the coarse sand of my own shore in Maine—sand largely made up of broken shell and rock, fragments of sea urchin spines, opercula of snails. I brought some of the purple sand to the house. When I put a pinch of it under the microscope I knew at once that this came from no plant—what I saw was an array of gems, clear as crystal, returning a lovely amethyst light to my eyes. It was pure garnet.

[20] The sand grains scattered on the stage of my microscope spoke in their own way of the timeless, unhurried spirit of earth and sea. They were the end product of a process that began eons ago deep inside the earth, continued when the buried mineral was brought at last to the surface, and went on through millennia of time and, it may be, through thousands of miles of transport over land and sea until, tiny, exquisite gems of purest color, they came temporarily to rest at the foot of a glacier-scarred rock.

[21] Perhaps something of the strength and serenity and endurance of the sea—of this spirit beyond time and place—transfers itself to us of the land world as we confront its vast and lonely expanse from the shore, our last outpost.

ANALYTICAL READING

1. What common misconception about the sea does the author try to change?

2. What is significant about the horseshoe crabs?

3. What is memorable about the early morning sea?

4. What essential characteristics do the beaches of Cape Cod, Peaked Hill Bars, and Buzzards Bay have in common, and why are these characteristics important?

5. What does the phrase "time stood still" at the end of the first sentence in paragraph 15 mean to you?

6. What point does Carson make about the purple color of the sand at the end of the selection? What does this incident reveal about her?

REFLECTING

Point: What purpose do all the descriptions of the various shores serve? Try to state in one sentence the central idea of the selection.

Organization: Outline the main sections. Do you find an organizational pattern, or just a series of loose associations?

Support: Which paragraph did you find most vivid and why? Which words or phrases were most suggestive? Discuss the effect of the following: "a spectacle that echoes" (paragraph 2); "primeval magic" (paragraph 2); "a curtain of fog" (paragraph 7); "communion" (paragraph 14). Explain the impact of the series of questions in paragraph 5.

Synthesis: In paragraph 8, Carson states that perhaps only Beethoven's Ninth Symphony could do justice to her experience. Do you sometimes share that feeling about the inadequacy of words and the superiority of music? Do you think that Carson does convey her feelings effectively in words, thus perhaps contradicting herself? Has your feeling about the sea changed as a result of having read the selection? On the basis of this selection, why do you think that Carson became a conservationist?

Evaluation: Do you experience the author's feelings and relive them with her? How clearly has she conveyed her ideas about something that she found difficult to express in words? How convincing has she been about the sea? What are the strengths of her writing? The weaknesses?

FROM READING TO WRITING

1. Describe some natural setting that has stirred you, awaking you in some manner to a new understanding of nature and your place in it.

2. Write about some building or painting or other object that has attracted or repelled you, being careful to describe it clearly.

Character Sketch —
An Individual

MY BEAUTIFUL GRANDMOTHER
Kathryn Stripling

BIOGRAPHICAL SKETCH

Kathryn Stripling, born in south Georgia, holds degrees from Wesleyan College and the University of North Carolina at Greensboro. She has studied writing with Allen Tate, Robert Watson, and A. R. Ammons. Her awards include poetry prizes from the Academy of American Poets and the Irene Leache Memorial Award. "My Beautiful Grandmother" recently won the first Amon Liner Award. Journals that have published her poems include the Iowa Review, Hudson Review, *and the* Southern Review. *Although she currently lives in North Carolina, she writes mainly about her childhood in Georgia.*

PRE-READING

1. What do the title and the first verse of the poem suggest about the subject and the situation?

2. How does the last verse reinforce your answer to question 1?

My Beautiful Grandmother

died ugly,
wasted with hunger,
her arms black and blue from the needles,
the last ones she took up
when she stopped embroidering pink cornucopias   5
on square after square of white cotton.
Nobody could coax her to eat after six years
of morphine. Not even my father.

FROM *The Greensboro Review*, Winter 1976–77, pp. 20–21. © 1976 by The University of North Carolina at Greensboro. Reprinted by permission of the author and *The Greensboro Review*.

She'd wanted to leave
for a long time, she wanted   10
the mountains, the cool
air, the sky coming down
like a good sleep, she wanted

to go back to where she had been
when she wore the red plume in her hat   15
and sat pointing the toe of her shoe
at the camera. Oh

she was a dashing one
all the men said, and say
still if you ask them. Her mind was as quick   20
as the stitch of a sparrow's wing.
Coming and going,
she made sure her petticoats rustled.
A flirt and a good one she was
and so square-jawed and German she looked   25
like the belle of some old-country tavern.
Her laugh was a yodel.

She wasn't the belle of that small town
in Georgia. But, stubborn,
she tried what she knew worked   30
a little while. She fell in love
with a young man whose letters she saved
in a hatbox. I opened one
once. It read: "Darling,
my heart counts the moments   35
until we are wed!" Then
it crumbled like stale bread.
The rats had gnawed whole words away.
Such a bride,
such a bride, all the townspeople said   40
and forgot her. I grew up remembering

I was her granddaughter. And it's been years
I've spent leaving that small town in Georgia
where my beautiful grandmother stayed.

ANALYTICAL READING

1. Explain the background of the poem. How long after the death of the grand-
    mother is the poem written? What probably caused the grandmother's death:

was she a drug addict or a sick person? Where did she die? What did she long for before her death?

2. What are some of the main impressions presented about the grandmother besides her beauty?

3. In the third verse, what is implied about the camera?

4. In line 24, does the designation of the grandmother as "a flirt" connote a favorable or unfavorable impression? Why?

5. Discuss the significance of lines 28–31. Do they suggest that perhaps the grandmother was truly beautiful? What is the meaning of "she tried what she knew worked"?

6. What is the effect of line 38, "The rats had gnawed whole words away"?

7. Explain lines 42–44: "And it's been years. . . ." What do they reveal about the poet?

REFLECTING

Point: Is the poem simply a character description of the grandmother, or does it suggest a more general observation about people and life?

Organization: Discuss the function of each verse, showing how it is related to the previous one. Then consider whether the entire poem follows some organizational pattern.

Support: How is contrast used effectively in the reference to "the needles" in the first verse? What is ironic about the mention of embroidering cornucopias? How do the details in the fourth verse support its opening line (line 18)? Identify and discuss some of the figures of speech.

Synthesis: Have you had an experience similar to that described in the poem, observing change in someone whom you idolized? Do you feel the adoration of the girl in the poem for her grandmother? How does the poem affect you—is it sad, angry, bitter, or what?

Evaluation: Can the poem be criticized for focusing only on the physical attractiveness of the grandmother instead of discussing her other qualities? Is contrast used effectively in providing images of ugliness and beauty? Is the introduction effective? The ending? Are sufficient details provided so that you can develop a sense of what the grandmother was like? Will you remember the poem and perhaps want to reread it? If so, why?

FROM READING TO WRITING

1. Write a poem or an essay about an older relative or family friend, contrasting the person's present with his or her past.

2. Write a character sketch in the form of a poem or an essay about someone who has recently died and whom you wish others to know as you did.

THE GREAT BABE
Leo Durocher

BIOGRAPHICAL SKETCH

Leo Durocher was born in 1906 in West Springfield, Massachusetts. He played with the New York Yankees in the late 1920's, but he was better known as the scrappy captain of the St. Louis Cardinals' "Gashouse Gang," where he starred in the mid-1930's after two years with the Cincinnati Reds. Traded to the Brooklyn Dodgers in 1937, Durocher was their manager from 1939 to 1946, when he was barred from baseball by Commissioner "Happy" Chandler for one year. He returned to the Dodgers in 1948, but soon afterward became manager of their arch-rivals, the New York Giants, and remained with the Giants until the early 1950's. Among the many highlights of his colorful career were playing in several World Series, receiving a Manager of the Year award, and piloting the 1952 Giants into a World Series victory. Few baseball players and managers were as capable and controversial, or were associated with as many famous players, as Durocher.

PRE-READING

1. How does the first line indicate the writer's thesis? In the opening paragraph, what shows the relationship between Ruth and Durocher at this time?

2. Which sentence in the first paragraph most clearly suggests how discussion of the subject, Babe Ruth, will be restricted or limited to one view or aspect of his life?

3. From the biographical sketch, would you expect Durocher to be a good judge of baseball players? Explain.

[1] Babe Ruth dominated that team totally. He dominated it on the field, and he dominated it even more off the field. He made more money by far than anybody else, and nobody resented it, because we knew he was putting money in all of our pockets. There has never been anything like Babe Ruth, because everything about him was bigger than life.

[2] As far as I am concerned, there is only one all-time home-run champ and that's Babe Ruth. All right, Henry Aaron went to bat 2,890 more times in order to hit one more home run. All you have to do is use your common sense. I'm not trying to take anything away from Henry Aaron. Long before anybody even thought he had a shot at the record I had been saying that they ought to put Henry Aaron in the Hall of Fame right now. While he was still playing. Henry Aaron is a great all-around ballplayer who, among his other

FROM Leo Durocher with Ed Linn, *Nice Guys Finish Last* (New York: Simon & Schuster, 1975), pp. 53–55. Copyright © 1975 by Leo Durocher and Ed Linn. Reprinted by permission of Simon & Schuster, a Division of Gulf & Western Corporation.

accomplishments, hit a lot of home runs. It you appreciate baseball in all its finer aspects, he has been a pleasure to watch.

³ Babe Ruth was *** The Sultan of Swat ***

⁴ Babe Ruth was *** THE BAMBINO ***

⁵ Babe Ruth was what you came to see!!!!

⁶ It was like going to a carnival, with Babe as both the star performer and the side-show attraction. Hell, that's what we called him: "You big ape." He was what a home-run hitter was supposed to look like. Wide, flat nose. Big feet. Little ankles. Belly hanging over his belt. All he had to do was walk on to the field and everybody would applaud. The air became charged with electricity. You just felt that something great was going to happen.

⁷ He'd twirl that big 48-ounce bat around in little circles up at the plate as if he were cranking it up for the Biggest Home Run Ever Hit—*you felt that*— and when he'd hit one he would hit it like nobody has hit it before or since. A mile high and a mile out. I can see him now, as I did so many times, just look up, drop the bat and start to trot, the little pitter-patter pigeon-toed, high-bellied trot that seemed to say, I've done it before and I'll do it again, but this one was for you. (Henry Aaron has a good home-run trot too, it's probably the most colorful thing about him. He holds his elbows up high, if you've ever noticed, and kind of swaggers from the waist up while he's kind of shuffling from the waist down.)

⁸ The Babe didn't even have to hit a home run to thrill you. He would hit infield flies that were worth the price of admission. The fielder would holler, "I got it," and he'd wait . . . and wait . . . and then he'd begin to stagger and finally he'd make a wild lunge. The ball would land fifteen feet away from him, and the Babe would be standing on second base with a big grin on his face.

⁹ You'll think I'm exaggerating when I say that it was a thrill to see him strike out. But not if you ever saw him. He would take that big swing of his and you could hear the whole stands go *Whooooosssshhhh!* And then break out into wild applause as he was walking back to the bench.

¹⁰ Charisma counts. Charisma is what takes a superstar and turns him into a super-superstar. I've never seen a charismatic ballplayer who didn't make the team better than it figured to be, for the same reason that a charismatic actor makes any play he is in better than it should be. There is just something about these people that carries everybody else along with them.

¹¹ There's no question about it, Babe Ruth was the greatest instinctive baseball player who ever lived. He was a great hitter, and he had been a great pitcher. The only thing he couldn't really do was run, but when he went from first to third—or stole a base for you—he invariably made it because he instinctively did the right thing.

ANALYTICAL READING

1. What does the author mean in paragraph 1 when he says that Ruth was not resented because "he was putting money in all our pockets"?

2. Why does Durocher compare Ruth with Henry Aaron? What is the point about Aaron's having gone to bat many more times than Ruth? Does Durocher belittle Aaron while glorifying Ruth?

3. Explain the statement in paragraph 4 that Ruth was "both the star performer and the side-show attraction."

4. In what ways was it thrilling to watch Ruth bat even if he didn't hit a home run?

5. Why does Durocher discuss charisma?

6. What seldom-mentioned but important fact about Babe Ruth is mentioned in the last paragraph?

7. What does Durocher mean when he refers to Ruth as an "instinctive" player?

REFLECTING

Point: Which sentence best indicates Durocher's thesis?

Organization: How does each paragraph contribute to that thesis? Do you find any organizational pattern?

Support: What facts are used and what is their purpose? How do descriptions make this character sketch more interesting and vivid? What is the effect of the three parallel sentences in paragraphs 3, 4, and 5? Do the sentence fragments in paragraph 6 serve some purpose? Do you approve of the coinage "super-superstar" in paragraph 10? Discuss the voice and tone of the writer.

Synthesis: Can you understand after reading the excerpt why some older fans rave about the Babe? Are there modern players with charisma? Do you think another Babe Ruth is likely to appear one of these days, or has big-league baseball changed too much?

Evaluation: Has the author delivered less than he promised in failing to show how Ruth "dominated" the team "even more off the field" and to explain how "everything about him was bigger than life" (paragraph 1)? Is there too much discussion of Henry Aaron, resulting in an unnecessary digression? Is Ruth's charisma sufficiently explained?

FROM READING TO WRITING

1. Write a character sketch about a living athlete, trying to explain what makes him or her so exciting.

2. Write a character sketch about a celebrity other than an athlete, trying to account for the person's charisma.

MISS MAY
Wilma Dykeman

BIOGRAPHICAL SKETCH

Wilma Dykeman was born in Ashville, North Carolina, in 1920. She earned a B.S. in 1940 from Northwestern University. Primarily a writer, she has lectured at universities and colleges and received the Thomas Wolfe Memorial Trophy in 1955 for her book about a river, The French Broad. *In 1958, along with her husband, James A. Stokely, Jr., she received the Hillman Award for* Neither Black Nor White. *In 1963, she was awarded a prize from the Chicago Friends of Writers for* The Tall Woman. *Most of her works involve the Great Smoky Mountain region, where she has spent most of her life.*

PRE-READING

What sentence early in this character sketch best suggests its direction?

¹ Every town needs a "Miss May." She was in essence a lady; she was in influence a leader. Any city or community can ill afford to lose the likes of her.

² I suppose there were those who thought Miss May was indestructible because she had given herself to so many succeeding generations. Her strength was not only physical. She gave with her hands, the lowliest manual labor—and with her head and her heart as well. And wherever she gave, it was to build.

³ I can see her now as she stood in the neat, attractive stone house she acquired in her later years (even helped construct, in part). Gracious and hospitable, yet surrounded by a certain sad reserve, she welcomed a guest to share her chicken and rice, or her needlework, or the ceramics she adopted as a hobby.

⁴ I can remember her as she stood before the handful in the graduating class of her school—head tilted slightly to one side, cheekbones high and prominent beneath the large brown eyes that searched each pupil's face for a spark of ambition, a flicker of the hope she had tried to kindle there.

⁵ I can visualize her before the congregation in her church—tall, erect, exemplifying reverence and dignity in a world that had too little of each, pleading for the pennies or dollars that would finally install a new heating plant, bring new benches, buy a new piano in this bare wooden room.

⁶ I can realize the unusual balance of pride and humility that gave Miss May her special grace, set her character apart. She stood upright with the strength of an oak when strength was needed, and she bent with grace and the ease of a willow when her help was needed.

⁷ Miss May never knew idleness. The fact that she was a Negro was incidental to her essential worth, but it was central to the limitations set on her by an indifferent, sometimes hostile, world. She knew hard work all her life. Who can estimate the costs, in extra labor, wounded pride, disappointed trusts, that she paid because of a fact of her birth? I cannot begin to make such an estimate.

⁸ She saw men die violently and needlessly. She saw young people waste their talents and fling away their lives as carelessly as cigarette stubs. She saw the leaders on whom she must depend for survival gouge and wrench and squeeze to make pennies out of another's sweat and dollars out of another's need. She saw it clearly and recorded it in memory. But she did not yield to the luxury of cynicism or to the ease of hate. She persisted. Occasionally she prevailed.

⁹ Her father died when she was small; her mother was left with nothing but a family of young children and the will to work. Work they did—on neighboring farms, in the fields and households, growing their own crops and securing their own survival from a few unproductive acres.

¹⁰ And with it all, Miss May was determined to educate herself. She did, and then she was determined to educate others. She did this, for forty-five years. From one-room country schools to a consolidated brick building in the county seat, she taught class after class.

¹¹ She married, but had no children of her own. So she took whatever surplus of food anyone would give her and she canned thousands of jars of fruits and vegetables so that her schoolchildren might have nourishing lunches in the winter, whether they could pay or not. She found shoes for some of the bare feet that came to her door. She provided discipline for those who had known only wayward abandon all the years of their childhood. Her searching eyes looked upon them with tenderness and mercy—and measured them for the size of jackets they might need and the size of ideas they might grasp.

¹² Many of those Miss May taught are teachers now themselves. Many of those for whom she fought on one battleground have long since fought for her, and all of us, on farther battlefields. Many of those with whom she worked failed her and themselves. Others succeeded. None will forget her.

¹³ In her own way Miss May taught us all. The whole community was her pupil. We can ill afford to lose her instruction.

ANALYTICAL READING

1. In what way did Miss May give with her hands, her head, and her heart?

2. In what ways was Miss May a traditional "lady"; in what ways a leader?

3. Did it make any difference that Miss May was "a Negro"?

4. Explain the meaning of the parallel phrases near the end of paragraph 8, "the luxury of cynicism or . . . the ease of hate."

5. What do you think is the significance of the description of Miss May's family background and later, the mention of the fact that she had no children of her own?

6. Discuss the meaning of the last paragraph: Had Miss May literally taught everyone in the community? How does the paragraph suggest that one person can indeed make a difference?

REFLECTING

Point: Is Miss May too perfect? Does this tribute to her go so far that she seems unreal? Or do you suppose that many in the community did not view Miss May as the heroic woman that Wilma Dykeman makes her but merely thought of her as a good person? What particular qualities does the writer find most praiseworthy?

Organization: How effective are the extremely short introductory and closing paragraphs? Point out the topic of each paragraph and determine the organization of the character sketch. Discuss why you think the author chose not to begin with the family history.

Support: Note that paragraphs 2, 3, 4, 5, and 6 open with sentences that start with "I." Afterward the "I" is seldom mentioned. Why this change? Point to paragraphs in which details are used effectively and paragraphs in which much is suggested but details are sketchy. What words or phrases or figures of speech add to this tribute to Miss May?

Synthesis: Can you share the writer's feeling for Miss May? What do you think was the relationship between the writer and her subject? Are there people like Miss May in your community? Are they teachers, community leaders, social workers, homemakers, or what?

Evaluation: Has the author succeeded in making Miss May come alive? Is she believable? Does it make much difference that she is not described physically? What stylistic skills permit us to see and value Miss May as Dykeman did?

FROM READING TO WRITING

1. Write a character sketch about some teacher or person whose life is dedicated to helping others.

2. Responding to an inquiry by the dean of admissions of a college about a high school friend of yours who is applying there, write a letter of recommendation.

THE WILD BOY AND THE CIVILIZED TEACHER

Harlan L. Lane

BIOGRAPHICAL SKETCH

Harlan Lane was born in Brooklyn, New York, in 1936. He received his under-graduate and master's degrees from Columbia University and his doctorate in psychology from Harvard. He also holds the Doctorat d'Etat, a French degree. He taught psychology at the University of Michigan, the Sorbonne, and the University of California at San Diego and served as the director of Michigan's Center for Research on Language and Language Behavior before accepting his present position as chairman of the psychology department at Northeastern University. He also has served as a consultant to the U.S. Office of Education and to UNESCO and has received several honors, including the American Speech and Hearing Association Award in 1971 for the article of highest merit. His research in linguistics and psychology has resulted in more than seventy articles published in scholarly journals in this country and abroad. Lane's interest in the education of deaf children led him to write the book from which this selection is taken, The Wild Boy of Aveyron, *whose main concern is the method developed to teach this boy.*

PRE-READING

This introduction to the book presupposes that the reader knows it is about an experiment to educate a boy found in the wilderness. But the opening paragraph suggests something more about the subject of the book. What is it, and which sentence best states it?

[1] The Luxembourg Gardens are an island of calm, of lawns, gravel paths, fountains, and statues, in the heart of left-bank Paris. On a summer's day in 1800, two young Frenchmen from the provinces met there for the first time and joined together their lives and futures. Although neither could have said so, each was engaged in a search whose success required the other.

[2] The first young man was well but not elegantly dressed in a long coat, drawn in at the waist, with full lapels. His curly hair fell in locks over a slanting forehead; his aquiline nose extended the plane almost as far as his jutting chin. Tightly drawn wide lips and large, dark brown eyes completed the Mediterranean features, set off by a broad white collar that rose funnel-like from his frilly white shirt. Jean-Marc-Gaspard Itard was twenty-six and had just become a doctor. He had left the barren village at the foot of the French Alps where he was raised and had come to Paris in search of a place for himself in the new social order that had emerged from the chaos of the Revolution. Paris at this time was vibrant: painting, theater, music, and literature

FROM Harlan L. Lane, *The Wild Boy of Aveyron* (Cambridge, Mass.: Harvard University Press, 1976), pp. 3–5. Copyright © 1976 by Harlan Lane. Reprinted by permission of the author and publishers.

were flourishing, abetted by the glittering salons of the very rich, the rendez-vous of the intellectual and social elite. Medicine was surging ahead; it had become possible to protect people against disease by giving them some of the disease itself, although no one really knew why. One of Itard's teachers, Phi-lippe Pinel, had just written the first book of psychiatric diagnosis, and had dramatically ordered inmates of the city's insane asylums to be unchained. The first anthropological society was formed, while expeditions returned with the flora, fauna, and inhabitants of Africa, Indonesia, and the New World, to the delight and fascination of naturalists, anatomists, and, above all, philos-ophers. Itard had left the relative isolation of the provinces in search of this excitement of senses and mind, to share in it, even to contribute to it if he could. His alliance with the strange boy rocking back and forth in front of him would surely bring him public attention; it might admit him to the ranks of the great doctors and philosophers of his time, or it might destroy his career right at its beginning.

3 The boy was twelve or thirteen years old, but only four-and-a-half feet tall. Light-complexioned, his face was spotted with traces of smallpox and marked with several small scars, on his eyebrow, on his chin, on both cheeks. Like Itard, he had dark deep-set eyes, long eyelashes, chestnut brown hair, and a long pointed nose; unlike Itard, the boy's hair was straight, his chin receding, his face round and childlike. His head jutted forward on a long graceful neck, which was disfigured by a thick scar slashed across his voice box. He was clothed in only a loose-fitting gray robe resembling a nightshirt, belted with a large leather strap. The boy said nothing; he appeared to be deaf. He gazed distantly across the open spaces of the gardens, without focus-ing on Itard or, for that matter, on anything else. That same day, he had ended a grueling week-long journey. By order of the Minister of the Interior, Napo-leon Bonaparte's brother, Lucien, the boy had come to Paris from a forest region in the province of Aveyron in southern France. This journey was the latest development in his search, which began a year before when he clam-bered out of the forests, worked his way across an elevated plateau in the bitterest winter in recent memory, and entered a farmhouse on the edge of a hamlet. He exchanged the freedom and isolation of his life in the forests of Aveyron, where he had run wild, for captivity and the company of men in society. He came without a name, so he was called the Wild Boy of Aveyron.

4 Perhaps Itard knew better than the savants of his time, who expected to see in the boy the incarnation of Rousseau's "noble savage," man in the pure state of nature; perhaps he did not. What he saw, he wrote later, was "a disgustingly dirty child affected with spasmodic movements, and often con-vulsions, who swayed back and forth ceaselessly like certain animals in a zoo, who bit and scratched those who opposed him, who showed no affection for those who took care of him; and who was, in short, indifferent to everything and attentive to nothing." The society of the eighteenth century had held both young men at bay, depriving the first of the best it had to offer, depriving the second of everything. Itard sought to master the ultimate skills of his cul-

ture—trained observation, persuasive language, social grace—the boy, their rudiments. So be it: they would help each other. Educating the boy would be a test of the new science of mental medicine and a proof of philosophy's new empiricist theory of knowledge. It would give still more justification for social reform by showing how utterly man depends on society for all that he is and can be. If the effort succeeded, the nineteenth century would give them their proper place, where the eighteenth had not.

ANALYTICAL READING

1. What was Itard's background? What does this information contribute to your understanding of the relationship between him and the boy?

2. What purpose is served by the description of Paris?

3. In what way was the influence of Pinel, Itard's teacher, important?

4. Compare and contrast the general appearance of Itard and the boy.

5. Are you familiar with the reference in paragraph 4 to Rousseau's "noble savage," or can you guess from the context what it means?

6. In what ways were both young men deprived by the society of their time?

7. What was Itard attempting to prove? If his work was successful, what implications would it have?

8. What pattern of comparison and contrast is used?

REFLECTING

Point: How do the first and final paragraphs present the thesis of the selection? How do the character sketches of Itard and the boy show their differences and yet establish a basic similarity?

Organization: Indicate the general organization of the selection. Point out where and why the second paragraph might have been divided into two parts.

Support: Indicate, by referring to words, phrases, allusions, and ideas, the kind of readers Lane is addressing. Explain the use of the colon in the middle of paragraph 2 after the statement that "Paris at this time was vibrant." Illustrate how the sentence in paragraph 3 about the boy's journey exemplifies the cumulative structure. Can you find several others?

Synthesis: Can you compare the challenge faced by Itard with the educational problems of today? Can you sense what motivated Itard? Was it self-interest or the desire to contribute to science or a combination of the two? Can you understand why the boy reacted as he did to those taking care of him? Is there some relationship between Itard and young people who today leave their home towns to seek success in New York, Hollywood, Nashville, or other places?

Evaluation: Are Lane's brief character sketches of the two young men effective? Is there more information about the wild boy than about Itard? Is this a weakness or not? Why? Has the writer pictured Paris of 1800 adequately? How successful has the writer been in introducing his book about the "wild boy"? What specifically contributes to his success or lack of it?

FROM READING TO WRITING

1. Write a character sketch comparing and contrasting two friends or other people you know, such as your mother and father, two uncles or aunts, teachers, coaches, or clergymen.

2. Write a paper comparing and contrasting the family black sheep with some other relative.

Character Sketch — A Type

FROM CONFESSIONS OF A BOOK REVIEWER

George Orwell

BIOGRAPHICAL SKETCH

George Orwell (1903–1950) was born in Motihari, Bengal, educated in England at Eton, and joined the Indian Imperial Police in Burma. Resigning in protest against British imperialism, he then worked as a dishwasher, private tutor, teacher, and bookstore assistant. As a communist, he fought and was wounded in the Spanish Civil War, but later became disillusioned with communism. He is well known for his essays—particularly "Politics and the English Language" and "Shooting an Elephant," which are among the most anthologized prose writings—and for his novels, particularly Animal Farm *and* Nineteen Eighty-Four.

PRE-READING

1. What does the title suggest, particularly the word *confessions?*

2. Do you know anything about or have you read George Orwell's most famous books? Could he be writing about his early writing days? Should his views about the subject be considered authoritative? Why?

[1] In a cold but stuffy bed-sitting room littered with cigarette ends and half-empty cups of tea, a man in a moth-eaten dressing-gown sits at a rickety table, trying to find room for his typewriter among the piles of dusty papers that surround it. He cannot throw the papers away because the wastepaper basket is already overflowing, and besides, somewhere among the unanswered letters and unpaid bills it is possible that there is a cheque for two guineas which he is nearly certain he forgot to pay into the bank. There are also letters with addresses which ought to be entered in his address book. He has lost his address book, and the thought of looking for it, or indeed of looking for anything, afflicts him with acute suicidal impulses.

FROM George Orwell, "Confessions of a Book Reviewer," in *The Collected Essays, Journalism and Criticism of George Orwell*, vol. 4, ed. Sonia Orwell and Ian Angus (New York: Harcourt Brace Jovanovich, 1968). Copyright © by Sonia Brownell Orwell. Reprinted by permission of Harcourt Brace Jovanovich, Inc.

2 He is a man of 35, but looks 50. He is bald, has varicose veins and wears spectacles, or would wear them if his only pair were not chronically lost. If things are normal with him he will be suffering from malnutrition, but if he has recently had a lucky streak he will be suffering from a hangover. At present it is half-past eleven in the morning, and according to his schedule he should have started work two hours ago; but even if he had made any serious effort to start he would have been frustrated by the almost continuous ringing of the telephone bell, the yells of the baby, the rattle of an electric drill out in the street, and the heavy boots of his creditors clumping up and down the stairs. The most recent interruption was the arrival of the second post, which brought him two circulars and an income-tax demand printed in red.

3 Needless to say this person is a writer. He might be a poet, a novelist, or a writer of film scripts or radio features, for all literary people are very much alike, but let us say that he is a book reviewer. Half hidden among the pile of papers is a bulky parcel containing five volumes which his editor has sent with a note suggesting that they "ought to go well together". They arrived four days ago, but for 48 hours the reviewer was prevented by moral paralysis from opening the parcel. Yesterday in a resolute moment he ripped the string off it and found the five volumes to be *Palestine at the Cross Roads, Scientific Dairy Farming, A Short History of European Democracy* (this one is 680 pages and weighs four pounds), *Tribal Customs in Portuguese East Africa*, and a novel, *It's Nicer Lying Down*, probably included by mistake. His review—800 words, say—has got to be "in" by midday tomorrow.

4 Three of these books deal with subjects of which he is so ignorant that he will have to read at least 50 pages if he is to avoid making some howler which will betray him not merely to the author (who of course knows all about the habits of book reviewers), but even to the general reader. By four in the afternoon he will have taken the books out of their wrapping paper but will still be suffering from a nervous inability to open them. The prospect of having to read them, and even the smell of the paper, affects him like the prospect of eating cold ground-rice pudding flavoured with caster oil. And yet curiously enough his copy will get to the office in time. Somehow it always does get there in time. At about nine pm his mind will grow relatively clear, and until the small hours he will sit in a room which grows colder and colder, while the cigarette smoke grows thicker and thicker, skipping expertly through one book after another and laying each down with the final comment, "God, what tripe!" In the morning, blear-eyed, surly and unshaven, he will gaze for an hour or two at a blank sheet of paper until the menacing finger of the clock frightens him into action. Then suddenly he will snap into it. All the stale old phrases—"a book that no one should miss", "something memorable on every page", "of special value are the chapters dealing with, etc etc"—will jump into their places like iron filings obeying the magnet, and the review will end up at exactly the right length and with just about three minutes to go. Meanwhile another wad of ill-assorted, unappetising books will have arrived

by post. So it goes on. And yet with what high hopes this downtrodden, nerve-racked creature started his career, only a few years ago.

⁵ Do I seem to exaggerate? I ask any regular reviewer—anyone who reviews, say, a minimum of 100 books a year—whether he can deny in honesty that his habits and character are such as I have described. Every writer, in any case, is rather that kind of person, but the prolonged, indiscriminate reviewing of books is a quite exceptionally thankless, irritating and exhausting job. It not only involves praising trash—though it does involve that, as I will show in a moment—but constantly *inventing* reactions towards books about which one has no spontaneous feelings whatever. The reviewer, jaded though he may be, is professionally interested in books, and out of the thousands that appear annually, there are probably fifty or a hundred that he would enjoy writing about. If he is a top-notcher in his profession he may get hold of ten or twenty of them: more probably he gets hold of two or three. The rest of his work, however conscientious he may be in praising or damning, is in essence humbug. He is pouring his immortal spirit down the drain, half a pint at a time.

ANALYTICAL READING

1. From the first two paragraphs, what overall impression do you get of the man being described?

2. Discuss the implications of Orwell's statement at the beginning of paragraph 3: "Needless to say this person is a writer."

3. What is the "howler" that the book reviewer might commit (paragraph 4)? What American word would you use as a synonym for this British one?

4. What does the book reviewer rely on to meet his deadline? How honest, reliable, and thorough will his reviews probably be?

5. What does Orwell think is the most miserable part of being a book reviewer?

REFLECTING

Point: To what extent has Orwell written a character sketch of a book reviewer and to what extent is he concerned with some broader issue? Discuss the main idea in the selection and several of the secondary ones.

Organization: What are the main sections of this character sketch? What does the last paragraph contribute?

Support: List the specific sights, sounds, and odors in the first two paragraphs. Select several of the British words in the essay and give their American synonyms or counterparts. Point out several figures of speech, such as the simile in paragraph 4 and the image in the last sentence. Select what you consider to be the most vivid sentence, the one that most aptly conveys the plight of the book reviewer.

Synthesis: Does Orwell make you sympathize with the reviewer, or do you feel that this man has sold out? Is there any relationship between the reviewer's attempt to meet his deadline and your own efforts to meet deadlines for your college papers and other assignments?

Evalution: Have you gained any new insight into reviewers? How would you extend the reviewer's predicament to that of other writers? What makes Orwell's character sketch particularly effective? Do you think that much of the material is autobiographical? Why or why not?

FROM READING TO WRITING

1. Write a character sketch about someone in a job or position that seems interesting or exciting, exposing how boring and frustrating it really is. You might draw upon your own job or high school experiences, or the experiences of your parents or friends.

2. Write just the opposite kind of character sketch, showing how a person in some job or position finds it to be more challenging and stimulating than most people think it is.

AN INDIVIDUALIST: THE MAINE LOBSTERMAN
Gordon A. Reims

BIOGRAPHICAL SKETCH

Gordon A. Reims was born in New York City in 1918 and spent most of his life in the Long Island suburbs before moving to Maine in 1968. He studied creative writing at New York University and then pursued a career in publishing, working twenty-two years for Doubleday & Company and seven for the International Marine Publishing Company in Camden, Maine. Reims has written some forty magazine articles, chiefly about Maine and marine subjects, and many of his photographs of Maine have also been published.

PRE-READING

1. There are two parts to the title; what does each suggest?

2. What do the first two paragraphs tell you about what this character sketch will focus on?

¹ The lobsterman is an indelible part of the atmosphere, flavor and mystique of the Maine coastal town. When travelers go "down" to the coast of Maine they are invariably attracted and intrigued by those special sights and

FROM *Travel*, September 1976, pp. 41–44. Reprinted by permission of the author and *Travel* Magazine.

articles that pertain to lobstering. To those who have never seen them, or to those who have been away for a time, the sight of many white lobster boats scattered at moorings across a cove, all neatly facing in the same direction at the dictate of tide or wind, never fails to enthrall. There is an austerity, tenacity, and innate love for things marine evident in the character of the old wharves bedecked with traps and pails and other gear, or in the long-unpainted bait sheds, reeking with fish odors in their dark interiors, their outer walls gayly festooned with brightly colored lobster buoys drying in the sun.

[2] The lobsterman himself is a symbol, a mystery person to many who do not know him. He is a man who must pilot a seagoing truck from dawn until mid-afternoon, work hard and fast through lonely hours on the open water, and constantly wend his way through chains of rocky islets, past dangerous ledges, and across narrow tidal rips, ever-watchful of weather, wind and current.

[3] The colorful implements of the lobsterman are, of course, simply the basic necessities of his trade. The brightly colored buoys are the floating markers of which each lobsterman must have at least one or two hundred— and their colors are not decorative but dictated by law.

[4] When a lobsterman scatters a hundred or more traps into the sea, dropping each to the bottom, he has to be able to find them again a day or two later. The obvious way, of course, is by fastening one end of a line to the trap, and the other to an object floating on the surface. The buoys are the floating objects, and in order that a lobsterman may recognize his own, he colors it with his personal color-scheme—usually a bright, two-color combination. These color combinations are registered with the state, so that each lobsterman has official right to the use of his colors. A painted insignia on his boat displays the color-scheme, so that all may see he hauls his own traps.

[5] The lobsterman's other conspicuous items are his traps, and again each lobsterman has need of hundreds. His spares are usually stacked on or near the wharves, and add measurably to the distinctive atmosphere of a lobster port. Virtually all lobster traps (or "pots," as they were once invariably called) are alike. Basically a slatted wooden cage with a rope net in the entrance, the traps are about a yard long and much stronger than they look. The wood is heavy and seasoned, not only to withstand constant submersion, but frequent hard blows against rocks, wharves, and the sides of boats. The rope netting, frequently a hemp product called "pot warp," is simply but ingeniously devised so that a lobster can easily enter the trap, but will become hopelessly entangled if he attempts to leave. Weights are added to keep the traps anchored to the bottom.

[6] The lobster boats themselves are distinctive, and certainly recognizable once you've seen a few of them. Riding at their moorings in many a Maine cove and bay, they are very much a part of the pictorial lobster scene. Almost universally white, the lobster boats are usually 30 feet or a little more in length, and are low and broad with a high prow. The lobsterman operates the boat standing up in a half-cabin just forward of center. His winch, his gaff

hook and his bait pails, along with other paraphernalia, are all close beside him in this half-cabin, so that he may work entirely alone if need be.

7 The lobsterman's task is not an easy one, and he's a hard worker. He must find his marker buoy, bobbing in the waves; maneuver the boat close alongside it, and then let go of the boat's controls in order to grasp the gaff hook and proceed with the hauling operation. While the lobster boat begins to bob and pitch and turn, with momentum and master gone, the lobsterman catches his rope line with the hook, loops it over a winch pulley, and hauls the trap up from the deep. While the bobbing boat, by now perhaps drifting broadside to the waves, tries best to hinder him, he must balance the trap on the rail, remove and peg legal-length lobsters, toss back crabs and "shorts," and then re-bait the trap and return it to the sea. All of the these things he does as fast as his hands can move, the slowest chore being perhaps the pegging—the placing of a short peg in the joint of the lobster's claw, to prevent him from damaging lobsters or humans during the course of his captivity. Finally, the lobsterman grips the wheel again, roars the throttle, and surges forward to seek the next marker. The problem of pausing in choppy waters for a least a full minute or two is the reason most lobstermen, particularly those who work alone, stay in port when seas are rough or the wind rises.

8 Lobstermen do fall overboard and drown in cold waters—usually because a slipper trap pulls a lone man from a pitching boat, or he becomes too daring in attempts to free a trap line that has fouled his propeller. Lobstermen also founder in stormy seas and freeze to death in blizzards when engines fail and cold winds force them seaward, but the tragedies are thankfully few and far between, limited generally to a comparatively reckless and mechanically unprepared few. The average lobsterman is capable but careful, heeds weather warnings and keeps his boat in shape, and will not place himself in danger.

9 In the movies and on television, the lobsterman is sometimes pictured as a taciturn individual, speaking to strangers in dry monosyllables, and living in a hermit-like shanty. In books he is often a rugged and fearless man who constantly battles storm and fog to bring back the coveted lobster. Actually, he's rarely either of these, and lobstermen differ from each other as greatly as in other walks of life. Some are quiet old men, clinging tenaciously to ways of the past; some are young, restless, and employ every modern device in an effort to bring in the largest hauls, and some are kids just out of high school, pulling traps by hand from an outboard launch. All who are experienced and work at lobstering steadily make a decent income from it.

10 If the various types of lobstermen do have any attributes in common, they are sharp eyes, deeply tanned and weather-beaten faces, strong arms and wrists, and a tendency to be gruff-voiced from repeatedly shouting across water. Psychologically, they are individuals—men for whom the pride of being one's own boss, in one's own boat, far outweighs the discomforts of the job. To rise before dawn and wrestle with pails and traps and rowing dinghies in the raw damp of a March morning is not always pleasant—but many a

lobsterman does it, month after month, year after year, sometimes until he is 80 or 90 years old.

[11] You can see the wharves and traps and bright buoys, along with lobstermen and their boats, at a hundred small towns and coves along Maine's coast. At New Harbor you can eat on the "upper deck" of a harborside restaurant and watch lobster boats come and go. At Friendship, where the sloops race each summer, there is a succession of weathered lobster wharves set against a backdrop of quiet water and green shores. At Tenants Harbor, Port Clyde, and Stonington there are similar views. Even at edges of the open sea, one may observe lobstermen at work. One or two lobstermen sink traps only a few yards from the granite ledges at Pemaquid Point, carefully maneuvering to keep the swells of the Atlantic from sweeping them to destruction. You can also see them lobstering close to shore at Camden Hills State Park, and along the bases of the cliffs at Acadia National Park. Wherever the colorful buoys dot the surface of bay or sea, a lobster boat will eventually come chugging along.

[12] The 1970s race along. Although new problems beset the lobsterman in these days of rising costs and sophisticated equipment, he still follows his traditional ways pretty much in the same manner—and if he has his way he'll never really change. The colorful sight of distinctive traps, buoys, boats and wharves will remain an important ingredient in the Down East scene.

ANALYTICAL READING

1. What does Reims mean by the "mystique of the Maine coastal town" in the first sentence?

2. What are the main tools of the lobsterman's trade? Describe each and explain its use and purpose. How do the descriptions of them contribute to Reims' characterization of the lobsterman?

3. What makes the lobsterman's job so difficult?

4. How do lobstermen differ from the way they are usually portrayed in books, television, and movies? Why do you think they have been stereotyped in this way? How does the author account for their individualism?

5. According to the author, how can a vacationer in Maine spot lobstering waters?

REFLECTING

Point: What particular point does the author make about lobstermen? What is its significance? Which sentence best expresses it?

Organization: Point out the main sections of the essay. What do the first and last paragraphs contribute? What is the point of paragraph 11? In view of the probable readers of the magazine, could it have been omitted?

Support: How much does the writer assume his audience knows about the subject? In answering, refer to particular passages. Illustrate how the last sentence in paragraph 1 is a cumulative sentence; point out several others. Select other sentences that you find especially effective. Pick out several colorful words or phrases that enhance this character sketch.

Synthesis: Does the essay enable you to experience and understand the Maine lobsterman's life. Does it offer an insight into other occupations that attract individualists?

Evaluation: Should the thesis idea have been stated and developed earlier? Should paragraphs 3 and 4 have been combined—why or why not? Is the opening paragraph too long and too difficult, perhaps appealing to people familiar with the coast but not to inlanders? Can you understand the lure of lobstering as a life's occupation and the nature of the men who pursue it? If so, what specific features of the essay are noteworthy?

FROM READING TO WRITING

1. Write a character sketch about a type of individualist you know, describing the routine activities and, if you wish, account for the desire for individualism.

2. Write about a person engaged in some little-known occupation or hobby, describing the individual and the work in detail.

THOSE GOOD OLE BOYS
Bonnie Angelo

BIOGRAPHICAL SKETCH

Bonnie Angelo was born in North Carolina and holds a B.A. from the University of North Carolina. Married, with one son, she is currently a Washington correspondent for Time *magazine. Her journalistic career has included work on the* Winston-Salem Journal *and* Sentinel, Newsday, *and the Newhouse National News Service. She is also news correspondent for WTTG–TV. For her reporting on civil rights she received the Paul Tobenkin Memorial Foundation award in 1971.*

PRE-READING

1. If you are from the South or know something about it, then you probably realize the subject of the article from its title. If not, would the spelling of *old* as *ole* suggest that this isn't an article about senior citizens?

2. How do the first and last paragraphs provide clues about the subject and even the writer's attitude toward it?

¹ It is Friday night at any of ten thousand watering holes of the small towns and crossroads hamlets of the South. The room is a cacophony of the ping-pong-dingdingding of the pinball machine, the pop-fizz of another round of Pabst, the refrain of *Red Necks, White Socks and Blue Ribbon Beer* on the juke box, the insolent roar of a souped-up engine outside and, above it all, the sound of easy laughter. The good ole boys have gathered for their fraternal ritual—the aimless diversion that they have elevated into a life-style.

² Being a good ole boy is not a consequence of birth or breeding; it cuts across economic and social lines; it is a frame of mind based on the premise that life is nothing to get serious about. A glance at the brothers Carter tells a lot. There is some confusion about why Billy Carter seems in many respects the quintessential good ole boy, while Brother Jimmy couldn't even fit into the more polished subspecies of conscious good ole boys who abound in small-town country clubs. Billy, amiable, full of jokes, his REDNECK POWER T shirt straining unsuccessfully to cover the paunch, swigs a beer, carefree on a Sunday morning, as Jimmy Carter, introspective, hard driving, teaches Sunday school. Jimmy sometimes speaks wistfully of Billy's good-ole-boy ease.

³ Lightheartedness permeates the good ole boy's life-style. He goes by nicknames like "Goober" or "Goat." He disdains neckties as a form of snobbery; when he dresses up, it is to wear a decorated T shirt with newish jeans or, for state occasions, a leisure suit with a colored shirt. If discussions veer beyond football toward substance, he cuts them off with funny stories.

⁴ The core of the good ole boy's world is with his buddies, the comfortable, hyperhearty, all-male camaraderie, joshing and drinking and regaling one another with tales of assorted, exaggerated prowess. Women are outsiders; when social events are unavoidably mixed, the good ole boys cluster together at one end of the room, leaving wives at the other. The GOB's magic doesn't work with women; he feels insecure, threatened by them. In fact, he doesn't really like women, except in bed.

⁵ What he really loves is his automobile. He overlooks his wife with her hair up in pink rollers, sagging into an upside-down question mark in her tight slacks. But he lavishes attention on his Mercury mistress, Easy Rider shocks, oversize slickers, dual exhaust. He exults in tinkering with that beautiful engine, lying cool beneath the open hood, ready to respond, quick and fiery, to his touch. The automobile is his love and his sport.

⁶ Behind his devil-may-care lightheartedness, however, runs a strain of innate wisdom, an instinct about people and an unwavering loyalty that makes him the one friend you would turn to, not just because he's a drinking buddy who'll keep you laughing, but because, well, he's a good ole boy.

ANALYTICAL READING

1. Analyze the first paragraph, pointing out how it generates interest, uses language creatively and effectively, appeals mainly to one of our senses, and

builds a particular viewpoint from which Angelo will describe this Southern type. Discuss how the viewpoint might have been changed by substituting *bars* for *watering holes, crude guffaws* for *easy laughter,* and *wasteful diversion* for *aimless diversion.*

2. In paragraph 2, which sentence did you underline for its importance? Why is Sunday a particularly effective day to select for contrasting the brother's philosophies of life?

3. Why do you think that the good ole boys feel insecure around women?

4. How do you account for the good ole boy's love of automobiles?

5. Is there an implied contradiction between the good ole boy's disdain for substantive conversations (paragraph 3) and the writer's statement that he possesses "a strain of innate wisdom, an instinct about people" (paragraph 6)?

REFLECTING

Point: Which sentence in the article best summarizes the character of the good old boy? Try to write such a summary statement in your own words without looking at the article.

Organization: Analyze paragraph 5, pointing out the purpose of the first and last sentences. How effective is paragraph 3? Might anything be added or deleted from it? Discuss the article paragraph by paragraph, pointing out how the author moves logically from one to another.

Support: Select several cumulative sentences, showing how details are piled upon details. Note the use of the semicolon in the second sentence of paragraph 2; discuss its effectiveness, and consider whether you would have used it or not. Focus on some of the language that particularly interested you—for example, what about *good ole boy, newish jeans* (paragraph 3), *hyperhearty* (paragraph 4), *the GOB's magic* (paragraph 4), *upside-down question mark* (paragraph 5), and *Mercury mistress* (paragraph 5).

Synthesis: Although the article describes a well-known Southern type, do you know people outside the South who are similar to the good ole boys? In what ways are those people similar and in what ways dissimilar? Does the article do more then describe the good ole boys so that you would recognize them? If so, what else? If you are a woman, do you find yourself reacting differently to the article then the men students in the class?

Evaluation: What do you think the writer's purpose is and how well is it accomplished? Has anything of importance been omitted? For example, would you like to know what work the good ole boys do, whether many are found outside of small towns, and what they talk about after they have worn out the topic of football?

FROM READING TO WRITING

1. Some people think that Billy Carter and similar good ole boys are a disgrace. Write a character sketch from that viewpoint.

2. Write a character sketch of a high school, town or college type: the apple polisher, the cheerleader, the jock, the rock star, the pool shark, the social

butterfly, the freak (any kind), the electronic or automobile nut. You may treat these favorably or unfavorably, but you should take some stand about them.

3. Compare this character sketch of a type with either the previous or the following one.

THE TYPICAL FOOTBALL FAN
Glenn Dickey

BIOGRAPHICAL SKETCH

Glenn Dickey was born in Virginia, Minnesota, in 1936 and later moved with his family to California, where he graduated from the University of California at Berkeley. He has been a sports reporter for several newspapers and was appointed sports columnist for the San Francisco Chronicle *in 1971. He is the author of three books on sports,* The Jock Empire, The Great No-Hitters, *and* Champs and Chumps: An Insider's Look at American Sports, *and has written more than fifty magazine stories and articles. Five of his stories have appeared in* Best Sports Stories, *an annual anthology of sports fiction.*

PRE-READING

Skim the opening paragraphs and the closing one. Where does the author reveal his attitude toward football fans?

¹ In the 1950s, there was a game between San Jose State and Washington State in Pullman, Washington which was memorable only for the cold. The temperature was well below the freezing mark, as players and coaches wondered: Is this game really necessary?

² The public address announcer, about to begin his recitation of the starting lineups, did a doubletake as he looked around the stadium. "Dear Sir," he began.

³ That solitary fan, watching a game of no significance in miserable weather in an otherwise empty stadium, epitomizes the college football fan. It may not be necessary to be crazy to be a football fan, but it helps. No, scratch that. It may be necessary. Even football fans admit they're looney. That is, if you ask a fan of Ole Miss, he'll certainly tell you that LSU fans are crazy.

⁴ College football is often considered part of the overall entertainment package, but there is no real comparison between your average football fan and a person of, say, opera, ballet or the theatre. The patron of the arts is

FROM *Touchdown*, 18 September 1976. Reprinted by permission of Touchdown Publications.

pampered and civilized, two adjectives which would never be applied to football fans. Consider a few comparisons:

[5] 1) Food and drink. At the opera, theatre, ballet and symphony, there are often small restaurants, dispensing real food. There are also bars, which can be a mixed blessing; the combination of a couple of stiff drinks and a Wagnerian opera has induced more deep slumber than any number of Sominex pills.

[6] At a football game, there are refreshments, too—warm soda and cold hot dogs. Passed from the aisle, both soda and mustard are usually slopped on the patrons in between vendor and customer.

[7] 2) Comfort. Patrons of the arts sit in well-padded seats. There are carpets on the floor, and usually fancy draperies as well. There are often elevators and escalators to the higher floors.

[8] The ultimate in comfort for a college football fan is a plastic seat. Older stadiums have only wooden benches. Each row is numbered for at least one more peson than can be accommodated. There are often long flights of stairs to climb to get into the stadiums. There are never enough rest rooms for those who have been drinking an elixir, which gives the fan a choice of standing in line for the entire halftime or sneaking out for three minutes at the start of the second quarter, during which time you can be sure that two touchdowns and a field goal will be scored.

[9] 3) Weather. At the ballet, customers sit in air-conditioned or heated buildings, depending on the season. College football fans are victims of the often capricious weather. In the midwest, a nice day for football is any day when it isn't snowing. In the northeast, you have to worry about the nor'easters. In the south, the heat and humidity can be stifling. In the northwest, rain can drive one away. Yet, fans subject themselves to such conditions willingly. It is difficult for me to feel to superior to them. In my youth, my father, uncle and I watched a game in a driving rainstorm, though we chickened out late in the third quarter and left; by then, our team was down, 42-0.

[10] It should be noted that all comments about college football fans and their ability to withstand the extremes of weather do not extend to fans in southern California. In southern California, fans stay at home if the temperature goes below 70 and go to the beach if it goes above 80.

[11] 4) The final difference between the arts and football is the commitment of the football fan. If the symphony orchestra has an off night, the audience still claps politely; people don't even wince at the obvious clinkers. An opera buff who is truly aroused will murmur, "Bravo."

[12] "Bravo, indeed. Your average college football fan, self-contained as he or she may be at other times, goes a little, well, yes, crazy at a game. Woe be to the coach who calls the wrong play or the quarterback who throws an interception; not polite applause but a cascade of boos will descend on them. Fans cheer their team, jeer the officials, cast aspersions on the birth of players on other teams . . . and it is all done at full throat.

[13] Sometimes, the fans are more interesting than the game itself. Texas A&M students, for instance, stand during the entire game. Arkansas fans salute their team with hog calls.

[14] College football is less a sport than a way of life. The madness that football induces extends beyond the playing field. The game itself may last only about three hours, but the foreplay and aftermath last much longer.

[15] Strong men fear to leave their homes in Dallas the weekend of a Texas–Oklahoma game, for instance. Sooner and Longhorn fans roam the streets the entire weekend, omitting such non-essentials as sleep. Eating just enough to keep body and soul together and imbibing rather more than that, they seek out fans of the opposing team to start minature wars of their own.

[16] Behavior that would be considered aberrant at any other time is passed off as normal during the week preceding a big game. Obscene comments on the University of Michigan football team are displayed prominently in Columbus, Ohio before a Buckeye–Wolverine game, and judges tolerantly excuse them.

[17] The day of the game, fans gather very early for parties in their cars, trucks and recreational vehicles. These parties are commonly called "tailgate parties" because the original idea was to let the tailgate down on a station wagon and put food and drink there. They have become more complicated in recent years, with multi-course meals being prepared, accompanied by the drink common to the area; in California, for instance, it is always wine. Occasionally, the party will be such a success that fans miss the opening kickoff, the first quarter and—in extreme cases—the entire game. This tends to happen more frequently in California where the priorities are somewhat different.

[18] The original rationale for tailgate parties was as a way of beating the traffic. Now, of course, the traffic is heaviest three hours before a game, when everybody rushes to beat the traffic.

[19] In each section of the country, fans are convinced that their football is the best, in some way or another. Often, this requires convoluted logic and a precise definition of what is best, much like radio stations which can prove that they are No. 1 by the way they define their market.

[20] In the East, for instance, Ivy League teams have long since opted out of the mad race for No. 1 in the polls, Ivy League schools do not give out athletic scholarships as such, though special ability is taken into account when scholarships are issued and some top athletes—Calvin Hill, Ed Marinaro—have qualified. Players sometimes miss games because there is a laboratory field trip that weekend. Fans know this, and they argue that this is the most sensible way to approach football. Since their approach is the best, their teams must be the best.

[21] In the midwest, fans of eight of the Big Ten teams dutifully watch their teams play for third place. Their game, they're convinced, is the best because it is what football is all about—knocking down other people. Indeed, players usually have no choice because teams in the midwest tend to use little finesse.

There are fans who could not define a forward pass, never having seen one.

[22] In the Southeastern Conference, fans are convinced that their football is the best because, year after year, there are more Southeastern Conference teams in bowl games than teams from any other conference. That they are there because the conference allows any team which gets an invitation to go and because conferences like the Big Ten and Pacific Eight have, until recently, only allowed their champion to go to a bowl, does not seem to make a dent in the fans' consciousness.

[23] The Pacific Eight Conference tends to be USC and seven teams fighting for second place more often than not. Still, fans believe that their football is the best because their representative usually wins the Rose Bowl by throwing a ball up in the air a few times, a maneuver which has taken Ohio State or Michigan by complete surprise.

[24] The college football madness culminates in the big games. There are two types of big games in college football. One is the kind of game on which a bowl bid rides: Oklahoma-Nebraska has been an example of that because, in recent years, the teams seem to be ranked 1–2 nationally every time they play. The fans' madness there is conventional, i.e., a belief that Winning Is Everything.

[25] Much more difficult to explain to visitors from other planets would be the traditional games—The Game (Harvard-Yale), The Big Game (California-Stanford), Army-Navy. These games are the social event of the year for many. There are parties all week, as classmates hold reunions to talk about how many of their friends have died during the year.

[26] It is often said of these games that you can forget about the teams' records during the year because the underdog often wins. That is not true. The favorite usually wins these games, as it does any others. It is the fans who forget their teams' records. There are many who truly do not care if their team goes 0–10 the rest of the season if it wins the traditional game. At these favored games, it makes no difference whether both teams have had great seasons, poor seasons, medium seasons; the attendance will still be the same, full house. It makes no difference to fans whether the teams are well-matched or poorly. It is, simply, the game to see.

[27] Yeah, you have to be crazy.

ANALYTICAL READING

1. In what ways does the average college football fan differ from the opera, ballet, or theater patron? How accurate is Dickey's comparison according to your experience? Does it apply to fans of professional as well as college football? To the same extent or more?

2. What does Dickey mean when he says that "college football is a way of life"?

3. How is it possible that fans in different sections of the country each consider their conference to be the best?

4. What two types of big games does Dickey mention? What myth about one of them does he try to dispel?

5. How serious do you suspect Dickey is in saying that football fans are crazy? Explain your answer. Is Dickey probably a fan himself?

REFLECTING

Point: Does the central idea suggest that football fans are really "crazy" or merely that they are passionately devoted to their team or something else? Are any reasons suggested in the article?

Organization: What device is used in the article's introduction to attract interest? To what extent does the article start in the middle of its subject, then flash back to the beginning, and finally jump to the end, in a modification of a chronological flashback technique?

Support: Determine the author's audience—is he writing to football fans or to a general audience? Justify your answer. What particular ideas has the author supported well with details? Where is definition used concisely and effectively? Where is humor used?

Synthesis: If you are a football fan, do you agree with most of Dickey's points? Do you think he has exaggerated anywhere? What other aspects of football besides the game itself contribute to its being classified as entertainment? If you are not a football fan, were you still interested in the article or in any of its ideas? Why or why not?

Evaluation: Is it fair to compare football fans with patrons of the arts? Why not compare football fans with baseball fans? Does the author adequately describe post-game activities? How appropriate is the author's voice and use of language? Evaluate by citing examples. Point out particularly effective sentences. Is there any reason for the switch to "you" in the final paragraph? Overall, how well has the author provided a character sketch of the typical football fan?

FROM READING TO WRITING

1. Write a similar paper about some other type of fan in sports or in other fields, such as the fan of baseball, string quartets, rock music, poker, television, movies, or cars.

2. Write a character sketch comparing the fanatical participant with the average one, such as a constant golfer with a once-a-month player, or a gourmet chef with an ordinary cook, or an opera buff with someone who goes to the opera only occasionally.

LIBRARIANS TODAY AND IN THE FUTURE

Richard Armour

BIOGRAPHICAL SKETCH

Richard Armour was born in San Pedro, California, in 1906. He completed his undergraduate work at Pomona College and received an M.A. and a Ph.D. from Harvard University. He has taught at several universities, including Texas and Northwestern, but has spent most of his academic career as an English professor and dean at Claremont College. Among his awards are a Ford Foundation Faculty Fellowship and a Harvard Research Scholarship. A popular lecturer and columnist, he has contributed more than 6,000 poems and prose pieces, most of them short and humorous, to over a hundred magazines in America and England. Among the more than fifty books that he has written or edited are Gold Is a Four Letter Word, American Lit Relit, *and* Going Around in Academic Circles.

PRE-READING

1. From the name of the book containing this selection, what approach do you suspect that the author will take toward his subject?

2. How is this inference confirmed in the opening paragraphs and the footnotes?

3. Does the information in the biographical sketch suggest the voice that you could expect to encounter in the essay?

[1] Librarians have come a long way since stone and baked clay tablets, hieroglyphics, Ashurbanipal, rolls of papyrus, parchment codices, Pisistratus, Tyrannion, the *scriptorium,* Gutenberg (or Gänsefleisch), Caxton, Manutius, incunabula, Benjamin Franklin, Andrew Carnegie, the founding of the A.L.A., and everything else treated so thoroughly[1] in the previous chapters. As Melvil Dewey would put it, "Hyly important chanjes hav been numerus."

[2] Of recent years, the image of the librarian as a little old lady in tennis shoes has changed drastically. She has come a long way. Now she wears shoes with high heels that enable her to reach the topmost shelf. Or, if she is really "with it," she may wear sandals.[2] More men are librarians and some are in subordinate positions, though not insubordinate. It is not enough to be merely a librarian, but one must be a reference librarian, a cataloger, a children's librarian, or an audio-visual specialist. Also a librarian can be in a university

---

[1] If not exhaustively, then exhaustingly.

[2] Secretly she may imagine herself in an ancient Roman library, hoping the Emperor will drop in and she can get his autograph.

library, a law library, a public library, a medical library, an armed services library, a prison library, and on and on or, for the part-time librarian, on and off.

[3] As with paramedical personnel, there are more and more paralibrarians, not to be confused with a pair of libarians. The paralibrarian has no library degree and, just as her medical counterpart is not permitted to perform surgery, should be careful about doing any reader's advisory or reference work. Presumably giving wrong advice might lead to a malpractice suit.

[4] The work of librarians has necessarily changed because of changes in libraries. College and university libraries, for example, now have carrels. These are unlike Christmas carrels in that they are used the year around.[3] There are also rooms for showing films and slides as well as soundproof recording booths and darkrooms for developing photographs. Some of these rooms have dual-purpose uses, a room for showing films also being useful for lectures and for putting on plays and puppet shows for children. However, the darkroom is not recommended as a place for reading.

[5] Extended services of some school and public libraries necessitate that librarians handle many items in addition to books: motion picture films, filmstrips, slides, transparencies, overlays, disc and tape recordings, projectors, record players, tape recorders, cassettes, viewers for individual use, multimedia kits, etc. Whereas formerly nothing could upset a librarian more than loss of a book, now there could be such disasters as breakdown of a film projector, finding a crack in a record, or discovering a gap or erasure in a tape.

[6] All of this means that a librarian is no longer fully prepared by Library School courses such as "Bibliography and Reference Sources," "Basic Cataloging and Classification," and "Administration of Libraries." Now the librarian must also take work in "How to Splice a Broken Film," "The Operation and Care of Tape Recorders," and "The Underlying Benefits of Overlays." Some librarians, proud of their open-mindedness, who were never shocked by a book, are shocked by a short circuit in the electronic equipment.

[7] Many librarians have been unionized. They may have joined the union of a library staff, or government employees, or of plumbers, carpenters, or electricians. They had long used the union catalog, but now they carry a union card as well.[4]

[8] Indeed the change has been so great of recent years that some libraries are no longer called libraries but are known as Learning Resource Centers or Media Centers. Librarians, however, are still generally known as librarians

---

[3] The word "carrel" for a small enclosure or alcove is also spelled "carol" by architects, and "carol" comes from the Middle English word for dancing accompanied by singing. In fact it goes back to the Latin *choraules*, a flute player who accompanied the choral dance. Librarians would, I am sure, discourage singing, dancing, and flute playing in the modern carrel.

[4] They joined a union either by choice or by being outvoted. "In the union there is strength," they were told by union officials.

and not yet as Learning Resourcists or Media Centerists, though this may be only a matter of time.

⁹ A twentieth-century development has been the bookmobile, which permits librarians to take books to those who are unable to get to the library. The bookmobile also makes it possible to get outdoors and go for a spin into rural areas, especially enjoyable in the spring and fall. Though I have been searching the police records, I have been unable to find the driver of a bookmobile booked (an appropriate term) for speeding or drunken driving. There must be something about that precious cargo that keeps librarians on the straight and narrow and, when necessary, on the curved and narrow.

¹⁰ So much for librarians of today, though no reference has been made, among other things, to the interlibrary loan, the *Library Journal,* or the *Horn Book.*⁵ Let us now turn briefly to libraries and librarians of the future. This, it must be confessed, is purely speculative, since even the most thoroughly researched reference books give no clear picture of what conditions will be like in another fifty or one hundred years.⁶ Even the foreseeable future is hard to foresee.

¹¹ The way things are going, however, it would seem that microfilms will become micro-micro-microfilms, and a page can be reduced to the size of the head of a pin. According the John David Marshall,⁷ an important service of the librarian will be to direct the library patron, before he peers at the micro-micro-microfilm screen, to the resident optometrist (or ophthalmologist) to secure the proper glasses. On leaving, the reader will be provided with a seeing-eye dog to help him home.

¹² But what will the librarian of the future be like? In order to cope with the minuscule microfilm books that have been forecast, the librarian also may have to be reduced to a comparable size, at least during working hours. This might be accomplished by scientific means or, more literarily, by using the technique Alice learned from the caterpillar in *Alice in Wonderland.* Thus the librarian before starting work would eat a piece of mushroom held in the right hand to become smaller, and at quitting time would eat a piece held in the left hand to become larger. Just who on the library staff or the Library Board would be identified with the White Rabbit, the March Hare, the Mad Hatter, and others will perhaps vary with the library.

¹³ This is assuming, however, that there will still be flesh-and-blood librarians amidst the microfilmed books in the computerized library or Center for Storage and Retrieval. It is possible that librarians will be robots, con-

---

⁵ This last will be a disappointment to anyone wishing information about the trumpet or the tuba.

⁶ One book in this field that seems accurate and soundly based is John David Marshall's *A Fable of Tomorrow's Library,* Peacock Press, 1965. This scholarly work runs to seven pages, including the title page and copyright page.

⁷ *Op. cit.*

trolled by Master Minds having mastery of a master computer at the Library of Congress.[8]

[14] Or there will be no libraries and no librarians, flesh-and-blood or otherwise. The onetime library patron will press a button and turn a dial on his TV, whereupon the requested book, in the desired language, will appear on the screen, the pages turning at the designated speed. The only interruptions will be commercials in which authors plug their latest books. These they will have produced with electronic typewriters that, when set to WRITE, will produce overnight a novel, biography, juvenile, or whatever the author has programmed.

[15] Then again, as some old-fashioned members of the literary community hope, authors will write much as they do now, books will be books, libraries will be libraries, and librarians will be librarians.

[16] Then science, helping but not taking over, can concentrate on finding a cure for the common cold, which sometimes keeps librarians away for a day or two from the work they love.

ANALYTICAL READING

1. In what respects has the image of librarians changed drastically, as Armour indicates?

2. Is it that librarians have changed or that libraries have changed, or both? Explain.

3. Is the author merely joking about such new courses as "The Underlying Benefits of Overlays," or is there an element of seriousness in his discussion of the new curriculum for library students? Explain.

4. Is there such a thing as a "union catalog" (paragraph 7)? What about the *Horn Book* (paragraph 10)? Check your dictionary.

5. In his discussion of micro-micro-microfilm (paragraph 11), Armour relies on a device called *reductio ad absurdum* that is used frequently in argument when someone attacks something by showing how absurd it would be if carried to its logical conclusion. Explain how Armour uses this device humorously.

6. What fun does the author have with science and mechanization?

7. Is Armour in favor of the many changes that have occurred and may occur, or would he like libraries and librarians to remain just about as they are today? Justify your answer.

REFLECTING

Point: Can you formulate the main idea in this character sketch about librarians? Does any such statement fail to do justice to the essay? Why?

[8] These Master Minds may, of course, also be robots, operated by a superior race on a distant planet.

Organization: What are the main divisions of the selection? Where do these divisions occur? Show how Armour moves easily back and forth from writing about librarians to discussing libraries.

Support: What purpose do the footnotes provide? Armour uses puns to supply humor. Puns are not necessarily the lowest form of humor, but often a clever play on words in which a word is used to mean several things at once. Point out several puns and discuss how they help support an idea he is discussing. Is there any pattern in the use of humor—does it appear at the end of paragraphs that begin with relatively serious information? What language tendency is Armour satirizing when he states that libraries are often called Learning Resource Centers? To what kind of audience is Armour writing—a general or specialized one? If specialized, what educational background do the readers probably have? Explain. Which sentences or concepts did you find most amusing?

Synthesis: What is your general impression of librarians? Have you seen changes in your school, community, or college library? What changes do you foresee in the future? Is there a possibility that television will be used in some fashion? Are computers being used in libraries? Is it possible that librarians will be replaced by robots? Do you approve of the new libraries, or do you prefer the old ones? Explain. What experiences have you had with librarians.

Evaluation: Has the author been successful in writing an amusing but informative account of librarians today and in the future, or is the humor too extreme? Is there too much about libraries instead of librarians? If so, is that justified?

FROM READING TO WRITING

1. Write a humorous character sketch of a type whose job may change because of future technology, such as the garbage collector, farmer, secretary, truckdriver, or supermarket checker. Let your imagination run rampant.

2. Write a sketch of the future parent, showing how roles may change, how raising children may differ, and what the effects might be.

3. Write a serious character sketch of a type that you know from your parents' acquaintances, from your own work, or from your experience. Suggestions: the school's bus driver, the high school basketball coach, the substitute teacher, the car salesperson, the barber or beautician, the carpenter.

Assessment of
Reading and Writing Skills:
Descriptive Writing

Step 1

Read the essay that follows with the aim of understanding and recalling the important ideas. When you finish, note how long it took you to read the selection. Then close your book and write a summary of the important information without referring again to the essay. Indicate also your impression of the tone and word choice of the writer. You will be allowed 7 to 10 minutes to write; your instructor will establish the limit and tell you when the time is up.

BEAUTIFUL DAY
Dave Kindred

The snow was the packing kind. Just reach down with a gloved hand and there you had it: a wonderful, marvelous, round and firm, throw-it-at-his-head, take-me-back-to-my-childhood SNOWBALL. On a hill across the street, the enemy waited: Dale and Steve, both about 15, both right-handers. They had the faces of angels, but I knew better.

The barrage of snowballs was remarkable on several counts. Dale and Steve threw hard and straight. So did my son, Jeff, 14, who was allied with The Old Man. For reasons I prefer not to think about, my throws described gentle arcs and tended to sail to the right of the target.

Soon enough Dale and Steve scored the victory they sought. As I turned my back to scoop up ammunition, an artillery round collided with my cap, knocking it off my head. Everybody thought that was pretty funny, even my blood ally, who was laughing his thermal underwear off.

Those gentle arcs I mentioned—they became rainbows. If in the days of Frankie Avalon and Annette Funicello a kid could throw snowballs all day—

FROM *Louisville Courier-Journal*, 25 January 1977, p. C1. Copyright © 1977, The Courier-Journal, Louisville, Kentucky. Reprinted with permission.

throw them at trees, mailboxes, cars, wandering dogs—the same kid in Elton John's time has maybe 30 or 40 throws before paralysis sets in. So I moved on, leaving the three boys.

Mary Kay is 7 years old. She wore a red snow suit and was on her knees. In front of her were the beginnings of two snowmen.

"I'm going to make BIG snowmen," she said.

"As big as you?"

"Real big."

"How big?" I said.

"No, no, not THAT big. I'm going to make them kinda big and kinda little."

I passed Mary Kay's house on the way to the little creek that runs behind our subdivision. It was a beautiful day. New snow covered the old. The sun shone. One of the charms of this city is that you can be a part of it, yet be apart from it. Hardly 15 minutes from my office, the world was white velvet and silence. . . . This [day] was for snowballs and snowmen and walking in the snow.

It was a foot and a half deep in the woods behind Mary Kay's house. No one had walked there recently enough to leave footprints. I felt like an explorer, moving into uncharted land. The new snow gave way under my feet with the gentle sound of old paper tearing. Then, coming over a knoll, I saw the creek at the bottom of the hill, a black ribbon lying across the velvet.

From a distance came the bark of a dog. A boy somewhere shouted to a friend, "Hey, Tom, c'mon." Then it was quiet again. The creek isn't much. Maybe five feet wide, never deeper than a foot or so. It winds through the woods, past the ash trees, the maples, wild cherries, the tall cedars and beautiful white birches. Snow lay on branches, disturbed only by an occasional rush of air that caused a puff of powder to float down to the creek.

Water moved in the creek. Where the snow hit the water, ripples were born, the circles finally touching snow on the creek banks. I saw a squirrel a hundred feet away, my only company, and I wondered if he minded this heavy-footed intruder.

The ducks did. I'd walked on, toward the squirrel, when an incomprehensible noise broke the silence. Then I saw the ducks, a dozen of them, making a hurried take-off from an island of ice in the creek. Wings flapping, quacking, the ducks flew away, nine of them to the left of a clump of trees, the other three going to the right. They joined forces again on the other side of the trees.

On the way back home, I walked past Mary Kay's again.

The two snowmen were gone.

"What happened?" I said.

"I ruined them," she said brightly.

"Did you make them too big?"

"One got bigger than the other one, and the other one got ruined."

She was on her knees, having a grand time pushing snow with her red gloves. "Are you going to make another one?"

"Yes, I am. I'm going to start right now."

Dale and Steve, the flame-throwing snowballers, were shoveling snow out of a driveway. "Got you working." I said, probably unable to hide my Old Man intimation of it's-about-time.

I was 50 feet away, my back turned, when I heard a snowball land next to my feet. I turned. Dale, smiling, pointed to Steve.

Step 2

Read the following essay as quickly as you can without sacrificing your comprehension of the material. You will have a maximum of 3 minutes, 25 seconds (200 words per minute) to glean as much information as you can. If you finish before time is called, note how long it took you to read the selection.

Again, close your book and write a summary of the essay, including a statement about the tone and word choice. You will have 7 to 10 minutes for this task.

THOUGH UNOFFICIAL, SPRING COMES EARLY IN SPOTS
James Kilpatrick

It is a well-known fact—at least it is well-known here in Rappahannock County—that spring lives in a small swampy area just east of the Shade Road; about a quarter mile south of the apple packing plant. On the evening of Friday, March 11, spring made her first appearance.

The event is especially worth marking this year, for many discouraged Rappahannockers had begun to think the lady had moved away.

Under the heading of Mean and Dirty Winters, our winter certainly was small potatoes compared to the winter in Buffalo, Fargo and Brainerd, but it was a mean and dirty one all the same.

The winter went on and on. It would not stop. Our whole country froze up like a tray of ice. Pipes burst and water pumps froze, and it was a back-breaking effort to get hay to the cattle. Nobody could remember anything like it.

But a few days into March, things began to thaw; and on this particular Friday evening, driving home from Washington, there was spring beside the Shade Road. How do I know? Because you could hear the peepers. They are the certain heralds of April on its way.

FROM *Lexington (Ky.) Herald-Leader*, 19 March 1977, p. A4. Reprinted by permission of the Washington Star Syndicate, Inc.

If you have never met a peeper, you should know that a peeper is a tree frog. He is not bigger than a minute—maybe three-quarters of an inch, greenish-brown, pop-eyed. His sole function is annually to announce the entrance of spring. This he does by puffing up his tiny throat, thrusting his head forward, and crying PEEP-er, PEEP-er, PEEP, PEEP, PEEP-er. The note is somewhere around B-natural above middle C; and after a winter like ours, it is the most welcome note ever sounded.

Spring turned up the next day, Saturday, in the great willow tree down at Woodville. Twenty-four hours earlier, the branches were bare. Now they had become a green cascade, a fountain of leaves as tiny as tears. People came to the Woodville Rural Independent Post Office to get their mail, and they looked at the willow across the road, and they all said the same thing: Spring!

After that, the lady turned up everywhere. The crocuses popped up, lavender and orange, and in the rock garden all kinds of tiny things began to lift their heads: Hepatica, aconite, dwarf daffodils.

The heather that had been given up for dead came back to life. The wild iris shouldered its sturdy frame above the ground. By Thursday, St. Patrick's Day, the fields were unmistakably green.

We hadn't seen a groundhog since October. Now, driving down the Rudasill's Mill Road, we saw four of them lumbering along: Four fat men out for a morning jog. They were sweating and complaining and saying, "Man, am I out of shape!" A dozen rabbits were on the lawn Wednesday evening, practicing sprints and hurdles. Chipmunks and squirrels appeared out of nowhere.

The past Tuesday, a pair of newly-wed bluebirds arrived, took one look at Apartment 4-D, our very best bluebird box, and promptly moved in. This is a truly elegant apartment, if you will forgive a little bragging, equipped with washer, drier, two ovens, air conditioning and wall-to-wall carpeting throughout. It rents promptly every spring.

A flock of 50 robins arrived. The killdeer is back, foolish bird, building a nest in a perilous spot right next to the driveway. Most of the juncos have gone, and the grosbeaks also, but we have a new visitor not registered before: A fox sparrow, and a handsome fellow he is.

With spring looking on, everyone has started plowing and planting and getting gardens ready. On the 12th, we planted onion sets and lettuce, and we raked up the backyard around the great chestnut oak that rules our hill. Once again we marveled at the sheer fecundity of nature. In an area perhaps 15 × 30 feet, we must have raked up—or pulled up—5,000 acorns. Half of them were trying to take root and turn into oak trees.

Down on your hands and knees, digging out these seedlings, you wonder what the chestnut oak knew what we didn't. A year ago, that tree saw the bitter winter coming; it produced more acorns that we ever have seen before, each fruitful with the germ of life. The winds of November scattered them, and the snow and ice watered them, and now spring warms them, and the wonder and the mystery all begin anew. Peepers and willows and bluebirds and groundhogs! The shut-in spirit opens like a crocus, lifting fragile petals to a welcome sun.

Step 3

Without looking back at the two essays, write a paragraph or two in which you evaluate them and explain how their ideas or issues are related. You may refer to your summaries, but not to the essays. Time: 10 minutes.

PART **3**

The
Explanatory Voice:
Expository Writing

The main purpose of exposition is to explain. Unlike personal and some descriptive writing, in exposition the writer usually tries to suppress strong personal or emotional involvement. The aim is to write objectively and clearly so that every reader understands exactly what the writer is saying. Even when expressing an opinion, the writer uses a rational approach, rather than strong emotional appeal. Thus, the emphasis changes from the writer-centered approach of personal writing to a reader-centered one. The audience is viewed not as a group of sympathetic, homogeneous friends sharing common interests and backgrounds, but as strangers, not necessarily hostile, but unknown and mixed—a conglomerate of many different people of all ages and of varying interests and backgrounds. Therefore, the writer is more formal, more precise, and more careful to choose words and grammatical usages that are generally approved. The personality of the writer may still be evident, but the voice used is businesslike, matter-of-fact, rather than folksy or intimate.

Because clarity is a main concern, form is significant in expository writing. Chronological or spatial organization is not usually suitable for writing that explains *why* a certain phenomenon happens, *how* an operation works, precisely *what* a word or term means, or *why* a certain opinion is held. These writing problems require logical techniques: explaining cause-and-effect relationships, making comparisons and contrasts, dividing items into their component parts, supporting a thesis or main idea. These rhetorical tactics are used not only in the essay's overall organization but also in individual paragraphs throughout. In the most effective expository writing, form and meaning work together—one enhances the other. To illustrate, let us look at the four forms of exposition: classification, definition, analysis, and opinion.

KINDS OF EXPOSITORY WRITING

CLASSIFICATION

Classification, definition, and analysis all involve a sorting-out process—the division of an item into its component parts. In classification, the main purpose is to subclassify an item whose general category has already been established. The writer does not need to define the term, but does need to find a basis for classifying it. For instance, an article about concert bands can assume that all readers will have similar definitions of the term *concert band,* but one writer might subclassify the band on the basis of instrument families—woodwinds, brass, tympani, and so on. Another writer might choose to subdivide it into "voices"—tenor, baritone, bass.

Or tone quality might serve as a third basis for classification. But once the basic criterion for classification is established, it must be used consistently throughout the paper. In "Blues, and Other Noises, in the Night" (pages 209–12), this consistency is clearly exemplified as John Rockwell subclassifies modern country music strictly according to its traditional influences— its cultural beginnings—not according to music style or lyric content or a mixture of the three.

DEFINITION

Although closely related to classification, definition must establish the general category (class) of an item before subdivision begins. As you know, a particular word may have many connotations, or shades of meaning. To classify an item precisely, writers must sort out their particular meaning from other possible meanings. Sometimes definition can be handled simply; a one-word synonym or a short descriptive phrase following the word may suffice. At other times the kind of sentence definition found in dictionaries is sufficient. But often terms require extensive discussion: one then not only sorts out the meaning of the word from other meanings, but also subclassifies the term into its component parts, using the skills of classification. Definition then becomes an aim in itself. For instance, if the intent is to define the word *Republican* and then to subclassify it into various kinds or subclasses of Republicans, the writer must first pinpoint an exact meaning. *Republican* can refer to a form of government, to a political party or its members, to a set of political beliefs and ideals, or to a particular social stance, so you can see the need to provide a basis for subclassifying. Before any discussion of subclasses can begin, the writer must establish a precise definition of the term, sorting out the intended meaning by revealing the features that distinguish it from other possible meanings. For instance, in a definition of *Republican* as one of the two major political parties in the United States, the writer would have to separate first that connotation of the word from the others and then would need to describe those distinguishing features of Republicanism that separate it from other political parties in the country. At that point the subclassification of *types* of Republicans could begin and the same procedures involved in writing classification would apply. A lengthy, well-developed definition is usually called an *extended definition*. Warren Boroson's "The Workaholic in You" (pages 229–34) is an extended definition that follows the pattern just outlined in defining *Republican*.

ANALYSIS

A third expository form that subdivides a subject into its component parts is analysis. In this process, the writer's purpose goes beyond dividing a whole into parts; the aim is also to examine and weigh the relationships of the parts to one another and to the whole. There are two basic kinds of analysis. The first is *process analysis,* which separates the steps involved in a procedure or operation. Because it describes a step-by-step procedure, as in L. Rust Hills' "How to Eat an Ice-Cream Cone" (pages 250–56), the basic organization of a process analysis is often chronological, unlike other modes of exposition that rely mainly on logical organization. But as in Hills' delightful breakdown of the process of eating an ice-cream cone, each step is further divided into its component parts and discussed in terms of cause-and-effect relationships.

The second form of analysis, *item analysis,* divides the subject into its component parts and then indicates the relationships of the parts. Because Margaret Lantis views the emergence of college symbols historically in her article on pages 273–80, there is an underlying chronological organization. But the primary organizational scheme involves outlining the types of symbols created by three generations of college students, linking the symbols with student behavior and ideals, and then explaining the attitudes of different generations. As you can see, the process is considerably more complex than simply subclassifying the subject, because it also involves discussing logical relationships among the parts.

OPINION

Another popular expository form is the stating and supporting of an opinion. It is close to argument (see Part Four) but differs in that the writer makes no strong attempt to counter opposing views or to persuade the reader to act or to adopt the same opinion. The writer simply says, "These are my opinions about this situation, and here are my reasons for believing as I do." For instance, in "Think Little" (pages 285–93), Wendell Berry expresses his frustration with big social movements and his conviction that real change must come through individual efforts. As in most articles of this sort, his opinion is first expressed as a *thesis,* or main idea, early in the essay. The rest of the paper offers support for that idea—the writer's reasons for holding the opinion.

Occasionally, writers prefer to express all the reasons or causes that have led to their opinion, saving the actual statement of opinion (thesis) until the final paragraphs. Milton Friedman's "Prohibition and Drugs" (pages 312–13) exhibits such organization, which is frequently used in presenting unpopular views.

Occasionally, a paper of opinion may present the writer's personal solution to a general problem—a solution that is stated strongly but not primarily aimed at changing the reader's views. There is certainly an aspect of this in both the Berry and the Friedman selections, as well as in others in this part of the book.

TACTICS FOR READING
EXPOSITORY WRITING

PRE-READING

Pre-reading expository writing requires rather specialized skills in addition to the suggestions offered earlier. In reading through the first and the last few paragraphs of a classification, a definition, or an analysis, try to determine not only the general subject of the paper but also the writer's basis for subdividing the subject as a whole into its component parts.

In pre-reading opinion papers, search the opening and closing paragraphs for the thesis statement—the sentence containing what seems to be the main idea. Remember also to use the title as a clue. Determining the thesis idea before you start to read gives you all the advantages that the writer had before writing—a focusing point for the discussion, a revelation of the purpose for writing, and an expression of the writer's attitude toward the subject.

ANALYTICAL READING

As we said in the Introduction to the book, form is extremely important in expository writing. Therefore, to understand explanatory material thoroughly, you should be generally aware of structure as you read. The demands of the processes involved in writing classification, definition, and analysis almost automatically dictate their organizational scheme. The brief outline below indicates the kind of organization you might expect in each:

DEFINITION
{
Discussion of other possible meanings (historical or current)

A brief, "dictionary"-type definition that clearly defines the limits of meaning to be used in the paper

Subclassification of a *class* into parts
}
CLASSIFICATION
ANALYSIS (with relationships)

But the organization of an opinion paper follows a somewhat different pattern that might be designated as SUBJECT, RESTRICTION, and ILLUSTRATION. The thesis idea, along with the title and the opening paragraphs, usually not only reveals the general SUBJECT but also indicates the RESTRICTION placed on the subject or aspect to be discussed. For instance, Daniel S. Greenberg, in his article on the science of the future (pages 317–25), uses *science* as his general SUBJECT, but RESTRICTS his

discussion to the future of research science. This restriction is well established by the time he states his thesis.

All the devices a writer uses to support a statement of opinion constitute ILLUSTRATION. This can involve presenting examples, discussing effects and their causes, comparing or contrasting one idea or situation to
another, or using factual information to support the opinion. If these devices are handled effectively, the reader should be constantly aware of
their relationship to both the subject and the restriction. When the writer
arranges the three in this usual order—SUBJECT, RESTRICTION, ILLUSTRA-
TION—a paper organized like the Berry article results. When the order is
reversed—ILLUSTRATION, RESTRICTION, SUBJECT—the paper follows the
Friedman model. The organizational scheme for an opinion paper might
look like this:

Background material ⎱   SUBJECT, RESTRICTION
Thesis Idea   ⎰

Supporting Idea I   ⎫
Supporting Idea II ⎬   ILLUSTRATION
Supporting Idea III ⎭

Individual paragraphs within a paper of opinion usually exhibit a similar pattern. Somewhere in the paragraph, usually close to the beginning, a
statement of the restricted subject of the paragraph—the topic sentence—
appears. The rest of the material in the paragraph expands or illustrates the
topic sentence. If the article is well written, the general subject of the
paragraph reasserts the general subject of the paper; the paragraph restriction acts as a supporting idea for the thesis of the paper. Again, if we look
at Greenberg's article, we find few paragraphs that do not refer to *science*
and *research* in their opening sentences, although each presents some new
material to support the various components of the thesis idea. Being aware
that the thesis idea recurs throughout the paper can not only help you in a
slow, careful reading and in underlining important points but can also
assist you in skimming through the material. This latter skill is often desperately needed by college students faced with massive reading assignments. By reading only the opening sentences of paragraphs, you can readily find the main ideas in the material. If it's supporting details you're
looking for, skim the center sections of the paragraphs. Obviously, maximum understanding is achieved only when you read the whole essay, but
there are times when shortcuts are necessary.

Another helpful structural device of writing that you should watch for
as you read is parallelism. This is simply the repetition of the opening
elements of sentences within a paragraph. An effective example is in paragraph 12 on page 289, where Wendell Berry repeats the opening "we are
going to have to . . ." several times in subsequent sentences; later in the

same paragraph, "We need . . ." is repeated three times! As Berry does here, writers use this device to indicate a series of main points of equal importance, so readers should be alert to such signals.

REFLECTING

This step in reading exposition involves close analysis of the relationship between form and meaning. The following series of questions to ask yourself will be useful:

Point. Is the writer's main idea the one that you had arrived at in the pre-reading stage? Where in the essay is the best single statement of the main idea?

Organization. Can you easily outline the essay? If so, is it effectively organized? You might profit from trying to analyze what transitional devices the writer used to link the ideas together.

Support. What kinds of support did the writer rely on—examples, comparison and contrast, cause-and-effect relationships? Which did you find most effective?

Synthesis. Did the essay express some of the ideas that you hold about the subject or its parts? Do you have similar or conflicting views on the subject? Did you find ideas that relate to other works that you have read?

Evaluation. How effectively was information given? Did the writer's organizational scheme, word choice, and paragraph structure aid you in understanding the material? Did you have to reread sections, or did the style sometimes interfere—confusing rather than clarifying? Also, was the explanation complete, or did it omit some important material?

FROM READING TO WRITING

If you follow the reading suggestions, you will become aware of how writers use form in achieving clarity in expository writing. As a writer of exposition, you have the same responsibility. Learning from the organizational schemes, the paragraph structure, sentence devices, and word choice of the models you read, you can adapt those insights to your own writing.

Most writers don't begin until they have devised some organizational format, and you as a writer should follow that practice. Prepare some kind of outline before you start to write: know the basis you will use in subdividing processes; the opinion you wish to express; and the ideas you will use to support them. Work out the logical relationships you intend to reveal before you start to write the first draft. You will find that preliminary planning, rather than hindering your writing, frees you for the creative aspects of writing—designing effective sentence structure, making decisions about word choice, experimenting with paragraph devices.

Classification

BLUES, AND OTHER NOISES,
IN THE NIGHT
John Rockwell

BIOGRAPHICAL SKETCH

John Rockwell was born in Washington, D.C., in 1940, but moved to San Francisco at the age of eight. Two of his childhood years were spent in Germany, where he developed a love for German opera. He graduated from Phillips Academy and from Harvard and received his Ph.D. from the University of California at Berkeley. His dissertation was on the Berlin opera of the 1920s. In 1969 he became a music and dance critic, first with the Oakland Tribune *and then with the* Los Angeles Times. *He is now a music critic with* The New York Times *and is the first staff critic to cover pop music for the* Times. *He has also contributed many articles to* Rolling Stone.

PRE-READING

1. From the title, what would you expect the article to deal with? Does the biographical sketch lead to different expectations?

2. In skimming the first few paragraphs and the last, what do you find the actual subject to be?

¹ Country music today is symbolized for most people by Nashville, and it's a fitting symbol without being an inclusive one. "Country music" suggests a music of the land. Nashville is a city and a bustling, growing one, and so, too, the mainstream country music of 1976 is a music by and for urbanized people who may come from the land and remember it with an idealized affection, but who also want to put the brute realities of rural poverty behind them. If much contemporary country music strikes purists as slick and false, that's because its hard-core fans want not so much a recollection of how it used to be out on the back forty as an aural Hallmark card.

² If Nashville is the symbol of modern country music, then the new Grand Ole Opry and Opryland are the symbols and the center of Nashville's

FROM *Saturday Review,* 4 September 1976, pp. 32 ff. Copyright © 1976 by the Saturday Review Corporation.

music life. No longer does the Opry, country music's principal concert hall and the site of weekly radio broadcasts, consist of a homely, dowdy old theater not that far removed from Depression-era photographs, with their barely regenerate crackers, fresh off the farm, sawing fiddles and banging skillets. Today the closer parallel is Las Vegas, and with their sequined cowboy suits and swooning string sections, today's country stars aspire as much to Vegas success as to personal or regional traditions.

3 That said, country music remains a loyalist phenomenon, and its audiences are characterized by a strong sense of self and of communality. To judge from the tour itineraries of the best-known country stars—and country stars tour steadily and continuously to innumerable obscure places, hundreds of nights a year—there has been a good deal of leakage beyond the home area of the Southeastern United States. Naturally one is tempted to trace the spread of country concerts and country radio stations to the Southwest and, in isolated pockets, all over the rest of the country to migrational patterns of white Southerners. But Northeastern, Midwestern, and Pacific Coast country fans are likely to be blue-collar enthusiasts with only the most tenuous spiritual connections to the actual South.

4 Thus the best-known established country stars—Roy Acuff, Chet Atkins, Glen Campbell, Johnny Cash, George Jones, Loretta Lynn, Dolly Parton, and Tammy Wynette—stick to themes and musical idioms that reaffirm their audiences' sense of the familiar. There are, of course, the passing fads—truck drivers and their woes are particularly popular these days. But underlying it all are the staples of broken hearts, whiskey, family, and God, couched in steadily thumping common time, vocal lines squarely confined within the range of untrained voices, and an instrumentation colored by electric, slide, and pedal steel guitars.

5 If country music, like soul and Latin music, remains a securely delineated subgenre within pop, there are signs of erosion of that purity. The hope, as well as the fear, in Nashville these days is the "crossover," or the leap of a country song onto the national pop sales charts, and hence from relatively modest success to the millions to be made when the big pop AM stations all over the country start playing and propagating a record. The hope is that a country singer can reach that wider acclaim. The fear is that, in so doing, the artist may dilute his style past recognizability. And, further, there is fear that the process can work the other way—the supposed country charts in recent years have often been topped by such artists as John Denver, Olivia Newton-John, and Linda Ronstadt. They may be singing outwardly country songs, but they are hardly country in either their biographies or their links to Nashville musical institutions. The whole crossover phenomenon provides an obvious musical metaphor for Southern culture and its relation to the rest of America: crossover success means recognition on a national level even as the indigenous roots that nourish that success are eroded.

6 Needless to say, many older forms of country music remain vital parts of our folk culture today. What distinguishes them from mainstream country

and what helps assure their traditional purity is their very freedom from commercialism. There are some established country stars who consciously revert to the Anglo-American folk tradition that underlies all country music.

[7] But the many folk festivals around the country are full of eager "string bands"—fiddle-dominated ensembles that trace their ancestry back through the crudely amplified fiddle groups of the Depression to the traditional country and mountain ensembles of the nineteenth century. This music goes by a variety of overlapping names—"mountain music," "old-timey music"—that often refer to similar music with only minor regional variants. The best-known form of such older music is bluegrass, popularized by Eric Weissberg with his music for the film *Deliverance*. Bluegrass is actually of fairly recent invention, for all its debts to older forms of folk-country, and its inventors, Bill Monroe and the Bluegrass Boys, are still regaling audiences with their blend of quick-stepping tempos, exuberant fiddle playing, and high, hard tenorizing. More recently, Earl Scruggs, once the banjo-playing half of the Flatt and Scruggs duo, has attempted to broaden bluegrass's appeal by allying it with quasi-rock instrumentation.

[8] In so doing, he has only followed the lead of the rockers themselves. "Rock" is a far more amorphous term than "country" or "bluegrass" and, at its loosest, can embrace any form of highly amplified popular music that appeals largely to young audiences. Rock owes much of its continued vitality to its willingness to absorb influences from the most diverse sources, and country music has long since become a staple of present-day rock, with such bands as the Byrds, the Eagles, the Grateful Dead, Poco, and the New Riders of the Purple Sage leading the way. Such homage has in turn led to a new form of crossover, and today the children of once anti-hippie red-necks have themselves embraced rock with a vengeance. The children of the New South are as likely to be long-haired, dope-smoking rock fans as they are to be crew-cut football players or Bible-toting 4-H'ers; often the football players go to church and wear their hair long and listen to rock all at the same time. In fact, the South has produced the most popular and interesting group of rock bands of any part of the country in recent years, from the Allman Brothers to Lynyrd Skynyrd to ZZ Top to Wet Willie to the Marshall Tucker and Charlie Daniels bands. And towns like Macon, Ga., and Muscle Shoals, Ala., have come to rival Nashville itself as centers for the recording and institutionalization of music. The Southern rock bands stick to their heritage with music that tends to be simpler and more basic than the artier forms of rock that have proliferated elsewhere.

[9] The children of the New South aren't limited in their musical choices to George Jones and Gregg Allman. There is a whole new wave of "progressive" country musicians to listen to, as well, and so many people are taking that option that such artists as Willie Nelson, Waylon Jennings, and Emmylou Harris are topping the charts regularly these days. The progressive country musicians, based in both Nashville and Austin, Tex., reflect the concerns of their younger, hipper listeners, and their music echoes national trends by

being louder, harder, and more rockishly electric than traditional Nashville music. But it's still unequivocally country, and that indebtedness is just as likely to express itself in a return to the thirties and forties modes as in a similarity to present-day Opry styles. Woody Guthrie, with his nasal folkishness and his leftist populism, is just as much the idol of Merle Haggard and James Talley as he was of Bob Dylan a decade ago.

[10] Country music today is thus a far more diverse tapestry than casual stereotypes might suggest. People of all ages create it and listen to it, and its influence extends directly and indirectly far beyond the geographical confines of the South. By any conventional measurement of an art's vitality and capacity for growth, country music is alive and rambunctiously well, and it's hard to see any hint that vitality will taper off in the immediate future.

ANALYTICAL READING

1. What is the significance to the rest of the article of the opening description of Nashville and the Grand Ole Opry?

2. How does Rockwell define *country music*?

3. What words in the article help to establish the regionalism of country music? What is the meaning of *crossover* (paragraph 5)?

4. Were you aware of the use of analogy or comparison as you read? Point out examples.

5. Do you think the inclusion of the names of singers adds to the article? How?

6. How many subclasses of country music are mentioned in the article?

7. Paragraph 5 is a good example of SUBJECT–RESTRICTION–ILLUSTRATION organization. Explain each and show where it is located in the paragraph. Can you find other paragraphs that follow this organizational scheme?

8. Do you think Rockwell is writing for a specialized audience of country music fans or for a general audience? Explain, citing evidence from the article.

REFLECTING

Point: The rhetorical form of the article is classification. Which sentence best sets up the *class* to be subdivided? Has it been hinted at earlier? What is the central idea of the article? Which sentence best expresses it?

Organization: Outline the article, showing Rockwell's subclasses of country music. Be sure you account for any subdividing within each subclass.

Support: Is the opening description of Nashville used to support any aspect of the article? Are the examples carefully chosen to justify Rockwell's subclasses? Discuss.

Synthesis: Are you familiar with most of the country stars the writer names? Are there any not mentioned that you think are more representative of a certain subclass? Is there a subclass of country music that you think should be added? To what extent is the article out of date?

Evaluation: How effectively do you think Rockwell handles classification and explanations? What aspects of the article do you think contributed most to its clarity?

FROM READING TO WRITING

Following Rockwell's model of classification, write a paper subdividing another kind of popular music, such as rock, folk, protest music, progressive jazz, or the like. Be sure to include specific performers or recordings that are representative of the different subclasses.

LETTER WRITERS
John Ciardi

BIOGRAPHICAL SKETCH

John Ciardi was born in Boston, Massachusetts, in 1916 and educated at the University of Michigan, where he received an M.A. degree. After teaching at Harvard, Rutgers, and several other universities, he became poetry editor of Saturday Review *from 1956 to 1972. Since then he has served as one of the magazine's contributing editors. Ciardi is known mainly for his many books of poetry, for which he has received numerous awards, but he has also written books of literary criticism, books for children, and an excellent translation of Dante's* Inferno.

PRE-READING

1. From the title and the opening lines, what is the item or class you expect to be subclassified in this essay?

2. What kind of voice is projected in the opening and closing paragraphs? Is the tone serious or sardonic, formal or informal, angry or slightly annoyed?

3. From the biographical sketch, what kind of letters would you expect John Ciardi to receive?

¹ Readers of this magazine [*Saturday Review*], as I have long since discovered, are Herculean letter writers. Whether to confirm or confound, the subscription list makes itself felt. Three qualified cheers for them! What is more disappointing for a writer than to drop his published words into a bottomless well of silence from which no echo is ever to be heard? But if only a man could wish for an echo without wishing-up a roar. I dare not count how many letters are at this moment spilling over my desk unanswered. They are unanswered

FROM John Ciardi, *Manner of Speaking* (New Brunswick, N.J.: Rutgers University Press, 1972), pp. 118–21. Copyright © 1972, Rutgers, The State University. Reprinted by permission of the author.

for the good reason that to answer them would not be a chore but a career. And because I have other work to do.

2 One good reason, of course, for answering mail is that it is fun to receive it. But there are even better reasons for not answering, and certainly the first among them is the fact that many letters ought not to have been written in the first place. In terms of any reasonable social contract, the writer should have known better.

3 In the first rank of such social misdemeanors I certainly place the scores of letters I have received from misguided students fumbling at a term paper, who have blandly asked me in effect to write it for them. At first—because I have myself put in too many years as a teacher—I used to reply with a mild avuncular scolding, along with a brief summary of basic reference works available in any good library, and the assurance that the writer would neither lose social standing nor be shot down by the librarian were he to pass quietly through the front door and look for himself.

4 But no more. I am persuaded we have reared an unmannerly generation unto ourselves. Not one of the young whelps I wrote to took the trouble to say thanks. (One mother did write to thank me for the scolding I had given her young whippersnapper.) Not one enclosed a self-addressed stamped envelope. And not one knew enough to frame a considered (which is to say answerable) question, but only such hopelessly hopeful casts as "Please tell me what you think of William Butler Yeats. I am doing my term paper on him." I must insist on assuming that one is absolved when bad manners are added to ignorance, and that there need be no social debt to answer such letters.

5 The second rank of letters that must be discarded at once is made up of those that come along with a batch of bad poems (they are always bad) and a request for a personal critique.

6 Certainly I understand why a writer wants someone else to read his work and to comment on it. I have sought such reading and comment all my life. "Well, isn't that a debt?" one hears the letter writer thinking. Yes it is, and I do my best to repay it to my students. I try to repay it there because, there, repayment is more or less possible. I *can* criticize their writing—for better or worse—but only after at least a month of setting forth principles, rules of thumb, and a vocabulary of criticism.

7 What happens, on the other hand, when the editor confuses himself with the teacher? If a student passes in a poem whose diction is random I can say, "Show me how the overtones of your words bear any relation to one another." Or in another case I can say, "Break the poem down into its mechanical and meaningful stresses and show me what you think happens between the two." The student—at least the good one—will understand because he has been to the lectures that set up those criteria and because he has done supervised exercises in analyzing those elements of the poem.

8 But suppose I mention overtones to a reader? Or mechanical and meaningful stresses? I have not answered the mail, I have only multiplied it. Back

comes another letter saying, "What is an overtone? And what is a mechanical and a meaningful stress?"

⁹ By that point the hour has struck. Nothing less than 10,000 words could begin to make sense. I compute that I am offered daily the opportunity to write roughly 500,000 such words, and I leave simple addition to attest that the answer must be no. Sorry, but no. And since that is the only possible answer, why answer at all?

¹⁰ The third rank in the army of the pestiferous carries a banner that reads "Chatty Pals." Between Bangor and San Diego there must be millions of literate and semiliterate people with nothing to do, and the itch to write long soul-searching single-spaced letters. To engage in two such correspondences would be a life work for an unfastidious Lord Chesterfield. Forgive me, dear leisured friends, but once again, the rest is silence.

¹¹ I suspect we are all overcivilized these days, and it does in fact cause an uneasy feeling (at first) to leave letters unanswered. But in time the calluses grow. And in the name of reason, is everyman's mistake a duty upon me once any given writer has bought a postage stamp?

¹² But to ask that question is a way of wheedling toward an easy self-justification. A writer has purer grounds within his own need. The Age of Public Relations is upon us all, and where is the executive, however majestic in his banker's eye, who has not established a routine for making some sort of acknowledgement of every scrap of mail? He has heard the legend that the busiest and most important men always find time to answer, and since he is obviously busy and obviously important, he will not disappoint his own legend of himself. After all, it takes only a standard-forms book and a secretary who knows her business—both of them deductible items.

¹³ No thanks. I shall rest with the writer's purer refusal. What need he care about the legends of importance? He has the holy right of his own selfishness. His attention belongs to himself and to his writing. He owes no private pieces of his mind to junior college students in Minnesota, to hopefully hopeless young writers on Long Island, or to chatty housewives in Tuscaloosa. What he has to say is best said within the formalities of his writing. Whatever he has written well is there to be received by anyone able to read it, and nothing he might scribble out of a misplaced sense of public relations will take its place.

¹⁴ In the name of that indispensable selfishness, therefore, and to ask of such readers as are willing to grant it, their mercy upon selfish need, I hereby sweep the desk clean of all letters I have lacked the courage to chuck out before, and for such amends as it may offer, I begin this column in which I shall try to answer, among other things, some of the questions that crop up in the mailbag, at least such as involve matters of general interest. I have some thought of getting down to occasional specific discussion of poetic techniques. And obviously—along with every other columnist—I must take a shot at saving the world now and then. At saving it or damning it.

[15] My plans are no more definite than that. Except to look at the mail when there is time, and to give most letter writers the fullest assurance that unless their letters are answered here they will not be answered at all.

ANALYTICAL READING

1. Is classification the main purpose of the paper, or does Ciardi have another aim? If so, what?

2. What is the effect of his play on the word *well* in the opening paragraph?

3. How does Ciardi use cause-and-effect reasoning in the article?

4. How many major subclasses does Ciardi indicate? Where does he include himself?

5. What devices in the opening and closing paragraphs help to establish the tone of the article? By what devices is the tone sustained throughout?

6. What kind of readers is Ciardi addressing? Discuss their age, schooling, and so on, referring to the article to support your conclusions.

7. Indicate word choices that you found especially effective.

REFLECTING

Point: What is the point of the article? Is classification the primary purpose, or is it secondary to something else? Discuss.

Organization: Can you construct an organizational scheme showing the subclasses Ciardi outlines? Is there any pattern in his ranking of letter writers?

Support: How do examples serve as support?

Synthesis: Could you sympathize with Ciardi's aversion to answering letters? What kinds of letters do you find particularly unrewarding to answer? Do you expect letters that you write to magazines and businesses to be answered?

Evaluation: If you had not already known from the biographical sketch, would you have found evidence in the writing style that Ciardi is a poet? Did you respond favorably or unfavorably to his sarcastic humor? Why? Does Ciardi make a convincing case for not answering letters?

FROM READING TO WRITING

1. Emulating Ciardi's essay, write a classification paper that also indicates a strong opinion. Suggestions for topics: people who wait on tables, bus or taxi drivers, telephone operators, questionnaires—anything with which you have had extensive experience.

2. Write a classification paper in which you subclassify the kinds of people you have telephone conversations with.

INEXPENSIVE STILL AND MOVIE CAMERAS

The Editors of *Changing Times*

PRE-READING

From the title and the opening sentence, what do you expect the article to do?

The Still Cameras

[1] In still cameras you have three basic choices.

[2] *Aim-and-shoot.* This is the seventies' version of the venerable box camera. It's pocket-size now and spiffier-looking in simulated gun metal and leather casing. It uses 110 film cartridges that you simply drop in. Prices run from about $20 to $50.

[3] The basic aim-and-shoot camera has a single shutter speed of about 1/80 or 1/100 second and a fixed aperture lens (from f:8 to f:11) that will produce a focused picture of your subject at a distance of from five feet to infinity. It uses either four-shot flashcubes or the new eight-shot flash bar. (This camera's predecessor is the 126-size, Instamatic-type camera now fast fading from the scene—just as 8 mm movie equipment gave way to the super 8 format some years ago. Film for 126 cameras should be available for some years to come, however.)

[4] The aim-and-shoot pocket camera will produce prints or slides of adequate quality, but the camera's fixed-focus slow lens and fast shutter speed diminish its capacity for taking subtle, dim-light photos, stopping action without blurring the subject, and achieving exceptional sharpness and other special effects that can make finished pictures more interesting.

[5] *Automatic.* For those qualities you'll need a more advanced model of the 110 pocket camera, usually described as an automatic 110. It's about the same size as its aim-and-shoot cousin, but it costs from $50 to $130, depending on the level of sophistication you want.

[6] Automatics have a built-in electric eye light-metering system; a range of shutter speeds, typically from 1/650 second to as much as 18 full seconds; electronic controls that automatically set up the best shutter speed and aperture stop combination for the scene you are shooting. Focusing is done through a split-image range finder or by scale or zone (you estimate the distance to your subject and set the focusing tab accordingly). These cameras commonly have electronic flash units, either built-in or attachable. Some will also take flashcubes and flash bars.

FROM *Changing Times*, December 1976, pp. 31–34. Reprinted with permission from *Changing Times* Magazine. © 1976 by Kiplinger Washington Editor, Inc., December 1976.

⁷ The newest twist in 110 pocket cameras is the "zoom" or telescoping lens system, actually a dual lens setup that enables you to take pictures from either a normal-angle or telephoto range at the press of a button. In price and sophistication these cameras lie somewhere between the aim-and-shoot and the automatic 110's. Most telescoping 110 cameras now on the market have a fixed focus and exposure range, which puts them in the aim-and-shoot category. Some have automatic exposure control, though, which would probably place them in the automatic class.

⁸ *Instant.* Polaroid originated the idea. Now Kodak has served up its instant camera. The newest models, like Polaroid's SX–70 and Pronto line and Kodak's EK series, flip out a picture card within three seconds after you press the shutter button, and in eight minutes you have a finished color snapshot.

⁹ All these instant cameras feature automatic electronic exposure control and deliver color prints automatically (except Kodak's basic model, which has hand-cranked delivery). Some Polaroid models also feature single lens reflex focusing and can be folded to about the size of a paperback book. Other Polaroid models and the Kodak cameras have rigid bodies and zone focusing. A new Kodak model due sometime in 1977, the EK–8, will have a fold-up body.

¹⁰ The original type of Polaroid cameras—in which you pull the exposed snapshot from the camera, wait about a minute for it to develop and then peel off a cover sheet—aren't as sophisticated as the newer lines, but they can cost a lot less, have automatic exposure control and scale focusing, and use a greater range of instant films, including black-and-white and the kind that produces both a print and a negative.

The Movie Cameras

¹¹ In Super 8 home movie cameras you have two choices: silent or sound. The latter type will take silent movies as well. Super 8 sound systems, a fairly recent development, are already close to matching silent cameras in sales.

¹² *Silent and sound.* Most good silent and sound cameras now have automatic electronic exposure control, adjustable focusing (either through the lens or by scale), and a lens system fast enough to permit filming in low-light conditions without movie lights (with ASA 160 film). They also have such things as built-in filters, which permit you to shoot movies indoors and out without changing the type of film, and low-light, end-of-film and other warning signals in the viewfinder. A silent camera costs $160 to $300, depending on the number of features; sound cameras run $250 to $350.

¹³ For the best results and widest range of use, your movie camera should also have a powered zoom lens—a wide-angle, telephoto and normal lens all in one—which enables you to close in on or back away from your subject without moving the camera. A camera that has only manual zooming requires a very steady hand to operate the zoom lens ring. Even a little movement

while filming is greatly exaggerated when the movie is projected. Zoom ratios (the relative difference between the longest and shortest focal lengths of the lens) run from about 2-to-1 up to 10-to-1.

[14] Other special features you might find worth paying extra for are a fade device, macro focusing, more than one filming speed and single frame advance. A fade-in allows you to have an image gradually emerge from a dark screen, or in a fade-out to gradually disappear. Macro focusing permits sharp focus for extreme close-ups of the smallest of subjects; when the film is projected, the subject appears extraordinarily large and detailed. Normal filming speed is 18 frames per second (fps). A camera that also films at 36 fps will produce movies in slow motion; at 9 fps, in Keystone Kops-style fast motion. Single frame advance lets you expose one frame of film at a time, as you would with a still camera. With this feature you can produce animation, which gives motion to inanimate objects, such as title lettering, and also time-lapse movies in which events that take hours or days to occur, such as the blooming of a flower, appear on screen to be happening within a few seconds or minutes.

[15] *Sound.* Sound cameras are essentially the same as silent ones with the addition of a miniature built-in tape recorder that registers a synchronized sound track on the film. Most sound cameras are equipped with a simple omnidirectional microphone and a transistor radio-type earphone for monitoring sound pickup. Many can also be equipped with directional boom-type microphones.

Shopping for Your Camera

[16] The best way to begin your search is to do what you're doing now— reading about different brands and types of cameras. It's a good way to learn about the variety of capabilities available and to decide which will be most useful for the kind of picture taking you usually do. You'll find a sampling of still and movie cameras in the accompanying tables.

[17] Consult photo buff magazines, such as *Popular Photography*, particularly the special editions in which the newest cameras and projectors are reviewed. Thumb through any photo equipment catalogs you can get your hands on, too. Sears has just produced its first special camera catalog, which you can get through a Sears store; it includes dozens of types and brands in a wide range of prices.

[18] When you've done your homework, visit some photo shops and departments to take a look at equipment you've read about. Be sure to handle the cameras you're interested in. Try to find a knowledgeable salesperson who can demonstrate how to use them and answer your questions.

[19] As you browse the camera counters, check out prices. Cameras commonly sell for less than the manufacturer's suggested list price. Keep an eye out for further reductions during special brand promotions and seasonal sales.

Particularly when shopping for a movie camera, you might save 10% to 15% by buying camera, projector and screen as an outfit.

[20] Good cameras can last a lifetime. Also, this year's new special feature tends to be part of next year's standard equipment. So don't try to save money by skimping on camera features unless you know you'll have no use for them. It's not worth paying a lot more for fancier casing, for instance, but it may be worth the additional dollars to get a better lens system or a greater array of special-effect features you'll enjoy.

ANALYTICAL READING

1. How many types of still cameras are dealt with? How many types of movie cameras?

2. How is description used in the article? Would you classify it as factual or personal description? Explain.

3. What techniques does the writer use to make the writing less "scientific" and more personal?

4. What does the article do besides classify cameras?

5. Do you think the article is aimed at camera buffs or at a general audience? Cite examples from the essay to support your answer.

6. Paragraph 9 is organized from the general to the specific. How is the technique of subclassification handled within this organizational scheme? Can you find other paragraphs that follow the same pattern?

7. The last five paragraphs shift from classification to process analysis. Explain.

REFLECTING

Point: What is the purpose of the article? Does the opening sentence provide the clue to this? Do you think the article is organized around the purpose?

Organization: Using *camera* as the *class,* draw a diagram of the subclassification scheme in the article. Does the diagram provide an organizational framework for the article?

Support: What part do the discussions of advantages and disadvantages play in the article? Do you think an opening paragraph that provides some background might have added support to the article? What would you include in such a paragraph? Why do you think the author probably decided to omit such a paragraph?

Synthesis: Compare the voice projected in this article with the one encountered in Ciardi's essay (pages 213–16). Why are they different?

Evaluation: How effective do you find the article as a source of quick information? What part does the organization, voice, and choice of language play in its effectiveness or lack of it? How helpful would the article be to someone who wishes to buy an inexpensive camera?

FROM READING TO WRITING

1. Write an opening paragraph that sets up the purpose of the article and that indicates something about the classification procedure.

2. Write a similar classification paper about some item that you know a lot about—tennis racquets, guns, violin strings, guitars, racing cars, boats—using description as in the article. The paper should serve as a source of information for a reader trying to decide what to buy.

Definition

INTRODUCTION TO *SPORTS WORLD*
Robert Lipsyte

BIOGRAPHICAL SKETCH

Robert Lipsyte was born in New York City in 1938 and graduated from Columbia University. For about fourteen years he wrote an internationally syndicated column, "Sports of the Times." He won several awards for distinguished reporting. Since he retired from journalism, Lipsyte has written three novels and three nonfiction works, including Nigger *(with Dick Gregory),* The Masculine Mystique, *and* SportsWorld: An American Dreamland.

PRE-READING

1. From the biographical sketch, what would you expect Lipsyte's attitude toward sports to be?

2. Before reading the opening paragraphs, try to explain what SportsWorld means to you.

3. From skimming the first two paragraphs and the last one, what do you think Lipsyte's attitude toward SportsWorld is?

¹ For the past one hundred years most Americans have believed that playing and watching competitive games are not only healthful activities, but represent a positive force on our national psyche. In sports, they believe, children will learn courage and self-control, old people will find blissful nostalgia, and families will discover new ways to communicate among themselves. Immigrants will find shortcuts to recognition as Americans. Rich and poor, black and white, educated and unskilled, we will all find a unifying language. The melting pot may be a myth, but we will all come together in the ballpark.

² This faith in sports has been vigorously promoted by industry, the military, government, the media. The values of the arena and the locker room have been imposed upon our national life. Coaches and sportswriters are

FROM Robert Lipsyte, *SportsWorld* (New York: Quadrangle/The New York Times Book Co., 1975), pp. ix–xv. Copyright © 1975 by Robert Lipsyte. Reprinted by permission of Quadrangle/The New York Times Book Co.

speaking for generals and businessmen, too, when they tell us that a man must be physically and psychologically "tough" to succeed, that he must be clean and punctual and honest, that he must bear pain, bad luck, and defeat without whimpering or making excuses. A man must prove his faith in sports and the American Way by whipping himself into shape, playing by the rules, being part of the team, and putting out all the way. If his faith is strong enough, he will triumph. It's his own fault if he loses, fails, remains poor.

[3] Even for ballgames, these values, with their implicit definitions of manhood, courage, and success, are not necessarily in the individual's best interests. But for daily life they tend to create a dangerous and grotesque web of ethics and attitudes, an amorphous infrastructure that acts to contain our energies, divert our passions, and socialize us for work or war or depression.

[4] I call this infrastructure SportsWorld. For most of my adult life, as a professional observer, I've explored SportsWorld and marveled at its incredible power and pervasiveness. SportsWorld touches everyone and everything. We elect our politicians, judge our children, fight our wars, plan our vacations, oppress our minorities by SportsWorld standards that somehow justify our foulest and freakiest deeds, or at least camouflage them with jargon. We get stoned on such SportsWorld spectaculars as the Super Bowl, the space shots, the Kentucky Derby, the presidential conventions, the Indianapolis 500, all of whose absurd excesses reassure us that we're okay.

[5] SportsWorld is a sweaty Oz you'll never find in a geography book, but since the end of the Civil War it has been promoted and sold to us like Rancho real estate, an ultimate sanctuary, a university for the body, a community for the spirit, a place to hide that glows with that time of innocence when we believed that rules and boundaries were honored, that good triumphed over evil, and that the loose ends of experience could be caught and bound and delivered in an explanation as final and as comforting as a goodnight kiss.

[6] Sometime in the last fifty years the sports experience was perverted into a SportsWorld state of mind in which the winner was good because he won; the loser, if not actually bad, was at least reduced, and had to prove himself over again, through competition. As each new immigrant crop was milled through the American system, a pick of the harvest was displayed in the SportsWorld showcase, a male preserve of national athletic entertainment traditionally enacted by the working class for the middle class, much as the performing arts are played by the middle class for the amusement of the upper class.

[7] By the 1950s, when SportsWorld was dominated by what are now called "white ethnics," the black American was perceived as a challenging force and was encouraged to find outlets in the national sports arena. Although most specific laws against black participation had already been erased, it took cautious, humiliating experiments with such superstars as Jackie Robinson and Larry Doby to prove that spectator prejudice could be deconditioned by a winning team. Within a few years, pools of cheap, eager black and dark Latin labor were channeled into mainstream clubs.

[8] So pervasive are the myths of SportsWorld that the recruitment of blacks has been regarded as a gift of true citizenship bestowed upon the Negro when he was ready. It has been conventional wisdom for twenty years that the black exposure in sports has speeded the integration of American society, that white Americans, having seen that blacks are beautiful and strong, became "liberalized."

[9] This is one of the crueler hoaxes of SportsWorld. Sports success probably has been detrimental to black progress. By publicizing the material success of a few hundred athletes, thousands, perhaps millions, of bright young blacks have been swept toward sports when they should have been guided toward careers in medicine or engineering or business. For every black star celebrated in SportsWorld, a thousand of his little brothers were neutralized, kept busy shooting baskets until it was too late for them to qualify beyond marginal work.

[10] The white male spectator who knew few ordinary black men to measure himself against may have had his awareness raised by watching such superior human beings as Frank Robinson, Jim Brown, Bill Russell, O. J. Simpson, and other highly merchandised SportsWorld heroes, but it also doubled his worst fears about blacks: added to the black junkie who would rip out his throat was the black superstud who could replace him as a man—in bed, on the job, as a model for his children.

[11] By the middle of the 1970s it seemed as though the black experience in SportsWorld might be recapitulated by women. SportsWorld seemed on the verge of becoming the arena in which women would discover and exploit their new "equality." It would be a complex test of adaptability for SportsWorld. The major sports were created by men for the superior muscles, size, and endurance of the male body. Those sports in which balance, flexibility, and dexterity are the crucial elements have never been mass-promoted in America. When a woman beats a man at a man's game, she has to play like a man.

[12] There were signs, however, that women may not embrace SportsWorld as eagerly as did the blacks, profiting from that sorry lesson as well as from their own greater leverage in American society. It is no accident that Billie Jean King, while still an active player, became an entrepreneur and an important voice in American cultural consciousness while Jackie Robinson was a Rockefeller courtier almost to the end of his life.

[13] A great deal of the angry energy generated in America through the coming apart of the 1960s was absorbed by SportsWorld in its various roles as socializer, pacifier, safety valve; as a concentration camp for adolescents and an emotional Disneyland for their parents; as a laboratory for human engineering and a reflector of current moral postures; and as a running commercial for Our Way of Life. SportsWorld is a buffer, a DMZ, between people and the economic and political systems that direct their lives; women, so long denied this particular playland, may just avoid this trap altogether.

[14] But SportsWorld's greatest power has always been its flexibility. Even as we are told of SportsWorld's proud traditions, immutable laws, ultimate

security from the capriciousness of "real life," SportsWorld is busy changing its rules, readjusting its alliances, checking the trends. SportsWorld is nothing if not responsive. Hockey interest lagging, how about a little more blood on the ice? Speed up baseball with a designated hitter. Move the football goal posts. A three-point shot in basketball. Women agitating at the college arena gates? Let 'em in. Give 'em athletic scholarships, "jock" dorms, and Minnie Mouse courses. How about a Professional Women's Power Volleyball League?

[15] Stars, teams, leagues, even entire sports may rise or fall or never get off the ground, but SportsWorld as a force in American life orbits on.

[16] Ah, baseball. Our National Pastime. An incredibly complex contrivance that seems to have been created by a chauvinistic mathematician intent upon giving America a game so idiosyncratic that it would be at least a century before any other country could beat us at it. And indeed it was. After a century in which baseball was celebrated as a unique product of the American character, Chinese boys began winning Little League championships, and young men from Latin America and the Caribbean began making a significant impact upon the major leagues. The highly organized Japanese, who had taken up the game during the postwar occupation of their country (perhaps as penance for yelling "To Hell with Babe Ruth" during banzai charges) were almost ready to attack again.

[17] But SportsWorld had spun on. That other peculiarly American game, football, declared itself the New National Pastime. Baseball and God were announced dead at about the same time, but the decision against baseball apparently is taking longer to reverse, thanks in the main to pro football's colossal public relations machine. The National Football League played its scheduled games on Sunday, November 24, 1963, because its historic television deal was pending and Commissioner Pete Rozelle was determined to prove that nothing, *nothing*, could cancel the show. But that winter, NFL sportscasters infiltrated the banquet circuit with the engaging theory—quintessential SportsWorld—that America had been at the brink of a nervous breakdown after President Kennedy's assassination and that only The Sport of the Sixties' business-as-usual attitude had held the country together until Monday's National Day of Mourning unified us all in public grief.

[18] Ten years later, though hopefully still grateful, America had grown bored with the cartoon brutality of pro football. America was boogieing to the magic moves and hip, sly rhythms of basketball, The Sport of the Seventies. We've had enough of pure violence, simulated or otherwise, went the SportsWorld wisdom, now we need something smooooooooth.

[19] There is no end to SportsWorld theories—of the past, the present, the future—especially now that a new generation of commentators, athletes, coaches, and fans feels free to reform and recast sports, to knock it off the pedestal and slide it under the microscope, giving it more importance than ever. SportsWorld newspapermen dare to describe to us action that we have seen more clearly on television than they have from the press box, and SportsWorld telecasters, isolated from the world in their glass booths, dare to ex-

plain to us what the players are *really* thinking. SportsWorld analysts were once merely "pigskin prognosticators" predicting the weekend football scores; now they may be as heavy as any RAND Corporation futurist. Is hockey an art form or is it a paradigm of anarchy, in which case are we obligated as concerned citizens to watch it? Is tennis more than just a convenient new market for clothes and building materials and nondurable goods? What will be The Sport of the Eighties? Will no sport ever again have its own decade? Will cable television and government-regulated sports gambling and the institutionalized fragmenting of society balkanize us into dozens of jealous Fandoms?

[20] SportsWorld, once determinedly anti-intellectual, has become a hotbed of psychologists, physicians, and sociologists questioning premises as well as specific techniques. Should lacrosse players really be eating steak before games, or pancakes? Why are the lockers of defensive linemen neater than those of offensive linemen? Does athletic participation truly "build character" or does it merely reinforce otherwise unacceptable traits? Should communities rather than corporations own teams?

[21] But very few people seem to be questioning SportsWorld itself, exploring the possibility that if sports could be separated from SportsWorld we could take a major step toward liberation from the false values, the stereotypes, the idols of the arena that have burdened us all since childhood.

[22] SportsWorld is not a conspiracy in the classic sense, but rather an expression of a community of interest. In the Soviet Union, for example, where world-class athletes are the diplomat-soldiers of ideology, and where factory girls are forced to exercise to reduce fatigue and increase production, the entire athletic apparatus is part of government. Here in America, SportsWorld's insidious power is imposed upon athletics by the banks that decide which arenas and recreational facilities shall be built, by the television networks that decide which sports shall be sponsored and viewed, by the press that decides which individuals and teams shall be celebrated, by the municipal governments that decide which clubs shall be subsidized, and by the federal government, which has, through favorable tax rulings and exemptions from law, allowed sports entertainment to grow until it has become the most influential form of mass culture in America.

[23] SportsWorld is a grotesque distortion of sports. It has limited the pleasures of play for most Americans while concentrating on turning our best athletes into clowns. It has made the finish more important than the race, and extolled the game as that William Jamesian absurdity, a moral equivalent to war, and the hero of the game as that Henry Jamesian absurdity, a "muscular Christian." It has surpassed patriotism and piety as a currency of communication, while exploiting them both. By the end of the 1960s, SportsWorld wisdom had it that religion was a spectator sport while professional and college athletic contests were the only events Americans held sacred.

[24] SportsWorld is neither an American nor a modern phenomenon. Those glorified Olympics of ancient Greece were manipulated for political and com-

mercial purposes; at the end, they held a cracked mirror to a decaying civilization. The modern Olympics were revived at the end of the nineteenth century in an attempt to whip French youth into shape for a battlefield rematch with Germany. Each country of Europe, then the United States, the Soviet Union, the "emerging" nations of Africa and Asia, used the Olympics as political display windows. The 1972 Arab massacre of Israeli athletes was a hideously logical extension of SportsWorld philosophy.

[25] SportsWorld begins in elementary school, where the boys are separated from the girls. In *Sixties Going on Seventies,* Nora Sayre recounts the poignant confrontation of a gay man and a gay woman at a meeting. She is banging the floor with a baseball bat, and he asks her to stop; the bat symbolizes to him the oppression of sports in his childhood. But to her the bat symbolizes liberation from the restraint that had kept her from aggression, from sports, in her childhood.

[26] By puberty, most American children have been classified as failed athletes and assigned to watch and cheer for those who have survived the first of several major "cuts." Those who have been discarded to the grandstands and to the television sets are not necessarily worse off than those tapped for higher levels of competition. SportsWorld heroes exist at sufferance, and the path of glory is often an emotional minefield trapped with pressures to perform and fears of failure. There is no escape from SportsWorld, for player or spectator or even reporter, that watcher in the shadows who pretends to be in the arena but above the fray.

ANALYTICAL READING

1. This article is an extended definition. Formulate a one-sentence "dictionary" definition of SportsWorld from the material in the first three paragraphs.

2. The following sentences from the essay contain elements that appear to be short definitions. Discuss the weaknesses of each as a logical definition that could serve as the basis for the essay.
    a. "SportsWorld is a sweaty Oz. . . . " (paragraph 5)
    b. "SportsWorld is not a conspiracy in the classic sense, but rather an expression of a community of interest." (paragraph 22)
    c. "SportsWorld is a grotesque distortion of sports." (paragraph 23)
    d. "SportsWorld is neither an American nor a modern phenomenon." (paragraph 24)

3. According to Lipsyte, what aspects of the ethic of SportsWorld have invaded our society?

4. What are the "myths" and characteristics of SportsWorld that Lipsyte finds especially dangerous? Why?

5. How does Lipsyte subclassify the various sports? To what causes does he attribute the changing of the "National Pastime" every decade? Is basketball displaying any of the traits he claims for football? What sport do you think is the most likely candidate for the sport of the 1980's?

6. Did you have trouble with the word *infrastructure* (paragraph 3)? Does the meaning become clear in context as you read, or would a brief definition help? If so, formulate a synonym or short definition for *infrastructure.*

7. Where does Lipsyte use words that might be classified as slang? What is their effect?

8. Is the voice sincere? Does it come across as one of almost angry conviction? Is sentence structure important in establishing the voice? Illustrate.

REFLECTING

Point: Lipsyte wrote this introduction as a definition of *SportsWorld,* a term he coined for his book. Do you also find an opinion expressed? If so, what?

Organization: Outline the article so that the "infrastructure" of Lipsyte's definition is revealed.

Support: Discuss how Lipsyte uses example, cause-and-effect relationships, and analogy to support his subclassifications. Cite specific examples of each technique.

Synthesis: Do you agree or disagree with many of his ideas about sports? Do some of the attitudes you encountered in Leo Durocher's essay (pages 165–66) illustrate or contradict any of Lipsyte's convictions? Can you provide examples for any of the claims made in paragraph 4?

Evaluation: How do you react to the article? Do you think it is effective and thoughtful, or do you think Lipsyte exaggerates the sports situation? Defend your answer by citing examples from the essay. How effectively has he stated and supported his points?

FROM READING TO WRITING

1. Write an extended definition of a term that you create, such as *DormWorld, RockWorld, SpectatorWorld.* Be sure that you follow the form given for definition on page 204.

2. Write an extended definition about an area that has collected a number of myths—the freshman English grading system, childbirth, marijuana, or some other subject.

3. Choose a term or idiom from a sports activity or a game that has made its way into the general language and write an extended definition of it: for instance, *throw a curve, behind the eightball, two strikes against you, stalemate, hazard, take a swan dive, touché, hold the line.*

THE WORKAHOLIC IN YOU
Warren Boroson

BIOGRAPHICAL SKETCH

Warren Boroson was born in New York City in 1935. He completed his under-graduate studies at Columbia University and did graduate work there, at the New School for Social Research, and at New York University, mainly in writing and editing. He has worked as a reporter and editor for several publications, including Trans-Action, *a social science periodical, and he has contributed articles to numerous magazines.*

PRE-READING

1. What is the basis for the coined word in the title?

2. After reading the opening paragraph, can you find Boroson's "dictionary" definition of *workaholic?*

3. This article appeared in *Money* magazine; what audience is it aimed at?

¹ Lots of Americans work hard and play hard. But some just work, either from the unquenchable love of it or from a compulsion beyond their control. Work lovers—the unquenchables—provide society with many leaders in business, politics, science and the arts. Those who overwork out of compulsion—the work addicts, or workaholics, of this world—are in trouble. Their addiction can lead to dead-end careers, to poor health, even to early death. They are so emotionally dependent on work that without it they start coming unglued. Though the purebred workaholic is rare, there is a little of him in almost everyone. It is well to know the warning signals and how to cope with them.

² Confusing workaholics with work lovers is a bit like confusing winos with oenophiles. Mark Twain was a work lover. In 1908, when he was nearly 73, he said he hadn't done a lick of work in over 50 years. Wrote Twain: "I have always been able to gain my living without doing any work; for the writing of books and magazine matter was always play, not work. I enjoyed it; it was merely billiards to me."

³ Psychiatrist Carl Jung once said that the difference between the recondite prose of James Joyce and the poetry of Joyce's insane daughter was that he was diving and she was falling. The work lover is diving. He works hard and long by choice. When he wants to, he can stop without suffering acute withdrawal pains. When work addicts go on vacation, however, it is not the natives but the tourists who are restless.

4 The work lover's work is also his play. The work addict's motives are mixed. In many cases, he is seeking the admiration of other people because he doesn't approve of himself. As Dr. Alan McLean, an IBM psychiatrist, points out, the healthiest people usually have various sources of satisfaction: they are lawyers, say, but they are also spouses, parents, friends, citizens, churchgoers, art lovers, stamp collectors, golfers and so forth. If such people lose their jobs, or if their work becomes less satisfying or its quality starts deteriorating, they have not lost their sole interest in life, the only prop to their self-esteem. Many compulsive workers, according to cardiologist Meyer Friedman of San Francisco, co-author of the bestselling book *Type A Behavior and Your Heart* (1974), "want status, and their status depends on what other people think of them." Eventually, many addicts manage to labor under the delusion that they are indispensable.

5 Guilt propels some workaholics. Several years ago, a theological seminary in the East had a problem with guilt-ridden students who kept working even when the school closed for vacations. To get them out, the school was finally forced to turn off the electricity and water and change all the locks during vacation periods.

6 Because of their diligence, work addicts in corporations tend to keep getting promoted; but a lack of imagination keeps them from reaching the top rungs. They make great salesmen and terrible corporation presidents. "Workaholics rarely become famous," says Dr. Frederic Flach, a New York psychiatrist who has treated many people with work problems. "Because they lack creativity, they rarely make an original contribution to the welfare of mankind. They usually end up in upper-middle management, giving grief to everyone around them."

7 Continual work, Dr. Flach notes, "violates one of the basic rules for coming up with original solutions—to move into another area and let the problem simmer." He adds that one reason workaholics work ten to twelve hours a day is that "they are not good at finding ways to think about something in a new fashion." Work addicts, says Robert F. Medina, an industrial psychologist in Chicago, like "the sureness and safety of processing endless details. Creativity is a little too scary. It looks like idleness to them."

8 As employees of large corporations, work addicts can have a hard time of it. The staff psychiatrist at a huge national manufacturing firm tells of an executive in the New York headquarters who came to him for help. Discussion brought out that the executive felt best when things were "impossible"— when he was being seriously tested and overworked. Free time made him uneasy and anxious. Many addicts like him end up self-employed so they can have expandable working time. (But even blue-collar workers can manage to become work addicts by taking second jobs or constantly volunteering for overtime.)

9 Wherever he earns his living, the workaholic is likely to work hard not just on the job but off duty too. "When his back is to the wall," says Dr. Howard Hess, a Western Electric corporate psychiatrist, "he may cut the lawn

with a vengeance or play a murderous game of tennis." A Chicago psychiatrist, Dr. Saul M. Siegel, recalls a work addict who had an extramarital affair. He kept working as hard as ever, though, and "wound up with both a nagging wife and a nagging mistress."

[10] While work addicts work hard, they tend to die easily. Time and again, researchers have found that the compulsively hard-working person is particularly prone to heart disease in middle age. Dr. Friedman and his cardiologist co-author, Dr. Ray H. Rosenman, divide the world into two working types. Hard-driving people are classified as Type A and low-pressure people as Type B. Both types can become workaholics, but in different ways. The Type-A person is excessively ambitious and competitive, and frequently hostile; he feels pressured by deadlines. Cardiologists have found that he is two or three times as likely to have a premature heart attack as a Type B, who is not so competitive and hard driving.

[11] Type-B workaholics are civil service types who lose themselves in dull paperwork or other routine activities. Wayne Oates, a Louisville psychologist, thinks that a Type-B work addict, unlike the individualistic Type A, tends to identify with the company he works for and "not have any selfhood of his own. The company is a flat earth to him. Everything beyond it is dragons and disaster."

[12] The domestic life of the workaholic is likely to be troubled. In some cases, addicts marry each other and go their own unmerry ways. More typically, the wife is a non-addict, resentful that her husband has so little time and energy to expend on the family. The addict himself may nonetheless expect his wife and children to be robotlike perfectionists. Although the typical work addict doesn't like to help around the house, he "may be a busybody poking into his wife's household affairs and telling her how inefficient she is with the cooking and the housecleaning," reports Dr. Nelson J. Bradley, a psychiatrist in Park Ridge, Ill. "He's too preoccupied with his own work goals to be sensitive to the needs of others" in the family.

[13] Going on a family vacation with a workaholic can be a hellish ordeal. Robert Medina, the Chicago psychologist, tells of the president of a midwestern company whose wife and daughter shanghaied him to Hawaii for three weeks on the beach. The man hadn't taken a vacation in 13 years. He made everybody so miserable by his compulsion to keep phoning the office that after four days his family was as frantic to get home as he was.

[14] A housewife can be a workaholic too. She may insist on doing so much that her children never learn everyday household skills. The daughters of such women "often grow up without knowing how to cook, sew, clean and decorate the home," says psychologist Wayne Oates.

[15] Sometimes a work addict can persuade himself as well as other people that he is really a work lover, the way an alcoholic can persuade himself and others that he doesn't have a drinking problem because all he drinks is vintage cognac. Reading someone's basic motives can be difficult. But it's very likely that a work lover—unlike a work addict—has a job that offers freedom

and diversity; he is well recognized and amply rewarded for his efforts. An obscure middle-aged heart surgeon or social reformer who works as hard as Dr. Denton Cooley or Ralph Nader is more likely to be a self-destructive work addict than those two men are. Nader scoffs at the notion that his ceaseless toil makes him a workaholic. "You wouldn't ask an Olympic swimmer or chess player why he works 20 hours a day," Nader says. People don't understand Nader "because we haven't a tradition which explains me."

[16] Without being workaholics, most people experience the addict's symptoms from time to time. "Anyone who's been busy and active," says Dr. Flach, the New York psychiatrist, "has a tendency to get locked in, to become dependent on his work." Examples are accountants in March and April, salesclerks during the Christmas rush, air traffic controllers all the time. When they are no longer so busy, they may suffer from a mild version of "postpartum depression," like women who have just given birth.

[17] Some people work too long and hard at times because they fear being fired or are bucking for promotion or cannot do their jobs as well as they know they should. Other people sometimes lose themselves in work to escape emotional problems—the loss of a loved one, a financial setback or some other worry. They use work to keep from breaking down completely. Occupational therapy is, after all, one of the very best painkillers and tranquilizers.

[18] These people differ from chronic addicts in that once they have stopped working for a while, their pain begins to ebb, their spirits perk up, and they are back to normal. But someone who has been temporarily habituated to hard work would be best advised to unwind slowly. People who suddenly switch from hard work to idleness tend to develop a variety of physical and psychological illnesses, heart disease in particular. Social psychologist Jerome E. Singer of the National Research Council in Washington, D.C. mentions how people often die shortly after retiring from important posts.

[19] For some work addicts, the realization that something is amiss comes only when they develop health problems. For Wayne Oates, author of *Confessions of a Workaholic* (1971), recognition came when his five-year-old son asked for an appointment to see him. (Oates probably coined the term "workaholic," though the editors of the Merriam-Webster dictionaries give the Wall Street Journal of Feb. 2, 1971 as the first source.) Someone who suspects he may be growing psychologically dependent on work should ask himself whether he can unwind readily over a weekend or during a vacation.

[20] Jerome Singer recommends that hard-working people generally avoid making abrupt major changes in their work habits. People who work frenetically all year long may suffer if they suddenly flop down on a beach in Hawaii for a few weeks. Instead, Singer suggests that hard workers would be better off taking frequent short vacations or easing into long vacations by cutting down gradually on their work.

[21] Recognizing the value of vacations, many companies (General Motors, for one) now require all employees to take the vacations they are entitled to instead of accumulating them from year to year. Dr. Nicholas A. Pace, medical

director of GM's New York executive offices, adds that employees who try not to take vacations "don't get brownie points any more. They're just looked upon as damn fools." But a vacation need not be long to be therapeutic. Dr. John P. McCann of the Life Extension Institute in New York, which gives physicals to executives, points out that for many people even a one-day vacation may constitute a refreshing change of pace.

[22] The ideal vacation, in the opinion of Dr. Ari Kiev, a New York psychiatrist and author of *A Strategy for Handling Executive Stress* (1974), is a foil to a person's occupation. Someone who does close, detailed work all year long, like an accountant, might take up something less exacting, like sailing. (Says Dr. Howard Hess: "A Caribbean vacation is not the solution to everyone's problems. Just mine and yours.") A person who sees in himself symptoms of workaholism should try developing interests outside of his job. Dr. Flach recommends returning to the hobbies of your adolescence—photography, stamp collecting or what have you. "Your early interests," he believes, "are perhaps the closest expression of you as a person." Wayne Oates suggests renewing old acquaintances, making new friends and reading books you don't have to read, like mysteries. It may be easier for those further along the path to addiction to switch to hobbies that, like work, have well-defined goals, such as woodworking or sports.

[23] To suppress temptations to expand your work load, Oates cautions, take a wary look at offers of promotions that would keep you from doing the things you like best about your present job. Lest he try to do two jobs at once, a salesman who enjoys selling might be best off turning down a promotion to sales manager; a teacher who loves teaching might refuse a department chairmanship. In his own case, to keep from taking on so much extra work, Oates put a ceiling on the extra income he wanted each month, and he has stuck to it—with periodic adjustments for inflation.

[24] Sometimes workaholism is thrust on people. There are workaholic companies, which may expect everyone to be at work early, to skip lunch, to work late and to think about office problems on weekends. Work addicts tend to wind up in such places; incipient addicts should escape while they easily can. Dr. Flach, for one, doesn't think the workaholic organization has a special edge over its competitors. Like work addicts themselves, such outfits may lack imagination. "The typical workaholic organization," he says, "may set up the most carefully thought-out way to distribute money into a project, for example, and miss the obvious point—like how all that money is going to get ripped off."

[25] The incipient addict with the hard-driving personality of a Type A should consider slowing down the general pace of his life. Dr. Friedman, a Type A himself (complete with heart attack), deliberately began dressing informally. He spent lunch hours examining the stained glass windows in a nearby cathedral; he began rereading the seven parts of Marcel Proust's interminable *Remembrance of Things Past*. He now avoids cocktail parties: "I found that all you do at them is shout, and no one cares whether you leave or stay."

And he keeps away from "people who readily bring out my free-floating hostility, because I've never been able to convince those sons of bitches about anything and they've never been able to convince me."

[26] To get advice from other well-known people who are reputed to work very hard, I wrote Harold S. Geneen, president of ITT, actor Elliot Gould, film director Robert Altman, Governor Jerry Brown of California and Dr. DeBakey, among others. A spokesman for ITT apologetically reported that Geneen could not reply because he had been very busy with management meetings recently and was out on the golf course. The others did not respond at all. Presumably they were too busy working.

ANALYTICAL READING

1. How does Boroson establish *workaholic* as a class in paragraphs 1–6? What features set workaholics apart from work lovers? What is the danger of being a workaholic?

2. How many subclasses does Boroson set up? What authoritative source does he use to set up the subclasses?

3. What are the distinguishing features of each of the subclasses? How does he present them?

4. How does he capitalize throughout the article on the analogy set up in the title? Does he refer only to men? Distinguish between temporary and chronic work addicts.

5. What is meant by "incipient addicts" (paragraphs 24–25)?

6. Discuss several paragraphs that you found effective in making comparisons and contrasts.

7. Point out some of the devices that Boroson uses to keep the definition from becoming too dry and technical.

REFLECTING

Point: Did you find another purpose in the article besides that of defining *workaholic?* If so, what?

Organization: Does the organizational pattern follow the one suggested in the Introduction to this section of the book? Demonstrate.

Support: How does the author use examples to support his subclassification? How does he use authority?

Synthesis: Do you know anyone who fits the definition? Do you think that you or one of your parents might be an "incipient workaholic"? [Could Highet's "liberal teacher" (pages 235–42) become a workaholic? Why or why not?] Are annual vacations the answer? Do you have any other solutions?

Evaluation: Did you find the article interesting? If so, what devices made it so? Is it merely a book review of *Type A Behavior and Your Heart?* Do you think you could identify a workaholic now?

FROM READING TO WRITING

1. Write an extended definition of a type of person you know who exhibits some compulsive behavior, such as addiction to tennis (tennisholic), bridge (bridga-holic), or fishing (fishaholic). Following Boroson's example, establish class by separating compulsive behavior from normal.

2. Do you know any students who are compulsive about their studies? If so, construct an extended definition of the study addict.

3. Write a reply to the maxim, "Hard work never hurt anyone."

THE LIBERAL TEACHER
Gilbert Highet

BIOGRAPHICAL SKETCH

Gilbert Highet was born in Scotland in 1906. He received an M.A. degree from Oxford, where he taught for several years. Later, he became an American citizen and taught Greek and Latin at Columbia University in New York. He died in January of 1978. He received numerous awards and honorary degrees, wrote many scholarly articles, and is well known for his books about the classics and about teaching and learning. Among his highly regarded works are The Classical Tradition, The Art of Teaching, Man's Unconquerable Mind, *and* The Anatomy of Satire.

PRE-READING

1. What does the information in the title, the opening paragraph, and the last line tell you of the approach to be taken in this essay?

2. From the biographical sketch, do you accept Highet as an authority on his subject? Do you expect him to be somewhat biased toward a particular form of teaching? Why?

[1] What should be the character of the ideal teacher? What kind of man or woman is best fitted to give a liberal education?

[2] This is a serious question, both for teachers and for the general public. Teachers are respected; not always admired. We are praised for regularity and a sense of duty; but most people do not necessarily expect us to be bright. Doctors are held in honor, and lawyers are esteemed for their sharp intelligence; but teachers are sometimes thought of as respectable drudges—like hospital nurses, or even like attendants in an asylum for the harmless insane.

FROM Gilbert Highet, *The Immortal Profession: The Joys of Teaching and Learning* (New York: Weybright & Talley, 1976), pp. 37–55. Copyright © 1976 by Gilbert Highet. Reprinted by permission of Longman, Inc., and the author.

Yet they have high ideals, and often suffer in pursuing them. The man in the street scarcely realizes that many forms of business, some major industries, and one or two minor professions could be completely abolished without gravely injuring American society; whereas the disappearance—or even what we see in some quarters, the continuous neglect and degradation—of the teaching profession must mean a disaster to the entire nation. If the average man can be made to understand that our careers, although ill rewarded, are not merely unsuccessful attempts to make money, but are endeavors to attain a difficult set of ideals, ideals valuable to the whole community, perhaps he will take us, and his responsibilities to us, more seriously than he and his elected representatives now do.

³ The question is serious, and well worth the effort involved in trying to find an answer to it. Yet it cannot be answered precisely. There is not even a single answer to it. The definition of the liberal educator is, and ought to be, different in different countries of the world. His or her task in India would be disparate from his task in Sweden, and that again from his task in Brazil. And it is highly possible that the ideal teacher would be different in different parts of the United States. . . . Different, the answers to the question may be; but we shall not expect to find them conflicting with one another. A good doctor in Calcutta is unlike a good doctor in Detroit; but ultimately the two have the same purpose in life. In the same way, even if the answers to this question are different in various countries, and even in various sections of the United States, we shall expect to find them convergent, rather than inharmonious or contrary. Basically, all liberal educators are trying to do the same thing.

⁴ We are searching, not for the ideal teacher of *any* subject under the sun (boxing, hydrostatics, nursing, logic), but for the ideal teacher of the liberal subjects: the teacher who is best capable of giving a liberal education. This is the type of education which does not necessarily fit a man or woman to earn money, but prepares them to do what is ultimately more important and more difficult—to live well, using *all* their capacities. . . . This distinction, oversimplified though it may be, illuminates the difference between liberal and technical education. There are all kinds of skills which can be taught, and which will help the men and women who acquire them to make a living; but if these men and women have not also a liberal education, they are little better than clever slaves. The word "liberal" means "fitted for a free man," one who is not a slave to a machine or to an office or to a single money-making skill.

⁵ It would be a mistake to set the teacher's ideal uncomfortably high: for it is terribly discouraging . . . to learn that the ideal teacher would be endowed with so many admirable qualities that no human being could possibly realize them all. We are looking for the optimum character and accomplishment which, with proper application and decent luck, could be attained by a teacher who saw it clearly in his mind. Therefore we begin with the essentials.

⁶ There are some qualities which every teacher ought to possess—or to train himself to possess. These are the qualities which he wants his pupils to acquire.

⁷ The young learn much (more than they realize) by the silent power of example. In all professions this is understood. A surgeon does not explain to his students that it is their duty to be deft and neat and economical of action. When he does an operation, he is deft and neat: he economizes on effort, and on motion, and on pain. By watching him, the learners realize that they must imitate him until they too possess these qualities. In the U.S. Marine Corps training course for officers, one of the most powerful lessons is never spoken aloud. It is instilled simply by the force of example. By watching senior officers, the young officer candidates learn that they are expected to become taut and keen and energetic; and yet easy in their manner. . . .

⁸ Obviously, therefore, a teacher must have regular habits: regular without being machinelike. Young people tend to be sloppy and even anarchical. . . . If their teachers are obviously living regularly and effectively and happily, the pupils will learn (then or later) to live in the same way. Many a boy whose home life was a morass of untidiness and improvisation, because his parents were not house trained, has escaped from it and shaped his own character and career satisfactorily, because he admired and imitated a teacher whose life was orderly and yet humane and satisfying.

⁹ The teacher ought also to believe in the power of the human will. The young are creatures of impulse. . . . Nearly all of them lack confidence in their own will power. Some of them scarcely understand how much can be achieved by the will, even if it is imperfectly trained. Many of them shrink from the effort involved in consistent living, recoil from it all through their careers, and drift from youth to middle age to death like a ship which is all sails and mast, without a rudder. Yet, if the teacher is a man or woman of strong will power, he/she will show them what can be achieved, even in adversity, by determination. Both by example and by precept it is the duty of the liberal teacher to instill in his pupils a conviction of the value and power of the controlled human will. The connection between will power and teaching, the connection between will power and intellectual work generally, has not always been recognized. In the present time, because of our dangerous slide into complete permissiveness both in the home and in the school, it tends to be ignored or denied. . . .

¹⁰ A liberal education is based largely on training the mind. Therefore the good teacher will let it be clearly seen that he believes in the power of the mind and the satisfactions of spiritual life. He will be an intellectual. He will enjoy books, and he will go on enlarging and refining his taste throughout his life. I remember that it was a revelation to me in my middle teens when I discovered, simply from observing the behavior of one of my teachers in the school library, that there existed what W. B. Yeats called "the fascination of what's difficult." Certain books, certain types of thought and emotion expressed in words, were (I realized) intended to be obscure; meant to be grappled with; would always present problems; and yet, in their very complexities and insolubilities, contained delight. A good teacher will be a man who is happy when he is alone in a library.

¹¹ Furthermore, a humane educator will delight in the fine arts, and will either practice religion or respect religion. He will not deliberately refrain from uttering the word "beauty" or the word "God." He need not be constantly proclaiming them, nor need he emphasize them and expound them at great length. . . . Even without long speeches, the young can very soon detect when one of their teachers is a man or woman who secretly despises art and history and literature and the life of the mind, and who thinks religion is at best a matter of formal observance. Though it is possible that they may merely scorn him or her for this, it is also a grave danger that they may come to imitate their teacher, and so deny themselves many of the highest satisfactions and exaltations of this life.

¹² Many theorists have written about education as if it were chiefly intended to teach young people to live in society. Of course that is one of its purposes. Social living is complex and difficult. Yet it is clear, when we look at young men and women, that they also need to be taught how to live with themselves. Many of the most important things in life happen to us in solitude. Intellectual discoveries, powerful emotional experiences, enlargements of the soul, come more commonly to a man or a woman alone in a quiet room or sitting in the heart of wild nature, than in the restless and noisy and often thoughtless group. (Is this one of the weaknesses of Protestantism as compared with Roman Catholicism, that it provides very little for those who need to be alone?) When it arrives, the good society will ensure every one of us both life in common, and the equally precious life of privacy. The teacher who wishes to open and expand the hearts of his pupils ought himself to show that he respects and enjoys both these complementary styles of life.

¹³ All these, and others too, are the moral and intellectual qualities which the good teacher will possess. The young teacher has few of them, if any. Yet, if he or she knows that it is his duty to acquire them and to learn how to practice them—in just the same way as he learns the niceties of his own special subject—he or she will do so; and, when he is mature, will exercise them with the same confidence an experienced surgeon enjoys when he operates, with something of the same devotion as that which fills the heart of a minister when he offers up a prayer.

¹⁴ Turn now to harder and more complex questions. Is it possible to define the attitude of the ideal teacher to society? to his subject? to his pupils?

¹⁵ We have been told, and some of us have believed, that in his attitude to society the teacher should be militant: that he ought to be a strong advocate of immediate change, the architect of a new world, and, in fact, something close to an active revolutionary. . . .

¹⁶ Is this principle justified by the careers of distinguished teachers of the past? Have they been politically active inside their classrooms? Have they been revolutionaries?

¹⁷ Usually they have not. Men and women who felt strongly that a radical political change was needed have usually detached themselves from education altogether, and have adopted the more direct methods of electioneering and

propagandizing among adult citizens. Some teachers have been convinced conservatives in politics. Some have stood utterly outside the distracting world of political change. Some have been, during their spare time, active in political organizations, but have said little or nothing of their work to their classes. Most good teachers have apparently felt that education and politics do not mix, at least in school, and have been reticent about current political issues.

[18] On the other hand many distinguished teachers have been devoted to the cause of social reform, to the abolition of unearned and unjustified privilege, to the fuller utilization of all the human resources of their countries. Even when they were convinced that it was desirable to maintain the political structure of their times, they were often eager to make it more flexible, to induce it to nurture and to employ talents which might otherwise be wasted. . . . It is in the field of social reform rather than politics that a teacher, if his interests lie in that direction, can be most effective. Take a simple but striking instance. Which has produced the more remarkable effects on our civilization: the political agitation that led to the establishment of votes for women, or the slower and less spectacular social and educational movement that caused the admission of women into every institution of higher education?

[19] It is well to make this point clear, because the word "liberal" has frequently been misused by political writers. It has even been suggested that a liberal education ought to be controlled by the principles of those political parties which preempt the word "liberal" in their titles or their programs. This is a mistake, and it is a dangerous mistake. The true liberal respects the maximum development of every human being. Necessarily, therefore, he is opposed to the regulation of every citizen's life by an all-embracing system of law and to the control of all his activities by the all-seeing (though not all-wise) state. The worship of government is not liberalism, and is in fact opposed to those principles which are truly liberal.

[20] Can we define the attitude of the ideal teacher to his subject? Surely we can. It seems clear that the liberal educator will have two beliefs, and demonstrate them constantly in word and act.

[21] The first is the firm conviction that the subject he or she teaches is genuinely and permanently important. The teacher of French who never reads a French book for pleasure, the teacher of history who does not enjoy visiting historic sites and examining original documents, are frauds; and their pupils soon detect their fraudulence. . . . Yet there are many teachers . . . who have no interest in their own subject and no respect for it. They teach it because it provides a salary and prepares for a pension; otherwise it bores and even disgusts them. Such an attitude also bores and disgusts their pupils—with the additional danger that the pupils may well come to be bored and disgusted with all education and with all intellectual activity. . . . No, the good teacher believes in his subject and is genuinely, unashamedly enthusiastic about it. He will not shrink from saying to his pupils:

> I give you the end of a golden string;
> Only wind it into a ball—
> It will lead you into Heaven's gate,
> Built in Jerusalem's wall.

[22] Here we must make a distinction which is not always recognized, but is vitally important. The subjects of a liberal education are valuable for two different reasons and ought to be taught for two different reasons.

[23] One is that they are precious parts of our culture. They must be kept alive in our minds, for their own sake. It would be a miserable country which neglected history so as to forget the meaning of its own past; or neglected languages so as to be unable to read the writings of other nations and to enter into their thoughts.

[24] But it is also important for the teacher to train other teachers—scholars and communicators who will continue to explore and to explain the subject to which he has devoted himself.

[25] In colleges and universities here and in Europe one sometimes sees that these two different principles are confused. There are some teachers who regard their own subject as though it could not possibly improve the mind of the average young man and woman or contain any intellectual interest for the public in general. Their sole interest, besides doing research, is to produce other researchers. This is mistaken. And it is equally mistaken to talk of a subject as though it were of broad general interest, but could not capture the attention of any student enough to make him devote his life to working in it. . . . The liberal educator will aim at maintaining the importance of his subject (whatever it may be) both by making it known to all his pupils as part of their cultural equipment, and by stimulating a few of them to make it their life's work.

[26] The second conviction which ought to fill the mind of the ideal teacher, with reference to his subject, is that it is broad rather than narrow, deep rather than shallow, infinite rather than limited. Only those who teach very young children should try to convince their pupils that everything can be found out and understood. Those who teach young men and women should let it be seen that they believe complete knowledge is desirable but unattainable.

·   ·   ·

[27] Accordingly the liberal educator will both encourage and discipline his pupils by explaining to them that their minds deserve every respect, and yet can attain only an approximation to the truth; that the world, or even their one particular subject, is greater than any single brain can ever grasp. This is one of the best lessons that any teacher can give his pupils: particularly nowadays, when so much imperfect knowledge and inadequately sifted data and prejudiced guesswork masquerade under the name of "science." So much harm has been done in the world by those who believed that they were in possession of the whole truth, and that those who differed from them were

absolutely and wickedly wrong. . . . The effective teacher of the humane subjects may acknowledge the imperfection of knowledge by confessing his own errors and oversights. He may even admit his own prejudices—no, not prejudices, but considered preferences. The teacher of algebra can scarcely show a preference for one type of equation over another; but the historian and other teachers of liberal subjects can with advantage make it clear that they believe one period more fertile, one creative artist more admirable than another. They should not expect their students to follow their choices blindly, but rather hope to stimulate them into criticism and creative disagreement.

[28] In his attitude to his subject, then, the ideal teacher will be a liberal traditionalist. He will explain to the students (and to himself) that the subject he teaches is important; that its central truths are reasonably well established; that it is in its totality beyond the range of human comprehension; but that it may interest some of them enough to become their life's work, and must improve and uplift all of them by becoming part of their spiritual capital.

[29] The third problem in the work of the liberal educator is his attitude to his pupils. And this can best be defined by examining what the best teachers of the past have done: what they have felt about their pupils, and how they have treated them.

[30] Almost universally we find that they have not had a single relationship to their pupils, but rather a double one. They have maintained a tension composed of complementary feelings; and the difficulty of being a good teacher is largely due to the fact that it is hard to maintain such a tension without suffering oneself or making the pupils suffer.

[31] For instance, the best teachers give their pupils both a sense of order, discipline, control; and a powerful stimulus which urges them to take their destinies in their own hands, kick over all rules, and transgress all boundaries. Sometimes their pupils complain that they do not know what is wanted: are they to be puppets? or original geniuses? partners? or subdued subservient apprentices? The answer is that their teachers want to accustom them to both the essential types of mental activity: self-surrender to an external aim and purpose, and free development of their individual talents.

. . .

[32] Another tension in teaching is that between the group and the individual. However much the teacher is tempted to treat the exceptional pupil (whether very good or very bad) as a special case and to devote to him or her a great deal of time and attention, he must remember that this is not his sole duty, and usually is not his main duty. His first obligation is to his class: to the group. Within the class, he should learn to bring out the personalities and answer the special needs of each of the young people who are his pupils: he must make them feel that they are understood as individuals. But at the same time he must make them realize that they are part of a larger organization, and in some ways subordinate to it.

[33] In our work there are many more of these tensions. Most of the mistakes committed in teaching are made by those who believe that no such tensions exist or ought to exist. But the relation between teacher and pupil is a human relationship, and no relationship between human beings is ever simple.

[34] In fact, there is a tension between antitheses in the entire process of education. Education means a recognition of the force and value of traditional knowledge; but it also means a will to create and to advance what is new. The liberal educator knows that there is a central core of transmitted knowledge and discernment, without which his pupils can scarcely exist as human beings; but he also knows that this body of transmitted beliefs must always be subject to criticism and revision, and will always profit from addition. Such development continues permanently through the existence of the human race.

[35] Still we have not mentioned nearly all the qualities which the liberal educator ought to have. We might suggest that he should be trained to eat grass and to grow a thick coat of fur: so that he could live on his meager salary, without wasting it on buying expensive food and clothing; or that he should have no wife and family but spend each summer as a rootless hitch-hiker, thereby becoming able (without going bankrupt) to visit the big libraries and the foreign lands which provide so much of his spiritual nourishment. . . . Teachers are not rewarded with . . . anything like the value of the time and effort which they expend.

[36] . . . The most important qualification of the liberal educator is neither helped nor hindered by his poverty: perhaps it is even encouraged by his being hard up. This is that he must be an individual. He must not be a machine. He must not be a rubber stamp. He must not repeat the thoughts of others. He must not even repeat his own thoughts. Life is change within permanence, and the individual therefore must change within a fixed pattern of ideals. The liberal teacher is not a type, but an individual. . . .

ANALYTICAL READING

1. Starting with the opening paragraph, Highet uses many questions. Is this device effective? Are the questions always answered? Illustrate. Might this extensive use of questions reflect his profession?

2. How does Highet use definition in paragraph 4?

3. What does the writer think is the importance of a liberal education? What distinction does he make between a liberal and a technical education?

4. According to Highet, what are the moral and intellectual characteristics the liberal teacher should have? the attitudes? What are Highet's major subclasses of attitudes?

5. How does Highet think liberal teachers should feel about their subject?

6. Does Highet often equate liberal teaching with "good" teaching? Point out some instances. How does this reveal his own bias about teaching?

7. What part does tension play in teaching? How does Highet subclassify *tension?* Do you agree with his points concerning this aspect of teaching and learning?

REFLECTING

Point: In your opinion, does Highet achieve any other purpose besides defining *liberal teacher?* If so, what?

Organization: Does Highet's extended definition follow the structure outlined in the introduction to expository writing (see page 204)? How does he establish *liberal teacher* as a class? Make an outline of his subclassification process.

Support: How does Highet use examples and comparison and contrast for support? Find some individual sentences in which Highet shows contrast between points. Discuss the sentence structures he uses for this purpose.

Synthesis: Have you had teachers who have some or most of the characteristics (distinguishing features) of Highet's liberal teacher"? As a student, how do you respond to such teachers? How do you remember them? In this essay, does Highet exhibit any of the traits of a liberal teacher? Could Highet's "liberal teacher" become one of Boroson's "workaholics" (pages 229–34)? Why or why not?

Evaluation: How did you react to the comparisons in paragraphs 2 and 17? Does Highet's article give you a better concept of a liberal education?" Why or why not? Has he stated his ideas clearly and supported them effectively? Explain.

FROM READING TO WRITING

1. Write an extended definition of an "unliberal" teacher.

2. The word *liberal* has many connotations. Starting from Highet's use of the word, write an extended definition of *liberal.*

Process Analysis

12 WAYS TO GET MORE OUT OF STUDYING

Judi R. Kesselman

BIOGRAPHICAL SKETCH

Judi R. Kesselman (1934–   ) is a native of New York City and has a B.A. from Brooklyn College. She has been an editor for a number of popular magazines and is currently an instructor in the Communications and English Programs of the University of Wisconsin Extension Services. But her true vocation is free-lance writing, and her publications include Stopping Out: A Guide to Leaving College and Getting Back In, *written with Franklynn Peterson (1976),* The Do-It-Yourself Custom Van Book *(1977), and many articles for such publications as* Seventeen, Playgirl, The New York Times, *and* McCall's. *She is currently preparing a book for students, tentatively titled* How to Get Your (Father's) Money's Worth Out of College, *which will provide hints for studying, for getting higher grades, and for budgeting time.*

PRE-READING

1. From the title and the opening paragraph, what do you expect the article to do? How would you classify such an article?

2. What devices does Kesselman use to attract reader interest and to establish authority in the first three paragraphs?

¹ Effective studying is the one element guaranteed to produce good grades in school. But it's ironic that the one thing almost never taught in school is how to study effectively.

² For example, an important part of studying is note-taking, yet few students receive any instruction on this skill. At best you are told simply, "You had better take notes," but not given any advice on what to record or how to use the material as a learning tool.

³ Fortunately reliable data on how to study does exist. It has been demonstrated scientifically that one method of note-taking is better than others

and that there are routes to more effective reviewing, memorizing and text-book reading as well. Following are twelve proven steps you can take to improve your study habits. We guarantee that if you *really* use them, your grades will go up.

⁴ 1. *Use behavior modification on yourself.* It works. Remember Pavlov's dogs, salivating every time they heard a bell ring? Just as association worked with them, it also can work with you. If you attempt, as nearly as possible, to study the same subject at the same time in the same place each day, you will find after a very short while that when you get to that time and place you're automatically in the subject groove. Train your brain to think French on a time-place cue, and it will no longer take you ten minutes a day to get in the French Mood. Not only will you save the time and emotional energy you once needed to psych yourself up to French or whatever else, but the experts say you'll also remember more of what you're studying!

⁵ 2. *Don't spend more than an hour at a time on one subject.* In fact, if you're doing straight memorization, don't spend more than twenty or thirty minutes. First, when you're under an imposed time restriction, you use the time more efficiently. (Have you noticed how much studying you manage to cram into the day before the big exam? That's why it's called *cramming.*)

⁶ Second, psychologists say that you learn best in short takes. (Also remember that two or three hours of study without noise or other distractions is more effective than ten hours trying to work amid bedlam.) In fact, studies have shown that as much is learned in four one-hour sessions distributed over four days as in one marathon six-hour session. That's because between study times, while you're sleeping or eating or reading a novel, your mind subconsciously works on absorbing what you've learned. So it counts as study time too.

⁷ Keep in mind that when you're memorizing, whether it's math formulas or a foreign language or names and dates, you're doing much more real learning more quickly than when you're reading a social studies text or an English essay.

⁸ 3. *Keep alert by taking frequent rest breaks.* The specialists say you'll get your most effective studying done if you take a ten-minute break between subjects. (Again, it's akin to behavior modification. Pavlov's dogs were taught to respond on cue by being rewarded with tidbits. The break is your reward.) Dr. Walter Pauk, director of the Reading and Study Center at Cornell University, suggests you take that short break whenever you feel you need one, so you don't fritter your time away in clock-watching and anticipating your break.

⁹ 4. *Study similar subjects at separate times.* Brain waves are like radio waves: if there isn't enough space between inputs, you get interference. The more similar the kinds of learning taking place, the more interference. So separate your study periods for courses with similar subject matter. Follow your hour of German with an hour of chemistry or history, not with Spanish.

[10] 5. *Avoid studying during your sleepy times.* Psychologists have found that everyone has a certain time of day when he or she gets sleepy. Don't try to study during that time. (But don't go to sleep either. It hardly ever refreshes.) Instead, schedule some physical activity for that period, such as recreation or instrument practice. If you have a pile of schoolwork, use that time to sort your notes or clear up your desk and get your books together or study with a friend.

[11] 6. *Study at the most productive time for your course.* If it's a lecture course, do your studying soon *after* class; if it's a course in which students are called on to recite or answer questions, study *before* class. After the lectures you can review, revise and organize your notes. Before the recitation classes you can spend your time memorizing, brushing up on your facts and preparing questions about the previous recitation. Question-posing is a good technique for helping the material sink in and for pinpointing areas in which you need more work.

[12] 7. *Learn the note-taking system the experts recommend.* Quite a bit of research has been done on note-taking, and one system has emerged as the best.

[13] Use 8½-by-11-inch loose-leaf paper and write on *just* one side. (This may seem wasteful, but it's one time when economizing is secondary.) Put a topic heading on each page. Then take the time to rule your page as follows:

[14] A. If the course is one in which lecture and text are closely related, use the 2-3-3-2 technique: Make columns of two inches down the left-hand side for recall clues, three inches in the middle for lecture notes and three inches on the right side for text notes, and leave a two-inch space across the bottom of the page for your own observations and conclusions.

[15] B. If it's a course where the lectures and the reading are not closely related, use separate pages for class notes and reading notes, following the 2-5-1 technique: two inches at left for clues, five in the middle for notes and an inch at the right for observations. (After a while you won't need to draw actual lines.)

[16] In the center section or sections belong your regular notes, taken in the form you've evolved during your years of schooling. Probably you have also evolved your own shorthand system, such as using a *g* for all *-ing* endings, an ampersand (*&*) for *and,* and abbreviations for many words (e.g., *govt.* for *government* and *evaptn.* for *evaporation*).

[17] The clue column is the key to higher marks. As soon as possible after you've written your notes, take the time to read them over—not studying them, just reading them. Check now, while it's all still fresh, to see whether you've left out anything important or put down anything incorrectly, and make your changes. Then, in that left-hand column, set down clue words to the topics in your notes. These clue words should not repeat information but should designate or label the kind of information that's in your notes. They're the kind of clues you would put on crib sheets. For example, to remember the information contained so far in this section on note-taking, you need just the following clues: 8½-by-11 loose-leaf, one side; 2-3-3-2; 2-5-1. As you can see, they're simply memory cues to use later on in your actual studying.

[18] Dr. Robert A. Palmatier, assistant professor of reading education at the University of Georgia, suggests that you study for tests in the following manner: Take out your loose-leaf pages and shift them around so the order makes the most sense for studying. Take the first page and cover up the notes portion, leaving just the clues visible. See if you can recall the notes that go with the clues, and as you get a page right, set it aside. If you're going to be taking a short-answer test, shuffle up your note pages so they're out of order. (That's why it's important to use just one side of the paper.) "This approach provides for learning without the support of logical sequence," Dr. Palmatier says, "thus closely approximating the actual pattern in which the information must be recalled." If you're going to be taking an essay test, you can safely predict that "those areas on which the most notes are taken will most often be the areas on which essay questions will be based."

[19] The beauty of the clue word note-taking method is that it provides a painless way to do the one thing proved to be most conducive to remembering what you've learned—actively thinking about your notes and making logical sense of them in your mind. If instead you just keep going over your recorded notes, not only will you get bored, but you'll be trying to memorize in the worst way possible.

[20] 8. *Memorize actively, not passively.* Researchers have found that the worst way to memorize—the way that takes the most time and results in the least retention—is to simply read something over and over again. If that's the way you memorize, forget it. Instead use as many of your senses as possible. Try to visualize in concrete terms, to get a picture in your head. In addition to sight use sound: Say the words out loud and listen to yourself saying them. Use association: Relate the fact to be learned to something personally significant or find a logical tie-in. For example, when memorizing dates, relate them to important events whose dates you already know. Use mnemonics: For example, the phrase "Every good boy does fine" is used for remembering the names of the musical notes on the lines of the treble clef. Use acronyms, like OK4R, which is the key to remembering the steps in the reading method outlined in point 9, below.

[21] 9. *Take more time for your reading.* It really takes less time in the long run! And read with a purpose. Instead of just starting at the beginning and reading through to the end, you'll really do the assignment a lot faster and remember a lot more if you first take the time to follow the OK4R method devised by Dr. Walter Pauk.

[22] *O. Overview:* Read the title, the introductory and summarizing paragraphs and all the headings included in the reading material. Then you'll have a general idea of what topics will be discussed.

[23] *K. Key ideas:* Go back and skim the text for the key ideas (usually found in the first sentence of each paragraph). Also read the italics and bold type, bulleted sections, itemizations, pictures and tables.

[24] *R1. Read* your assignment from beginning to end. You'll be able to do it

quickly, because you already know where the author is going and what he's trying to prove.

25 *R2. Recall:* Put aside the text and say or write, in a few key words or sentences, the major points of what you've read. It has been proven that most forgetting takes place immediately after initial learning. Dr. Pauk says that *one minute spent in immediate recall nearly doubles retention of that piece of data!*

26 *R3. Reflect:* The previous step helps to fix the material in your mind. To really keep it there forever, relate it to other knowledge: Find relationships and significance for what you've read.

27 *R4. Review:* This step doesn't take place right away. It should be done for the next short quiz, and then again for later tests throughout the term. Several reviews will make that knowledge indelibly yours.

28 *10. Devise a color and sign system* for marking your personal books. Dr. Palmatier suggests red for main ideas, blue for dates and numbers, yellow for supporting facts. Circles, boxes, stars and checks in the margins can also be utilized to make reviewing easy.

29 *11. Clue your lecture notes* too. Underline, star or otherwise mark the ideas that your teacher says are important, thoughts that he says you'll be coming back to later, items that he says are common mistakes. Watch for the words—such as *therefore* and *in essence*—that tell you he's summarizing. Always record his examples. In fact, in such subjects as math your notes should consist mainly of the teacher's examples.

30 Pay closest attention in your note-taking to the last few minutes of class time. Often a teacher gets sidetracked and runs out of time. He may jam up to a half-hour's content into the last five or ten minutes of his lecture. Get down that packed few minutes' worth. If necessary, stay on after the bell to get it all down.

31 *12. Beware the underlined textbook.* Of course, if the book doesn't belong to you, you won't be underlining at all. But if you underline, do it sparingly. The best underlining is not as productive as the worst note-taking.

32 Over-underlining is a common fault of students; only the key words in a paragraph should be underlined. It should never be done in ink (something you think is important at the time may not seem so in retrospect), and it should be done only after you've finished the "OK" part of your OK4R reading.

33 If you're buying your books secondhand, *never* buy one that has already been underlined. You would tend to rely on it—and you have no idea whether the hand that held the pencil got an *A* or an *F* in the course!

34 Research has proven that it's not how much time you study that counts but how well. In fact, in at least one survey students who studied more than thirty-five hours a week came out with poorer grades than those who studied less. Use your study time wisely, and you too will come out ahead.

ANALYTICAL READING

1. What audience is the article directed to? Other than subject matter and the magazine it was published in, what clues to the audience can you find?

2. How does the article use cause-and-effect relationships? Cite some that attracted you particularly as you read.

3. Did any of the suggested study techniques surprise you? Which ones? How does this method contrast with your usual way of studying?

4. What reasons does the writer give for using clue words in your notes? Do you think it might be a useful studying device? If so, elaborate.

5. How are mnemonics and acronyms helpful? Explain with your own examples, if possible.

6. What suggestions involve an awareness of form—paragraph, sentence, thesis?

7. Is underlining encouraged? Discuss.

REFLECTING

Point: What is the main purpose of the analysis? Do you think that the purpose is kept before the reader throughout? Are the introduction and conclusion helpful in accomplishing the purpose?

Organization: Although the organization does not follow the usual chronology of a process analysis, the article still qualifies as one. Is there anything important in the sequence of the steps—for example, from most valuable to least, from most unusual to least?

Support: What devices does Kesselman use to give added weight to her suggestions? Discuss the effectiveness of the numbering system and the instructions in italic type.

Synthesis: As you read the suggestions, did you find some that you have already developed? What bad habits of studying (according to the article) are you guilty of? How do they relate to the reading method set forth in this text?

Evaluation: How effectively do you think Kesselman handles the material? Does she sound "bossy" or condescending? How does she temper the "dos and don'ts" quality of the article?

FROM READING TO WRITING

1. Write a process analysis on "_____ Ways to Keep from Studying."

2. Write a process analysis outlining the method of "cramming."

3. Write a process analysis describing the sequence of steps involved in learning a new skill, such as driving, changing oil in a car, roofing a house, or applying makeup.

HOW TO EAT AN ICE-CREAM CONE
L. Rust Hills

BIOGRAPHICAL SKETCH

L. (Lawrence) Rust Hills was born in Brooklyn, New York, in 1924. He received a B.S. degree from the Merchant Marine Academy, then earned B.A. and M.A. degrees from Wesleyan University. He has taught at several colleges, including Carleton, Columbia, and the New School for Social Research. In addition to being a former editor of Esquire, *the* Saturday Evening Post, *and* Audience *magazines, Hills has edited several anthologies, the best known being* How We Live *(with Malcolm Cowley). Currently a freelance writer, his articles, reviews, interviews, and humorous sketches have appeared in* The New Yorker, Esquire, McCall's, Harper's, *and other magazines.*

PRE-READING

1. What words in the title indicate the purpose of the essay?

2. What tone is established in the opening and closing paragraphs? Do you expect it to be a serious discussion? What might you expect from the fact that the article was first published in *The New Yorker?*

3. To what readers is the essay directed? Explain.

¹ Before you even get the cone, you have to do a lot of planning about it. We'll assume that you lost the argument in the car and that the family has decided to break the automobile journey and stop at an ice-cream stand for cones. Get things straight with them right from the start. Tell them that after they have their cones there will be an imaginary circle six feet away from the car and that no one—man, woman, or especially child—will be allowed to cross the line and reënter the car until his ice-cream cone has been entirely consumed and he has cleaned himself up. Emphasize: Automobiles and ice-cream cones don't mix. Explain: Melted ice cream, children, is a fluid that is eternally sticky. One drop of it on a car door handle spreads to the seat covers, to trousers, to hands, and thence to the steering wheel, the gearshift, the rearview mirror, all the knobs of the dashboard—spreads *everywhere* and lasts *forever*, spreads from a nice old car like this, which might have to be abandoned because of stickiness, right into a nasty new car, in secret ways that even scientists don't understand. If necessary, even make a joke: "The family that eats ice-cream cones together sticks together." Then let their mother explain the joke and tell them you don't mean half of what you say, and no, we won't be getting a new car.

FROM L. Rust Hills, *How to Do Things Right* (New York: Doubleday, 1972), pp. 76–86. Reprinted by permission of Doubleday and Company, Inc. The article first appeared in *The New Yorker*, copyright © 1968 by The New Yorker Magazine, Inc.

² Blessed are the children who always eat the same flavor of ice cream or always know beforehand what kind they will want. Such good children should be quarantined from those who want to "wait and see what flavors there are." It's a sad thing to observe a beautiful young child who has always been perfectly happy with a plain vanilla ice-cream cone being subverted by a young schoolmate who has been invited along for the weekend—a pleasant and polite visitor, perhaps, but spoiled by permissive parents and scarred by an overactive imagination. This schoolmate has a flair for contingency planning: "Well, I'll have banana if they have banana, but if they don't have banana then I'll have peach, if it's fresh peach, and if they don't have banana or fresh peach I'll see what else they have that's like that, like maybe fresh strawberry or something, and if they don't have that or anything like that that's good I'll just have chocolate marshmallow chip or chocolate ripple or something like that." Then—turning to one's own once simple and innocent child, now already corrupt and thinking fast—the schoolmate invites a similar rigmarole. "What kind are *you* going to have?"

³ I'm a great believer in contingency planning, but none of this is realistic. Few adults, and even fewer children, are able to make up their minds beforehand what kind of ice-cream cone they'll want. It would be nice if they could all be lined up in front of the man who is making up the cones and just snap smartly when their turn came, "Strawberry, please," "Vanilla, please," "Chocolate, please." But of course it never happens like that. There is always a great discussion, a great jostling and craning of necks and leaning over the counter to see down into the tubs of ice cream, and much interpersonal consultation—"What kind are *you* having"—back and forth, as if that should make any difference. Until finally the first child's turn comes and he asks the man, "What kinds do you have?"

⁴ Now, this is the stupidest question in the world, because there is always a sign posted saying what kinds of ice cream they have. As I tell the children, that's what they put the sign up there for—so you won't have to ask what kinds of ice cream they have. The man gets sick of telling everybody all the different kinds of ice cream they have, so they put a sign up there that *says*. You're supposed to read it, not ask the man.

⁵ "All right, but the sign doesn't say strawberry."

⁶ "Well, that means they don't have strawberry."

⁷ "But there *is* strawberry, right there."

⁸ "That must be raspberry or something." (Look again at the sign. Raspberry isn't there, either.)

⁹ When the child's turn actually comes, he says, "Do you have strawberry?"

¹⁰ "Sure."

¹¹ "What other kinds do you have?"

¹² The trouble is, of course, that they put up that sign saying what flavors they have, with little cardboard inserts to put in or take out flavors, way back when they first opened the store. But they never change the sign—or not often

enough. They always have flavors that aren't on the list, and often they don't have flavors that *are* on the list. Children know this—whether innately or from earliest experience it would be hard to say. The ice-cream man knows it, too. Even grownups learn it eventually. There will always be chaos and confusion and mind-changing and general uproar when ice-cream cones are being ordered, and there has not been, is not, and will never be any way to avoid it.

¹³ Human beings are incorrigibly restless and dissatisfied, always in search of new experiences and sensations, seldom content with the familiar. It is this, I think, that accounts for people wanting to have a taste of your cone, and wanting you to have a taste of theirs. *"Do* have a taste of this fresh peach—it's delicious," my wife used to say to me, very much (I suppose) the way Eve wanted Adam to taste her delicious apple. An insinuating look of calculating curiosity would film my wife's eyes—the same look those beatiful scary women in those depraved Italian films give a man they're interested in. "How's *yours?"* she would say. For this reason, I always order chocolate chip now. Down through the years, all those close enough to me to feel entitled to ask for a taste of my cone—namely my wife and children—have learned what chocolate chip tastes like, so they have no legitimate reason to ask me for a taste. As for testing other people's cones, never do it. The reasoning here is that if it tastes good, you'll wish you'd had it; if it tastes bad, you'll have had a taste of something that tastes bad; if it doesn't taste either good or bad, then you won't have missed anything. Of course no person in his right mind ever *would* want to taste anyone else's cone, but it is useful to have good, logical reasons for hating the thought of it.

¹⁴ Another important thing. Never let the man hand you the ice-cream cones for the whole group. There is no sight more pathetic than some bumbling disorganized papa holding four ice-cream cones in two hands, with his money still in his pocket, when the man says, "Eighty cents." What does he do then? He can't hand the cones back to the man to hold while he fishes in his pocket for the money, for the man has just given them to *him.* He can start passing them out to the kids, but at least one of them will have gone back to the car to see how the dog is doing, or have been sent round in back by his mother to wash his hands or something. And even if papa does get them distributed, he's still going to be left with his own cone in one hand while he tries to get his money with the other. Meanwhile, of course, the man is very impatient, and the next group is asking him, "What flavors do you have?"

¹⁵ No, never let the man hand you the cones of others. Make him hand them out to each kid in turn. That way, too, you won't get those disgusting blobs of butter pecan and black raspberry on your own chocolate chip. And insist that he tell you how much it all costs and settle with him *before* he hands you your own cone. Make sure everyone has got paper napkins and everything *before* he hands you your own cone. Get *everything* straight before he hands you your own cone. Then, as he hands you your own cone, reach out and take it from him. Strange, magical, dangerous moment? It shares some-

thing of the mysterious, sick thrill that soldiers are said to feel on the eve of a great battle.

[16] Now, consider for a moment just exactly what it is that you are about to be handed. It is a huge, irregular mass of ice cream, faintly domed at the top from the metal scoop, which has first produced it and then insecurely balanced it on the uneven top edge of a hollow inverted cone made out of the most brittle and fragile of materials. Clumps of ice cream hang over the side, very loosely attached to the main body. There is always much more ice cream than the cone could hold, even if the ice cream were tamped down into the cone, which of course it isn't. And the essence of ice cream is that it melts. It doesn't just stay there teetering in this irregular, top-heavy mass; it also melts. And it melts *fast*. And it doesn't just melt—it melts into a sticky fluid that *cannot* be wiped off. The only thing one person could hand to another that might possibly be more dangerous is a live hand grenade from which the pin had been pulled five seconds earlier. And of course if anybody offered you that, you could say, "Oh. Uh, well—no thanks."

[17] Ice-cream men handle cones routinely, and are inured. They are like professionals who are used to handling sticks of TNT; their movements are quick and skillful. An ice-cream man will pass a cone to you casually, almost carelessly. Never accept a cone on this basis! Too many brittle sugar cones (the only good kind) are crushed or chipped or their ice-cream tops knocked askew, by this casual sort of transfer from hand to hand. If the ice-cream man is attempting this kind of brusque transfer, keep your hands at your side, no matter what effort it may cost you to overcome the instinct by which everyone's hand goes out, almost automatically, whenever he is proffered something delicious and expected. Keep your hands at your side, and the ice-cream man will look up at you, startled, questioning. Lock his eyes with your own, and *then*, slowly, calmly, and above all deliberately, take the cone from him.

[18] Grasp the cone with the right hand firmly but gently between thumb and at least one but not more than three fingers, two-thirds of the way up the cone. Then dart swiftly away to an open area, away from the jostling crowd at the stand. Now take up the classic ice-cream-cone-eating stance: feet from one to two feet apart, body bent forward from the waist at a twenty-five-degree angle, right elbow well up, right forearm horizontal, at a level with your collarbone and about twelve inches from it. But don't start eating yet! Check first to see what emergency repairs may be necessary. Sometimes a sugar cone will be so crushed or broken or cracked that all one can do is gulp at the thing like a savage, getting what he can of it and letting the rest drop to the ground, and then evacuating the area of catastrophe as quickly as possible. Checking the cone for possible trouble can be done in a second or two, if one knows where to look and does it systematically. A trouble spot some people overlook is the bottom tip of the cone. This may have been broken off. Or the flap of the cone material at the bottom, usually wrapped over itself in that funny spiral construction, may be folded in a way that is imperfect and leaves an opening. No need to say that through this opening—in a matter of perhaps

thirty or, at most, ninety seconds—will begin to pour hundreds of thousands of sticky molecules of melted ice cream. You know in this case that you must instantly get the paper napkin in your left hand under and around the bottom of the cone to stem the forthcoming flow, or else be doomed to eat the cone far too rapidly. It is a grim moment. No one wants to eat a cone under that kind of pressure, but neither does anyone want to end up with the bottom of the cone stuck to a messy napkin. There's one other alternative—one that takes both skill and courage: Forgoing any cradling action, grasp the cone more firmly between thumb and forefinger and extend the other fingers so that they are out of the way of the dripping from the bottom, then increase the waist-bend angle from twenty-five degrees to thirty-five degrees, and then eat the cone, *allowing* it to drip out of the bottom onto the ground in front of you! Experienced and thoughtful cone-eaters enjoy facing up to this kind of sudden challenge.

[19] So far, we have been concentrating on cone problems, but of course there is the ice cream to worry about, too. In this area, immediate action is sometimes needed on three fronts at once. Frequently the ice cream will be mounted on the cone in a way that is perilously lopsided. This requires immediate corrective action to move it back into balance—a slight pressure downward with the teeth and lips to seat the ice cream more firmly in and on the cone, but not so hard, of course, as to break the cone. On other occasions, gobs of ice cream will be hanging loosely from the main body, about to fall to the ground (bad) or onto one's hand (far, far worse). This requires instant action, too; one must snap at the gobs like a frog in a swarm of flies. Sometimes, trickles of ice cream will already (already!) be running down the cone toward one's fingers, and one must quickly raise the cone, tilting one's face skyward, and lick with an upward motion that pushes the trickles away from the fingers and (as much as possible) into one's mouth. Every ice-cream cone is like every other ice-cream cone in that it potentially can present all of these problems, but each ice-cream cone is paradoxically unique in that it will present the problems in a different order of emergency and degree of sensitivity. It is, thank God, a rare ice-cream cone that will present all three kinds of problems in exactly the same degree of emergency. With each cone, it is necessary to make an instantaneous judgment as to where the greatest danger is, and to *act!* A moment's delay, and the whole thing will be a mess before you've even tasted it (*Figure 1*). If it isn't possible to decide between any two of the three basic emergency problems (i.e., lopsided mount, dangling gobs, running trickles), allow yourself to make an arbitrary adjudication; assign a "heads" value to one and a "tails" value to the other, then flip a coin to decide which is to be tended to first. Don't, for heaven's sake, *actually* flip a coin— you'd have to dig in your pockets for it, or else have it ready in your hand before you were handed the cone. There isn't remotely enough time for anything like that. Just decide *in your mind* which came up, heads or tails, and then try to remember as fast as you can which of the problems you had assigned to

the winning side of the coin. Probably, though, there isn't time for any of this. Just do something, however, arbitrary. Act! *Eat!*

Figure 1   Figure 2

[20] In trying to make wise and correct decisions about the ice-cream cone in your hand, you should always keep the objectives in mind. The main objective, of course, is to get the cone under control. Secondarily, one will want to eat the cone calmly and with pleasure. Real pleasure lies not simply in eating the cone but in eating it *right*. Let us assume that you have darted to your open space and made your necessary emergency repairs. The cone is still dangerous—still, so to speak, "live." But you can now proceed with it in an orderly fashion. First, revolve the cone through the full three hundred and sixty degrees, snapping at the loose gobs of ice cream; turn the cone by moving the thumb away from you and the forefinger toward you, so the cone moves counterclockwise. Then, with the cone still "wound," which will require the wrist to be bent at the full right angle toward you, apply pressure with the mouth and tongue to accomplish overall realignment, straightening and settling the whole mess. Then, unwinding the cone back through the full three hundred and sixty degrees, remove any trickles of ice cream. From here on, some supplementary repairs may be necessary, but the cone is now defused.

[21] At this point, you can risk a glance around you. How badly the others are doing with their cones! Now you can settle down to eat yours. This is done by eating the ice cream off the top. At each bite you must press down cautiously, so that the ice-cream settles farther and farther into the cone. Be very careful not to break the cone. Of course, you never take so much ice cream into your mouth at once that it hurts your teeth; for the same reason, you never let unmelted ice cream into the back of your mouth. If all these procedures are followed correctly, you should shortly arrive at the ideal—the way an ice-cream cone is always pictured but never actually is when it is handed to you *(Figure 2)*. The ice cream should now form a small dome whose circumference exactly coincides with the large circumference of the cone itself—a small skullcap that fits exactly on top of a larger, inverted dunce cap. You have made order out of chaos; you are an artist. You have taken an unnatural, abhorrent, irregular, chaotic form, and from it you have sculpted an ordered, ideal shape that might be envied by Praxiteles or even Euclid.

²² Now at last you can begin to take little nibbles of the cone itself, being very careful not to crack it. Revolve the cone so that its rim remains smooth and level as you eat both ice cream and cone in the same ratio. Because of the geometrical nature of things, a constantly reduced inverted cone still remains a perfect inverted cone no matter how small it grows, just as a constantly reduced dome held within a cone retains *its* shape. Because you are constantly reshaping the dome of ice cream with your tongue and nibbling at the cone, it follows in logic—and in actual practice, if you are skillful and careful—that the cone will continue to look exactly the same, except for its size, as you eat it down, so that at the very end you will hold between your thumb and forefinger a tiny, idealized replica of an ice-cream cone, a thing perhaps one inch high. Then, while the others are licking their sticky fingers, preparatory to wiping them on their clothes, or going back to the ice-cream stand for more paper napkins to try to clean themselves up—*then* you can hold the miniature cone up for everyone to see, and pop it gently into your mouth.

ANALYTICAL READING

1. In most process analyses, the paper starts with the first step in the actual process. What advantage does Hills gain by starting at the planning stage? Would you recommend this for every process analysis? Why or why not?

2. How does Hills use cause-and-effect reasoning in the essay? Cite examples.

3. Point out places where you noticed effective uses of metaphor.

4. Where does Hills use exaggeration (hyperbole) to create humor?

5. Does Hills show the relationship of one step of tackling an ice-cream cone to the next? Discuss.

6. Where does he describe the process in terms of playing a game?

7. Do we get any hint of Hills' family relationships? Or his personality? How?

REFLECTING

Point: Why do you think Hills wrote the article (other than for money!)? Does it contain serious advice, or is it just an amusing account?

Organization: Make a topic outline of the process as he describes it. Is the organization chronological of spatial? Explain.

Support: Point out how the writer's descriptions and analogies help to support his subdivisions. Why is dialogue handled differently in paragraph 3 and paragraphs 5–11?

Synthesis: Did this remind you of times you have gone for ice-cream cones with your own family? Did you take the family dog with you? If so, what steps could you add to Hills' process analysis?

Evaluation: Did you enjoy reading the article? Why or why not? Discuss word choices that you found especially delightful. Does Hills forget about the children late in the essay?

FROM READING TO WRITING

1. Hills is able to see the ritual in ice-cream eating. What other foods did you eat as a child that became rituals—milkshakes, popcorn, watermelon, cotton candy, cookies? Write a similar humorous process analysis paper about eating one of these foods.

2. Write a process analysis explaining how to do something that you have done so often that it has become a ritual, such as how to get the family car; how to walk in the rain; how to go camping or picnicking; how to skip a day of high school; or how to use a skateboard.

SIMPLIFIED TECHNIQUES FOR CLEANING AND STORING PAINT BRUSHES

Bernard Gladstone

BIOGRAPHICAL SKETCH

Bernard Gladstone (1921–   ), a native of New York City, has attended Miami University, the City College of New York, and New York University. Before joining the staff of The New York Times, *he was a free-lance writer. His books include* Complete Book of Garden and Outdoor Lighting, Tips and Hints for the Handyman, *and* The New York Times Complete Manual of Home Repair. *In addition, he has written hundreds of "how-to" articles for* Better Homes and Gardens, Popular Science, American Home, Popular Mechanics, *and other magazines. He is the recipient of the Lawrence Tiefer Award for service to the building industry.*

PRE-READING

1. How would you characterize the title? What kind of voice would you expect in an article with such a title?

2. What appeal to the reader is made in the first paragraph? Has the author taken the reader's interest for granted?

[1] It is suprising how many do-it-yourself home painters will buy top quality paints, varnishes or other finishes, and then purchase an inexpensive, low quality, so-called "throwaway" paint brush or roller cover to put it on with.

[2] Buying cheap paint brushes or rollers is not only more expensive in the long run (a new tool must be purchased for each job), it also makes it difficult, and sometimes impossible, to get a really smooth, professional looking finish

that will stand up the way it should. All paint manufacturers agree that no matter how carefully they formulate their product, unless it is properly applied with a good quality brush, roller or other applicator, it is highly improbable that a smooth, uniform finish will be achieved.

³ Thus, it makes sense to buy top quality paint brushes and roller covers, and then clean them thoroughly after each use so they will be ready when needed again. Contrary to what some people think, thorough cleaning of a brush or roller cover does not take a lot of time and does not require using gallons of thinner—as long as the job is tackled promptly after each use.

⁴ The first step in cleaning either of these painting tools is to try and get as much of the paint out of the fibers or bristles as possible. The more paint removed before cleaning is begun, the less there will be to rinse or wash out.

⁵ To remove excess paint from a brush, start by wiping it vigorously across the rim of the can several times so that excess paint runs back into the can. Next, rub the brush out on scrap material such as old lumber, scrap pieces of plasterboard or plywood, or even on sheets of cardboard. Don't just rub the tips of the brush; hold it almost flat against the surface and rub the full length of the bristles against the surface.

⁶ If the brush was used with a latex (water-thinned) paint, then wash under running water if possible. While letting water run over the bristles, rub back and forth against the bottom of the sink or pail, and be sure the bristles are spread apart so that the water gets in near the heel to flush out paint that is caked there.

⁷ Where running water is not available, use a pail of water, but work the bristles vigorously under the water with your fingers. Pour the dirty water out, then replace with fresh water and repeat. Three or four rinses may be required before the water runs clear after the brush is washed in it.

⁸ If the brush was used in a solvent-thinned paint, then use a small container such as a coffee can or plastic food container which is only slightly wider than the brush to rinse it in. Pour about half an inch of solvent or thinner into this container, then work the brush vigorously against the bottom of the container by pressing down hard on the handle, and by turning the brush over each time. Then wipe the brush across the rim of the can to remove excess liquid and pour the dirty solvent away.

⁹ Add about the same amount of fresh solvent to the can again and repeat the process twice more, for a total of three rinses. Since only a small amount of solvent is used each time, all three rinses will require only a few ounces of liquid. If desired, the dirty solvent can be poured into a separate container and allowed to settle, then only the dirty portion at the bottom thrown away after the top is poured off and saved.

¹⁰ When a brush will be used again the next day, this cleaning will be sufficient. However, if the brush will be stored for some time, then one more step is advisable. Rinse the brush in a warm solution of detergent and water, or use one of the water-washable brush cleaning solutions sold in most paint stores. This final rinse should be followed by a clear water rinse, then the

brush is dried and wrapped before storing. To dry the brush hold the handle between the palms of your hands with the bristles pointing down inside a can or bucket. Now spin back and forth between the palms of the hands by twirling the handle rapidly. This will spin all water or solvent out of the bristles, but the spattering will be contained inside the can.

[11] Brushes that are heavily caked with paint, or those whose bristles get tangled and knotted when spinning or twirling them, will benefit from being combed out with a steel-tooth comb which is sold for this purpose in most paint and hardware stores. Lay the brush almost flat on a piece of old wood or a stack of paper, then comb the bristles out. . . .

[12] A good paint brush should always be wrapped in paper or thin cardboard when it is to be stored for any length of time. This not only keeps dirt and dust out of the bristles, it also helps retain the shape of the brush so bristles don't curl or flare. The original wrapper can be used if still intact, or ordinary brown wrapping paper can be used.

[13] First wrap at least once all the way around the bristles and ferrule, then fold over and crease at the tip. . . . Use a rubber band or string to hold the wrapping tight, and store flat on a shelf or in a drawer. Never allow brushes to stand on end—even for a few hours. That is a sure way to cause bristles to develop a permanent curl.

ANALYTICAL READING

1. What are the steps suggested in cleaning a brush? Which is most important?

2. Point out places where Gladstone uses definition.

3. What information does the writer supply that indicates that he assumes his audience to have had no experience with cleaning brushes?

4. Would his instructions apply only to one kind of painting or cleaning situation? Explain.

REFLECTING

Point: Is the main purpose of the paper to tell people how to perform an operation? Explain.

Organization: Is the paper arranged chronologically, spatially, or both? Discuss.

Support: What rhetorical devices does the writer use to move the reader from one step to another? Illustrate.

Synthesis: Would any aspect of the article have helped you solve a problem you have encountered during a paint clean-up? How does Gladstone's advice relate to the environmentalist movement? Do you expect to encounter more articles of this sort in the future? Why or why not? Can you add any advice?

Evaluation: How effective is the article as an objective description of a process? Would you have responded better to it if it had been written in the style of Hills' article on eating an ice-cream cone (pages 250–56)? Why or why not? Is the advice clear, practical, reasonable, convincing? Explain. Would the article have been improved if the equipment or tools needed had been listed at the beginning?

FROM READING TO WRITING

Write an objective process analysis, telling a general audience how to perform some sequential task, such as fixing a carburetor; planting a garden; making pickles; changing a flat tire; restringing a tennis racquet. Either avoid using jargon or be sure to define terms with specialized meanings.

GO TIE A FLY

J. A. Maxtone Graham

BIOGRAPHICAL SKETCH

J. A. Maxtone Graham is a native of Streatley, England, a town on the Thames River about fifty miles west of London, but he spends much of his time at his fishing cottage in southern Scotland. He describes himself as a "free-lance fisherman" who must work as a free-lance writer to support his true vocation. His articles have appeared in such magazines as Signature, Sports Afield, McCall's, *and* Lithopinion. *This article is a segment of a longer piece that appeared in the latter publication.*

PRE-READING

1. If you knew nothing about fishing, would you be able to tell from the title what the article is about? Would the final paragraph give you a clue? What word play is possible on the imperative structure of the title?

2. What tone is established in the first paragraph of this selection? What kind of person is revealed? Do you expect serious, objective instructions?

¹ . . . I drifted into fly-tying by mistake. While at school, I studied the clarinet and at some concert or other won first prize in the clarinet division— not surprising, since I was the only entrant. They gave me a bookshop certificate worth 10 shillings and sixpence, doubtless imagining I would buy an advanced book on clarinet-playing with it. What I bought was L. Vernon Bates's *Tackle-making for Anglers.* Bates taught his readers to make rods, reels, bobbers, nets, sinkers, spinning-reels—and flies. I couldn't afford to buy all the proper materials, so I simply stole: My younger brother and sister still haven't forgiven me my assaults on their possessions when I was inventing the

FROM *Lithopinion,* Spring 1975, pp. 43–45. Reprinted by permission. Original drawings by Betty Fraser.

Red Indian and Golliwog, a somewhat gaudy fly that did indeed catch a trout or two. Through the goodwill of farmers, poulterers, drapers, and older friends of mine who had guns, I built up a fair stock of birds and animals.

2 Then, during some wartime move, I somehow lost my precious box of materials and it wasn't until 20 years later, when a horse-racing acquaintance gave me four tips for that afternoon at the local track, that I resumed my interest in fly-tying. I hadn't bet for years, but I lashed out in a complicated parlay of mixed doubles. Three of the horses won, and I was the richer by nearly $40. I didn't want to do anything foolish with that windfall, like save it; so the next day I went to the tackle shop, bought a vise and quite a good basic lot of materials. I found the old skill nearly gone, but I struggled through the making of one fly, and pretty awful it was. I took it to the river, tied it to the nylon leader, cast it to a rising trout, which ate it first shot. The fish weighed nearly two pounds. I knew that every fisherman in the area had been after it for weeks—and I can only suppose that it had never seen anything quite like the terrible concoction I threw at it.

3 Since then, I haven't bought a single fly; but, of course, I found the original $40 went nowhere. I have to stock thousands of hooks in three-dozen shapes and sizes; over 30 colors of wires and tinsels; feathers from 40 or 50 different types of birds; furs and skins from seal, deer, rabbit, squirrel and mole. A junk dealer wouldn't give me a dollar for the lot, yet I suppose they must have cost me the price of a third-hand car. By the end of my life, I might be showing a small profit.

4 Many materials are just not to be bought. A farmer I know owns a rooster whose neck feathers (which provide the hackle, the fibers flaring out around the eye of the hook) are of a delicate and desirable greenish-olive shade. He has promised them to me, but the wretched bird seems destined to live forever.

5 One day, I read of an ancient fly-dressing which demanded, for the body of the fly, some pinkish fur obtained from the underbelly of a half-grown hedgehog, a material that sounds like what suitors of princesses in fairy tales have to dig up. No one—not surprisingly—in the fly-material trade seemed to stock it. Then, my attention was caught by the words of the barmaid in the local pub. Her children had found this baby hedgehog, she said, and were trying to raise it at home, on milk and stuff. "Listen, Valerie," I whispered to her when I got her alone in the corner of the bar. "Valerie, I've got to speak to you . . . Please remember, if anything should happen to that animal . . ." Knowing about my hobby, she looked at me suspiciously. "Listen you," she said through clenched teeth for all to hear, "you keep your hands off my hedgehog!"

6 The experienced flytier is characterized by constant dissatisfaction with his past efforts. You manufacture a superb imitation of the Blue-Winged Olive: Its three tails, its brown-olive body, its slate-blue hackles and wings look just right, and you catch your limit of fish on Wednesday. On Thursday, perhaps through some subtle change in the sun's light, or a difference in the

clarity of the water, the trout ignore it. Back to the drawing board: Friday's fly has a touch more orange than olive, and the hackles are enriched by a few fibers of brown. Come Saturday, when the fish won't look at either, the flytier feels he may have been on the wrong track after all. A few months later, after his formal release from the mental home, he starts all over again.

[7] There is little doubt that some thoughtful psychiatrist will have advised him to take up some therapeutic hobby, something skilled but relaxing, like maybe tying flies . . .

[8] Want to try fly-tying? Except for the hook, the materials are at hand in every household. The instructions that follow will enable you to make a very simple fly that is certainly capable of catching a trout: your child, or parent or spouse cannot fail to be impressed.

[9] You need: a fishhook, with a ring or eye at the blunt end (which can be bought at any tackle shop—ask for size 8), about three-quarters of an inch long; a foot of sewing thread, silk preferred; the stub of a candle; a small piece of aluminum foil, about three-eighths by one-half inches; a feather from a pillow, one of those long ones with fibers about half-an-inch long, a pair of small sharp scissors; and nail polish.

[10] Wax the thread by drawing it through the candle several times. Hold the hook at the bend, in the fingers of the left hand.

[11] Lay a short length of the thread along the shank, or straight part, of the hook. Starting about one-eighth inch from the eye, wind the rest of the thread over the short length, making each successive turn farther to your *left*.

[12] Continue winding to your *left* until you reach the start of the hook's bend.

[13] Tie a half-hitch (the simplest form of knot) around the shank. This gives the thread a firm grip and provides a surface on which you can build the rest of the fly.

[14] Take the aluminum foil and wrap it as best you can round the now thread-covered shank, leaving the loose end of the thread uncovered. Wind the thread in spaced turns (about six times) around the aluminum, to form a ribbing that protects the aluminum from the teeth of the innumerable trout that will soon be irresistibly drawn to your new lure. Make another half-hitch at the right-hand end of the aluminum, about an eighth-inch from the eye of the hook.

[15] Strip from the feather any fluffy bits at the stem's thick end. Hold the tip of the thin end between forefinger and thumb of the left hand. With the fingers of the right hand, brush back the remaining fibers of the feather until they stick out at right angles to the stem. This will form a "neck" between the brushed and unbrushed fibers.

[16] With the stem of the feather pointing to your left, apply the "neck" to the place of your last half-hitch. Tie in place with four turns of thread; tie a half-hitch.

[17] Cut off the extreme tip of the feather, which should be protuding over the eye of the hook. Next, holding the shank with your left hand, start winding the feather round the hook, making sure that each turn is to the *right* of the previous one. The fibers will splay outward, at right angles, to the shank. Give the feather three turns round the hook, then tie it down with four turns of thread. (This is the part where you wish you had three hands.)

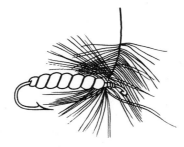

[18] Make one more half-hitch. Cut off any surplus stem of the feather. Then make two or three more half-hitches near the eye of the hook. (There is a more professional way of finishing off, but it's quite difficult, and you may have suffered enough already.) Paint a little nail polish over the last visible turns of thread and allow to dry. Trim thread.

[19] You have now made a basic trout-fly. Tell someone to go catch a fish with it.

ANALYTICAL READING

1. What information about fly-tying does the reader gain from the first seven paragraphs? What can the reader infer about the availability of materials? What would be lost if these paragraphs were omitted?

2. Why is paragraph 9 a good device for a process analysis paper?

3. Could you follow each step without its accompanying illustration? Why or why not?

4. Where is irony used in the article? Does it have a use other than revealing the writer's personality?

REFLECTING

Point: What does the reader learn besides how to tie a fly? Does the essay say something about hobbies?

Organization: Is the process arranged chronologically? How does the sentence structure help to reveal the organization?

Support: How do the very specific instructions dealing with direction help the reader in duplicating the process? Refer to a particular example.

Synthesis: Were you reminded of an unusual hobby you have? How does this essay relate to Hills' "How to Eat an Ice-Cream Cone" (pages 250–56)? Even if you don't fish, did you enjoy the essay?

Evaluation: Did you find the article entertaining as well as informative? Why or why not? Are the instructions clear and simple enough for anyone to follow? Why or why not?

FROM READING TO WRITING

Write a paper about an unusual skill you have, giving instructions that will enable another person to repeat the process. Examples: making kites, blowing glass, making ceramic pots, knotting macramé, cooking crêpes. If you like, you might give a few paragraphs explaining how you became interested in this hobby. Note that Graham's article is restricted to one kind of fly.

Item Analysis

DO AS I SAY, NOT AS I DO
Amitai Etzioni

BIOGRAPHICAL SKETCH

Amitai Etzioni was born in Cologne, Germany, in 1929. He received B.A. and M.A. degrees from Hebrew University and a Ph.D. from the University of California at Berkeley. He has been a professor of sociology and chairman of the Department of Sociology at Columbia University, and is currently the Director of the Center for Policy Research. Among his honors was a Guggenheim Fellowship and an appointment as a Fellow at the Center for Advanced Study for Behavioral Studies. In addition to serving on the editorial board of Science *magazine and writing numerous articles in professional journals, he is the author of twelve books, including* Modern Organizations, Studies in Social Change, The Active Society, *and* Genetic Fix.

PRE-READING

1. The title is a familiar maxim; what does it indicate to you about the subject matter?

2. Skim the first and last paragraphs. What do you think the subject and the writer's attitude toward it are?

3. From the biographical sketch, do you accept Etzioni as an authority?

¹ The hottest new item in post-Watergate curriculums is "moral education," an attempt by educators to instill moral values in youngsters by using newly designed teaching methods. With many believing that people in the United States do not live as moral and honest lives as they used to, according to Gallup, moral education is now favored by four out of every five Americans.

² But moral education means rather different things to different people— from teaching respect for the law as embodied in police officers and other authority figures, to instilling "good manners," to developing the capacity to form one's own standards and judgments. Though the goals of moral educa-

FROM *The New York Times Magazine*, 26 September 1976, pp. 44, 65–66. © 1976 by The New York Times Company. Reprinted by permission.

tion are at best contradictory, a significant number of the nation's public schools are nonetheless forging ahead.

[3] Progressive educators are keenly aware that preaching ethics in the classroom is not likely to meet with much success. They also know that assigning "morals" readings in textbooks, the way children are taught, say, geography, is not likely to be anywhere near as productive for character building as such techniques are for developing factual understanding. In the search for an appropriate way to get moral value across, a variety of approaches are being tried.

[4] In 1970, Jane Elliott, a teacher at Community Elementary school in Riceville, Iowa, wanted to teach her third-grade students the injustice of discrimination, but sensing that just talking about the arbitrariness and unfairness of race prejudice would be too academic to have much impact, her inspiration was to appeal directly to the children's capacity for emotional experience and empathetic insight by declaring a day of discrimination against the blue-eyed. She began by "explaining" the innate superiority of the "cleaner, more civilized, smarter" brown-eyed. When the children were, at first, disbelieving, she snapped sarcastically at a blue-eyed child, "Is that the way we've been taught to sit in class?" and then moved all the blue-eyed to the back of the room. To snickers from the brown-eyed, she then informed the blue-eyed that they would not be permitted to play on the big playground at recess and could only play at all if invited by a brown-eyed child. Throughout the day she was conspicuously more tolerant of mistakes made by brown-eyed children. The brown-eyed quickly started to enjoy lording it over the blue-eyed, who soon showed signs of growing insecurity and loss of confidence.

[5] After reversing the roles for a day, Mrs. Elliott had every child write about how it felt to be discriminated against. Though to many adults her procedure may sound heavy-handed, as far as her students were concerned the experience "took." That it made a profound impression is apparent from such comments as "I felt dirty, left out, thought of quitting school." The children were not shy about saying how "rotten" it felt to be labeled inferior and how relieved they were to be equal again.

[6] In the context of the current moral-education drive, what Jane Elliott did in 1970 is of particular interest because despite the successful results she was reported to have achieved, few schools have followed her lead.

[7] One Monday morning, the students in a Pittsburgh junior high school started their civics class not with a rehash of government branches, the meaning of "checks and balances," or that pragmatic addition of recent years, how to fill out Form 1040A, but with a brief "moral dilemma": "Sharon and Jill were best friends. One day they went shopping together. Jill tried on a sweater and then, to Sharon's surprise, walked out of the store with the sweater under her coat. A moment later, the store's security officer stopped Sharon and demanded that she tell him the name of the girl who had walked out. He told the storeowner that he had seen the two girls together, and that he was sure

that the one who left had been shoplifting. The storeowner told Sharon that she could really get in trouble if she didn't give her friend's name."

8 "Should Sharon tell?" the teacher asked. One student suggested that Sharon should deny knowing Jill. The teacher wanted to know if the student approved of lying for a friend. "Yah," was the answer. The teacher then inquired, "What is going to happen to all of us if everyone lies?" This elicited the following pupil observation: "If everyone goes around shoplifting, do you know what kind of life that would be? Everybody would just be walking around stealing everybody else's stuff." Another student interjected, "But everybody doesn't steal and everybody wouldn't, and, anyway, the storeowner probably has a large enough margin of profit to cover the few rip-offs." The first stuck to his guns: "But the store can't exist if everybody is stealing, there are so many people, and it is getting worse every day." A third student felt it was "like stealing from the rich and giving to the poor."

9 What educators who favor this moral-dilemma approach stress is that, first of all, it elicits a discussion in which the teacher tolerates free expression of student viewpoints and, second, such give-and-take improves student awareness of moral issues, and leads to higher levels of moral reasoning.

10 According to Harvard's Lawrence Kohlberg, most often cited by moral-dilemma advocates, children move from an amoral stage toward concern for the needs and feelings of others. It is useless, he argues, to try to get children at the most primitive stage of moral development—in the early years where they only do what is right to avoid punishment or to gain approval—to suddenly understand principles or modes of reasoning at the highest level. But it is possible, through proper classroom dialectics, to help children move toward a point where they wish to be ethical because they themselves think it's right.

11 Just as in past years many whites who referred to adult black men as "boys" did not fully comprehend the offense they were giving, in numerous other situations many youngsters (and adults) simply do not perceive the moral issue at stake. Nearly 20 years ago, following the "$64,000 Question" quiz-show scandal, in which it was discovered that TV personnel had provided some contestants with the answers, Kurt and Gladys Lang asked a class of New York University students to rank various behaviors according to their relative unethicality. A year ago I used their questionnaire with Columbia University undergraduates and obtained similar results. One of the main findings of both surveys was that students tend to have a difficult time perceiving behavior as unethical if they can not identify individual victims. Thus, the Langs found, for example, that the students considered the behavior of a land speculator who made millions on a tip-off from city hall less unethical than that of a student who cheated on an exam—or of Charles Van Doren, the "cheating professor" of "$64,000 Question" fame.

12 The students reasoned that a student who cheats gains an unfair competitive advantage over other students and that Van Doren had "let down" television viewers who believed in him, but they could not see that the land

speculator had harmed anyone. They had a hard time conceiving of the community—or business or government—as the victim of unethical conduct.

[13] By far the most prevalent method of classroom ethics teaching today is paper-and-pencil assignments. The main champion of this approach is Prof. Sidney B. Simon of the University of Massachusetts. One of the more than 1,000 schools using his "values-clarification kits" is the William W. Niles Junior High School in the Bronx. According to Claudia Macari, assistant principal for guidance, and Mildred W. Abramowitz, principal, who were responsible for introducing values clarification at William W. Niles, an example of the technique is as follows:

[14] Exercise one: "Write down 20 things you love to do." Pause. "Now that you have all made your lists, state *the five* things you love to do *best of all*. Check the things you love to do alone; X the things you love to do with other people; . . . things that cost less than $3 to do."

[15] Macari and Abramowitz explain that the purpose of having the students choose the five out of 20 things they like best is to make them aware of what it is they value. The whole idea of values clarification is *not* to instill or introduce any particular values, new or old, but to help students discover those they already have. Having to decide which 15 items to leave out, which five to include, leads the youngsters to an understanding of how values work, the choices inevitably involved.

[16] The items relating to gregariousness and money help the student gain insight into why he values what he does, and foster greater self-awareness.

[17] Values-clarification exercises differ from most other work-book assignments in one way: Any and all answers are considered "right" as long as one can give a reason for them. Asked whether a youngster might not, therefore, end up reaffirming "wrong" values, such as intolerance or thievery, the designers of the approach reply: "Our position is that we respect his right to decide upon that value."

[18] Some claim that it is precisely its amorality that makes the values-clarification package so popular in the public schools—it protects them from having to choose *whose* values to teach.

[19] Actually, despite the "rules" of such programs, when sensitive issues like abortion, women's rights and discrimination against minorities are discussed in the classroom, it is difficult for teachers to hide their feelings. Body language, tone of voice, allotment of more speaking time to children who have the desired point of view, will indicate to the student where his teacher stands.

[20] Whatever method of teaching morals is employed—there is not yet enough data available to support the superiority of any one technique—there are other ways schools communicate moral values.

[21] It has long been understood that children learn from their parents by emulation—as is acknowledged in the well-known saw: "Do as I say, not as I do!" The same notion is equally applicable to the ethics taught in school: The

way teachers, administrators, coaches and other school officials interact with the children teaches ethical values by example. Mrs. Elsa Wasserman, a counselor to the Cambridge, Mass., public schools, explains: "The governance structure of many schools teaches students that in school they have no significant control over their lives; that they must conform to arbitrary rules or be punished; and that they should go along with what the majority thinks and does even when they disagree." This is the "hidden curriculum."

22 Talking to students, one finds that the core of the hidden curriculum revolves around grades, athletics and student behavior. The attitudes and actions students observe on the part of school officials with regard to these are not often ones which convey the importance of standing up for ethical principles.

23 For example: In one Eastern Pennsylvania school, administrators became aware that some black pupils had formed gangs which collected 25 cents a day in "protection money" from younger, mainly white children. For a long time, these officials looked the other way. Why? Well, they said, they were afraid that active efforts to find out which children were in the extortion ring and to punish them would expose them to charges of "police tactics." The principal's main concern was that it was a "no-win" situation.

24 When some gang members were finally caught, he first suspended the extortionist pupils, then, when black parents protested, had them reinstated, then, when white parents were outraged, sent them to an experimental school, then, when the black parents charged "exile," had them returned. He felt no need to apologize for setting policy according to which ethnic group was protesting most. The main issue, as he saw it, was not what to do about extortion, or how his failure to do anything credible about it would affect the students, but how to negotiate a political tightrope.

25 In marked contrast to the idealism of a few years back that sought to replace grades with more meaningful evaluations, many of today's students believe their life's fate hangs on getting into the "right" college—which in turn depends on getting high grades. Thus, for quite a few students the notion that cheating on exams or term papers is a serious ethical issue is about as quaint as the medieval scholastic debate over how many angels can stand on the head of a pin.

26 Among the students with whom I have spoken, attitudes seem to be less cynical toward sports than toward grades. But each sport has its own "informal" rules of fair play. Basketball players, for instance, say they are trained to keep a keen eye on the referee and to push another player out of the way when the referee is not looking, although "really digging your elbow into the other guy" is considered going too far. Football seems to be the focus of the most intense pressures to win—and, therefore, the greatest temptations to win at any price.

27 Traditionally, one of the major justifications for lavishing large sums on school sports programs—especially competitive team-sports programs—has been that athletics are "character-building." And, indeed, they very likely are.

The question that needs greater attention, however, is what kind of character are they building?

[28] The hidden-curriculum emphasis on high grades and winning in sports suggests that grades and sports are still considered important tools for instilling the American "success ethic" and that stimulating the drive for success is still a major mission of the American school. The success drive has ethics-undermining side-effects, however, if built into its creed is the attitude conveyed by the late football coach Vince Lombardi's oft-quoted motto: "Winning is not the most important thing, it's the only thing." Unbounded competition is incompatible with ethical codes because it puts self (or one's team) above the rules of the game.

[29] Of all the approaches to moral education, the one which focuses on reform of the hidden curriculum is likely to be both the most relevant and the most difficult to accomplish, because teachers and students are less aware of its moral implications than they are of the formal curriculum, and because its roots lie in the community. It is thus far from accidental that when Professor Kohlberg tried to apply his ideas about how best to foster higher levels of moral reasoning in the schools, he ended up having to set up an experimental, "alternate," school, in which 72 students selected from four high-school classes in the Cambridge High and Latin school, together with a volunteer staff, became a school-within-a-school run on principles of student participation. In Kohlberg's "just school," each student and each staff member has one vote and "no major decision or commitments are made without consulting the entire community."

[30] Most of America is probably far from ready for such a radically egalitarian approach in the public schools. But most schools may be ready for limited reforms to bring the hidden curriculum more in line with what is taught in ethics classes—awarding grades on the basis of merit rather than on conformity to the teacher's views or docility in the face of authority, emphasizing respect for the rules in sports rather than just playing to win.

[31] The objection may be raised that schools structured to produce more ethical youth would fail in their major mission of adequately preparing their students for later life, in which "success" often entails bending, if not violating, the rules. One could counter this criticism by maintaining that it is the schools' job to educate their students morally—over and above the prevalent societal standards. At the very least, then, the students will have some principles to compromise later on; and though their standards may become eroded, nonetheless they will not become as unethical as they would have had they started out with no scruples at all. True, most schools cannot proceed very far in promoting values not shared by the community at large. Before the schools can effectively provide moral education, the surrounding society must work to reform itself so that its members are less concerned with success and material achievements, and more concerned about quality of life and individual conduct.

ANALYTICAL READING

1. In item analysis, classification is used. How do the first three paragraphs set up the basis for the classification in this article? What is it?

2. List in one-sentence summaries the subclasses of "approaches to teaching moral values."

3. What factors seem to be most important in making value judgments? Your answer should be an inference that you have drawn from reading the examples given in the article.

4. Do you agree with the contention in paragraph 19? Can you cite some personal experience?

5. In what ways are grades and sports compared and related?

6. From reading the article, can you define the "hidden curriculum," giving its characteristics? Is it a positive or negative influence on students?

7. How might emphasis on ethics interfere with students' success in the world?

8. Does Etzioni think that the schools can do an effective job of teaching morality? Why or why not? How is his opinion on this revealed?

REFLECTING

Point: What else is achieved in the article besides listing methods of teaching moral values? How appropriate is the title for the essay?

Organization: Using the list you made in answer to question #2, work up an organizational scheme for the article, indicating the relationships involved. Show how many sections of the essay follow the ILLUSTRATION–RESTRICTION–SUBJECT pattern.

Support: Do the examples act as support to the subclassification process? Explain. How are authorities used?

Synthesis: Have you had experience with any of the moral dilemmas dealt with in the article, such as shoplifting or cheating? Have you been encouraged to discuss controversial subjects that involve moral issues in your classrooms? Discuss. Are there nonreligious reasons for doing what is ethical? Compare Etzioni's views about sports with those expressed by Lipsyte in the selection from *SportsWorld* on pages 222–27.

Evaluation: What element of the essay did you find most effective? Why? Do you think the subject is an important one? Do you agree or disagree that schools should attempt to teach ethics? How much influence can teachers and principals have?

FROM READING TO WRITING

1. Pick a topic about which people hold differing opinions, such as athletic scholarships, abortion, school discipline, open dorms. Write an item analysis, not simply listing these opinions, but showing some relationship they share.

2. Write an item analysis about attitudes toward the grading system.

AS TIMES CHANGE, SO DO SIGNS, SIGNALS ADOPTED BY YOUTH
Margaret Lantis

BIOGRAPHICAL SKETCH

Dr. Margaret Lantis, retired professor of anthropology at the University of Kentucky, has long been interested in young people and their activities. Although she spent many years serving as a social-science analyst for numerous government agencies, she regularly took "vacations" as a visiting professor at various colleges in the United States and Canada. In addition to the contact with student attitudes that her teaching gave her, she habitually visited campus bookstores while attending scholarly conferences to determine what "symbols" the students were currently buying.

PRE-READING

1. What organizational plan does the title imply?

2. From reading the biographical sketch and the opening paragraph, what can you say of Lantis as an authority?

3. From the second paragraph and the biographical sketch, what do you infer about Lantis' attitude toward understanding young people by noting their symbols and signs?

4. Judging from the last paragraph, what do you think the writer's attitude toward the student movement is?

[1] In looking back to the great youth upheaval of the Sixties, we generally think it all started in Berkeley, California. Because I was there in 1964–65 as a visiting member of the university faculty, and because one of my interests is America-watching, I began to look at what became—on and off campus—a great national passing show. Let's watch it, passing step by step from the scene and mood of Berkeley then to the mood of anywhere this year. A momentous ten-year trip it is, some years bitter, some enlivening and exhilarating, and to many parental sideline observers, puzzling.

[2] The epidemic of sit-ins and teach-ins—and of violence—did not happen to us unforewarned. We should not have been surprised—although we were—at what "good" kids were doing in the early 1960s. If we had looked more wisely at the graphic materials that were becoming symbols of the period, the signs and gestures created to express real emotional needs, we might have sensed the students' mood.

[3] (Perhaps now we are more aware. This summer the Smithsonian's Renwick Gallery in Washington has an exhibition titled "Signs of Life: Symbols in the American City." It shows the evolution of symbolism in the 19th-century city, in the home, and on the modern commercial strip.)

FROM *Smithsonian*, September 1976, pp. 74–80. Copyright 1976 by the Smithsonian Institution.

4 Back in the 1950s, on ashtrays and wall plaques we had "People Are No Damned Good," muttered by a dour figure in a box shutting himself off from people. By 1962 Jules Feiffer, whose cartoons appeared in publications that students read, already was playing the role of bitter-humorous social critic. And through that whole period there was "poor old Charlie Brown," who wanted, expected and tried to win, yet lost every ball game: Charlie Brown, characterized on the 20th anniversary of *Peanuts* in 1970 as "a basic reflection of his time." His creator, Charles M. Schulz, has said, "When I first started Charlie Brown, I didn't know he was going to lose all the time." "I think the security blanket really was *the* major breakthrough . . . suddenly these kids were being identified with many kids around the country." In 1963, Linus' security blanket was featured. The theme was always a need for real accomplishment, always frustration and, as we'll see, the resulting thumb in mouth and security or fantasy or hostility.

5 The October 1961 issue of *Harper's* magazine had a special supplement on *The College Scene*, with articles on sex (*The Problem Colleges Evade*), religion, young black rebels, and inadequate teaching (*The Wasted Classroom*). Although accompanying photographs show that both boys' and girls' hair was short, one picture shows students listening to a young soapbox speaker who was motioning toward a sign, "Columbia students for a sane nuclear policy." That should remind us: what became the familiar "peace symbol" was originally "Ban the Bomb."

6 One of those who *were* paying attention to the signs of the time, Philip Rieff, wrote in that issue: "What of the young themselves? My own experience of them . . . indicates to me that they are well aware of the role into which they have been cast. They have been told, often, that their elders have become both disenchanted with ideologies and lacking in ideals. And, for this good reason, they refuse to listen to anything else we have to say. . . . They neither heed . . . their fathers, nor destroy them. Lacking continuing leadership, they play a fickle game of father figures." Their professors concurred that students had no interest in or sense of history. To them, the past was irrelevant to their modern world. Students, however, were willing to be compelled by John Kennedy, an older-brother sort of age-peer. Then he was assassinated. Later came Robert Kennedy and Eugene McCarthy, and the young did identify with political parties, without success.

7 For Berkeley students in the mid-Sixties, leadership, with the essential accompanying slogans, did not come from their potential father figure, Clark Kerr, president of the massive University of California, whose article, *The Multiversity*, got much attention in 1963. President Kerr was, above all, an administrator, the top man in a knowledge industry; he had some understanding of and sympathy for its human products, but in the students' opinion one of the things wrong with U.C. was that it *was* a huge multiversity, like a Washington bureaucracy or a multinational industry. Instead, leadership developed internally, on a free-speech issue. This concerned, first, tables with placards and signs representing various "causes" and political parties that stu-

dents and evidently some nonstudents set up at the most-used entrance to the campus and, later, signs bearing a then unmentionable word.

[8] To many local people, the unexpected sit-in in the fall of 1964 looked like an overreaction to denial of a minor demand. Some of the students, however, reacting against their own feeling of uselessness, had been seeking to do something worthwhile by fighting for personal rights—other people's rights if not their own. SNCC [Student Nonviolent Coordinating Committee], CORE [Congress of Racial Equality], and Students for a Democratic Society were in place in 1963, putting many students through rehearsals for the big scene.

[9] Across the country at Columbia University, according to a former student, "we started off gently, joining the Peace Corps, going on freedom rides into the South. But [in 1968] after several years of this, those of us who stayed active weren't so gentle anymore."

[10] The transfer of activism from Southern roads and Northern city streets to the campuses did not begin solely at Berkeley. In the spring of 1965, some University of Michigan faculty held an all-night seminar to discuss with students the question of U.S. involvement in the Vietnam war. Soon many universities held teach-ins and Dr. Benjamin Spock, Senator Ernest Gruening (the first Senate dove), Norman Thomas, Dick Gregory, Joan Baez and others participated.

[11] The many who congregated as onlookers, or who set up their tables or carried placards, were rather quiet and thoughtful, and the "in" signs were, frankly, not very graphic. The stark upraised fist, which needed no words, had not yet appeared. Some signs were wordy, others succinct, such as "Impeach Lyndon Johnson!" But still not the dove of peace nor the two fingers in the V-for-Victory sign. It was much too early for even a hope of success.

[12] Compared with the next year, 1966 simmered: it occasionally boiled but did not explode. In 1966, what became a universal subject of youth protest— the Vietnam war—was not yet taken as the prime target. College-age people were symbolically shooting in many directions at once.

[13] The Beatles, who had entranced the young in the earlier Sixties, were still touring; the musical *Hair* was proliferating; and the shagginess of these two was becoming on nearly every young head the defiant pennant of the youth revolt. Along with the supposedly new realism there was, however, fantasy.

[14] From 1964 to 1967, Snoopy all but monopolized *Peanuts*. Although there was the pathetic fantasy of Linus' Great Pumpkin, this could not be sustained the year around, while Snoopy's imagined characters could be assumed day after day. He tried out various roles of accomplishment and heroics until, as "the World War I flying ace," pitted against the Red Baron, he hit the right note in 1967, just when war became hateful. As with Charlie Brown's earlier attempts to win which ended in the reality of an incompetent team, so from 1965 to 1969 fantasy was fun—until reality intruded. The big concern of so many young men (and their girl friends) was how to stay in school to avoid the

draft. The war was a personal threat. The wry message that young people sensed but their elders did not receive: wartime heroics are laughable.

15 In 1966 and 1967, all the lines of growth flowered in buttons. Here is a sample:

I ate my Draft Card	Send a Cop to Camp
i is ignorant	LET'S GROW HAIR
Organize an Orgy	Let's Eliminate Monday
Kiss now—worry later	ABOLISH KIDS
NIXON FOR NOTHING	Pass the Pill
I am a Peace Monger	I CAME I SAW I LEFT

16 The crescendo was played in 1967, the climax in 1968 and 1969. The terrible ghetto riots occurred in 1967. These were not symbols as we usually define them; the riots were the real thing.

17 On the national chart, as one line of interest rose toward its peak, another was starting locally and much farther down. Summer 1967 was the "Summer of Love" in San Francisco with the burgeoning of the Haight-Ashbury hippie community. This interest would spread and rise, merging with the ecology movement.

18 But the next year was grim. By June 15, 1968, there had been, by National Student Association count, 221 major demonstrations at 101 colleges, with the Columbia University sit-in "by far the most spectacular." Most sobering of all, both Martin Luther King, Jr., and Robert Kennedy were assassinated. The confrontation of New Left activists (the Yippies of the Youth International Party, the Mobe of National Mobilization Committee to End the Vietnam War, and others) with the Chicago police at the Democratic convention was, as we all remember, violent. Young people reacted by taking one of two courses; they became grim, cynical, more violent, or they turned to "Flower Power," not yet fully identified as such, but growing.

19 In 1969 graphics appeared all over. The peace sumbol and the upraised fist were now common, in many forms. And posters! The variety was astonishing. They presented not only "Ban the Bomb"—they presented L O V E, at times the Beatles, of course pinup girls (generally featuring large breasts), psychedelic geometrics entitled "Gates of hell," "Trips," "Out of step," "No exit," "Target." There were reproductions, now given a new meaning, such as the old poster of Uncle Sam pointing and saying "I WANT *YOU* FOR U.S. ARMY." Among art posters, Picasso was prominent and enduring: his *Don Quixote, The Dove, Harlequin, Les Petit Fleurs* (sic). Finally, mandalas (Hindu or Buddhist symbols of the universe), advertised as "sacred meditation symbols," appeared.

20 Perhaps the most subtly revealing was the old photo of W.C. Fields, hatted and gloved, peering in a secretive and calculating way over a hand of cards. The old, roguish iconoclast made defiance of the mores appear amusing. The kids would have been merely impudent or smug like Fields if they hadn't

been so earnest about their waywardness. Anyway, he became one of their symbols.

²¹ Pullover shirts with large designs that made them look like posters appeared. One company offered four: Peace ("our best seller"); clenched fist under STRIKE ("official Harvard strike shirt"): YOUR THING; and a woman's zodiac nightshirt ("it's lucky to wear your sign"). Note the zodiac nightshirt: because of the song in *Hair*, Aquarius behavior became a theme. Aquarius in that period was defined as "calm, introverted and seldom angry, you are freedom-loving, and like defying popular opinion with your unpredictable ways."

²² There was liberal use of the national flag by supporters of Richard Nixon, who was opposing the antiwar movement (they also used bumper stickers: LOVE IT OR LEAVE IT). Soon, however, there were flags on the seats of bluejeans.

²³ Within the youth society, vibrations for the ears, as well as the eyes, drew protesters together. They moved on pounding waves of sound. Periodically, hundreds and even thousands got high as a rocking sleepless mass, benumbed by wine or beer, marijuana or LSD, and always by music. Like the signs, music was symbolic and a means of communication as well as a justification for congregating and communing.

²⁴ Except for *We Shall Overcome*, there were in the Sixties noticeably few rousing songs that became well known to the older public. Did television induce the protesters unconsciously to present their mood and message graphically to their parents, to their critics? With their hand-lettered placards, were they not so much telling themselves as telling the world?

²⁵ The moon flight in the summer of 1969 excited and inspired for a while, but a trip to the moon was soon regarded as something very carefully planned and controlled. Life for most young people was just the opposite. It was filled with uncertainty, some of it exciting, some anxiety-producing: chancy efforts to escape the draft; experiments with psychedelic drugs; brushes with police, at times ending in being "busted"; and experiments in new living arrangements.

²⁶ Earlier in the decade the poor people and blacks had carried to Washington their protests against disadvantage. Then the students moved from campus to capital. The defiance became serious and strong.

²⁷ In November of 1969, 250,000 people rallied and marched in Washington to protest the Vietnam war. The nation read on the nightly TV newscasts the signs they carried: "Not one more dead" and "Vietnam Vets for Peace." We looked at the casual dress and the hostile or triumphant gestures of the marchers.

²⁸ If the first earthquakes occurred in 1969, then the Kent State University deaths in 1970 set off other severe shocks that swept through the colleges as fast as seismic waves. At the University of Kentucky, where I was then, an old frame building assigned to the ROTC was burned and similar lurid events occurred elsewhere. The tragic explosion in the physics laboratory at the Uni-

versity of Wisconsin was not by any means the only bomb explosion that year.

[29] Two movements, one growing, the other reaching a climax, moved along together: environmental awareness teach-ins and seminars and (in April) National Vietnam Week activities. In May came the unplanned reaction to Kent State. There was a third movement: women's rights. Its symbol, used for example by the women's movement at Yale, was the fist combined with the medical symbol for female.

[30] By the end of the year, the ecology movement had added nature to the themes. "Save Our Earth" was the slogan in 1971. Pictures of woodland scenes and love pictures of the arms-around-each-other type were appearing separately and combined.

[31] In 1972 and 1973 there was a beneficent mood: the Jesus Movement, with its misnamed Jesus Freaks, the generally harmless play-acting witchcraft (there were student covens), yoga, new meditation or chanting cults, student volunteerism in welfare and education, the collecting of old newspapers and cans, cleaning riverbanks, attending local hearings on dams or rezoning or anything affecting the Earth's face. And the well-meant but overworked exhortation "Have a nice day" which even appeared on bumper stickers. The ancient Egyptian symbol of life, the ankh (*crux ansata*), became popular as a pendant and on rings.

[32] The graphic symbol that swept nearly all others off the student bookstore shelves was the Happy Face: round, simple, bland, without any individuality. How could those vociferous young people of three years before, who had enjoyed the angry or impish or Establishment-taunting phrases and gestures, buy and wear this smiling stereotype? Having run the course of rebellion, having accomplished something by expressing many Americans' reaction against the war, now blandness evidently was what they needed and wanted.

[33] As usual, many students wanted only to survive. They were not hitting the highways; they stayed in school. But they were not revved up by ambition. Get through the courses, get the degree, and get out. Regarding other than professional courses, I heard them saying, "It's a drag. You don't learn anything useful. But if you've gone this far, you might as well stick it out." Smile. Endure. One animal poster that was becoming popular in 1972–73 expressed it: a simple photo of a bewildered kitten hanging by its front paws on a bar, with the caption, "Hang in there, Baby."

[34] By the end of the 1972–73 school year, the smiling face was no longer acceptable on campus although it survived a while in the commercial world. (In 1974, the manager of one student bookstore told me, "If you think it isn't dead, look at all the T-shirts with the smiling face that we can't sell now.") Although college youth had no part in the Watergate exposé and legal action, there was a feeling—as with the remainder of the citizenry—that solemn, very sobering events had occurred. The mood had changed again.

[35] What is acceptable ten years after Ann Arbor and Berkeley? Of the forms that we have been considering—comic strip characters, abstract sym-

bols, semiabstract forms like the peace dove, and the drawings and photographs on the posters—there developed through 1974 into 1975 a meaningful new combination of very old forms among abstract and semiabstract symbols.

[36] During the Christmas season in my university town, "Hang in there, Baby" remained popular in the largest boutique, but most in demand was a picture of a baby sitting in an adult-size toilet bowl, with the caption, "Life's A Bummer!" Said the cashier, "We couldn't keep enough in stock!"

[37] This followed the period of the first big energy crisis, the automobile sales slump and employee layoffs. Many people had a sinking feeling—like the baby, they were in something too big for them.

[38] In that winter, enlightenment—regarding the current type of symbols and their expressive power—came to me in the jewelry stores. In different sizes of shops in various towns, the story was the same. Among bracelet charms and neck pendants, the big sellers during the Christmas season were crosses and zodiac signs. In answer to my query, one salesman exclaimed, "Crosses! All kinds! Zodiac signs—very popular!"

[39] Next in popularity came St. Christopher medals ("not only Catholics have been buying these") and the Italian horn, the latter originally a counter-charm to protect one from the evil eye. There was some demand for the fisherman's or Ichthys cross, also for good luck and protection; the Star of David, the Hand of Fatima, Southwest Indian jewelry, even a few star and crescent pendants, and small gold mezuzahs but without the scroll that a real mezuzah should contain.

[40] We are interested in both form and meaning. All these forms are unquestionably very old. For most of the modern users, the meanings probably are basically the old ones, although the symbols may have a more generalized meaning of protection, of good, provided by Christ or Providence or the stars, rather than protection in special circumstances. In periods like the recent pervasive economic insecurity and of general anxiety, people turn to what "is known to have had" power in the past, magical or spiritual. As Max Lerner has written, "A heritage is at any moment a selection of symbols out of the past."

[41] In 1975–76, there were mottos not only on wall plaques but also on boxes, tiles, even coffee mugs, usually combined with pictures of little girls in sunbonnets, pinafores and high shoes. Flowers and house plants in decorative pots became a big thing. There was much talk of nostalgia, of going back to the Fifties when life was, supposedly, simpler and more secure. In movie tastes and clothing styles, young Americans turned to even earlier times. The return to the past has been literally spelled out on the plaques. Whether one calls it sentiment or wisdom, it radiates from flower-and-scroll bordered reminders like these:

May we always have old memories and young hopes. Live for Today, Dream for Tomorrow, Learn from Yesterday. Lord help me to be slow—slow to anger—slow to condemn—slow to walk that I may not pass one who needs me.

[42] It appears that the youngsters, and some not so young, being faced for the first time with the anxieties of their grandparents, were trying, without conscious intent, to re-create in a small way what they thought was their ancestors' world, wild West or staid East.

[43] While violence has appeared to be growing in many high schools, the colleges have been quieter. At my university a bookstore manager said: "The students' attitudes have changed, too. They don't look so scruffy. They don't rip me off as they used to." A professor's statement of satisfaction: "I've had good attendance and good response in class. This is happening generally."

[44] Symbols are not fads even though they wax and wane, unless one thinks that life is just a series of fads. I don't think that. The changes that create new symbols or revive old ones are important changes in the circumstances of our lives and in our responses.

[45] To use an erstwhile common phrase, when they "got it all together," students could write on the wall, "Life's a bummer, but hang in there. We'll survive, with luck and love and—a little effort." In no small way they prepared the nation to accept and enjoy the Bicentennial celebration. We'll just have to wait to find out what may be germinating for the next period.

ANALYTICAL READING

1. The title gave you a hint of the subject to be analyzed. Where does the author first set up the relationship between the signs and behavior? What does she have to say about it?

2. What kinds of "signs" does Lantis deal with in the article? What sentence sums up most of them?

3. According to Lantis, how has the comic strip *Peanuts* reflected student attitudes?

4. What relationship does she see between "signs" and student behavior—is it a cause-and-effect relationship? Explain.

5. What sequence in attitudes does the author see in the kinds of signs that students display? Illustrate.

6. How do the signs and attitudes displayed by students reflect the concerns of adults in the political, the economic, the social, the religious, and other areas?

7. How does the article illustrate Lantis' belief that the trends she outlines are not "fads"?

REFLECTING

Point: What point does Lantis make in the article?

Organization: What part does chronological sequence play in the organization? How would you characterize the subclasses Lantis establishes? Point to paragraphs using the ILLUSTRATION–RESTRICTION–SUBJECT structure.

Support: Does the writer use examples only for support, or do they serve another purpose in reference to the organization?

Synthesis: What signs are currently popular on your campus? Using Lantis' assumptions, what would you hypothesize about the kind of student behavior these signs might reflect? Are car bumper stickers considered to be signs? What ones are popular today and what do they indicate?

Evaluation: Did you find the article interesting and thought-provoking? Why or why not? Did the attitude you noticed in the last paragraph at the pre-reading stage pervade throughout? Discuss. Has Lantis changed your attitude toward signs? Do you, therefore, find her article to be convincing? If so, what in particular makes it effective? If not, why not?

FROM READING TO WRITING

1. Could students' clothes be considered a sign? If you think so, write an item analysis in which you classify the various kinds of clothing now popular on campus and what they signify.

2. Using Lantis' article as a model, write an item-analysis about current signs on campus.

SHAPE UP, BIONIC WOMAN!

Ann Pincus

BIOGRAPHICAL SKETCH

Ann Pincus was born in Little Rock, Arkansas, in 1937. After graduating from Vassar College, she worked for Glamour *magazine, then served as correspondent in Washington for the Ridder publications, and afterward wrote features for the* New York Post. *She has edited a cookbook and currently does freelance writing for the* New York Times Magazine, Potomac Magazine, Washington Monthly, *and others. Until recently, she also wrote a regular column for* Working Woman *magazine.*

PRE-READING

1. What can you tell from the title about the subject and the writer's tone of voice?

2. What can you determine from the opening and closing paragraphs, besides the subject of the analysis?

3. From the biographical sketch, what would you expect Pincus' stance toward the women's movement to be?

[1] My daughter Battle is 6 years old. Her brothers, Adam and Ward, are 8½ and 10 years old, respectively. They watch a lot of TV programs. The boys even draw their make-believe heroes from the tube. A couple of years ago, their idols were Batman and Robin; last year they switched to Captain Kirk and Mr. Spock. More recently, they've been imitating "The Fonz" and Kotter. They identify closely with these larger-than-life heroes.

[2] Who is there for my daughter to identify with? Lieutenant Uhura? Laverne and Shirley?

[3] My answer is: THERE IS NO ONE. There is not one larger-than-life heroine worth mentioning, or one female life-style worth imitating. There aren't any at 7 o'clock at night and there wouldn't be any if I let her stay up seven nights a week until the 11 o'clock news.

[4] Someone may say, "Oh, that's not at all true any more!" There's Wonder Woman and the Bionic Woman, even Police Woman. There's Mary Tyler Moore and Rhoda and Maude and Phyllis. This fall there's even Charley, the female protagonist in Norman Lear's new sitcom, "Alls' Fair."

[5] True, these are shows about women. But are these women drawn from life? Are any of them heroines? Would anybody want to be like any of them? For that matter, *should* anybody want to be like any of them? Let's examine the kind of images they project.

[6] Mary Tyler Moore, the duenna of television sitcoms, started out six years ago as an assistant producer in name, but a girl Friday in fact, at a Minneapolis television studio. A couple of years ago, she got promoted to a full-fledged producer (a crumb dropped to the feminist movement), but her real function in the program—to play Ann Landers to her TV colleagues—has not changed.

[7] The private life of TV's Mary Richards would demoralize the real Ann Landers. Despite the fact that she's had at least a dozen boyfriends over the years, she still has trouble telling a man what she thinks about him. She must be close to 40 in TV age, yet when a man makes a pass at her, she manages to put on the "oh, gee whiz, golly, what'll I do" routine.

[8] It may be great entertainment but she's not a great role model.

[9] Rhoda has trouble with her job (and her husband) because she's so neurotic, Phyllis can't keep a job (or a man) because she's too dumb. Maude, who clearly is more intelligent and has more on the ball than her husband—a little wart named Walter—stays at home while her husband botches up their bank accounts at the office. Maude also suffers from being on the verge of hysteria all the time. Perhaps that's the reason she doesn't get a job.

[10] Mary Hartman doesn't count, but Charley of "All's Fair" does because she has a real-life job. She is a photographer for a newsweekly, yet she is hopelessly dizzy, offensively aggressive and stupid. She couldn't get a job selling Instamatic cameras, much less using a Leica.

[11] What kind of role model is that?

[12] Angie Dickinson as Police Woman certainly landed a good job with the LAPD. It apparently pays well because she wears clothes that would make Jackie O green with envy. I may be wrong, but it seems to me she got her job

by playing up to the boss. She certainly is a flirt. She does tote a gun and go along with the boys to track down the bad guys, but she tends to get caught by the villains—due to mistakes such as tripping over a twig or some other clever move—and has to be rescued by her colleagues.

[13] Wonder Woman has possibilities. But her only motivation to right wrongs appears to be to save her beloved Major Trevor from harm. That leaves only the Bionic Woman, the Eve-like offshoot of the Six Million Dollar Man who miraculously manages to be weaker than he even though they have the same machines in their mechanical legs.

[14] Now, you will say (alas, my husband has already said it) that the male-role models seen on television are not positive either, that some men are portrayed as bigots and most act like klutzes. But you are wrong. And my husband is wrong. Men in television, whether in sitcoms or dramatic series, ordinarily are the Decision Makers, the Problem Solvers. It is their wit or wisdom or *savoir-faire* that tricks the villain. Just look at Columbo or Kojak or Starsky and Hutch or Steve Austin, the guys in "Switch" or "M*A*S*H" or "Hawaii Five-O," or Raymond Burr in any of his incarnations.

[15] There have, of course, been women on TV who dealt with "life." Good or bad, they quickly disappeared. Remember Faye, the gay divorcee? Kate McShane was another *involved* woman. She was a lawyer, and by inference a good role model. Unfortunately she couldn't make a move without consulting her brother, the priest, or her father, the mentor. "McNaughton's Daughter" was much better. She, too, was a lawyer who fought injustice, and she managed to be self-sufficient. She didn't even last one season.

[16] It must be said that true heroines are hard to find in any kind of fiction. Tom Sawyer was brave and daring while Becky Thatcher had hysterics in the cave. And my favorite schoolgirl idol, Jo March of "Little Women," finally disappointed me. It was fine and noble to run a school for the needy. But why did it have to be a school mainly for boys? What about the girls?

[17] There was at least one role model for young girls to identify with on the radio 25 or 30 years ago. Her name was Lorelei Kilbourne and no doubt she inspired a whole generation of women to become journalists. She was the intrepid girl reporter who, with Steve Wilson, tracked down many a miscarriage of justice on "Big Town." She was wonderful. She had a real job. She was paid for her work. She was good at it. She made difficult decisions and, as far as I know, she didn't quit to get married.

[18] Why can't television create someone like that? A more accurate question is: why can't *American* television create someone like that? British television created just such a character in "The Avengers" about fifteen years ago.

[19] At least television programs should have women in them who are wives, mothers and working women. More and more American women juggle all three jobs; why shouldn't the television screen reflect that?

[20] We've had the Bionic Woman. Now let's try for a Three-Dimensional Woman.

[21] Burbank, can you hear me?

ANALYTICAL READING

1. Do you agree with the charge about television characters made in the first three paragraphs? Why or why not? Has Pincus omitted any important regular programs?

2. What are the three major subclasses in the article? How is each subdivided? Can you add some that the writer leaves out?

3. How does Pincus relate the contention in the opening paragraphs to the subclasses she set up? Give examples.

4. Do you think that there is current evidence that female TV roles are changing? If so, state the evidence.

5. Did you write any remarks in the margins?

REFLECTING

Point: Although basically an item analysis, the article also is persuasive in character. State Pincus' recommendation as a summary. How does the author refute a counter-argument about men's roles?

Organization: Outline the classification scheme in the article, showing all the subclasses. Do you think it could serve as a good model for writing an analysis? Why or why not?

Support: How does Pincus use examples? What tone pervades the article, and how is it achieved? Does it help to support the contentions made?

Synthesis: Have you reacted negatively to certain types portrayed on television or in movies? Other writers have accused children's books of the same sex-role stereotyping. In your school textbooks, how were women portrayed? men? old people? teen-agers?

Evaluation: Do you think the article is effective? Why or why not? Does the tone add or detract from its effectiveness? Discuss.

FROM READING TO WRITING

1. Using the article as a model, write an item analysis of types of teen-agers or parents portrayed on television.

2. Write an item analysis of the images of animals portrayed on television over the last ten years.

Opinion

THINK LITTLE
Wendell Berry

BIOGRAPHICAL SKETCH

Wendell Berry was born in Henry County, Kentucky, in 1934. He received his B.A. and M.A. degrees from the University of Kentucky, where he is currently a professor of English. He has written many books, including novels (A Place on Earth, The Memory of Old Jack); books of poetry (The Broken Ground, The Country of Marriage); and essay collections (A Continuous Harmony, The Long-Legged House). In addition, he has been active in farming and conservation efforts, working his own farm and contributing to such publications as The Whole Earth Catalog. He has also been prominent as a local and regional spokesman for the Sierra Club and the Friends of the Earth.

PRE-READING

1. What device has been used to make the title interesting? Skim the first two and the last two paragraphs. What opinions do you find there? What key sentence would you underline?

2. From the biographical sketch, what would you expect Berry's environmental attitudes to be?

[1] First there was Civil Rights, and then there was The War, and now it is The Environment. The first two of this sequence of causes have already risen to the top of the nation's consciousness and declined somewhat in a remarkably short time. I mention this in order to begin with what I believe to be justifiable skepticism. For it seems to me that the Civil Rights Movement and the Peace Movement, as popular causes in the electronic age, have partaken far too much of the nature of fads. Not for all, certainly, but for too many they have been the fashionable politics of the moment. As causes they have been undertaken too much in ignorance; they have been too much simplified; they have been powered too much by impatience and guilt of conscience and short-

term enthusiasm, and too little by an authentic social vision and long–term conviction and deliberation. For most people those causes have remained almost entirely abstract; there has been too little personal involvement, and too much involvement in organizations which were insisting that *other* organizations should do what was right.

2 There is considerable danger that the Environment Movement will have the same nature: that it will be a public cause, served by organizations that will self-righteously criticize and condemn other organizations, inflated for a while by a lot of public talk in the media, only to be replaced in its turn by another fashionable crisis. I hope that will not happen, and I believe that there are ways to keep it from happening, but I know that if this effort is carried on solely as a public cause, if millions of people cannot or will not undertake it as a *private* cause as well, then it is *sure* to happen. In five years the energy of our present concern will have petered out in a series of public gestures—and no doubt in a series of empty laws—and a great, and perhaps the last, human opportunity will have been lost.

3 It need not be that way. A better possibility is that the movement to preserve the environment will be seen to be, as I think it has to be, not a disgression from the civil rights and peace movements, but the logical culmination of those movements. For I believe that the separation of these three problems is artificial. They have the same cause, and that is the mentality of greed and exploitation. The mentality that exploits and destroys the natural environment is the same that abuses racial and economic minorities, that imposes on young men the tyranny of the military draft, that makes war against peasants and women and children with the indifference of technology. The mentality that destroys a watershed and then panics at the threat of flood is the same mentality that gives institutionalized insult to black people and then panics at the prospect of race riots. It is the same mentality that can mount deliberate warfare against a civilian population and then express moral shock at the logical consequences of such warfare at My Lai. We would be fools to believe that we could solve any one of these problems without solving the others.

4 To me, one of the most important aspects of the environmental movement is that it brings us not just to another public crisis, but to a crisis of the protest movement itself. For the environmental crisis should make it dramatically clear, as perhaps it has not always been before, that there is no public crisis that is not also private. To most advocates of civil rights racism has seemed mostly the fault of someone else. For most advocates of peace the war has been a remote reality, and the burden of the blame has seemed to rest mostly on the government. I am certain that these crises have been more private, and that we have each suffered more from them and been more responsible for them, than has been readily apparent, but the connections have been difficult to see. Racism and militarism have been institutionalized among us for too long for our personal involvement in those evils to be easily apparent to us. Think, for example, of all the Northerners who assumed—

until black people attempted to move into *their* neighborhoods—that racism was a Southern phenomenon. And think how quickly—one might almost say how naturally—among some of its members the peace movement has spawned policies of deliberate provocation and violence.

⁵ But the environmental crisis rises closer to home. Every time we draw a breath, every time we drink a glass of water, every time we eat a bite of food we are suffering from it. And more important, every time we indulge in, or depend on, the wastefulness of our economy—and our economy's first principle is waste—we are *causing* the crisis. Nearly every one of us, nearly every day of his life, is contributing *directly* to the ruin of this planet. A protest meeting on the issue of environmental abuse is not a convocation of accusers, it is a convocation of the guilty. That realization ought to clear the smog of self-righteousness that has almost conventionally hovered over these occasions, and let us see the work that is to be done.

⁶ In this crisis it is certain that every one of us has a public responsibility. We must not cease to bother the government and the other institutions, to see that they never become comfortable with easy promises. For myself, I want to say that I hope never again to go to Frankfort [Kentucky] to present a petition to the governor on an issue so vital as that of strip mining, only to be dealt with by some ignorant functionary—as several of us were not so long ago, the governor himself being "too busy" to receive us. Next time I will go prepared to wait as long as necessary to see that the petitioners' complaints and their arguments are heard *fully*—and by the governor. And then I will hope to find ways to keep those complaints and arguments from being forgotten until something is done to relieve them. The time is past when it was enough merely to elect our officials. We will have to elect them and then go and *watch* them and keep our hands on them, the way the coal companies do. We have made a tradition in Kentucky of putting self-servers, and worse, in charge of our vital interests. I am sick of it. And I think that one way to change it is to make Frankfort a less comfortable place. I believe in American political principles, and I will not sit idly by and see those principles destroyed by sorry practice. I am ashamed and deeply distressed that American government should have become the chief cause of disillusionment with American principles.

⁷ And so when the government in Frankfort again proves too stupid or too blind or too corrupt to see the plain truth and to act with simple decency, I intend to be there, and I trust that I won't be alone. I hope, moreover, to be there, not with a sign or a slogan or a button, but with the facts and the arguments. A crowd whose discontent has risen no higher than the level of slogans is *only* a crowd. But a crowd that understands the reasons for its discontent and knows the remedies is a vital community, and it will have to be reckoned with. I would rather go before the government with two men who have a competent understanding of an issue, and who therefore deserve a hearing, than to go with two thousand who are vaguely dissatisfied.

[8] But even the most articulate public protest is not enough. We don't live in the government or in institutions or in our public utterances and acts, and the environmental crisis has its roots in our *lives*. By the same token, environmental health will also be rooted in our lives. That is, I take it, simply a fact, and in the light of it we can see how superficial and foolish we would be to think that we could correct what is wrong merely by tinkering with the institutional machinery. The changes that are required are fundamental changes in the way we are living.

[9] What we are up against in this country, in any attempt to involve private responsibility, is that we have nearly destroyed private life. Our people have given up their independence in return mostly for the cheap seductions and the shoddy merchandise of so-called affluence. We have delegated all our vital functions and responsibilities to salesmen and agents and bureaus and experts of all sorts. We cannot feed or clothe ourselves, or entertain ourselves, or communicate with each other, or be charitable or neighborly or loving, or even respect ourselves, without recourse to a merchant or a corporation or a public service organization or an agency of the government or a style-setter or an expert. Most of us cannot think of dissenting from the opinions or the actions of one organization without first forming a new organization. Individualism is going around these days in uniform, handing out the party line on individualism. Dissenters want to publish their personal opinions over a thousand signatures.

[10] The Confucian *Great Digest* says that the "chief way for the production of wealth" (and he is talking about real goods, not money) is "that the producers be many and that the mere consumers be few. . . ." But even in the much publicized rebellion of the young against the materialism of the affluent society, the consumer mentality is too often still intact: the standards of behavior are still those of kind and quantity, the security sought is still the security of numbers, and the chief motive is still the consumer's anxiety that one is missing out on what is "in." In this state of total consumerism—which is to say a state of helpless dependence on things and services and ideas and motives that we have forgotten how to provide ourselves—all meaningful contact between ourselves and the earth is broken. We do not understand the earth either in terms of what it offers us or what it requires of us, and I think it is the rule that people inevitably destroy what they do not understand. Most of us are not directly responsible for strip mining and extractive agriculture and other forms of environmental abuse. But we are guilty nevertheless, for we connive in them by our ignorance. We are ignorantly dependent on them. We do not know enough about them; we do not have a particular enough sense of their damage. Most of us, for example, not only do not know how to produce the best food in the best way—we don't know how to produce any kind in any way. And for this condition we have elaborate rationalizations, instructing us that dependence for everything on somebody else is efficient and economical and a scientific miracle. I say, instead, that it is madness, mass produced. A man who understands the weather only in terms of golf is participating in a

chronic public insanity that either he or his descendants will be bound to realize as suffering. I believe that the death of the world is breeding in such minds much more certainly and much faster than in any political capital or atomic arsenal.

[11] For an index of our loss of contact with the earth we need only to look at the condition of the American farmer—who must in our society, as in every society, enact man's dependence on the land, and his responsibility to it. In an age of unparalleled affluence and leisure, the American farmer is harder pressed and harder worked than ever before; his margin of profit is small, his hours long; his outlays for land and equipment and the expenses of maintenance and operation are growing rapidly greater; he cannot compete with industry for labor; he is being forced more and more to depend on the use of destructive chemicals and on the wasteful methods of haste and anxiety. As a class, farmers are one of the despised minorities. So far as I can see farming is considered marginal or incidental to the economy of the country, and farmers, when they are thought of at all, are thought of as hicks and yokels, whose lives do not fit into the modern scene. The average American farmer is now an old man, whose sons have moved away to the cities. His knowledge, and his intimate connection with the land are about to be lost. The small independent farmer is going the way of the small independent craftsmen and storekeepers. He is being forced off the land into the cities, his place taken by absentee owners, corporations, and machines. Some would justify all this in the name of efficiency. As I see it, it is an enormous social and economic and cultural blunder. For the small farmers who lived on their farms *cared* about their land. And given their established connection to their land—which was often hereditary and traditional as well as economic—they could have been encouraged to care for it more competently than they have so far. The corporations and machines that replace them will never be bound to the land by the sense of birthright and continuity, or by the love which enforces care. They will be bound by the rule of efficiency which takes thought only of the volume of the year's produce, and takes no thought of the slow increment of the life of the land, not measurable in pounds or dollars, which will assure the livelihood and the health of the coming generations.

[12] If we are to hope to correct our abuses of each other and of other races and of our land, and if our effort to correct these abuses is to be more than a political fad that will in the long run be only another form of abuse, then we are going to have to go far beyond public protest and political action. We are going to have to rebuild the substance and the integrity of private life in this country. We are going to have to gather up the fragments of knowledge and responsibility that we have parceled out to the bureaus and the corporations and the specialists, and we are going to have to put those fragments back together again in our own minds and in our families and households and neighborhoods. We need better government, no doubt about it. But we also need better minds, better friendships, better marriages, better communities.

We need persons and households that do not need to wait upon organizations but who can make necessary changes in themselves, on their own.

13 For most of the history of this country our motto, implied or spoken, has been Think Big. I have come to believe that a better motto, and an essential one now, is Think Little. That implies the necessary change of thinking and feeling, and suggests the necessary work. Thinking Big has led us to the two biggest and cheapest political dodges of our time: plan-making and law-making. The lotus-eaters of this era are in Washington D.C., Thinking Big. Somebody comes up with a problem, and somebody in the government comes up with a plan or a law. The result, mostly, has been the persistence of the problem, and the enlargement and enrichment of the government.

14 But the discipline of thought is not generalization; it is detail, and it is personal behavior. While the government is "studying" and funding and organizing its Big Thought, nothing is being done. But the citizen who is willing to think little, and, accepting the discipline of that, to go ahead on his own, is already solving the problem. A man who is trying to live as a neighbor to his neighbors will have a lively and practical understanding of the work of peace and brotherhood, and let there be no mistake about it—he is *doing* that work. A couple who make a good marriage, and raise healthy, morally competent children are serving the world's future more directly and surely than any political leader, though they never utter a public word. A good farmer who is dealing with the problem of soil erosion on an acre of ground has a sounder grasp of that problem, and *cares* more about it, and is probably doing more to solve it than any bureaucrat who is talking about it in general. A man who is willing to undertake the discipline and the difficulty of mending his own ways is worth more to the conservation movement than a hundred who are insisting merely that the government and the industries mend *their* ways.

15 If you are concerned about the proliferation of trash, then by all means start an organization in your community to do something about it. But before—*and while*— you organize, pick up some cans and bottles yourself. That way, at least, you will assure yourself and others that you mean what you say. If you are concerned about air pollution, help push for government controls, but drive your car less, use less fuel in your home. If you are worried about the damming of wilderness rivers, join the Sierra Club, write to the government, but turn off the lights you're not using, don't install an air conditioner, don't be a sucker for electrical gadgets, don't waste water. In other words, if you are fearful of the destruction of the environment, then learn to quit being an environmental parasite. We all are, in one way or another, and the remedies are not always obvious, though they certainly will always be difficult. They require a new kind of life—harder, more laborious, poorer in luxuries and gadgets, but also, I am certain, richer in meaning and more abundant in real pleasure. To have a healthy environment we will all have to give up things we like; we may even have to give up things we have come to think of as necessities. But to be fearful of the disease and yet unwilling to pay for the cure is not just to be hypocritical; it is to be doomed. If you talk a good line

without being changed by what you say, then you are not just hypocritical and doomed; you have become an agent of the disease. Consider, for an example, the President [Richard Nixon], who advertises his grave concern about the destruction of the environment, and who turns up the air conditioner to make it cool enough to build a fire.

¹⁶ Odd as I am sure it will appear to some, I can think of no better form of personal involvement in the cure of the environment than that of gardening. A person who is growing a garden, if he is growing it organically, is improving a piece of the world. He is producing something to eat, which makes him somewhat independent of the grocery business, but he is also enlarging, for himself, the meaning of food and the pleasure of eating. The food he grows will be fresher, more nutritious, less contaminated by poisons and preservatives and dye, than what he can buy at a store. He is reducing the trash problem; a garden is not a disposable container, and it will digest and re-use its own wastes. If he enjoys working in his garden, then he is less dependent on an automobile or a merchant for his pleasure. He is involving himself directly in the work of feeding people.

¹⁷ If you think I'm wandering off the subject, let me remind you that most of the vegetables necessary for a family of four can be grown on a plot of forty by sixty feet. I think we might see in this an economic potential of considerable importance, since we now appear to be facing the possibility of widespread famine. How much food could be grown in the dooryards of cities and suburbs? How much could be grown along the extravagant rights-of-way of the Interstate system? Or how much could be grown, by the intensive practices and economics of the small farm, on so-called marginal lands? Louis Bromfield liked to point out that the people of France survived crisis after crisis because they were a nation of gardeners, who in times of want turned with great skill to their own small plots of ground. And F.H. King, an agriculture professor who traveled extensively in the Orient in 1907, talked to a Chinese farmer who supported a family of twelve, "one donkey, one cow, . . . and two pigs on 2.5 acres of cultivated land"—and who did this, moreover, by agricultural methods that were sound enough organically to have maintained his land in prime fertility through several thousand years of such use. These are possibilities that are very readily apparent and attractive to minds that are prepared to think little. To Big Thinkers—the bureaucrats and businessmen of agriculture—they are quite simply invisible. But intensive, organic agriculture kept the farms of the Orient thriving for thousands of years, whereas extensive—which is to say, exploitive or extractive—agriculture has critically reduced the fertility of American farmlands in a few centuries or even a few decades.

¹⁸ A person who undertakes to grow a garden at home, by practices that will preserve rather than exploit the economy of the soil, has set his mind decisively against what is wrong with us. He is helping himself in a way that dignifies him, and that is rich in meaning and pleasure. But he is doing something else that is more important: he is making vital contact with the soil and

the weather on which his life depends. He will no longer look upon rain as an impediment of traffic, or upon the sun as a holiday decoration. And his sense of man's dependence on the world will have grown precise enough, one would hope, to be politically clarifying and useful.

¹⁹ What I am saying is that if we apply our minds directly and competently to the needs of the earth, then we will have begun to make fundamental and very necessary changes in our minds. We will begin to understand and to mistrust *and to change* our wasteful economy, which markets not just the produce of the earth, but also the earth's ability to produce. We will see that beauty and utility are alike dependent upon the health of the world. But we will also see through the fads and the fashions of protest. We will see that war and oppression and pollution are not separate issues, but are aspects of the same issue. Amid the outcries for the liberation of this group or that, we will know that no person is free except in the freedom of other persons, and that man's only real freedom is to know and faithfully occupy his place—a much humbler place than we have been taught to think—in the order of creation. And we will know that of all issues in education the issue of relevance is the phoniest. If life were as predictable and small as the talkers of politics would have it, then relevance would be a consideration. But life is large and surprising and mysterious, and we don't know what we need to know. When I was a student I refused certain subjects because I thought they were irrelevant to the duties of a writer, and I have had to take them up, clumsily and late, to understand my duties as a man. What we need in education is not relevance, but abundance, variety, adventurousness, thoroughness. A student should suppose that he needs to learn everything he can, and he should suppose that he will need to know much more than he can learn.

²⁰ But the change of mind I am talking about involves not just a change of knowledge, but also a change of attitude toward our essential ignorance, a change in our bearing in the face of mystery. The principle of ecology, if we will take it to heart, should keep us aware that our lives depend upon other lives and upon processes and energies in an interlocking system which, though we can destroy it completely, we can neither fully understand nor fully control. And our great dangerousness is that, locked in our selfish and myopic economics, we have been willing to change or destroy far beyond our power to understand. We are not humble enough or reverent enough.

²¹ Some time ago I heard a representative of a paper company refer to conservation as a "no-return investment." This man's thinking was exclusively oriented to the annual profit of his industry. Circumscribed by the demand that the profit be great, he simply could not be answerable to any other demand—not even to the obvious needs of his own children.

²² Consider, in contrast, the profound ecological intelligence of Black Elk, "a holy man of the Oglala Sioux," who in telling his story said that it was not his own life that was important to him, but what he had shared with all life: "It is the story of all life that is holy and it is good to tell, and of us two-leggeds sharing in it with the four-leggeds and the wings of the air and all

green things. . . ." And of the great vision that came to him when he was a child he said: "I saw that the sacred hoop of my people was one of many hoops that made one circle, wide as daylight and as starlight, and in the center grew one mighty flowering tree to shelter all the children of one mother and father. And I saw that it was holy."

ANALYTICAL READING

1. What relationship does Berry think the environmental movement has to other movements of the past decade or so? Is there a classification scheme involved? Is there a cause-and-effect relationship?

2. Where does the writer establish the public-versus-private idea? How is it sustained throughout? Is there a conflict between his view about public political protests and private responsibilities?

3. What does Berry think about the institutionalization of every aspect of life? What examples does he use?

4. What points does he make in the discussion of farmers?

5. This article was first given as an Ecology Day speech before a group of University of Kentucky students. Do you think Berry has a sense of his audience? If so, illustrate.

6. What is the function of the first sentence in paragraph 12? Did you underline it?

7. How does Berry use comparison and contrast in paragraph 15? Note the sentence structure and parallelism.

8. Berry uses many SUBJECT–RESTRICTION–ILLUSTRATION paragraphs. Point out some that you found especially effective in using form to promote meaning.

9. What basic change in attitude does Berry say is necessary? Explain.

REFLECTING

Point: What is the main idea of the essay? Which one sentence do you think is the most effective statement of it?

Organization: The essay has basically a SUBJECT–RESTRICTION–ILLUSTRATION organization. Where is the subject and illustration introduced? Does the ending reflect the restriction of the paper? What kinds of illustration devices are used?

Support: How does Berry relate his personal example to his thesis idea?

Synthesis: This article was written in 1970. Do you think the ideas expressed here are becoming more widespread? If so, illustrate. How have the energy crisis and inflation affected our thinking?

Evaluation: Did you find the article effective? If so, what aspects of it did you find most appealing? In terms of the occasion and the audience, was quoting Black Elk at the end a good writing device? Why or why not?

FROM READING TO WRITING

1. Write a paper illustrating how one person can make a difference in improving the quality of life.

2. Explain in a paper how critical the need to solve environmental problems is.

3. Do you agree with Berry that "we have nearly destroyed private life" (paragraph 9)? Respond in a paper.

4. Write a paper entitled "Think Big," taking issue with Berry.

5. Most city dwellers have no land for small gardens. Write a paper explaining what they can do in thinking little about the environment.

AFTER ALL, IT'S A SMALL, SMALL WORLD
Raymond F. Betts

BIOGRAPHICAL SKETCH

Raymond Betts was born in Bloomfield, New Jersey, in 1925. He graduated from Rutgers and earned a Ph.D. from Columbia University. He has taught at Bryn Mawr College and Grinnell College and is presently a professor of history at the University of Kentucky. He has edited and written six books, including The False Storm: European Imperialism in the Nineteenth Century, *and his articles on social and cultural values have appeared in* Newsday *and the* Lexington Herald. *A specialist in French history, Betts has studied and taught in France and has also written several articles on aspects of French history. In addition, he has written and acted in several plays.*

PRE-READING

1. What relationship do you see between the title and the opening paragraph?

2. What opinion is expressed in the final paragraph?

3. From the information in the biographical sketch, what do you expect Betts' approach to be?

¹ Future historians may single out the new Chevrolet Chevette as the significant artifact marking the decline of the popular fascination with giantism that has characterized American progress for the last century-and-a-half. Proudly proclaimed because of its diminutive size, the Chevette even sports a model title of "Scooter," a name in itself constituting an act of defiance cast against a Detroit tradition of poetic expressions about power and length of wheelbase.

FROM *Newsday*, 30 November 1975, p. 7. Reprinted by permission of the author.

[2] For generations the American public has been culturally conditioned to believe that size mysteriously expresses value: The bigger the better, or the biggest the best. Whatever its form—from horsepower generated to number of PhD's granted in a given year—the more impressive the resultant figure the worthier the item or institution is considered to be. That the word "imperial"—a word politically shrouded in negative connotations these days—could have been enthusiastically assigned to the model of an automobile or selected as the brand name of a margarine and a motel chain is a very obvious indication of the persistent appeal that grandeur enjoys.

[3] Now that size, like so much of our industrial waste, is being compacted, we might well ask why the almost metaphysical principle of giantism spread so widely in the first place.

[4] The popular interest in immensity is an outcome of industrial democracy. Technological developments, particularly in the fields of energy and engineering, enabled the western world to undertake both the conquest of distance and the imprisonment of space. Among the structural wonders of the last hundred years, consider only the Eiffel Tower, the *Titanic* and Pennsylvania Station, and we, as today's observers, can gain an appreciation of the excitement felt at the time over the monumental accomplishments made possible through the release of human imagination by technological ingenuity.

[5] From a psychological perspective, this intense concern with the oversized reflected the widespread interest in the organization of mass, whether that be of inert building materials, or of urban space, or even of human beings, as demonstrated, for instance, by the Nazis who magnificently arrayed thousands during party rallies. Observing such developments, critics since the time of Alexis de Tocqueville have remarked that an industrial democratic social order makes all individuals equally insignificant but imparts to their totality an importance and idea of greatness not expressed in other societies. Perhaps this is the ultimate explanation of the Pentagon and the Astrodome as spatio-cultural phenomena: Both are the settings in which well-organized activities engage vast numbers of participants who are individually assigned an essentially passive role.

[6] Yet what has really differentiated industrial democratic monumentalism from that of previous social systems—such as ancient Egypt with its pyramids—is the nature of power, of the controlled energy giving rise to it. Not in its buildings, but in its mechanism does American giantism express indigenous form. The jet aircraft, of which the Boeing 747 is the awesome model, proudly demonstrates collective effort at its technological best, just as the roar of its engines at take-off humbles passengers into a realization of their own weakness, their limited energy.

[7] However, we have all been able to ignore this latter personal and social condition because of the innumerable concepts and forms translated symbolically and practically into units that we can individually grasp. At the "pop" or ridiculous end of the spectrum is the series of names given detergents and cleansers with which household chores can be heroically and dramatically

subdued: "Bold," "Dynamo," "Drive," "Dash," and "Drain Power," for instance. At the bright end are the many items of industrial hardware designed to fill our leisure time. Outboard motors, trail bikes, stereophonic equipment, even CB transmitters help provide each of us with the power to manipulate our environment: to force space through changes in speed and sound, to conform to our immediate wishes.

[8] Above and beyond all, of course, is poised the motor car, the personal valet answering our unarticulated demands. Symbol and reality of American industrial prowess and the gigantic results it has attained, the automobile has reinforced our cultural indoctrination of respect for giantism as a social and ethical principle. Why else own a Cadillac or—and notice the incongruity of names—a Lincoln Continental, unless to possess some measurable amount of the power and grandeur generated by modern technology?

[9] Of course we are all aware of the obvious reason for which the Chevette has appeared: the energy crisis. But place this realization in a broader historical setting, and the further meaning becomes clear. The age of boundlessness—of the incessant expansion which the spirit of giantism encouraged—is now over. True, it is doubtful that an expression like "think small" will replace the traditional "think big," but democratic principles and cultural pretensions will surely be readjusted. Perhaps at that time the word "Eldorado" will no longer be scrolled in chrome but simply confined to the magnificent dream city far beyond the radius of the Scooter and the values it will convey.

ANALYTICAL READING

1. What reasons does Betts give for the American emphasis on bigness? How are they expressed in terms of cause-and-effect relationships?

2. What contrast does the writer make between current "giantism" and the Egyptian pyramids (paragraph 6)? What point does he make with this brief comparison?

3. According to Betts, how do brand and model names reflect our social attitudes?

4. Why do you think he places strongest emphasis on the automobile?

5. Explain the meaning of the last sentence.

REFLECTING

Point: Is the opinion in the final paragraph the thesis idea for the paper? Summarize the author's opinion in one sentence.

Organization: How does Betts handle SUBJECT–RESTRICTION–ILLUSTRATION organization? Does the restriction come at the beginning or end of the essay?

Support: Discuss how Betts uses examples, cause-and-effect relationships, and citing of authority to support his thesis.

Synthesis: How does this essay relate to Wendell Berry's "Think Little" (pages 285–93)? Given a choice, would you prefer to own a small car, a big car, or no car at all? What forces do you think have influenced your choice? Why are CB radios so popular?

Evaluation: What features of the article do you think are most effective? Why? Do you think Betts is trying to persuade his audience or merely to explain a current situation? Explain.

FROM READING TO WRITING

1. Using Betts' thesis that modern Americans are conditioned to bigness, write an opinion paper discussing the changes in camping equipment over the last twenty years or so.

2. Referring to Betts' article and Robert Lipsyte's "SportsWorld" (pages 222–27), write an opinion paper about sports in the United States.

3. Write an opinion paper illustrating a trend you see in American society that indicates a shift from "thinking big" to "thinking small."

MARRIAGE IS NOT A PERSONAL MATTER
John Finley Scott

BIOGRAPHICAL SKETCH

John Finley Scott was born in California in 1934. He did his undergraduate work at Reed College and earned M.A. and Ph.D. degrees from Stanford University. Presently a professor of sociology at the University of California at Davis, he has written numerous articles and a book, Internalization of Norms.

PRE-READING

1. What do you think the rather enigmatic title means?

2. From skimming the first and last paragraphs, what would you guess the subject and the writer's opinion to be?

[1] The newest wrinkle in the old game of courtship is match-making by computer. It goes something like this: a young man lists in a "data bank" what he most desires in a prospective female companion and supplies information

FROM *Women: Their Changing Roles,* ed. Elizabeth Janeway (New York: Arno Press, 1973), pp. 516–19. Originally printed in *The New York Times Magazine.* © 1966 by The New York Times Company. Reprinted by permission.

about his own characteristics. The computer compares the qualities and interests desired against those of an . . . inventory of candidates who have also put themselves on file. After some adjustment and compromise, our young man is presented with the name, address and telephone number of a "Miss Just-Right-and-very-nice-too." Since electronic match-making is not quite yet an exact science, he may also be informed of a few alternates . . . in case something goes wrong and he doesn't quite hit it off with Miss Just-Right.

² The fact that many "computerized introduction services" are pretty much fly-by-night operations does not mean that computer match-making is unworkable in principle. If marital felicity can be accurately defined, then it would seem that a compatible marriage partner would more likely be found among the thousands of candidates to which a computer could refer than among the handful that any one person could ever meet face to face.

³ But the problem is identifying "marital felicity"; what on earth *is* a successful marriage? Can any kind of successful matching be based on the verbal responses of the largely adolescent segment of the population that is on the verge of matrimony? Any programmer will tell you that a computer is no better than the information put into it. In many respects, the verbal professions of persons facing marriage are the last things on which to base predictions about the future condition of the families thus formed. That a number of marriages—a minority, to be sure, but a substantial one—will terminate in divorce within three years will hardly be revealed through polling the expectations of brides-to-be.

Excerpts from the sort of questionnaire a person in search of a date or mate might fill out for processing by computer.

For Men

1. Which of the following activities most appeals to you?
   (1) skindiving in Montego Bay
   (2) touring the Rijksmuseum in Amsterdam
   (3) watching a bullfight in Seville
   (4) mountain climbing in Lausanne
   (5) eating leberkase and drinking dark beer in a brauhaus in Munich

2. With which of the following cars can you most readily identify?
   (1) Rolls Royce
   (2) Mustang
   (3) Cadillac
   (4) Jaguar XKE
   (5) Maxwell (vintage)
   (6) Volkswagen

For Women

1. In which of the following situations would you feel most comfortable?
   (1) exploring Vesuvius and the ruins of Pompeii
   (2) sipping cappucino on the Via Veneto (Rome)
   (3) boating off the island of Mykonos (Greece)
   (4) conversing with peasants in Skoplje (Yugoslavia)
   (5) visiting the Uffizi Galleries (Florence)

2. Of the following, which would you prefer?
   (1) loving a man who did not love you
   (2) being loved by a man you could not love
   (3) neither loving nor being loved until the feeling was mutual, regardless of how long it took to come about

For Men

3. You are at a party where you don't know anyone. You would very likely:
   (1) *leave early*
   (2) *find a comfortable chair in a corner*
   (3) *join a conversation about sports*
   (4) *introduce yourself to the women*
   (5) *introduce yourself to the men*

4. Which of the following fields are you most closely associated with or interested in?
   (1) *medicine and research*
   (2) *law*
   (3) *education*
   (4) *social services*
   (5) *advertising–public relations*
   (6) *science and technology*
   (7) *military service*
   (8) *sales*
   (9) *finance and industry*

5. Your fiancée informs you that she has had relations with another man. You would probably:
   (1) *break the engagement*
   (2) *marry her despite grave misgivings*
   (3) *tell her it doesn't matter*
   (4) *tell her of your own amorous adventures*
   (5) *feel that her experience would make for a more successful marriage*

6. Which of the following would probably give you the greatest personal satisfaction?
   (1) *working for the welfare of others*
   (2) *traveling extensively*
   (3) *being elected to public office*
   (4) *earning a fortune*
   (5) *raising a family*

7. You've taken her out to dinner three or four times, but when you ask her to prepare the next meal herself, she informs you that she can't cook. You would most likely feel:
   (1) *angry*
   (2) *dejected*
   (3) *relieved*
   (4) *indifferent*
   (5) *hungry*

For Women

3. How well can you cook?
   (1) *expertly, exotic dishes and proper wines*
   (2) *quite well, but nothing fancy*
   (3) *hit or miss*
   (4) *TV dinners and canned soup*
   (5) *can-openers are for picture-hanging*

4. Which of the following fields are you most closely associated with or interested in?
   (1) *nursing*
   (2) *secretarial*
   (3) *modeling or fashion*
   (4) *sales or purchasing*
   (5) *fine arts or design*
   (6) *education*
   (7) *business administration*

5. Your date has spent his money on an electronic fish-finder, but you had wanted him to escort you to a concert. You would most likely:
   (1) *pay your own way*
   (2) *lend him money*
   (3) *find another date and let him go fishing*
   (4) *treat him*
   (5) *go fishing with him*

6. You are with your friends when an argument develops about the evening's activity. You would:
   (1) *remain silent*
   (2) *compromise*
   (3) *go along with the majority*
   (4) *insist upon your choice*
   (5) *go off alone*

7. Which of the following date ideas most appeals to you?
   (1) *dining and dancing*
   (2) *horseback riding*
   (3) *a picnic in the country*
   (4) *watching TV*
   (5) *attending a concert*

8. How important is it that your match own and drive a car?
   (1) *very important*
   (2) *moderately important*
   (3) *he can borrow mine*

Questions reprinted courtesy of Data-Date, Inc.

[4] Part of the problem is that marriage, though often regarded as an intensely personal affair, is one of the least individualistic of all social institutions. The family . . . has evolved not because it satisfies individual preferences but because it is socially useful. It combines the functions of reproduction, child care, sexual gratification and economic cooperation with an over-all efficiency that no alternative arrangement has so far been able to match. Since marriage is such a good thing from the society's point of view, it is convenient to make young people want to get married by teaching them that marriage satisfies their *own* needs, and to soft-pedal the demands of the larger society. This is why marriage . . . is easier to enter than to leave. Young people are recruited to matrimony, but at the same time their hopes come to depend on frequently unrealistic aspirations, and their ability to predict what lies ahead becomes limited.

[5] Here lies the problem with any scheme of matchmaking that relies solely on the expressed preferences of the young people involved. This is hardly anything new: many parents, and most professional matchmakers . . . have known it for years. It would be interesting to see what kind of matches a computer would arrange if it interviewed parents as well as their eligible children.

[6] We live in a society where unprecedented numbers of young people, aided by rapid social change, higher education, urbanization and widespread geographical and social mobility, negotiate marriages on their own, without the help of kith and kin. But the notion that the process as a whole is primarily an individual matter is a myth. When two people date who did not know each other beforehand, it is called a "blind date"—a name which stresses the fact that most dates are not blind. Wherever dating customs are studied closely—from church socials to Army barracks—intermediaries and "fixer-uppers" are found busily at work, pairing off the boys and girls in roughly the same way as the new computers. Considering the cost involved, it is economical for persons who date to rely on some outside help. For a young man, expected to take the initiative, dating is one of the most ruthless and unprotected forms of competition in which he can engage. He must put himself up for acceptance or rejection, and rejection can produce severe psychic wounds.

[7] For a young woman, masculine attention in dating and courtship is the greatest social reward she will ever receive, and she therefore desires it to an extreme degree. But for her to accept dates indiscriminately is to run a variety of risks from boredom to sexual assault. The services of intermediaries, who present young men with invitations already accepted and young women with escorts already screened, are therefore greatly appreciated and widely practiced. . . . When young people today talk in all sincerity about their freedom to date anybody they please, they simply are not describing the entire process, of whose many controls they are often artfully kept unaware.

[8] One very general answer can be given to the question of who marries whom: Most people marry someone pretty much like themselves. . . . But

scientific and garden-variety curiosity alike concentrate on the unexpected and unlikely combinations. . . .

⁹ Unexpected marriages . . . catch our attention when they deviate from social norms. The salient thing about marriage in this society—indeed, in any society with an organized system of kinship—is that it is regulated by the kinship-based groups which it affects. On the one hand, rules against incest drive young adults out of their own families; yet everywhere these young adults are expected to marry someone from a quite similar family. The anthropologist A. R. Radcliffe-Brown put the matter well when he referred to marriage as a "crisis."

¹⁰ Norms of mate selection—as sociologists rather coarsely phrase it—can be looked at as a classification of social groups in some of which marriage is to be preferred and in others is to be avoided. The practice of marriage within a group is called endogamy. All large groups formed by inheritance—what we call "ethnic groups"—will prefer endogamy to some degree. Since two parents who share the same ethnic traditions can pass them on more consistently than two whose backgrounds differ, endogamy makes a good deal of sense if one wishes to preserve traditions. And the more traditions are cherished, the stronger is the urge toward endogamy. American Jews, for example, voice great concern over the extent of Jewish exogamy—the opposite of endogamy—although, from a comparative point of view, it is amazingly small— probably less than 10 percent of all marriages involving a Jew. But it seems that the only way for Jewish traditions to survive is through lifelong training of persons born into the group. . . . Jewish control of endogamy is therefore remarkably strong, and the democracy and indulgence that seem characteristic of Jewish family life usually end abruptly when the prospect of intermarriage looms. Similar rules can be found among American Oriental population groups, the Mormons and, in weaker form, Roman Catholics (who more willingly accept converts).

.   .   .

¹¹ Predicting whether a certain proportion of marriages will be endogamous or exogamous actually depends on a few rather obvious variables. The relative numbers of the two sexes—the "sex ratio"—is one of the most obvious. It is historically important because men are more likely to migrate than women. This is largely why American, as a land of migrants, has been as much of a melting pot as it has. Many immigrant men who felt strongly about "marrying a nice (Jewish-Polish-Irish-Armenian, etc.) girl" found there wasn't enough of the kind they wanted to go around. Faced with the choices of marrying out or not marrying at all, many of them married out. The same thing goes on inside America today because men migrate to one place and women to another (there are usually more unmarried women than men in big cities, for example), so that rules for some sort of endogamous marriage get slighted in the competition for anyone to marry at all.

¹² Another factor is the degree of parental control. This is important because it is the older generation that most respects the traditional rules of endogamy, while young people are easily swayed by personal attractions. Here residence is important. A young lady who lives at home and receives her suitors there cannot easily entertain young men of whom her parents strongly disapprove. Even when she is given much freedom, the elders can still influence her choice. Daughters can hardly fall in love with unsuitable men they never meet, and the chances of their not meeting them are greatly increased if the parents happen to have moved (for the children's sake, of course) to a class-homogeneous suburb. When a girl becomes infatuated with a boy beneath her station, her parents can use the old strategem of inviting him to a rather formal dinner, the better that his incorrigible unfitness for symbolically important occasions will be forced on the daughter's attention.

¹³ Today, however, parental control faces the peculiar threat of college education. When children live at home, parents can keep track daily of whom they are dating. But college often requires "dependent" and "irresponsible" children to live away from home. To be sure, a few young people have been going away to college for generations. But three trends combine to make college today a major threat to endogamy: (1) More persons of college age are in college (currently about 40 per cent); (2) An increasing proportion of students are women; and (3) The average age at marriage has dropped (especially for women) to a point where it falls for many in the traditional undergraduate years.

¹⁴ College and matrimony thus combine to render the campus the most active marriage market of modern times. Even when children live at home while attending college (a growing trend as new campuses and junior colleges are built), the dating situation on the campus is hard for parents to control. Student bodies tend to be large and heterogeneous, and almost any of the many campus activities can be used for making contacts and thus beginning the process of dating and courtship. Not that parents have not fought back. College fraternities, and especially sororities, embody many ingenious arrangements whereby the courtship of young persons is kept in line with the desires of an older generation. Yet it is safe to predict that an increasing number of American marriages will be between persons who meet in college, and they are likely to meet under conditions largely indifferent to older rules of endogamy.

¹⁵ A third factor affecting the maintenance of endogamy is social mobility—the process by which members of a generation achieve a higher class position than that into which they were born. In America this movement is ultimately related to higher education, for we widely believe that upward mobility is a good thing and that higher education contributes to it. But to the extent that young people start moving up before they are married, and that boys move up in different ways, or at different rates, than girls, then the traditional ways of pairing them off endogamously no longer work.

¹⁶ The most basic difference here is that a man gains his status mainly through his job, whereas a woman's status is mainly conferred on her by her husband. We often speak as if occupational success were equally inportant for both sexes, but actually it is much less important for women. Women *can* gain a tolerable status through work, but a better one can usually be gained more easily through marriage. Where men move up most directly by competing for good jobs, women move up mainly by marrying men who move up. Marriage thus becomes the means of mobility for women. Insofar as she responds to the American dream of upward mobility, every unmarried American girl has a bit of the gold-digger in her.

¹⁷ Consider the situation of American Catholics. Catholic girls are expected to marry Catholic boys, but they also want to marry successful men. And it just so happens that, for most of the country, Protestant men on the average hold higher-ranked positions than do Catholic men. If the Catholic girl marries up, she is likely to marry out. And evidently this does occur, because more Catholic women marry outside their faith than do Catholic men. Among Jews, however, the situation is reversed. Men in this group are eminently successful and are "good catches" for girls of any faith who want to marry up. Evidently they do get caught, for many more Jewish boys marry gentiles than do Jewish girls.

¹⁸ The pressure for marrying up among women produces a kind of imbalance in marital bargaining, to the advantage of high-status men and low-status women and the disadvantage of low-status men and high-status women. A low-status man has little wealth or prestige to offer a wife. In addition, he must compete for a wife not only with others in his own station but with higher-ranked men as well.

¹⁹ A well-born woman, if she is to maintain through marriage the status conferred on her by her parents, must marry a man at least equally well-born—but for such men she faces a deadly competition from lower-status female rivals who also regard them as desirable husbands. As a result, low-status men are more likely to remain bachelors, and high-status women are more likely to remain spinsters. . . .

²⁰ If a sociologist is so artlessly blunt as to ask young women whether they marry for money or for love, he will be lucky to escape with his questionnaire forms. Love, the girls indignantly tell us, conquers all. Lovable personal qualities eclipse Philistine wealth. But this is too simple by far.

²¹ On the one hand, there is a strong statistical tendency for women to marry up. If our hypothetical sociologist returns, suitably chastened, with a subtler set of questions on what makes men lovable, he will receive a list of characteristics of which many—urbane good manners, sensitivity, sophisticated good taste, interesting conversation, and so on—depend on expensive education and are thus associated with wealth. . . .

²² On the other hand, there probably never has been a society in which all lovable attributes were monopolized by one class. Love thus becomes a poten-

tially random factor in marriage, one contrary to all rules of endogamy. In societies with stronger rules of endogamy than our own, love is not unknown, but it is strongly controlled and is regarded as irrelevant in the choice of marital partners.

23 The emotions of love are strong, but they are also ambiguous and volatile, and are therefore subject to deception and fraud. This places an emphasis on sincerity, but sincerity in love is very hard to assess. Young women are besieged with professions of love which they suspect are voiced simply to facilitate a quick seduction—and this is not what "love" means to most of them.

24 Especially where courtship tends to be individualistic, so that suitors cannot be effectively held to account for their promises, young women tend to measure the love of a young man not simply by what he says, but also by what he invests in the relationship. Often this is his money, but more often it is his time. Because any marriage market involves a wide age range of men competing for the smaller range of women in the years when they are young and pretty, the investment required in courtship gets bid up to a high level. Feminine nubility, thus rewarded, becomes a veritable institution in its own right. The extravagance of attention that young girls expect, however, paradoxically limits their chances for marrying well. Regardless of his income, the *time* of a successful man is always dear, while the adult male who is "still finding himself" is the one with the leisure to invest in courtship.

25 This applies also at the college level, where the pre-professional student who is going places occupationally has little time for dating and leaves most of the social life to the less ambitious campus playboys. This means that women who expect their suitors to spend a great deal of time in dating are likely to marry men of modest achievement in other areas.

26 Now: How can all this be put in a matchmaking computer? It would be easy to specify the information that would be required, but awfully hard to find any way of digging it up. Getting it by simple interrogation—which is what the computers use now—would make the money-or-love question look like a masterpiece of diplomacy.

·   ·   ·

27 The marriage practices of human society embody both ancient traditions and novel responses to changing times. The broad patterns of marriage—movement across class lines, the age at which it occurs, its impact on education and work—can be pretty well predicted, and in fact are predicted by sociologists, demographers and insurance actuaries. But the narrow practical questions—"Will he marry her?" or "Will they be happy together?"—are likely to remain inexplicable, at least to the people involved. And the mystery is what gives these questions their abiding appeal. Successful computer matching—unlikely, anyway—would only spoil the fun.

ANALYTICAL READING

1. What purpose does the opening discussion about computer courtship have? What is the function of the first sentence of paragraph 4?

2. What social reasons does Scott give for the evolution of marriage?

3. In what ways are young people programmed for marriage? Explain *endogamy* and the importance of a woman's residence.

4. How does Scott classify the "norms of mate selection" (paragraph 10)?

5. What reasons does he give for women using marriage as a device of "upward mobility?" This article was written in 1966; to what extent do you think women still do this?

6. What does Scott have to say about love as a basis for marriage?

7. Does the writer think computer selection could work? Why or why not? What are the difficulties?

REFLECTING

Point: What opinion is the writer expressing? Is he against love?

Organization: How does the writer employ classification in this opinion paper? Is it the main organizational scheme? Discuss.

Support: How are classification and comparison and contrast used to support the opinion expressed?

Synthesis: Have any societal attitudes changed since this article was written? Do the marriages in your own family reflect Scott's opinions about the way we select mates?

Evaluation: Did you find the essay effective? Why or why not? Did you disagree with any points the writer made? Why?

FROM READING TO WRITING

1. Fill in the questionnaire and compare answers with your classmates. Then write an opinion paper in which you suggest an approach for collecting information from people for computer matchmaking.

2. What role do sororities and fraternities play in mate selection?

3. What are the advantages and disadvantages of blind dates?

THE STAGES OF DYING
Elisabeth Kübler-Ross

BIOGRAPHICAL SKETCH

Elisabeth Kübler-Ross was born in Zurich, Switzerland, in 1926. A doctor of psychiatry, she has received degrees from a number of universities, including the University of Zurich, Smith College, and Albany College of Medicine. She has been a practitioner, a teacher, and a consultant in psychiatry since 1959. Although her professional interests include children's emotional problems and psychosomatic medicine, her main concern has been with the psychological adjustment to dying. Besides On Death and Dying, *from which this selection is taken, her publications include* Death: The Final Stage of Growth *and* Questions and Answers on Death and Dying.

PRE-READING

1. From the title of the book and the opening paragraph, what do you think will be the author's attitude toward dying?

2. Does the opening paragraph help to allay your aversion to reading about death? If so, how?

3. From the biographical sketch, what do you assume about Kübler-Ross as an authority on the subject?

¹ In a time of uncertainty, of the hydrogen bomb, of the big rush and the masses, the little small, personal gift may again become meaningful. The gift is on both sides: from the [dying] patient in the form of the help, inspiration, and encouragement he may give to others with a similar predicament; from us in the form of our care, our time, and our wish to share with others what they have taught us at the end of their lives.

² One reason perhaps for patients' good response is the need of the dying person to leave something behind, to give a little gift, to create an illusion of immortality perhaps. We acknowledge our appreciation for their sharing with us their thoughts about this taboo topic, we tell them that their role is to *teach* us, to help those who follow them later on, thus creating an idea that something will live perhaps after their death, an idea, a seminar in which their suggestions, their fantasies, their thoughts continue to live, to be discussed, become immortal in a little way.

³ A communication has been established by the dying patient who attempts to separate himself from human relationships in order to face the last separation with the fewest possible ties, yet is unable to do this without help from an outsider who shares some of these conflicts with him.

⁴ We are talking about death—the subject of social repression—in a frank, uncomplicated manner, thus opening the door for a wide variety of discussions, allowing complete denial if this seems to be necessary or open talk about the patient's fears and concerns if the patient so chooses. The fact that *we* don't use denial, that we are willing to use the words death and dying, is perhaps the most welcomed communication for many of our patients.

⁵ If we attempt to summarize briefly what these patients have taught us, the outstanding fact, to my mind, is that they are all aware of the seriousness of their illness whether they are told or not. They do not always share this knowledge with their doctor or next of kin. The reason for this is that it is painful to think of such a reality, and any implicit or explicit message not to talk about it is usually perceived by the patient and—for the moment—gladly accepted. There came a time, however, when all of our patients had a need to share some of their concerns, to lift the mask, to face reality, and to take care of vital matters while there was still time. They welcomed a breakthrough in their defenses, they appreciated our willingness to talk with them about their impending death and unfinished tasks. They wished to share with an understanding person some of their feelings, especially the ones of anger, rage, envy, guilt, and isolation. They clearly indicated that they used denial when the doctor or family member expected denial because of their dependency on them and their need to maintain a relationship.

⁶ The patients did not mind so much when the staff did not confront them with the facts directly, but they resented being treated like children and not being considered when important decisions were made. They all sensed a change in attitude and behavior when the diagnosis of a malignancy was made and became aware of the seriousness of their condition because of the changed behavior of the people in their environment. In other words, those who were not told explicitly knew it anyway from the implicit messages or altered behavior of relatives or staff. Those who were told explicitly appreciated the opportunity almost unanimously except for those who were told either crudely in hallways and without preparation or follow-up, or in a manner that left no hope.

⁷ All of our patients reacted to the bad news in almost identical ways, which is typical not only of the news of fatal illness but seems to be a human reaction to great and unexpected stress: namely, with shock and disbelief. Denial was used by most of our patients and lasted from a few seconds to many months. . . . This denial is never a total denial. After the denial, anger and rage predominated. It expressed itself in a multitude of ways as an envy of those who were able to live and function. This anger was partially justified and enforced by the reactions of staff and family, at times almost irrational and a repetition of earlier experiences. . . . When the environment was able to tolerate this anger without taking it personally, the patient was greatly helped in reaching a stage of temporary bargaining followed by depression, which is a stepping-stone towards final acceptance. The following diagram demon-

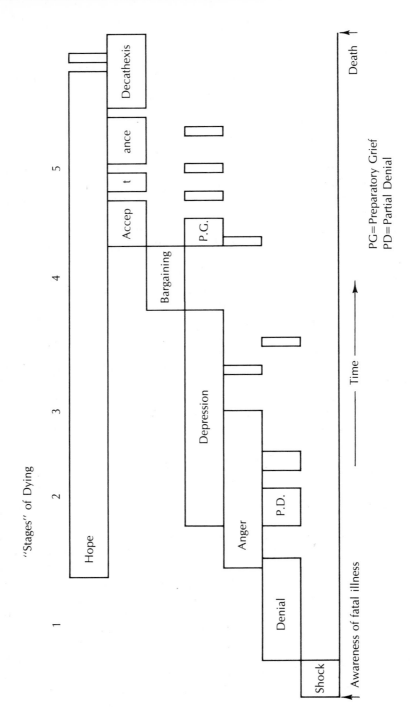

"Stages" of Dying

PG = Preparatory Grief
PD = Partial Denial

strates how these stages do not replace each other but can exist next to each other and overlap at times. The final acceptance has been reached by many patients without any external help, others needed assistance in working through these different stages in order to die in peace and dignity.

[8] No matter the stage of illness or coping mechanisms used, all our patients maintained some form of hope until the last moment. Those patients who were told of their fatal diagnosis without a chance, without a sense of hope, reacted the worst and never quite reconciled themselves with the person who presented the news to them in this cruel manner. As far as our patients are concerned, all of them maintained some hope and it is well for us to remember this! It may come in the form of a new discovery, a new finding in a research laboratory, a new drug or serum, it may come as a miracle from God or by the discovery that the X-ray or pathological slide really belongs to another patient. It may come in the form of a naturally occurring remission, . . . but it is this hope that should always be maintained whether we can agree with the form or not.

[9] Though our patients greatly appreciated sharing their concerns with us and talked freely about death and dying, they, too, gave their signals when to change the topic, when to turn to more cheerful things again. They all acknowledged that it was good to ventilate their feelings; they also had the need to choose the time and the duration for this.

[10] Earlier conflicts and defense mechanisms allow us to predict to a certain degree what defense mechanisms a patient will use more extensively at the time of this crisis. Simple people with less education, sophistication, social ties, and professional obligations seem in general to have somewhat less difficulty in facing this final crisis than people of affluence who lose a great deal more in terms of material luxuries, comfort, and number of interpersonal relationships. It appears that people who have gone through a life of suffering, hard work, and labor, who have raised their children and been gratified in their work, have shown greater ease in accepting death with peace and dignity compared to those who have been ambitiously controlling their environment, accumulating material goods, and a great number of social relationships but few meaningful interpersonal relationships which would have been available at the end of life. . . .

[11] Religious patients seemed to differ little from those without a religion. The difference may be hard to determine, since we have not clearly defined what we mean by a religious person. We can say here, however, that we found very few truly religious people with an intrinsic faith. Those few have been helped by their faith and are best comparable with those few patients who were true atheists. The majority of patients were in between, with some form of religious belief but not enough to relieve them of conflict and fear.

[12] When our patients reached the stage of acceptance and final decathexis, interference from outside was regarded as the greatest turmoil and prevented several patients from dying in peace and dignity. It is the signal of imminent

death and has allowed us to predict the oncoming death in several patients where there was little or no indication for it from a medical point of view. The patient responds to an intrinsic signal system which tells him of his impending death. We are able to pick up these cues without really knowing what psycho-physiological signals the patient perceives. When the patient is asked, he is able to acknowledge his awareness and often communicates it to us by asking us to sit down *now*, since he knows that tomorrow will be too late. We should be keenly aware of such insistence on the part of our patients, as we may miss a unique chance to listen to them while there is still time.

. . .

¹³ At this time in a patient's life the pain ceases to be, when the mind slips off into a dreamless state, when the need for food becomes minimal and the awareness of the environment all but disappears into darkness. This is the time when the relatives walk up and down the hospital hallways, tormented by the waiting, not knowing if they should leave to attend the living or stay to be around for the moment of death. This is the time when it is too late for words, and yet the time when the relatives cry the loudest for help—with or without words. It is too late for medical interventions (and too cruel, though well meant, when they do occur), but it is also too early for a final separation from the dying. It is the hardest time for the next of kin as he either wishes to take off, to get it over with; or he desperately clings to something that he is in the process of losing forever. It is the time for the therapy of silence with the patient and availability for the relatives.

¹⁴ The doctor, nurse, social worker, or chaplain can be of great help during these final moments if they can understand the family's conflicts at this time and help select the one person who feels most comfortable staying with the dying patient. This person then becomes in effect the patient's therapist. Those who feel too uncomfortable can be assisted by alleviating their guilt and by the reassurance that someone will stay with the dying until his death has occurred. They can then return home knowing that the patient did not die alone, yet not feeling ashamed or guilty for having avoided this moment which for many people is so difficult to face.

¹⁵ Those who have the strength and the love to sit with a dying patient in the *silence that goes beyond words* will know that this moment is neither frightening nor painful, but a peaceful cessation of the functioning of the body. Watching a peaceful death of a human being reminds us of a falling star; one of a million lights in a vast sky that flares up for a brief moment only to disappear into the endless night forever. To be a therapist to a dying patient makes us aware of the uniqueness of each individual in this vast sea of humanity. It makes us aware of our finiteness, our limited lifespan. Few of us live beyond our three score and ten years and yet in that brief time most of us create and live a unique biography and weave ourselves into the fabric of human history.

The water in a vessel is sparkling; the water in the sea is dark.
The small truth has words that are clear; the great truth has great silence.
                    —Rabindranath Tagore, from *Stray Birds*, CLXXVI*

ANALYTICAL READING

1. What relationship has the mention of the "small, personal gift" in paragraph 1 to the discussion of dying that follows?

2. What reasons does Kübler-Ross give for dealing openly with dying patients?

3. How does the author use classification in her discussion of the stages of dying? What are they?

4. What recommendations does she make about the initial informing of patients that they have a terminal illness? What personality characteristics should a doctor develop?

5. What does she have to say about religious beliefs? Did this surprise you? Why?

6. How would you define the *silence that goes beyond words* (paragraph 15) and *decathexis* (paragraph 12)?

7. What philosophy about human life is revealed in the last paragraph? Does it appear in other parts of the essay? Where?

REFLECTING

Point: State in one sentence the opinion thesis of the selection. Where is it first stated?

Organization: Outline the organizational scheme of the selection. Is there a SUB-JECT–RESTRICTION–ILLUSTRATION format?

Support: How does the author's classification of the stages of dying help to support her thesis idea?

Synthesis: What have been your own experiences with death? Have family deaths been shielded from you? Do you agree with Kübler-Ross that we should become more open about dying and death? If so, what are some means of achieving that aim? Do you think a terminal cancer patient should be informed? Why or why not?

Evaluation: Did you find the essay effective and thought-provoking? How would you characterize the writer's voice? Does the voice contribute to the effectiveness of the selection? Discuss.

FROM READING TO WRITING

1. Write an opinion paper in which you formulate a thesis statement concerning whether or not children should be exposed to death in other ways than by watching violent television programs and movies.

2. Write an opinion paper relating the ecology movement to the attitude toward dying reflected in Kübler-Ross' essay.

*Copyright 1916 by Macmillan Publishing Co., Inc. Renewed 1944 by Rathindranath Tagore.

PROHIBITION AND DRUGS
Milton Friedman

BIOGRAPHICAL SKETCH

Milton Friedman was born in New York City in 1912. He received a Ph.D. from Columbia University and holds seven honorary degrees. Awarded the Nobel Prize for economics, he has had a distinguished career as a columnist (currently for Newsweek), government advisor to Republican Presidents, and scholar and teacher of economics at the University of Chicago. He has been president of the American Economic Association and is a member of the National Academy of Sciences. Best known as the founder of the monetarist "Chicago School" of economics, Friedman has written about a wide variety of social and political subjects, crusading tirelessly and vigorously for freedom from government controls in all fields. His innumerable articles and fifteen books include the epic A Monetary History of the United States *(with Anna J. Schwartz).*

PRE-READING

1. Having read the biographical sketch, are you surprised to find Friedman writing about drugs? What position do you think he will take?

2. Skim the opening and closing paragraphs. What opinion do you expect Friedman to express in the essay?

¹ "The reign of tears is over. The slums will soon be only a memory. We will turn our prisons into factories and our jails into storehouses and corn-cribs. Men will walk upright now, women will smile, and the children will laugh. Hell will be forever for rent."

² This is how Billy Sunday, the noted evangelist and leading crusader against Demon Rum, greeted the onset of Prohibition in early 1920. We know now how tragically his hopes were doomed. New prisons and jails had to be built to house the criminals spawned by converting the drinking of spirits into a crime against the state. Prohibition undermined respect for the law, corrupted the minions of the law, created a decadent moral climate—but did not stop the consumption of alcohol.

³ Despite this tragic object lesson, we seem bent on repeating precisely the same mistake in the handling of drugs.

⁴ On ethical grounds, do we have the right to use the machinery of government to prevent an individual from becoming an alcoholic or a drug addict? For children, almost everyone would answer at least a qualified yes. But for responsible adults, I, for one, would answer no. Reason with the potential addict, yes. Tell him the consequences, yes. Pray for and with him, yes.

FROM Milton Friedman, *There's No Such Thing as a Free Lunch* (LaSalle, Ill.: Open Court Publishing Co., 1975), pp. 227-29. The article was originally published in *Newsweek*, 1 May 1972. Copyright 1972 by Newsweek, Inc. Reprinted by permission.

But I believe that we have no right to use force, directly or indirectly, to prevent a fellow man from committing suicide, let alone from drinking alcohol or taking drugs.

⁵ I readily grant that the ethical issue is difficult and that men of goodwill may well disagree. Fortunately, we need not resolve the ethical issue to agree on policy. *Prohibition is an attempted cure that makes matters worse—for both the addict and the rest of us.* Hence, even if you regard present policy toward drugs as ethically justified, considerations of expediency make that policy most unwise.

⁶ *Consider first the addict.* Legalizing drugs might increase the number of addicts, but it is not clear that it would. Forbidden fruit is attractive, particularly to the young. More important, many drug addicts are deliberately made by pushers, who give likely prospects their first few doses free. It pays the pusher to do so because, once hooked, the addict is a captive customer. If drugs were legally available, any possible profit from such inhumane activity would disappear, since the addict could buy from the cheapest source.

⁷ Whatever happens to the number of addicts, the individual addict would clearly be far better off if drugs were legal. Today, drugs are both incredibly expensive and highly uncertain in quality. Addicts are driven to associate with criminals to get the drugs, become criminals themselves to finance the habit, and risk constant danger of death and disease.

⁸ *Consider next the rest of us.* Here the situation is crystal-clear. The harm to us from the addiction of others arises almost wholly from the fact that drugs are illegal. A recent committee of the American Bar Association estimated that addicts commit one-third to one-half of all street crime in the U.S. Legalize drugs, and street crime would drop automatically.

⁹ Moreover, addicts and pushers are not the only ones corrupted. Immense sums are at stake. It is inevitable that some relatively low-paid police and other government officials—and some high-paid ones as well—will succumb to the temptation to pick up easy money.

¹⁰ Legalizing drugs would simultaneously reduce the amount of crime and raise the quality of law enforcement. Can you conceive of any other measure that would accomplish so much to promote law and order?

¹¹ But, you may say, must we accept defeat? Why not simply end the drug traffic? That is where experience under Prohibition is most relevant. We cannot end the drug traffic. We may be able to cut off opium from Turkey—but there are innumerable other places where the opium poppy grows. With French cooperation, we may be able to make Marseilles an unhealthy place to manufacture heroin—but there are innumerable other places where the simple manufacturing operations involved can be carried out. So long as large sums of money are involved—and they are bound to be if drugs are illegal—it is literally hopeless to expect to end the traffic or even reduce seriously its scope.

¹² In drugs, as in other areas, persuasion and example are likely to be far more effective than the use of force to shape others in our image.

ANALYTICAL READING

1. Why is the quotation from Billy Sunday an effective way to open the paper?

2. Did you note the use of parallel structure in paragraph 4? What is the effect?

3. What effects does Friedman claim drug prohibition has had? How does he classify the effects?

4. What is his main reason for legalizing drugs? Is it a persuasive one? Does he attempt to present opinions other than his own?

5. What solutions does the author recommend? Has he examined all the possibilities? Is his solution practical? Would it be publicly and politically effective?

REFLECTING

Point: Did you underline the sentence that contains the thesis idea? Where does it occur?

Organization: How does Friedman indicate to the reader the pattern of his organization?

Support: How does the writer use cause-and-effect reasoning and the example of alcohol to support his ideas?

Synthesis: Do you agree with Friedman, or do you think he ignores other factors? Has ending alcohol prohibition eliminated all our problems with liquor? How does the information about the writer's economic philosophy given in the biographical sketch relate to the attitudes expressed in the article?

Evaluation: Do you find the article convincingly written? To what extent is it persuasive?

FROM READING TO WRITING

1. In an opinion paper in which you utilize cause-and-effect relationships, agree or disagree with Friedman's thesis.

2. Write an opinion paper about the decriminalization (as distinct from the outright legalization) of marijuana, heroin, or cocaine.

HELPING THINGS GROW

James Cass

BIOGRAPHICAL SKETCH

James Cass was educated at Ohio Wesleyan and at Columbia University. After serving nine years as director of research and secretary of the National Citizens Council for Better Schools, he became education editor of the Saturday Review. *Over the years, Cass, along with Max Birnbaum, has written a number of comparative guides to various institutions of higher learning, which are revised annually to provide the latest information to students seeking a college. Perhaps the best known of these works is their* Comparative Guide to American Colleges.

PRE-READING

1. From the title, what do you expect the article to be about?

2. After reading the opening and closing paragraphs, what do you think the subject is?

¹ One of life's great pleasures is watching things grow, especially when one has had a hand in their nurture. When the first red blush begins to appear on the tomatoes, when the eggplant begins to set fruit, and the butternut squash seems to double in size overnight, I know that I have done something right. The Swiss chard and zucchini have already graced our dinner table, and last night the first mess of snap beans was a tender delight. Everything is more fruitful this year, but my triumph has been the lettuce.

² Two years ago I hit an all-time low. The few lettuce seeds that germinated put out stunted leaves that rapidly disappeared. My wife, out of her superior wisdom, advised me to lime the garden. "Haven't you heard," she asked, "that Long Island's soil is acid and that the acid rains of the East Coast are making it more so? You need to sweeten the soil." So I bought a soil-testing kit, and as usual, she was right. The soil tested out at roughly the acidity level of lemon juice. A generous application of lime did sweeten the soil enough last year so that all our salad greens were not purchased at the supermarket, but our success was qualified, at best. This year I decided that if some lime was good, more would be better. And so I went back to the nursery for another hundred pounds so many times that I considered buying stock in a limestone quarry. But I'll wager that I ended up with the sweetest soil—and the most succulent lettuce—on Long Island. Even my daughter Julia's marigolds are blooming more happily this year.

³ Now I'm reminded that by the time this column appears in print, one growing season will be drawing to a close, and another will be just getting

FROM *Saturday Review*, 6 September 1975, p. 52. Copyright © 1975 by the Saturday Review Corporation.

under way as the schools open for the coming year. I am reminded, too, that children, like many other growing organisms, do not flourish in an acid environment. They may "germinate" easily enough; but their growth can be stunted, and all too often they never have a chance to achieve the fruitful growth of which they are capable. They, too, need the "soil" in which they may grow sweetened—with kindness, compassion, and, above all, understanding.

⁴ But the process of nurturing growth—either in the classroom or in the garden—requires much more than merely caring. Many years ago, in my father's garden, we used to plant the seeds, throw on a little evil-smelling fertilizer when the plants appeared, control the weeds, and accept what the earth offered. Our expertise, such as it was, came from experience rather than from theoretical knowledge. Today, we know much more about the stages of development in growing things, when to stimulate root growth and when to spur the formation of fruit, when to treat either plants or children tenderly and when to give them freedom to go it on their own.

⁵ We know, too, that plants, like children, differ in their requirements: they grow at different rates, they need different kinds of stimuli at different times, they respond in widely varying ways to different degrees of freedom and restraint. And we know that no single formula is best for all. Nurturing, in other words, takes time, thought, and energy—as well as understanding. Sometimes—when we run short of time and find that we have been thoughtless or that our energy has simply given out—we pay a price in the development of the things we are growing.

⁶ But one big difference distinguishes the process of growing things in the garden and in the classroom. Each spring, when the seed catalogs arrive, we can forget past failures and accept all over again the challenge we posed for ourselves in the fall: "Just wait till next year." In the classroom one season's failure cannot be retrieved the following year: the opportunity is gone forever, and the children will forever pay the price. To be sure, some circumstances we can't control, but we do what we can to overcome the vagaries of nature—and society—for the rewards are great when we do our gardening right.

⁷ I would like to write more about helping things grow. But my deadline is tomorrow morning, and right now I have to go out and plant my brussels sprouts in the hope that, though late, they will mature before the frost.

ANALYTICAL READING

1. What is the actual subject of the paper? What rhetorical device is the writer using in the paper?

2. In how many ways does Cass compare children and plants?

3. What is the main difference between growing plants and teaching children?

4. Discuss how Cass sets up the comparison between plants and children in paragraphs 3–6. How does sentence structure help?

REFLECTING

Point: Summarize in one sentence the main idea of the article. Does the writer ever formulate it precisely? Discuss.

Organization: Discuss how Cass uses one rhetorical device to unify the paper.

Support: What features of gardening does Cass use to support his opinion?

Synthesis: In what ways do you think children require more than "merely caring" (paragraph 4) from their parents? For all our knowledge about child development (from Spock, Gessell, Salk, and other experts), is there any proof that children are growing up better or learning more?

Evaluation: Did you find the rhetorical device effective? Would it have limitations in a longer paper? Discuss. Is the essay more convincing about gardening than about raising or teaching children? To what extent is it true that "one season's failure cannot be retrieved" in the following school year (paragraph 6)?

FROM READING TO WRITING

1. Write a paper comparing the learning of two dissimilar skills, such as playing tennis and the piano.

2. Write a paper about watching two dissimilar things grow or change, such as a plant and a younger brother or sister, or the decorating of a room and a person dressing for a formal dance or party.

3. Compare the changes in nature during a particular season and the changes in school atmosphere, activities, and attitudes that take place at the same time.

SCIENTISTS WANTED—PIONEERS NEEDN'T APPLY; CALL A.D. 2000
Daniel S. Greenberg

BIOGRAPHICAL SKETCH

Daniel S. Greenberg was born in New York City in 1931. He graduated from Columbia University and worked as a reporter for several newspapers. In addition to being the author of The Politics of Pure Science, *he is the publisher of* Science and Government Report *and a contributor of articles about science to many magazines.*

PRE-READING

1. Does the name of the magazine in which this essay appeared mean anything to you? If so, what do you infer the essay will deal with?

FROM *Smithsonian*, July 1976, pp. 60–67. Copyright 1976 by the Smithsonian Institution.

2. What approach to the subject do you expect to find after reading the title skimming the first paragraph and the last two?

[1] Science continues to mold our future, but what of the future of science itself? It seems impossible to predict what the most exciting frontiers of physics or biology will be in another quarter of a century, but we can be surprisingly confident of what life will be like in the American scientific community. With a very unscientific time machine, we can collect two eminent scientists from the last turn of the century and transport them into this future, letting their experiences define the changes.

[2] The first scientist, a young man with a mediocre academic record, used good family connections to obtain a job in the Swiss Patent Office in 1902. A one-time high school dropout who had been told by a teacher that "You will never amount to anything," he had relied heavily on borrowed lecture notes to get his undergraduate degree. But he had aspirations beyond patent applications.

[3] Now imagine the time machine has transported him to the last quarter of this century. Envision the young clerk anxiously opening a letter from a foundation to which he had applied for a graduate fellowship to study physics. Disappointment shrouds his face as he reads the response:

[4] Dear Mr. Einstein:

We are in receipt of your application for financial assistance to pursue graduate studies in physics. Having examined your academic record and references from former teachers, we regret to inform you that your preparation is inadequate for the rigorous requirements of the course of study that you wish to follow. Therefore, we are unable to act favorably on your application.

Sincerely,
The Graduate Fellowship Committee

[5] To meet a second time-traveler, turn back to 1900. An Army surgeon holds the unorthodox notion that yellow fever, then epidemic in an American protectorate, Cuba, is transmitted by mosquitoes. Since there is no way to test this hunch on animals, he proposes to test it on humans. Suddenly he, too, finds himself in the final quarter of this century. Submitting his plan to his superiors, he is rewarded with the following memorandum:

[6] From: Surgeon General, U.S. Army
To: Dr. Walter Reed
Subject: Human Experimentation, Regulations Concerning

As we are sure you are aware, any experimentation involving human subjects must conform to the informed-consent regulations that the Department of the Army has adopted from the Department of

Health, Education and Welfare in accordance with directives of the Federal Council for Science and Technology. As a preliminary step toward fulfilling the requirements for application for issuance of a human-experimentation permit, it will be necessary for you to submit a detailed protocol of animal studies. In conjunction with regulations concerning animal welfare, it will also be necessary for you to provide evidence that the preliminary studies cannot be accomplished without the use of animals.

[7] Failure to comply with this memorandum will result in disciplinary action.

[8] The addressees are real, but the correspondence, of course, is mythical. Patent Clerk Albert Einstein was spared any such rebuff when he sought a graduate fellowship. Working at theoretical physics in his spare time, he quickly published five papers, including the special theory of relativity, and was awarded a doctorate by the University of Zurich.

[9] And Dr. Walter Reed simply followed the honorable tradition of using himself and his research-team colleagues as experimental subjects, without encountering the present-day committees that are concerned with animal-welfare regulations and informed consent of human subjects. Some of his co-workers died, but Reed proved his point. The mosquitos were eradicated and the number of yellow fever cases dropped to zero.

[10] Our heroes of the past thrived in what might be called the frontier days of scientific research. Vast and open territories of the scientific unknown lay before any investigator, and virtually all that was required for plunging ahead was the wit and the will to do so, plus relatively minor sums for equipment and supplies. How different it is today, and how much more so it will be tomorrow!

[11] Peering ahead to the turn of the century, I see a crowd of people concerned with science—but surprisingly few of them are wearing lab coats.

[12] The crowd is mainly composed of legislators, lawyers, economists, diplomats, budget planners, aptitude testers, bookkeepers, labor union officials, technology assessors and lots of anxious citizens. Few of them can distinguish an electron microscope from an automatic olive pitter. Their presence in the heart of the scientific enterprise signifies the blossoming of a theme that is already with us: namely, science is too potent, costly, dangerous and valuable to be wholly entrusted to mere scientists.

[13] During the next quarter of a century, research will thrive in terms of expenditures, scientists and technicians at work, ambitious projects and costly facilities. But it will do so as a tightly reined captive of the surrounding society, and in an atmosphere of caution and thrift. Most important, opportunities for scientific research will no longer be judged in the traditional terms of knowledge being a desirable goal in itself regardless of the purposes to which it might be applied.

[14] Scientists and research administrators will find that whole regions of research and technological application have been declared off limits, shunned as economically unworthy of pursuit or legally prohibited as too dangerous to be entrusted to frail humans and their unpredictable social and political institutions.

[15] Research in many, if not most, fields will be actively encouraged, for the thickening problems of mankind on a crowded globe will demand scientific and technological solutions. But the choice of what to research will not be left entirely to the people who perform the research. Rather, it will receive the scrutiny and require the approval of a wide-ranging assortment of nonscientists who are concerned with costs, priorities, social impact, public safety and political significance. The "Everest Complex" will no longer be sufficient reason for undertaking many research projects. Scientists will find that "because it's there" isn't a convincing argument to use on the keepers of the administrative cage in which science is confined.

[16] The next 25 years will also produce further changes in the internal affairs of the scientific community, largely as the result of the progressive mechanization of scientific research. The conduct of most kinds of research is impossible without the use of highly expensive facilities—computers, particle accelerators, space satellites, oceanographic vessels, huge banks of experimental animals. There is and always will be a market for the breakthrough genius, but without the assistance of sophisticated apparatus, genius will be to science as expert archery is to modern military affairs—admirable, but ineffective by itself. Theoreticians may still use their traditional tools, paper and pencil, but to test their work they like to have a powerful computer which can race through calculations that would require weeks, even years, of hand computation.

[17] Big science thus means big organizations. The machinery of modern science spawns a cast of characters that includes budget planners, technicians, maintenance people, and so forth. Schedule makers reign supreme when the lineup of would-be users overwhelms the available time on a machine. Big organizations mean layers of administrators, divisions of labor, and tendencies to assign people to preconceived duties rather than permit them to flourish according to their individual abilities.

[18] When a few test tubes and a microscope constituted a "laboratory," research could be done in a spare room as a spare-time occupation. (Our patent clerk did his research on a kitchen table!) But when the tools required for research are million-dollar rockets and atom smashers, the number of persons who are professionally capable of using the tools will always be in surplus supply; patent clerks with abysmal academic records need not apply. These conditions will be particularly onerous to the freewheeling pioneers who people the history of science and technology. Charles Lindbergh picked himself to fly the Atlantic, but committees of physicians and psychologists selected the astronauts who went to the moon. The turn-of-the-century scientist will have to harmonize with his societal and professional setting. To put it

bluntly, the scientist will, with rare exception, be a member of a scientific and technological proletariat, well trained and competent, but no more distinguished from the mass of his colleagues than is, for example, an automobile assembly worker of today.

[19] How confident can we be of this scenario? Very, because the changes are already taking place. The aspects of science and technology that we have been considering are governed by a powerful inertia; as we move into the last quarter of the century, the forces of change are gradually gathering momentum. Among people who feel that science and technology are at least as much a bane as a blessing, there is an axiom that says the products of research tend to take on a life of their own, that they almost inevitably spread through society and elude control. (Often cited as an example of this is the airplane, which, for the convenience of a few, creates a nuisance for the many.) What does not get much attention is the fact that in recent years some rather serious curbs have been applied. Decisions on technical projects have been increasingly made for political, economic or at least nontechnical reasons.

[20] Consider the American effort to build a supersonic transport. Technically, it was a manageable task—as the Anglo-French and Soviet SSTs demonstrate. We could have done it, but we didn't. And the reason we didn't turn thousands of scientists, engineers, and technicians loose on the task was simply that Congress and the public concluded that the SST was a poor investment. So here we see politics and business determining that something that can be done should not be done. There have been other cases along these lines (drilling into the Earth's mantle, manned flight to Mars) and as the outsiders tighten their grip on science and technology, there will be more of them.

[21] Consider the case of nuclear explosives for peaceful earth-moving purposes. Known as Project Plowshare, the peaceful use of nuclear devices is described by advocates as a safe, highly economical and unmatchable technique for digging canals, moving mountains and loosening mineral and gas resources from deep inside the earth. Though a few small tests have been conducted, the method is politically taboo and is unlikely ever to come into large-scale use in the United States. This is not only because Plowshare runs the risk of releasing radioactivity in violation of the atmospheric nuclear test ban treaty to which the United States is a party; it is also because public fears of nuclear power are so extensive that no matter how great the benefits and minuscule the risks, peaceful explorations are—at least for now—politically out of bounds.

[22] For another example of politics thwarting what is scientifically and technically doable, consider biological, or germ, warfare. Waging war with microorganisms is such a chancy business that both the United States and the Soviet Union probably felt they had little to lose when they formally renounced biological warfare under the Biological Weapons Convention that went into effect last year. (The United States, in fact, gave it up unilaterally in 1969.) Prior to the renunciations, however, a large and amply supported com-

munity of biological warfare researchers filled a major Army laboratory at Fort Detrick, Maryland. As far as they were concerned, biological weapons merited a serious and continuing research effort, and there can be little doubt that if the decision had been left to them, they would still be at it.

²³ These cases all involve the inhibition of science and technology by outside forces. What also must be considered is a relatively new, but rapidly expanding, process of the scientific and technical communities attempting to stay one step ahead of societal restraint by setting limitations for themselves. Last year, genetics researchers from several nations voluntarily agreed to an unprecedented moratorium; they were afraid certain gene transplantation experiments might result in highly dangerous disease-producing strains. The moratorium was partially lifted earlier this year following agreement on safety procedures and the development of microorganisms that are said to be unable to survive outside a controlled laboratory environment. The significance of this episode in voluntary scientific restraint cannot be exaggerated. For the principal figures in the story are all basic researchers, and, historically, if there is any basic tenet to basic science, it is that all of nature's secrets are fair game. The temporary moratorium did not conflict with that rule, but it did have the effect of delaying a good many research projects for social rather than scientific reasons. And that's something new in the life of science.

²⁴ Along these lines, a blend of inside and outside concerns has produced uncertainty and turbulence over the use of human subjects in experimentation. The maze of regulations that has ensued from these concerns would astonish Dr. Walter Reed—just as they often astonish, and thwart, many of his scientific descendants today. What it all adds up to is that in response to pressures from the outside world, the scientific community is now seriously restricted when it wants to test pharmaceutical drugs and other substances on human beings, even when those human beings want to serve as test subjects.

²⁵ Recommendations that are likely to have a profound effect on the conduct of research over coming decades are now being drafted by the National Commission for the Protection of Human Subjects of Biomedical and Behavioral Research. The commission, which advises Congress and the Department of Health, Education and Welfare, has already provided the advice that the Secretary of HEW followed in changing rules for experimentation on fetuses. The moratorium on fetal research instituted by Congress in July 1974 was lifted in August 1975 after guidelines for the conduct of such research were tightened in response to commission recommendations. Now it is looking at the problems involved in experimenting on institutionalized mental patients, children and prisoners. One step ahead of the commission, however, the U.S. Bureau of Prisons has banned the use of prisoners in medical research on the grounds that the potential for abuse and manipulation is too great when a prisoner is invited to "volunteer" to take part in an experiment. The irony of it is that in testimony before the commission prisoners have insisted that they wish to retain the option to take part in experiments. They say they like the financial and psychological rewards that accompany participation. Drug re-

searchers say that the ban will impede the development of valuable pharmaceuticals, since prisoners, living in environments where nutrition and other factors can be controlled, are ideal experimental subjects.

²⁶ Many scientists support the new rules, but many others feel that society is clumsily imposing rules that will ultimately be to the detriment of society. All agree, however, that the days are gone when such matters were exclusively the business of science.

²⁷ Today the federal government pays for about half of all the research and development performed in the United States. Over the first three decades of the postwar period, the amount of federal money for research and development grew so rapidly—from $918 million in 1946 to $24 billion in 1976—that it really was an era in which the doable usually stood a very good chance of getting done. This was a period in which the Air Force spent over $1 billion in a futile effort to construct a nuclear-powered airplane, oblivious of warnings that the weight of the shielding on the reactor would result in a plane that would be huge and slow, and of little military use. Because of the ever-present danger of a crash that would almost certainly spread radioactivity, the plane would not have been permitted to fly over populated areas. Nevertheless, more than a billion dollars was put into the venture and more would have followed if the Kennedy Administration had not stopped it in 1962.

²⁸ From today's perspective, the striking aspect of the atomic aircraft project was that it got under way and flourished with virtually no public notice and scant congressional attention. Today, the scientific landscape in Washington is dotted with organizations that scrutinize research projects. Private organizations on the periphery of government, such as the Arms Control Association and the Federation of American Scientists, bring together prestigious scientists and engineers to examine the Defense Department's research programs and testify about them in Congress. Laden with Nobel laureates and former high-level officials of the department itself, they work in close alliance with the press and several-score congressmen and senators to throw light on weapons planning. Their main objective is arms control, which means they tend to be naysayers—definitely a minority position on military research and development. But their effect has been powerful in getting the issues out in the open and making the Defense Department less free-wheeling in its weapons programs. For example, the department has been trying for years to obtain funds for the production of a new type of poison gas projectile known as a "binary" in which two gases, nontoxic themselves, are joined to become a lethal weapon at the critical moment. Congress, mainly at the urgings of nongovernment critics of the weapon, has so far refused to put up the money.

²⁹ The Congress itself has taken the unusual step of setting up its own organization, the Office of Technology Assessment, to attempt to look over the horizon and anticipate the impact of scientific and technological developments. OTA went into operation in 1974 and, though still a fledgling, has conducted a wide assortment of studies, ranging from the environmental effects of offshore drilling to the effectiveness of pharmaceutical drugs.

[30] Meanwhile, government is increasingly relying on the use of impact statements to attempt to foresee the consequences of federal projects. The widest and best known use is in environmental matters. Before any federal agency can turn a spade of soil, it must now carefully analyze the cost effectiveness of its plans, the available alternatives and the environmental consequences. In effect, it must serve up reams of material that can be used by opponents of the project, which is one reason that the development of nuclear power in the United States is tied up in legal knots. The environmental impact statements have been cited in the court proceedings as evidence that the projects are unsafe, environmentally unsound or uneconomical.

[31] In other nations, nuclear power plants are built where the nuclear power authorities choose to build them, with virtually no interference from dissenting parties. This process once prevailed in the United States, but today outsiders have a powerful say.

[32] While the government's research programs have come under a variety of constraints, research conducted by private industry is also going through a transformation that is likely to extend for decades. Perhaps the most striking aspect of this transformation is that American industry—once the world's pioneer in innovation—has become extremely cautious about investing its money in research and development, so much so that some economists are expressing concern about where the new products will come from to spur the economy of the 1980s and 1990s. The increasing corporate timidity about research comes from a number of factors, among them the high costs and uncertainties of getting new products on the market, consumer conservatism in an inflationary period, and a tangle of government regulations concerning product safety. E.I. duPont de Nemours & Co., traditionally a pioneer in turning research into profitable products, typifies the new development. Irving S. Shapiro, chairman and chief executive of the giant chemical company, recently noted the changed attitude toward research projects when he said, "Where we had 24 a couple of years ago, I feel more comfortable with, say, five or six." Other industrial executives say that their firms have concluded that it is safer and more profitable to refine existing products than it is to start from the ground up with new ones.

[33] The effect of this caution is likely to spread throughout the entire research enterprise, starting with university training of scientists and engineers. If industry pulls back from innovation, its manpower requirements will have to be changed accordingly. With the academic job market already saturated and offering few employment opportunities for teachers, the trend is already toward warning prospective students that the future may be grim in many scientific and engineering specialties. Thus, a committee of the National Academy of Sciences last year recommended that university astronomy departments carefully advise interested students that the job market in astronomy has virtually collapsed. Even the medical profession is facing the possibility of saturation in some specialties; another Academy committee, studying the

problem at the request of Congress, concluded that the United States has an oversupply of surgeons.

[34] The maturing of the American scientific and technical communities has also been accompanied by several developments that would have been considered utterly remote just a decade ago. With employment opportunities declining and job security weakening, union membership is no longer a novelty among university scientists and engineers. Meanwhile, professional scientific societies have departed from their traditionally exclusive concern with substantive professional matters and have organized to protect their members' jobs. The American Chemical Society, for example, has established a legal defense fund to provide low-cost loans for members who feel their rights have been violated. The American Association for the Advancement of Science is in the process of encouraging its approximately 200 constituent societies to set up committees to protect the "scientific freedom and responsibility" of their members.

[35] What, then, will the life of the scientific community be like in, say, 1998? My expectation is that it will be cautious in what it goes about researching; many possibilities will arise for researching this or that, but the final choices will be filtered through scrutiny processes that will examine costs, societal value, potential benefits and hazards. The researchers will enter the profession through a fine-screen selection process and their performance will be closely monitored. The situation is not likely to be favorable for late bloomers or innovators who need a decade to produce results.

[36] The situation I foresee is not especially attractive in comparison with the frontier days of science. It is heavily organized, bureaucratized, reasonably productive, relatively safe and probably quite dull in its ultimate output.

[37] The Albert Einsteins and Walter Reeds of the next turn of the century won't like it.

ANALYTICAL READING

1. What is the purpose of the opening two illustrations about Einstein and Reed? Which paragraph states this purpose? Did you mark that paragraph?

2. What is meant by the statement that "science is too potent, costly, dangerous and valuable to be wholly entrusted to mere scientists" (paragraph 12)? Does the author offer examples to support these views? Where? How does he say scientists feel about this idea?

3. What does the author mean by the "Everest Complex" (paragraph 15), and what is the significance of this term in the essay?

4. How does the opening sentence of paragraph 16 signal a change in the direction of the ideas expressed?

5. What is the purpose of the reference to the atomic aircraft project (paragraphs 27–28)?

6. What are "impact statements" (paragraph 30), and what has been their effect?

7. Did you underline the opening sentence of paragraph 30? What purpose does it serve?

8. What effects may the predicted changes have on students? On present and future scientists and technicians? Will the change be for the better or the worse? Why?

REFLECTING

Point: State the thesis of the article in a single sentence, trying to weave together most of the causes as well as the effects.

Organization: Write a brief outline of the essay. Discuss how examples, such as that of the SST, might have been located elsewhere. Would this change in position have been more effective?

Support: Greenberg is on dangerous ground in trying to predict what science will be like in about twenty-five years. How does he make a reasonably convincing case for his views?

Synthesis: In your community, your reading, or other experiences, have you come in contact with some of the restrictions that Greenberg mentions? What are your feelings about scientific research: has it worked to humanity's advantage or disadvantage, or both? Explain with specific examples.

Evaluation: How typical are Einstein and Reed as examples of past scientists? Are any scientists working in much the same manner today? What about inventions such as the Xerox machine and the Polaroid camera? Why did the United States finance expensive space research? Is Greenberg's analysis of present conditions complete and convincing? Can you quarrel with his technique of projecting from the present to the future?

FROM READING TO WRITING

1. Write an opinion paper, based on current developments, to indicate what some sport, such as professional baseball, will be like twenty years from now.

2. Many people point to creeping government controls or influence in fields other than science. Write a paper about how government may be a significant factor in some field, such as education or medicine, in future years. Support your ideas by pointing to present trends.

3. Write an opinion paper about the changes you foresee in the use of drugs, restrictions on television, changes in family life, the nature of cars and transportation, the composition of the armed forces, the status of women, or some other subject. Consider changes resulting from both external and internal factors. Support your prediction by citing recent changes.

Assessment of Reading and Writing Skills: Expository Writing

Step 1

Read the essay that follows with the aim of understanding and recalling the important ideas. When you finish, note how long it took you to read the selection. Then close your book and write a summary of the important information without referring again to the essay. Indicate also your impression of how the writer used form or structure to clarify meaning. You will be allowed 7 to 10 minutes to write; your instructor will establish the limit and tell you when the time is up.

NO MORE ISOLATION IN THE NUCLEAR FAMILY AND MONOTONOUS SUBURBS ... A RELAXING OF POLITICAL FRONTIERS

Margaret Mead

Changes in methods of child rearing are important not only because they contribute to changes in the character of the future citizens of the planet but because making changes in the way children are raised affects the character of those who raise them—parents, teachers, physicians, legislators. How children will be raised in the year 2000 can only be a more or less informed guess by someone who has specialized in the relationship of child rearing to other aspects of culture. But how we should raise our children is necessarily a program for a better future and a citizenry that can better deal with the great issues of the next century.

I hope that they will be raised in neighborhoods where they have warm relationships with many older people—grandparents or surrogate grandparents, teen-agers, currently unmarried adults, who have time to teach children special skills. I hope that such contacts will mean that children will no longer be confined to the isolated nuclear family in suburbs and housing develop-

FROM *Saturday Review*, March 1973, p. 30. Copyright © 1973 by the Saturday Review Corporation.

ments, where all of the families are of the same class and ethnic group and have children of approximately the same age.

I hope that we will have redesigned our cities and suburbs so that there is a real outdoors for all little children's play, so that they can experience the unpredictability and endless fascination of growing things and be rescued from their current boredom with only-too-predictable toys and school tasks.

I hope that men and women will have come to design their married lives as parents who share, in many different styles, both the domestic tasks of homemaking and the tasks that contribute to the public life of the country, with all division of labor based on temperament and skill rather than on sex membership. Providing such an upbringing for children is the easiest and most efficient way to bring up children who will be persons first—individuals able to use their full potentialities—and members of one sex or the other second.

I hope that children can be raised with the recognition that since war can no longer protect any country, it is no longer appropriate to raise boys who will someday be asked to kill and die and girls who will concur in these activities. If boys are not raised to be soldiers, it will be easier to relax those political frontiers that are now powerless to protect us against the new enemies: nuclear death, overpopulation strangulation, ecological death of sea and air. We can relax the lines around the small family and around the state and raise children in continually widening circles of affection for family, community, country, and planet—children who will care enough for each circle to be willing to make any sacrifice for its well-being and who will not find life stale and meaningless, as they so often do now, but will find it exacting, exhilarating, and significant.

Step 2

Read the following essay as quickly as you can without sacrificing your comprehension of the material. You will have a maximum of 2 minutes, 45 seconds (200 words per minute) to glean as much information as you can. If you finish before time is called, note how long it took you to read the selection. Again, close your book and write a summary of the essay, including a statement about the organization. You will have 7 to 10 minutes for this task.

A CONCERTED EFFORT TO ELIMINATE ALL THE GIANT AND SUBTLE WAYS OF DETERMINING HUMAN FUTURES BY CASTE

Gloria Steinem

The year 2000. It has a hopeful, science-fiction ring, so perhaps we can predict that by then there will be an understanding of how caste functions in our child-rearing operations, that there will be a concerted effort to eliminate all the giant and subtle ways in which we determine human futures according to the isolated physical differences of race or sex.

That statement may sound simple or unnatural to many of us reading it now. Simple—to those of us who accept the fact that individual differences far outstrip the group differences based on race or sex. Unnatural—to those of us who assume that physical differences pervade and shape all human capabilities. But it seems to me that the problem of caste is the most profound and revolutionary of the crises we must face. Only by attacking the patriarchal and racist base of social systems of the past—tribal or industrial, capitalist or socialist—can we begin to undo the tension and violence and human waste that this small globe can no longer afford, and that the powerless, castemark majority of this world will no longer tolerate.

By the year 2000 we will, I hope, raise our children to believe in human potential, not God. Hopefully, the raising of children will become both an art and a science: a chosen and a loving way of life in both cases. Whether children are born into extended families or nuclear ones, into communal groups or to single parents, they will be wanted—a major difference from a past in which, whatever the sugar coating, we have been made to feel odd or unnatural if we did not choose to be biological parents. Children will be raised by and with men as much as women; with old people, as well as with biological or chosen parents; and with other children. For those children of single parents or nuclear families, the community must provide centers where their peers and a variety of adults complete the human spectrum. For those children born into communal groups or extended families, the community must provide space to be alone in and individual, one-to-one teaching. The point is to enlarge personal choice, to produce for each child the fullest possible range of human experience without negating or limiting the choices already made by the adults closest to her or to him.

It used to be said that this country was a child-centered one. Nothing could be further from the truth. Children have been our lowest priority, both in economic and emotional spending. They also have been looked upon as a caste, although a temporary one. And that caste has been exploited as labor by relatives as well as by business people. It has been used as a captive audience or a way of seeking social status. It has finally been reduced to the status of object—a possession of that caste known as adults.

By the year 2000 there should be no one way of raising children; there should be many ways—all of them recognizing that children have legal and social rights that may be quite separate and different from the rights or desires of the adults closest to them. At last we should be nurturing more individual talents than we suppress.

Step 3

Without looking back at the two essays, write a paragraph or two in which you evaluate them and explain how their ideas or issues are related. You may refer to your summaries, but not to the essays. Time: 10 minutes.

PART 4

The
Argumentative Voice:
Persuasive Writing

ontrary to the popular understanding of the word *argument* as synonymous with *quarrel,* argument as a rhetorical form means persuasion, not pugnacity. An argument is an opinion with verbal salesmanship added. In an opinion paper, the writer presents one particular point of view on a subject; in argument, or persuasive writing, the writer attempts to "sell" an idea or solution to an audience that is indifferent or only slightly interested at best, openly hostile and opposed at worst. Therefore, merely laying out an opinion is not sufficient to persuade such a varied audience; instead, the writer must anticipate all possible objections or counter-arguments. In argument, the writer consciously makes an appeal to the readers: to their sense of reason and fairness; to their ethical convictions; to their human sympathies and sometimes to their emotions.

KINDS OF PERSUASIVE WRITING

EMOTIONAL ARGUMENT

When the last is the aim—to appeal primarily to the readers' feelings of pity, their sense of outrage, or to their anger—an emotional argument is the result. In emotional argument, more attention may be given to the tone of voice and to examples than to refutation of counter-arguments. Russell Baker's "Bad Study Habits" (pages 343–45) illustrates a common type of emotional argument that relies heavily on the writer's tone—a satirical treatment of a situation that requires examination and change. The writer's tone and his use of examples play a major role in Michael Mewshaw's "Irrational Behavior or Evangelical Zeal?" (pages 346–49), in which an ethical appeal is made to Americans' idealism regarding religious freedom.

LOGICAL ARGUMENT

Logical argument, however, as its name implies, makes extensive use of argumentative devices, such as syllogistic reasoning and refutation of opposing viewpoints. In its strictest form a syllogism consists of three statements: the first two serve as premises and establish the necessary relationships; the third logically follows as a "therefore" conclusion. Sometimes in an argument paper all three parts are readily apparent. For instance, in Bud Shuster's article on seat belts (pages 388–91) the underlying syllogism could be stated as follows:

A law that cannot be easily enforced is a bad law.
The seat belt law cannot be easily enforced.
Therefore, the seat belt law is a bad law.

All parts of this syllogism appear someplace in the article. Other points that he makes about the appropriateness of laws can also be stated as a syllogism.

More frequently, however, only a portion of the syllogism is stated; the rest is implied or assumed (so it is called a hidden assumption) and must be supplied by the reader. Looking again at the Shuster's article, we find such a situation in the final paragraph. He speaks of the evil of letting big government control our lives and then moves to a plea for individual choice in using safety belts. The reader then supplies the logical relationships, the missing premise that takes the reader from a very general statement to a conclusion about a particular subject—in this case, seat belt laws.

Government regulation from Washington is evil.

Therefore, seat belt regulation is evil.

Obviously, the omitted step must state something like, "Seat belt regulation is government regulation from Washington."

Writers employ syllogistic reasoning because it adds to the persuasive force of the argument, providing an orderly, logical framework when all the syllogistic parts are included and subtly flattering the reader's intelligence when a missing part must be supplied. As a reader, you should be aware that because of this persuasiveness, syllogistic reasoning can be abused—to present arguments that seem reasonable and logical but are actually fallacious in some way.

Another element that adds to the persuasive force is the treatment of refutations. Stating and negating an opponent's viewpoints not only counteracts them but establishes the writer as a careful, thorough, knowledgeable person. It establishes readers' confidence in the writer because it shows that he or she has considered other possibilities before arriving at a conclusion.

MIXED ARGUMENT

Combining the elements of logical and emotional argument can also add persuasive force; that approach we call mixed argument. It is most effective when logical argument is presented first and then the conclusion either appeals to the ethical standards or the emotions of readers or attempts to arouse them to action. The latter is the device used in the last paragraph of Lisa Shillinger's "Kill the Metric!" (pages 422–24), which ends with a series of questions couched in emotionally charged language designed to goad readers into action—which was her purpose in writing the article. How much emotional persuasion is used to enhance or temper a logically presented argument depends largely on the writer's purpose, the audience being addressed, and the seriousness of the subject matter.

TACTICS FOR READING ARGUMENT

PRE-READING

The special pre-reading skills for reading and understanding argumentative writing build on the suggestions made in earlier sections. In reading argument, as in reading exposition, you should search for the main idea before tackling the whole assignment. But in argument, you need to determine not only the subject but also the writer's recommendations about it, the stand the writer takes, and the purpose of the argument. It helps, also, to analyze your own feelings about the subject: do you agree or disagree with the writer's viewpoint? Before you read beyond the opening paragraph, try to list mentally the arguments you might present on the subject. Then as you read through the article, you can judge how well the writer deals with those points—either using them as support or refuting them as opposing views. Also, if you are hostile to the writer's viewpoint, you may need to discipline yourself to read as objectively as possible so that you will give the writer's argument a fair hearing.

ANALYTICAL READING

An awareness of the organizational form of argument can greatly increase your understanding. Ordinarily, arguments are organized around a proposition-thesis having a form like that of the following examples: "Seat belts *should not* be required by law"; "Young people *should* have the right to make their own religious choices"; "The U.S. *can* solve the automobile problem." The proposition may be stated early in the opening paragraphs, followed by supporting materials (similar to the organizational scheme outlined for expository writing on pages 206–07). This results in deductive organization—movement from a general statement to specifics, from SUBJECT to RESTRICTION to ILLUSTRATION. Because most arguments follow this order, you can usually find the writer's proposition or proposal in the opening paragraphs.

But occasionally, particularly when the writer's ideas are highly controversial, the supporting materials may be presented first and the proposition stated in the closing paragraphs. This order is also often evident in problem-solution arguments—the writer first outlines the problem, its causes and effects, and then states the solution as a proposition. In either case, the organization is inductive—it moves from specific to general, from ILLUSTRATION to the statement of the SUBJECT and its RESTRICTION. So to find the writer's main point, you must look at the end of the article. Ann Roiphe's "Why More Than One?" (pages 382–87) exhibits inductive organization.

In addition to being aware of the organizational scheme as you read, you should also be alert to the rhetorical devices that writers use to support their arguments. Does the writer use comparison and contrast, comparing one situation with another, the present time with a previous era, one solution with another? Does the writer set up causal relationships, talking of effects and how they result from specific causes? Or perhaps the writer uses analogy, explaining a situation by finding logical relationships to a similar situation, as Bud Shuster (page 389, paragraph 10) does in his analogy between the prohibition of cigarette smoking and the mandatory wearing of seat belts.

In reading persuasive writing, you should be especially alert to the writer's bias about the subject. Word choice is instrumental in establishing the writer's viewpoint and determining whether the argument is presented objectively and logically or emotionally. For instance, the language in Lisa Shillinger's argument ("Kill the Metric!," pages 422–24) about metric conversion being "sheer madness" leaves little doubt as to her subjective attitude toward her topic.

Another caution to keep in mind as you read argument is to beware of the hidden assumption. As we pointed out earlier, persuasive technique often utilizes syllogistic reasoning which may omit one of the premises or the conclusion itself. Make sure that you are aware of the missing element and decide whether you accept its truth and validity. As an example, the hidden assumption in the opening paragraph of Edward M. Kennedy's argument for gun control (pages 411–16) is that "people who possess firearms are more apt to commit murder." Before you can intelligently evaluate his arguments, you must decide whether you accept or reject that unstated premise.

REFLECTING

In argument, this stage of reading involves discerning not only the relationship of form to meaning but also the significance of form to the persuasive force of the argument. As you work your way through the POSSE approach, keep these questions and considerations in mind.

Point. Do you need to restate the proposition that you developed in the pre-reading stage? Where in the article is the writer's purpose best stated?

Organization. Is the organization inductive or deductive? How does the sequence of material serve the persuasive force of the argument? the writer's purpose? Does the thesis-proposition follow logically from the main arguments in the paper? from a "therefore" relationship?

Support. What devices does the writer use to develop and support the main points: example, citing of authority, cause-and-effect relationships, statistics, reasons, comparison and contrast, analogy? Does the choice of one of these work especially well in making the point clear and persuasive?

Synthesis. Do you agree or disagree with the writer's viewpoint and proposition? Does the writer deal adequately with your counter-arguments and with those of other viewpoints you may have encountered? Were you convinced by any of the arguments, or did the article reinforce your own attitudes toward the subject?

Evaluation. How effective do you find the argument to be? Are refutations tactfully and thoroughly handled? Is the tone offensive or persuasive? Does the writer effectively couple emotional or ethical appeal with logical argument? Does the author avoid fallacious argument? How valid do you find the writer's argumentative devices—syllogistic reasoning, analogy, causal relations, authoritative evidence? If a solution is proposed, is it practical, better than other solutions, and not likely to create more problems?

FROM READING TO WRITING

If you have developed an awareness of the form used for the articles you read, you can model your own organizational pattern after them. One word of caution, however. Remember that in writing an argument paper, you need to take into account the reading audience, the sensitive nature of the subject, and the purpose for writing. All of these influence your ordering of the paper—your decision to use deductive organization, stating your proposition early and following it with your main arguments and support, or your decision to use inductive organization because you feel that the subject matter is so controversial that the supporting evidence should be presented first, helping to temper the effect of your proposition at the end. Even within the paper, the audience, subject, and purpose may influence your decisions about the order in which to present your supporting points. Thus, you see, you should avoid slavishly following any particular model, but should adapt it to your own writing situation.

Whether you plan to write an emotional or a logical argument, spend some time organizing your paper before you start. Argument works best when there is syllogistic reasoning involved in the organizational scheme; this adds persuasive force to your paper. To achieve that, you should see that your thesis serves as a conclusion of a syllogism and that your supporting arguments serve as premises that lead logically to the conclusion-thesis: "Point A is true; *therefore* thesis."

Also before writing, you should give some thought to the ways that you might treat the supporting evidence. Here are some suggestions for ways to handle your supporting ideas:

Comparison and contrast. There are two basic methods for organizing a comparison of several items. One is to deal with each item separately, discussing all the points to be made about it. The second is to handle each item in turn in reference to each point. These outlines may help to illustrate the two methods:

First Method	Second Method
Item A	Point 1
Point 1	Item A
Point 2	Item B
Item B	Point 2
Point 1	Item A
Point 2	Item B

Cause-and-effect analysis. As in reading, before you write you need to determine what are causes and what are effects. Traffic congestion, for instance, can be an effect; its causes might include rush-hour traffic, poorly coordinated traffic lights, lack of left-turn arrows, and so forth. But traffic congestion in another discussion might be a cause. In a paper arguing against constructing another shopping center in a particular district, traffic congestion might only be one of the causes resulting in the effect of an undesirable situation.

Again, you have at least two choices for arranging your material:

From Effect to Cause	From Cause to Effect
Effect	Cause A
↑	Cause B
Cause A	↓
Cause B	Effect

Other writing devices. Before writing, you should also determine whether you will find other devices useful for presenting evidence. These could include illustration or example, the citing of authority, or the use of statistical evidence. All these can effectively add weight and authority to your argument. Also, if you are planning a logical argument, give some thought to handling refutations of opposing views. Sometimes it is more effective to deal with all of them in the beginning; other times you may want to use them at places throughout the paper where they are related to a point you are making.

Another important consideration in writing argument is to avoid fallacious reasoning. After writing, you can often spot faulty reasoning by checking to see if you have been guilty of sweeping generalizations that you have skimpily supported, or whether you have stated a faulty conclusion—one based on too small a sample. Finally, test your points: see that they are logically supported by evidence.

Because most of us are stimulated by controversy, we find satisfaction in reading an argument, and even greater satisfaction in writing one. Persuasive writing gives us a chance not only to sharpen our views on a subject but also to exert an influence over other people—a chance to test the old adage that the pen is mightier than the sword.

Emotional Argument

THE NIGHTMARE OF LIFE WITHOUT FUEL

Isaac Asimov

BIOGRAPHICAL SKETCH

Isaac Asimov was born in Petrovichi, Russia, in 1912 and moved to the United States in 1923. Since receiving a Ph.D. from Columbia University, he has been an indefatigable writer, having produced over 165 books. They range from science fiction to pure science, history, religion, literature, and geography. Among them are such classics as I Robot, the Foundation *trilogy, and* Asimov's Guide to Science. *His recent novel,* The Gods Themselves, *won several awards. One recent work is* Murder at the ABA, *his first mystery novel in eighteen years. Asimov has also written innumerable articles and appeared on many television talk shows.*

PRE-READING

1. Combining your biographical knowledge of Asimov and his previous writings with the title, what do you speculate he might be attempting to deal with in this essay?

2. What does skimming the first paragraph add to your previous ideas about the essay?

3. Do the final short four paragraphs indicate a purpose to Asimov's view of the world of 1997?

[1] So it's 1997, and it's raining, and you'll have to walk to work again. The subways are crowded, and any given train breaks down one morning out of five. The buses are gone, and on a day like today the bicycles slosh and slide. Besides, you have only a mile and a half to go, and you have boots, raincoat and rain hat. And it's not a very cold rain, so why not?

[2] Lucky you have a job in demolition too. It's steady work. Slow and dirty, but steady. The fading structures of a decaying city are the great mineral mines and hardware shops of the nation. Break them down and re-use the

FROM *Time*, 25 April 1977, p. 33. Reprinted by permission from TIME, The Weekly Newsmagazine. Copyright by Time Inc. 1977.

parts. Coal is too difficult to dig up and transport to give us energy in the amounts we need, nuclear fission is judged to be too dangerous, the technical breakthrough toward nuclear fusion that we hoped for never took place, and solar batteries are too expensive to maintain on the earth's surface in sufficient quantity.

³ Anyone older than ten can remember automobiles. They dwindled. At first the price of gasoline climbed—way up. Finally only the well-to-do drove, and that was too clear an indication that they were filthy rich, so any automobile that dared show itself on a city street was overturned and burned. Rationing was introduced to "equalize sacrifice," but every three months the ration was reduced. The cars just vanished and became part of the metal resource.

⁴ There are many advantages, if you want to look for them. Our 1997 newspapers continually point them out. The air is cleaner and there seem to be fewer colds. Against most predictions, the crime rate has dropped. With the police car too expensive (and too easy a target), policemen are back on their beats. More important, the streets are full. Legs are king in the cities of 1997, and people walk everywhere far into the night. Even the parks are full, and there is mutual protection in crowds.

⁵ If the weather isn't too cold, people sit out front. If it is hot, the open air is the only air conditioning they get. And at least the street lights still burn. Indoors, electricity is scarce, and few people can afford to keep lights burning after supper.

⁶ As for the winter—well, it is inconvenient to be cold, with most of what furnace fuel is allowed hoarded for the dawn; but sweaters are popular indoor wear and showers are not an everyday luxury. Lukewarm sponge baths will do, and if the air is not always very fragrant in the human vicinity, the automobile fumes are gone.

⁷ There is some consolation in the city that it is worse in the suburbs. The suburbs were born with the auto, lived with the auto, and are dying with the auto. One way out for the suburbanites is to form associations that assign turns to the procurement and distribution of food. Pushcarts creak from house to house along the posh suburban roads, and every bad snowstorm is a disaster. It isn't easy to hoard enough food to last till the roads are open. There is not much in the way of refrigeration except for the snowbanks, and then the dogs must be fought off.

⁸ What energy is left cannot be directed into personal comfort. The nation must survive until new energy sources are found, so it is the railroads and subways that are receiving major attention. The railroads must move the coal that is the immediate hope, and the subways can best move the people.

⁹ And then, of course, energy must be conserved for agriculture. The great car factories make trucks and farm machinery almost exclusively. We can huddle together when there is a lack of warmth, fan ourselves should there be no cooling breezes, sleep or make love at such times as there is a lack of light—but nothing will for long ameliorate a lack of food. The American population isn't going up much any more, but the food supply must be kept high even though the prices and difficulty of distribution force each American

to eat less. Food is needed for export so that we can pay for some trickle of oil and for other resources.

[10] The rest of the world, of course, is not as lucky as we are. Some cynics say that it is the knowledge of this that helps keep America from despair. They're starving out there, because earth's population has continued to go up. The population on earth is 5.5 billion, and outside the United States and Europe, not more than one in five has enough to eat at any given time.

[11] All the statistics point to a rapidly declining rate of population increase, but that is coming about chiefly through a high infant mortality; the first and most helpless victims of starvation are babies, after their mothers have gone dry. A strong current of American opinion, as reflected in the newspapers (some of which still produce their daily eight pages of bad news), holds that it is just as well. It serves to reduce the population, doesn't it?

[12] Others point out that it's more than just starvation. There are those who manage to survive on barely enough to keep the body working, and that proves to be not enough for the brain. It is estimated that there are now nearly 2 billion people in the world who are alive but who are permanently brain-damaged by undernutrition, and the number is growing year by year. It has already occurred to some that it would be "realistic" to wipe them out quietly and rid the earth of an encumbering menace. The American newspapers of 1997 do not report that this is actually being done anywhere, but some travelers bring back horror tales.

[13] At least the armies are gone—no one can afford to keep those expensive, energy-gobbling monstrosities. Some soldiers in uniform and with rifles are present in almost every still functioning nation, but only the United States and the Soviet Union can maintain a few tanks, planes and ships—which they dare not move for fear of biting into limited fuel reserves.

[14] Energy continues to decline, and machines must be replaced by human muscle and beasts of burden. People are working longer hours and there is less leisure; but then, with electric lighting restricted, television for only three hours a night, movies three evenings a week, new books few and printed in small editions, what is there to do with leisure? Work, sleep and eating are the great trinity of 1997, and only the first two are guaranteed.

[15] Where will it end? It must end in a return to the days before 1800, to the days before the fossil fuels powered a vast machine industry and technology. It must end in subsistence farming and in a world population reduced by starvation, disease and violence to less than a billion.

[16] And what can we do to prevent all this now?

[17] Now? Almost nothing.

[18] If we had started 20 years ago, that might have been another matter. If we had only started 50 years ago, it would have been easy.

ANALYTICAL READING

1. According to Asimov, what has happened to the sources of energy? How plau-

sible are his speculations about coal, nuclear fission, nuclear fusion, solar energy, and oil?

2. Is Asimov serious about the advantages of critical fuel shortages? Do you think he is suggesting some possible present reforms, or is he just portraying the future as he sees it?

3. How does Asimov move from a narrative beginning about a demolition worker to a world view of life in 1997?

4. What are the top priorities in this country in 1997? Explain.

5. What points is Asimov making about the population decline, undernutrition, and the armies? Are these ideas pertinent today?

6. How effective are the closing series of questions and the answers to them in the final three paragraphs?

7. Is Asimov's essay the development of a conclusion he reaches from current facts about the petroleum supply? Explain.

REFLECTING

Point: Why would you consider Asimov's essay to be an argument? What are some of the minor points he makes in his projection of future life with little fuel? How does the author's voice contribute to his purpose?

Organization: What are the main divisions in the essay? Do you find a logical organizational structure? Is the argument organized inductively or deductively? Explain and suggest the advantage of this plan.

Support: How does Asimov use the narrative to support the major points in his argument? What logical evidence does he provide?

Synthesis: Do you think that Asimov has painted either too grim or too favorable a picture? How do your views of life in the future differ from his? Explain the different assumptions you may have about fuel and population. What specific ideas do you agree with? Which ones do you disagree with?

Evaluation: How plausible are Asimov's basic assumptions? Given these assumptions, does Asimov make an effective case for the nature of life in 1997? To what extent does his projection suggest the simple, healthy, carefree life that existed before the industrial age and that some people today are seeking in commune living? Does he weaken his argument by allowing television to operate for three hours a night, by providing for some movies and books, and by apparently not restricting sports and other forms of leisure? Overall, how effective is this scenario as an emotional argument? And how skillfully and convincingly does Asimov use this device? Explain.

FROM READING TO WRITING

1. Using analogy or satire, write an argument about the future types and uses of cars in view of the fuel problem. You might draw upon Raymond Betts' article (pages 294–96) for some ideas.

2. The cost of medical and hospital care has increased rapidly during the past five years. Write an argument against these huge increases by projecting a view of medical treatment in the future.

3. Follow Asimov's opening paragraph and the following three sentences with a portrayal of one day in the life of this person, using your ideas, Asimov's or both.

4. Strike out on your own by using Asimov's futuristic argumentative device to argue your case for or against something that you favor or oppose.

BAD STUDY HABITS
Russell Baker

BIOGRAPHICAL SKETCH

Russell Baker, a graduate of Johns Hopkins University, was born in 1925 in Loudoun County, Virginia. After working as a reporter for the Baltimore Sun *and the* New York Times, *in 1962 he became the author of a nationally syndicated humorous column, "The Observer." He has been awarded honorary degrees by Princeton and several other universities. Among his six books are two novels and several collections of his essays, including* All Things Considered *and* Baker's Dozen. *In addition, he has contributed witty and satirical essays to numerous magazines, such as* Ladies' Home Journal, Sports Illustrated, Holiday, *and* McCall's.

PRE-READING

1. What information in the biographical sketch suggests the probable tone of the essay?

2. How is this tone revealed in the opening paragraph?

3. What does the final paragraph indicate about the general subject and Baker's attitude toward it?

¹ Had the Government simply refused to watch 58 women cook three meals a day for a week, no reasonable citizen would have complained, for the Government is terribly busy. But the Government did not refuse. This, after all, was a study, and if there is one thing the Government loves, it is a study.

² And so it assembled 58 women in a kitchen at the National Bureau of Standards and told them to start cooking. They cooked and they cooked. And while they cooked, the Government watched them on television cameras and through one-way mirrors.

FROM *The New York Times Magazine,* 5 June 1977, p. 12. © 1977 by The New York Times Company. Reprinted by permission.

3 They were not told why they were cooking, and so they did not know that their cooking habits were being scrutinized to determine the energy efficiency of the typical American cooker. The results are now in, and a more unexciting batch of results I have rarely seen.

4 For example, the women tended to cook on their stoves' right front burners, even when these were the biggest burners on the stove. What's more, many of the women left their oven doors open while they peeled potatoes.

5 The Government's conclusion is that Americans waste a lot of gas and electricity through bad cooking habits. This differs substantially from my own conclusion, which is that the Government wastes a lot of money and energy through bad study habits.

6 Any government half as efficient as ours wants its cooking citizenry to be would have nipped this study in the bud. It would have said, "Look here, you're not only proposing to tie me up for a week watching 58 women who don't know why they're being watched, but you're also asking me to spend a lot of money on television cameras, one-way mirrors, psychologists, tabulators, report writers and similar gewgaws. And all you're going to learn is that people cook indiscriminately on the right front burner."

7 "How can you be so sure?" the study director might have asked.

8 To which a sagacious government would have replied, "Because most people are right-handed, and because Americans are a people who don't like to put things on the back burner."

9 Our Government does not operate this way. Americans don't like to put things on the back burner, and the Government doesn't like to pass up the chance to conduct a study that will confirm what everyone has always known. A few years ago it conducted a study that discovered kissing transmits colds.

10 As for the discovery that many people leave the oven door open while peeling potatoes, this is almost certainly wrong. The error in all probability results from elevating cookery to a laboratory enterprise.

11 Every cook at some point in his or her development has left the oven door open while peeling potatoes. But only once. In a normal kitchen with its cramped space, an open oven door leads inexorably to cracked shinbone, perhaps broken leg and possibly severe burn. After the first encounter with an oven door in the typical American kitchen, the neophyte Escoffier rarely, if ever, leaves it open again while dealing with the spuds.

12 The women who did so in the Government's test probably had good reasons. Perhaps the Government's kitchens were as commodious as its purse and gave them a luxurious sense of spaciousness which allowed them to indulge a vice denied them in their homes. More likely, I suspect, since the women were kept in the dark about why they were cooking in this laboratory, some of them tried to outguess the experimenters.

13 If I were taken to the National Bureau of Standards and told to cook three meals daily for a week under close observation, and utterly without explanation, I might very well conclude that the Government was trying to discover whether I was wasting potatoes by peeling off too much potato with

the skin. Under the intense strain of struggling to keep my potato peels paper thin, I might easily forget such normal kitchen habits as keeping the oven door closed.

[14] The Government doesn't pounce on this sensible explanation of why the oven doors were left open. Instead, it proposes to inflict yet another buzzer on the national nervous system. This buzzer would sound off with each opening of the oven and, of course, in the natural development of buzzers, acquire a mind of its own which would set it off whenever it became peevish, at all hours of the day and night, whether the oven is open or shut.

[15] We need only one more buzzer in America. This should go off in the Government's ear every time somebody proposes to study whether water is wet and whether fleas like dogs.

ANALYTICAL READING

1. What sentences in paragraphs 2, 3, and 5 indicate the author's attitude toward the Government study? Analyze how their structure achieves this effect.

2. Why is the word *government* not capitalized in the first sentence of paragraph 6? Can you rewrite this sentence to make it clearer?

3. Is the pun on *back burner* (paragraph 8) a logical or humorous statement in this context? What is the relationship between the statement about the back burner and the results of the study? What is the effect of this point and of Baker's imagined conversation between the Government and the study director?

4. Could you guess at the meaning of the allusion to *Escoffier* (paragraph 11), or did you look it up? How appropriate is the simile in paragraph 12? What specific words in the essay did you find particularly delightful and most effective in maintaining the tone?

5. How knowledgeable is Baker about cooking? On what evidence do you base your conclusion?

6. How does Baker render absurd a serious Government recommendation about adding a buzzer to stoves to save wasted energy? Is his argument logical or not? And to what extent is it aided by the final paragraph?

7. Is the analogy in the last sentence logically appropriate?

REFLECTING

Point: Is the article mainly concerned with a particular study, most Government studies, Government waste of money, or all three? Answer this question by writing a summary statement of the essay.

Organization: Indicate how the essay is divided into its respective parts. Could the order of these parts have been changed without affecting the essay? Could any part have been omitted?

Support: Does Baker offer sufficient examples to illustrate the nature of the Government study? Does he clearly explain his reasons for feeling that the study was unnecessary, the results inconclusive, and the recommendation impractical?

Synthesis: Do you agree with Baker about the study? What case can be made for it? Do you think that the 58 women watched under the conditions mentioned would have acted normally or would have been more careful than usual about leaving oven doors open and cooking on the most efficient burner? Is there any value in determining whether kissing transmits colds? Whether great amounts of saccharin produce cancer in laboratory rats?

Evaluation: How effective is Baker in presenting his argument? Describe the voice he uses and indicate whether it contributes to or detracts from his essay. Is the essay written clearly, interestingly, and convincingly?

FROM READING TO WRITING

1. Write an essay about a high school study of homework, dating, driving, or some other student habits, showing how ridiculous the methodology, conclusions, or recommendations are.

2. If some campus rule, procedure, or proposal irritates you, write a letter to your college newspaper, emulating Baker's voice and tone.

3. Write an emotional argument against some community, state, or federal government policy that appears absurd to you. Use ridicule as your weapon; avoid expressing your anger or annoyance directly.

IRRATIONAL BEHAVIOR OR EVANGELICAL ZEAL?
Michael Mewshaw

BIOGRAPHICAL SKETCH

*Michael Mewshaw was born in Washington, D.C., in 1943 and holds a B.A. from the University of Maryland and a Ph.D. from the University of Virginia. Besides his four novels—*Man in Motion *(1970),* Walking Slow *(1972),* The Toll *(1972), and* Earthly Bread *(1976)—he has published many articles and reviews.* Earthly Bread *is about a young Catholic priest who helps to "deprogram" a "Jesus freak"; Mewshaw's research for this novel stimulated his interest in such "deprogramming."*

PRE-READING

1. What do the title and the biographical sketch prepare you for?

2. When the first paragraph provides inadequate clues about an article, as this one does, then you should read on until you gain more insight into the subject.

FROM *The Chronicle of Higher Education,* 18 October 1976, p. 32. Copyright © 1976 by Editorial Projects for Education, Inc. Reprinted by permission of the author and *The Chronicle of Higher Education.*

How far do you have to read before you feel reasonably confident that you know the subject of this essay?

3.   The title poses an either-or question. From skimming the last paragraph, how do you suppose the author would answer the question?

[1] As the radio ads have announced—to the accompaniment of spooky music, shrieks, and the burble of green pea soup—*The Exorcist* is back. But one wonders whether it ever went away. Judging by the recent spate of books and movies dealing with demonic possession, it seems to have spawned clones and provided a self-replenishing resource for publishing and film companies.

[2] This phenomenon, odd as it is, would deserve no more than a footnote in a pop-culture thesis if it weren't for the fact that grotesque parodies of exorcism are performed whenever pentecostal Christians, Moon people, and Hare Krishna chanters are kidnapped, confined for days with little food and sleep, and badgered into recanting their beliefs.

[3] Euphemistically called "deprogramming," the process amounts to little more than a methodical and sometimes violent attempt to exorcise not Satan, but unpopular, misunderstood, or inarticulate notions about God.

[4] During the last four years as I researched, wrote, and published a novel concerning this subject, I ran into very few people—except for direct participants—who had much substantive knowledge about deprogramming. Although most victims of these systematized efforts at brainwashing are college or graduate students, or members of the free-floating communities that congregate around universities, my academic colleagues were either oblivious to the situation or else felt that evangelical Christianity wasn't intellectually respectable and therefore its *dévotés* deserved whatever they got. At the start, I myself was ill-informed, and, though a practicing Catholic, I scarcely qualified as a pentecostal or charismatic believer. Yet driven by curiosity and convinced of the basic decency of the "born-again" Christians in my classes, I decided to take a closer look at the problem.

[5] What I learned surprised and dismayed me. Much as I might disagree with the theology of certain evangelical groups, they struck me as no more deluded or neurotic than others on campus. Yet from parents I repeatedly heard the same justification of deprogrammings. They claimed their children were misguided, distressingly inclined to give away money, incapable of making mature decisions, maybe even demented. In cases where the "children" turned out to be college graduates in their 20's and 30's and sometimes mothers and fathers themselves, the charges grew more dramatic. The "kids," I was told, had been abducted, hypnotized, or—shades of Patty Hearst—forced into joining a cult which then held them captive against their will.

[6] Just recently a distraught mother confronted me and tearfully asked what I would do if my own son had joined a religious group and would no longer communicate with me. Wouldn't I consider kidnapping him and trying to talk sense to him? It was only after I had sympathized with her that she

revealed that her son was 26, a Phi Beta Kappa graduate of Notre Dame, and a former student at the Sorbonne. I suggested that since he sounded like a gifted, responsible boy she should perhaps try to understand and accept his decision. Our conversation was then broken off by hysterical sobs and her accusation that I didn't know what I was talking about.

[7] The woman may have been right; I may be wrong. But I must say I never encountered any of the irrational, robot-like zealots I heard about, and, to my knowledge, none of the sensational allegations against unorthodox religious groups has ever stood up in court.

[8] Gradually I've come to believe the problem may be semantic as much as anything else. For example, what parents call propaganda and coercion the religious groups invariably call evangelical zeal. After all, don't Catholics and Protestants also send out missionaries? What the parents see as irrational behavior the groups say is ritualized devotion. Don't most religions encourage ideas and rites that strike outsiders as bizarre, if not insane? What the parents interpret as extortion or embezzlement the groups view as voluntary charity. Don't all organized churches accept—and in some instances demand—contributions?

[9] Yet, while parents have failed to prove their charges, they have managed to convince a crucial segment of the media and the public that their children are in danger. Thus young people continue to be captured, imprisoned, and physically and emotionally abused because of their beliefs. Civil libertarians have shown no great eagerness to get involved, and some local police forces have admitted that they actually encouraged and assisted deprogrammers. There have been a few cuts and bruises, broken bones, and chipped teeth. Fortunately no one has been killed or maimed so far, but substantial damage has been done to our constitutional guarantees of religious freedom.

[10] All of this prompts questions about America's commitment to the First Amendment and to human rights in general. While the country retains its capacity for selective indignation, it often appears to relinquish one old liberty for each new one it wins. For instance, recent court rulings have affirmed the right of adolescent girls, regardless of age, to undergo abortions without parental approval. Yet both by their decisions and by their refusal to hear certain cases, the courts have suggested that the same young girl who has gained complete control over her body might have to accept familial interference with her soul. And this interference won't necessarily end when she reaches 21. Even marriage offers no sanctuary, for many people have paid to have their spouses kidnapped and deprogrammed.

[11] Frequently I have been asked questions by students and young people who have been harassed because of their theology, their dress, and their behavior. Why have "born-again" Christians been singled out? Why aren't dope dealers or pornographers kidnapped and deprogrammed? How would the public respond if a Protestant pulled his son out of a seminary and kept him incommunicado until he gave up his vocation? What would the Vatican do if

a Catholic dragged his daughter from a convent? How would the Black Muslims react if their congregation was picked off one by one? Would Jews consider it just if Reform members grabbed Orthodox believers and put them through a crude form of behavior modification?

[12] These questions, I think, deserve careful consideration—and honest answers. As a country committed to the separation of church and state and to freedom of worship, we may not always approve of what others believe or the way they express their beliefs, but we have no moral or legal right to intervene except in the most extreme circumstances. It would be a shame . . . if America was not mature and wise enough to insist upon that religious liberty that was one of its founding principles and is still one of its greatest claims to international respect.

ANALYTICAL READING

1. What was Mewshaw's attitude before he began research for his novel, and how did other professors feel about deprogramming?

2. Why do you suppose parents are so upset about their children joining evangelical religious groups?

3. What does the author mean when he says that "the problem may be semantic" (paragraph 8)?

4. According to the author, how do many people feel about deprogramming? Do you agree with his appraisal?

5. What is so ironic about the rights that courts have granted and denied to young people?

6. Does Mewshaw believe in the absolute right of religious freedom, or does he suggest that some restriction might be placed upon it? If so, what kind of restriction might be imposed and why?

REFLECTING

Point: What is the main idea in Mewshaw's essay? Where do you find it best expressed? What do you suppose was his purpose in writing the essay?

Organization: What is accomplished by the linking of deprogramming with exorcism in the opening paragraphs? How is the rest of the essay organized? Does a change begin at paragraph 9? Discuss the development of paragraph 10. Write a syllogism to illustrate the argument in the essay.

Support: Does Mewshaw load his argument by associating exorcism with deprogramming, or is this a sound analogy? Does the author's voice reveal him to be a fair, reasonable, and sympathetic person? Why or why not? Do you feel that the abortion and deprogramming analogy in paragraph 10 adds valid support? What about the analogies implied in the rhetorical questions in paragraph 11? Does Mewshaw deal with the rights of parents or of spouses?

Synthesis: What do you know personally of this problem? Should young people over twenty-one have the right to join any religious cult? Since in many states young people can drive at sixteen, vote at eighteen, and buy liquor at twenty-one, might it not be wise to give them unlimited religious freedom, which may call for greater emotional and intellectual maturity, at twenty-five?

Evaluation: Does Mewshaw appear to have treated the problem fairly, fully, and logically? Could it be argued that his research experiences were not typical? How convincing would he be to parents? What audience do you think he is writing to? How convincing do you think he would be with this audience? Why?

FROM READING TO WRITING

1. Write a letter to the editor of a local newspaper, arguing for the freedom of young people to make their own religious choices.

2. Write for or against a California plan (struck down by a higher court) that allowed parents to have custody for a thirty-day period of their children, who were followers of the Reverend Sun Myung Moon. (It might interest you to know that of five, who ranged in age from twenty-one to twenty-five, three chose to return to their parents, two returned to Moon's Unification Church.)

3. In a letter to *Newsweek,* Carol Mays, Director of Christian Education in Blacksburg, Va., commented that it is fortunate Mary did not have Jesus deprogrammed for leaving a promising career as a carpenter and following his conscience. Write an argument agreeing or disagreeing with Ms. Mays' statement.

FROM BANANA RIVER
Charles A. Lindbergh

BIOGRAPHICAL SKETCH

In May 1927 Charles A. Lindbergh (1902–1974) completed the first solo transatlantic flight, from New York to Paris, in 33½ hours. With this feat, he began the era of modern aviation. An international hero, "Lucky Lindy" lost some of his popularity during World War II by joining the isolationist America First Committee which opposed U.S. aid to Great Britain. When the United States entered the war, Lindbergh volunteered his services, trained fighter pilots in the Pacific, and participated in over fifty combat missions himself; he was eventually commissioned as a brigadier general in the U.S. Air Force Reserve. In his later years, he turned to ecology and environmentalism. He died of cancer in 1974 and by his request was buried on the Hawaiian island of Maui. The following selection appears in his recently published book, which consists of material from his unpublished 1,000-page memoir.

FROM Charles A. Lindbergh, *Banana River,* a part of *Autobiography of Values* (New York: Harcourt Brace Jovanovich, 1976), pp. 13–22. Copyright © 1976 by Harcourt Brace Jovanovich, Inc. and Anne Morrow Lindbergh. Reprinted by permission of the publisher.

PRE-READING

1. Do you know anything about the author besides the information furnished in the biographical sketch? What general subject do you believe he would write about? Does the title give any indication of the subject?

2. What sentence in the first paragraph seems to suggest the particular subject?

3. What does the last paragraph suggest about Lindbergh's viewpoint toward the subject?

[1] Man feels he must conquer space. He works sometimes in the interests of pure science, sometimes for the practical needs of war. His reason may be convenient to his motive, but the spirit of adventure is beyond his power to control. Our earliest records tell of biting the apple and baiting the dragon, regardless of hardship or of danger, and from this inner drive, perhaps, progress and civilization developed. We moved from land to sea, to air, to space, era on era, our aspirations rising with our confidence and knowledge. Wheels and hulls and wings changed our present environment. Where will missiles fit in the human scale of values as they may be recorded ten centuries from now?

[2] I look at the faces around me: the civilians at instrument benches, the general at a window, the colonel and the captain with their check lists, the guards and workmen who have come inside for shelter, all intent on a missile and its mission—years of dreaming, designing, building brought to this moment, about to be tested by a firing. Their minds are concentrated on mechanical perfection. Who has time to think of what that rocket signifies in human values of the future? . . .

[3] "X minus two minutes?" One feels the tenseness in the blockhouse although every man is trying to show an attitude of calm. A cigar tip accentuates the trembling of lips and a paper's flutter tattles on a hand.

[4] "X minus sixty seconds!" Words of command grow sharp, terse. Multiple recorders click in the background.

[5] "X minus ten seconds! Nine! Eight! Seven! . . . Zero! Rocket away!"

[6] A muffled roar, then flame, and great clouds of smoke burst outward from the tailpipe. The rocket thunders, rising slowly, as though uncertain of its strength, yet firm and erect with no sign of instability. It moves faster, leaps suddenly upward, streaks out of sight beyond the range of blockhouse windows. Steel doors are thrown open. Men shout, joke, laugh with success. The tension is broken, the responsibility has passed to other hands. The Control Center has taken over, and instruments will from now on tell the missile's story.

[7] I think of the long, sleek vehicle streaking out through space, far above our atmosphere's layer of interference. It is the prototype of man-made meteors that can be directed to atomize any spot on earth: Moscow, London, Tokyo, Rome, cities that can become a series of figures. Select your missile's

destination, read the digits, set the dials. A cannon shell is sluggish, moving at a medieval pace, compared to this projectile in flight.

⁸ Millions of lives, centuries of labor, can be wiped out by words of command spoken more than an ocean-width away! It is theoretical, so separate from the senses. Enclosed within a concrete blockhouse, your mind tells you the significance of what has taken place; but your flesh and bone do not feel it. There is no deafening scream, no hurricane of wind against the check, no sight of blood to assault the eye. You deal in contrivances, in ideas and imagination: a button pressed, a lever pulled, a city will disappear. I watched a cup of cold coffee tossed into a sink.

⁹ A ballistic missile orbits dozens of miles outside our world: the dream of science and dread of man; the culmination of military power and ultimate in civilized destruction. I step through the open doorway and look up to a tranquil sky. How can a modern airman comprehend the devastation he causes? And how often that question has churned my mind before—at Wotje and Tarawa; at Jefman and Samate; at Rabaul and Kavieng. And yes, at Kavieng.

¹⁰ Eyes of memory still see it clearly, the bombed city of Kavieng on New Ireland's northern coast. My vision shifts from Florida to South Pacific seas. Kavieng looked like an ant hill when I approached in my fighter-bomber on May 29, 1944. I was flying in a three-plane patrol from Major Joseph Foss's Marine Corsair Squadron VMF-115, Major Marion Carl and Lieutenant Rolfe F. Blanchard flanking me. My mind slips back easily through the stream of time, into that Corsair's cockpit. I feel the stick's vibration in my hand, and the pedals against my feet. My thumb has the power of TNT and my finger controls six machine guns.

¹¹ A few miles ahead, fifteen thousand feet below my altitude, a scorched-brown texture between blue of sea and green of jungle is our target—so minute, so apparently trivial compared to the limitless expanse of land and water that rolls to the horizons. Careful scanning of the earth informs me that Kavieng, situated on the top of a peninsula, is sheltered from the sea by two islands and their reefs, and that the hulks of several sunken ships obstruct the harbor. Minute circles on the ground warn of enemy antiaircraft cannon. Group Intelligence officers told us to be wary of those gunners: "The 'Nips' have none better in the South Pacific."

¹² My exact target is an area of city in which Japanese troops are stationed. I want to kill some of those troops. In fact, I want to kill as many as possible. But when I tell myself I am going to kill, the idea somehow does not take hold inside me. I never have the feel of killing as I move the controls of my plane. Whenever I fly in my fighter-bomber, I seem to lose relationship to earth's community of men.

¹³ Everything is quiet on the ground and in the sky. It is hard to realize that we can strike with deadly force across such a magnitude of space, that we have come to toss five-hundred-pound bombs at humans down below, and

that at any moment black blooms in air around us will symbolize the hostility of our reception.

¹⁴ An airman separates himself from the earth and its people when he follows a warplane's orbit. There are moments when the planet he is bound to seems as unrelated to his actions as does the moon, moments when he is completely isolated from the world's problems, its happiness and its sufferings, when the calculations of his mission appear as bloodless as the digits of astronomy. He guides his plane along independent courses through a space of air, watching dials, moving levers, caring no more about the lives he crushes than he would if the city below were an ant hill. How well I know the irresponsibility of the bomb's red button, and how often I have pressed it: in the Marshalls, over Noemfoor, in the Bismarks, above Kavieng. . . .

¹⁵ The wings of Corsair 1 are rocking. We drop our dive brakes, purge our wing tanks, brighten gun sights. Corsair 1 peels off; it is Carl. Corsair 2 follows; it is Blanchard. I pull into a wingover, putting the sun behind my back, and nose steeply to the dive. I see the two Corsairs well below me, screaming toward the ground. My controls tighten, the altimeter needle touches ten thousand feet, air howls, wings tremble. At seven thousand feet I make a final adjustment to the trim tabs; six thousand feet, steady on the rudder; pipper beyond the target. Fifty-five hundred feet. NOW. My thumb presses, my arm pulls back. I kick right rudder toward the sea, reverse bank to throw off enemy ack-ack, reserve again, and look down to check my marksmanship.

¹⁶ There was no sense of combat on that mission; it was like an exercise in aerial calisthenics. I saw no flashes on the ground to challenge my attack. I did not feel the bomb drop. One moment it was held firmly in its rack, completely under my control. Then my thumb moved ever so slightly against a small red button on the stick and death went hurtling earthward. I caught one glimpse of the bomb falling after I dropped my wing—cylindrical, inert, awkward, irretrievably launched on its mission; certain to destroy itself and the first object that it touched. In another second it was lost to sight. No power of man could countermand my action. If there was life where that bomb would hit, I had taken it; yet that life was still thinking, breathing when the bomb was still falling: there was still eternal seconds. Nothing had changed in my cockpit; nothing in my sky.

¹⁷ The little puff of smoke—the pebble-splash of debris—was centered in a row of buildings near the beach, an area where antiaircraft guns had been reported. What a slight scar it left! I could not even find it with my eyes after the smoke drifted away. So far as I could tell, Kavieng was no worse off for our visit. But in reality were there torn and writhing bodies in that pinprick I had made in the ground? Were they already out of sight behind me? Was a machine-gun nest wiped out? Had I eliminated a score of soldiers from the war? Was some child without a mother, a mother without a child? I felt no responsibility for what I had done. It was too far away, too disconnected.

¹⁸ How can an airman comprehend the devastation he causes? He must stand on the rubble of a destroyed city to sense the power of the bomb's red

button. He must see flashing concussion waves tear across the ground, debris vomiting through air, and great columns of smoke billowing. He must take the hammer blows on his chest, the thunder against his ears, hear the cries of terror. When you look down at two human heads above a single body, at bones protruding from a mass of flesh a dozen feet away; when you stand at some cross street on a pile of brick and let your eyes travel its four directions over block after block of fire-blacked, shattered walls; when you watch clouds redden with the flames beneath them, and feel after a bombardment the white dust of death that settles over everthing—then your thumb's contact with the bomb button transmits significance.

[19] Hiroshima lies flat and peaceful between plum-tinted mountain ranges and the island-studded beauty of Japan's Inland Sea. It is December 1947. I am in an Air Force transport plant, circling at three thousand feet. Two years have passed since the bomb was dropped. The aged mountains, the nestling city, the calm sea, all the crystal tranquility beneath me—it seems impossible that the people here witnessed the horror of that August day when an airplane soared overhead, barely specking the sky, yet leaving behind it excruciating pain and devastation. There is no sign to mark the gigantic mushroom cloud that once towered in the sky, no sign except, when I look more carefully, the shades on earth below.

[20] To see the terror of past war, an airman's eye must translate shadings. A city, like a human face, can show the pallor of death. A gray-ash saucer, a mile or so in width, marks the blasted, radiated, and heat-shriveled earth of Hiroshima. Surrounding it is a black halo of undamaged roots on the outskirts. The straw-colored stippling which glints now and then in sunlight, as we bank, is caused by the unpainted lumber of the newly built dwellings that have sprung up like fungi. Inside that gray saucer more than seventy thousand men, women, and children were killed, and that many more were burned and mangled. Over one hundred and forty thousand casualties from a single bomb—from words of command—from the pressure of buttons.

[21] Since I flew over Hiroshima we have developed bombs of more than a thousand times the power. The kilotons and hours we used in our calculations at the end of World War II have been replaced by figures representing megatons and minutes. In planning for the possibility of an all-out nuclear conflict we discuss casualties running into tens of millions, huge uninhabitable areas caused by fallout. Will half or three-quarters of a continent's population be wiped out?

ANALYTICAL READING

1. What is the point of the scene in the Control Center? Which paragraph best conveys that point?

2. The first two paragraphs are linked by their references to missiles. In what other significant way are they related?

3. What is the connection between the account of the missile's launching and Lindbergh's own bombing run at Kavieng?

4.   Analyze paragraph 8 closely. How does Lindbergh use comparison and contrast effectively to make his point? What is accomplished by the reference to the cold cup of coffee?

5.   Discuss Lindbergh's thoughts about killing in paragraph 12. Does he want to kill or not? Is there a feeling that he must kill or be killed? What different effect might have been created by mention of Pearl Harbor and the many American deaths caused by Japanese soldiers?

6.   How does he feel after the bombing run? What is the rhetorical effect in paragraph 17 of his concern for a child and its mother?

7.   Note how Lindbergh describes his bombing experience, moving back and forth from vivid description to generalizations about the experience. Did you find this distracting? Why or why not? Is it appropriate in view of Lindbergh's purpose?

8.   What emotions is Lindbergh appealing to in the description of his flight over Hiroshima?

9.   What does Lindbergh mean at the beginning of paragraph 20 when he states that "an airman's eye must translate shadings"? Analyze the structure of that paragraph.

REFLECTING

Point: Is Lindbergh making a statement only to airmen and those involved in launching missiles, or is he appealing to a larger audience? Formulate his purpose in a sentence or two.

Organization: What are the main divisions in this essay? How are they linked? Would it have been more effective to have started with his bombing experience instead of the missile launching? Why or why not?

Support: What emotions does Lindbergh appeal to? Which of his examples best convey those emotions? How does he maintain interest? Discuss the tone and its appropriateness to the subject. Analyze the effect of the "ant hill" image in paragraph 10, point out where it is used again, and discuss any other images.

Synthesis: What significance does the essay have for you? What practical argument can be used against Lindbergh's discussion of future weapons? To what extent can Lindbergh's argument be extended into everyday life, to actions like shoplifting, vandalizing a school building, or stealing a hubcap from an unknown person's car?

Evaluation: Does Lindbergh make his point clearly and convincingly? Does he leave you as troubled as he is, or can you remove yourself from his strong emotional appeal and look only at the practical side of war? Is his language forceful and thought-provoking? Select specific sentences that you felt were powerful and compelling. Do you think that you are likely to remember the essay? Why or why not?

FROM READING TO WRITING

1.   On the basis of incidents in your school career, write an emotional argument for or against cheating on exams and out-of-class assignments.

2. Write an emotional reply to Lindbergh's argument.

3. Referring to specific examples, write an emotional argument for or against raising or lowering the present legal driving or drinking age in your state.

THE MOTHER
Gwendolyn Brooks

BIOGRAPHICAL SKETCH

Gwendolyn Brooks was born in Topeka, Kansas, in 1917, graduated from Wilson Junior College, and since then has received ten honorary doctorates from various colleges and universities. She has lectured at numerous colleges. Among her many literary awards are the Pulitzer Prize in poetry for Annie Allen, *two Guggenheim fellowships, and a prize from the Academy of Arts and Letters. Brooks has written a novel (*Maud Martha*), her autobiography, and numerous books of poetry, including one for children. Most of her best-known poems appear in* The World of Gwendolyn Brooks. *Her latest volume of poetry is entitled* Beckonings.

PRE-READING

1. Judging from the title and the first few lines of the poem, what is the subject and what view of the subject do you expect to find in the poem?

2. How is this view confirmed in the final lines?

Abortions will not let you forget.
You remember the children you got that you did not get,
The damp small pulps with a little or with no hair,
The singers and workers that never handled the air,
You will never neglect or beat   5
Them, or silence or buy with a sweet.
You will never wind up the sucking-thumb
Or scuttle off ghosts that come.
You will never leave them, controlling your luscious sigh,
Return for a snack of them, with gobbling mother-eye.   10

I have heard in the voices of the wind the voices of my dim killed children.
I have contracted. I have eased
My dim dears at the breasts they could never suck.
I have said, Sweets, if I sinned, if I seized
Your luck   15

And your lives from your unfinished reach,
If stole your births and your names,
Your straight baby tears and your games,
Your stilted or lovely loves, your tumults, your marriages, aches, and your
    deaths,
If I poisoned the beginnings of your breaths,   20
Believe that even in my deliberateness I was not deliberate.
Though why should I whine,
Whine that the crime was other than mine?—
Since anyhow you are dead.
Or rather, or instead,   25
You were never made.
But that, too, I am afraid,
Is faulty; oh, what shall I say, how is the truth to be said?
You were born, you had body, you died.
It is just that you never giggled or planned or cried.   30
Believe me; I loved you all.
Believe me, I knew you, though faintly, and I loved, I loved you
All.

ANALYTICAL READING

1. Explain the paradox in line 2 about "the children you got that you did not get."

2. How do you account for the change from the use of the second-person *you* in the opening stanza to the first-person *I* in the second?

3. What is the meaning in line 21 of the statement, "even in my deliberateness I was not deliberate"?

4. What is the truth that the poem states about the relationship between the mother and her aborted children?

5. Does the poem present an argument against abortion, or does it confine itself to a statement of a mother's sense of guilt? How could the mother have loved these children?

REFLECTING

Point: Is the poem a personal expression of a mother (not necessarily or even probably the poet herself), or is it an argument? Write a statement summarizing the subject of the poem.

Organization: Point out the main divisions of the poem and explain the subject of each.

Support: Do you feel that the "I" of the poem is a young girl or older woman? Has she had living children? Does she sentimentalize parenthood? Do you feel that the poem is indeed a "whine" (line 22)? If so, how is this effect created? Which lines did you find most moving?

Synthesis: How did you feel about abortion before reading the poem and afterwards? If the mother really loved her children, how do you account for her having aborted them?

Evaluation: To what extent is the argument in the poem emotional? Should reasons for the abortions have been mentioned in the poem? How effective is the poem in presenting one aspect of the abortion controversy that is not frequently mentioned? Should all women contemplating abortion be urged to read this poem?

FROM READING TO WRITING

1. Write a poem or paper consoling women who have had abortions and feel guilty. Do not argue logically; appeal mainly to the problems that the children might have encountered.

2. Write a prose argument to women who are considering abortion, using mainly the material from the poem. If you wish, you may make it an emotional argument.

A NON-EXHORTATION
Joan Mondale

BIOGRAPHICAL SKETCH

Joan Mondale was born in 1930 in Pennsylvania and received a B.A. in history with minors in art and French from Macalester College in St. Paul. During her years in college and for several years afterward, she worked at the Minneapolis Institute of Arts; for two of those years she served as Assistant in Education. In 1955 she married Walter Mondale, former senator from Minnesota and now Vice-President of the United States. She has pursued her interests in art, conducting weekly tours for public school children at the National Gallery of Art in Washington, writing a book, Politics in Art, *and actively promoting art throughout the country. This speech was delivered at Macalester College when she was given an honorary doctor of humane letters degree.*

PRE-READING

1. In view of the occasion for Joan Mondale's speech, what does the title suggest to you? What is an exhortation?

2. What do the last three paragraphs tell you about the subject and main idea of her commencement address?

FROM *The New York Times,* 29 May 1977, p. E15. © 1977 by The New York Times Company. Reprinted by permission.

[1] Alice in Wonderland must have been delighted when she was introduced to the concept of the un-birthday. After all, it was explained to her, each of us has only one birthday a year, whereas there are 364 un-birthdays to celebrate!

[2] I mention that inspired notion because it is my purpose to deliver an un-Commencement Speech. I have heard a great many commencement speeches and most of them left me feeling vaguely dissatisfied.

[3] The typical commencement speaker, for example, says to his young, captive audience: "You are the best educated, the most intelligent, the most skilled and able generation in history."

[4] Well, I'm not so sure.

[5] I don't want to take anything away from the Class of 1977. But the ancient Greeks were rather impressive, don't you think? And the Renaissance—I seem to remember some skill and intelligence there.

[6] When I was told that my generation was the best educated, the most intelligent, et cetera, I shifted uncomfortably in my seat. I don't feel terribly brilliant or skilled or accomplished. I felt eager and excited and uncertain. And very green.

[7] So I won't patronize you. As an un-Commencement speaker, I will say simply that you have in your lives a marvelous opportunity: the opportunity to become educated, intelligent, skilled and able. It will probably take the rest of your life, and you may never feel that you've completely succeeded. But the effort, if you keep at it, will make your life very rich indeed. And it will help you to enrich your world.

[8] You know the next chapter of the Commencement Speech: It is that "our troubled world needs you"—needs you, that is, to repair all the damage done by the older generation. Well, heaven knows, the world is troubled. And, heaven knows, the older generation has made some incredible mistakes. But it occurs to me that the "older generation"—several older generations—deserve a good word or two of praise. For we have also done some things right.

[9] We pass along to you a lively, working democracy—a bit battered, perhaps, but essentially intact. A record of breathtaking scientific and technical achievements. A wealth of cultural and educational institutions that have their faults, but also do great good.

[10] Of course, your world needs you. It needs you not only to correct, but also to continue, what your parents have done.

[11] If the future is anything like the past, you, too, will make mistakes—many of them, but you will also achieve great things. And you may live to see your children's generation coming of age, flowing with the confidence of youth, certain that they can do a better job than yours.

[12] Finally, but by no means least, the typical commencement speaker urges you to get involved—to plunge up to your neck into politics or public service, stuffing back into Pandora's Box all the plagues that she unleashed so many years ago.

[13] To which I, the un-Commencement speaker, reply: All right, Get involved if you want to. If it is right for you. But only *if*.

[14] For it occurs to me that many great things indeed have been achieved by those who chose not to leap into the mainstream. Things like novels and symphonies and paintings, for example: works achieved by people who stood aside, for a while or for a lifetime, from the practical, problem-solving world.

[15] One of my abiding preoccupations is art in America: art in all its unpredictable richess and diversity. I spend some of my time going about encouraging artists—and encouraging our citizens to support and enjoy the arts. Again and again I am struck by how much we owe to those who enrich our lives without "solving problems."

[16] These people work in quiet isolation, in lofts and studios; they pay little attention to headlines or clocks or schedules. We are infinitely the richer for their noninvolvement—and I will defend to the last barricade their right, and yours, to let the world go by.

[17] To be sure, your joyful moments of noninvolvement need not produce high art. I have spent some of my happiest hours at a humming potter's wheel, with light slanting down through the window and the clamoring world at bay, creating objects that please me, but perhaps no critic.

[18] That is, after all, one of the freedoms this land affords us: the freedom to choose one's own path to fulfillment.

[19] For some, that path may be along a crowded way; for others a quiet place.

[20] No matter! It is my un-Commencement hope for each of you that you will find that path—and take it—*that* is, I think, and I hope your teachers will agree, the aim of your liberal education here: to help you gain the wisdom to find that path—and the courage to take it. In doing that, you will find the wholeness and unity of purpose that are the real meaning of integrity.

ANALYTICAL READING

1. How do the opening two paragraphs establish the voice, tone, and general direction of the speech?

2. What is the effect of the single sentence in paragraph 4?

3. How does Mondale establish rapport with her audience in paragraph 6?

4. What is achieved in paragraph 11 by the reference to the children of the graduating class?

5. Examine the untraditional sentence structure in paragraphs 13 and 14; comment on the appropriateness and effectiveness of these sentences.

6. Does Mondale recommend that people get involved or not? Explain. Does she establish a false either-or dilemma that might be refuted by referring to her own public and private life.

7. Discuss the sentence in the last paragraph about "the aim of your liberal education." How does it differ from the popular view of education? In what sense does Mondale use the final word, *integrity*?

REFLECTING

Point: The address is composed of a series of refutations and counter-statements. What are Mondale's key ideas, and which is the main one?

Organization: Is Mondale's argument organized deductively or inductively? What is the advantage of this structure? How does her "un-commencement" approach provide the organizational structure?

Support: In what specific ways does Mondale refute each point? How convincing is her use of evidence? For which point does she provide the most detail? To what extent does she depend on personal opinion rather than factual or logical evidence?

Synthesis: Compare Mondale's stereotype of the typical commencement speech with the one given at your high school graduation. Then consider her concept of a college education. Is it education for career or vocation, for citizenship, or for self-fulfillment? Do her views agree with those of your parents and others? In what sense does art (music, painting, and literature) require involvement in life? In what sense may art be viewed as non-involvement? Do you agree with Mondale that we "owe much" to those who pursue the arts? Explain. Is her address really a "non-exhortation"?

Evaluation: How interesting, clear, well organized, and effective is Mondale's argument? Do her voice and tone play a major role in persuading readers to accept or consider seriously her ideas? Explain. How would you evaluate her speech in view of her audience, the occasion, and her personal history?

FROM READING TO WRITING

1. Assume that you have been invited to give the graduation address at your high school. Emulate Mondale by writing an interesting argument to present as an un-commencement address.

2. Assume that you have been asked by the Rotary Club, the PTA, the League of Women Voters, or some other organization to give a talk about the freshman year at college. Write the speech, remembering that you should strive to gain and maintain the audience's interest. As the basis of your argument, try to correct some false impression you think your audience may have about college and college students.

3. Write a speech for new freshman attending a summer orientation program given at your college. Follow the structure of Mondale's speech in refuting erroneous impressions these students may have.

THAT DISTINCTIVELY AMERICAN CHRISTMAS
Newspaper Editorial

PRE-READING

1. Does the title raise any suspicions about the author's treatment of the subject?

2. Can you point to any statement in the first paragraph that sheds light on the viewpoint of the editorial?

3. What does the last paragraph reveal about the tone of the writer? Is it serious or satirical? Does it demonstrate the use of irony (a figure of speech used in argumentation to discredit something by appearing to approve of it)?

¹ Christmas is being celebrated all over the world today, in the cathedral towns of Europe, in the squalid slums of Latin American metropolises, in the steaming jungles of Africa and on the overpopulated plains of India. But the diverse peoples of those distant lands, however worthy and devout they may be in other respects, do not understand the true meaning of Christmas, as we do. Our Christmas is a uniquely American product quite distinct in spirit and tone from lesser Christmases. In these uncertain times, when most of our institutions are suspect, it remains a source of national stability and pride.

² Let the flighty sophisticates of France and Belgium observe the winter solstice with their feasts and frivolity and midnight Masses. Let the Christian converts of Japan and Indonesia rejoice over the nativity of Our Lord. In our country, Christmas is, as it should be, a deadly serious business enterprise, a time for encouraging the combativeness of young men, and an ennobling ordeal. From the first appearance of plastic greenery in the department stores just before Halloween until the final hoarse cheer echoes across the Rose Bowl on New Year's Day, it is a splendid, glorious, incomparable festival that reflects the enduring strengths and values of our great land.

³ Christmas traditions have had their origins in many parts of the world. The ancient Romans first came up with the idea of a late December bash, which later merged with Christian ceremonies imported from the Mideast. The Teutonic tribes of central Europe added the evergreens, the wassailing and the yule log. Many of our favorite carols came from Britain and France. But Americans have made the greatest contributions, using their native ingenuity and technological skills to devise a Christmas celebration for the rest of the world to admire, envy and wonder at.

⁴ It was the business community of the United States, after all, that fully realized the potential of Christmas as a stimulus to commerce and trade. And

FROM *Louisville Courier-Journal and Times,* 25 December 1973, p. A10. Copyright © 1973 by The Courier-Journal and Times, Louisville, Kentucky. Editorial reprinted with permission from the Opinion page.

it was the advertising industry of our native land that introduced parents to the pleasures of investing their annual savings in mountains of breakable toys for their deprived offspring, and that aroused the natural longings of infant children for battery-operated, three-speed blooper blappers.

⁵ The people who plan our Christmas seasons were the first in the world to recognize the harmonious relationship between hymns of peace and games of violence. Where else is it possible to combine family togetherness during the holidays with non-stop viewing of an immense number and variety of athletic contests?

⁶ Think of what our educational system has done to make Christmas pleasurable. The primary school teachers of America have singlehandedly made Christmas the mainstay of their curriculums for a full four weeks before the holiday, sending their pupils home with an endless succession of hand-crafted Santa Clauses and snowmen, and helping to generate the frantic excitement and whining insolence that parents so value in their young.

⁷ And we can claim credit for so many other innovations that will eventually spread across the seas and bring cheer and good will to billions of people all over the world. In our suburbs, for instance, the decoration of homes and yards has developed into a competitive sport, momentarily side-tracked by an energy shortage that frowns on conspicuous waste. The mass feeding of family and relatives has been elevated into a joyous opportunity for young wives to demonstrate their culinary skills. Where else is it possible to satisfy one's need to be charitable to the lonely and under-privileged simply by shedding tears over the sentimental slosh of television's Christmas specials? Moreover, Americans have wisely incorporated traditional pre-Lenten promiscuity into their Christmas celebrations, making it perfectly acceptable for a tipsy executive to lunge at his secretary while the wife is home making cookies.

⁸ Nor should we overlook the role that our American Christmas has played in the advancement of psychiatry. The inevitable feelings of guilt, depression and unfulfilled expectations that follow Christmas often require extensive treatment, opening up an entire new industry for the medical profession. It is now rumored that a new disorder, tentatively known as the Reverse Scrooge Syndrome, has been identified. Its victims, normally kind, decent and generous people, are said to burst into uncontrollable rages when a small child looks up from his or her $7,000 electric train, which took an entire night to assemble, and says: "Is that all, daddy?"

⁹ Christmas in our country is never static, never stays the same. Each year brings new delight and new excitement. This year, for instance, the women's liberationists have thoughtfully helped us to recognize that the careless selection of toys can cause our daughters to grow up to be as passive, vacuous and helpless as their mothers, and our sons to become as insensitive, militaristic and obnoxious as their fathers.

¹⁰ Is there any way that Christmas in America can be made more rewarding? A few dissident pseudo-intellectuals, it is true, argue that the holiday

season should be shorter and simpler and should have a narrower focus, with, perhaps, a greater religious orientation. Fie on them, we say. Washington may be awash with corruption, family life may be disintegrating and belief in God may be declining. But Christmas is a symbol of the rationality and essential virtuousness of our people and must remain pure and undefiled.

ANALYTICAL READING

1. What sentence in the second paragraph might you have underlined because of its importance?

2. According to the writer, what primarily caused the distinctive American celebration of Christmas?

3. What other groups have contributed to the American Christmas? Do you agree with the writer's selection of all these special groups?

4. What point is made about American psychiatry? If you had any doubt about whether the writer's intent was serious or not, what specific statements in paragraph 8 would clearly settle the question?

5. Explain the reference to the women's liberation movement in paragraph 9. Do you agree with this point or not?

REFLECTING

Point: What do you think the author's purpose is? Do you think the emotional method used is more effective than a more logical, direct argument would have been? Explain.

Organization: Discuss the point of each paragraph. Then determine whether the writer has followed a particular plan. Could the sequence of certain paragraphs be changed without spoiling the effect? How does the essay follow a SUBJECT–RESTRICTION–ILLUSTRATION plan?

Support: What assumption does the writer make? How does the writer appeal to readers to change the way Christmas is celebrated? Point to specific statements suggesting practices that should be changed. Also, point out phrases that are particularly delightful or effective.

Synthesis: How do you feel about the distinctive way that Americans celebrate Christmas? Do you agree with the author's ideas about the roles of business, advertising, the schools, home decorations, and feasts? Is this subject—or the approach to it—new? Where else has the subject been discussed? Are our celebrations of Christmas getting better or worse? Explain.

Evaluation: How convincing is the editorial? Does it gain most of its persuasiveness from the approach it takes? Is it more or less likely to affect people than a sermon on the subject? Are any points not pertinent? Could some additions be made? If you are familiar with Jonathan Swift's "A Modest Proposal," relate this editorial to that classic.

FROM READING TO WRITING

1. Write an ironic argument, using this indirect form of attack instead of the direct form. You might, for example, point out why women shouldn't be paid the same as men, why people should litter, why more violence should be presented on television, or some such subject. Have fun with your paper just as the author of this editorial did.

2. Read or reread Swift's "A Modest Proposal" and write a proposal of your own for solving some current political or other problem. Your plan should be seriously presented but be utterly inhumane or preposterous, such as killing all convicted criminals or requiring all students with low grades to be sterilized.

Logical Argument

WHAT'S RIGHT WITH SIGHT-AND-SOUND JOURNALISM

Eric Sevareid

BIOGRAPHICAL SKETCH

Eric Arnold Sevareid was born in the small town of Velva, North Dakota, in 1912. He graduated from the University of Minnesota and worked as a reporter for several newspapers before embarking on a career as a radio and television commentator, originally abroad and then as a regular editorialist for CBS. The recipient of Peabody Awards for distinguished reporting in 1949, 1964, and 1968, Sevareid was generally acknowledged to be the dean of American broadcasters before his retirement in 1977. He is the author of five books and is a frequent contributor to magazines.

PRE-READING

1. What does the title state about the subject and direction of the article?

2. How does the biographical sketch establish the writer as an authority?

3. What ideas does the opening paragraph suggest the article will deal with?

4. Although the ending is personal, what logical point can you infer from it?

¹ A kind of adversary relationship between print journalism and electronic journalism exists and has existed for many years. As someone who has toiled in both vineyards, I am troubled by much of the criticism I read. Innumerable newspaper critics seem to insist that broadcast journalism be like *their* journalism and measured by their standards. It cannot be. The two are more complementary than competitive, but they *are* different.

² The journalism of sight and sound is the only truly new form of journalism to come along. It is a *mass* medium, a universal medium; as the American public-education system is the world's first effort to teach everyone, so far as that is possible. It has serious built-in limitations as well as advantages,

FROM *Saturday Review*, 2 October 1976, pp. 18–21. Copyright © 1976 by the Saturday Review Corporation.

compared with print. Broadcast news operates in linear time, newspapers in lateral space. This means that a newspaper or magazine reader can be his own editor in a vital sense. He can glance over it and decide what to read, what to pass by. The TV viewer is a restless prisoner, obliged to sit through what does not interest him to get to what may interest him. While it is being shown, a bus accident at Fourth and Main has as much impact, seems as important, as an outbreak of a big war. We can do little about this, little about the viewer's unconscious resentments.

3 Everybody watches television to some degree, including most of those who pretend they don't. Felix Frankfurter was right; he said there is no highbrow in any lowbrow, but there is a fair amount of lowbrow in every highbrow. Television is a combination mostly of lowbrow and middlebrow, but there is more highbrow offered than highbrows will admit or even seek to know about. They will make plans, go to trouble and expense, when they buy a book or reserve a seat in the theater. They will not study the week's offerings of music or drama or serious documentation in the radio- and TV-program pages of their newspaper and then schedule themselves to be present. They want to come home, eat dinner, twist the dial, and find something agreeable ready, accommodating to *their* schedule.

4 For TV, the demand-supply equation is monstrously distorted. After a few years' experience with it in Louisville, Mark Ethridge said that television is a voracious monster that consumes Shakespeare, talent, and money at a voracious rate. As a station manager once said to a critic, "Hell, there isn't even enough mediocrity to go around."

5 TV programming consumes eighteen to twenty-four hours a day, 365 days of the year. No other medium of information or entertainment ever tried anything like that. How many good new plays appear in the theaters of this country each year? How many fine new motion pictures? Add it all together and perhaps you could fill twenty evenings out of the 365. As for music, including the finest music, it is there for a twist of the dial on any radio set in any big city of the land. It was radio, in fact, that created the audiences for music, good and bad, as nothing ever had before it.

6 Every new development in mass communications has been opposed by intellectuals of a certain stripe. I am sure that Gutenberg was denounced by the elite of his time—his device would spread dangerous ideas among the God-fearing, obedient masses. The typewriter was denounced by intellectuals of the more elfin variety—its clacking would drive away the muses. The first motion pictures were denounced—they would destroy the legitimate theater. Then the sound motion picture was denounced—it would destroy the true art of the film, which was pantomime.

7 To such critics, of course, television is destroying everything.

8 It is destroying conversation, they tell us. Nonsense. Non-conversing families were always that way. TV has, in fact, stimulated billions of conversations that otherwise would not have occurred.

⁹ It is destroying the habit of reading, they say. This is nonsense. Book sales in this country during the lifetime of general television have greatly increased and well beyond the increase in the population. At the end of a program with Hugo Black, we announced that if viewers wanted one of those little red copies of the Constitution such as he had held in his hand, they had only to write to us. We received about 150,000 requests—mostly, I suspect, from people who didn't know the Constitution was actually down on paper, who thought it was written in the skies or on a bronze tablet somewhere. After my first TV conversation with Eric Hoffer, his books sold out in nearly every bookstore in America—the next day.

¹⁰ TV is debasing the use of the English language, they tell us. My friend Alistair Cooke, for one. Nonsense. Until radio and then TV, tens of millions of people living in sharecropper cabins, in small villages on the plains and in the mountains, in the great city slums, had never heard good English diction in their lives. If anything, this medium has improved the general level of diction.

¹¹ The print–electronic adversary relationship is a one-way street. Print scrutinizes, analyzes, criticizes us every day; we do not return the favor. We have tried now and then, particularly in radio days with "CBS Views the Press," but not enough. On a network basis it's almost impossible because we have no real national newspapers—papers read everywhere—to criticize for the benefit of the national audience. Our greatest failure is in not criticizing ourselves, at least through the mechanism of viewers' rebuttals. Here and there, now and then, we have done it. It should have been a regular part of TV from the beginning. The Achilles heel of TV is that people can't talk back to that little box. If they had been able to, over the years, perhaps the gas of resentment could have escaped from the boiler in a normal way; it took Agnew with his hatchet to explode it, some years ago. The obstacle has not been policy; it has been the practical problem of programming inflexibilities—we don't have the fifteen-minute program anymore, for example. If we could extend the evening news programs to an hour, as we have wished to do for years, we could do many things, including a rebuttal period from viewers. It is not the supposedly huckster-minded monopolistic networks that prevent this; it is the local affiliates. It was tough enough to get the half-hour news; apparently it's impossible to get an hour version.

¹² I have seen innumerable sociological and psychological studies of TV programming and its effects. I have never seen a study of the quality—and the effect—of professional TV criticism in the printed press.

¹³ TV critics in the papers tell us, day in and day out, what is wrong with us. Let me return the favor by suggesting that they stop trying to be Renaissance men. They function as critics of everything on the screen—drama, soap operas, science programs, musical shows, sociological documentaries, our political coverage—the works. Let the papers assign their science writers to our science programs, their political writers to our political coverage, their drama critics to the TV dramas.

¹⁴ Let me suggest also that they add a second measurement to their critiques. It is proper that they judge works of fiction—dramas, for example—entirely on the basis of what they see on the little screen because in that area the producers, writers, and performers have total control of the material. If the result is wrong, *they* are wrong. News and documentaries are something else—especially live events, like a political convention. Here we do not have total control of the material or anything like it. On these occasions, it seems to me, the newspaper critic must also be a reporter; he must, if he can, go behind the scenes and find out why we do certain things and do not do other things; there is usually a reason. In the early days such critics as John Crosby and Marya Mannes would do that. A few—Unger on the *Christian Science Monitor*, for example—still do that, but very few.

¹⁵ Let me suggest to their publishers that a little less hypocrisy would become them. Don't publish lofty editorials and critiques berating the culturally low common denominator of TV entertainment programming and then feature on the cover of your weekly TV supplements, most weeks of the year, the latest TV rock star or gang-buster character. Or be honest enough to admit that you do this, that you play to mass tastes for the same reason the networks do—because it is profitable. Don't lecture the networks for the excess of violence—and it *is* excessive—on the screen and then publish huge ads for the most violent motion pictures in town, ads for the most pornographic films and plays, as broadcasting does not.

¹⁶ Now, at this point the reader must be thinking, what's this fellow beefing about? He's had an unusually long ride on the crest of the wave; he's highly paid. He's generally accepted as an honest practitioner of his trade. All true. I have indeed been far more blessed than cursed in my own lifework.

¹⁷ But I am saying what I am saying here—I am finally violating Ed Murrow's old precept that one never, but never, replies to critics—because it has seemed to me that someone must. Because the criticism exchange between print and broadcasting is a one-way street. Because a mythology is being slowly, steadily, set in concrete.

¹⁸ Why this intense preoccupation of the print press with the broadcast press and its personae? Three reasons at least: broadcasting, inescapably, is the most personal form of journalism ever, so there is a premium on personalities. The networks are the only true national news organs we have. And, third, competition between them and between local stations is intense, as real as it used to be between newspapers.

¹⁹ So the searchlight of scrutiny penetrates to our innards. Today we can scarcely make a normal organizational move without considering the press reaction. Networks, and even some stations, cannot reassign a reporter or anchorman, suspend anyone, discharge anyone, without a severe monitoring in the newspapers. Papers, magazines, wire services, don't have to live with that and would very much resent it if they did.

²⁰ We live with myths, some going far back but now revived. The myth that William L. Shirer was fired by Ed Murrow and fired because he was

politically too liberal. He wasn't fired at all; but even so good a historian as Barbara Tuchman fell for that one. The myth that Ed Murrow was forced out of CBS. At that point in his great career, President Kennedy's offer to Ed to join the government, at cabinet level, was probably the best thing that could have happened to him. The myth that Fred Friendly resigned over an issue of high principle involving some public-service air time. There are other such myths, and a new generation of writers are perpetuating them in their books, which are read and believed by a new generation of students and practitioners of journalism.

[21] We have had the experience of people leaving, freely or under pressure, then playing their case in the papers to a fare-thee-well; they are believed because of that preconceived image of the networks in the minds of the writers. What does a big corporation do? Slug it out with the complainant, point by point, in the papers? Can it speak out at all when the real issue is the personal character and behavior of the complainant, which has been the truth in a few other cases? It can't. So it takes another beating in the press.

[22] There is the myth that the CBS News Division—I am talking about CBS of course, because it is the place I know and because it is the network most written about these days—has been somehow shoved out to the periphery of the parent corporation, becoming more and more isolated. What has happened is that it has achieved, and been allowed, more and more autonomy because it is fundamentally different from any other corporate branch. Therefore it is more and more independent.

[23] There is the myth that the corporation is gradually de-emphasizing news and public affairs. In the last sixteen years since CBS News became a separate division, its budget has increased 600 percent, its personnel more than 100 percent. It does *not* make money for the company; it is a loss leader, year after year. I would guess it spends more money to cover the news than any other news organization in the world today. This is done because network news servicing has become a public trust and need.

[24] There is the myth that since the pioneering, groundbreaking TV programs of Murrow and Friendly, CBS News has been less daring, done fewer programs of a hard-hitting kind. The Murrow programs are immortal in this business because they were the *first*. Since then we have dealt, forthrightly, with every conceivable controversial issue one can think of—drugs, homosexuality, government corruption, business corruption, TV commercials, gun control, pesticides, tax frauds, military waste, abortion, the secrets of the Vietnam War—everything. What shortage has occurred has been on the side of the materials, not on the side of our willingness to tackle them.

[25] In case I had missed something myself, I have recently inquired of other CBS News veterans if they can recall a single case of a proposed news story or a documentary that was killed by executives of the parent organization. Not one comes to anyone's mind. Some programs have been anathema to the top executive level, but they were not stopped. Some have caused severe heartburn at that level when they went on the air. Never has there been a case of

people at that level saying to the News Division, "Don't ever do anything like that again."

²⁶ For thirteen years I have done commentary—personal opinion inescapably involved—most nights of the week on the evening news. In that time exactly three scripts of mine were killed because of their substance by CBS News executives. Each one by a different executive, and none of them ever did it again. Three—out of more than 2,000 scripts. How many newspaper editorialists or columnists, how many magazine writers, have had their copy so respected by their editors?

²⁷ There is the perennial myth that sponsors influence, positively or negatively, what we put on the air. They play no role whatever. No public-affairs program has ever been canceled because of sponsor objection. Years ago, they played indirect roles. When I started doing a six P.M. radio program, nearly thirty years ago, Ed Murrow, then a vice-president, felt it necessary to take me to lunch with executives of the Metropolitan Insurance Company, the sponsors. About fourteen years ago, when I was doing the Sunday-night TV news, a representative of the advertising agency handling the commercials would appear in the studio, though he never tried to change anything. Today one never sees a sponsor or an agency man, on the premises or off.

²⁸ There is the myth, which seems to be one of the flawed premises of so successful a reporter as David Halberstam, that increased corporate profitability has meant a diminished emphasis on news and public affairs. The reverse, of course, is the truth.

²⁹ There is the new myth, creeping into print as writers rewrite one another, that an ogre sits at the remote top of CBS Incorporated, discouraging idealistic talents down the line, keeping the news people nervous, if not cowardly. His name is William S. Paley, and the thesis seems to be that the tremendous growth of CBS News in size and effectiveness, its unmatched record of innovation and boldness in dealing with public issues, its repeated wars with the most powerful figures of government and business, have all taken place over these forty years or more in spite of this man's reluctance or downright opposition. The reverse is much closer to the truth. *Only* with a man of his stripe could all this have been done. Think what it is to sit up there all those years, whipped by gales of pressures from every public cause group, politicians, Presidents, newspapers, congressional committees, the FCC, affiliates, stockholders, and employees, individually and organized. To sit up there under unrelenting pressures of an intensity, a massiveness, rarely endured by any print publisher and still keep the apparatus free and independent and steady on its long course. After all, in this country networking might at its inception have become an appendage and apparatus of government; it might have gone completely Hollywood. It did neither. It grimly held to every freedom the law allows, and it fights for more. This has not been accomplished by weak or frightened men at the top.

³⁰ I am no appointed spokesman for William Paley. We are not intimates. I owe him nothing; I have earned my keep. I have not got rich. I have had my

differences with him, once or twice acutely. I have been a thorn in his side a number of times. But we had our differences out, and never once was his treatment of me less than candid and honorable. He is now in the evening of his career; I am now pretty much the graybeard of CBS News. I must soon go gently into that good night of retirement. But I shan't go so gently that I shall not say what I think of the mythologists who now surround us, what I think of these ignorant assaults on Paley. It would be cowardly of me not to say that many of these critics are simply wrong—wrong in their attitude, wrong in their premises, repeatedly wrong in their facts.

³¹ We are not the worst people in the land, we who work as journalists. Our product in print or on the air is a lot better, more educated, and more responsible than it was when I began, some forty-five years ago, as a cub reporter. This has been the best generation of all in which to have lived as a journalist in this country. We are no longer starvelings, and we sit above the salt. We have affected our times.

³² It has been a particular stroke of fortune to have been a journalist in Washington these years. There has not been a center of world news to compare with this capital city since ancient Rome. We have done the job better, I think, than our predecessors, and our successors will do it better than we. I see remarkable young talents all around.

³³ That's the way it should be. I will watch them come on, maybe with a little envy, but with few regrets for the past. For myself, I wouldn't have spent my working life much differently had I been able to.

ANALYTICAL READING

1. What distinctions does Sevareid make between print journalism and electronic journalism? Why does he make these distinctions?

2. What charges do the critics of television make? How does Sevareid refute these charges? Do you agree with him? Is his evidence sufficient?

3. What does Sevareid mean in stating that "the Achilles heel of TV is that people can't talk back to that little box" (paragraph 11)? Can people talk back to newspapers? How?

4. In what ways does Sevareid criticize the TV critics and their publishers? Do you think that he is justified in pointing out their hypocrisy?

5. Why do you suppose that Ed Murrow, one of the first great radio and television journalists, felt that critics should be ignored? For what three reasons has Sevareid violated this precept?

6. If you saw the movie *Network*, to what extent do you think Sevareid would have agreed or disagreed with its portrayal of television?

7. What are some of the myths about television journalists or CBS that Sevareid refutes? Do you accept his evidence? Why or why not?

8. In what ways do you think Sevareid is right in saying that journalists affect the times (paragraph 31)? Refer to specific events.

9. Note that in the closing paragraphs, Sevareid links print and electronic journalists. How does this support a concept stated in the opening paragraph? What is the effect of this association at the end of his argument?

REFLECTING

Point: What audience is Sevareid addressing? How does that influence his purpose? What is his specific purpose besides defending television journalism? Formulate in a sentence or two the main points in his argument.

Organization: How does paragraph 16 link two sections of the article? What are these sections? What is Sevareid's main strategy throughout the article in defending television journalism?

Support: Sevareid uses the first person throughout. Why is this particularly effective here? Is his tone angry, annoyed, even-tempered, or what? How effective is the repetitive use of the word *nonsense* in paragraphs 8, 9, and 10 twice as a one-word sentence? What do you think of the repetitive use of myths in the topic sentences of many of the paragraphs from 20 to 29? Where and how is comparison and contrast used effectively? What justification is there for the single sentence in paragraph 7?

Synthesis: What is your general criticism about television news? Has Sevareid made you aware of factors that you had not considered previously? If so, what are they? Do you think that television has interfered with your family conversations, reduced your reading time, or affected your use of the English language? If so, how? How do you reconcile Sevareid's claim that television stimulates book sales with the general criticism that TV interferes with students' reading?

Evaluation: Does Sevareid portray television journalism too favorably? Has he overlooked any significant criticism of either television programming or news reporting? Are his refutations of criticisms and myths convincing? Is his writing clear and interesting? Does his argument gain from his own reputation as a respected TV journalist? Is there any reason to think that CBS is not a typical network and that the others operate less responsibly?

FROM READING TO WRITING

1. Write a paper entitled "What's Right with _____," using some of Sevareid's strategy.

2. Write a paper attacking, defending, or modifying some of the points mentioned by Sevareid, such as the importance of studying TV schedules instead of watching indiscriminately; the need to allow viewer response; or the criticism of newspapers for their hypocritical appeal to low tastes.

STANDARDIZED TESTS: THEY REFLECT THE REAL WORLD
Robert L. Ebel

BIOGRAPHICAL SKETCH

Robert Louis Ebel was born in Waterloo, Iowa, in 1910. He received a B.A. from Northern Iowa University and an M.A. and Ph.D. from Iowa University. After teaching and serving as a school superintendent in Michigan, he was vice-president of the Educational Testing Service for six years before joining the faculty at Michigan State University, where he is now a professor of educational psychology. He has also served as a consultant for various school systems and educational associations in this country and others. Ebel's writing includes several books and numerous scholarly articles, mainly about testing and its reliability and social consequences.

PRE-READING

1. What does the title imply to you after a reading of the first paragraph?

2. What does the final paragraph reveal about the subject?

¹ Are standardized tests headed for extinction? To judge from news reports, magazine articles and some popular books the answer might seem to be yes. A variety of charges have been laid against them, and there is substance to some. But the effects are neither so overpowering nor so harmful as the critics imply. On balance the case for standardized tests is persuasive.

² A common accusation is that some pupils have, and others lack, a special talent for taking tests and that tests end up measuring this ability rather than academic achievements. Only on a carelessly or ineptly constructed test, though, can a pupil inflate his score by special test savvy. Most widely used standardized tests have been constructed carefully by experts. Unfamiliarity with the item types or response modes employed in a standardized test can indeed handicap a naïve examinee. But that kind of naïveté can be removed quite easily by careful instructions and practice exercises.

³ Bear in mind that the test score reports only the level of knowledge the pupil possesses, not how frequently or how effectively he makes use of it. It reports what the pupil can do, not what he typically does. What a pupil does, and how well he does it, depends not on his knowledge alone. It depends also on his energy, ambition, determination, adroitness, likableness and luck, among other things. A pupil's knowledge as measured by a standardized or any other test is one ingredient—but only one—of his potential success in life.

⁴ The simplicity with which answers to multiple-choice questions can be recorded on an answer sheet, and the objectivity and speed with which correct

FROM *The New York Times*, 1 May 1977, Sec. 12, pp. 1 ff. © 1977 by The New York Times Company. Reprinted by permission.

answers can be detected and counted by modern scoring machines, offends some devotees of the other common type of examination, the written essay. They confuse the simplicity of the process of recording an answer with the complexity of the process of figuring it out. Some of them charge that multiple-choice questions test only rote learning, or superficial factual information. That is clearly not true. Consider this question:

> The sides of a quadrilateral having two consecutive right angles are consecutive whole numbers. The shortest side is one of the two parallel sides. What is the area of the quadrilateral in square units? (a) 11 (b) 18 (c) 25 (d) 36 (e) Not given

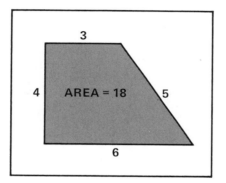

[5] Multiple-choice questions can be trivial or irrelevant. They need not be.

[6] Critics of tests and testing sometimes provide examples of questions that seem to be ridiculously trivial or impossibly ambiguous. In some cases their criticisms are justified. Bad questions have been written and published. But few of these come from professionally constructed standardized tests of achievement. In other cases the criticism is not justified. The objection is based on a possible but unlikely interpretation different from the clearly intended sense of the question. One who sets out to discover how a question might conceivably be misconstrued is likely to find some way to misconstrue it. Language, after all, is not a flawless means for the precise communication of thought.

[7] Another charge is that standardized testing harms children. It is said that the tests threaten and upset pupils, that if a pupil gets a low score he will be seriously damaged and that standardized testing is incompatible with educational procedures designed to support the child.

[8] There is, no doubt, anecdotal evidence to support some of these claims. However, common sense suggests that the majority of pupils are not harmed by testing, and as far as I know there is no substantial survey data that would contradict common sense on this matter. The teachers I talk with seem much more often to be concerned with pupils who don't care enough how well or

how poorly they do on such tests, than with the relatively rare instances of pupils who care too much.

⁹ It is normal and biologically helpful to be somewhat anxious when facing any real test, regardless of one's age. But it is also a necessary part of growing up to learn to cope with the tests that life inevitably brings. Of the many challenges to a child's peace of mind, caused by such things as angry parents, playground bullies, bad dogs and shots from the doctor, standardized tests must surely be among the least fearsome. Unwise parental pressure can in some cases elevate anxiety to harmful levels. But usually the child who breaks down in tears at the prospect of a test has problems of security, adjustment and maturity that testing did not create and that cannot be solved by eliminating tests.

¹⁰ A pupil who consistently gets low scores on tests of what that pupil has tried hard to learn is indeed likely to become discouraged. If this does happen, the school cannot claim to be offering a good educational program, and the teacher cannot claim to be doing a good job of teaching. Most low scores on tests, however, go to pupils who, for one reason or another, have not tried very hard to learn. In the opinion of the teachers of such pupils, it is the trying rather than the testing that is most in need of correction.

¹¹ It is sometimes charged that tests distort school curriculums by causing schools to teach to the tests and by thus hampering curricular innovation.

¹² A school that is teaching what the tests test will surely teach many other things besides. Even in the basic areas that the test does sample, there will be time and cause to venture into areas of learning not covered by the standardized tests. Standardized tests can dominate local curriculums only to the extent that school administrators and school teachers allow them to.

¹³ There are, of course, some programs of open education that are satisfied merely with maximum pupil freedom, trusting nature alone to do what others employ the art and science of teaching to help nature do. To say that standardized tests of achievement are inappropriate for such programs may imply more criticism of the programs than of the tests.

¹⁴ Standardized tests are also charged with encouraging harmful comparisons of one pupil with another. Let a pupil measure his achievements against his potential, or against his own past performance, say the cr̹tics, not against his classmates.

¹⁵ I believe they are wrong. What they should criticize is unwise reactions to comparison, not comparison itself. For those who are interested in excellent education find it difficult to believe that comparisons of educational achievement are irrelevant or unnecessary. No proud parent believes it. No capable teacher believes it. It simply is not true.

¹⁶ The only basis for judging a human performance excellent, acceptable, or inferior is in comparison with other human performances. The only basis for setting reasonably attainable objectives for pupil learning is knowledge of what similar pupils have been able to learn. Of course it is good for a pupil to compare his present performance with his own past performance. But that is

no substitute for comparing his present performance with the present performances of his classmates. Surely it is cold comfort to a pupil when his arithmetic teacher says, "For you, five out of ten is quite good."

[17] Only in some eyes have tests lost favor. Quite clearly they are not headed for extinction. They are much too useful to the competent, concerned educator. They are much too essential to the pursuit of excellence in education.

ANALYTICAL READING

1. Does Ebel effectively refute the accusation that some students have special skills for taking standardized tests?

2. What importance does he place on such tests?

3. What is the purpose of Ebel's example of a multiple-choice question? How typical is this example?

4. How satisfactorily does Ebel refute the contention that standarized tests are damaging to low-scoring children? Explain.

5. Explain and discuss Ebel's statement at the end of paragraph 12 to the effect that teachers and administrators determine the extent to which standardized tests dictate curriculums.

6. Does Ebel point out the positive value of standardized tests? If so, where? Can you formulate a syllogism of this point? If so, do you agree with the basic assumption?

REFLECTING

Point: What is the purpose of the article? How is it accomplished? In one or two sentences, state the main points of the argument.

Organization: Is the article organized deductively or inductively? Why do you think Ebel chose this form? In a paragraph-by-paragraph analysis, explain his strategy as reflected in the article.

Support: What is the role of voice and tone in the article? What evidence does Ebel use to refute most of the claims made by opponents of standardized tests?

Synthesis: How do you feel about standardized tests? Do such tests seem fair? Do you know students who have been harmed by them? Do you think that essay tests are preferable to multiple-choice tests? Do the tests seem to rate you and your friends as your teachers do? Do you agree with Ebel's final statement that standardized tests "are much too essential to the pursuit of excellence in education"?

Evaluation: How effective are the examples or reasons? How thoroughly has Ebel refuted counter-arguments? How convincing is he? Explain.

FROM READING TO WRITING

See the suggestions after the essay by Taylor and Lazarus (pages 381–82).

STANDARDIZED TESTS: THEY DON'T MEASURE LEARNING

Edwin P. Taylor and Mitchell Lazarus

BIOGRAPHICAL SKETCH

Edwin Taylor was born in Oberlin, Ohio. He graduated from Oberlin College and earned M.A. and Ph.D. degrees in physics from Harvard. After teaching at Wesleyan University for about twelve years, he became a senior research scientist in the Education Research Center at the Massachusetts Institute of Technology. He has published numerous articles in scholarly journals, mainly about subjects related to mechanics, special relativity and quantum physics, and computer-assisted learning.

Mitchell Bernard Lazarus was born in Montreal in 1942, received a B. Eng. degree from McGill University and an S.M. in electrical engineering, and a Ph.D. in psychology from Massachusetts Institute of Technology. In addition to teaching at MIT, Lazarus taught at George Mason College and Northern Virginia Community College before becoming associated first with MIT's Education Research Center and then with the Education Development Center at Newton, Massachusetts, where he is currently a senior staff associate. His articles about the teaching of mathematics, testing, and educational television have appeared in educational journals.

PRE-READING

1. This essay is also concerned with standardized testing. What is the purpose of the title?

2. How do the opening and closing paragraphs add to your knowledge of the argument?

[1] The controversy over achievement testing starts from a simple fact: Achievement tests reward test-taking skills as much as they reward achievement. Different children who know a subject equally well can still receive very different scores on a multiple-choice achievement test.

[2] Some children work fast, not taking time to think deeply: they may make quick conventional guesses on some questions, be tidy and accurate in shading boxes on answer sheets and have suburban, middle-class backgrounds—useful for quickly grasping the words and pictures on most tests. These children get credit, perhaps, for what they know about the subject matter.

[3] Other children may work slowly, think through too many possibilities, be too insecure to guess fast or be sloppy with the answer sheet. Children

come from a variety of cultural and linguistic backgrounds. Thus many children's test scores will probably not reflect their grasp of the subject, even if they know the subject well.

⁴ And nearly every achievement test is a reading test first, before it is a test of anything else.

⁵ Neatness, accuracy, speed and good reading are useful skills, worth encouraging in children. But as long as test scores depend so much on skills that supposedly are not being tested, the results are bound to be inaccurate.

⁶ All questions on standardized achievement tests are multiple choice. The child must (1) read the question and (2) think of the answer—but not write it down! Instead, he or she must (3) try to find this answer among those given; (4) and when it is not there, pick one that is; (5) keep track of its number or letter, and (6) shade in the correct little box on the answer sheet. Only two of these six steps concern the subject being tested. The other four help the computer grade the test.

⁷ Multiple-choice questions distort the purposes of education. Picking one answer among four is very different from thinking a question through to an answer of one's own, and far less useful in life. Recognition of vocabulary and isolated facts makes the best kind of multiple-choice questions, so these dominate the tests, rather than questions that test the use of knowledge. Because schools want their children to perform well, they are often tempted to teach the limited sorts of knowledge most useful on the tests.

⁸ Questions are often badly worded, confusing, or downright wrong. For many questions, the thoughtful or imaginative student can see several acceptable answers among those given.

⁹ There is an easy defense against the charge of poor question quality: make the questions better. But after many decades of testing, the proportion of defective questions seems about the same—enough so that missing the defective ones can change a first-rate performance into a mediocre score. For at least two reasons—test secrecy and use of multiple-choice questions—the proportion of defective questions is unlikely to go down in the future.

¹⁰ Aside from the content of the tests, there is the fact that some children are intimidated by the testing procedures—vastly different from ordinary classroom activity—and perform poorly.

¹¹ "Keep quiet. Sit with an empty row of desks between you and your neighbor. Listen hard to the instructions. Don't mind the teacher stalking up and down between the rows during the test. Remember how much your future depends on your score—but don't be nervous. Imagine what your folks will say if you land in a low percentile. If you tighten up under pressure, you are in real trouble. Hurry. Stay calm. Hurry. Stay calm."

¹² There are many stories of children breaking down during a test or being physically ill the night before. But life is full of trials and fears; why should we protect children? Because they are children; because we want to find out, for example, how well they are learning rather than how well they

stand stress, and because those children already hobbled by insecurity, past failure or discrimination will be the most vulnerable in a vicious cycle.

[13] Once the tests are administered and scored, the purpose to which the results are put—comparing children using numbers—is of no use.

[14] Every person is complicated, everyone has unique skills and difficulties. But each test score reduces the pattern of a child's strengths and weaknesses to a single number. Why? To compare the child with others around the country. Why? To tell if the schools are doing their job. But the single numbers and averages carry no hints about how to improve either the schools or individual children.

[15] Healthy competition encourages excellence. But competition in standardized tests encourages intellectual narrowness and triviality.

[16] Society does need to measure people's achievement and school performance, and could do so in much better ways. Imagine school tests set up like the test for a driver's license, each test matched to the skills under test and each child doing "well enough" or not, with a chance for those who did not to try again later. In judging a school, attention would focus on the fractions of its children who passed various tests at various ages.

[17] Your children's future depends in part on tests you are not allowed to see. There is growing expert opinion that this violates your rights and those of your children. It also puts the test publishers beyond public criticism—and that's one reason the tests remain so bad.

[18] The publishers say that the tests must be secret so children cannot prepare for them. But if the tests were good, preparing for them would be a fine idea. Everyone knows the range of questions that will be on the driver's license tests, and by practicing and preparing for them, it is possible to become a better driver. Children could become better thinkers in much the same way if they were given good, open tests.

[19] In the past we developed an unjustified faith in numbers, and then in computers. Objectivity and statistical analysis became major virtues; automatic data analysis often replaced thoughtful evaluation. Now we are learning that numbers can misrepresent children and can lead to wrong decisions about their lives. There can be no true objectivity in a heterogeneous society, and all data analysis is subject to the GIGO principle: garbage in, garbage out.

[20] The task is to find out how well children are learning. The present standardized multiple-choice achievement tests are doing it badly, sometimes destructively. There are better ways to find out, without compressing children into uniform molds that misrepresent their accomplishments.

ANALYTICAL READING

1. What is the meaning of the reference to "middle-class backgrounds" in paragraph 2?

2. Why do Taylor and Lazarus contend that "many children's test scores will probably not reflect their grasp of the subject" (paragraph 3)?

3. Explain what Taylor and Lazarus mean by their claim that multiple-choice questions "fail to test the use of knowledge" (paragraph 7)?

4. To what extent do you think that the authors would find essay tests more acceptable than multiple-choice tests?

5. Do you think paragraph 11 provides a representative or exaggerated example of the testing procedure? Support your answer with references to your own experience.

6. If the purpose of school is to prepare children for life, why do Taylor and Lazarus feel that they should be protected from stress and tension?

7. Do Taylor and Lazarus state that it is important to evaluate students and their schools? How do they propose that it be done, if not by standardized tests?

REFLECTING

Point: What are the main ideas in this argument against standardized tests?

Organization: What are the main divisions of the essay? Can you find an organizational pattern in the first section?

Support: What group of readers is the article addressed to? Do you think they would agree with the point that test questions are poorly worded? What is the purpose of the analogy between achievement tests and driver's license tests? How appropriate is this analogy?

Synthesis: What role has reading ability played in the standardized tests you have taken? Do you feel that some or many children are intimidated by such tests? Would the fact that the average score of one high school's students on ACT or SAT tests was higher than another school's average indicate that the former was better than the latter? Is there any way to prepare for the tests? Don't such tests provide the simplest and easiest way to evaluate student learning?

Evaluation: Which points have the authors argued most convincingly? Least convincingly? Explain. How clear and practical are their solutions? How effective are their examples? Why would their audience probably agree or disagree with them?

FROM READING TO WRITING

1. Write an argument stating which article (pro or con achievement tests) is better, and why.

2. Write an argument as if you were the dean of admissions in a college or university with more students applying than you could accept, explaining and defending your procedure for choosing students.

3. Argue for or against standardized testing.

4. Write a letter to high school seniors, trying to persuade them to sign up for the special study course offered by your company to help them raise their ACT or SAT scores.

5. Write a letter to your former high school principal, suggesting some change in the use or application of standardized tests.

6. Write a problem-solution argument discussing measures other than standardized test scores that might be used in evaluating schools.

7. In paragraph 10 of his essay, Ebel contends that only students who do not try very hard to learn receive low scores on standardized tests. Write an argument agreeing or disagreeing with or modifying this view.

WHY HAVE MORE THAN ONE?
Anne Roiphe

BIOGRAPHICAL SKETCH

Anne Roiphe was born in New York in 1935. She graduated from Sarah Lawrence College and also studied in Munich, Germany. After working in public relations and business research, she turned to writing novels about the condition of modern women. Her novel Up the Sandbox *was made into a motion picture; her other works include* Digging Out, Long Division, *and* Torch Song. *Roiphe is a frequent contributor to periodicals, particularly* Vogue *and* The New York Times.

PRE-READING

1. What significance does the title have for you?

2. What cause-and-effect relationships are set up in the opening paragraph?

3. From the biographical sketch, what viewpoint about having children would you expect from Roiphe? What viewpoint is revealed in the last paragraph?

[1] Images of man's future that have us standing on our allotted one square foot of space or waiting on infinite lines for a cup of desalinated water; women's new-found drive for self-realization, for doctoral degrees and executive secretaries of their own; concern about holocaust, revolution, depression—these cause many young couples to pause before conceiving a second child. What rational reason could there be for having another baby? The first, after all, has made them parents, has given them the experience of process, of wonder, of exhaustion, of change in life style. Their firstborn has succeeded in muting their egotism and shifting the marriage from mere romance to the earnest discipline of baby sitters, tuition plans and Saturdays spent at the zoo. What more could the second child do or be? What vacuum remains for it to fill? Isn't *one* of nature's miracles and all the complications that follow enough? Apparently not. For nearly 50 percent of the parents in the labor rooms in

FROM *The New York Times Magazine*, 5 June 1977, pp. 49–50 ff. © 1977 by The New York Times Company. Reprinted by permission.

New York Hospital last month, one child was only the beginning. There may be fewer new families being started in America nowadays. Many more young people are delaying or deciding against having children altogether, but for those young Americans who have decided to become parents, the majority still plan on that second baby and maybe more.

² The most frequent reason given for the second baby, prior to its birth, is that it will be company for the first, that the first child needs a friend, needs a competitor, should not be the only apple of its parents' eye—it's more normal for the child to have a brother or sister. This reason for conception is one of those harmless rationalizations we use as we climb about our lives. Without dwelling on how ungrateful the first child usually is for this particular gift of normality, it's hardly a decent thing to bring a life into the world in order to make another life better, happier, more normal. Furthermore, it's an idea that only exists while the second child remains a vague suggestion without particular form. Once the second baby has arrived, its need to be burped, have an allowance and attention paid to its nightmares, its clay ashtrays, will erase all previous considerations of its worth as a companion for the first child. For better or worse, 'til death do us part, it is a life unto itself.

³ Several young couples expecting a second baby said that they wanted to be sure that at least one of their children would survive. These couples were pushed by some drive toward the immortality of their DNA, some stake in the endurance of their personal helixes. Of course, with infant mortality down so dramatically since the turn of the century and the common childhood illnesses all but defeated, the odds of any particular American child surviving to adulthood are so enormous that one really doesn't have to take a double flier for one success. In actuality, the second child doubles the jeopardy of suffering the incredible pain a loss through birth defect, cancer or accident can bring. The parent of two or more children is more exposed—double the odds—to the haunting visions of catastrophe that, realistic or not, lie dormant just beneath the gay nursery wallpaper.

⁴ It used to be, when people had children to help on the farm or to bring in money, that parents thought of their children as some form of high-premium insurance against future isolation and poverty. Now, of course, most of us know that this land of mobility may very well take our children into universes, psychologically or culturally or physically far distant from ours. Therefore, very few are counting on a second child to increase the chances of a comfortable old age.

⁵ Some of the expectant young couples I spoke to were hoping their second child would be of a different sex from their first. They expressed a real desire for a child of each gender. However, they were all quick to say they wanted a healthy baby. They were not having the baby just for sexual variety among the offspring. They would welcome a child of either sex. Since there are as yet no foolproof methods of guaranteeing a baby's sex, one would have to be mad to conceive that second child for reasons of sexual diversity. The chances of disappointment are too great, and while a spouse who turns out in

an unexpected or unpleasant way can be discarded, a child is a commitment of another sort.

⁶ So then, if none of the reasons people give each other for that second birth seem in and of themselves very convincing, there must be some other, perhaps not entirely conscious, reason that explains it. It must after all have to do with an image of family, an almost unconscious expectation of what that word "family" means—an expectation that goes quite beyond anything a man and woman can reasonably discuss over their after-dinner coffee. Maybe it comes from images of Dick and Jane and Spot in those influential early readers. Maybe it comes from all the weight of the stories of the past, from fairy tales where brothers and sisters vied for the crown, from Bible stories of inheritances stolen, of coats of many colors, from lists of names of sons and daughters that rumble through the Old Testament, the "Odyssey," the "Iliad," the stories of Roman gods. Maybe, on the other hand, our sense of what a family should be comes from some unconscious connection of ourselves with the rest of the animal world, where lion and lioness are standing in the veld, surrounded not by cub but by cubs. Maybe our need to create family comes not only from some need to make life, but to test our quality, our worth, in nurturing it. Or it could be that the second child is a peculiarly unconscious act of faith, a religious act on the part of the parent who says, "If God made more than one living creature, I should, too."

⁷ Whatever is valid among these speculations, the fact is that families continue to be created at as fast a rate as they fall apart, and a disappointment and a sense of personal failure racks almost every divorced parent as he anguishes over the end of a not even clearly articulated dream of what the family meant to him.

⁸ What really happens when the second child is born? Immediately, most parents experience guilt for having created the jealousy quickly apparent in the first child. That marks the beginning of the balancing of the needs of one against the other and the tensions that are routine in family life. Soon after the new arrival is absorbed into the fabric of the household, the parents become involved in the truly fascinating game of watching the similarities and differences in their offspring. Late at night they begin discussions on nature versus nurture that may last 40 years. They begin to worry if this one's crankiness, that one's allergies, this one's fear of spiders and that one's resistance to dinner are outward manifestations of something wrong in themselves. Equally, they soar with exultation when one child learns to read prematurely and another has perfect pitch.

⁹ There is a kind of family joy when one's offspring is talking back to "Sesame Street" and the neighbor's only babbles to his bottle. This has already been experienced with the first, but with the second comes an additional risk of failure and an additional chance to buttress one's self-pride and self-worth. Perhaps the second will be an athlete or a ballet dancer or a tough guy or a poet, fulfilling some parental ambition that the first didn't. Of course, it's equally possible that the second will be thrown out of school for pushing

dope, will wash out, be laid-back, drop out or drift away. The game is played for emotionally high stakes because we are not birds that nudge our young out of the nest and then forget. We know we can be held, we hold ourselves, responsible.

[10] Within the larger family, patterns of behavior can have more variety. The several children of the family, whether of the same sex or not, take into their separate psyches the differing, sometimes conflicting character traits and childhood experiences of their parents. This one is always good and conforming, his anger like nuclear wastes buried underground. That one is just like her mother, defiant, courting catastrophe at every turn. In the making of their new family both parents bring a mixed bag of memories from their old. Unconsciously and consciously they repeat patterns of the past. The son is better loved or the daughter always sickly. Sometimes parents try to undo what was done to them as children, often creating traumas in the opposite direction: "I give my youngest a lot of attention because my older sister was preferred."

[11] The children also shape themselves in response to each other. This one gives up violin lessons because her brother is so good at the cello. That one loves to cook because his sister hates it, and each eyes the other with that mixture of rancor and love, opposition and imitation that becomes, like orange juice and Oreo cookies, the daily fare of family life. In cases where the balance of love and hate dips way to the negative side, the terrible Cain and Abel drama is recreated, to be chewed over and over and regretted endlessly in later years.

[12] When the children reach adolescence, the family dream is subjected to its greatest strain. The children are pulling away and the parents are adjusting both to the ending of their nurturing years and the reality of what they and their genes have wrought. Some may see their own faults, their own failures imitated in their children's gestures. They may have hoped for some degree of human happiness in their children that unfortunately has not been achieved. They repeat through their children the anguishes of their own uncertain acne days. Two children increase the risks all around. No matter what feelings of love and compassion bind the family together, they are strained by the new elements of disenchantment. Illusions fade and expectations (Johnny will pass math next year), (Dad will curb his temper), (Mom will understand me), (Sister will be a tennis champion) die. The wonder that was family life can turn to wormwood, to rue, to ulcers, to compromise, to prune instead of plum. With two children, more possibilities exist that the family playroom can turn into a storage space full of albums never looked at because of painful memories.

[13] On the other hand, if there is only one child, the drama is heightened, the pulling away is more difficult and more terrible. In the multichild family, each child will feel less pressure to stay, but the odds are one or the other will keep some emotional closeness. Sister may be a revolutionary after daddy's heart while brother is a Wall Street lawyer whose name is never spoken. Second sister may be kind or vicious, whatever is the opposite of her sibling,

and parents can patch up the family dream being bewildered, bemused, ashamed and proud at the same time.

[14] Ridiculous as it is, the idea of family stays with us and lurks even in those who would change its form, or outward shape. It is absurd, this giving of love to beings that can never return it because family relationships become tainted with such complex psychological interactions that love itself becomes a word to hide behind.

[15] To father and mother a family is to expose one's most vulnerable flank to certain attack. The hurt when one's child is hurt is unlike any other torture extant. To find oneself even momentarily hating one's own child is a terror of the highest order. To be the object of the anger of one's child, to experience the occasional coldness of his or her eyes, is to be in a special circle of hell. No one can marshal rational arguments against those young people who steer clear of the family encounter entirely, saving their money for skiing weekends in Vermont and their psyches for work and pleasure that depend only on themselves. For the rest of us, who have cornered ourselves into creating families, which may split and re-form in different ways, who, in this way, have dared fate to humiliate us with pain or defeat—we have to recognize that this two-parent, multichild family image at the core of our lives, while preposterous, is still amazingly dear.

[16] There are grand things to say about the sanctity of birth and the grace of nature. I could go on about the bravery of the human spirit that risks disaster in searching for an ideal of family, of generational responsibility. But the last impenetrable line of defense is in certain images shared in a variety of forms by most of us, images that are a part of the parenting experience whether there is one child or many, but if there are more than one, they occupy more internal space, reflect more external time and account for more of what we might call our individual souls. Images of balls thrown in the park, of wheels turning, bikes, skates, hoops, the thumping of jump ropes, the call at dusk of moving shadows, "allee, allee in free," images of birthday parties, of victories over the shoelace, the clock, the written word, images of a tone-deaf mother hearing her daughter sing at the school assembly, of a father teaching a child to swim, comforting a child crying over a broken bicycle or a lost friendship, of nights spent worrying about a child's school failure, about a sore throat that wouldn't go away, images of a man and woman trying to find the money for a scout trip, or medical school, images of hours spent in the pediatrician's waiting room, in the dentist's waiting room, in the shoe store, at the barber's, of games of Monopoly and Walt Disney movies. Image after image floats up of time spent enmeshed in the seemingly trivial work of family life which, if things go well enough, can make us less alone, can hide from us the vastness of the universe and the insignificance of our individual place in it.

[17] The conventional family dream will have to do some changing. Too many of us don't stay married. Too many of our children end up repudiating our life styles and selected goals. Too many children grow up damaged or

abused and pass on this damage to the family of their own making. But the care of children, the dream of family life must be repaired. We may be riding in a blimp that leaks and is highly flammable, but at the moment we have no other transportation.

[18] I spoke the other day to a man in his 60's who had eight children, one after another, right after World War II. "I had a need," he explained, "to replace the lives that were lost in the war, to replenish the globe." "Now that your children are grown," I asked, "would you do it all over again? Would you have all eight?" "Of course," he replied. "They've made me the man I am." "What about overpopulation," I asked, "aren't you concerned?" "Oh, you're right," he answered. "If I were young today I would really only have two children. But which two?" He looked bewildered. "I could never choose!"

ANALYTICAL READING

1. What is the subject of the article? How does Roiphe tie the subject to the cause-and-effect relationship outlined in the opening paragraphs?

2. Discuss her use of "causes" in the paragraphs 2–5 as arguments. How does she refute them?

3. What contrast does she make between the traditional ideas of family and contemporary changes in that idea.

4. In paragraph 6, Roiphe lists the possibilities for underlying motivations. What are they? How does she use parallelism to help the reader?

5. In paragraph 10, Roiphe sets up a comparison and contrast. Make a brief outline of the paragraph that reveals the method of comparison and contrast used.

6. In paragraph 11, the writer refers to "the terrible Cain and Abel drama." Why is that allusion pertinent to her discussion?

7. Roiphe packs many specific details into paragraph 16. Analyze the structure of the sentences in the paragraph. How does she help the reader to keep the subject in mind?

8. In paragraph 16, is she arguing for or against having more than one child per family? Explain.

9. Is the last paragraph simply an emotional appeal to the audience? Explain.

REFLECTING

Point: What is Roiphe's main point? Can you summarize it in one sentence? To what audience is Roiphe writing?

Organization: Is the article organized inductively or deductively? Why do you think Roiphe chose this method of organization? Indicate the main divisions of the article.

Support: How does she use each of the following to support her main argument: comparison and contrast, causal relationships, and specific detail?

Synthesis: Do some of Roiphe's descriptions of sibling relationships remind you of your own family? What is your image of family life? Do you plan to have children? If so, how many? Give reasons for this decision.

Evaluation: How effective is the argument? Does Roiphe solve the problem, or is it impossible for one person to find a solution? Are you able to discern whether she has strong feelings for or against large families? Use specific points from the article to support your opinion.

FROM READING TO WRITING

1. As a future parent, write an argument in favor of having no children, one, two, or more. Try to refute any possible counter-arguments.

2. As a sibling, write a paper arguing for or against having one brother or sister or more than one.

3. Agree, disagree, or qualify Roiphe's statement in paragraph 12 that "the family dream is subjected to its greatest strain" when the children are adolescents.

SHOULD SEAT BELTS BE MANDATED BY LAW? CON
Bud Shuster

BIOGRAPHICAL SKETCH

Representative E.G. (Bud) Shuster was born in 1932. He has a B.S. from the University of Pittsburgh, an M.B.A. from Duquesne University, and a Ph.D. from American University. After working as a business executive and serving in the U.S. Army, he was elected to Congress from the Ninth District of Pennsylvania. Shuster also serves as a trustee of the University of Pittsburgh.

PRE-READING

1. Shuster's title is so formal because it was originally printed as part of a pro-and-con discussion of the subject. However, it does state both his subject and his viewpoint toward it. What are they?

2. What do you learn from the final paragraph about Shuster's general political views and their relationship to this specific subject?

1 The Swedish car manufacturer Volvo found in a recent study of 28,000 auto crashes that the fastening of both shoulder and lap belts increases your chances of surviving an accident tenfold.

FROM *Motor Trend*, August 1976, pp. 41–42, 99. Reprinted by permission of Petersen Publishing Company.

² A General Motors study estimates that 7700 lives can be saved each year if only three-quarters of us would buckle up.

³ The U.S. Department of Transportation estimates that between 10,000 and 15,000 lives can be saved each year if we *all* use safety belts.

⁴ The statistics make a telling point, one that should be central to the driving experiences of Americans: Seat belts save lives.

⁵ There are those who take this point one step further and add: "If seat belts save lives, then the government should make the wearing of them mandatory."

⁶ I disagree.

⁷ I think that any person who operates or rides in a motor vehicle and who fails to use the safety belts provided by the manufacturer is foolish. But I also think that, in a free society, people have a right to do dumb things. And I further believe that legislation is a totally inappropriate remedy for this particular type of foolishness. Highway fatalities and injuries are a bad problem for our society—but they will not be solved by passing a bad law.

⁸ In order for a law to be appropriate it must do three things: fit the situation or ill that it is intended to correct; be effective in correcting it; and not create additional problems which outweigh the intended benefits. A mandatory safety-belt usage law would satisfy none of these requirements.

⁹ As a general rule, we make behavior subject to criminal liability only if it adversely affects other members of the society. If others' rights are not impaired by an individual's behavior, we do not hold the individual guilty— even if he does something which is harmful to his own health or well-being.

¹⁰ We allow individuals to take all sorts of liberties with their health. As a society, we tolerate smoking, drinking, overeating, overconsumption of caffein and any number of other excesses visited upon individuals by themselves. But no one seriously expects to pass laws prohibiting smoking—except as it infringes upon the rights of non-smokers. No one that I know has proposed a law to limit our caloric intake, although obesity contributes to heart disease and other illnesses. The government tried to curb drinking during Prohibition, and it was a disaster . . . and I defy anyone to legislate a sudden stop to the consumption of caffein in this coffee-, tea- and cola-saturated society.

¹¹ All these are matters which the individual should share only with his conscience. For the government to pass laws prohibiting self-destructive behavior is, in effect, for the government to say, "We know what is good for you." There is, I think, a direct analogy here to the use of safety belts.

¹² I submit that the failure to wear safety belts does not harm society at large, any more than the aforementioned abuses. Of course, it can be said that injuries resulting from an accident in which the passenger was not wearing a belt have effects beyond the individual himself—after all, someone will have to pay for the cost of his medical care and tend to his children if he is left impaired.

¹³ But I feel very strongly that these are matters for which the individual, and not the state, must assume responsibility.

¹⁴ There should be a distinction drawn, when considering legislation, between those actions by an individual which directly risk the safety and welfare of other members of the society, and those actions which affect primarily the individual, with only indirect consequences to the rest of the community. Legislation should not be a bludgeon employed by the government to eradicate every evil; rather, it should permit the government's intervention in human affairs only when absolutely necessary, and for very particular remedies. It is inappropriate to make a criminal offense of an action which risks the safety of only the individual, if by doing so he does not *directly* risk the safety of others.

¹⁵ And it seems obvious that the failure to wear safety belts does not cause such a direct risk. The wearing of safety belts, after all, does not decrease the chances of an accident. It only decreases the chances of an injury to the individual wearer. A driver's failure to fasten his safety belt will not impair his ability to drive the car—and forcing a bad driver to wear a safety belt won't make him any less of a threat to the other motorists.

¹⁶ So it is clear, then, that legislation is not the right solution to the problem at hand. But let's assume for a moment that Congress passed a law making it mandatory to wear safety belts. Would it work? Could it, as I asked previously, be effective?

¹⁷ It's apparent that enforcement of such a law would be difficult at best. Proponents of this legislation often draw an analogy between it and drunk-driving laws: If a car were stopped and the driver were found not to be wearing a belt, a penalty would result.

¹⁸ But there is no analogy, really. Drunk driving contributes to speeding, weaving and other infractions that alert authorities to the need to stop the car in question. Safety belts do not cause such recklessness. So how could the "offense" be checked out?

¹⁹ Do we expect policemen, observing a flow of traffic, to be able to spot each driver or passenger not fully harnessed? Or would we resort to sophisticated monitoring devices? And how would detection be possible at night?

²⁰ I know for certain that the American people will not stand for the interruption of their driving by buzzers and bells telling them to buckle up. The outcry against mandatory seat-belt interlock devices—which I opposed on the floor of the House in 1974—was too great.

²¹ The difficulty of enforcement raises another very serious question.

²² During the debate on safety belt legislation in the British Parliament on March 1 of this year, the Minister for Transport claimed that he would be satisfied with a wearing rate of 80% resulting from the law he proposed. I expect that proponents of a similar law in this country would likewise be happy with 80% compliance, given the enforcement problem.

²³ But in a nation with over 100 million registered autos, that means that roughly 20 million persons a day would be violating the law!

²⁴ I can only ask what it would do to respect for the law in general if so large a number of citizens regularly disobeyed a law. There are few things

more disruptive to the lawful order of society, and to relations between citizens and authorities, than the passage of a bad law easily ignored. Again, I point to Prohibition as an example.

25 As one who has authored several pieces of highway safety legislation, I realize the crying need for people to use safety belts. I know that, as a nation, we have not done nearly enough to promote their usage, and I accept the notion that government has a responsibility to join in the fight—not through coercive and unworkable legislation, but through persuasion and education.

26 Some more feasible means of reaching our goal of universal safety belt usage, by the enlistment of all sectors of the public, should be explored. They include:

27 • Educational programs in schools and educational aids at licensing and renewal time.

28 • A major media campaign, wherein all broadcast and print media would flood the public with information on the value of safety belts, both in "public service" formats and during news programs.

29 • Legislative endorsements—resolutions in the national and state legislatures promoting seat belt usage, with concurrent publicity.

30 • A road sign program to remind motorists to buckle up—for example, access ramps to major highways could be marked with signs saying "Please fasten safety belts before entering roadway."

31 • Development of more comfortable belts by manufacturers, facilitating their use.

32 Along with these measures, research should continue into alternative means of preventing auto injuries. Passive restraints, such as air bags, should be developed and marketed so that their reliability is improved and their cost brought into reasonable equivalence with that of safety belts.

33 In this election year, we are hearing much about the evils of big government and regulation from Washington of our daily lives. It's well to remember that big government will continue to exert ever-greater influence on us as long as we relinquish to it our responsibility for our own health and safety. For this reason, I say we should let every individual make the wise choice to wear a safety belt.

ANALYTICAL READING

1. What three conditions does Shuster think are necessary for a law to be appropriate? How does he handle this information so that it forms the basic structure for his argument?

2. What is the importance of Shuster's point that "the failure to wear safety belts does not harm society at large" (paragraph 12)? Does he deal adequately with the possible counter-arguments to this? Can you offer some others?

3. What reasons does Shuster give for his belief that the enforcement of a safety belt law would be difficult? Does Shuster believe that anything difficult to enforce should not become a law? Support your answer from statements in the article.

4.   Shuster estimates that about 20 percent of all drivers would probably ignore a safety belt law. What does he find wrong with that? Do you agree or disagree? Is he guilty of a statistical fallacy? Why or why not?

5.   What solutions does Shuster offer instead of a safety belt law? How effective would these be? Have similar suggestions been made about smoking? How effective are they?

6.   Does Shuster believe in the concept of "the less government, the better"? Why or why not?

REFLECTING

Point: Write a statement about the purpose of the essay, incorporating Shuster's concern about the highway death rate, his objection to a safety belt law, and his general proposals. Be as informative but as concise as possible, limiting yourself to a sentence or two.

Organization: What are the main divisions of the essay? State how the organization of the essay follows the form of a syllogism. What does the author accomplish in his introductory paragraphs? What is the purpose of paragraph 8? What is the function of paragraphs 26–33?

Support: Shuster uses a number of persuasive devices to support his main argument. They include analogy, statistical evidence, and refutation of opposing views. Where in the essay does he use each of these techniques?

Synthesis: Do you wear safety belts? Why or why not? Do you agree with Shuster's general political views? Would you abide by a safety belt law? Would you ignore it because others did? What role would peer pressure play in your using safety belts? How has reading Shuster's essay influenced your ideas about wearing safety belts, passing such a law, and prohibiting government interference in matters of health and safety that allegedly do not affect others? Shuster has introduced a resolution in Congress to overturn the government's regulation that air bags be made mandatory in 1984. What arguments would you expect him to offer?

Evaluation: Does Shuster state his case clearly, and is his argument easy to follow? How would you characterize his voice and tone? Can you find flaws in his logic? Does he provide solutions that would be practical and effective? Would his proposals be preferable to a safety belt law? Do you think that he himself uses a safety belt, and if so, how does this fact help his argument? How effective and appealing is his conclusion, particularly the last sentence?

FROM READING TO WRITING

1.   Write a paper with the title "Should Seat Belts Be Mandated by Law? Pro."

2.   Using Shuster's line of argument, write a paper in defense of marijuana, prostitution, gambling, or some other activity that is illegal but perhaps does not harm society or is unenforceable.

3.   To what extent should the government ban drugs or products that will affect the health and safety of citizens?

THE OTHER INFLATION
"Aristides"

BIOGRAPHICAL SKETCH

Aristides, a second-century Athenian philosopher, is the pen name of Joseph Epstein, editor of the American Scholar. *Born in Chicago in 1937, Epstein graduated from the University of Chicago and has been a visiting lecturer in the English department at Northwestern University. His articles, mainly about students, faculty members, and academic subjects, appear frequently in* The American Scholar, The New Yorker, Harper's, Commentary, *and the* New York Review.

PRE-READING

1. How informative and interesting is the title?

2. From the fact that the article was written for *The American Scholar,* at what audience would you expect the essay to be aimed?

3. Skim the opening paragraph; what do you infer to be the subject of the essay and the viewpoint of the author?

4. What argument does the final paragraph indicate?

    [1] The other inflation is grade inflation, the label affixed to the indisputable rise in the grade-point averages of undergraduates at public and private, elite and community colleges and universities across the country. The metaphor of inflation—borrowed from economics, which had earlier borrowed it from physical mechanics—is apt. Economic inflation, defined by Lord Robbins as "the general rise in prices or the decline in the purchasing power of money," has an exact intellectual equivalent in grade inflation: where grades generally rise, their intrinsic value goes down. "When a building catches fire," Colin Clark has written, "it is the combustion of one object which generates the heat required to ignite the next. Unless counter measures are taken, the fire spreads further and further, becoming more and more difficult to control, until there is nothing left. It is exactly the same with inflation. . . ." Professor Clark writes as an economist, but his analogy holds for grade inflation as well.

    [2] That the building is ablaze is not any longer arguable. Although further statistical studies are still being done, the phenomenon of grade inflation has thus far been fairly well documented. According to an article in the *Chronicle of Higher Education,* from "the early 1960's to the early 1970's, the number of A's awarded at a group of major universities more than doubled, while the number of C's fell by not quite half. . . ." At Union College, in Schenectady, New York, on a scale of 4.0, the median accumulated grade-point average of seniors went from 2.38 in 1966 to 3.11 in 1975. At Harvard some 70 percent of the

FROM *The American Scholar,* 45:4, Autumn 1976, pp. 492–97. Copyright © 1976 by the United Chapters of Phi Beta Kappa. Reprinted by permission of the publishers and the author.

total grades given in the fall 1975 term were As and Bs. The University of Massachusetts, where the collective grade-point average rose from 2.364 in 1966–67 to 2.93 in 1973–74, then fell back slightly to 2.91, seems to reflect what looks to be the national trend. In his summary remarks to a study of grades at twenty-three American colleges and universities, Sidney Suslow, director of the Office of Institutional Research at the University of California at Berkeley, notes that grades have shown a persistent increase since 1963, "from 2.49 that year to 2.94 in 1974" ("A Report on an Interinstitutional Survey of Undergraduate Scholastic Grading, 1960s to 1970s").

[3] An academic subject, grade inflation, academic in both the literal and unhappy senses of the word. And yet one wonders. The issues and questions connected with grade inflation have to do with standards; and standards, it is not priggish to insist, are never wholly an academic matter. Careers—hence lives—hinge on such things as grades; and although teachers may forget this, students whose careers and lives are at stake do not. Grades have long been crucial, not merely to academic success but to launching careers in law, medicine, business, and many other occupations. But they have now become swollen, misshapen, deformed to the point where few people any longer know what their true meaning is.

[4] I had my own first inkling of how confused the matter of grades had become when a young woman, a student in two courses I have taught, told me that she had hoped to do graduate work in clinical psychology but had not been accepted by any of the graduate schools to which she had applied. She was a shy student, not easy to draw out in classroom discussion, but her written work was nonetheless superior, and upon it she had floated to a solid A in each of the two courses she had taken with me. Perhaps she had not done so well in her other courses. But when I asked about her grade-point average, she said it was 3.76, which meant better than three As for every B and no Cs whatever. Possibly she had done less than magnificently on her Graduate Record Examination. Possibly because she is shy she was not able to get strong recommendations from professors in psychology, her major. Still, a 3.76 average seemed to me impressive—I, her professor, had had nowhere near so high an average as an undergraduate—and I knew from her work that she was in fact impressive. Evidently a great many students with an average as high as hers must be walking the campuses; and, just as evidently, so high a grade-point average is today no great badge of honor. Such a badge as it is, she now wears it, when last I heard, doing clerical work of a kind well beneath her ability.

[5] Victim does not seem an extreme term to describe this young woman's predicament. But victim of what? Of strange circumstances, but how strange becomes apparent only when one begins to seek out the reasons for the inflation of grades in recent years. Multivarious these reasons turn out to be; but many and (often) discrepant though they are, taken together they form the basis for a question of great moment: What kind of society do we in America want?

⁶ To look on the possibly cheery side first, is the chief reason for the inflation of grades that students today are more intelligent—mentally quicker, better prepared, more mature in intellectual judgment—than they were, say, ten or fifteen years ago? How comforting for the short-term evolutionists among us if it were so, but, as it turns out, it apparently is not so. Nationally, we are told, the Scholastic Aptitude Test scores for students entering college in 1975 were lower than the scores of thirteen years before, and in fact lower than similar scores of only five years before.

⁷ But test scores, however objective they are said to be, cannot be the last word, especially tests that measure aptitude rather than performance under the pressure of day-to-day academic challenge. Is it, then, possible that the rise in grades is owing to the fact that undergraduates today work harder than did undergraduates of five or ten years ago? Some undergraduates, now as in the past, work furiously hard; and no one is more appalled by stories of grade inflation then the undergraduate who has arduously striven for his As. He is appropriately appalled, moreover, for he—to revert yet again to the economic analogy—is in the position of the man who has worked hard all his life to achieve his pension, only to find, upon retirement, that it is nearly worthless.

⁸ But the notion that grades have risen in proportion to an increase in undergraduate effort, giving off as it does pleasant thoughts of a finely just world, is not ultimately persuasive. It does not persuade because other items are more persuasive. Not least among them has been the advent, in colleges and universities around the nation, of what is known as the "pass-fail option" in grading procedures. The pass-fail option means that at some schools a student can take as many as one-quarter of his courses without grade conse-quence; that is, he receives, in lieu of an ABCDF grade, either a pass (credit) or fail (no credit) for his effort. The boom period for the installation of the pass-fail option—according to Professor Arvo E. Juola of Michigan State University, and author of "Grade Inflation (1960–1973): A Preliminary Report"—was dur-ing the years 1967–1971. These were the years of the great student tumult, and the pass-fail option seems to have been a student demand everywhere acceded to.

⁹ Still, the pass-fail option had much to recommend it. Under its benefi-cence, a certain leeway in the selection of courses could be allowed those most competitively engaged in the academic marketplace. Twenty years ago, for example, most premedical students dared not risk taking an intellectually ad-venturous course outside their field of study—one in philosophy, say, or mod-ern literature—lest they receive a C or worse, causing their grade-point aver-age to drop, and the door to medical school to slam shut upon them. Consequently, the physicians of that generation tend to be among the most narrowly educated group ever to have passed through a university. Pass-fail, had it been in force, might have made possible an undergraduage life of greater intellectual breadth for such students.

¹⁰ In practice, though, the pass-fail option seems to be used today less to extend frontiers of learning than to protect the flanks of students. The major-

ity of undergraduates who use it do so, it seems, for those courses (including required courses) that seem to them most threatening—most threatening, that is, to end in a grade below a B. Whether or not taking a course pass-fail reduces the intensity of a student's intellectual effort by removing the competitive element is not altogether clear. (On occasion, students who have taken my courses pass-fail have done A work. More often, in my limited experience, students enrolled pass-fail have tended to perform in the middle range between C and B.) More to the point, the pass-fail option has had the result of raising grade-point averages, if only by removing some of the more strenuous courses—courses that might once have produced numerous Cs, Ds, and Fs—from the machinery of grading.

¹¹ Another mechanical contrivance that has caused the raising of grade-point averages is the greater leniency of rules permitting students to withdraw from courses. Withdrawals were always possible, but formerly the conditions under which a student could withdraw from a course were rather stringent, and the decision to seek a withdrawal had to be made fairly early in the term. Now withdrawals can not only be made fairly late in the term at most schools, but no reason for the withdrawal need be given. Frequent (if unstated) reasons for withdrawals are that a professor is too dull, the reading load in a course is too heavy, or the student finds himself out of his depth and calls for the withdrawal as for a life preserver to pull him to safety. Used as a means of avoiding boredom, strenuous work, and failure, withdrawals can only have further contributed to the inflation of grades.

¹² But more significant is the simple fact that higher grades—more As and Bs, fewer Cs and Ds—are now awarded than previously. Why should this be so? Not long ago I heard a student remark that he thought professors now gave higher grades to students as a form of bribery; higher grades, his reasoning ran, were the tacit payoff for undergraduate political quiescence. When queried further on the point, he said he was not prepared to argue that this was done consciously by professors—he was inclined to think it was done unconsciously—but he had not the slightest doubt that grade inflation was tied to politics. Not the least interesting aspect of this observation is that the student who made it is not himself notably political.

¹³ When a pattern is so clear, a trend so undeniable, the temptation is to look for causes commensurate in clarity to effects. And the pattern of grade inflation is astonishingly clear, the trend undeniable. Professor Juola, in his report, asks: "Are grades in higher education undergoing inflation? The answer is an emphatic 'Yes!'" In "Whither Grades?," a roughly 1,300-page department-by-department longitudinal study of grades at the University of Minnesota, Gary Engstrand has shown that not only have grades risen cumulatively at his school but they have done so pretty much across the board. As and Bs are up and Cs and Ds down, not only in the College of Liberal Arts but in the College of Veterinary Medicine and in the College of Business Administration. Everybody, as the old popular song has it, is doing it.

[14] When the causes come to be considered, they turn out, in the three studies I have looked at, to be manifold. Sidney Suslow speculates upon no fewer than thirty "factors responsible for grade inflation." Divided into four categories (Student Behavior, Faculty Behavior, Changes in Grading Policies, Other Influences or Changes), and running from "intense competition for admission to professional programs" to "adoption of permissive standards for educationally disadvantaged students [that] has resulted in their adoption for all students," no one of Mr. Suslow's factors seems in any way irrelevant.

[15] Yet for all the soundness of Mr. Suslow's particular factors, in a more general way grade inflation seems the logical consequence of the contradictions of our thinking about higher education. Going no further than language, consider the phrase "higher education" itself. The belief in education—the more, the better—is endemic to Americans. But as greater and greater numbers of students go off to college, that adjective "higher" grows less and less accurate. Behind the hope of getting as many people as possible into college is the hope of changing the situation of those we think of as the disadvantaged and underprivileged. But change it to what—a situation that finds them privileged or advantaged? Can everybody be advantaged and privileged? On the face of it, this is an impossibility. Yet one way to meet our extravagant expectations is to lower our standards.

[16] A mocking tone has crept into that paragraph, but who has not felt the pull of the goal of a society in which everyone is well educated? When children make the climb out of the slums or out of narrowly ethnic neighborhoods to succeed at a university and thence at a graduate or professional school, it is most impressive. Ability, ambition, discipline made possible their rise, excellence has been duly rewarded, and what we are pleased to call "the system" appears to have worked once again.

[17] Grades have long been an integral part of this same system, though at various times they have been under attack. In the latter half of the 1960s students made a great pretense to nonchalance about grades, but behind that nonchalance was a serious interest in getting the highest grades possible. Complication of a moral kind set in when, during the Vietnam War, grades became crucial to student deferment from the draft. Many professors who did not believe in the rightness of the war did not believe they ought to aid it in any way—and so, in an act of academic sabotage of the war effort, some of them gave all their students As. The entry of large numbers of minority students into the universities on a programmatic basis also had a consequence for grades. A heavy emotional investment of hope was placed in these students, an investment with a built-in self-fulfilling aspect: one so wanted these students to succeed that it was frequently difficult not to nudge them along with a helping hand. Not many professors spoke openly about it, but the contemporary equivalent of the old "gentleman's C" in many schools became the black's B.

[18] Grades were simultaneously played down in theory and raised up in practice. Concurrently, at many universities and colleges the curriculum

seemed to loosen up, if not cave in, in the attempt to make way for relevance and with-it-ry. Student interests began to be catered to more than ever before. In the cliché of the day, many courses became less "structured." This, too, had consequences for grading. If one is offering a course entitled "Women and the Media" or "The Space of Intimacy," how, in such a course, can one award grades? Can a student get a C in "Theories of Play" or an A in "Deviant Behavior"? (These are the titles of actual college courses; their names have not been changed lest the guilty be protected.)

¹⁹ Grade inflation would soon become a student problem, but it is a problem brought on by faculty behavior. For reasons various and sundry, the obligation of honor in grading has been relinquished. When, for example, it became evident that the great boom in education was over, and that for persuasive demographic reasons enrollments were down and would not soon rise again, professors and administrators did not see it as a splendid time to invoke standards. Could a good small school, suffering under rising costs and declining students, afford to flunk many out? In larger schools, with emoluments on the line—higher salaries, lighter teaching loads—it was scarcely the time to frighten students off to other departments by severity of grading. Some teachers graded loosely to ensure the regard of their students as well as high enrollments in their own classes. During this same period, students would be asked to evaluate their teachers. For younger faculty members, contract renewal and sometimes tenure might hinge on these evaluations. A young teacher enforcing firm grading standards just might have the same firm standards applied by his students to him. All these factors were scarcely an inducement to academic rigor.

²⁰ Even if one has felt none of these pressures as a teacher, something of the atmosphere of grade inflation can still seep through to affect the way one awards grades. Anecdotes fill faculty lounges, about students unhappy over getting merely Bs, about others withdrawing from a course after getting a C on a first paper or examination. A professor defends what he takes to be his own implacably high standards by remarking that in a class of seventeen he has given six Cs. Ds and Fs are simply no longer spoken about. Word meanwhile creeps up and down the student grapevine about which professors are tough and which easy graders; "fair grader" is a term almost never heard. As classrooms become less formal, firmness in grading becomes more difficult. With distance between teacher and student eliminated, a low or even a middling grade can seem, not a judgment on performance, but a personal comment, and as such nothing less than an insult.

²¹ Assuming a professor is impervious to all this as well, he is still left with a question of some ethical nicety. Is it fair to employ serious standards in grading when almost no one else does? On the one hand, not to do so is to give students an exaggerated sense of their abilities, which can have harsh consequences in the world outside the university. On the other hand, in the eyes of the graduate and professional school admissions directors an honest assessment is likely to have the look of condemnation, a C being akin to the

blackball that keeps a young student out of the club. Much the same conditions apply to the letter of recommendation, the language of which, like grades, has been subject to considerable inflation. Any professor called upon to write a letter of recommendation for a decent but not truly exceptional student knows that the first order of such a task is the suppression of candor, without which one is likely to write a recommendation that would read something like the following:

> Mr. Brompton is industrious, dependable, and reasonably serious. Because of his habits of perseverance, I think it likely that he will, with great strain, get through your law school. While I cannot confidently predict that he will be an ornament to his chosen profession, neither does he figure to disgrace it.

But of course no one but a knave would think of writing a recommendation of that kind for poor Mr. Brompton. Instead the likelihood is that he would get a recommendation that, were it written about him, would make Hegel blush.

[22] Lost in all this is the restricted but nonetheless significant meaning of grades. Grades, as has often been said, do not measure learning, but academic performance. They supply a rough but still ready measure of the extent to which a student's talent is joined to industry in bookish things. Except in a most limited sense, grades do not measure character, general intelligence, or even one's chances for success in the great world. Of many wretched measures of academic performance, grades appear to be least inadequate.

[23] For decades, grades have been under criticism, their limitations discussed from every point of view. Yet they do—or until recently did—serve as a useful differentiating tool. Interestingly enough, precisely because of their function of differentiating students according to academic performance, grades have come under attack. For those who saw their influence as baneful, something of the taint of elitism clung to grades, or at least to the idea of sorting people out by academic performance. To eliminate grades thus seemed a long stride on the road to equality. Yet where grades were eliminated the experiment tended not to be a happy one. Students apparently liked to know where they stood academically, and this, for better or worse, grades told them. But grade inflation has turned out to be a vast improvement on all such experiments. By raising all grades it has simultaneously eliminated the differentiating function of grades while carrying the extra advantage of convincing all students to believe themselves academically masterful.

[24] The rub is that differentiation goes on—and in a way that is intrinsically more elitist than the opponents of grades may ever have dreamed. With grades no longer an adequate measure, with letters of recommendation increasingly useless, where may graduate and professional schools look in choosing their students? Up to now they have tended preponderantly to look at an applicant's scores on standardized examinations and at what they take to

be the quality of his undergraduate school. Yet relying on standardized examinations and the prestige of certain colleges and universities can only freeze American society further by closing off what has long been a traditional and heavily trafficked form of social mobility in America—that available through academic performance. If grade inflation is not reversed, if grades are not restored to their former function, the time will soon come when students not from upper-middle-class homes, or from a handful of special schools, or from select minority groups, will be locked out of American life. Such are the potential consequences of grade inflation. Less immediate than those of economic inflation, over the long haul they could be much more troublesome.

ANALYTICAL READING

1. Why is the metaphoric use of the term *inflation* appropriate? What analogy is used?

2. What is the point of the author's example about his student with a 3.76 grade-point average (paragraph 4)?

3. What evidence does the author present to refute the possibilities that students today are either more intelligent or work harder than former students?

4. What causes for grade inflation does Aristides consider? Which of these causes are outdated? Which may still prevail at your school? Explain how the author uses classification in the cause-and-effect paragraphs (13–14).

5. Does the author blame students, faculty, or both for grade inflation? Support your answer with references to the essay. Does Aristides use classification techniques in this discussion?

6. What are the author's views about the validity of grades as an accurate measurement of student ability?

7. Does the author believe that grades should be eliminated?

8. Why is Aristides concerned about grade inflation? What harm does he claim it does?

REFLECTING

Point: Is the purpose of this essay to point out a problem, offer a solution, focus on causes, or what? State the purpose in one or two sentences.

Organization: What is the initial concern of the author in the essay, how does he establish this point, and why is it vital to the organization of the rest of the essay? Is the essay organized inductively or deductively? Explain. Discuss the main divisions of the essay and whether or not it is organized effectively.

Support: What kinds of evidence does Aristides offer to support his argument? What role does voice play in the argument? Describe the voice and tone used. Discuss the effectiveness of the analogies: grade inflation to economic inflation, a C being akin to social blackballing (paragraph 21), and others. Point out effective use of language and the semantic argument involved in the discussion of the phrase "higher education" (paragraph 15).

Synthesis: Do you think that there was grade inflation in your high school? If so, what were the probable causes and the effects? What do you know about grade inflation in your college? Should teachers lower standards for minority students because of their educational handicaps? To what extent are students attracted to departments or teachers who grade easily? Are students' grades a factor in their evaluations of instructors? Would you like to see grades eliminated or to have more courses available on a pass-fail basis? Why? How does this article pertain to the Ebel and Taylor-Lazarus articles on achievement-test scores (pages 374–80)?

Evaluation: Does Aristides convince you of the existence and seriousness of the problem? Is his writing interesting and clear? Does his evidence support his conclusions about probable causes? Has he treated the problem fairly from the viewpoints of both students and faculty members? Are there any flaws in his logic? Is the dilemma posed at the end a valid one?

FROM READING TO WRITING

1. Make a case for or against giving high grades to a student who studies diligently, attends class regularly, submits all assignments on time, but performs only average work.

2. Write a paper about the extent that you think grades are an effective measurement of student ability. Either argue for the present grading system, in high school or college, or suggest some other plan for evaluating student achievement.

3. Study your school's policy on pass-fail options or course withdrawal. Select one of these subjects, explain the policy, and defend or denounce it, using cause-and-effect arguments.

4. Write an editorial for your school newspaper, agreeing or disagreeing with Aristides' argument about the importance of reducing grade inflation. Rely on logical arguments, including examples or comparisons, to support your points.

Mixed Argument

GIVE THE PEOPLE A VISION
Rev. Jesse L. Jackson

BIOGRAPHICAL SKETCH

Jesse Louis Jackson was born in Greenville, North Carolina, in 1941. He earned a B.A. in sociology from the Agricultural and Technical College in North Carolina and did postgraduate work at the Chicago Theological Seminary, from which he later received an honorary degree. A Baptist preacher and close friend of Martin Luther King, Jr., he was active in the civil rights movement for many years, particularly as one of the leaders of Operation Breadbasket, a Chicago organization devoted to increasing jobs for black people. Recently, Jackson, as head of the Chicago-based Operation PUSH (People United to Save Humanity), has launched a national crusade to improve black schools and students.

PRE-READING

1. While the title is interesting and inviting, it does not indicate the direction of the article. But when you add the title to the information in the first paragraph, what do you know about Jackson's subject and purpose?

2. Does the last paragraph specifically indicate Jackson's "vision"? If so, what is it?

¹ It is time, I believe, to reexamine the causes of the social and economic plight in which black Americans—and particularly the poor blacks of the Northern cities—still find themselves, despite the legal advances of the 60's. Since so many past analyses of this problem have failed to bring about satisfactory improvement, I think it is time to suggest some new approaches, based largely on new values. It is my view that such a fresh start offers the best hope not only of lifting up the black people but of saving America's cities.

² I also believe that it is fruitful to think of these problems within a larger context—the relationship between the United States and the third world. For the white racist attitudes that are part of the problem at home have also been an often unconscious element in the policy failures of the white political leadership via-à-vis the emerging nations, most recently in Africa. And the natural

FROM *The New York Times Magazine*, 18 April 1976, pp. 13, 71–73. © 1976 by The New York Times Company. Reprinted by permission.

pride of American blacks in the achievement of black leaders abroad is a factor in their own struggle.

[3] As a starting point, let us take a noteworthy statistic: There are now 130 black mayors in the United States. We blacks have populated the cities; we must now learn to run them. The need is urgent. The ethical collapse, the heroin epidemic, the large numbers of our people who are out of work and on welfare, and the disruptive violence in our schools all indicate that the cities may be destroying us.

[4] The thrust of my argument is that black Americans must begin to accept a larger share of responsibility for their lives. For too many years we have been crying that racism and oppression have kept us down. That is true, and racism and oppression have to be fought on every front. But to fight any battle takes soldiers who are strong, healthy, spirited, committed, well-trained, and confident. This is particularly true when the enemy is as tough and elusive as American racism. I don't believe that we will produce strong soldiers by moaning about what the enemy has done to us.

[5] It is time, I think, for us to stand up, admit to our failures and weaknesses and begin to strengthen ourselves. Here are some of the things I am talking about:

[6] There is a definite welfare mentality in many black communities that derives perhaps from slavery but that must now be overcome.

[7] We have beome politically apathetic. Only 7 million out of 14 million eligible black voters are registered to vote. Yet politics is one key to self-development. In terms of votes, we have more potential strength than labor or any other single bloc. We have responsibility to use it to the full.

[8] We too often condemn blacks who succeed and excel, calling them Toms and the like, when the ideal ought to be for all of us to succeed and excel.

[9] We are allowing a minuscule minority of criminals in our midst to create disorder, ruin our schools and sap the energy we need to rebuild our neighborhoods and our cities.

[10] Many leaders who are black, and many white liberals, will object to my discussing these things in public. But the decadence in black communities— killings, destruction of our own businesses, violence in the schools—is already in the headlines; the only question is what we should do about it. Others will object that to demand that we must meet the challenge of self-government is to put too much pressure on the victims of ancient wrongs. Yet in spite of these objections, in spite of yesterday's agony, liberation struggles are built on sweat and pain rather than tears and complaints.

[11] In facing up to the new reality of black concentration in the Northern cities, the flight of whites to the suburbs, and the decay of the inner cities— particularly their black communities—in many parts of the country, many black and white leaders demand Federal aid as the only solution. More Federal aid is certainly needed, but money alone, or in combination with minor reforms, will not significantly change the welfare system, reduce crime, build

enough new houses, improve education, restore stable families or eliminate drug abuse. A multitude of Federal antipoverty and urban-renewal programs should have proved that by now. But if more Federal money will not solve the problem, what will?

¹² I believe we should look to the third world for an answer. The message from there is clear: Through the proper use of money and a positive attitude, we can stimulate self-development and give the people a vision. It has been fascinating for me to observe what has happened in South Vietnam in the past year. The new Saigon leaders have spent little time talking about the Americans who carpet-bombed and defoliated their country. Instead, they have concentrated on rebuilding, putting people to work, inculcating new values and attitudes. They did it with military authority and a liberated attitude. We black Americans can rebuild our communities with moral authority. We need a blueprint, such as an urban Marshall Plan, but at its base there must be moral authority and sound ethical conduct.

¹³ This is not unrealistic. It was the moral authority of the civil-rights movement, not the Federal marshals—who stood back initially and let whites have their way with the demonstrators—that changed the face of the South. It was a disciplined struggle—and such a struggle can be waged again, to good purpose, in the cities of the North.

¹⁴ We need to tell our young people in those cities: "All right, we'll get all the state and Federal money that we can; but first and foremost, we need to put your hands and your bodies and your minds to work building our communities." What we must do for our young people is challenge them to put hope in their brains rather than dope in their veins. What difference does it make if the doors swing wide open if our young people are too dizzy to walk through them?

¹⁵ I often wonder what would happen if Coleman Young, the Mayor of Detroit, who has inherited a city of much moral and economic decay, were to go into one of Detroit's stadiums and had 50,000 or 60,000 people in there— just as Jomo Kenyatta has done, and Castro, and President Samora Machel of Mozambique—and delivered a resounding State of Detroit message.

¹⁶ "All right, people" he could say, "Detroit needs 200 doctors in the next 10 to 15 years, and here is what we will do to make certain that it happens. And we will need 200 lawyers and 400 electricians and 250 nurses, and here is what we will do to make sure it happens. I cannot pass a law about these things, but I am appealing to you parents and you children to cooperate. Parents, you must keep your children at home every night from 7 to 9 to study, and get them into bed by 10. Every morning the city will provide physical-training directors in city parks. We will close off one block in every neighborhood for half an hour every morning for exercise—we want you out there getting your bodies healthy for this struggle for independence."

¹⁷ I have been visiting major cities across the country, preparing for a crusade next fall that will stimulate people along these lines. Everywhere I go, from Washington to Los Angeles, I meet young people in schools that the

politicians have given up on. I frequently find myself addressing 3,000 or 4,000 young people in a rundown assembly hall. Each time I suggest a program of self-development, they respond with overwhelming enthusiasm. Black teen-agers—some of the roughest, most street-wise dudes you will ever meet—respond to that appeal.

[18] There is another parallel with the third world that is very much to the point. The emerging countries have had to proceed by stages—from a situation in which they were outright colonies, and their white rulers simply grabbed up the countries' natural resources; to a state of neocolonialism, in which the people attained nominal independence but the former colonizers remained in de facto control of the resources, which they continued to exploit primarily for their own benefit; to a situation of real independence in which the people take over control of their resources and work out mutually beneficial production arrangements with the former colonizers.

[19] We black Americans feel we have been exploited, too, although the natural resources we had to offer were not minerals in the ground or produce in the field but the human resources of brain and brawn. And we feel we are at a stage at which we can emulate the third-world countries by moving from "neocolonialism," as it were, to real "independence." The lessons, of course, must be applied to situations that often are vastly different from those facing the leaders of the economically underdeveloped countries of Africa, Asia and Latin America, but the principle of self-reliance in place of dependency is the same.

[20] Let me give a practical example. In the 60's, many black leaders, myself included, were picketing in front of Sears and A. & P. and other supermarkets in the black neighborhoods, demanding more and better jobs for blacks and more equitable financial arrangements with the community. And we succeeded. Some of these stores began to appoint black managers, put products of black companies on their shelves, hire black contractors for building new stores, and place their accounts in black-controlled banks. But today we find ourselves in Chicago, East Orange, N.J., and elsewhere, lying down at Sears' back doors begging the man not to fire us all and close down.

[21] We want those white-owned branches, with the services and jobs they provide, to stay, but if they want to go, we should not be left with nothing to take their place. The point is that if we had pulled together in the intervening decade, if we had not lost so many good minds to the jails and the drug culture, if we had taken the pooling of our money more seriously, we would today have the ready capital and trained managers and communal organization to buy out those white-controlled stores that want to close down, direct all black business to them, and make them economically successful. But that takes discipline and purpose and dedicated leadership at many levels, and that is where I think the experience of the third-world countries can be of help to us.

[22] It is bad to be in the worst slums in the country; it is even worse if those slums are internalized, become part of you. Hence the therapeutic effect of the

Black Power symbolism of the 60's. But some black students became so caught up in the symbolism of black nationalism and black liberation that they forgot about such basic skills as reading, writing and thinking.

[23] God knows that I recognize the need for black self-pride. But that monument must be built on a solid foundation; we must not, as Dr. Martin Luther King, Jr. used to say, confuse symbolism with substance. When I stand in front of an audience of 3,000 black high-school or college students and we chant back and forth, "I am somebody, I am somebody," I can feel them tell me: "I need to be told I am somebody, I need to know I am somebody." But shouting "I am somebody" is only the first small step toward independence.

[24] In the last 10 to 12 years, many of us missed the chance to grow intellectually and chased Superfly instead. Many of us spent more time on lottery and luck than looking for a job. Many of us did not use the opportunities we had. But it is time to cut that now. That backward trend goes against our own best traditions. Africa's great leaders, from Nkrumah to Machel, have all been learned men.

[25] Preoccupation with symbolism has also made it hard for many of us to dintinguish service from servility.

[26] As I travel around the country, I often eat in restaurants run by the Nation of Islam. One reason is that the waiters are the most courteous and prompt you will find anywhere. They enjoy serving black people: you will never find a Muslim waiter with an "attitude." Unfortunately, the same is not true of all blacks. I know of black contractors who have gone out of business because their black workers were not prompt or had negative attitudes. I know young black workers who talk with pride about going to work any hour they feel like it, taking a day off when they feel like it, wearing Apple Caps on the job, playing loud portable radios on the assembly line. They're rebelling against the system, they say: they're exhibiting their independence. (There are many white workers, it should be added, who do the same.) What they're really exhibiting is ignorance of a tradition of work in the black community that is one of our proudest legacies.

[27] Slavery is over now, but you can't free a man who still has a slave mentality, just as you can't enslave a man who has a free spirit. We don't need to carry chips on our shoulders, fearing we are being treated in a servile manner. This does not mean we cannot be angry and loud and ornery on occasion, as all mortals have a way of being, but we should always try to use the power that derives from true courtesy.

[28] The process of "internalizing" conditions that should instead be banished has another tragic effect.

[29] According to black historian Lerone Bennett Jr., the first black people arrived in America in 1619. That means that black people have been in this land for 357 years. For 244 of those years we were slaves; for 113 years we have been technically free; but real freedom has only just come since the turn of the 20th century. Although welfare was set up mainly to aid poor whites,

and two-thirds of the recipients today are white, our history of slavery and oppression, and the decades of forced dependency, do seem to have carried over into what I call the welfare mentality. There are black families that have not had an opportunity to be independent of a white-controlled system of one kind or another for as many generations back as they can account for. It is time for that syndrome to end. We cannot afford it any longer.

[30] My own approach to the welfare situation is mixed. We need all the reforms the progressives argue for—guaranteed minimum income; an end to the humiliating spying and investigating by case workers; passage of the Humphrey-Hawkins full-employment bill now before Congress; an end to the "make a dollar, take a dollar" regulations that penalize people on welfare who get part-time jobs; incentives to encourage people on welfare to go to school and improve themselves. On the other hand, as the job market expands, we must inspire people to get off that debilitating welfare system and say to them: "We need you to help us rebuild our communities." Then we must supply the tools for the urban poor to work with. We need jobs, for self-esteem, self-confidence and character—not just money.

[31] The greatest potential for self-development is to be found in the public schools in our cities. That is also where there is now the greatest potential for explosions. Predominantly black schools in most urban areas with high concentrations of black people—New York, Washington, Detroit, Chicago, Los Angeles, St. Louis, Boston—are largely out of control. Violence against students and teachers, perpetrated by students, is steadily and dangerously increasing. Drug abuse is an accepted fact of life; pushers operate freely in many schools, and police patrol the corridors. Discipline has broken down. In a number of New York schools, teachers complain that the places are run not by the principals but by the gangs. We need to change this because it is morally right, because it is necessary for our development, and because no one else is going to do it for us.

[32] The principals are not alone: Parents, teachers, superintendents, school boards have all failed to impose discipline and create a proper atmostphere for learning. And if our young people are not learning today, we will not have the doctors, engineers, lawyers, mechanics, nurses, clerks and accountants that we will need to manage the cities.

[33] A few years ago there was sizable movement for community control of the public schools. But the community-control movement never did seriously address the problem of control of the students by their parents. Many black students turned the movement into a cynical rebellion against any authority—black or white, sympathetic or unsympathetic, healthy or destructive. A people seeking independence cannot tolerate that.

[34] A related problem is the misconception, perpetrated on many parents, that a parent with little formal education is in a position to dictate on pedagogical matters to teachers and educators. Parents have something more fundamental to offer: motivation, love, care, discipline—and sometimes chastise-

ment. Children cannot be allowed to play the game of "teach me if you can catch me." Children must be taught that they have a responsibility to learn as well as a right to an education. Busing is absolutely necessary, but without a will to learn, busing is irrelevant.

35 With all that in mind, PUSH (People United to Save Humanity), the organization that I direct from Chicago, has begun a national program, "PUSH for Excellence," to address urban problems, beginning with the public schools. The models for this project are in Washington, Los Angeles and Chicago, but we have already found great interest in the approach in other cities.

36 We have begun in Washington by stimulating high-school students to organize a city-wide Council Against Drugs, Racism and Violence and for Discipline. A student conference will be held by this council in the spring. We have had large numbers of students turn out for planning meetings, and we have aroused substantial mass support at high-school assemblies. Parallel and sometimes coordinated meetings have been held with teachers, athletic coaches, superintendents and school boards. Mayor Walter Washington has shown great interest—as have Mayors Maynard Jackson of Atlanta, Coleman Young of Detroit, Richard Hatcher of Gary, Ind., and Thomas Bradley of Los Angeles for similar initiatives in their cities.

37 Our program is simple. We want to get black men from the neighborhoods to replace the police in patrolling the school corridors and the street corners where the dope pushers operate. We want all parents to reserve the evening hours of 7 to 9 for their children's homework. We want student leaders and athletes to help identify and solve discipline problems before they get out of control. We want the black-oriented media to find ways to publicly reward achievers. We want the black disc jockeys, who reach more black kids than the school principals, to inform and inspire as well as entertain.

38 A crucial element in our program is the black church. The church is the most stable influence in the black communities. It is the only place where all segments of the community come together, once a week. An estimated 11 to 13 million men, women and children are members of black churches. Historically, the black church has been involved in or behind every black movement of any significance. I have been involved with high schools in Washington, Chicago and Los Angeles that are working with churches, and if there is anything the experience has shown me, it is that black ministers still carry moral authority with our people, except for a hard-core few, and most people want moral authority.

39 America is in the midst of a crisis, both in regard to its cities and in regard to its position in the world. Black Americans, inheritors of the role of the restless and disenfranchised minorities of the past who helped make America strong, have a historic opportunity to show that the cities can be saved. We can do so by stimulating change in the schools and the communities we control.

40 Also by virtue of our special empathy for the colored peoples of the

third world, and particularly Africa, black Americans can contribute to the foreign-policy debate by exposing the racism at the root of some of our Government's worst domestic and foreign blunders. It would be tragic if our nation lost its potential for true greatness by letting racist legacies deflect it from its proper course.

[31] Vital though this second task may be, it must, for the moment, take second place. The first and immediate task for American blacks is to rise up from the decadence in which we too often find ourselves in the cities, and to do so by the force of our will, our intellect, our energy and our faith in ourselves. It is a historic opportunity we cannot afford to miss.

ANALYTICAL READING

1. What problems concern Jackson? Have political changes taken place that allow for the possibility of new solutions to these problems in the United States?

2. Why are the old solutions inadequate? Have they failed completely?

3. What four specific failures does Jackson point out early in his essay? Which one do you think concerns him most?

4. What objections to his argument does Jackson note, and how does he refute them?

5. Why is Jackson confident about relying on moral authority and sound ethical conduct? Does he base his appeal on morality or group self-interest?

6. Why does Jackson look to the Third World as an example? Do these African countries face some of the problems of American blacks? What solutions does he find that might be adopted by American blacks?

7. What did Dr. Martin Luther King, Jr., mean by the statement that blacks should not "confuse symbolism with substance" (paragraph 23)? Does Jackson believe that black symbolism is of some importance? Why or why not? Does it present any problems? Explain.

8. How does he use cause and effect to discuss "slave mentality"?

9. Whom does Jackson blame for the problems in the schools? What solutions does he propose?

10. If, as Jackson states, the church in black communities is such a stabilizing force, why have the churches been so ineffective in helping to improve the circumstances of their members?

REFLECTING

Point: Jackson's article originally appeared in the *New York Times Magazine*. What audience is he addressing? Would he write differently for a general public periodical than for a black magazine, such as *Ebony*? What is his thesis and what do you suppose is his purpose?

Organization: After the first two introductory paragraphs, Jackson starts his argument with a statistic. Is this effective? Why or why not? How does he handle the four failures he mentions near the beginning of the essay? What is the persuasive advantage of (1) downplaying the currently favored solution to black problems—more federal money—early in the essay and (2) saving his specific proposals for near the end? Discuss the overall organization of the article.

Support: What examples does Jackson use? How pertinent and effective are they? What role do statistics play in his argument? What evidence is offered to show that his plan is practical? Write a syllogism that you feel provides the basis for the main argument in the article. Be prepared to explain how Jackson supports the premises, realizing that at times he might believe that some points in his argument are self-evident and do not require proof. What part does his analogy to the Third World play in supporting his arguments?

Synthesis: To what extent is Jackson's argument applicable to whites? Why is it important to whites? From your personal experience in urban or other schools, do you agree with his assessment of many black students? How do you feel about discipline in the schools? Do you agree with his ideas about the role of parents in the schools? Do you think his plan will work? Why or why not?

Evaluation: Are you convinced that a problem exists? Do you accept Jackson's contention that present solutions are inadequate? Does he offer evidence that his solution is practical enough to appeal to teenagers, or do you believe it is too idealistic? Is his argument weakened or strengthened by his reference to the Third World? Does Jackson write clearly and convincingly?

FROM READING TO WRITING

1. Write a letter to your high school principal arguing that the schools themselves, rather than black students, are at fault for learning failures. Use examples to support your contentions.

2. Write an argument about the influence of the church today, either in the black or white community, or with black or white young people.

3. Write an argument about the influence parents have on their children, either blaming them for failing to discipline and provide a model for their offspring or relieving them of the major blame for the faults of their children.

4. Write a letter to your mayor favoring, modifying, or repudiating Jackson's PUSH program.

THE NEED FOR GUN CONTROL LEGISLATION

Edward M. Kennedy

BIOGRAPHICAL SKETCH

Edward M. Kennedy, born in 1932, is the youngest son of Joseph P. and Rose Kennedy and the brother of the late President John Kennedy and Senator Robert Kennedy. He holds a B.A. from Harvard University (1954) and a law degree from the University of Virginia. Married to Joan Bennett Kennedy and father of three children, he has been a Democratic Senator from Massachusetts since 1962 and held the position of majority whip from 1969 to 1971. Kennedy's publications include Decisions for a Decade *and* In Critical Condition. *He has been active in volunteer community work and has received numerous awards for his services on behalf of children's hospitals and the fine arts.*

PRE-READING

1. What do the title and the first paragraph indicate about the subject of the article and Kennedy's stand on it?

2. What do the last two paragraphs state about possible general solutions to the problem indicated in the title and opening paragraph?

¹ The case for effective firearms legislation can be logically and clearly explained on the basis of the daily tragedies reported in our nation's newspapers. Over 25,000 Americans die each year because of shooting accidents, suicides and murders caused by guns, primarily because too many Americans possess firearms. When guns are available, they have proved to be a far too easily accessible tool for the destruction of human life. Because of the senseless deaths and injuries caused by guns I strongly support the public demand for legislation to provide a uniform, nationwide system to control the abuse and misuse of firearms. A brief review of the conditions involving firearms in this country makes it clear that the proliferation of firearms, particularly handguns, must be halted.

² My interest in the need for effective firearms legislation goes back at least to 1963. I have introduced firearms bills in the Senate on several occasions. I offered gun control amendments to pending legislation on the Senate floor. Since I have been in the Senate, I have heard much of the testimony presented by nearly 200 witnesses, during more than 40 days of hearings on gun control. The issues never change. The arguments never vary. The statistics never recede. In 1963, handgun murders totaled 4,200. Eleven years later, in 1974, handguns were used to murder 11,000 Americans. The tragic toll of

FROM *Current History*, July/August 1976, pp. 26, 27, 28, 31. Reprinted by permission of the publisher.

handgun suicides and accidental handgun deaths pushes the annual figures well beyond reasonable limits for a society that claims to respect life and personal security.

[3] Gun manufacturers produce more guns each year, and American gun deaths increase right along with the output of firearms. Advocates for stronger controls are understandably alarmed by production figures showing that the annual output of handguns increased from 568,000 in 1968 to over 2.5 million in 1974.

[4] Many experts insist that a gun, and particularly a handgun, is such a viciously lethal weapon that no citizen deserves to wield the awesome power of a gun. Our complex society requires a rethinking of the proper role of firearms in modern America. Our forefathers used firearms as an integral part of their struggle for survival. But today firearms are not appropriate for daily life in the United States.

[5] The arguments used to oppose gun controls are old and hackneyed. The same lament has been used in one of the following forms time and time again:

First.   Gun controls cannot limit the supply of guns enough to reduce violence.

Second.   The Constitution protects the citizen's right to bear arms.

Third.   There is no need to ban guns because guns are not killers; people do the killing.

Fourth.   Criminals will always find a way to obtain guns. Thus, controls will only disarm those who obey the law.

Fifth.   Registration and licensing procedures are so cumbersome and inconvenient that they would create unfair burdens for legitimate gun owners.

[6] Opponents of effective gun controls believe that these objections are valid. But a thorough examination of each of these claims reveals that not one of them is well founded.

[7] First, can laws limit the supply of guns enough to reduce violent crime?

[8] Of course, such laws, properly enforced, can reduce the availability of handguns. In 1968, when importers anticipated the enactment of a new gun law, about 1.2 million handguns were rushed into the American market. In 1969, pistol and revolver imports fell to less than 350,000 and have not risen substantially above that total since then.

[9] Today, nearly three million new handguns enter the American market every year because handgun parts are still legally imported and because American manufacturers are still authorized to produce them. The legislation I have introduced would not only reduce the number of handguns assembled from imported parts, but it would also drastically curtail the output of domestically manufactured handguns.

[10] In June, 1934, President Franklin D. Roosevelt signed the National Firearms Act, which outlawed civilian ownership of machineguns. Perhaps this is the law that best illustrates the way in which legislation can effectively restrain

the availability of firearms. Since enactment of that measure over 40 years ago, machineguns have been virtually eliminated in the United States. Obviously, a machinegun has no legitimately useful place in a civilized society. Easily concealed pistols and revolvers are also out of place in today's highly urbanized and complex society.

[11] Opponents of handgun control insist that it is impossible to prevent a criminal from obtaining a handgun. But if a criminal has to steal a gun before he can use a gun, he will use a gun much less frequently.

[12] An effectively enforced ban on the output of these deadly devices is the most direct way to reduce the deaths and injuries caused by guns.

[13] Second, it is claimed that the second amendment to the constitution protects the citizen's right to bear arms. Anyone who believes that "the right to bear arms" is guaranteed in the constitution has conveniently ignored the language of the second amendment, which provides that:

> A well regulated militia being necessary to the security of a free state, the right of the people to keep and bear arms shall not be infringed.

[14] The United States Supreme Court has repeatedly said that this amendment has nothing to do with the right to personal ownership of guns but only with the right of a state to establish a militia.

[15] In perspective, the purpose of the second amendment emerges clearly. Debates in the first and second Congresses were naturally affected by the recently won independence of the new government. And in Massachusetts it was bitterly recalled that the British Crown had quartered its troops but forbade the organization of a colonial militia. Congressional debates of early Congresses support the view that the second amendment was designed to protect and preserve the state militias. No mention was made of any individual's "right" to possess, carry, or use arms, and there is no indication of any concern with the need to do so. The new government was far more interested in maintaining state militias to defend the hard-won liberty. That fledgling government feared the establishment of a federal standing army as a threat to the basic authority of the several states.

[16] Indeed, in December, 1791, when the Bill of Rights was ratified, all but one of the 14 states of the Union adopted a constitution or a declaration of rights under which their people were governed.

[17] Rhode Island still operated under its charter of 1663, which authorized the colony to organize a militia. But there was no mention of any "right" to bear arms.

[18] Eight states—Delaware, New Jersey, Connecticut, Georgia, South Carolina, Maryland, New Hampshire, and New York—operated under constitutions that made no mention of any "right" to bear arms, although each authorized a state militia.

[19] Three states—Massachusetts, North Carolina, and Virginia—expressly recognized the right of the people to bear arms for the defense of the state.

[20] Two states—Pennsylvania and Vermont—included language in their constitutions which acknowledged that:

> The people have a right to bear arms for the defense of themselves and the State.

[21] However, that sentence was included in a paragraph that was concerned with the prohibition against a standing army and the guarantee of civilian control of the militia. Considering the history of the right to bear arms, reason defines the phrase "defense of themselves" as referring only to collective defense. That phrase did not include individual defense.

[22] It appears, therefore, that both the states and the Congress were preoccupied with the distrust of standing armies and the importance of preserving state militias. It was in this context that the second amendment was written and it is in this context that it has been interpreted by the courts.

[23] Third, a common refrain against firearm controls is that "guns do not kill, people do." This argument contends that people who use guns to commit crimes should be dealt with severely but that efforts to control weapons are not necessary. Yet, a glance at the statistics and common sense tell us that it is when guns are in hand that two-thirds of the people who kill other people do so; it was when guns were in hand that over 250,000 robberies were committed in 1973; it was when guns were in hand that one-fourth of the nation's 400,000 aggravated assaults were committed in 1973.

[24] Murder is usually committed in a moment of rage. Guns are quick and easy to use. They are also deadly accurate, and they are all too often readily accessible. It is estimated that there are over 35 million handguns in private ownership in this country. Each year, 2.5 million new handguns are introduced into the marketplace for civilian use. Because handguns are available people use them.

[25] An attacker makes a deliberate choice of a gun over a knife. But because the fatality rate of knife wounds is about one-fifth that of gun wounds, it may be concluded that using a knife instead of a gun might cause 90 percent fewer deaths.

[26] Fourth, others argue that because criminals have guns, gun control will simply disarm law-abiding citizens. Lawless citizens, according to that argument, will not feel obliged to abide by gun restrictions.

[27] Perhaps there is truth in this argument. And for this reason, I am convinced that gun restrictions can be effective in limiting the wholesale misuse of firearms. Strict gun restrictions will aid in disarming anyone who fails to register his weapons or to obtain a license for ownership. Indeed, the enforcement of licensing and registration laws will isolate precisely those citizens who flaunt the law, because such legislation makes it a crime merely to possess an unregistered firearm. The commission of a crime with such a weapon compounds the wrong of any criminal action.

^{28} Fifth. It may be that the greatest number who protest gun controls do so because the administrative requirements for registration are cumbersome and inconvenient. Since 1969, Congress has attempted several times to remove the 1968 gun control law's record-keeping requirements with regard to sales of .22 caliber ammunition.

^{29} I have repeatedly objected to any move that would eliminate the requirement that sales of such ammunition must be recorded. Between 6 billion and 7 billion rounds of ammunition are produced in this country each year. At least 85 percent of those bullets are .22 caliber. Records maintained to control the sale of ammunition may be useful in restricting access to those gun owners who intend to use their weapons for legitimate purposes.

^{30} I believe that any measure that will substantially reduce the misuse of firearms will at the same time enhance whatever pleasures may be derived from the so-called recreational pursuits of gun ownership.

^{31} Among the nations of the world, the United States stands in the bloodiest pool of deaths by gunfire. Americans are not only ranked No. 1, but No. 2 lags so far behind that a tally of gun deaths in all civilized nations probably would not equal the excessive fusillade Americans train on their fellow citizens.

^{32} In 1973, the total gun murder rate in the United States was 6.2 per 100,000 population. Thus, even the United States handgun murder rate was 62 times the rate in Scotland, the Netherlands, and Great Britain and Japan, 31 times the rate in Denmark, France, Sweden, and Switzerland, and 20 times the rate in New Zealand, Germany and Italy. (See Table 1.)

Table I: Total Number of Homicides and Rate per 100,000 Population

Country (year is the latest for which figures are available)	Total Homicide		Gun Homicide	
	Number	Rate	Number	Rate
United States, 1973	19,510	7.5	11,249	6.2
Australia, 1970	190	1.5	71	.6
Denmark, 1971	48	1.0	12	.2
England and Wales, 1972	384	.8	41	.1
France, 1970	373	.7	124	.2
German Federal Republic, 1971	802	1.3	203	.3
Ireland, 1972	21	.7	—	—
Italy, 1970	442	.8	239	.4
Japan, 1971	1,380	1.3	20	.0
Netherlands, 1972	72	.5	13	.1
New Zealand, 1971	25	.9	8	.3
Scotland, 1972	73	1.4	3	.1
Sweden, 1971	76	.9	19	.2
Switzerland, 1972	57	.9	12	.2

Source: International Statistical Classification of Diseases, Injuries and Causes of Death (Geneva: World Health Organization, 1971, 1972, 1973, 1974).

[33] Among civilized societies that have acted to control guns the United States is a glaring exception. In Italy, West Germany, France, Britain, and the Soviet Union, "the right to bear arms" is a strictly regulated privilege. In Japan, private gun ownership is all but prohibited. Five European countries totally prohibit the private possession of handguns. A 1968 State Department survey of 102 of its diplomatic posts revealed that 29 European countries require either a license to carry a firearm or registration of the ownership or sale of each privately owned firearm, or both.

[34] Legislation to control the violence caused by firearms is essential in a national campaign to reduce handgun deaths. At the same time, public education and ongoing research in the relationship between firearms and violence is also important.

[35] The gun mystique fascinates and excites the imagination. Films, novels and dramatic presentations that depict gun violence are enjoyed and readily understood by all members of our society. The role of the handgun in American society has been distorted. A complete reform of the role of the handgun is needed. It is clearly not a weapon of entertainment, and only rarely is it used for sporting purposes. Many Americans insist that a handgun provides comfort and security in a menacing environment where assailants threaten the weak, the helpless, and the lonely. Yet the proliferation of handguns seems to involve a vicious cycle that sees more and more people buying guns to protect themselves from more and more people who have guns.

[36] I am convinced that this national evil of handgun roulette must be interrupted before the two-gun family becomes as common as the two-car family.

[37] In April, 1976, the House of Representatives' Subcommittee on Crime reported a bill to begin to establish controls on the use of handguns. If this measure is enacted, it will establish the foundation for a full system of controls that can stem the unbridled flow of firearms violence.

[38] From other sources, it has also been recommended that handgun production quotas must be imposed upon the nation's firearms producers. Because the American people have repeatedly expressed the demand for an end to firearms violence, I look forward to the enactment of effective and enforceable controls on the use of firearms.

Sources

Bakal, Carl. *The Right to Bear Arms.* New York: McGraw-Hill, 1966.

Newton, George D. and Franklin Zimring. *Firearms and Violence in American Life—Staff Report to the National Committee on the Causes and Prevention of Violence.* Washington, D.C.: U.S. Government Printing Office, 1968.

Senate Subcommittee on Juvenile Delinquency. "Hearing on the Saturday Night Special." Washington, D.C.: U.S. Government Printing Office, 1971.

Sherrill, Robert. *Saturday Night Special.* New York: Charterhouse Books, 1973.

ANALYTICAL READING

1. What is the effect of Kennedy's mention in paragraph 2 of his personal in-volvement in gun control legislation?

2. Is the machinegun analogy in paragraph 10 valid? Why or why not?

3. Are the conclusions Kennedy bases on the figures in Table 1 acceptable? How would you reply to the counter-argument that the United States has a much greater population than all the other countries cited, so it inevitably has more handgun murders?

4. How does Kennedy refute the argument that the Constitution guarantees "the right to bear arms"?

5. Consider the following analogy: cars do not kill, people do; thus we need not safer cars and highways, but better education for drivers. Similarly, guns do not kill, people do; hence we need better education of people. Do you agree? Why or why not?

6. How does Kennedy reply to the slogan, "When guns are outlawed, only out-laws will have guns"?

7. Does Kennedy respond directly, indirectly, or not at all to the argument that gun controls would be "cumbersome and inconvenient"? Explain.

8. Why does Kennedy refer to restrictive policies in other countries? Aren't Americans different by tradition, upbringing, and environment?

9. What does Kennedy find wrong with the fact that more and more people are buying guns to protect themselves from criminals? Do you agree or disagree? Discuss.

10. Is there a "gun mystique" in the United States (paragraph 35)? What does this phrase mean, and how do you feel about this theory?

REFLECTING

Point: Write a statement about the purpose of Kennedy's article, but do not try to incorporate each of the five arguments he refutes. Instead, summarize them in some way and show what the article contains besides these refutations. What single sentence states the thesis of his argument?

Organization: What is the function of the first four paragraphs? What other major divisions do you find in the article? Explain the general purpose of each and discuss the effectiveness of this organization. Write a syllogism showing the framework of Kennedy's argument. Discuss the short paragraphs, pointing out where some could have been combined and indicating why Kennedy perhaps did not combine them.

Support: What does Table 1 contribute to the argument? Does Kennedy let the facts speak for themselves, or does he discuss the information given in the table? Do you think that Kennedy's argument would have been aided by a direct reference to the assassination of his two brothers? Why do you suppose he did not refer to them? Describe the voice and tone used. What is the effect of the concession Kennedy makes at the beginning of paragraph 27? Are the references to "handgun roulette" and "the two-gun family" (paragraph 36) in keeping with the style of the article? Are they effective or not?

Synthesis: Do you or your family or friends have any firearms or handguns? What are your feelings about the article? Does your church take a position on handguns? Should it? Do you feel comfortable or more secure with a gun in the house? Explain. Polls show that more than 70 percent of Americans favor a registration and licensing law similar to the ones for automobiles. Why do you think that little has been done to comply with the wishes of the majority of Americans?

Evaluation: How thorough is Kennedy in treating his subject? Has he failed to consider all the objections, and has he adequately refuted the ones he does mention? Has he conveyed a sense of the seriousness of the problem? Does the need for a solution appear to be urgent? Do his proposed solutions seem to be practical? Would they raise other serious problems? Has he presented his argument clearly, logically, and effectively? Why or why not?

FROM READING TO WRITING

1. Write a letter to your minister or rabbi, pointing out that he or she should speak out and act in favor of gun control. Or, if you feel otherwise, urge this person not to take such a stand.

2. Write a reply to Kennedy's argument, opposing gun control. Use logical argument, rather than relying on emotional persuasion. Before writing, put your argument into syllogistic form and use it as the basis for your organization.

3. As of December 8, 1976, handgun sales were prohibited in San Francisco. Write a letter to your community newspaper, urging that your city council and state legislature either enact or reject a similar law.

IS IT TIME TO STOP LEARNING?
David S. Saxon

BIOGRAPHICAL SKETCH

David Stephen Saxon was born in St. Paul, Minnesota, in 1920. He earned B.S. and Ph.D. degrees in theoretical nuclear physics from Massachusetts Institute of Technology in 1944 and spent several years working in research laboratories. Since then, he has served as professor of physics, dean of physical sciences, and executive chancellor before being appointed president of the University of California at Los Angeles in 1975. He has written many scholarly articles, has received a Guggen-

FROM *Newsweek,* 28 June 1976, pp. 12–13. Copyright 1976 by Newsweek, Inc. All rights reserved. Reprinted by permission.

heim fellowship and a Fulbright lectureship, and has been a consultant for several electronic and aerospace companies.

PRE-READING

1. What possibilities does the title suggest?

2. How do the first two paragraphs restrict the meaning of the title?

3. What viewpoint does the final paragraph reveal?

¹ A strange new term has recently crept into our national vocabulary: overeducation. It is a term that would have confounded most Americans in every generation up to this Bicentennial year. For them, education was a social necessity to be provided, an individual good to be sought and an end to be sacrificed for. The only limits were the abilities and aspirations of students and the resources of the community.

² What has happened in society today that gives rise to talk of overeducation? Have we actually reached and even passed the socially useful and individually rewarding limits of learning in America? Or have we somehow mislaid our proper measure of the broader values of education in a democratic society?

³ Let's examine this curious new term, overeducation. Overeducation for *what?* For a full and satisfying life? For a lifetime of changing careers in a rapidly changing world? For active participation in the affairs of a modern democratic government?

⁴ No, the term generally means that a person has received more learning, or other learning, than is required for his or her first major job. It may be a perfectly valid description of a person's education in relation to that particular circumstance. But that circumstance, though important, is not the whole of life. And the tendency to measure the value of education against this single, limited yardstick is disastrously shortsighted for both the individual and society.

⁵ Throughout our history, American education has been built to other measures, and the results have had a tremendous influence on the nation's development. One such measure has been the need for leadership based on ability and talent rather than rank. The Pilgrims, after just sixteen years of colonizing the New World wilderness, established Harvard College, declaring that "one of the next things we longed for, and looked after was to advance learning and perpetuate it to posterity; dreading to leave an illiterate ministry to the churches, when our present ministers shall lie in the dust." And Thomas Jefferson called for the education of "youth of talent" without regard for their social or economic status as "the keystone of the arch of our government."

⁶ Another measure has been the importance of universal education to a democratic society. Benjamin Franklin wrote that "nothing is of more impor-

tance for the public weal, than to firm and train up youth in wisdom and virtue. Wise and good men are, in my opinion, the strength of a state; much more so than riches and arms." A third measure has been the advantage of merging the practical and liberal arts. When Abraham Lincoln signed the land-grant college legislation of 1862, he set America on its course toward a distinctive model of higher education, not for the few but for the many, not as a cloister but as the active partner of agriculture and industry and all the other segments of a developing society.

⁷ And when Johns Hopkins University in 1876 joined undergraduate education with the most advanced graduate instruction and research, American education was extending its reach toward the farthest frontiers of scientific and scholarly discovery.

⁸ Building to these measures has produced in America an educational system that is in many ways unparalleled in history, and this is a healthy perspective from which to view our present shortcomings and the problems that lie ahead.

⁹ Certainly education in the United States is unmatched in its accessibility to the highest levels for the broadest cross-section of the citizenry, though we have much farther to go in this respect. Our total educational structure is unequaled in its diversity—public and private institutions, religious and secular, local and statewide—and this rich diversity is our protection against control or conformity in the realm of ideas. And nowhere else has there been a more rapid transfer of scholarly discoveries through basic research to practical application.

¹⁰ But have we now, finally, reached the useful limits of our educational resources for many of our citizens? Can we now say to some of them, "You won't need any more formal learning for *your* role in society"? And to *which* Americans shall we say that their future working careers or their cultural horizons or their prospects for civic or political leadership don't seem to warrant the cost of a broad education beyond their immediate occupational needs?

¹¹ I am painfully aware that academic leaders have themselves too often resorted to strictly economic appeals for support because these seemed easier to explain and justify than the less tangible purposes of learning. We have too often promised more than we could deliver on investments in research, and so have invited disappointed expectations and some disillusion with what education can offer in exchange for its considerable cost. But neither education nor society in general will benefit from a continuing rebuff for these sins.

¹² To the extent that the level of education and society's ability to put it to use are out of balance, then what a peculiarly negative solution—what a tragic waste of human potential—to limit education and learning. Wouldn't it make far better sense to concentrate on how to use the full capacity of all of our citizens?

¹³ We need that capacity now. I think we are more in need of wisdom today than at most earlier stages of our history. A broad liberal education is

not the only ingredient of wisdom, but it is an essential one. We need all the knowledge we can muster to meet our technological and scientific problems. We need all the accumulated experience and understanding of humanity we can absorb to meet our social problems. And I believe we can ill afford the risk of foreclosing the maximum cultivation of that knowledge and understanding simply because it seems not to be required for immediate vocational purposes.

[14] America's vision for 200 years has been longer than that. Overeducation is an idea whose time must never come.

ANALYTICAL READING

1. Judging from paragraphs 3 and 4, what do you think Saxon means by *education*? How does this differ from what he believes most people mean by the term?

2. Does Saxon refer to three or to four historical measures of education? Explain each. What purpose does this historical survey serve?

3. In what ways does Saxon state American education is unique? Discuss.

4. Does Saxon answer the questions in paragraph 10? What purpose do they serve?

5. Why is Saxon critical of educational leaders?

6. What solution does Saxon propose to the so-called problem of overeducation?

7. Why does Saxon stress the role of the liberal arts?

REFLECTING

Point: What problem is Saxon addressing in his essay? What do you think is his purpose in writing the essay? In a sentence or two, write a statement that expresses his main ideas about overeducation.

Organization: What effect is created by starting with a definition? How is this definition linked to the section about the measures of education? What effect is created by not dividing paragraph 6 into two paragraphs? Where might it have been divided? What is the function of paragraph 8? Relate the purpose of each of the three sections to the thesis.

Support: How does Saxon define his use of the term *education?* What role does the testimony of authorities play in the essay? Do you find adequate support for his statement that we need wisdom more today than in earlier periods (see paragraph 13)? What audience is Saxon addressing, and to what extent does this intended audience influence the nature of and the need for support?

Synthesis: Are you familiar with the term *overeducation?* How have you heard it used? How did you resolve this problem in deciding to attend college? To what extent does Saxon deal with the purpose of a college education? Explain. Do you agree with his views?

Evaluation: How satisfactorily does Saxon answer those who believe overeducation is a problem? To what extent would his response placate a recent graduate in history, psychology, or journalism who couldn't find a job? Are any parts of Saxon's essay unnecessary, unclear, or unconvincing? Has he developed his ideas sufficiently? Has he merely stated the obvious, or has he written an essay that many people might profit from reading? Is his voice appropriate and helpful to his argument? Discuss.

FROM READING TO WRITING

1. Write an argument addressed to high school seniors about why they should or should not attend college.

2. Agree or disagree with Saxon's statement about the great need for wisdom today.

3. Write an argument for or against one of the points about American education in paragraph 9.

4. Assume that your parents are uncertain about financing your college education. Write a letter trying to make them realize the importance of your going to college. Use some of Saxon's ideas and some of your own.

KILL THE METRIC!
Lisa Shillinger

BIOGRAPHICAL SKETCH

Lisa Shillinger graduated from the University of Illinois School of Journalism in 1965. Since then, she has been a technical/promotional writer and graphic designer for several colleges and universities. She currently works for Purdue University's School of Engineering. Her publications include a book she co-wrote, Men and Ideas in Engineering, *and an article that appeared in* Journalism Quarterly, *"British and American Press Coverage of the Bolshevik Revolution."*

PRE-READING

1. What information can you glean from the title? What bias?

2. What argument does Shillinger dispose of in the first paragraph that might be used by some people in writing about the adoption of the metric system in the United States?

3. What viewpoint does the writer reveal in the final paragraph that suggests the aspect she is most concerned with?

[1] Miss Horsefield introduced me to the metric system in her third-grade class at DuBois School in Springfield, Ill., 25 years ago. I didn't find it awesome

or difficult to understand then, and I don't now. The interrelationship of distance, volume and weight is impressive. What a pity the United States didn't adopt it 100 years ago when we joined in the signing of the International Metric Convention.

[2] Now, however, I wonder with growing horror what lunacy propels us to go metric at this late date. Thanks to the Metric Conversion Act of 1975, . . . the metric wave is scheduled to engulf this country over the next ten years.

[3] Whereas conversion to the metric system (or International System of Units) was accomplished by Napoleonic decree in France and accompanied political upheavals in the Soviet Union, China and Latin America, the United States is relying on a seventeen-member Board of Metrics and public indifference to usher in the conversion.

[4] It's "The Emperor's New Clothes" and Prohibition all over again. To oppose the metric system in the United States is to oppose progress, we are told. As soon as we learn our conversion factors and overcome our reactionary fears we shall rise up and join the great brotherhood of metric man.

[5] Well, I disagree. Conversion to the metric system in this country is simply an exorbitantly expensive experiment in inconvenience. The primary victim, as usual, will be the American consumer.

[6] Point one: let us accept the inherent superiority of the ISU over the English system. It is more logical and easier to learn. For Europe, which gave birth to it during the French Revolution and matured with it, the metric system has served very well. For developing nations emerging from tribal cultures, why not? But for the United States, the most industrialized and standardized nation in the world, to convert to another system of measure is sheer madness.

[7] Point two: the American public is under the delusion that the effects of conversion will primarily hit industry and science. Media reports on conversion costs and schedules are almost exclusively concerned with heavy industry. The average American has been led to believe the primary effect upon his own life will be the obsolescence of a few old saws and literary expressions ("A miss is as good as 1.6 kilometers")—hoo-hah. What is being overlooked is the devastating effect the conversion to metrics will have on the everyday life and pocketbook of the American consumer.

[8] Point three: examples abound. We are going to have to invest in gram scales and measures to weigh out our flour, sugar, rice, cocoa, etc. That's merely an inconvenient adjustment housewives will have to make. But what about the millions of dollars of cookbooks now on the market and in our homes, not to mention those favorite old recipes? They'll soon be obsolete. If your recipe calls for the traditional cup of whipping cream you will have to settle for a .2- or .3-liter size, since it would be a bit ridiculous to come up with a .23656-liter carton to equal our current 1-cup carton. That's not real efficient. That, of course, goes for all those convenient packages that now happen to match what a recipe calls for—like the familiar 3-ounce package of cream cheese and the fifth of wine that goes into your holiday punch. Thousands of recipes are coordinated with food items that have been commercially pack-

aged in quarts, pints, ounces and pounds in the United States since the Year One. And, by the way, who do you think is going to absorb the cost of repackaging? It isn't General Foods.

⁹ What if you want to reframe that fine old family portrait into a new nonexistent 9- by 12-inch frame? Or perhaps you'll want to hang a mirror on the wall. Finding the studs is no big problem since studs in American homes built in the last 50 years are standardized at 16 inches apart. That means you mark off the distance in handy increments of 40.64 centimeters. Of course in the new post-metric homes we'll probably round that off to 40 centimeters and in a few years that could result in a lot of excitement when you try to locate your studs to install new wiring, insulation or whatever.

¹⁰ Down on the farm, the south 40 (acres) becomes the south 16.1874 (hectares). It'll be up to the farmer to figure out how many kilos of fertilizer to buy per hectare. And what about all the land and property titles to be converted?

¹¹ And in the business world, we may say goodbye to the 8½- by 11-inch paper that fits your file folders and lines up with all those existing sheets. The post office can scrap all its ounce-calibrated scales and postal meters. And since the metric system will hit our printing industries with a real wallop, you may even have a slightly larger- or smaller-size *National Geographic* to file away with all those your grandfather saved for you.

¹² Finally, a nice little touch for travelers. Europeans vacationing in this country frequently remark on the convenience of the English system, which allows one to figure a town 45 miles away is just about 45 minutes away. I won't even attempt to convert that.

¹³ The examples of the idiocy of conversion to the metric system are infinite and all-pervasive. They permeate every phase of our lives, creating costly obsolescence in everything from shot glasses to storm doors—items that we never considered vulnerable before.

¹⁴ Let the scientists and industrialists continue to use whatever system they choose to carry out their international dealings. For the rest of us, let's stick with our English system. Conversion is exorbitantly expensive, inconvenient and pointless. What's more, like Prohibition, it won't work.

¹⁵ Where were *we* when they pushed this one through? Who's making the bucks on this one? Where is the consumer uproar? Where are our crusaders now that we need them? I say, *"Vive la différence!"*

ANALYTICAL READING

1. Explain the references to "The Emperor's New Clothes" and Prohibition in paragraph 4.

2. Does Shillinger cite three points against the metric system? What are they? Discuss whether in actuality they comprise two or three.

3. What does Shillinger have to say about the convenience of the metric system for Europeans visiting this country? Do you accept her statement?

4. What basic assumption probably motivates her to ask "Who's making the bucks on this one?" (paragraph 15)?

5. Explain the last sentence. Do you have to know French to understand it?

REFLECTING

Point: The author's main idea is quite obvious. In what sentence is it best expressed? What do you think the purpose of the essay is?

Organization: The essay is divided into four sections. Are these divisions logical, or do they simply break up the essay into convenient sections? Does Shillinger consider or imply arguments favoring conversion to the metric system? If so, where?

Support: Is any evidence presented to support the "sheer madness" statement at the end of paragraph 6 or the statement in paragraph 14 that, like Prohibition, conversion to metric won't work? Is it logically acceptable? Discuss the voice and tone of the writer. Does it contribute to or detract from the effectiveness of her argument?

Synthesis: What are your own feelings about conversion to the metric system? Do you know the arguments in its favor? Do you think that you could adapt to it? What do you think of Shillinger's examples? Which ones would give you the most trouble? Do you think her examples of the disadvantages are petty in comparison with the advantages?

Evaluation: How clear, complete, and logical is the argument? Is the support adequate to convince someone who knows little about the metric controversy? Are the voice and tone appropriate? Is the writing lively, interesting, forceful?

FROM READING TO WRITING

1. Write an argument replying to the one advanced in this essay. Combine logical and emotional persuasive techniques.

2. Write an argument against some campus, community, national, or international proposal for change.

3. Write a letter to your high school principal or to a department head or dean at your college, urging that some policy course, program, or behavior code be abolished.

LOVE IS A FALLACY
Max Shulman

BIOGRAPHICAL SKETCH

Max Shulman was born in St. Paul, Minnesota, in 1919, and graduated from the University of Minnesota. He has written fiction, nonfiction, plays, a television series, and film scripts. Among his eight novels are Barefoot Boy with Cheek *and* Rally 'Round the Flag, Boys. *The former was adapted to the stage and was a success on Broadway, as were two other plays,* The Tender Trap *and* How Now, Dow Jones. *Also popular was his television series,* The Many Loves of Dobie Gillis. *The best of Shulman's essays are collected in two anthologies,* Guided Tour of Campus Humor *and* Large Economy Size.

PRE-READING

1. What tone does the writer set in the opening paragraph? Does it give any hint of the subject?

2. From the title and the closing paragraphs, what do you think the subject of the paper is?

3. On the basis of the biographical sketch, how would you expect Shulman to handle any subject?

¹ Cool was I and logical. Keen, calculating, perspicacious, acute and astute—I was all of these. My brain was as powerful as a dynamo, as precise as a chemist's scales, as penetrating as a scalpel. And—think of it!—I was only eighteen.

² It is not often that one so young has such a giant intellect. Take, for example, Petey Burch, my roommate at the University of Minnesota. Same age, same background, but dumb as an ox. A nice enough fellow, you understand, but nothing upstairs. Emotional type. Unstable. Impressionable. Worst of all, a faddist. Fads, I submit, are the very negation of reason. To be swept up in every new craze that comes along, to surrender yourself to idiocy just because everybody else is doing it—this, to me, is the acme of mindlessness. Not, however, to Petey.

³ One afternoon I found Petey lying on his bed with an expression of such distress on his face that I immediately diagnosed appendicitis. "Don't move," I said. "Don't take a laxative. I'll get a doctor."

⁴ "Raccoon," he mumbled thickly.

⁵ "Raccoon?" I said, pausing in my flight.

⁶ "I want a raccoon coat," he wailed.

⁷ I perceived that his trouble was not physical, but mental. "Why do you want a raccoon coat?"

FROM *The Many Loves of Dobie Gillis* (Garden City, N.Y.: Doubleday and Company, 1953). Copyright Max Shulman, 1951. Reprinted by permission of Harold Matson Co., Inc.

[8] "I should have known it," he cried, pounding his temples. "I should have known they'd come back when the Charleston came back. Like a fool I spent all my money for textbooks, and now I can't get a raccoon coat."

[9] "Can you mean," I said incredulously, "that people are actually wearing raccoon coats again?"

[10] "All the Big Men on Campus are wearing them. Where've you been?"

[11] "In the library," I said, naming a place not frequented by Big Men on Campus.

[12] He leaped from the bed and paced the room. "I've got to have a raccoon coat," he said passionately. "I've got to!"

[13] "Petey, why? Look at it rationally. Raccoon coats are unsanitary. They shed. They smell bad. They weigh too much. They're unsightly. They—"

[14] "You don't understand," he interrupted impatiently. "It's the thing to do. Don't you want to be in the swim?"

[15] "No," I said truthfully.

[16] "Well, I do," he declared. "I'd give anything for a raccoon coat. Anything!"

[17] My brain, that precision instrument, slipped into high gear. "Anything?" I asked, looking at him narrowly.

[18] "Anything," he affirmed in ringing tones.

[19] I stroked my chin thoughtfully. It so happened that I knew where to get my hands on a raccoon coat. My father had had one in his undergraduate days; it lay now in a trunk in the attic back home. It also happened that Petey had something I wanted. He didn't *have* it exactly, but at least he had first rights on it. I refer to his girl, Polly Espy.

[20] I had long coveted Polly Espy. Let me emphasize that my desire for this young woman was not emotional in nature. She was, to be sure, a girl who excited the emotions, but I was not one to let my heart rule my head. I wanted Polly for a shrewdly calculated, entirely cerebral reason.

[21] I was a freshman in law school. In a few years I would be out in practice. I was well aware of the importance of the right kind of wife in furthering a lawyer's career. The successful lawyers I had observed were, almost without exception, married to beautiful, gracious, intelligent women. With one omission, Polly fitted these specifications perfectly.

[22] Beautiful she was. She was not yet of pin-up proportions, but I felt sure that time would supply the lack. She already had the makings.

[23] Gracious she was. By gracious I mean full of graces. She had an erectness of carriage, an ease of bearing, a poise that clearly indicated the best of breeding. At table her manners were exquisite. I had seen her at the Kozy Kampus Korner eating the specialty of the house—a sandwich that contained scraps of pot roast, gravy, chopped nuts, and a dipper of sauerkraut—without even getting her fingers moist.

[24] Intelligent she was not. In fact, she veered in the opposite direction. But I believed that under my guidance she would smarten up. At any rate, it was

worth a try. It is, after all, easier to make a beautiful dumb girl smart than to make an ugly smart girl beautiful.

25 "Petey," I said, "are you in love with Polly Espy?"

26 "I think she's a keen kid," he replied, "but I don't know if you'd call it love. Why?"

27 "Do you," I asked, "have any kind of formal arrangement with her? I mean are you going steady or anything like that?"

28 "No. We see each other quite a bit, but we both have other dates. Why?"

29 "Is there," I asked, "any other man for whom she has a particular fondness?"

30 "Not that I know of. Why?"

31 I nodded with satisfaction. "In other words, if you were out of the picture, the field would be open. Is that right?"

32 "I guess so. What are you getting at?"

33 "Nothing, nothing," I said innocently, and took my suitcase out of the closet.

34 "Where are you going?" asked Petey.

35 "Home for the weekend." I threw a few things into the bag.

36 "Listen," he said, clutching my arm eagerly, "while you're home, you couldn't get some money from your old man, could you, and lend it to me so I can buy a raccoon coat?"

37 "I may do better than that," I said with a mysterious wink and closed my bag and left.

38 "Look," I said to Petey when I got back Monday morning. I threw open the suitcase and revealed the huge, hairy, gamy object that my father had worn in his Stutz Bearcat in 1925.

39 "Holy Toledo!" said Petey reverently. He plunged his hands into the raccoon coat and then his face. "Holy Toledo!" he repeated fifteen or twenty times.

40 "Would you like it?" I asked.

41 "Oh yes!" he cried, clutching the greasy pelt to him. Then a canny look came into his eyes. "What do you want for it?"

42 "Your girl," I said, mincing no words.

43 "Polly?" he said in a horrified whisper. "You want Polly?"

44 "That's right."

45 He flung the coat from him. "Never," he said stoutly.

46 I shrugged. "Okay. If you don't want to be in the swim, I guess it's your business."

47 I sat down in a chair and pretended to read a book, but out of the corner of my eye I kept watching Petey. He was a torn man. First he looked at the coat with the expression of a waif at a bakery window. Then he turned away and set his jaw resolutely. Then he looked back at the coat, with even more longing in his face. Then he turned away, but with not so much resolu-

tion this time. Back and forth his head swiveled, desire waxing, resolution waning. Finally he didn't turn away at all; he just stood and stared with mad lust at the coat.

⁴⁸ "It isn't as though I was in love with Polly," he said thickly. "Or going steady or anything like that."

⁴⁹ "That's right," I murmured.

⁵⁰ "What's Polly to me, or me to Polly?"

⁵¹ "Not a thing," said I.

⁵² "It's just been a casual kick—just a few laughs, that's all."

⁵³ "Try on the coat," said I.

⁵⁴ He complied. The coat bunched high over his ears and dropped all the way down to his shoe tops. He looked like a mound of dead raccoons. "Fits fine," he said happily.

⁵⁵ I rose from my chair. "Is it a deal?" I asked, extending my hand.

⁵⁶ He swallowed. "It's a deal," he said and shook my hand.

⁵⁷ I had my first date with Polly the following evening. This was in the nature of a survey; I wanted to find out just how much work I had to do to get her mind up to the standard I required. I took her first to dinner. "Gee, that was a delish dinner," she said as we left the restaurant. Then I took her to a movie. "Gee, that was a marvy movie," she said as we left the theater. And then I took her home. "Gee, I had a sensaysh time," she said as she bade me good night.

⁵⁸ I went back to my room with a heavy heart. I had gravely underestimated the size of my task. This girl's lack of information was terrifying. Nor would it be enough merely to supply her with information. First she had to be taught to *think*. This loomed as a project of no small dimensions, and at first I was tempted to give her back to Petey. But then I got to thinking about her abundant physical charms and about the way she entered a room and the way she handled a knife and fork, and I decided to make an effort.

⁵⁹ I went about it, as in all things, systematically. I gave her a course in logic. It happened that I, as a law student, was taking a course in logic myself, so I had all the facts at my finger tips. "Polly," I said to her when I picked her up on our next date, "tonight we are going over to the Knoll and talk."

⁶⁰ "Oo, terrif," she replied. One thing I will say for this girl: you would go far to find another so agreeable.

⁶¹ We went to the Knoll, the campus trysting place, and we sat down under an old oak, and she looked at me expectantly. "What are we going to talk about?" she asked.

⁶² "Logic."

⁶³ She thought this over for a minute and decided she liked it. "Magnif," she said.

⁶⁴ "Logic," I said, clearing my throat, "is the science of thinking. Before we can think correctly, we must first learn to recognize the common fallacies of logic. These we will take up tonight."

⁶⁵ "Wow-dow!" she cried, clapping her hands delightedly.

⁶⁶ I winced, but went bravely on. "First let us examine the fallacy called Dicto Simpliciter."

⁶⁷ "By all means," she urged, batting her lashes eagerly.

⁶⁸ "Dicto Simplicter means an argument based on an unqualified generalization. For example: Exercise is good. Therefore everybody should exercise."

⁶⁹ "I agree," said Polly earnestly. "I mean exercise is wonderful. I mean it builds the body and everything."

⁷⁰ "Polly," I said gently, "the argument is a fallacy. *Exercise is good* is an unqualified generalization. For instance, if you have heart disease, exercise is bad, not good. Many people are ordered by their doctors *not* to exercise. You must *qualify* the generalization. You must say exercise is *usually* good, or exercise is good *for most people*. Otherwise you have committed a Dicto Simpliciter. Do you see?"

⁷¹ "No," she confessed. "But this is marvy. Do more! Do more!"

⁷² "It will be better if you stop tugging at my sleeve," I told her, and when she desisted, I continued. "Next we take up a fallacy called Hasty Generalization. Listen carefully: You can't speak French. I can't speak French. Petey Burch can't speak French. I must therefore conclude that nobody at the University of Minnesota can speak French."

⁷³ "Really?" said Polly, amazed. *"Nobody?"*

⁷⁴ I hid my exasperation. "Polly, it's a fallacy. The generalization is reached too hastily. There are too few instances to support such a conclusion."

⁷⁵ "Know any more fallacies?" she asked breathlessly. "This is more fun than dancing even."

⁷⁶ I fought off a wave of despair. I was getting nowhere with this girl, absolutely nowhere. Still, I am nothing if not persistent. I continued. "Next comes Post Hoc. Listen to this: Let's not take Bill on our picnic. Every time we take him out with us, it rains."

⁷⁷ "I know somebody just like that," she exclaimed. "A girl back home— Eula Becker, her name is. It never fails. Every single time we take her on a picnic—"

⁷⁸ "Polly," I said sharply, "it's a fallacy. Eula Becker doesn't *cause* the rain. She had no connection with the rain. You are guilty of Post Hoc if you blame Eula Becker."

⁷⁹ "I'll never do it again," she promised contritely. "Are you mad at me?"

⁸⁰ I sighed deeply. "No, Polly, I'm not mad."

⁸¹ "Then tell me some more fallacies."

⁸² "All right. Let's try Contradictory Premises."

⁸³ "Yes, let's," she chirped, blinking her eyes happily.

⁸⁴ I frowned, but plunged ahead. "Here's an example of Contradictory Premises: If God can do anything, can He make a stone so heavy that He won't be able to lift it?"

⁸⁵ "Of course," she replied promptly.

⁸⁶ "But if He can do anything. He can lift the stone," I pointed out.

[87] "Yeah," she said thoughtfully. "Well, then I guess He can't make the stone."

[88] "But He can do anything," I reminded her.

[89] She scratched her pretty, empty head. "I'm all confused," she admitted.

[90] "Of course you are. Because when the premises of an argument contradict each other, there can be no argument. If there is an irresistible force, there can be no immovable object. If there is an immovable object, there can be no irresistible force. Get it?"

[91] "Tell me some more of this keen stuff," she said eagerly.

[92] I consulted my watch. "I think we'd better call it a night. I'll take you home now, and you go over all the things you've learned. We'll have another session tomorrow night."

[93] I deposited her at the girls' dormitory, where she assured me that she had had a perfectly terrif evening, and I went glumly home to my room. Petey lay snoring in his bed, the raccoon coat huddled like a great hairy beast at his feet. For a moment I considered waking him and telling him that he could have his girl back. It seemed clear that my project was doomed to failure. The girl simply had a logic-proof head.

[94] But then I reconsidered. I had wasted one evening; I might as well waste another. Who knew? Maybe somewhere in the extinct crater of her mind, a few embers still smoldered. Maybe somehow I could fan them into flame. Admittedly it was not a prospect fraught with hope, but I decided to give it one more try.

[95] Seated under the oak the next evening I said, "Our first fallacy tonight is called Ad Misericordiam."

[96] She quivered with delight.

[97] "Listen closely," I said. "A man applies for a job. When the boss asks him what his qualifications are, he replies that he has a wife and six children at home, the wife is a helpless cripple, the children have nothing to eat, no clothes to wear, no shoes on their feet, there are no beds in the house, no coal in the cellar, and winter is coming."

[98] A tear rolled down each of Polly's pink cheeks. "Oh, this is awful, awful," she sobbed.

[99] "Yes, it's awful," I agreed, "but it's no argument. The man never answered the boss's question about his qualifications. Instead he appealed to the boss's sympathy. He committed the fallacy of Ad Misericordiam. Do you understand?"

[100] "Have you got a handkerchief?" she blubbered.

[101] I handed her a handkerchief and tried to keep from screaming while she wiped her eyes. "Next," I said in a carefully controlled tone, "we will discuss False Analogy. Here is an example: Students should be allowed to look at their textbooks during examinations. After all, surgeons have X–rays to guide them during an operation, lawyers have briefs to guide them during a trial, carpenters have blueprints to guide them when they are building a

house. Why, then, shouldn't students be allowed to look at their textbooks during an examination?"

[102] "There now," she said enthusiastically, "is the most marvy idea I've heard in years."

[103] "Polly," I said testily, "the argument is all wrong. Doctors, lawyers, and carpenters aren't taking a test to see how much they have learned, but students are. The situations are altogether different, and you can't make an analogy between them."

[104] "I still think it's a good idea," said Polly.

[105] "Nuts," I muttered. Doggedly I pressed on. "Next we'll try Hypothesis Contrary to Fact."

[106] "Sounds yummy," was Polly's reaction.

[107] "Listen: If Madame Curie had not happened to leave a photographic plate in a drawer with a chunk of pitchblende, the world today would not know about radium."

[108] "True, true," said Polly, nodding her head. "Did you see the movie? Oh, it just knocked me out. That Walter Pidgeon is so dreamy. I mean he fractures me."

[109] "If you can forget Mr. Pidgeon for a moment," I said coldly, "I would like to point out that the statement is a fallacy. Maybe Madame Curie would have discovered radium at some later date. Maybe somebody else would have discovered it. Maybe any number of things would have happened. You can't start with a hypothesis that is not true and then draw any supportable conclusions from it."

[110] "They ought to put Walter Pidgeon in more pictures," said Polly. "I hardly ever see him any more."

[111] One more chance, I decided. But just one more. There is a limit to what flesh and blood can bear. "The next fallacy is called Poisoning the Well."

[112] "How cute!" she gurgled.

[113] "Two men are having a debate. The first one gets up and says, 'My opponent is a notorious liar. You can't believe a word that he is going to say.' . . . Now, Polly, think. Think hard. What's wrong?"

[114] I watched her closely as she knit her creamy brow in concentration. Suddenly a glimmer of intelligence—the first I had seen—came into her eyes. "It's not fair," she said with indignation. "It's not a bit fair. What chance has the second man got if the first man calls him a liar before he even begins talking?"

[115] "Right!" I cried exultantly. "One hundred percent right. It's not fair. The first man has *poisoned the well* before anybody could drink from it. He has hamstrung his opponent before he could even start. . . . Polly, I'm proud of you."

[116] "Pshaw," she murmured, blushing with pleasure.

[117] "You see, my dear, these things aren't so hard. All you have to do is concentrate. Think—examine—evaluate. Come now, let's review everything we have learned."

[118] "Fire away," she said with an airy wave of her hand.

[119] Heartened by the knowledge that Polly was not altogether a cretin, I began a long, patient review of all I had told her. Over and over and over again I cited instances, pointed out flaws, kept hammering away without let-up. It was like digging a tunnel. At first everything was work, sweat, and darkness. I had no idea when I would reach the light, or even *if* I would. But I persisted. I pounded and clawed and scraped, and finally I was rewarded. I saw a chink of light. And then the chink got bigger and the sun came pouring in and all was bright.

[120] Five grueling nights this took, but it was worth it. I had made a logician out of Polly; I had taught her to think. My job was done. She was worthy of me at last. She was a fit wife for me, a proper hostess for my many mansions, a suitable mother for my well-heeled children.

[121] It must not be thought that I was without love for this girl. Quite the contrary. Just as Pygmalion loved the perfect woman he had fashioned, so I loved mine. I determined to acquaint her with my feelings at our very next meeting. The time had come to change our relationship from academic to romantic.

[122] "Polly," I said when next we sat beneath our oak, "tonight we will not discuss fallacies."

[123] "Aw, gee," she said, disappointed.

[124] "My dear," I said, favoring her with a smile, "we have now spent five evenings together. We have gotten along splendidly. It is clear that we are well matched."

[125] "Hasty Generalization," said Polly brightly.

[126] "I beg your pardon," said I.

[127] "Hasty Generalization," she repeated. "How can you say that we are well matched on the basis of only five dates?"

[128] I chuckled with amusement. The dear child had learned her lessons well. "My dear," I said, patting her hand in a tolerant manner, "five dates is plenty. After all, you don't have to eat a whole cake to know that it's good."

[129] "False Analogy," said Polly promptly. "I'm not a cake. I'm a girl."

[130] I chuckled with somewhat less amusement. The dear child had learned her lessons perhaps too well. I decided to change tactics. Obviously the best approach was a simple, strong, direct declaration of love. I paused for a moment while my massive brain chose the proper words. Then I began:

[131] "Polly, I love you. You are the whole world to me, and the moon and the stars and the constellations of outer space. Please, my darling, say that you will go steady with me, for if you will not, life will be meaningless. I will languish. I will refuse my meals. I will wander the face of the earth, a shambling, hollow-eyed hulk."

[132] There, I thought, folding my arms, that ought to do it.

[133] "Ad Misericordiam," said Polly.

[134] I ground my teeth. I was not Pygmalion; I was Frankenstein, and my monster had me by the throat. Frantically I fought back the tide of panic surging through me. At all costs I had to keep cool.

135 "Well, Polly," I said, forcing a smile, "you certainly have learned your fallacies."

136 "You're darn right," she said with a vigorous nod.

137 "And who taught them to you, Polly?"

138 "You did."

139 "That's right. So you do owe me something, don't you, my dear? If I hadn't come along you never would have learned about fallacies."

140 "Hypothesis Contrary to Fact," she said instantly.

141 I dashed perspiration from my brow. "Polly," I croaked, "you mustn't take all these things so literally. I mean this is just classroom stuff. You know that the things you learn in school don't have anything to do with life."

142 "Dicto Simpliciter," she said, wagging her finger at me playfully.

143 That did it. I leaped to my feet, bellowing like a bull. "Will you or will you not go steady with me?"

144 "I will not," she replied.

145 "Why not?" I demanded.

146 "Because this afternoon I promised Petey Burch that I would go steady with him."

147 I reeled back, overcome with the infamy of it. After he promised, after he made a deal, after he shook my hand! "The rat!" I shrieked, kicking up great chunks of turf. "You can't go with him, Polly. He's a liar. He's a cheat. He's a rat."

148 "Poisoning the Well," said Polly, "and stop shouting. I think shouting must be a fallacy too."

149 With an immense effort of will, I modulated my voice. "All right," I said. "You're a logician. Let's look at this thing logically. How could you choose Petey Burch over me? Look at me—a brilliant student, a tremendous intellectual, a man with an assured future. Look at Petey—a knothead, a jitterburg, a guy who'll never know where his next meal is coming from. Can you give me one logical reason why you should go steady with Petey Burch?"

150 "I certainly can," declared Polly. "He's got a raccoon coat."

ANALYTICAL READING

1. How does Shulman establish the rationality of the narrator—his concern with logic and reason?

2. What logical fallacies does Shulman present? How does he make them interesting? Define each briefly and cite the paragraphs in which they are mentioned. (Your instructor may want to substitute other names for them.)

3. How much character development is in the article? How does this contribute to Shulman's argument?

4. How does Shulman use irony to develop humor in relation to the fur coat, to Polly Espy and logic, and to the narrator's logic?

5. Do you think the article reveals the weakness of logic or of human nature? Discuss.

6.   How do the events of the story change the reader's attitudes toward the narra-
     tor portrayed in the opening paragraphs?

REFLECTING

Point: If Shulman had a stated proposition–thesis, what would it be?

Organization: What advantage is gained by the narrative, chronological order? Is
     there another organizational scheme buried within the narrative—prob-
     lem–solution, argument? Try to outline the article in two ways.

Support: How are the fallacies themselves used to support Shulman's contention
     about logic and human behavior? What part does language play, especially
     metaphor and slang?

Synthesis: Can you think of other situations in which humans seem unable to act
     logically and rationally? Could the thesis of Shulman's article be applied to any
     of the subjects discussed in this section of the book—for example, religion,
     gun control, grades, abortion? Explain.

Evaluation: How effective do you think the essay is? Does Shulman succeed in
     making a dull subject interesting? Is Shulman himself guilty of a fallacy—
     stereotyping? Discuss.

FROM READING TO WRITING

1.   Using the proposition "People cannot live by logic alone," write a paper that
     illustrates how human behavior reflects logical fallacies. For example, you
     might write a narrative about someone you know who believes staunchly in
     superstitions, or someone who is blind to the fallacious reasoning in advertis-
     ing. Try to establish a satirical tone.

2.   Write an argument paper exposing and condemning the use of one of the
     article's logical fallacies in the advertising of a particular product.

3.   Write an argument for your college newspaper in favor of or against some
     current fad.

Assessment of Reading and Writing Skills: Persuasive Writing

Step 1

Read the essay that follows with the aim of understanding and recalling the important ideas. When you finish, note how long it took you to read the selection. Then close your book and write a summary of the important information without referring again to the essay. Include a discussion of the persuasive techniques the writer uses. You will be allowed 7 to 10 minutes to write; your instructor will establish the limit and tell you when the time is up.

NO RETREAT ON ABORTION
John D. Rockefeller III

It is ironic that in this Bicentennial year there is a strong effort across the nation to turn the clock back on an important social issue. Ever since the Supreme Court legalized abortion in January 1973, anti-abortion forces have been organizing to overturn the decision. They have injected the issue into the campaigns of 1976, including the appearance of a Presidential candidate who ran on the single issue of opposition to abortion.

There have been efforts within the Congress to initiate a constitutional amendment prohibiting abortion. There is litigation being pressed in state courts and appeals to the Supreme Court. Last November the National Conference of Catholic Bishops issued a "Pastoral Plan for Pro-Life Activities" calling for a wide-ranging anti-abortion effort in every Congressional district, including working to defeat any congressman who supports the Supreme Court decision.

Those who oppose abortion have won the battle of the slogans by adopting "Right to Life" as theirs. And, by concentrating on the single issue of the fetus, they have found abortion an easy issue to sensationalize. Thus, they have tended to win the publicity battle, too.

In contrast, those who support legalized abortion—and opinion polls demonstrate them to be a majority—have been comparatively quiet. After all, they won their case in the Supreme Court decision. Legalized abortion is the law of the land. It is also in the mainstream of world opinion. The number of countries where abortion has been broadly legalized has increased steadily, today covering 60 percent of the world population.

In this situation, there is a natural tendency to relax, to assume that the matter is settled and that the anti-abortion clamor will eventually die down. But it is conceivable that the United States could become the first democratic nation to turn the clock back by yielding to the pressure and reversing the Supreme Court decision. In my judgment, that would be a tragic mistake.

The least that those who support legalized abortion should do is try to clarify the issue and put it in perspective. The most powerful arguments about abortion are in the field of religious and moral principles—and this is where the opposing views clash head-on. Abortion is against the moral principles defended by the Roman Catholic Church, and some non-Catholics share this viewpoint. But abortion is *not* against the principles of most other religious groups. Those opposed to abortion seek to ban it for everyone in society. Their position is thus coercive in that it would restrict the religious freedom of others and their right to make a free moral choice. In contrast, the legalized abortion viewpoint is non-coercive. No one would think of forcing anyone to undergo an abortion or forcing doctors to perform the procedure when it violates their consciences. Where abortion is legal, everyone is free to live by her or his religious and moral principles.

There are also strong social reasons why abortion should remain legalized. In a woman's decision to have an abortion, there are three key considerations—the fetus, the woman herself, and the future of the unwanted child. Abortion opponents make an emotional appeal based on the first consideration alone. But there is steadily growing understanding and acceptance of a woman's fundamental right to control what happens to her body and to her future. In the privacy of her own mind, and with whatever counseling she seeks, she has the right to make her decision, and no one is better qualified. If she is denied that right, the result may well be an unwanted child, with all the attendant possibilities of abuse and neglect.

Finally, as a practical matter, legalization of abortion is a much more sound and humane social policy than prohibition. Banning abortions does not eliminate them; it never has and it never will. It merely forces women to go the dangerous route of illegal or self-induced abortions. Even worse, it makes abortion a "rich–poor" issue. At a high price, a well-to-do woman can always find a safe abortion. But, unable to pay the price, the poor woman all too often finds herself in incompetent hands.

Experience in three Catholic countries of Latin America that I visited provides dramatic evidence of a high incidence of abortion even when it is against the law. Estimates are that there is one abortion for every two live births in Colombia, and that more than half a million illegal abortions are performed every year in Mexico. In Chile, hospital admissions caused by illegal abortions gone wrong exceed 50,000 per year.

In contrast, the access to safe procedures in the United States has resulted in a drastic decline in deaths associated with abortion. In the period 1969–74, such deaths have fallen by two-thirds. Statistics also strongly suggest that about 70 percent of the legal abortions that have been performed would still have occurred had abortion been against the law. The only difference is that they would have been dangerous operations instead of safe ones.

When you combine the religious, moral and social issues raised above with the fact that women need and will seek abortions even if they are illegal, the case for legalized abortion is overwhelming. We dare not turn the clock back to the time when the religious strictures of one group were mandatory for everyone—not in a democracy.

We must uphold freedom of choice. Moreover, we must work to make free choice a reality by extending safe abortion services throughout the United States. Only one-fourth of the non-Catholic general hospitals and one-fifth of the public hospitals in the country now provide such services. It is still extremely difficult to have a legal and safe abortion if you are young or poor or live in a smaller city or rural area.

On a broader front, we must continue the effort to make contraceptive methods better, safer and more readily available to everyone. Freedom of choice is crucial, but the decision to have an abortion is always a serious matter. It is a choice one would wish to avoid. The best way to do that is to avoid unwanted pregnancy in the first place.

Step 2

Read the following essay as quickly as you can without sacrificing your comprehension of the material. You will have a maximum of 5 minutes, 36 seconds (200 words per minute) to glean as much information as you can. If you finish before time is called, note how long it took you to read the selection. Again, close your book and write a summary of the article, including a statement about the persuasive tactics used by the writer. You will have 7 to 10 minutes for this task.

DISCRETIONARY KILLING
George F. Will

It is neither surprising nor regrettable that the abortion epidemic alarms many thoughtful people. Last year there were a million legal abortions in the U.S. and 50 million worldwide. The killing of fetuses on this scale is a revolution against the judgment of generations. And this revolution in favor of discretionary killing has not run its course.

That life begins at conception is not disputable. The dispute concerns when, if ever, abortion is a *victimless* act. A nine-week-old fetus has a brain, organs, palm creases, fingerprints. But when, if ever, does a fetus acquire another human attribute, the right to life?

The Supreme Court has decreed that *at no point* are fetuses "persons in the whole sense." The constitutional status of fetuses is different in the third trimester of pregnancy. States constitutionally can, but need not, prohibit the killing of fetuses after "viability" (24 to 28 weeks), which the Court says is when a fetus can lead a "meaningful" life outside the womb. (The Court has not revealed its criterion of "meaningfulness.") But states cannot ban the killing of a viable fetus when that is necessary to protect a woman's health from harm, which can be construed broadly to include "distress." The essence of the Court's position is that the "right to privacy" means a mother (interestingly, that is how the Court refers to a woman carrying a fetus) may deny a fetus life in order that she may lead the life she prefers.

Most abortions kill fetuses that were accidentally conceived. Abortion also is used by couples who want a child, but not the one gestating. Chromosome studies of fetal cells taken from amniotic fluid enable prenatal diagnosis of genetic defects and diseases that produce physical and mental handicaps. Some couples, especially those who already have handicapped children, use such diagnosis to screen pregnancies.

New diagnostic techniques should give pause to persons who would use a constitutional amendment to codify their blanket opposition to abortion. About fourteen weeks after conception expectant parents can know with virtual certainty that their child, if born, will die by age 4 of Tay-Sachs disease, having become deaf, blind and paralyzed. Other comparably dreadful afflictions can be detected near the end of the first trimester or early in the second. When such suffering is the alternative to abortion, abortion is not obviously the greater evil.

Unfortunately, morals often follow technologies, and new diagnostic and manipulative skills will stimulate some diseased dreams. Geneticist Bentley Glass, in a presidential address to the American Association for the Advancement of Science, looked forward to the day when government may require what science makes possible: "No parents will in that future time have a right to burden society with a malformed or a mentally incompetent child."

At a 1972 conference some eminent scientists argued that infants with Down's syndrome [Mongolism] are a social burden and should be killed, when possible, by "negative euthanasia," the denial of aid needed for survival. It was the morally deformed condemning the genetically defective. Who will they condemn next? Old people, although easier to abandon, can be more inconvenient than unwanted children. Scientific advances against degenerative diseases will enable old people to (as will be said) "exist" longer. The argument for the discretionary killing of these burdensome folks will be that "mere" existence, not "meaningful" life, would be ended by euthanasia.

The day is coming when an infertile woman will be able to have a laboratory-grown embryo implanted in her uterus. Then there will be the "surplus embryo problem." Dr. Donald Gould, a British science writer, wonders: "What happens to the embryos which are discarded at the end of the day—washed down the sink?" Dr. Leon R. Kass, a University of Chicago biologist, wonders: "Who decides what are the grounds for discard? What if there is another recipient available who wishes to have the otherwise unwanted embryo? Whose embryos are they? The woman's? The couple's? The geneticist's? The obstetrician's? The Ford Foundation's? . . . Shall we say that discarding laboratory-grown embryos is a matter solely between a doctor and his plumber?"

But for now the issue is abortion, and it is being trivialized by cant about "a woman's right to control her body." Dr. Kass notes that "the fetus simply is not a mere part of a woman's body. One need only consider whether a woman can ethically take thalidomide while pregnant to see that this is so." Dr. Kass is especially impatient with the argument that a fetus with a heartbeat and brain activity "is indistinguishable from a tumor in the uterus, a wart on the nose, or a hamburger in the stomach." But that argument is necessary to justify discretionary killing of fetuses on the current scale, and some of the experiments that some scientists want to perform on live fetuses.

Abortion advocates have speech quirks that may betray qualms. Homeowners kill crabgrass. Abortionists kill fetuses. Homeowners do not speak of "terminating" crabgrass. But Planned Parenthood of New York City, which evidently regards abortion as just another form of birth control, has published an abortion guide that uses the word "kill" only twice, once to say what some women did to themselves before legalized abortion, and once to describe what some contraceptives do to sperm. But when referring to the killing of fetuses, the book, like abortion advocates generally, uses only euphemisms, like "termination of potential life."

Abortion advocates become interestingly indignant when opponents display photographs of the well-formed feet and hands of a nine-week-old fetus. People avoid correct words and object to accurate photographs because they are uneasy about saying and seeing what abortion is. It is *not* the "termination" of a hamburger in the stomach.

And the casual manipulation of life is not harmless. As Dr. Kass says: "We have paid some high prices for the technological conquest of nature, but none so high as the intellectual and spiritual costs of seeing nature as mere material for our manipulation, exploitation and transformation. With the powers for biological engineering now gathering, there will be splendid new opportunities for a similar degradation of our view of man. Indeed, we are already witnessing the erosion of our idea of man as something splendid or divine, as a creature with freedom and dignity. And clearly, if we come to see ourselves as meat, then meat we shall become."

Politics has paved the way for this degradation. Meat we already have become, at Ypres and Verdun, Dresden and Hiroshima, Auschwitz and the

Gulag. Is it a coincidence that this century, which is distinguished for science and war and totalitarianism, also is the dawn of the abortion age?

Step 3

Without looking back at the two essays, write a paragraph or two evaluating them and explaining how the arguments are related. You may refer to your summaries, but not to the essays. Time: 10 minutes.

5

The Critical Voice: Writing About Literature, Television, and Film

I n critical writing, the writer analyzes a work of literature, such as a novel, movie, or television program, and then evaluates it. Sometimes the writer assesses the work on its own qualities, sometimes on its strengths and weaknesses in comparison with similar works, sometimes with regard to generally recognized standards of excellence. As in opinion and argument papers, the critical writer presents the ideas of the work clearly and logically, discusses certain aspects of it, expresses a strong opinion, and supports it with evidence from the work. But in critical writing, a new dimension is added—one that derives from the author's critical reading skills and experience—that is, the interpretation of the work. This interpretation requires an ability to read beyond the surface, literal meaning, trying to understanding what the emotional, imaginative, and intellectual qualities of the work mean not only to you but to other intelligent readers. A critical essay then is not a statement of personal preferences or a plot summary, but a re-viewing of a work, an analysis of its qualities as a work of art, as a form of entertainment, as a commentary about life and people, or perhaps all of these.

ASPECTS OF CRITICAL ANALYSIS

Certainly, the plot or action is an important part of a narrative, and some attention is usually paid to the structure of the work in all critical reviews. But other aspects may be scrutinized by a critic, especially these: the characters, setting, time, theme, technique. All contribute to the overall effectiveness of any work. A critical writer may choose to focus on only one of these topics or may discuss several. To help you in reading, let's look briefly at some of the main considerations that critics may take into account in writing reviews. For a fuller discussion you should consult a rhetoric or introduction to literature text.

CHARACTER

Characters fall into three main categories: those who are central to the plot (for example, Archie Bunker in *All in the Family*), those with supporting roles (Archie's sidekick, Stretch Cunningham), and those who play minor or background roles (the old people in Edith's nursing home). Examining the ways in which central characters interact with others helps the critic to determine the function of each: whether they complement each other by revealing certain personality traits, or whether they act as foils to create a contrast or dramatic tension. Edith Bunker's goodness and innocence, for instance, complement Archie's bigotry and cynicism; the liberal Mike, by contrast, acts as a foil for Archie's ultra-conservatism—a major factor in the tension created in most episodes of *All in the Family*.

In evaluating the characters and their functions, the critical reader-writer will also be aware of how well the work reveals the characters' motivations, whether the characters are consistent (that is, do not change without sufficient motivation), and whether they are complex, lifelike individuals rather than flat, stock stereotypes.

SETTING

The function of setting can vary: it may be merely a place in which the action occurs, or it may be an essential element in the plot or the revelation of character. In the movie *Rocky,* for example, the filth and poverty of Rocky's Philadelphia slum add to his characterization as a pug fighter and born loser. If the setting plays an important role, its relationship to characterization or plot may well be an appropriate topic for a critical review.

TIME

Like autobiographical narrative, most fictional plots move in normal chronological time from the beginning of the narration to the end. But writers can handle time in other ways: for instance, there may be numerous flashbacks to earlier occasions; at the beginning the story may jump from the time of the concluding situation back to an historical account of the events leading up to it; or time may be psychological—moving inside the narrator's head from one event to another, not because of a logical time order, but because of the mental associations the narrator makes between events. If the handling of time is innovative or significant to the understanding of a work, then it can serve as the subject of a critical paper. In Arthur Miller's play *Death of a Salesman,* for example, time is psychological; in J. D. Salinger's novel *The Catcher in the Rye,* a flashback is used: the story opens with Holden in a mental institution, and the rest of the narrative deals with how he got there. Remembering this flashback is important in understanding *The Catcher in the Rye.*

THEME

A theme in a narrative is a central idea or viewpoint that pervades and unifies the work. To use a television program as an example, the recurring theme of *Star Trek*—and one that may account for its continuing popularity—is the optimistic view that, even in outer space, humans can solve social problems peaceably and rationally. Many critical articles have been written on the theme of the human will pitted against forces of nature, a common theme in modern works such as Hemingway's novel *The Old Man and the Sea.* Joy Gould Boyum's review of the movie *Bound for Glory* (pages 482–84) deals with themes common to both the film and Woody Guthrie's music.

TECHNIQUE

Technique involves many aspects of a work, among them the language, the tone or mood, the narrative devices. In relation to language, for instance, a critic may be interested in whether its use by different characters reflects regional or social differences. For that reason, several critical studies have been made of the dialect variation in Mark Twain's *Huckleberry Finn.* The critic's interest might also center on whether the figurative language—such as metaphor, simile, or symbol—contributes in a significant way to the narrative. The critical article dealing with *All in the Family* (pages 456–59) discusses the function of Archie Bunker's misused words and coinages in his characterization.

Another technical consideration might involve what the tone or mood of the work is, how it is achieved, and how it functions in the narrative. If the purpose of a work is to ridicule or expose some social condition, the tone may be satirical or ironic; the critic would then be interested in analyzing the techniques the writer used to achieve that effect. Both language and situation may be involved in creating a satirical tone: Hawkeye, the cynical doctor of *M*A*S*H*,* satirizes the Korean War, its senseless carnage, and the Army through his constant stream of crazy puns and absurd, Groucho Marx-like jokes and quips.

Another aspect of technique involves the narration of the story. Is it told by an unknown narrator? Does the story simply unfold as a plot (as in most movies and television shows), or does one of the characters narrate the story? If the latter is true, the critical writer may wish to discuss the narrator's function and credibility. One character whose accuracy has been analyzed is Chief Bromden, the narrator of Ken Kesey's novel *One Flew Over the Cuckoo's Nest.* Psychotic and hallucinatory, he is hardly an objective, believable storyteller.

TYPES OF CRITICAL WRITING

Because of the variety of possible subjects and approaches, critical writing can take many forms. Papers describing particular characters and their functions are character sketches, similar in format to those discussed in Part 1 of this book, on personal writing. Expository and argumentative forms may also be used. The writer may formulate an opinion-thesis and support it with evidence from the work; or the writer may present an argument, urging the reader to accept a particular interpretation of a work and refuting others. Many critical reviews are analysis papers, which break the work down into its parts and discuss their relationships. Or the writer might use a classification process to discuss the characters as to their types or functions in the narrative before discussing them in detail. The characters in M*A*S*H*, for instance, might be divided into those who are army professionals, those who view their army service as a patriotic duty, and those who hate war on humanitarian grounds.

In addition, many rhetorical strategies may be used. One character may be compared and contrasted to another or one work to another. The writer may set forth an effect that a work has had and discuss possible causes for that effect, as in the discussion of *Roots* (pages 465–68).

As you can see, critical writing calls upon all the skills of other forms of writing, and reading it makes similar demands on the audience. The main difference is that usually the evidence to support the writer's thesis is drawn from the work itself, rather than the writer's personal experience or research in the library.

TACTICS FOR READING CRITICAL WRITING

PRE-READING

As a critical reader, you should continue to apply the pre-reading techniques discussed earlier in this book. Before tackling a critical article, try to discover the author's subject and purpose for writing from the title and the opening and closing paragraphs. (Often in critical writing, however, the title may be intended mainly to attract readers rather than to inform them.) Also, in pre-reading, you should try to identify the writer's attitude toward the subject. Does the voice betray a biased critic, one so prejudiced for or against the author or work that the critical statements are likely to be too emotional, too irrational? Or is the voice rational and authoritative, that of someone you can trust? Sometimes the biographical sketch can help you in determining the nature and qualifications of the critical writer.

ANALYTICAL READING

Reading critical writing really involves two separate analytical tasks: one is to gain an understanding and knowledge of the work being discussed, the other is to follow the points that the critic is making about it. Thus, you should usually expect the writer to provide enough information about the plot so that even those readers who have not read or seen the work will be able to understand the reviewer's ideas about it. You, as the reader, however, must be alert as to whether the plot summaries and quotations help to support the critic's points or are unnecessary digressions.

Also, you should make yourself aware of the strategies the writer uses. If a comparison is made, be sure that you understand the significance and scope of the comparison; if cause and effect is used, note how the plot discussion discloses the relationships the writer is trying to reveal; if the review contains opinion or argument, determine whether the evidence cited is valid, significant, and convincing.

REFLECTING

In this final step in the process of reading critical reviews, add these suggestions to those offered earlier.

Point. After reading, you should be able to summarize the writer's main point about the work, and you should have some knowledge of the work itself—what ideas it deals with and what it is about.

Organization. You should be able to perceive the rhetorical methods used: whether the article takes the form of opinion-thesis, argument-thesis, comparison and contrast, cause-and-effect relationships, classification, or analysis.

Support. You should be aware of the kinds of support used: the citing of specific examples or quotations from the work, comparisons with other similar works, the citing of the opinions of authorities.

Synthesis. If you have read or seen the work being reviewed, you should weigh your appraisal of it against the one presented. Decide whether you strongly disagree with some points made in the essay and why. Ask yourself whether you gained new insights about the work. If you have not read or seen it, analyze the reasons why you liked or disliked the review and the extent to which you think it would contribute to your understanding and enjoyment of the work.

Evaluation. In weighing the effectiveness of critical writing, remember that criticism can be destructive, "picky," and unfairly subjective, or it can be soundly reasoned, constructive, and concerned with important points. Obviously, the latter type of review will be most effective in satisfying the greatest variety of readers.

FROM READING TO WRITING

Once you have determined the approach you will take to a particular work, you need to give some thought to your purpose before you decide on the form your critical paper will take. If you intend to write about a single character, you would probably prefer to write a character sketch. If you decide to compare several characters or several events, then obviously comparison and contrast will work best. If you plan to discuss all the characters in the work, a classification or analysis strategy is necessary. Before you write, determine which organizational method will work best for your purpose and then give some thought to what materials you might include.

In critical writing, there are certain pitfalls to avoid. These include:

1. *Too much plot summary.* Short summaries of particular episodes or even the entire work are usually sufficient to support your main points. How much plot summary you need depends on your audience. If you have been instructed to write for a teacher or classmates studying the work, even a small amount of plot summary may be too much. However, if you imagine your audience to be composed of intelligent people who are familiar with, but may not have read, the work recently, you will want to support your points with some references to the overall plot or to a particular episode.

2. *Overuse of quotations.* Citing quotations is certainly a necessary method of offering supporting details, but try to develop ways to integrate only the parts that are relevant to your discussion. Often a phrase or even a single word provides sufficient evidence and saves your readers from having to read lengthy, distracting, irrelevant chunks of the work being analyzed.

3. *Faulty punctuation of quotations.* Be sure that everything quoted directly is enclosed in quotation marks; this includes even single words lifted out of context. If you must use a long quotation, separate it from your own words by indenting on the left side and single-spacing (and then you need not use quotation marks). It also generally helps to indicate in parentheses the page number on which the quotation appears, even when you are not required to furnish a full footnote (see Warren French's essay, pages 476–80).

One last word. A good critical essay or review is one that helps readers to understand, enjoy, and appreciate a particular work or art form. Even if the critic finds fault, readers learn from a good review how to establish and develop critical standards. In a sense, when you take upon yourself the role of critic, you become a teacher, instructing readers and helping them to learn more and derive more enjoyment from books, films, plays, poems, television programs, paintings, ballets, concerts, and other artistic works. Consequently, while writing reviews is certainly demanding, it is also an important and fulfilling endeavor.

Critical Analysis of Character

A REVIEW OF *ROCKY*
Pauline Kael

BIOGRAPHICAL SKETCH

Pauline Kael was born in Petaluma, California, in 1919. She graduated from the University of California at Berkeley, and in recent years she has received honorary doctorates from Smith, Reed, Haverford, and several other schools. Formerly the film critic for McCall's *and then for* New Republic, *she has been writing for* The New Yorker *since 1968. Among Kael's honors are a Guggenheim fellowship and the George Polk Memorial Award for her film criticism. In addition, she has given many lectures at colleges and universities, served as judge at many film festivals, and appeared on innumerable television talk shows. Kael is the author of four books:* I Lost It at the Movies, Kiss Kiss Bang Bang, Going Steady, *and* Deeper into Movies *(which won a National Book Award). These books consist mainly of the articles she published previously in the magazines mentioned above and in such others as* Vogue, Atlantic, Harper's, Film Quarterly, *and* Partisan Review.

PRE-READING

1. As often occurs with critical writing, the title provides little helpful information, so the reader must turn to the first paragraph. What does it suggest about the movie and the probable emphasis of the review?

2. How does the final paragraph reinforce or modify this emphasis?

¹ Chunky, muscle-bound Sylvester Stallone looks repulsive one moment, noble the next, and sometimes both at once. In "Rocky," which he wrote and stars in, he's a thirty-year-old club fighter who works as a strong-arm man, collecting money for a loan shark. Rocky never got anywhere, and he has nothing; he lives in a Philadelphia tenement, and even the name he fights under—the Italian Stallion—has become a joke. But the world heavyweight champion, Apollo Creed (Carl Weathers), who's a smart black jester, like Muhammad Ali, announces that for his Bicentennial New Year's fight he'll give an unknown a shot at the title, and he picks the Italian Stallion for the

FROM *The New Yorker*, 29 November 1976, pp. 154–55. Reprinted by permission. © 1976 by The New Yorker Magazine, Inc.

racial-sexual overtones of the contest. This small romantic fable is about a palooka gaining his manhood; it's Terry Malloy finally getting his chance to be somebody. "Rocky" is a threadbare patchwork of old-movie bits ("On the Waterfront," "Marty," "Somebody Up There Likes Me," Capra's "Meet John Doe," and maybe even a little of Preston Sturges' "Hail the Conquering Hero"), yet it's engaging, and the naïve elements are emotionally effective. John G. Avildsen's directing is his usual strictly-from-hunger approach; he slams through a picture like a poor man's Sidney Lumet. But a more painstaking director would have been too proud to shoot the mildewed ideas and would have tried to throw out as many as possible and to conceal the others— and would probably have wrecked the movie. "Rocky" is shameless, and that's why—on a certain level—it works. What holds it together is innocence.

² In his offscreen bravado, Stallone (in Italian *stallone* means stallion) has claimed that he wrote the script in three and a half days, and some professional screenwriters, seeing what a ragtag of a script it is, may think that they could have done it in two and a half. But they wouldn't have been able to believe in what they did, and it wouldn't have got the audience cheering, the way "Rocky" does. The innocence that makes this picture so winning emanates from Sylvester Stallone. It's a street-wise, flowers-blooming in-the-garbage innocence. Stallone plays a waif, a strong-arm man who doesn't want to hurt anybody, a loner with only his pet turtles to talk to. Yet the character doesn't come across as maudlin. Stallone looks like a big, battered Paul McCartney. There's bullnecked energy in him, smoldering; he has a field of force, like Brando's. And he knows how to use his overripe, cartoon sensuality—the eyelids at half-mast, the sad brown eyes and twisted, hurt mouth. Victor Mature also had this thick sensuality, but the movies used him as if it were simple plushy handsomeness, and so he became ridiculous, until he learned— too late—to act. Stallone is aware that we see him as a hulk, and he plays against this comically and tenderly. In his deep, caveman's voice, he gives the most surprising, sharp, fresh shadings to his lines. He's at his funniest trying to explain to his boss why he didn't break somebody's thumbs, as he'd been told to; he's even funny talking to his turtles. He pulls the whiskers off the film's cliché situations, so that we're constantly charmed by him, waiting for what he'll say next. He's like a child who never ceases to amaze us.

³ Stallone has the gift of direct communication with the audience. Rocky's naïve observations come from so deep inside him that they have a Lewis Carroll enchantment. His unworldliness makes him seem dumb, but we know better; we understand what he feels at every moment. Rocky is the embodiment of the out-of-fashion pure-at-heart. His macho strut belongs with the ducktails of the fifties—he's a sagging peacock. I'm not sure how much of his archaism is thought out, how much is the accidental result of Stallone's overdeveloped, weight lifter's muscles combined with his simplistic beliefs, but Rocky represents the redemption of an earlier ideal—the man as rock for woman to cleave to. Talia Shire plays Adrian, a shy girl with glasses

who works in a pet store; she's the Betsy Blair to Stallone's Marty. It's un-
speakably musty, but they put it over; her delicacy (that of a buttonfaced
Audrey Hepburn) is the right counterpoint to his primitivism. It's clear that
he's drawn to her because she isn't fast or rough and doesn't make fun of him;
she doesn't make hostile wisecracks, like the other woman in the pet store, or
talk dirty, like the kids in the street. We don't groan at this, because he's such
a *tortured* macho nice-guy—he has failed his own high ideals. And who doesn't
have a soft spot for the teen-age aspirations congealed inside this thirty-year-
old bum?

⁴ Stallone is the picture, but the performers who revolve around him are
talented. Carl Weathers, a former Oakland Raiders linebacker, is a real find.
His Apollo Creed has the flash and ebullience to put the fairy-tale plot in
motion; when the champ arrives at the ring dressed as Uncle Sam, no one
could enjoy the racial joke as much as he does. Adrian's heavyset brother
Paulie is played by Burt Young, who has been turning up in movies more and
more frequently in the past three years and still gives the impression that his
abilities haven't begun to be tapped. Young, who actually was a professional
fighter, has the cracked, mottled voice of someone who's taken a lot of punishment in the sinuses; the resonance is gone. As Mickey, the ancient pug who
runs a fighters' gym, Burgess Meredith uses the harsh, racking sound of a man
who's been punched too often in the vocal cords. The director overemphasizes
Meredith's performance (much as John Schlesinger did in "The Day of the
Locust"); Meredith would look better if we were left to discover how good he
is for ourselves. I found "Marty" dreary, because the people in it were sapped
of energy. But Stallone and Talia Shire and the others here have a restrained
force; you feel that they're being pressed down, that they're under a lid. The
only one who gets a chance to explode is Paulie, when, in a rage, he wields a
baseball bat, and it's a poor scene, out of tune. Yet the actors themselves have
so much more to them than they're using that what comes across in their
performances is what's under the lid. The actors—and this includes Joe Spinell
as Gazzo, Rocky's gangster boss—enable us to feel their reserves of intelligence; they provide tact and taste, which aren't in long supply in an Avildsen
film.

⁵ "Rocky" is the kind of movie in which the shots are underlighted,
because the characters are poor and it's wintertime. I was almost never convinced that the camera was in the right place. The shots don't match well, and
they're put together jerkily, with cheap romantic music thrown in like cement
blocks of lyricism, and sheer noise used to build up excitement at the climactic
prizefight, where the camera is so close to the fighters that you can't feel the
rhythm of the encounter. And the film doesn't follow through on what it
prepares. Early on, we see Rocky with the street-corner kids in his skid-row
neighborhood, but we never get to see how these kids react to his training or
to the fight itself. Even the bull mastiff who keeps Rocky company on his
early-morning runs is lost track of. I get the feeling that Avildsen is so impa-

tient to finish a film on schedule (or before, as if it were a race) that he hardly bothers to think it out. I hate the way "Rocky" is made, yet better might be worse in this case. Unless a director could take this material and transform it into sentimental urban poetry—a modern equivalent of what Frank Borzage used to do in pictures such as "Man's Castle," with Spencer Tracy and Loretta Young—we're probably better off with Avildsen's sloppiness than with careful planning; a craftsmanlike "Rocky" would be obsolete, like a TV play of the fifties.

⁶ Stallone can certainly write; that is, he can write scenes and dialogue. But as a writer he stays inside the character; we never get a clear outside view of Rocky. For that, Stallone falls back on clichés, on an urban-primitive myth: at the end, Rocky has everything a man needs—his manhood, his woman, maybe even his dog. (If it were rural-primitive, he'd have some land, too.) In a sense, "Rocky" is a piece of innocent art, but its innocence doesn't sit too well. The bad side of "Rocky" is its resemblance to "Marty"—its folklorish, grubby littleness. Unpretentiousness shouldn't be used as a virtue. This warmed-over bum-into-man myth is unworthy of the freak macho force of its star; talking to turtles is too endearing. What separates Stallone from a Brando is that everything Stallone does has one purpose: to make you like him. He may not know how good he could be if he'd stop snuggling into your heart. If not— well, he may be to acting what Mario Lanza was to singing, and that's a form of bumminess.

ANALYTICAL READING

1. What is the point of Kael's reference to other movies in the first paragraph?

2. What does Kael accomplish in the second paragraph by referring to Stallone as "a waif" and "a child"?

3. What does Kael mean in paragraph 3 by stating that Adrian, Rocky's girl friend, is "the right counterpoint to his primitivism"?

4. To what extent does Kael feel that Stallone makes the picture effective? Without him as actor would it be unsuccessful?

5. What faults in technique does Kael find with the film? What other faults?

6. Explain Kael's statement at the end of paragraph 5: "we're probably better off with Avildsen's sloppiness than with careful planning; a craftsmanlike 'Rocky' would be obsolete . . ."?

7. What is Kael's attitude toward Rocky's innocence? To what extent does she praise or condemn it?

REFLECTING

Point: To what audience is Kael writing—one that has seen the film, one that is knowledgeable about films? Summarize Kael's overall evaluation of Rocky. What one sentence might serve as the thesis of the essay?

Organization: What is the function of the opening paragraph? How is the second paragraph related to the first? Explain how the opening sentence of paragraph 4 functions as a transitional sentence. What is the function of the final paragraph?

Support: How does Karl support her contention that "Stallone is the picture" (paragraph 4)? Does she explain adequately what she means by "the mildewed ideas" of the film (paragraph 1)? Discuss. What is gained by the comparison between Brando and Stallone? How does the comparison of Stallone with Mario Lanza at the end of the essay indicate her perception of her audience?

Synthesis: If you have seen *Rocky,* what do you agree or disagree with in Kael's review? What appealed to you about the movie? How did you feel about Adrian (Rocky's girl friend) and Mickey (Rocky's trainer)? Did you notice and object to the technical flaws that Kael mentions? Is Apollo Creed a satire on Muhammad Ali? Discuss.

Evaluation: You may disagree with Kael's criticism, but you should be objective in evaluating her review. How effectively does she support her ideas? How adequately does she give her audience a sense of the film? How completely does she deal with the film's many aspects? Is her writing interesting, detailed, and clear? Does she seem to be informed, perceptive, and fair in her criticism?

FROM READING TO WRITING

1. If you saw *Rocky* and remember it well, write a critique of Kael's review, assuming that your readers have also both seen the movie and read Kael's review.

2. Analyze the plot of a film, television drama, or book that you have read recently, explaining how it uses worn-out devices and is similar to many other works, as Kael says *Rocky* is. Assume that your readers are not familiar with the work.

3. Write a review of a movie you have seen recently, recommending it to readers (members of your class) because of the appeal of the leading character.

ARCHIE BUNKER, LENNY BRUCE, AND BEN CARTWRIGHT: TABOO-BREAKING AND CHARACTER IDENTIFICATION IN *ALL IN THE FAMILY*

Dennis E. Showalter

BIOGRAPHICAL SKETCH

Dennis E. Showalter was born in Delano, Minnesota, in 1942. He received an undergraduate degree from St. John's University and M.A. and Ph.D. degrees in history from the University of Minnesota. After teaching there, he joined the faculty at Colorado College, where he has remained since 1969. Showalter has received grants from the Ford Foundation and the National Endowment for the Humanities. His special area of interest is Prussian history, particularly its military aspects, about which he has published several scholarly articles.

PRE-READING

1. Sometimes the name of the periodical and the date of original publication can help in understanding an article. *The Journal of Popular Culture,* in which this essay first appeared, is written mainly by and for a scholarly audience; consequently it is carefully footnoted. The year of publication, 1975, is useful as a warning that some of the statements may be outdated. Do you think that the title is different in structure from many others in this book because of the readers it is addressed to? Explain.

2. Who was Lenny Bruce, and what is meant by "taboo-breaking"? Do the answers to these questions suggest what Showalter's essay is concerned with?

3. What main point about the essay is revealed in the first few sentences of the second paragraph?

4. From a reading of the final paragraph, what other major trend does the essay describe?

 [1] Television's first family of five years' standing, Archie and Edith, Gloria and Mike, has evoked as much controversy as anything coming over the airwaves since Lucille Ball's advancing pregnancy regaled fans of "I Love Lucy" during the 1950s. In the first year of their existence the Bunkers received the accolade of a *Newsweek* cover story and were attacked in the columns of the *Ladies' Home Journal* by no less a pop authority figure than Doctor Theodore Rubin. "All in the Family" was described as an insult to blue-collar America and an accurate picture of the silent majority. It was called good clean fun and an insidious legitimation of bigotry. It established a model for series featuring ethnic insults, right-on dialogue, and family infighting. Whether originally

FROM *Journal of Popular Culture,* 9:3, Winter 1975, pp. 618–21. Reprinted by permission.

developed as spinoffs, counter-attacks, or imitations, programs such as "Maude" and "The Jeffersons," "Sanford and Son" and "Lotsa Luck," "Hot L Baltimore" and "Chico and The Man," are all part of Archie's extended family. And if discussion of the series' message and meaning no longer occupies a prominent place in the media's entertainment columns, "All in the Family" continues to attract attention from other sources. It is presented as a source of pop theology, with Edith as a "little Christ."[1] It has been linked with classical drama, with Mike described as descending from the glutton figure of the Greco-Roman stage.[2] It is even the subject of at least two doctoral dissertations.

[2] In the process of incorporating "All in the Family" into the intellectual establishment, it becomes increasingly easy to forget the fact that the show is a reflection of two major trends in American popular entertainment. The first is shock value: Archie Bunker is a legitimate successor to Lenny Bruce. Of course there are substantial differences between the stage personality of Bruce and the scriptwriters' creation animated by Carroll O'Connor—who from the beginning took careful and successful pains to separate himself from the role. Yet both Archie and Lenny utter the unspeakable, both contemplate the unthinkable, with relish. It may be a truism to suggest that bigotry in all its forms has replaced sex as a taboo subject, yet the generalization is accurate. In the permissive 1970s accusations of an overt Oedipus complex became mere opening shots in a spirited political dialogue. The stage nudity of *Oh! Calcutta!* evolved into the multiple presentation of the sex act before increasingly jaded audiences. Yet at a time when exploiters of the new sexual freedom are increasingly concerned over what to do for an encore, what Michael Novak calls "the rise of the unmeltable ethnics" has created new forbidden fruits. "Black" is capitalized by journalists as well as militants. "Polish Power" is a slogan vital enough to have given ex-teen idol Bobby Vinton a second career. The women's movement has swept away much of the "take my wife—please!" genre of sexist humor, and the Gray Panthers attack Johnny Carson's Aunt Blabby as a tasteless slur on the elderly.

[3] Without debating the intrinsic merit of this new taboo, it is certain that like its predecessor, it exists to be broken. The delicious sense of participation in the forbidden as Lenny Bruce said "fuck" in a 1960 cabaret was felt by a new generation as Archie Bunker growled "nigger" on coast-to-coast television in 1971. But Archie's is taboo-breaking with a difference. The new age of militancy and permissiveness puts strains on the middle-class white American who sincerely wants to do the right thing and feel the right emotions. As the grandfather developed avoidance mechanisms to avert sexual response at the sight of an exposed ankle, so the grandson suppresses or sublimates nega-

[1] Edward McNulty, "The Gospel According to Edith Bunker," *Christian Century*, March 27, 1974, 346–47.

[2] John L. Wright, "Tunie-In: The Focus of Television Criticism," *Journal of Popular Culture*, VII (1974), 891.

tive reactions to behavior patterns *he* finds obnoxious. Yet the commuter jostled by a black in the subway, the businessman involved in an acrimonious dispute with a Jewish associate, the professor who has had one too many relevant students, can find release as Carroll O'Connor echoes his own subconscious. On the other hand, Archie's blue-collar vulgarity prevents the kind of excessive identification which disturbs the viewer's equilibrium and incites him to change channels. Indeed Archie's character relates uniquely to the possibility of such identification. His incongruous command of ideas and phrases, his glib flights of verbal fancy, his "Bunkerisms," those made-up words and malapropisms which provide much of the show's ongoing humor, reflect pretension as well as prejudice.[3] They convey the idea of an ignoramus vainly trying to rise above himself. They are not necessary to the character; Redd Foxx and Jack Albertson play broadly similar roles without them. Bunkerisms are rather an educated person's image of the way someone like Archie *ought* to use words of more than two syllables. Archie is in fact an intellectual's *Doppelgänger*, an academician's Mr. Hyde. His degenerate verbalizations offer the opportunity to alleviate lingering guilt by indulging one's superior learning at Archie's expense and therefore, by extension, reaffirming one's superior moral sense as well.

[4] It is not necessary, however, to explain "All in the Family's" ambiguous appeal strictly in terms of pop psychology. Simply put, in five years Archie's character has mellowed and those of his family have developed. This pattern is common in American television, particularly in programs with several regularly-featured players. Such a series usually begins with sharply-delineated characters, and scripts emphasizing conflicts among them. If the show survives, a combination of changed script structure and growing familiarity of the actors with each other and the characters they portray often results in a softening of interpretations, a blurring of outlines.[4] The dominant pattern of interaction between Alan Alda's Hawkeye and Loretta Swit's Hot Lips in "M.A.S.H." has changed from hostility to affection since the initial episodes. In the western series "The High Chaparral," tensions among the patriarchal rancher, his ineffectual son, and his scapegrace brother dominated the first seasons' scripts. The relationship between the rancher and his Mexican wife was hardly less strained. By the time the show was cancelled the Cannons were one big happy family, with conflicts among them played as comedy rather than drama. But the best example of this process remains that long-time prime-time favorite, "Bonanza." It requires a real effort of memory to recall the days when Little Joe carried an epée, Ben Cartwright pronounced anathemas on wrongdoers, and there were three brothers who fought each other almost as fiercely as they battled external enemies. How many viewers

[3] Alfred F. Rosa and Paul A. Eschholz, "Bunkerisms: Archie's Suppository Remarks in 'All in the Family,' *ibid.*, VI (1972). 275.

[4] This can also be done by network or producer's fiat, as illustrated by the rapid mellowing of Jack Albertson's Ed Brown in response to Chicano criticism of "Chico and the Man."

even of syndicated reruns know that Adam's mother was a Yankee, Little Joe's a southern belle, and Hoss's a Swedish immigrant? And how many can remember when those distinctions were important to "Bonanza's" plots?

[5] It is possible similarly to trace the evolution of Archie Bunker from a faintly malevolent embodiment of bigotry into an avuncular Chester Riley whose bark bears little relationship to his bite. Apart from the scripts, which generally show Archie as ridiculous or ineffectual in any role he tries to perform, the process was furthered by his appearance. Caroll O'Connor has never managed to make Archie *look* threatening or vicious, an important characteristic in a visual medium. The swaggering walk, the clenched teeth, and the ever-present cigar are belied by the pudgy body and the perpetual expression of bewilderment at the complexities of present-day life. Moreover, as the secondary characters have become personalities in their own right, the series no longer focusses so strongly on Archie and his rhetoric. Indeed he vanished entirely from several recent episodes during a recent contract dispute. Gloria's increasing maturity, her search for an identity, Mike's male chauvinism, Edith's emerging assertiveness, are at least as interesting and amusing as Archie's undifferentiated prejudices—perhaps even more so, because there are only a limited number of ways to say "Hebe." To a new viewer, or an old one willing to suspend his sense of outrage, "All in the Family" can be seen as developing into just another situation comedy. Archie's racial and religious slurs fit the pattern of Felix Unger's fussiness in "The Odd Couple," or Maude Finley's stridently liberal rhetoric. They represent a method of character identification and an aid to comedy—nothing more. As "All in the Family" begins its new season, Lenny Bruce has given way to Ben Cartwright.

ANALYTICAL READING

1. How is Showalter's statement that "bigotry . . . has replaced sex as a taboo subject" (paragraph 2) important in his article?

2. What role does Archie's misuse of words or creation of new ones ("malapropisms" or "Bunkerisms") play in the audience's response to his character?

3. What does Showalter mean by the "ambiguous appeal" of *All in the Family* (paragraph 4)?

4. What is the function of paragraph 4 in the development of Showalter's ideas?

5. What is the importance of the point that Showalter makes about Carroll O'Connor's physical appearance?

6. What does the last sentence do for the meaning and the organization of the essay?

7. In paragraph 5, replace the following words with appropriate synonyms: *malevolent, embodiment, avuncular, ineffectual, rhetoric, undifferentiated.* Try to find words more familiar to a general audience and note the difference in tone achieved by these substitutions.

REFLECTING

Point: What is the purpose of Showalter's historical approach to his subject? What two major trends embody his thesis? Write another title for the essay, indicating these two trends more clearly. Would you classify the essay as an argument? Why or why not?

Organization: What is the function of the opening paragraph? Would it make any difference if Showalter had discussed the trend involving Ben Cartwright before the one involving Lenny Bruce? Discuss the way that he organizes the comparison and contrast of Lenny Bruce and Archie Bunker (paragraphs 2 and 3).

Support: Should any statements have been footnoted besides the ones that are? Discuss. How does Showalter support his contention about the changes that take place in series like *All in the Family?* In what ways does the author reveal that he is writing to a highly educated audience, not to a general one? How does footnote 4 differ from the others?

Synthesis: How do you react to Archie—with annoyances, sympathy, or mixed feelings? Explain. To what do you attribute the success of the series? Do you agree with Showalter's point about the changes that occur in series that have numerous characters? Discuss, referring to more recent programs. Is Showalter's criticism outdated? Would he have included *Mary Hartman, Mary Hartman* in his article? According to his analysis, do you think that *All in the Family* will continue for years? Why or why not?

Evaluation: How knowledgeable does Showalter appear to be about television programs like *All in the Family?* Does he adequately support his main points? Is his essay well organized, informative, and convincing? Is his analysis of Archie thorough, perceptive, and clear? How appropriate are the voice and tone of the writer? Has he overlooked anything significant about *All in the Family* or Archie that would weaken his thesis?

FROM READING TO WRITING

1. Write a review of examples of certain kinds of television programs, showing how their appeal may be attributed to taboo-breaking. For example, you might examine the popular "celebrity roasts," the late-evening "adult" or interview discussions, or a particular show such as Franco Zeffirelli's *Jesus of Nazareth* presented on Palm Sunday and Easter Sunday.

2. Write a critical review of a popular, long-running series other than *All in the Family,* showing how it has or has not changed over the years.

3. Compare and contrast the series originated by Norman Lear that are mentioned in paragraph 1 (and any newer ones), paying particular attention to the reasons for their success or failure.

4. To what extent has violence replaced both sex and bigotry as the main attraction of television? Write a paper on this theme, referring to several televisions programs.

MORE LONELY THAN EVIL: A REVIEW OF WILLIAM TREVOR'S *THE CHILDREN OF DYNMOUTH*

Joyce Carol Oates

BIOGRAPHICAL SKETCH

Joyce Carol Oates was born in Lockport, New York, in 1938. She earned a B.A. from Syracuse University and an M.A. in English from the University of Wisconsin. She is currently a professor of English at the University of Windsor in Canada. Oates has received a Guggenheim fellowship, the Rosenthal Foundation award of the National Institute of Arts and Letters, and the Lotus Club Award of Merit. She has written seven novels, seven volumes of short stories, two volumes of critical essays, four volumes of poetry, and two plays produced in New York. Among her novels are Them *(a National Book Award recipient);* Do with Me What You Will *(a Literary Guild selection);* The Assassins *(an alternative Literary Guild selection); and the recently published* Childwold.

PRE-READING

1. What does the title of this review suggest to you about the author's approach to the subject of the book?

2. What information about *The Children of Dynmouth* do you gain from the opening paragraph?

3. What do the final paragraph and, especially, the final sentence add to your knowledge about the book and the emphasis of the review?

[1] James Joyce once said that he could have written two conventional novels a year, but that it would not have been worth it. And it has been said by Anthony Burgess that the writer who refuses to acknowledge Joyce is like a person who, living near the foot of a mountain, pulls down his blinds and stubbornly refuses to look out. Nevertheless, it has been the case for decades that English novelists continue to work in a realistic and conventional tradition that looks back not to the great Modernists (Joyce, Woolf, Mann, Lawrence, Gide), but to the late 19th century: to a common-sense vision of the world that is adequately expressed in terms of beginnings, middles and ends, and in language that is pragmatic and unadorned. Within such limitations (which are perhaps primarily those of English publishers), a surprisingly rich and humanly engaging literature has been developed, and it is possible to read certain outstanding English novelists of our time—among them Iris Murdoch, V. S. Naipaul and William Trevor—as "experimentalists" in a special sense. They are far less concerned with formal virtuosity than their American coun-

FROM *The New York Times Book Review*, 17 April 1977, pp. 13, 36. © 1977 by The New York Times Company. Reprinted by permission.

terparts, and far more explicitly concerned with the moral dimensions of their art. It may safely be said that they are more readable; and many readers might argue that they are more entertaining.

[2] William Trevor is the author of three collections of short stories, the most recent and most impressive being "Angels at the Ritz" (1976), and six novels, among them "Elizabeth Alone" (1974) and "Miss Gomez and the Brethren" (1971). In these novels and in his current novel, Trevor evokes potentially tragic situations that do not develop into tragedy: He gives life to quite ordinary people—men, women and children—who find themselves locked together by a single event and who are forced to reassess themselves and, as a consequence, their relationships.

[3] The lonely, divorced heroine of "Elizabeth Alone" enters a London hospital for a hysterectomy and enters as well the varied lives of her ward-mates. When she is discharged from the hospital, she is a changed women, braver, more content with her fate, as a result of her confrontation with a naïvely religious older woman. Miss Gomez of "Miss Gomez and the Brethren" is a young Jamaican woman who becomes converted to an evangelical Christian sect, and whose fervent prayer may or may not have prevented an act of murder from being committed by an emotionally unstable man—Trevor does not force his readers to any clear-cut conclusions. What is unmistakable is his faith in his characters and his exuberant talent in bringing those characters alive in succinct, unsensational terms.

[4] "The Children of Dynmouth" is Trevor's finest novel so far. At its core is a memorable creation—an aimless, sadistic 15-year-old boy named Timothy Gedge who, having no father and virtually no mother, wanders about the seaside town of Dynmouth trying to connect himself with other people. He turns up at every funeral, knocks on every door, greets everyone he encounters in the street, always with the same insouciant, brainless, shrewd smile; he is tolerated by everyone and liked by no one; by the novel's end he has come close to destroying several people. Timothy's malice arises from his chronic aloneness, so that it isn't possible, as the vicar recognizes, to see the boy as evil. He is a fact of life in Dynmouth, a testimony to Dynmouth's inexplicable failure. The boy wants more than anything to participate in a talent show, so that his gift for comic impersonations will be discovered and his career launched. But in order to mount his performance he needs the aid of several people, each of whom he attempts to blackmail: an aging homosexual whose marriage he nearly destroys; an adulterer who has been having an affair with Timothy's own mother; a 12-year-old boy and his stepsister whose friendship he brutally damages. Trevor has basically a comic imagination, though he deals with very serious subjects; his novels, for all their anxious moments, manage to end more or less happily.

[5] One comes to detest Timothy Gedge, with his sharp cheekbones, his mocking, moronic conversation and utterly selfish concerns; yet at the same time one is forced to experience Timothy as a natural event—or an Act of

God, like flood or famine. He is mean, vicious, silly, idle, tiresome, but he will not go away. He is always underfoot in Dynmouth. For some weeks he is buoyed along by his fantasy of winning great applause with a comedy routine based on a famous London murderer named George Joseph Smith; his fantasizing allows him to forget temporarily that he is, like many of his school classmates, really on his way to a lifetime of work in the Dynmouth sandpaper factory.

⁶ At the end of the novel he is unmasked and his power over his victims is taken from him. He surrenders the hope of becoming a famous comedian, but then takes up, pathetically, rather crazily, the fantasy of being the son of a couple more attractive than his own parents.

⁷ Timothy's connections with the people of Dynmouth are achieved only through the violation of their privacy and through the violation of his own sanity; in fact he remains utterly alone, one of those deprived, debased individuals who commit terrible crimes without possessing the depth of feeling required to know what they are doing. "The boy would stand in courtrooms with his smile. He would sit in the drab offices of social workers. He would be incarcerated in the cells of different gaols. By looking at him now you could sense that future, and his eyes reminded you that he had not asked to be born," Trevor's young vicar thinks. But what is to be done with Timothy? He exists, and he stumbles into his own forlorn future.

⁸ Yet such is Trevor's optimism that there may be a place in the pattern of lives even for Timothy; the vicar's wife, who has been unable to have a son, comes to see in Timothy the son who had not been born to her. And so there is the possibility of redemption; or, if not redemption, at least a place in the community. But it is all very tenuous, very problematic. The novel ends abruptly and ironically, and nothing is really resolved.

⁹ "The Children of Dynmouth" is a skillfully written novel, a small masterpiece of understatement. Where "Elizabeth Alone" sags and nearly buckles beneath the weight of too many incidental characters and their whimsical lives, "The Children of Dynmouth"—like the powerful "Miss Gomez and the Brethren"—manages to give life to a surprising variety of people, linking them together in the rhythms of a community as well as in the more urgent rhythms of a suspenseful narrative. It is a sensitive and honorable achievement, a work of rare compassion.

ANALYTICAL READING

1. In the opening paragraph, discuss the effectiveness of the first sentence, the reason for the reference to the Modernists, and point out the sentence that best indicates the main concern of Trevor's works.

2. What is achieved by Oates' discussion of two other novels by Trevor?

3. Paragraph 4 might have been divided into two paragraphs. Discuss where it could have been split and the advantages and disadvantages of not dividing it.

4. What does Oates mean at the end of paragraph 4 when she states that "Trevor has basically a comic imagination"? What function does this sentence perform in the paragraph?

5. What appears to be the purpose of paragraph 7 and of the quotation in it?

6. What is the overall picture conveyed by Oates about Trevor's Timothy Gedge— is he evil or not? Explain. How does Oates manage to give plot information in the context of a character sketch (see paragraph 4)?

REFLECTING

Point: Why do you think the novel is entitled *The Children* rather than *The Child?* Is Oates' review favorable or not? What special quality of the book does she emphasize? Try to write a statement summarizing her review.

Organization: Explain the overall organization of the review. Discuss the funnel-like structure of the opening paragraph. How are paragraphs 3 and 8 organized—SUBJECT-RESTRICTION-ILLUSTRATION or ILLUSTRATION-RESTRICTION-SUBJECT?

Support: One characteristic of Oates' writing style is her use of the semicolon to add details instead of presenting them by means of shorter sentences. Discuss this practice in paragraph 4. Examine how she supports her generalizations about Trevor (paragraph 2) and her characterization of Timothy Gedge as "a memorable creation" (paragraph 4). What difference would result if the final sentence were rewritten this way: "It is a work of rare compassion, a sensitive and honorable achievement"?

Synthesis: Are you interested in reading the book? Why or why not? Does this story about a boy in a small English town pertain to anything in your life or in American society today? Why do you think Oates does not condemn the indefinite, unresolved ending? Do you like endings to be resolved? Explain.

Evaluation: Has Oates conveyed sufficient information about the novel to inform a reader and suggest her evaluation of it? Does she support adequately her main point about the work? Is her writing clear, interesting, and specific? As she describes him, does Timothy seem a plausible, lifelike, and fully developed character? Explain.

FROM READING TO WRITING

1. Write a review of a film, book, or television play, focusing on the main character and discussing whether this person is credible, adequately motivated, generally consistent, and more of an individual than a stereotype.

2. Compare and contrast two characters in a film, play or book, pointing out their differences—especially, if possible, their distinctive reactions to some person or situation.

3. Write a review of Joyce Carol Oates' review, describing and documenting its strengths and weaknesses.

Critical Analysis of Theme

ROOTS: WHY WHITEY WATCHED
William Greider

BIOGRAPHICAL SKETCH

William H. Greider was born in Cincinnati, Ohio, and graduated from Princeton University with a B.A. in English and American Civilization. He began his newspaper career at the Wheaton, Illinois, Daily Journal, *moved to the Louisville* Times, *became Washington correspondent for the* Times *and the Louisville* Courier-Journal, *and then in 1968 joined the Washington* Post, *where he is currently a reporter on the national staff. Greider has won recognition for his coverage of the Apollo 11 moon landing and for his reporting of the trial of Lt. William Calley, for which the Washington-Baltimore Newspaper Guild awarded him a grand prize.*

PRE-READING

1. From the title, what aspect of *Roots* do you think Greider will focus on—plot, character, setting, theme, or some other? Why?

2. How helpful are the opening and closing paragraphs in revealing his specific critical emphasis?

¹ Something awesome happened in America this winter, more awesome than all the storms. Without quite defining it, we know intuitively that the television series called "Roots" was a shared crossing over deep water, a stunning passage in the mass culture of America.

² To grasp this, merely consider 30 million American families, nearly half of our population, gathering in their living rooms for eight evenings, children and parents, to watch an eight-part melodrama on our greatest national disgrace. Black people groaning in the hold of the white man's slave ship. This TV set in your living room is a powerful preacher.

³ Or try to imagine the reasons why this gruesome story, so long suppressed or excluded from our orthodox history, should not enthrall us. What made the ugly truth so compelling to America's popular audience?

FROM *Louisville Courier-Journal and Times,* 13 February 1977, p. D3. © The Washington Post. Reprinted by permission of The Washington Post Company.

[4] It will take a long time (and probably many arguments, from many different viewpoints) to define the message of "Roots" and its impact on ourselves. In obvious ways, it was a very crude history lesson and critics will enumerate the benign falsehoods and wholesale simplifications. As a sequence of eight dramas, it was better than most TV but still clumsy and blatant, in the manner of TV melodrama.

[5] Low history, bad art. These complaints are still only footnotes, I think, which do not really reduce the social phenomenon of "Roots." It has glorious implications for the future of the nation, an obvious suggestion that the self-enriching process that built the American culture remains alive and inventive. "Roots" is a little frightening, too, as a dramatic example of how our mass mythologies can be defined or altered so effectively, so swiftly, by a small number of citizens—the people who control television broadcasting.

[6] The social implications become clearer and more impressive, if one assumes the worst about those TV people, if we assign the most cynical motives to their endeavor.

[7] Assume ABC did not gamble on "Roots" out of some deep yearning to promote racial justice, but from a deep yearning to sell soap and hamburgers to the largest possible audience. Assume also that these TV people know what they're doing, if not as artists or historians, then as packagers of massive audiences, as manipulators of images that draw people to their TV sets.

[8] In that sense, the profound social message of the "Roots" phenomenon is contained in this simple fact: White America did not switch to another channel.

[9] I think the effect of "Roots" was, ironically, to make the story of slavery, the truth about it, accessible for white Americans for the first time. This TV series, so artfully put together, allowed—even forced—white people to look upon slavery-and-freedom as their story too. Yes, even their triumph.

[10] That possibility might rankle some black people who have tried for generations to get white Americans to focus on the black memory of our history. It's a bit much to suggest that white folks are not prepared to embrace it as their own.

[11] Still, I think that roughly describes what happened during the showing of "Roots." For 100 years—actually for much longer—white Americans have always heard this story told in terms of their own moral redemption. "Uncle Tom's Cabin" established the literary frame: good white folks struggling with evil white folks over the fate of simple, hapless black creatures, idealized beyond recognition as human beings.

[12] Now this TV series called "Roots" trampled the old mythology into the dust, relentlessly tore it up. The first six shows offered a series of white characters who might "do good" for the black folk—the conscience-stricken ship captain, the gentle plantation owner, the master's daughter who taught Kizzy to read—and each became a creature of treachery, betraying friendship, inflicting random pain, tearing away Kunta Kinte's heritage.

[13] If the white audience felt a bit giddy, it was an eccentric form of suspense—they kept waiting unconsciously for the white hero to emerge. After all, for generations this has been the familar dramatic convention for us and, especially on television, we expect the conventions to be honored. This time, each potential white hero (and heroine) became in turn a part of the evil.

[14] Finally, in Part VII, there emerged a pale substitute (pardon the expression), but it is not what the white audience had been waiting for. The white sharecropper, "Old George," and his wife are less than heroic—they are incompetent, dependent, grateful for the aid the black slaves so freely offer.

[15] In fact, "Old George" is a neat mirror image of that black stereotype from the old mythology—a helpless creature, good-hearted but none too bright, willing to learn, gushingly grateful for the good that is done for him. In short, not very believeable.

[16] So what kept so many white people at their sets? Why didn't they switch to something more satisfying on another channel? For one thing, "Roots" was exciting, with plenty of television's bread-and-butter—violence.

[17] In the process, without any special controversy, the series introduced a number of once-taboo images to national television, in vivid terms. Half-naked women. Black seduction. White-on-black rape. These racial-sexual motifs have always been powerful theater and, based on the success of "Roots," you can be sure the TV networks will do more of them, until perhaps familiarity renders them as stale as other TV themes.

[18] Even so, I think the mature sex and racial violence were secondary attractions to something much more important that "Roots" was doing. For these programs managed to cast the black story of slavery in totally familiar images—comfortable images that white people could recognize and identify with. So, during the course of eight programs, bombarded with evil white characters, any sensible white viewer identified with the familiar heroes—the black heroes.

[19] Kunta Kinte's village was portrayed as a pristine Eden where natural man flourished before the invasion of civilization. This is a very old dream, of course, going back to Rousseau, and white Americans have seen it often themselves—in the sympathetic movies about American Indians.

[20] The young black warrior even seemed at times to talk like our mythical version of the Indian—an expressive language of natural imagery, rich in such noble abstractions as courage and honor.

[21] Torn away from his Eden, the black warrior struggles virtuously in another familiar mode. He and his kin are the classic pioneer family determined to be free and to survive. Instead of battling the cruel elements of nature and hostile Indians, they must struggle against wicked white men and the institution of slavery.

[22] In every chapter, those familiar American qualities reverberate so strongly in the story that racial differences become less and less important and another message—more conventional and satisfying for everyone—becomes the powerful theme.

²³ This is the American story "Roots" proclaims, in every qualitative dimension. This story of slaves struggling for freedom is the orthodox story of American values. Their virtues—courage, honor, family, mercy—are the American virtues, the ones we need to believe in as Americans. In short, the dramatic marvel of "Roots" is that it allows white Americans to watch that terrible racial history and instead of taking on guilt, they are encouraged to say to themselves—"Hey, that's my story too."

²⁴ So one might say that the TV craftsmen were providing a clever substitution—destroying the long-familiar moral framework through which whites have always looked at slavery and other racial questions, replacing it with comfortable images that are totally familar to all Americans. In that sense, "Roots" is the direct descendant of a thousand Hollywood movies and 10,000 TV shows, the homogenized pop culture that idealizes our lives and our society.

²⁵ The final montage of family snapshots, which shows the subsequent generations of Alex Haley's family, is outside the drama—and perhaps the most controversial distortion of history. It ends with Haley himself a national literary hero now and, as every viewer knows, a very rich man.

²⁶ The implicit message is, of course, that the American dream works for blacks too. Every child can make it to the top. That is a fundamental article of faith and an important one for all of us. But those rapid snapshots blur over 100 years of bitter history rather easily, erasing for mythology's sake the truth of that long, slow struggle toward racial equality.

²⁷ "Roots" might have ended with a more troubling message for us. It might have suggested, as so many viewers noted for themselves, that many vestiges of the dreadful past are still evident in this American society, expressed indirectly in custom, legal process, economic status. That might have been a more authentic reporting of our shared racial history but, to be fair, TV is not a historian. It packages audiences by manufacturing popular myths.

²⁸ Some people may regard all this as frivolous, but it is the most serious event one can imagine. The beginning of genuine racial equality must surely involve white people, against all their training, choosing black heroes.

ANALYTICAL READING

1. Explain the function and meaning of the opening sentence fragment in paragraph 5.

2. Why does Greider find that the implications of *Roots* are "glorious" and yet "a little frightening" (paragraph 5)?

3. What is *Uncle Tom's Cabin* about (check a plot summary in the library, if necessary)? What myth does Greider state it established? How does *Roots* differ from that myth and also from the portrayal of blacks in *Gone with the Wind?*

4. What does Greider point out about the treatment of the white characters in *Roots?* Why are these observations important in his analysis?

5. Why is the treatment of sexual taboos and violence considered to be "second-ary attractions" (paragraph 18)? Why do you suppose Greider even mentions them?

6. According to Greider, white viewers did not assume guilt. Why not? What did they substitute for it? Do you find any irony in this situation?

7. In the final paragraphs, Greider comments on the theme of *Roots* suggesting that television might have presented a more accurate picture instead of prepet-uating a popular myth. Explain what he means both here and in the final sentence about white people choosing black heroes.

REFLECTING

Point: What is the purpose of Greider's article? What is the main point he makes? Where is this idea best expressed?

Organization: Greider's essay has an effect-to-cause organization—that is, he moves from the popularity of the TV version of *Roots* as an effect to conditions that he considers its causes. Outline these causes as presented in the article, noting how the paragraphing aids in the organization. Where is the thesis statement of the effect? Is the essay organized inductively or deductively—from effect to causes or from causes to effect?

Support: How does Greider support his views about the black and white charac-ters? Is he writing for an audience who has seen *Roots* or for a wider audi-ence? How do the opening paragraphs contribute to his discussion of *Roots*? What purpose is accomplished by linking the blacks to the American Indians?

Synthesis: If you saw *Roots,* did you derive the same ideas from it that Greider mentions? Do you agree with his belief that the television series corrected the myth about slaves and their white owners? What view of slavery were you taught in American history class in high school? How do you feel about Grei-der's reference to *Roots* as melodrama? What do you think is the impact of *Roots?*

Evaluation: Should Greider have stated his main idea earlier? Why or why not? Does he adequately support his explanation of the theme of *Roots?* Has he omitted or inadequately discussed any important ideas? Is his commentary at the end pertinent, significant, and convincing?

FROM READING TO WRITING

1. Account for the popularity of some recent film, television program, or book because of the appeal of its theme.

2. Analyze the theme of a play, novel, television drama, or film, showing how it is developed and commenting on it.

3. Analyze and comment on the theme of a nonfictional work, such as a biogra-phy, essay, or documentary.

HOLDEN AND HUCK: THE ODYSSEYS OF YOUTH

Charles Kaplan

BIOGRAPHICAL SKETCH

Charles Kaplan was born in Chicago in 1919. He received an undergraduate degree from the University of Chicago and M.A. and Ph.D. degrees in English from Northwestern University. He has taught at Roosevelt College and Los Angeles State College, and since 1959 he has been professor and chairman of the Department of English at California State University in Northridge. He has been awarded a Fulbright lectureship, has been co-author of a textbook, Technique of Composition, *and has written several other books, including* Literature in America: The Modern Age. *Kaplan has also written numerous articles on American literature and literary criticism.*

PRE-READING

1. How does the biographical sketch establish Kaplan as an authority?

2. Do both the title and the quotation from Thoreau relate to the thesis stated in the opening paragraph? From these, what do you expect the essay to deal with?

3. Does the final paragraph go beyond the scope of the first? Explain.

4. From the language used in the opening paragraph, what kind of audience do you think Kaplan is addressing?

¹ Henry Thoreau, himself an interior traveler of some note, says in *A Week on the Concord and Merrimac Rivers:* "The traveller must be born again on the road, and earn a passport from the elements, the principal powers that be for him." In Mark Twain's *Adventures of Huckleberry Finn* (1884) and in J. D. Salinger's *The Catcher in the Rye* (1951) we meet two young travelers—travelers in their native land and also in the geography of their souls. Their narratives are separated in time by almost seventy years, but the psychic connection between them eliminates mere temporal distance: Huck Finn and Holden Caulfield are true blood-brothers, speaking to us in terms that lift their wanderings from the level of the merely picaresque to that of a sensitive and insightful criticism of American life.

² Each work, to begin with, is a fine comic novel. Each is rich in incident, varied in characterization, and meaningful in its entirety. In each the story is narrated by the central figure, an adolescent whose remarkable language is both a reflection and a criticism of his education, his environment, and his

FROM *College English,* 18 (November 1956), 76–80. Copyright © 1956 by the National Council of Teachers of English. Reprinted by permission of the publisher and the author.

times. Each is fundamentally a story of a quest—an adventure story in the age-old pattern of a young lad making his way in a not particularly friendly adult world. An outcast, to all intents without family and friends, the protagonist flees the restraints of the civilization which would make him its victim, and journeys through the world in search of what he thinks is freedom—but which we, his adult readers, recognize to be primarily understanding. Society regards him as a rogue, a ne'er-do-well whose career consists of one scrape after another; but the extent to which he is constantly embroiled with authority is exactly the index of his independence, his sometimes pathetic self-reliance, and his freedom of spirit. He is a total realist, with an acute and instinctive register of mind which enables him to penetrate sham and pretense—qualities which, the more he travels through the adult world, the more he sees as most frequently recurring. He has somehow acquired a code of ethics and a standard of value against which he measures mankind—including, mercilessly, himself. There are people and things—not many, however—that are (in Holden's term) "nice"; there are many more that are "phony." He does not understand the world, but he knows how one should behave in it. The comic irony that gives each novel its characteristic intellectual slant is provided by the judgments of these young realists on the false ideals and romanticized versions of life which they encounter on their travels.

³ The slangy, idiomatic, frequently vulgar language which Twain and Salinger put in the mouths of their heroes is remarkable for the clarity of the self-portraits that emerge, as well as for the effortless accuracy of the talk itself. F. R. Leavis describes Huck's colloquial language as a literary medium that is "Shakespearian in its range and subtlety." Likewise, Holden's twentieth-century prep-school vernacular, despite its automatic and somehow innocent obscenities and its hackneyed coinages, also manages to communicate ideas and feelings of a quite complex sort within its sharply delimited boundaries. The language, in each case, is personal, distinctive, and descriptive of character. Holden and Huck are moralists as well as realists: each has a deep concern with ethical valuation, and each responds fully to the experiences which life offers him. It is the tension between their apparently inadequate idiom and their instinctively full and humane ethics that both Twain and Salinger exploit for comic purposes.

⁴ "The traveller must be born again," said Thoreau; and Huck's voyage down the Mississippi is a series of constant rebirths, a search for identity. Beginning with the elaborately staged mock murder which sets him free from the clutches of Pap, Huck assumes a series of varied roles, playing each one like the brilliant improviser that he is. Twain counterpoints Huck's hoaxes against the villainous or merely mercenary pretenses of the Duke and the Dauphin; the boy's sometimes desperate shifts are necessary for his survival and to both his moral and physical progress. The series reaches a climax in the sequence at the Phelps farm, when Huck is forced to assume the identity of Tom Sawyer—when, for the first time, he cannot choose his own role.

⁵ This, it seems to me, is a significant variation, pointing to the world which begins to close in upon Huck toward the end of the novel. Not only is an identity forced upon him, but with the appearance of the real Tom Sawyer upon the scene, Huck surrenders the initiative in planning and, in effect, loses control of his own fate. This is the tragedy of Huckleberry Finn: that he has gone so far only to surrender at the end to the forces which have been seeking to capture him. For despite the apparent similarities, there is a vital difference between Huck and Tom: Tom behaves "by the book"; Tom relies on historical precedent; Tom operates within the conventions of the civilized world, accepting its values and standards, and merely play-acting at rebellion—Tom, in short, is no rebel at all, but a romanticizer of reality. Huck's term to describe Tom's method of doing things is that it has "style." Style it may have, but it lacks design. Huck's willingness to let Tom take over Jim's rescue indicates Twain's final acquiescence to the world which has been criticized throughout. True, Huck is going to light out again, he tells us in the last lines: "Aunt Sally she's going to adopt me and sivilize me, and I can't stand it. I been there before." But, despite the expression of sentiments pointing to another future escape—and the fact that the limiting article is not part of Twain's title—Huck, by the end of the novel, has been trapped. I should like to add my bit to the perennial debate concerning the artistic validity of the final sequence, and suggest that it is both ironical and true to life. Tom's play-acting before Huck sets off down the river—his ambuscade of the "A-rabs," for example—seems innocent and amusing; but the rescue of Jim seems, as I think it is meant to seem, tedious and irrelevant. After all, something has happened to Huck—and to us—between chapters 3 and 43.

⁶ Huck is trapped by a society whose shortcomings he sees, and he says, "I can't stand it." Holden's terminology is "It depresses me" and "It kills me." Ironically, he is revealed as telling us his narrative from an institution of some kind—psychiatric, we are led to suspect—having also been trapped by the people who want to "sivilize" him.

⁷ Holden's instinctive nonconformity asserts itself early in the novel. He has been told by one of the masters at Pencey Prep, from which he is about to be dismissed, that life is a game. "Some game," Holden comments. "If you get on the side where all the hot-shots are, then it's a game, all right—I'll admit that. But if you get on the *other* side, where there aren't any hot-shots, then what's a game about it? Nothing. No game." At the age of seventeen he has learned to suspect the glib philosophies of his elders, and to test the coin of experience by determining whether it rings true or false for him, personally.

⁸ Like Huck, Holden is also a refugee. He flees the campus of Pencey Prep before he is formally expelled, and returns to New York City to have three days of freedom before rejoining his family. Pencey Prep is merely the most recent in a series of unsatisfactory academic experiences for him. "One of the biggest reasons I left Elkton Hills was because I was surrounded by phonies. That's all. They were coming in the goddam window. I can't stand that stuff. It drives me crazy. It makes me so depressed I go crazy."

⁹ Also like Huck, Holden assumes a series of guises during his lone wanderings. "I'm the most terrific liar you ever saw in your life. It's awful. If I'm on the way to the store to buy a magazine, even, and somebody asks me where I'm going, I'm liable to say I'm going to the opera. It's terrible." In a sequence which reminds one forcibly of Huck Finn, Holden finds himself in conversation with the mother of one of his classmates, Ernie Morrow, whom he describes as "doubtless the biggest bastard that ever went to Pencey, in the whole crumby history of the school." But Holden, adopting the name of "Rudolf Schmidt" (the janitor), tells her what she wants to hear about her son, to her wonder and delight. Holden's comment is: "Mothers are all slightly insane. The thing is, though, I liked old Morrow's mother. She was all right." His imagination rampant, Holden tells her a cock-and-bull story which includes an impending brain operation and a trip to South America to visit his grandmother, but he stops just short of revealing himself completely. It is a wonderfully funny scene, showing Holden in several aspects: his instinctive evaluation of the mother's "rightness" overcoming his profound distaste for her son, his adolescent imagination in a frenzy of wild invention, and his own awareness of the limits to which he can act his suddenly-adopted role of Rudolf Schmidt.

¹⁰ Huck's tortured decision not to "turn in" Jim is made on the basis of his own feelings, which he automatically assumes to be sinful since they have so often put him at odds with society. His personal moral code seems always to run counter to his duty to society, a conflict which serves to confirm him in the belief that wickedness is in his line, "being brung up to it." In the crucial moral act of the novel, Huck must "decide, forever, betwixt two things, and I knowed it. I studied a minute, sort of holding my breath, and then says to myself, 'All right, then I'll *go* to hell.' " Huck's humanity overcomes the so-called duty to society. Holden, also, is "depressed" by the notion that he is somehow a misfit, that he does strange, irrational things, that he is fighting a constant war with society—but his awareness of his own weaknesses (his compulsive lying, for example) is the result of his searching honesty.

¹¹ The yardstick which Holden applies to the world is a simple one—too simple, perhaps, too rigorous, too uncompromising, for anyone but an adolescent (or, as the popular phrase has it, "a crazy mixed-up kid") to attempt to apply to a complex world: it is the test of truth. The world is full of phonies— so Holden dreams of running away and building his own cabin, where people would come and visit him. "I'd have this rule that nobody could do anything phony when they visited me. If anybody tried to do anything phony, they couldn't stay."

¹² Huck's world, realistically depicted as mid-America in the middle of the nineteenth century, is also the world where the established codes are penetrated as being either hypocritical or superficial; Huck finds peace and reassurance away from the haunts of man, out on the river. After the waste and folly of the Grangerford-Shepherdson sequence, for example, Huck retreats to the river:

Sometimes we'd have that whole river all to ourselves for the longest time. Yonder was the banks and the islands, across the water; and maybe a spark—which was a candle in a cabin window; and sometimes on the water you could see a spark or two—on a raft or a scow, you know; and maybe you could hear a fiddle or a song coming over from one of them crafts. It's lovely to live on a raft.

But the idyll is interrupted shortly thereafter with "a couple of men tearing up the path as tight as they could foot it"—the Duke and the Dauphin imposing their unsavory world upon Huck's.

[13] Holden's world is post-war New York City, from the Metropolitan Museum to Greenwich Village, during Christmas week, where, in successive incidents, he encounters pompous hypocrisy, ignorance, indifference, moral corruption, sexual perversion, and—pervading all—"phoniness." Holden's older brother, a once promising writer, is now a Hollywood scenarist; the corruption of his talent is symptomatic to Holden of the general influence of the movies: "They can ruin you. I'm not kidding." They represent the world at its "phoniest" in their falsification of reality; in addition, they corrupt their audiences, converting them into people like the three pathetic girls from Seattle who spend all evening in a second-rate night club looking for movie stars, or like the woman Holden observes at the Radio City Music Hall. She cries through the entire picture, and "the phonier it got, the more she cried. . . . She had this little kid with her that was bored as hell and had to go to the bathroom, but she wouldn't take him. . . . She was about as kind-hearted as a goddam wolf."

[14] Holden's awareness of sham sensitizes him to its manifestations wherever it appears: in the pseudo-religious Christmas spectacle at Radio City ("I can't see anything religious or pretty, for God's sake, about a bunch of actors carrying crucifixes all over the stage"); in ministers with "Holy Joe" voices; in magazine fiction, with its "lean-jawed guys named David" and "phony girls named Linda or Marcia"; and in the performance of a gifted night-club pianist as well as that of the Lunts. His reactions to the performances of all three is a comment on the relationship between virtuosity and integrity: "If you do something *too* good, then, after a while, if you don't watch it, you start showing off. And then you're not as good any more." Both mock humility and casual bravura are dangerous to the integrity of the individual: Holden finds no "naturalness" in the finished and most artistic performers in his world. His world, he comes to feel, is full of obscenities, both figurative and actual; even a million years would be inadequate to erase all the obscenities scribbled on all the walls. His week-end in New York reminds him of the time an alumnus of Pencey visited the school and inspected the doors in the men's toilet to see if his initials were still carved there. While he searched for this memento of his past, he solemnly gave platitudinous advice to the boys. The glaring disparity between what even "good guys" say and what they do is enough to make Holden despair of finding anyone, except his sister Phoebe, with whom he can communicate honestly.

¹⁵ A few things Holden encounters on his voyage through the metropolis make him "feel better." Like Huck, who has to retreat regularly to the river, to reestablish his contacts with his sources of value, Holden several times meets perfectly "natural" things which delight him: the kettle-drummer in the orchestra, who never looks bored, but who bangs his drums "so nice and sweet, with this nervous expression of his face"; a Dixieland song recorded by a Negro girl who doesn't make it sound "mushy" or "cute"; and the sight of a family coming out of church. But these incidents merely serve to reveal in sharper contrast the phoniness and the tinsel of the adult world which seeks to victimize Holden, and which, in the end, finally does. Like Huck, he finds himself at the mercy of the kindly enemy. The realist's sharp perceptions of the world about him are treated either as the uncivilized remarks of an ignorant waif or—supreme irony!—as lunacy.

¹⁶ In addition to being comic masterpieces and superb portrayals of perplexed, sensitive adolescence, these two novels thus deal obliquely and poetically with a major theme in American life, past and present—the right of the nonconformist to assert his nonconformity, even to the point of being "handled with a chain." In them, 1884 and 1951 speak to us in the idiom and accent of two youthful travelers who have earned their passports to literary immortality.

ANALYTICAL READING

1. Explain the phrase "the level of the merely picaresque" (paragraph 1).

2. On what bases does Kaplan compare the two novels?

3. How does Kaplan integrate into his essay the quotation from Thoreau in the opening paragraph? What evidence does he offer from each book to illustrate the quote?

4. What points in the essay might be viewed as contrasts between the two books?

5. What points has Kaplan made throughout the essay that lead the reader to accept his contention that the books illustrate "the right of the nonconformist to assert his nonconformity" (paragraph 16)?

REFLECTING

Point: Using the information in the opening and closing paragraphs, write a one-sentence summary of Kaplan's thesis.

Organization: Would you classify the paper as an opinion-thesis paper, a comparison-and-contrast paper, or a combination of the two? Support your answer with a brief outline of the paper. What comparison-and-contrast scheme does Kaplan follow?

Support: Indicate places where Kaplan uses quotations from the two novels as support. Discuss the variety of ways that he uses them. How do his comparison-and-contrast paragraphs support his thesis about the two books? Does his thesis demand a comparison-and-contrast approach? Explain.

Synthesis: If you have not read the books, did you find the information complete enough to enable you to identify with the two heroes? If so, at what points? If you have read one or both works, did you agree or disagree with any of Kaplan's points?

Evaluation: Do you think the writer handles the comparisons effectively? Are they easy to follow? Why or why not? What transitional devices do you find especially effective? Why? Has Kaplan supported his thesis adequately and written about the two books clearly, interestingly, and convincingly? Has he included any unnecessary material?

FROM READING TO WRITING

1. Write a critical paper comparing and constrasting two works—novels, short stories, TV shows, movies—that have similar themes.

2. Write a critical paper comparing and contrasting two characters in a single work and how they relate to the themes in the work. Try to relate your discussion of the characters to real life, as Kaplan does.

FROM THE EDUCATION OF THE HEART: JOHN STEINBECK'S THE GRAPES OF WRATH
Warren French

BIOGRAPHICAL SKETCH

Warren G. French was born in Philadelphia in 1922. He did his undergraduate work at the University of Pennsylvania and received M.A. and Ph.D. degrees in English from the University of Texas. He has taught at the universities of Kentucky, Stetson, Florida, and Kansas State. Since 1970 he has been chairman of the Department of English at Indiana-Purdue University at Indianapolis. French has written and edited many books, including critical biographies about John Steinbeck, Frank Norris, and J. D. Salinger, and several anthologies of American fiction, poetry, and drama of the 1930's, 1940's, and 1950's.

PRE-READING

1. What does the title suggest? What kind of clues would be provided by a different title, such as "The Education of the Head"?

2. How does the first paragraph add to the meaning suggested by the title? How does it indicate the probable ideas and emphasis of the rest of the essay?

3. Does the final paragraph support your previous ideas? How?

FROM Warren French, *John Steinbeck* (New York: Twayne Publishers, 1962), pp. 107–112. Reprinted with the permission of Twayne Publishers, A Division of G. K. Hall & Co., Boston.

¹ *The Grapes of Wrath* is not a period piece about a troublesome past era. The allegory of the Joads applies, for example, to the problems we face today as we strive for a world government. It is an allegory that is applicable wherever prejudice and a sense of self-importance inhibit co-operation, and the message of the book is that co-operation can be achieved only through the willingness of individuals of their own volition to put aside special interests and work towards a common purpose.

² The emphasis on individualism and the willing co-operation of individuals explains why the book has been attacked by special interest groups of all kinds. In the course of the narrative, Steinbeck examines and finds fault with four "organized" methods of solving problems: organized charity, organized religion, organized government, organized private enterprise. He rejects two alternatives quickly. Organized charity, symbolized by the Salvation Army, he rejects as distasteful and degrading. At Weedpatch Camp another migrant tells Ma Joad, "Fella tol' us to go to the Salvation Army. . . . We was hungry— they made us crawl for our dinner. They took our dignity. They—I hate 'em. . . . I ain't never seen my man beat before, but them—them Salvation Army done it to 'im" ([page] 432). Earlier Tom Joad has questioned the organization's methods. He tells Casy:

> "Las' Christmus in McAlester, Salvation Army come an' done us good. Three solid hours a cornet music, an' we set there. They was bein' nice to us. But if one of us tried to walk out, we'd a-drawed solitary. That's preachin'. Doin' good to a fella that's down an' can't smack ya in the puss for it" (128).

Steinbeck evidently sympathized with Thoreau's statement in *Walden* that "if I knew for a certainty that a man was coming to my house with the conscious design of doing me good, I should run for my life. . . ."

³ Organized religion with its preoccupation with sin Steinbeck gives equally short shrift. As in most of his other books, he treats the church not with hostility but condescension; perhaps that is why religious organs have criticized his works violently—even institutions that thrive on persecution wince at contempt. The most pious figure in the book is Mrs. Sandry at the Weedpatch Camp, who moans, "They's wicketness in that camp. . . . The poor is tryin' to be rich," and of whom the camp manager says simply, "Try not to hit her. She isn't well. She just isn't well" (437–39). Steinbeck suggests elsewhere in the novel that religion is a kind of affliction. When Muley Graves is trying to get Tom to hide from the deputy sheriff who comes to inspect the deserted Joad farm, he tells Tom, "You can easy tell yourself you're foolin' them lyin' out like that. An' it all just amounts to what you tell yourself" (79).

⁴ Casy has evidently given up preaching when he has come to view religion as amounting to what one tells one oneself. Sin is, as he sees it, a matter of the way one looks at things: "There ain't no sin and there ain't no virtue. There's just stuff people do" (32). He expands this view when he later talks to

Uncle John about his wife's death. "For anybody else," Casy says, "it was a mistake, but if you think it was a sin—then it's a sin. A fella builds his own sins right up from the groun' " (306).

⁵ This relativistic view of sin leads Steinbeck into a philosophical mire from which he fails to emerge satisfactorily. Casy goes on to say, "Some of the things folks do is nice, and some ain't nice, but that's as far as any man got a right to say" (32). Who determines, however, what's "nice" and what isn't? Steinbeck does not, as some critics seem to think, evade this question completely. As Walter Fuller Taylor points out in his essay in *Mississippi Quarterly* (Summer, 1959) Steinbeck acknowledges in Chapter Seventeen (265) that certain "rights" must be respected and others destroyed or else the little world of the migrant camps "could not exist for even a night."

⁶ Steinbeck never attempts, however, to codify these rights or to explain how a system for seeing that they are observed will operate; neither, however, had other transcendentalists, all of whom seemed to assume that man in his natural state, uncorrupted by civilized institutions, tended to do the right thing. What should be emphasized again, however, is that *The Grapes of Wrath* is a novel, not a tract—art, not sociology or philosophy. As an artist Steinbeck is concerned with depicting not prescribing man's behavior. He feels that if people develop the proper attitude they will be able to govern themselves. He tries to help them see themselves as they are, but he is not a law-giver.

⁷ He does feel that traditional religion no longer enables man to see himself as he is, that its laws are not applicable to the situation in which contemporary man finds himself. Steinbeck's attitude is that this religion is all right for those who can afford it, but that in critical times it becomes an unconscionable luxury. This disdainful attitude is suggested by Pa Joad's telling Uncle John, who begins moaning when Tom gets into trouble, "We ain't got the time for your sin now." Ma simply observes, "Uncle John is just a-draggin' along" (535–36). Conventional religious attitudes are clearly represented as hindrances rather than helps in solving the urgent problems of life under unprecedented conditions.

⁸ Steinbeck is much more sympathetic toward the government, as is shown by his depiction of the opportunities to recover self-respect offered the migrants at the Weedpatch Camp. "Why ain't they more places like this?" Tom asks (393) and obviously speaks for the author. Yet even though he pictures the camp attractively, Steinbeck does not suggest that the whole burden of solving the problem should or even can be placed upon the government. He never suggests that the migrants should have remained in Oklahoma and sought federal relief, since he is arguing not that the government solve problems but that individuals should learn from experience. The trouble with the Weedpatch Camp is that it provides the migrants with everything but work. The dream of these migrants is not to be supported, but to work land of their own. Steinbeck is definitely no collectivist.

⁹ The treatment of organized private enterprise is more complex, since, although Steinbeck criticizes "the ridiculousness of the industrial life" (385)

and depicts the companies as "machines and masters" and the employees as "slaves" (43), his objection is primarily that the corporations have become too remote and impersonal and do not "love the land." He definitely advocates private ownership of property. One of the tenant farmers muses, for example:

> "Funny thing, how it is. If a man owns a little property, that property is him, it's part of him, and it's like him. . . . Even if he isn't successful, he's big with property. . . . But let a man get property he doesn't see, or can't take time to get his fingers in, or can't be there to walk on it—why then the property is the man . . . he's the servant of his property" (50–51).

Later Casy says in the discussion of a property that is obviously the late William Randolph Hearst's vast San Simeon ranch, "If he needs a million acres to make him feel rich, seems to me he needs it 'cause he feels awful poor inside hisself" (282). In Steinbeck's analysis of "the crime . . . that goes beyond denunciation," he praises the skill of scientists and producers and levels his charges at failures in the system of distributing the product (477). Steinbeck's objection is never to the private enterprise system, but to the irresponsibility of big business. His idea at the time he wrote *The Grapes of Wrath* was that the solution to the nation's ills lay in a system based upon small landholdings.

[10] It is particularly interesting, in view of the attitudes expressed in *The Grapes of Wrath*, to examine an explanation by an American of the modern corporation in one of Steinbeck's latest books, *The Short Reign of Pippin IV*. The son of a California egg-king is talking to a king of France:

> ". . . here's the funny thing, sir. You take a big corporation in America, say like General Motors or Du Pont or US Steel. The thing they're most afraid of is socialism, and at the same time they themselves are socialist states. . . . Why, if the US Government tried to do one-tenth of what General Motors does, General Motors would go into armed revolt. . . . They don't do it out of kindness, sir. It's just that some of them have found out they can produce and sell more goods that way. They used to fight the employees. That's expensive."

This description of corporations isn't as strange as it sounds from the author of *The Grapes of Wrath*. It should be remembered that in one of the interchapters in the novel, Steinbeck tried to explain the significance of the migration and commented, "If you who own things people must have could understand this [growing unity], you might preserve yourself" (206). As some of those not blinded by "fambly" prejudices perceived even at the time of the novel's publication, *The Grapes of Wrath* is not an external attack upon the American economic system, but an internal demand for its reform. Yet Stanley Edgar Hyman is also wrong when he says in his notes on Steinbeck in the *Antioch Review* (June, 1942) that the central message of the novel is an appeal to

the class that controls the economy to behave; its main point is that the workers, too, must reform their views if there is to be any real improvement. At
bottom, Steinbeck believes, like his great predecessor, Hawthorne, that the
only lasting and meaningful reforms originate in the individual human heart.

ANALYTICAL READING

1. French's strategy in writing should be apparent from a reading of the first two
   paragraphs. What does he say that Steinbeck affirms? What does Steinbeck
   reject?

2. According to French, what is Steinbeck's view of sin in *The Grapes of Wrath?*
   What is the importance of this attitude about sin in the discussion of the
   novel?

3. How does French support his statement that Steinbeck is not "a lawgiver" but
   "an artist . . . concerned with depicting not prescribing man's behavior" (paragraph 6)? How does he reconcile this statement with the point in paragraph 1
   about the message of *The Grapes of Wrath?*

4. Why does French believe that the novel rejects government relief for the poor
   migrants?

5. To what extent does he view *The Grapes of Wrath* as an attack upon the
   capitalist system?

6. According to French, what faults does Steinbeck find in society and what
   changes does he recommend?

REFLECTING

Point: Which sentence best expresses Steinbeck's thesis? Why does French discuss
   the four "organized" methods of solving the problems of poor people?

Organization: Excluding the opening and closing paragraphs, how is the essay
   organized? Where is this structure signaled? How are most paragraphs organized?

Support: What evidence is offered to support French's interpretation of Steinbeck's
   thesis about the reformation of the human heart? Point out the two techniques that French uses to support his points with quotations. Explain the use
   and purpose of the series of three or four periods in the quotations. Why does
   French refer to Walter Fuller Taylor (paragraph 5) and Stanley Hyman (paragraph 10)? Point out sentences and paragraphs where the form adds to effectiveness (for example, paragraph 6).

Synthesis: Do you agree with French's statement that *The Grapes of Wrath* deals
   not only with the plight of Oklahoma farmers during the drought of the 1930's
   but also with today's problems? Explain. How do you feel about Steinbeck's
   attitude toward the Salvation Army, sin, government aid, the need to work, the
   irresponsibility of big business? Do you think that Steinbeck would favor
   unions of migrant laborers, such as the United Farm Workers?

Evaluation: Is French's analysis organized well and presented clearly? Does he support his ideas with sufficient evidence? Does he explain why Steinbeck's novel has been attacked by many special-interest groups? Is his introduction interesting and meaningful? Is his conclusion effective? Explain. Does he generally provide an insight into the ideas discussed in the book and make a convincing case for his interpretation of the novel's theme?

FROM READING TO WRITING

1. Write a paper discussing the theme of a book, film, or television program. Assume that your audience is familiar with the work.

2. If you have read *The Grapes of Wrath* recently, explain how its ending supports or refutes French's interpretation. Briefly summarize the ending for readers unfamiliar with the work.

3. Discuss how the theme of an essay or sermon differs from the theme of a novel, play, film, or television drama. Be certain to use at least two or three examples in your paper.

Critical Analysis of Technique

"THIS LAND IS YOUR LAND": A REVIEW OF *BOUND FOR GLORY*

Joy Gould Boyum

BIOGRAPHICAL SKETCH

Joy Gould Boyum was born in New York in 1934. She received a B.A. from Barnard College and M.A. and Ph.D. degrees in English from New York University. After teaching at Jersey City State College, she joined the faculty at New York University, where she is currently a professor of English. In addition, since 1971 she has been the film critic for the Wall Street Journal. *Boyum is co-author of a textbook,* Film as Film, *and the author of numerous articles about films and critical approaches to film in such publications as* Scholastic Teacher, *and* World Yearbook, *and the* Encyclopaedia Britannica.

PRE-READING

1. What statement in the second paragraph suggests Boyum's main interest in the film?

2. What do you find in the last paragraph that would alert you to the main ideas in her critique?

¹ "This Land Is Your Land." "So Long, It's Been Good to Know You." "Union Maid." "This Train Is Bound for Glory." Most of us have heard these songs even if we haven't heard of the man who wrote them: Woodrow Wilson Guthrie or, as he was better known, "Woody." To folklorist Alan Lomax he was "the best ballad-maker to come down the American 'pike." To critic Clifton Fadiman, "a modern Walt Whitman," to others "a dusty-voiced Homer."

² Whatever else he may have been, Woody Guthrie was a genuine folk poet, writing simple lyrics set to simple tunes that told of the people and were for the people. But though his songs have universal appeal and have inspired a generation of singers and composers in the folk tradition—Bob Dylan, Judy

Collins, his son Arlo among them—Guthrie and his music remain very much rooted in a specific time and a specific atmosphere.

[3] Born in Oklahoma in 1912, living in Texas during the great dust storms of the '30s, Guthrie joined with other dust bowl refugees in the great trek Westward. And it was about these storms, this journey and the disappointments California held for those without the "Do Re Mi" that Guthrie mostly wrote and sang.

[4] It is also this world of Depression America that is recreated in "Bound for Glory," the majestic and moving film about Woody Guthrie. The film, in fact, tells a very small part of Guthrie's story, that period from 1938 to 1940 when Guthrie, travelling the hobo route along dusty high-ways and in crowded box cars from Texas to California, literally lived the saga immortalized by John Steinbeck's "The Grapes of Wrath." It was during this period, too, that Guthrie, much like Steinbeck's hero Tom Joad, went through his political and social apostleship, involved in early efforts to unionize the migrant workers and using his music to carry his protest and commitment.

[5] "Wherever little children are hungry and cry/Wherever people ain't free,/Wherever men are fightin' for their rights/That's where I'm gonna be," goes the final verse of Guthrie's ballad, "Tom Joad"—a verse which describes not only what motivated Steinbeck's hero but what impelled Guthrie as well. But though the film delineates the shaping of an individual and distinctive sensibility, its focus is not really on the man himself. Rather, it is on the sources of his sentiments. And since these lie above all in the American landscape and in the poverty and social injustice that marred it during the '30s, "Bound for Glory" is less a portrait of an artist than a picture of that artist's world.

[6] And what a magnificent picture it is! Rendering the whole in subdued, almost sunbleached tones, cinematographer Haskell Wexler has invested image after image with the kind of compassion and eloquence that makes the visual texture of "Bound for Glory" of a piece with the photographs of Walker Evans and the paintings of Ben Shahn. The parched and windswept Texas town where we first meet Guthrie, and the terrifying dust storm that descends upon it (spectacularly dramatized by special effects man Albert Whitlock), tell us all we need to know about what drove the Okies and others like them from their land.

[7] The vast horizons seen from freight trains speeding Westward are radiant with the sense of hope that these people must have felt. But it is not only the landscape that is visualized so powerfully. Michael Haller's production designs, William Theiss's costumes, and Lynn Stalmaster's casting have all combined with Wexler's cinematography to make everything and everyone in this movie more than merely authentic, but vividly alive and intensely expressive.

[8] Epic in scope, "Bound for Glory" is clearly no standard Hollywood biography. And viewers expecting a more conventional kind of movie may very well be put off by the film's refusal to meet their expectations. They may,

for example, find the sensitive interpretation of Guthrie by David Carradine (whose father John, incidentally, was one of the stars of "The Grapes of Wrath") a bit too internalized, a bit too understated. They may be frustrated, too, by the tendency of director Hal Ashby to treat his camera as a quiet observer, to keep us at a distance from character and action, thereby making his hero a figure in a landscape.

[9] Viewers may also be disoriented by the film's deliberate pace, its low-keyed rendition of even its most potentially charged moments. Except in a few sequences near the end, treating the breakup of Woody's marriage and radio career, where Robert Getchell inserts the conventional scenes and clichés he has elsewhere resisted, the film carefully eschews the traditional kinds of movie drama, opting instead for the drama inherent in its social view.

[10] Yet even here there is a distinctively muted quality to the film. As if taking its clues from Guthrie's music (which, by the way, is used in the movie with the same restraint that characterizes the whole, heard only in suggestive fragments until the very end), politics have here been elegized and softly romanticized, expressed as a lyric celebration of the land and people. Still, sometimes the most simple sentiments can also be the most moving.

[11] At the end of the movie we hear Woody Guthrie's actual voice saying, "I hate a song that makes you think that you're not any good . . . that makes you think you are just born to lose . . . that pokes fun at you on account of your bad luck or hard travellin'. . . . I am out to sing songs that will prove to you that this is your world . . . that make you take pride in yourself and in your work." In the background, Odetta and the Weavers are singing "This Land Is Your Land." And we cannot help but be overcome with what I suppose are essentially populist emotions. Nevertheless, by giving us this sense of affinity with the common man, "Bound for Glory" manages to make itself not simply an historic document but a movie for our time.

ANALYTICAL READING

1. Is the audience Boyum is addressing familiar with Woody Guthrie? One that has seen the film? One that is quite well educated? Justify your answers.

2. Is the essay helped by its brief comparison of *Bound for Glory* to Steinbeck's *The Grapes of Wrath?* Explain.

3. What does Boyum mean by the statement in paragraph 5 that the film's "focus is not really on the man himself," but on "the sources of his sentiments"? How does the sentence structure help to emphasize that point?

4. According to Boyum, what role does the setting play in creating an appropriate atmosphere for the film?

5. Why does Boyum view the movie as more than a historical document?

REFLECTING

Point: Does Boyum recommend the film or not? If so, to what viewers? What does she find to be its most appealing feature?

Organization: What purpose does the introductory paragraph serve? Point out the main divisions of the essay and discuss the effectiveness of their order. What is the function of the final sentence? Show how Boyum links each paragraph to the one preceding it.

Support: What do the quotations from Woody Guthrie's songs achieve? How does Boyum develop her main point about the film? How does she show the unusual artistic nature of the film? What words function as both description and evaluation?

Synthesis: After reading the essay, would you like to see the film? Why or why not? Does Boyum's review tell enough about the plot, too much, or too little? When you are watching a film, do you notice the camera use? Do you prefer the camera to be "a quiet observer" (paragraph 8), or do you prefer special camera effects, such as slow motion, sudden zoom shots, or fuzzy pictures? Do special effects, such as the dust storm mentioned by Boyum, add to your enjoyment of films?

Evaluation: Has Boyum conveyed a clear sense of the film? Has she indicated clearly and convincingly what she liked and disliked about it? Has she demonstrated what is noteworthy about it? Does she capture for readers some of the quality of the film and of Woody Guthrie? Explain.

FROM READING TO WRITING

1. Write a film or television review in which you emphasize some technique, such as camera work, setting, acting, sound, or special effects. Assume that your readers have seen the work.

2. Write a review explaining why a recent film or television play was a run-of-the-mill production, composed mainly of clichés. Assume that your readers are unfamiliar with the work.

3. Write a review for your college newspaper urging other students either to see or to skip a film being shown on campus or in the neighborhood.

4. If you saw *Bound for Glory* and disagree with Boyum's views, write her a letter explaining how your interpretation and evaluation differ from hers.

5. Compare and contrast a book with its film or television version. Assume that your readers are unfamiliar with the book but have seen the movie or TV show.

Assessment of
Reading and Writing Skills:
Critical Writing

Step 1

Read the essay that follows with the aim of understanding and recalling the important points it makes about the work. When you finish, note how long it took you to read the selection. Then close your book and write a summary of the important information without referring again to the essay. Include a discussion of the writer's interpretation of the work and how the examples contribute to that interpretation. You will be allowed 7 to 10 minutes to write; your instructor will establish the limit and tell you when the time is up.

THE IMAGES IN SHAKESPEARE
Cathy A. Stovall

In the play *Macbeth*, Shakespeare's use of imagery helps the reader to see or feel a more vivid, forceful image of the characters, their moods, and the atmosphere around them.

Shakespeare employs clothing images mainly to describe Macbeth's character and how other people feel about him. In Act I, Macbeth speaks of people honoring him by saying, "Golden opinions from all sorts of people,/Which would be worn now in their newest gloss,/Not cast aside so soon." Then in Act III this type of imagery is applied again when Macduff tells Ross,

> Well, may you see things well done there, Adieu!
> Lest our old robes sit easier than our new!

Finally in Act IV, Angus says, "Now does he feel his title/ Hang loose about him like a giant's robe/ Upon a dwarfish thief." Through this image Shakespeare shows that Macbeth is declining in the people's opinion, and that Angus thinks Macbeth is not as good a king as Duncan was. This speech is

FROM *Kentucky English Bulletin*, Student Writing Issue, 25:3, Spring 1976, pp. 20–22. Reprinted by permission of the author and the publisher.

related to the first clothing image used in Act I, where Macbeth asks, "Why do you dress me in borrowed robes?" because the people are now aware that Macbeth is indeed in "borrowed robes," for he gained the throne by devious means and is unworthy of the position. In each of these cases the speeches are made poetic and picturesque by Shakespeare's words, and they also give the reader insight to Macbeth's character.

Disorder images intensify the prevailing gloom of the drama by including unnatural happenings. In Act II, scene 4, Ross and an old man are talking about all the strange things that happened a few days earlier, such as Duncan's horses breaking out of their stalls, and then eating each other. This adds a dramatic and supernatural atmosphere because it was just before this scene that Macbeth had murdered Duncan.

More examples of disorder images appear in Act IV, scene 1, when Macbeth commands the witches:

> Though you untie the winds and let them fight
> Against the churches, though the yesty waves
> Confound and swallow navigation up, . . .
> Though palaces and pyramids do slope
> Their heads to their foundations, . . .
> Even till destruction sicken, answer me
> To what I ask you.

This is a dramatic and effective way of showing Macbeth's moral decline, for his speech indicates that he doesn't care what happens to the world as long as he receives what he desires.

In Act IV Shakespeare again employs disorder images in these words of Ross:

> But cruel are the times, when we are traitors
> And do not know ourselves; when we hold rumor
> From what we fear, yet know not what we fear,
> But float upon a wild and violent sea
> Each way and move.

This occurs during an emotional scene between Lady Macduff and Ross. Lady Macduff is both frightened and angry because her husband has left Scotland without telling her why. This reference to "Wild . . . violent sea" heightens the emotional intensity of this scene, for it reflects the turbulence Lady Macduff feels.

Images involving sleep and animals reveal the characters' innermost feelings and their moods. In Act II, after murdering Duncan, Macbeth cries out, "Wake Duncan with thy knocking! I would thou coulds't!", thus showing guilt and remorse for his evil deed. In Act III he says,

> ... Better be with the dead,
> Whom we, to gain our peace, have sent to peace,
> Than on the torture of the mind to lie
> In restless ecstasy. Duncan is in his grave;
> After life's fitful fever he sleeps well.

This picture of sleep emphasizes Macbeth's inability to rest. Another more prophetic picture occurs in Act II when Macbeth tells Lady Macbeth, "Methought I heard a voice cry, 'Sleep no more! Macbeth does murder sleep.' " This shows the troubled state and fears of Macbeth's mind.

An animal image is used when Lady Macbeth speaks of a croaking raven which signifies death. Through this phrase Lady Macbeth reveals that murdering Duncan is on her mind. In Act III, a vivid picture of the agony in Macbeth's mind is painted for the reader when Macbeth tells Lady Macbeth, "O full of scorpions is my mind, dear wife!" Shakespeare combines animal and disorder imagery here. In Act III Ross tells Macduff that Lady Macduff and her babes have been killed and describes them as "deer," thus stressing their defenselessness and innocence. This image makes the reader react emotionally with Macduff.

By using different kinds of imagery, Shakespeare has added to the play's value because imagery appeals to the reader's senses, and is fitted into the characters' speeches without being awkward or stiff. Shakespeare's usage of images in *Macbeth* creates more colorful and poetic speeches, thus capturing the reader's imagination and his sense of excitement.

Step 2

Read the following essay as quickly as you can without sacrificing your comprehension of the material. You will have a maximum of 2 minutes, 56 seconds (200 words per minute) to glean as much information as you can. If you finish before time is called, note how long it took you to read the selection. Again, close your book and write a summary of the article, including a statement about the interpretation and how it is supported. You will have 7 to 10 minutes for this task.

THE IRONY IN *MACBETH*
Kimberley Messer

By Shakespeare's use of irony, the reader or viewer of *Macbeth* becomes more interested and involved in the drama as he is more aware of the outcome of events than the characters are.

FROM *Kentucky English Bulletin*, Student Writing Issue, 25:3, Spring 1976, pp. 18–19. Reprinted by permission of the author and the publisher.

Even in the first scenes, dramatic irony is used to link Macbeth with his downfall. He echoes the witches' paradox, "Fair is foul, and foul is fair," when he says, "So foul and fair a day I have not seen." Here Shakespeare shows that supernatural or evil forces have already acted on Macbeth. Yet, he does not know how foul a day this will prove to be for him as it leads to a foul life.

As the character of Macbeth is developed, irony reveals how he lets his desire for the kingship override his concept of right and wrong. Duncan, whom he murders, speaks of Macbeth as a noble and trustworthy kinsman. He even describes the castle where he is to be murdered as a pleasant place since he is not aware of Macbeth's plans. When Macbeth speaks of Duncan's virtues, he refers to the "deep damnation" of the murderer. After Duncan's murder, Macbeth's own actions and words begin to turn against himself.

Then, continuing in a dramatically ironic tone, Lady Macbeth comments to Macbeth that they must not dwell on what has been done. To do so, she says, will make them mad. Thus, Lady Macbeth, in Act II, foretells her own madness. This use of irony provides a clue of her eventual mental collapse and gives some evidence of Macbeth's greater emotional stability. She had called upon night to come and hide their deed, but toward the end of the play, she goes to sleep. She had told Macbeth that a little water would clear them of the deed, but now in her sleep she continually washes her hands, seeking to get the blood off them. Her broken utterances, repeating what she has said before, are highly ironic. She had tried to make Macbeth forget his crime with the statement, "What's done is done," but we see that what is done continues to be re-lived and repeated.

The clever use of tragic irony in the porter's scene gives the reader or viewer a break from the tension of the murder having just been committed. However, the porter's pretending he is the keeper at hell gate is truer than he realizes. The castle of Macbeth has been transformed into an evil place with the murder of Duncan.

In Act IV, the three apparitions, especially the third one, make Macbeth think his throne is secure because they tell him that he will never be defeated until the Great Birnam wood moves up Dunsinane hill. But by use of camouflage or some similar technique, Malcolm and Macduff's men do move trees up the hill. With this ironic situation, the reader or viewer is prepared for the inevitable conclusion, Macbeth's doom.

A final example of irony is portrayed in the hardened character that Macbeth becomes. He had been closely joined to his wife in love and common ambition. She had wanted him to become a "real" man so that he could kill Duncan and attain the throne. By the end of the drama, Macbeth seems to be without any feelings. The news of Lady Macbeth's death does not cause him to grieve. He dismisses it with the observation that she had to die some time. Life has become meaningless, and ironically he has brought his own downfall upon himself. In his pursuit of the kingship, he fails to listen to his conscience, and thereby loses all of the characteristics that had brought him greatness. He has become a mere shadow of his former self, the brave, strong, courageous Macbeth.

Step 3

Without looking back at the two essays, write a paragraph or two evaluating them and explaining how they are related. You may refer to your summaries, but not to the essays. Time: 10 minutes.

INDEX OF AUTHORS AND TITLES

9
C 0
D 1
E 2
F 3
G 4
H 5
I 6
J 7